Springer Series on Cultural Computing

Founding Editor

Ernest Edmonds, De Montfort University, Leicester, UK

Series Editor

Craig Vear, De Montfort University, Leicester, UK

Editorial Board

Paul Brown, University of Sussex, Brighton, UK

Nick Bryan-Kinns, Queen Mary University of London, London, UK

David England, Liverpool John Moores University, Liverpool, UK

Sam Ferguson, University of Technology, Sydney, Australia

Bronač Ferran, Birkbeck, University of London, London, UK

Andrew Hugill, University of Leicester, Leicester, UK

Nicholas Lambert, Ravensbourne, London, UK

Jonas Lowgren, Linköping University, Malmo, Sweden

Ellen Yi-Luen Do, University of Colorado Boulder, Boulder, CO, USA

More information about this series at http://www.springer.com/series/10481

Fotis Liarokapis · Athanasios Voulodimos ·
Nikolaos Doulamis · Anastasios Doulamis
Editors

Visual Computing
for Cultural Heritage

 Springer

Editors
Fotis Liarokapis
Faculty of Informatics
Masaryk University
Brno, Czech Republic

Nikolaos Doulamis
National Technical University of Athens
Athens, Greece

Athanasios Voulodimos
University of West Attica
Athens, Greece

Anastasios Doulamis
Department of Electrical
and Computer Enineering
National Technical University of Athens
Athens, Greece

ISSN 2195-9056   ISSN 2195-9064   (electronic)
Springer Series on Cultural Computing
ISBN 978-3-030-37193-7   ISBN 978-3-030-37191-3   (eBook)
https://doi.org/10.1007/978-3-030-37191-3

This Springer imprint is published by the registered company Springer Nature Switzerland AG
The registered company address is: Gewerbestrasse 11, 6330 Cham, Switzerland

Preface

Cultural heritage is a priceless, non-renewable resource, which constitutes one of the core elements of peoples' identities. As such, the preservation, archival, comprehension, and study of cultural heritage is of utmost significance at local, national, and international levels and a key to the deeper understanding of our contemporary cultural and societal context. The advent of affordable imaging devices combined with the technological advancements in terms of computing and storage capabilities has contributed to the soaring interest of the broader scientific community of visual computing in cultural heritage. In the last decades, visual computing researchers have contributed a growing set of tools for cultural heritage, thereby offering valuable support to the preservation and promotion of cultural heritage. This interest has in turn uncovered a new series of research challenges to be addressed by the community.

Visual computing encompasses all computer science disciplines dealing with digital images and 3D models. In fact, image and video processing, computer vision and photogrammetry, 3D modeling, computer graphics, virtual and augmented reality technologies are nowadays widely employed to capture, analyze, conserve, virtually or physically restore, document, classify, recognize, and render cultural artifacts. These include historic buildings and monuments, archaeological sites and finds, artworks such as paintings, sculptures, etc., manuscripts, photograph, films, and other entities of artistic, historical, or archaeological importance.

The aim of this edited volume is to provide a point of reference for the latest advancements in the different fields of visual computing applied in Digital Cultural Heritage research, covering a broad range from visual data acquisition, classification, analysis and synthesis, 3D modeling and reconstruction, to new forms of interactive presentation, visualization and immersive experience provision via VR/AR, serious games, and digital storytelling. This book brings together and targets researchers, professionals, and students from the domains of computing, engineering, archaeology, and arts, and aims at underscoring the potential for cross-fertilization and collaboration among these communities.

In particular, the book reviews comprehensively the key recent research into visual computing for both tangible and intangible cultural heritage. It goes into details to explain how to make use of visual computing for both tangible and intangible cultural heritage. To illustrate the capabilities as well as the limitations of digital heritage technologies, the book provides a number of case studies.

The chapters of this book are organized in six main parts: Computer Graphics, Computer Vision and Photogrammetry, Extended Reality, Serious Games, Storytelling, and Preservation and Reconstruction.

In terms of computer graphics and visualization, three chapters illustrate ways that computer graphics and visualization can be leveraged to showcase cultural heritage assets and delve into the past. In respect to computer vision and photogrammetry methods are provided to interpret, represent, classify, summarize, and comprehend cultural heritage content. AR, VR, games, and storytelling demonstrate innovative examples of accessing and interacting with cultural assets. Finally, in terms of preservation and reconstruction, different approaches are presented showcasing the effectiveness of the techniques in both tangible and intangible cultural heritage.

Brno, Czech Republic   Fotis Liarokapis
Athens, Greece   Athanasios Voulodimos
Athens, Greece   Nikolaos Doulamis
Athens, Greece   Anastasios Doulamis

Contents

Part I   Computer Graphics

1   Computer Graphics for Archaeology   3
Filipe Castro and Christopher Dostal

2   Studying Illumination and Cultural Heritage   23
J. Happa and A. Artusi

3   High Dynamic Range in Cultural Heritage Applications   43
Demetris Marnerides, Vedad Hulusic and Kurt Debattista

4   Procedural Modeling for Cultural Heritage   63
António Coelho, Augusto Sousa and Fernando Nunes Ferreira

Part II   Computer Vision and Photogrammetry

**5   Providing Access to Old Greek Documents Using Keyword
Spotting Techniques**   85
Anastasios L. Kesidis and Basilis Gatos

**6   Machine Learning for Intangible Cultural Heritage:
A Review of Techniques on Dance Analysis**   103
Ioannis Rallis, Athanasios Voulodimos, Nikolaos Bakalos,
Eftychios Protopapadakis, Nikolaos Doulamis
and Anastasios Doulamis

7   Classification and Detection of Symbols in Ancient Papyri   121
Alexandros Haliassos, Panagiotis Barmpoutis, Tania Stathaki,
Stephen Quirke and Anthony Constantinides

**8   Image-Based Underwater 3D Reconstruction for Cultural
Heritage: From Image Collection to 3D. Critical Steps
and Considerations**   141
Dimitrios Skarlatos and Panagiotis Agrafiotis

Part III Extended Reality

9   Virtual Reality Reconstruction Applications Standards for Maps,
     Artefacts, Archaeological Sites and Monuments   161
     Anastasios G. Bakaoukas

10   Using Augmented Reality, Gaming Technologies, and
     Transmedial Storytelling to Develop and Co-design Local
     Cultural Heritage Experiences   177
     Lissa Holloway-Attaway and Lars Vipsjö

11   Tackling Problems of Marker-Based Augmented Reality
     Under Water.   205
     Jan Čejka and Fotis Liarokapis

12   A True AR Authoring Tool for Interactive Virtual Museums.   225
     Efstratios Geronikolakis, Paul Zikas, Steve Kateros, Nick Lydatakis,
     Stelios Georgiou, Mike Kentros and George Papagiannakis

Part IV Serious Games

13   Transforming Heritage Crafts to Engaging Digital Experiences . . .   245
     Nikolaos Partarakis, Xenophon Zabulis, Margherita Antona
     and Constantine Stephanidis

14   Everyone Is not a Gamer! Developing Cultural Heritage
     Experiences for Diverse Audiences   263
     Ulf Wilhelmsson and Per Backlund

15   Beyond Virtual Museums: Adopting Serious Games
     and Extended Reality (XR) for User-Centred Cultural
     Experiences   283
     Stella Doukianou, Damon Daylamani-Zad
     and Ioannis Paraskevopoulos

16   Fostering Engagement with Cultural Heritage Through
     Immersive VR and Gamification.   301
     Stuart O'Connor, Simon Colreavy-Donnelly and Ian Dunwell

Part V Storytelling

17   Exploring the Potential of Visually-Rich Animated Digital
     Storytelling for Cultural Heritage   325
     Akrivi Katifori, Fay Tsitou, Myrsini Pichou, Vassilis Kourtis,
     Evangelos Papoulias, Yannis Ioannidis and Maria Roussou

18   Digital Storytelling   347
     Selma Rizvic, Vensada Okanovic and Dusanka Boskovic

**19 Storytelling in Virtual Museums: Engaging A Multitude
    of Voices** 369
    Stella Sylaiou and Panagiotis Dafiotis

Part VI Preservation and Reconstruction

**20 Analyzing Spatial Distribution of Photographs in Cultural
    Heritage Applications** 391
    Florian Niebling, Jonas Bruschke, Heike Messemer, Markus Wacker
    and Sebastian von Mammen

**21 Relict–Interpolated–Extrapolated–Speculative: An Approach
    to Degrees of Accuracy in Virtual Heritage Reconstruction** 409
    Marleen de Kramer

**22 Preserving and Presenting Cultural Heritage Using
    Off-the-Shelf Software** 423
    Eike Falk Anderson, David John, Richard Mikulski, Adam Redford
    and Mario Romero

Part I
Computer Graphics

Chapter 1
Computer Graphics for Archaeology

Filipe Castro and Christopher Dostal

Abstract Archaeologists reconstruct past human activity from material culture remains. Recording, representing and reconstructing artifacts or contexts is a long, morose, and often expensive process. Computers have radically changed traditional methodologies and are creating opportunities to develop more eloquent images or graphic files that convey compressed information and engage the public in a more participative way. Archeological reconstructions are thinking tools that allow us to reason better and faster about our past and present, and computer graphics can replace the traditional long texts and orthographic images with a rich learning environment that transforms the learning experience into an active and critical mental process. This chapter analyses the current methodologies and evaluates the cost-benefits of the best off-the-shelf software packages and their potential to improve the recording, representing, reconstructing, and sharing archaeological contexts and artifacts.

1.1 Introduction

Computers are changing the world fast and radically, and they appear to archaeologists as exceptional tools to increase the social value of archaeology. In the past years we have been repeating the idea, advanced by the American philosopher Daniel Dennett, that certain bits of knowledge—what he calls thinking tools, or apps we upload to our 'necktops'—make us think faster and better (Dennett 2013). There are good reasons to believe that knowledge makes us smarter, and that knowledge about the past is a very important part of who we are. This is one of the most important reasons to preserve the planet's cultural heritage: educated societies are stronger, healthier, happier, and smarter. The social importance of archaeology is undebatable. We exist in a time frame that is impossible to ignore, and we are all interested in our condition. French historian Fernand Braudel explained how cultural change happens at different paces (Braudel 1958) and if we want to better understand who we are, where we come from, where we are going, and what can we know, studying the past

F. Castro (✉) · C. Dostal
Nautical Archaeology Program, Texas A&M University, College Station, USA
e-mail: fvcastr@tamu.edu

© Springer Nature Switzerland AG 2020
F. Liarokapis et al. (eds.), *Visual Computing for Cultural Heritage*, Springer Series on Cultural Computing, https://doi.org/10.1007/978-3-030-37191-3_1

is a good first step. Preserving, studying, protecting, and curating material remains of past human activity is important to everybody. As archaeologists say: few among us would throw away their family photo albums.

Computers offer a vast array of solutions to capture, archive, preserve, curate, and share our cultural heritage. As life in society becomes more complex, the pace of innovation accelerates, and we are confronted with new moral quandaries, sometimes posed by seemingly trivial developments, like the possibility of sharing one's DNA online. Intellectuals are more than ever called to help society navigate the intricate web of knowledge necessary to sustain our social reality. Economies are irreversibly interconnected worldwide, and their problems require partial solutions, which generate new problems, often unforeseen. Modern society is an organism whose survival depends on a large number of educated people, with a wide range of technical, cultural, historical, and philosophical skills. Few people would be able to survive alone in the present world: all of our artifacts are made through a long chain of skills, working like a functional organism, made of people with different knowledges, and computers are one of the best metaphors for this situation. More than half of the planet's population is connected to the internet, and computers are creating opportunities to transfer knowledge in ways that would be unthinkable only one generation ago.

In this chapter we propose to use two communities of domain experts—in computer science and archaeology—to produce and share narratives of the planet's past, and build into them the possibility to add voices that previously were not considered, such as those of women, minorities, the peoples that were colonized, or invaded, or lost conflicts and found themselves on the wrong side of history.

As already mentioned above, archeology is becoming increasingly important to our understanding of culture change, politics, conflicts, and solutions. As the world becomes smaller and more homogeneous, the diversity of cultures and ways of life that could be found around the planet two generations ago are disappearing, and archaeology is presenting itself as one of the best sources for understanding the thick and rich patterns of culture that characterized each region of the planet. Diversity is becoming a thing of the past, and the old pledge that archaeology should be anthropology or it is nothing is as relevant as ever. But we propose a new pledge in this paper: that archaeology is public or it is nothing. The age of an archaeology almost exclusively for archaeologists is ending. The world needs and wants information about its past and it is no longer possible to sustain an archaeology—preferably paid for with taxpayers' money—that is not based on the full publication of all primary data. Moreover, as illiteracy diminishes worldwide and middle classes grow globally—mostly due to their fast rise in Asia—we expect to witness a rise in the demand for cultural products. Museums, libraries, concerts, movies, documentaries, magazines, and books are an integral part of the lives of middle classes everywhere, and archaeological discoveries are already a frequent theme in the media.

Combined with the rise of a diverse and international middle class, the rise of a more diverse and international body of archaeologists promises to break away with the basic tenets of the traditional Western discipline that characterized the 19th and 20th centuries, and will bring about more diverse narratives of the past, including voices that traditionally were not heard. Archaeology has been largely a European invention, and the growing geographical and cultural diversity in the field promises to offer us different points of view, different narratives, and different interpretations of archaeological data. This trend is increasing the social value of archaeology, making it public, participatory, and incomparably richer than it has ever been.

Computers will certainly play increasingly important roles in this process, and we believe that social media can turn archaeology into a dynamic, public, and exciting discipline, helping specialists to construct and deconstruct new and better narratives, accelerate the iterative process of interpretation of archaeological data, and yield more complete and diverse reconstructions of the planet's common past. Our perception of who we are is built on memories and amnesias, more often than not based on narratives developed by the winners in the historical process, the conquerors, the upper classes, religious leaders, or majorities. Archaeology can give a voice to the people without history, those whose voices were never heard, or recorded in historical documents.

Computers and social media are excellent vectors for the diffusion of new ideas. New ideas can of course be good or bad, accurate or fabricated, and enlighten us or fuel conspiracy theories. Like it always happens with all forms of communication, it is up to us to build the trust of the public, make our points clearly and eloquently, and stand corrected when we find out that we were wrong on any issue. There are also opportunities for computer science to help develop a reliable online peer-review processes, and perhaps even resolve some of the problems of structural injustice or asymmetry posed by gate keepers' networks in the peer-review journal business, but these are not within the scope of this paper.

As maritime archaeologists, we present here a particular set of relatively simple applications for maritime archaeology—applicable to any other sub-disciplines of archaeology—and propose a methodology to simplify and standardize the description of ship's hull remains.

1.2 Maritime Archaeology

It is difficult to find a person on the planet that is not interested in ships and boats, the history of seafaring, maritime travels and adventures, migrations, shipwrecks, piracy, or any other subject connected to seafaring. Ships are fascinating artifacts, and maritime archaeology is concerned with their conception, construction, and handling. Maritime archaeologists study maritime communities and their artifacts, including boats and ships. The range of emotions and thoughts that ships and boats evoke is vast and exciting. There is something poetic about ships, either sailing on a landscape, against the margins of a lake or a river, or a coast, or sailing on the sea, an immense desert that covers a large part of the planet.

This dichotomy between the ships that sail against a landscape, and those that cross the oceans was best described by Barthes (1957), who saw ships simultaneously as a mobile environment from which one could perceive the amazing diversity of the world—inspired by Rimbaud's poem "Drunken Boat"—and as a safe, closed environment that protect human life from the dangers and the isolation of the sea, as in Jules Verne's Captain Nemo and his submarine *Nautilus*.

As Barthes puts it, "The image of the ship, so important in his mythology, in no way contradicts this. Quite the contrary: the ship may well be a symbol for departure; it is, at a deeper level, the emblem of closure. An inclination for ships always means the joy of perfectly enclosing oneself, of having at hand the greatest possible number of objects, and having at one's disposal an absolutely finite space. To like ships is first and foremost to like a house, a superlative one since it is unremittingly closed, and not at all vague sailings into the unknown: a ship is a habitat before being a means of transport. And sure enough, all the ships in Jules Verne are perfect cubby-holes, and the vastness of their circumnavigation further increases the bliss of their closure, the perfection of their inner humanity. The *Nautilus*, in this regard, is the most desirable of all caves: the enjoyment of being enclosed reaches its paroxysm when, from the bosom of this unbroken inwardness, it is possible to watch, through a large window-pane, the outside vagueness of the waters, and thus define, in a single act, the inside by means of its opposite."

Conrad (1897) called ocean-going ships "dark and wandering places of the earth." As so many other authors, Conrad was fascinated with the culture of the ship's crews. He wrote: "Old Singleton, the oldest able seaman in the ship, sat apart on the deck right under the lamps, stripped to the waist, tattooed like a cannibal chief all over his powerful chest and enormous biceps. (…) He was intensely absorbed, and, as he turned the pages an expression of grave surprise would pass over his rugged features. He was reading 'Pelham.' The popularity of Bulwer Lytton in the forecastles of Southern-going ships is a wonderful and bizarre phenomenon. What ideas do his polished and so curiously insincere sentences awaken in the simple minds of the big children who people those dark and wandering places of the earth?"

Another example of ship's wide interest in cultural studies is that of Foucault (1984), who wrote that "the boat is a floating piece of space, a place without a place, that exists by itself, that is closed in on itself and at the same time is given over to the infinity of the sea and that, from port to port, from tack to tack, from brothel to brothel, it goes as far as the colonies in search of the most precious treasures they conceal in their gardens, you will understand why the boat has not only been for our civilization, from the sixteenth century until the present, the great instrument of economic development, but has been simultaneously the greatest reserve of the imagination. The ship is the heterotopia *par excellence*. In civilizations without boats, dreams dry up, espionage takes the place of adventure, and the police take the place of pirates."

There are endless literary examples of the importance of ships and boats in our imaginary. George Bass used to remind us that "long before there were farmers, there were sailors." Our relationship with the sea and other bodies of water runs deep in our veins and has inspired many artists and intellectuals. An important part of maritime archaeologists' work is, however, to patiently and tirelessly describe and classify all known types of ships and boats, to understand how they were conceived and put together, handled and lost. To understand Conrad's "dark, wondering places" and Rimbaud's "drunken boats" we need to approach each archaeological site with a solid methodology to record and interpret every piece of information, starting by the artifact itself, which is one of the most complex artifacts produced by our species.

As land archaeologists proposed for vernacular architecture, ships can be analyzed from four different viewpoints: as objects (*object-oriented*), as part of the life of a society (*socially-oriented*), as products of a particular culture (*culturally-oriented*), or as objects that have symbolic meanings for the peoples that use them, interact with them, or see them (*symbolic-oriented*) (Upton 1983).

Our first, basic approach to the study of ships or boats is generally *object-oriented*, concerned with the ships as artifacts. In this case we want to know when were these ships built, how they were built, by whom, if they suffered changes during their existence, or why. We look at each vessel as a particular artifact that is the product of a long and diverse list of factors—some serendipitous—which go from where did the knowledge to build them reside to the price and availability of materials, to the specificities of the function each one was designed to fulfil, to the taste of the shipwright and the beliefs and fashions of the people for which it was built. More technical and perhaps more specialized, this approach is intimately connected to the history of technology and is based on detailed descriptions of the hull remains under study. Archaeologists must measure and describe each vessel as if they were going to be destroyed forever. Capturing the curves that define a hull shape is one of the goals of this approach. It is paramount to understand how each type was conceived of and built, what ranges of sizes were considered, how the space was distributed, occupied, transformed, and when possible, what the characteristics were that defined a particular type in a particular period and region (e.g. caravels, cogs, galleons). The other goal is to describe the ship's structure in detail, registering the ship's construction sequence and recording each timber, its scarves, fasteners, tool marks, coatings and paints, and carpenter marks. As we will show, computers have considerably simplified these tasks and set much higher standards for archaeologists: as tools become more accurate, the demand for operator's precision increases.

The second way to look at these ships, as *socially-oriented* objects, takes them as "a part of everyday existence and [...] as evidence for aspects of the past that can be known imperfectly from other kinds of evidence" (Upton 1983). As social objects vessels are considered artifacts, and though the technical characteristics of the ship like size and shape are important, they are important from the viewpoint of how these characteristics impacted the social use of the vessel. Depending on their sizes and functions, archaeologists try to understand how the spaces were used and by whom, when, and for what purposes. Social stratification, gender, labor specializations, and function defined the shape and content of each ship or boat, its decorations, equipment, and sturdiness. The occupants of a ship can be first divided between crew and passengers, and then hierarchies, generally separated for each of the groups. For instance, throughout the early modern period in the Western World, ocean-going ships were spaces where social mobility was accepted with naturality. In the Spanish New World routes it was normal for apprentices to become sailors and later, if they were competent, masters or even pilots. In the 15th-century Venetian galley trade a rower could rise to much higher positions. The unwritten rules regulating social mobility, freedom of association, and acquisition of knowledge or working experience, to cite only a few, applied to crews, passengers, and everybody on the shore, effectively all of the inhabitants of the maritime communities and landscapes where ships were built, sailed, and lost. Anthropologists are interested in understanding culture change. As Braudel (1958) wrote, social change happens at different speeds and influences our lives in different ways, and ships are excellent subjects of study, for they reflect changes in social organization, subsistence modes, division of labor, fashion, and the history of the ideas.

The third approach, *culturally-oriented*, looks at construction features (*memes*) related to the different cultures at play, something that Ole Crumlin-Pedersen called 'cultural fingerprints', and Eric Rieth calls 'architectural signatures' (Crumlin-Petersen 1991; Rieth 1998). Upton (1983) defines culture as "learned behavior that embodies the enduring values and deepest cognitive structures of a social group," and archaeologists look at ship and boat remains as means of retrieving ideas, gestures, practices, and tastes that may allow them to better reconstruct the political, technical, and cultural environment in which they were built. The history of wooden shipbuilding is an important part of the history of technology because ships tend to be rather complex machines. The *culturally-oriented* approach tries to select and systematize the characteristics and solutions of ships and boats that are specific to a particular culture or region, and trace their paths as they cross-pollinate along the shores of the planet. Ships were vectors of culture and technological change because they carried people, merchandises, and ideas. To trace the evolution of shipbuilding and the convergence of shapes, sizes, and design and construction solutions is one of the main concerns of maritime archaeology. It aims at understanding both the material folk culture and the higher-end scientific understanding of the maritime cultures, their theoretical boundaries, and the dynamic processes through which these were reinterpreted, adapted, changed, and evolved from region to region and through time. In this context, archaeologists collect ethnographies, catalog and organize artifacts to understand in which ways they embody local cultures, and describe design and construction solutions, trying to trace the paths through which knowledge travelled and changed. The end-result of this approach is the proposal of models of evolution based on taxonomies and cultural processes by which they change. Linguistics play an important role in these studies, and the collection of vocabulary and elaboration of glossaries are integral to any *culturally-oriented* look at ships, crews, harbors, and routes. Computers are particularly useful in these studies, namely because they are the perfect tools to design databases or ontologies.

The fourth and last approach, *symbolic-oriented*, focuses on decorative and aesthetic elements, as well as the symbolic character of architectural solutions and the images and emotions that ships evoke(d) in peoples' minds (Bachelard 1957). Trying to reconstruct and understand the *meaning* of ships and boats is not an easy task. Ships and boats mean different things to those who design, build, operate, inhabit, or watch them from the shore. The archaeological symbolic approach is concerned with the more pedestrian, functional aspects of the ships, such as how they address the demands and tastes of those who ordered their construction or bought them, and with more personal and complex aspects such as aesthetics. Ships have been portrayed in a variety of ways to evoke different emotions, from delicate lines and landscapes eliciting gentle beauty, to imposing hulls with an imposing armament displayed, projecting military might. Again, Upton guides us through the theoretical definitions of his four approaches, mentioning semiotics—the study of the lives of symbols in our lives—and proposing that ships' formal elements can be recorded as systems of signs with particular meanings to different social groups. Ship's appearances can be obvious in the objective conveyance of power, dignity, elegance, or strength, but they can also trigger subjective feelings through their size, shape, internal division, decoration, rigging, or construction materials (Eriksson 2014).

All four of these approaches—also barely described above—help archaeologists understand each particular vessel studied, and create a narrative that may explain the economic and social role of each vessel type, define what features they have in common, and what variations in shape and size are allowed before it compromises the definition of a particular type in a particular cultural environment. Perhaps more important, these four approaches call for a creative set of informatic tools—based on ontologies—that will allow archaeologists to share their discoveries and separate descriptions from interpretations so that other persons can reinterpret the data and construct and deconstruct new and old narratives.

Before we even look at the social and economic role of a ship, however, there are shapes, scantlings, scarves, connections, fasteners, timber species, tree morphology, construction sequences, geometric aids, and a vast array of other characteristics that we use to describe and classify boats and ships. And that is just one of the ways in which computers come in handy.

In this chapter we propose a methodology to record, store, and publish shipwrecks with hull remains. Although maritime archaeology is over half a century old, there are no generally accepted formats for the recording and publication of shipwreck remains (Castro et al. 2018). We find the increasing use of computers an excellent opportunity to change this situation and propose a series of steps and off-the-shelf software packages to record and publish ship's hull. Even though it is likely that the software packages will change or be replaced, we believe that it is easy and desirable to establish a standardized methodology to record, store, and share the primary data in ways that simplify comparative studies.

1.3   Surveying

The first step we want to address in this chapter is the survey process. The primary goal of a survey is to assess an underwater archaeological site and estimate its area and limits, and the secondary goal is to generate a description of the archaeological context or object. Remote sensing devices have simplified these tasks considerably, and they have made large, previously unreachable areas accessible, such as those below the professional diving depths. Magnetometers, side scan sonars, multi-beam sonars, and sub-bottom profilers are constantly evolving and can be towed behind a boat or deployed in remotely operated and autonomous vehicles (ROVs and AUVs).

Remote sensing has been around for a long time. Devices to measure magnetic fields created by submerged or buried metal masses, and devices to record the shape of the bottom of a body of water with sonar technology have evolved considerably in the past 50 years, together with sub-bottom profiling, which also uses ranges of frequencies to probe differences in rigidity of the sediments and other objects they main contain. The present challenges are related to the coordination and representation of these heterogeneous sources of data, and a good amount of energy is being aimed at synchronizing and representing it.

Filming and photography have also evolved for over a century now and archaeologists have better lenses, better cameras, digital imaging, and constantly evolving software to interpret and reconstruct images, as well as increasingly smaller, cheaper, or more sophisticated remotely operated vehicles (ROVs) to capture images. Unmanned vehicles—autonomous underwater vehicles (AUVs), and autonomous surface vehicles (ASVs)—can be programed to perform all sorts of tasks and return to harbor or to the vessel from which they were deployed with the data acquired. In some cases it is possible to retrieve these data remotely. All the data generated by these vehicles is stored in digital formats and can be represented on a computer screen.

The first step of a publication is a location map and an undisturbed site plan. Traditionally developed on paper with a variety of measurements, offsets, and sketched descriptions, site plans are now more often than not developed from remote sensing data, or from video or photography images, which can be treated with single-image photogrammetry software to produce point clouds or meshes that represent the surface of a site before disturbance. The shift toward digital documentation to produce site plans has resulted in a massive increase in the amount of data accumulated at each stage of documentation. The storage of all these data is a complex problem, and there are no cheap and easy to use software packages that streamline the archaeological site plan development in a way that directly addresses these problems. The first step to even aspire to have such computer capacities is to define the basic chain of processes that form an archaeological survey (Fig. 1.1).

All files generated in each one of these processes need to be stored and assigned metadata with basic information: date, location, keywords. Geographical Information Systems (GIS) are a perfect environment for the storage and synthesis of layered information.

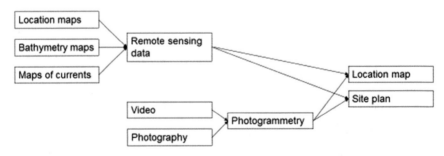

Fig. 1.1 Chain of processes required to produce a location map and a site plan

1.4 Recording

Starting in the 1980s, J. Richard Steffy proposed that computers were the most promising tools for the study of shipbuilding. Comparative studies being the natural way to understand shipbuilding as a particular type of human behavior, he proposed that the first step was inventorying and comparing construction features. Steffy fully understood that this was not an easy project. In 1990 he mentioned the absolute lack of a standard to publish ship hull remains and wrote: "we must admit to an unbridled confusion in the recording and publication of our vessels. Of the forty-four subjects considered for this study, little more than half of them have been reported formally. Of the eighteen categories I chose for comparison, only a few wrecks filled all of the columns, even though the information must have been available on many others. I am not criticizing the way in which anyone documents their shipwrecks, because we have differing priorities and varying opinions about what is and what is not important. But I do think that in the future we must take a clue from the older artifact disciplines and all record the same basic features where they survive" (Steffy 1990).

In a 1994 paper archaeologist Roger Hill proposed a set of development lines for the application of computer technology to archaeology (Hill 1994). He noted that the data are preserved in the ground in different conditions, having been deposited there by a range of dynamic processes, and that time and human activity have made the ground "a database in which an imperfect memory of those processes is retained." According to Hill, the purpose of archaeological recording "is to transfer the ground-based record system into a form accessible not just to the site archaeologist, but to all potential users." As we have written elsewhere, the most important part of Hill's seminal paper is a call to understand that the nature of the output generated by computers is the primary concern in the adoption of computers to record archaeological sites: "the technology used to record the data (…) is central to the activity of archaeology properly considered" (Yamafune et al. 2017). Hill proposed a paradigm change in archaeology by making the possibilities of digital technology the base for a new philosophy "for planning and managing the recovery of the soil database, recording deposited materials," and modeling the site formation process.

The year after, in 1995, Steffy—following his seminal 1990 paper—wrote a second call for standardization in the study of shipwrecks, and argued that computers were going to change maritime archaeology in a drastic way—noting that archaeology was entering "the computer age, bringing with it expanded possibilities for examining data and analyzing hull structures. More than ever before, we must document our finds more completely to take advantage of this new medium. At the same time, we must reevaluate the ways in which we have been considering our hull remains and take new approaches to these old problems. (…) In the past, theories [about the ways in which shipwrights projected and controlled hull shapes] have ranged from the use of standing control frames to the haphazard assembly of planks, but I am not convinced that any of them are accurate and certainly none of them are complete" (Steffy 1995).

Being an outstanding field archaeologist, Steffy did not mention the recording process of individual components of ship's hull, which he had described and established as a standard in his 1994 book (Steffy 1994). In it, he explained that archaeological recording requires precision and accuracy. The first depends on the tools, and the second on the skill of the archaeologists involved. It is paramount that archaeologists are trained both in archaeological and anthropological methods and theory. Archaeologists typically have only one shot at a site. Excavating is destroying.

Recording is a process that entails therefore two complementing tasks: measuring and describing. Measurements can be taken directly, with tools, or indirectly, with photographs or scaled 3D models, like those produced with computer vision photogrammetry. Photogrammetry has been around since the 19th century, but the recent development of computer software to represent and process digital images has simplified the process and increased the precision of the measurements obtained from a collection of scaled images.

Describing a site requires a different type of knowledge. Archaeologists must know what they are describing and select a number of characteristic measurements that defines each feature or component of an archaeological site.

The excavation process typically entails a cycle of four tasks: digging, cleaning, tagging and recording. All these tasks need to be recorded for each cycle, both through images, measurements, and descriptions, and multi-image photogrammetry provides accurate surfaces of each stage of an excavation. This is an extremely useful tool, because the exposed surfaces of wooden structures often erode during the excavation process, and the software utilized to store and manage the excavation processes will save the fresh surfaces exposed in each excavation cycle. In the Nautical Archaeology Program at Texas A&M University we have been using *Agisoft Metashape* with good results.

Artifacts are traditionally tagged, bagged, and positioned before being lifted, and subsequently entered in a database designed to keep their provenance, main dimensions, images, characteristics, and conservation treatment steps. At A&M we have been using both *FileMaker Pro* and *Microsoft Access* with similarly good results to not only track each artifact through the conservation treatment steps, but to house all metadata for each artifact to streamline study and analysis.

Hull timbers are treated differently. When they can be raised, we scan them with a FARO ScanArm laser scanner to create a point cloud for each individual timber. The ScanArm is a fixed-base coordinate measuring machine (CMM), meaning that as the arm is moved, the position of the scanner relative to the base remains known, which allows for highly accurate data capture. CMM arms can be used with a probe attachment or a laser scanner, the former being a contact measuring device and the latter being a non-contact measuring device. Using the laser scanner instead of a probe attachment means that for each timber, millions of data points are collected, capturing every tool mark, fastener, and wood grain detail. These details are of course captured with manual probing by tracing the details on the surface of the wood with the probe, but the laser scanning captures more detail in substantially less time. Working on a project with the city of Alexandria, VA, two researchers with Texas A&M's Conservation Research Laboratory were able to scan, process, virtually arrange, and 3D print an entire disarticulated vessel (207 timbers, with hull remains approximately 15.6 m long by 2.8 m wide) in six weeks.

Each timber is scanned in sections, with enough overlap between sections to allow for alignment during the processing phase. For ship timbers, the data is collected as a point cloud with an average point spacing of 0.25 mm. This is a higher resolution than is needed for virtual arrangement or 3D printing, but the high resolution is collected to 'future proof' the data; or, perhaps merely to slightly delay its obsolescence. The point clouds for each timber side/section are saved as separate files for maximum redundancy of data, and then later combined into a single, aligned point cloud, that we mesh using *Design X*. With each timber saved as a water-tight mesh, they are then exported as an .stl file, which is a cross-platform, non-proprietary file time that allows the meshes to be used in a wide variety of programs. An additional lower resolution mesh is made from this full-resolution mesh, by 'decimating' the files to <200 MB. The decimating process is essentially lengthening the sides of the polygons that make up the surface of the mesh, which lessens the details visible in the model, but reduces the file size. Often the difference in detail is negligible to the naked eye. The decimated files are then saved as separate .stl files. The 200 MB threshold works both as a way to keep the file sizes manageable by our assembly software, and also to allow us to upload each timber file to the online 3D model hosting site Sketchfab.com, where each file can be made available as a free download to the public to maximize open access to our data. The hull remains are then assembled in *Rhinoceros* and generally 3D printed to a 1:10 or 1:12 scale for preliminary analysis and observation.

For publication purposes we treat the 3D files with rendering software *plug-ins* for *Rhino*ceros like *Penguin*, which allows the development of non-photorealistic drawings, ideal for technical publications. Traditional timber drawings can be produced by using *Rhinoceros* to outline the timbers at each elevation, and then these outlines can be exported to other programs like *AutoCAD* for easy markup and layout. It is increasingly important to ensure that the implementation of rapidly evolving computer programs does not eclipse the past century of recorded archaeological data sets. Though arguably superior data can be obtained by published the digital models, failure to produce data sets that can be directly compared to older methods of documentation make holistic understanding of the archaeological record impossible.

When possible, a set of tentative lines is developed from the surviving hull in *Rhinoceros*. Once the disarticulated timbers are imported and arranged in Rhinoceros, data points are taken on the exterior portion of the framing timbers, where they would meet the exterior planking. The data points collected along the frames can then be connected, forming the basis for a set of ships lines. By connecting the data points along the water lines, station lines, and the buttock lines, a complete set of partial lines can be developed from the 3D model. Once those lines are established, they can be printed on paper and extrapolated using traditional naval architecture drafting techniques to elucidate the original dimensions and shape of the hull. If available, we use coeval iconography, or similar archaeological remains.

Other types of software—such as *AutoDesk Maya* and *SideFX Houdini*—have been used in the treatment and reconstruction of shipwreck hull with impressive results (Figs. 1.2 and 1.3). The problem is that the sophistication of these software packages requires the involvement of domain experts, which are not always available. *AutoDesk Maya* has been used to model shipwreck hulls and explore issues like interior space use because it allows the construction of VR models (Fig. 1.4), which can be used to provide full immersion experiences and acquiring a better understanding of the full-size reconstructions (Wells 2008; Castro et al. 2010; Suarez et al. 2019). *Maya* is also an excellent tool for creating animations and dynamic models that allow for better immersion into the data, though the program is incredibly expensive for non-academics. Other applications associated with the outreach phase of a project will be addressed below.

Houdini is perhaps the most promising package, for its versatility and flexibility. Again, this is not a software package for archaeologists and all projects developed in this environment need a domain expert (Saldaña 2015). We have experimented with *Houdini* to create a procedural model of a lower hull from a typical early modern European merchantman with very promising results (Suarez et al. 2019). The goal of this project was to reduce the large investment of time and expertise that is currently required to create 3D reconstruction models for nautical archaeological research

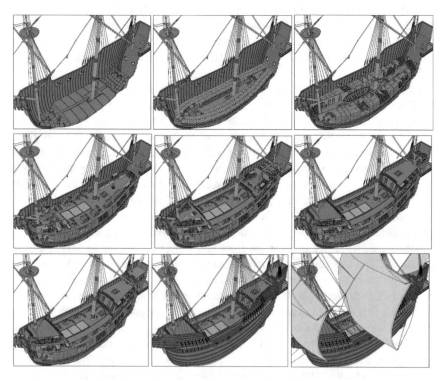

Fig. 1.2 Virtual model of a 17th century Portuguese Indiaman, based on a reconstruction of the Pepper Wreck, 1606 (Wells 2008)

Fig. 1.3 Virtual model of the Audrey Wells reconstruction represented on Fig. 1.2. It can be downloaded from https://texag64.itch.io/nossa-senhora-dos-martires-wreck (Josh Hooton, Jacob Stafford, Cody Leuschner, Thomas Sell, and Bruce Gooch, 2016)

Fig. 1.4 A Bluetooth virtual visit to Audrey Wells' 17th century nau (Troy Edwards, Josh Higginbotham, Humayun Syed, Mitchell Blowey, and Bruce Gooch, 2017)

using typical modeling methods. Our strategy was an approach leveraging computer-based modeling, both parametric- and rule-based. We developed a procedural model of the lower hull of a 16th century European merchant ship through an iterative process of prototype implementation. The resulting model was flexible and versatile, and could be iterated through parametric controls, greatly reducing the traditional change and revision time. The results of this project provided evidence of the time-saving effectiveness of a procedural approach to create 3D models as research tools.

Once procedural models are created, they provide both accessible and powerful means for researchers to create and test multiple interpretations of the archaeological data. Although the development of a procedural model requires skilled computer operators and a significant investment in design, construction, and trouble-shooting, these problems are outweighed by the flexibility the models offer.

The generic hull model developed could be easily changed by changing its parameters, and adapted to the scantlings, shapes, sections, scarves, and connections of a set of timbers from a 16th century ship—designated Belinho 1—that we were recording and studying at the time.

1.5   Sharing

The only purpose of archaeology is to produce knowledge that can be shared and enjoyed by as wide an audience as possible. The best form of archaeology is communal archaeology, which involves the audience from the first steps and strives to include as many stakeholders and as many viewpoints as possible (Hodder 2006, 2013).

In the past archaeologists have not, however, been famous for sharing their data (Bass 2011). In the western world archaeologists do not publish all the sites they excavate (and therefore destroy), and it is difficult to imagine this situation changing, at least as long as we don't change the technological paradigm. In fact, a number of studies suggest that over the last 50 years less than 25% of the materials and results of professional archaeological excavations have been properly published (Boardman 2009), 70% of the Near East excavations have not been published (Atwood 2007; Owen 2009), and that perhaps 80% of all Italian archaeological materials remain unpublished (Stoddart and Malone 2001). It is difficult to argue that the situation in maritime archaeology is better than those mentioned above.

The reasons for this are many, starting with the difficulty of making data available in many different formats, from the diving slates to the daily diving sheets, to the evolving sketches and the notes from the daily excavation debriefings. But the recording process can be organized and streamlined to simplify the excavation and recording process. Like and engineering project, archaeological excavations are organized in consecutive tasks, some of which are repetitive (e.g. digging, cleaning, tagging, photographing, measuring, describing, and sometimes raising), others have preceding activities, and others can be carried out in parallel, at the same time.

Documenting is a responsibility. Archaeologists destroy the sites they dig, and recording every step of the way is an ethical obligation. Interpreting and reconstructing are perhaps the most interesting phases of an archaeological project, but they are often not completed, and many excavations never see the final publication (Bass 2011). The perceived problem of people stealing credit from one archaeologist and publishing it behind there back will always happen, but it is much less frequent than people have assumed in the past. The harsh reality is that even when one puts all their source data freely online, the biggest hurtle to overcome is attracting any attention at all. There are more items online, both academic and not, competing for our attention than ever before. The days of a handful of archaeological projects dominating the public eye are long over. Even the biggest discoveries vanish from the public eye in a matter of days today, because there are so many people learning and sharing so many new things.

We see the implementation of digital data and online file sharing as the antidote to the long-standing practice of hoarding data. Younger generations of archaeologists are far less likely than their mentors to shun the idea of freely sharing data amongst one another. This openness with data may be in part due to the societal erosion of personal privacy over the last several decades; as a society, we have happily traded privacy for convenience. This tradeoff may well have disastrous consequences for personal liberty in the future, but the long-term impact on academic work and intellectual property is proving to be incredibly healthy. Whatever the cause, more and more archaeological data is being freely and openly shared online.

3D model hosting sites such as sketchfab.com have massive collections of archaeological models, and academics, museums, and state agencies are nearly all moving towards a model of sharing digital models of their collections online and encouraging public engagement of their data. With so many new and exciting projects being undertaken around the world, openness and collaboration, combined with effective use of digital data and computer driven organization, are the only effective ways to manage and interpret all the data being collected.

1.6   Reconstructing

The interpretation phase of an archaeological project is arguably the most interesting component and it cannot, by definition, be separated from the measurement and description phase. When excavating, cleaning, tagging, measuring and describing an archaeological site, archaeologists have an idea of what they are representing, and their drawings, measurements, pictures, and descriptions are informed by that idea. No excavation should start without a good idea of its outcomes and deliverables.

The reconstruction phase depends on the amount and quality of the information acquired during excavation. The implementation of digital documentation techniques like laser scanning and photogrammetry allow archaeologists to create ever more informed and convincing interpretations of sites. Computer-aided extrapolation of even the slightest impressions can tease out long lost shape and details that might have otherwise been missed. Statistical analysis of the shapes of certain timbers across many ships can help us develop methodologies for identifying de-contextualized fragments from future ships (Castro et al. 2018). Additionally, animating reconstructions can help convey the mystique of the ship, and to create a tantalizing connection to our past through the scant remains we are lucky enough to happen across.

While this is almost entirely a positive shift, care must be taken to ensure that the distinction between interpretation and primary data is always made clear. Jeffery Clark wrote that an emphasis on reconstruction has been detrimental to the discipline of archaeology because the false sense of knowledge a reconstruction might present can make it difficult to entertain competing interpretations of data (Clark 2010). This is especially true with the power modern computer graphics have in conveying realism. Without a consistent methodology for emphasizing what is based on evidence and what is based on interpretation in a model, there is a real danger of building future studies on a faulty foundation.

Pencil and paper, wooden models, and even cardboard approximations have been used to represent shipwrecks and shipwreck sites, and to propose reconstructions. Marrying these traditional techniques with the newest technologies helps us refine what we have been able to accomplish in the past and expand the impact our reconstructions can have on the public for whom we work. At Texas A&M, we have been combining traditional ship modeling, naval architecture, 3D modelling, and 3D printing to build models of disarticulated ships that integrate each of the best aspect of the different techniques.

European shipwrecks of the early modern period can be interesting to reconstruct due to the existence of written sources describing design and construction processes. When archaeologists can date a ship being excavated with some degree and certainty and identify its origin, it is sometimes interesting to try reconstructing the design process. In the 15th and 16th century some European ships were built following recipes that have been recorded in technical documents. In fact, the earliest shipwreck to have been reconstructed having in mind the relations between its dimensions was the 11th century Serçe Limanı shipwreck, excavated in Turkey by the Institute of Nautical Archaeology. Texas A&M professor and McArthur grant recipient J. Richard Steffy published a seminal paper describing the construction measurements and proving that it was built with a modular dimension precisely equivalent to a Bizantine Foot (Steffy 1982). This paper was later completed and refined in the ship's final publication (Steffy 2003). There are a handful of ship reconstructions based on the ship's dimensions and on sometimes clearly defined units (Castro 2003; Pevny 2017). This aspect is particularly important when archaeologists have access to procedural reconstruction tools, such as *Houdini*, for instance (Suarez et al. 2019).

In 2019, the timbers from the disarticulated hull of an 18th-century shipwreck discovered in Alexandria, VA were each laser scanned and modelled using the techniques described above. During the lengthy conservation of the timbers at the Conservation Research Laboratory, each of the timbers was temporarily removed from its vat and laser scanned with a CMM arm, the FARO ScanArm, with a laser line probe attachment using. The resolution of the scans was set to 0.25 mm spacing between the points, which was fine enough to capture details such as fastener positions, wood grain, and too marks, but not so fine that the files produced would be too large to quickly process (Dostal 2017). The point cloud models of each timber were then meshed, and the mesh models were imported into the computer graphics program Rhinoceros 6.

Each of the timbers were then virtually arranged in Rhinoceros using fastener patterns, excavation photos, and tool marks. An in situ photogrammetric model made during the excavation of the vessel proved to be a useful touchstone for the arrangement, though the goal of arranging the timbers in Rhinoceros was to correct for

Fig. 1.5 Wooden, metal, and resin model of the Alexandria, VA shipwreck (Christopher Dostal and Glenn Grieco)

the deformation of the hull shape that had occurred over the centuries it remained buried. Once the arrangement was complete, a set of preliminary ships lines were pulled from the model by tracing the exteriors of select framing timbers at predefined stations. Those lines were extrapolated out virtually, and then printed out on paper and curves were extrapolated by hand to establish a plausible shape for the vessel. Extrapolating the lines virtually produced perfectly acceptable results, but tracing them out by hand allows for a more traditional means of verification. Comparing the lines established with this technique with archival sources, a draft of a ship was located that matched the general shape, size, and curvature of the vessel, and this draft was used as a basis to inform the reconstruction of the vessel beyond what remained of the timbers. Each timber was then 3D printed, reassembled, and oriented in a physical wire frame that was built to show the reconstructed shape of the vessel (Fig. 1.5). This helped contextualize the remains and point future researchers in the right direction to understand what that ship might have looked like.

Again, computers are simplifying this process by allowing archaeologists to make better, scalable models that are capable of being experienced either in person, on a computer screen, or even with VR masks.

1.7   Conclusion

We understand that it is not possible to propose a definite methodology to record, share, and reconstruct archaeological sites. There are too many variables between scholars for a one-size-fits-all approach to this problem, including varying skillsets, differing availabilities of resources, finances, and time. Despite this, the general shift towards comprehensive 3D documentation and an openness and willingness to share and collaborate internationally will continue to help push towards a much-needed standardized methodology. The more open we are and the more we work together, the greater the need for data compatibility, and this standardization will likely occur organically.

Although computers are not evolving as fast as they once were, their processing capacity is slowly increasing and allowing for more sophisticated software packages to be developed. Every time a new technology is adapted by the archaeological community it might seem like the end-all be-all way of preserving our collective cultural heritage that should be immediately adopted and standardized, but it is useful to remember that nobody could have conceived of computer image photogrammetry being used the way it is today just 30 years ago. It is important that as technology changes, we as archaeologists change with it and adopt the techniques that allow us to preserve history as thoroughly and efficiently as possible. While we do this, it is also important that we maintain backwards compatibility with the techniques that have proceeded us, so that a continuous chain of past knowledge can be maintained as we move forward.

In this chapter we propose several software packages, which we believe are suitable for the tasks necessary to achieve plausible and flexible reconstructions.

References

Atwood R (2007) Publish or be punished: Israel cracks down of delinquent diggers. Archaeology 60(2):18, 60, 62

Bachelard G (1957) La poétique de l'espace. Presses Universitaires de France, Paris

Barthes R (1957) The *Nautilus* and the drunken boat. In: Mythologies. Vintage 2009, London

Bass G (2011) Introduction. In: Catsambis A, Ford B, Hamilton D (eds) The Oxford handbook of maritime archaeology. New York

Boardman J (2009) Archaeologists, collectors, and museums. In: Cuno J (ed) Whose culture? The promise of museums and the debate over antiquities. Princeton

Braudel F (1958) Histoire et Sciences Sociales. La longue durée. Ann Hist Sci Soc 13(4):725–753

Castro F (2003) The Pepper Wreck, an early 17th-century Portuguese Indiaman at the mouth of the Tagus River, Portugal. Int J Naut Archaeol 32(1):6–23

Castro F, Fonseca N, Wells A (2010) Outfitting the Pepper Wreck. Hist Archaeol 44(2):14–34

Castro F, Bendig C, Bérubé M, Borrero R, Budsberg N, Dostal C, Monteiro A, Smith C, Torres R, Yamafune K (2018) Recording, publishing, and reconstructing wooden shipwrecks. J Marit Archaeol 13(1):55–66

Clark J (2010) The fallacy of reconstruction. In: Forte M (ed) Cyber archaeology. Archaeopress, Oxford, pp 63–73

Conrad J (1897) The Niger of the Narcissus. Heinemann, London

Crumlin-Pedersen O (1991) Aspects of maritime Scandinavia, Proceedings of the Nordic seminar on maritime aspects of archaeology, Roskilde 1989. The Viking Ship Museum, Roskilde

Dennett D (2013) Intuition pumps and other tools for thinking. W.W. Norton & Company Inc., New York

Dostal C (2017) Laser scanning as a methodology for recording archaeological ship timbers: a case study using the world trade center ship. Dissertation, Anthropology, Texas A&M University, Texas

Eriksson N (2014) Urbanism under Sail. Elanders, Stokholm

Foucault M (1984) Dits et écrits 1984, Des espaces autres - conférence au Cercle d'études architecturales, 14 mars 1967. Architecture, Mouvement, Continuité (5):46–49

Hill R (1994) A dynamic context recording and modeling system for archaeology. Int J Naut Archaeol 23(2):141–145

Hodder I (2006) The leopard's tale: revealing the mysteries of Catalhoyuk. Thames & Hudson, London

Hodder I (2013) Archaeological theory today. Polity Press, Cambridge, UK

Owen D (2009) Censoring knowledge: the case for publication of unprovenanced cuneiform tablets. In: Cuno J (ed) Whose culture? The promise of museums and the debate over antiquities. Princeton University Press, Princeton, NJ

Pevny T (2017) 7. Capturing the curve: underlying concepts in the design of the hull. In: Bruseth J, Borgens A, Bradford J, Ray E (eds) La Belle: the archaeology of a seventeenth-century vessel of new world colonization. Texas A&M University Press, pp 131–202

Rieth E (1998) Construction navale à Franc-Bord en Méditerranée et Atlantique (XVIe-XVIIe) et «Signatures Architecturales»: une première approche archéologique. In: Méditerranée Antique. Pêche, navigation, commerce, Sous la direction d' Éric Rieth. [S. l.]: Éditions du CTHS, pp 177–187

Saldaña M (2015) An integrated approach to the procedural modeling of ancient cities and buildings. Digit Sch HumIties 30(1):148–163

Steffy JR (1982) The reconstruction of the 11th century Serçe Liman vessel. Int J Naut Archaeol 11(1):13–34

Steffy J (1990) Problems and progress in dating ancient vessels by their construction features. In: Tzalas H (ed) Tropis II, Proceedings of the 2nd international symposium on ship construction in antiquity, Athens, pp 315–320

Steffy JR (1994) Wooden shipbuilding and the interpretation of shipwrecks. Texas A&M University Press, College Station

Steffy J (1995) Ancient scantlings: the projection and control of ancient hull shapes. In: Tzalas H (ed) Tropis III, Proceedings of the 3rd international symposium on ship construction in antiquity, Athens, pp 417–428

Steffy JR (2003) Chapter 10, Construction and analysis of the vessel. In: Bass G, Matthews S, Steffy JR, van Doorninck F (eds) Serçe Limanı, an eleventh-century shipwreck, vol 1. Texas A&M University Press, College Station, pp 153–170

Stoddart S, Malone C (2001) Antiquity. Editorial 75(288):233–246

Suarez M, Parke F, Castro F (2019) A procedural approach to computer-aided modeling in nautical archaeology. In: McCarthy JK, Benjamin J, Winton T, Duivenvoorde W (eds) 3D recording and interpretation for maritime archaeology. Springer/UNITWIN, Cham, pp 123–134

Upton D (1983) The power of things: recent studies in American vernacular architecture. Am Q 35(3):262–279

Wells A (2008) Virtual reconstruction of a seventeenth century Portuguese Nau. MS thesis, Visualization Sciences, Texas A&M University

Yamafune K, Torres R, Castro F (2017) Multi-image photogrammetry to record and reconstruct underwater shipwreck sites. J Archaeol Method Theory 24(3):703–725

Chapter 2
Studying Illumination and Cultural Heritage

J. Happa and A. Artusi

Abstract Computer graphics tools and techniques enable researchers to investigate cultural heritage and archaeological sites. They can facilitate documentation of real-world sites for further investigation, and enable archaeologists and historians to accurately study a past environment through simulations. This chapter explores how light plays a major role in examining computer-based representations of heritage. We discuss how light is both documented and modelled today using computer graphics techniques and tools. We also identify why both physical and historical accuracy in modelling light is becoming increasingly important to study the past, and how emerging technologies such as High Dynamic Range (HDR) imaging and physically-based rendering is necessary to accurately represent heritage.

2.1 Introduction

The application of empirically grounded digital capture of our material culture and visualization is becoming increasingly important for preservation, educational and research purposes. These digital surrogates are used by academics, industry, museums and the media to represent the physical appearance of our cultural heritage throughout time. As digital technologies advance, there is a growing need for techniques to represent real-world historical sites and materials, as well as to investigate ways to better share this captured and subsequently interpreted data.

Computer graphics enables researchers to document and investigate cultural heritage and archaeological sites using computer-based models. Specifically, we use computer graphics for the creation, storage, maintenance, analysis and dissemination of computer-based (oftentimes referred to as *virtual* or *synthetic*) representations of real-world objects in order to facilitate archaeological study. A *digital surrogate* is a virtual representation of a real-world object that may be used to gain insight into

J. Happa (✉)
Information Security Group, Royal Holloway, University of London, London, UK
e-mail: jassim.happa@rhul.ac.uk

A. Artusi
DeepCamera MRG Group, RISE Ltd, Nicosia, Cyprus

© Springer Nature Switzerland AG 2020   23
F. Liarokapis et al. (eds.), *Visual Computing for Cultural Heritage*, Springer Series
on Cultural Computing, https://doi.org/10.1007/978-3-030-37191-3_2

its function and historical relevance. Through simulations in virtual environments, we can study and propose hypotheses about an object, and ask questions related to how it, or a site was used in the past, and how it may have changed over time. These digital surrogates need to be based on existing evidence and expert interpretation available today (Badler and Badler 1978; Reilly 1991; Happa et al. 2012).

An important aspect of creating digital surrogates to study the past is their appearance, both today and in the past. *Light* and *illumination* both play essential roles in the appearance of objects. Light is made up of photons, an elementary particle, that exhibits properties of both particles and waves. As light hits the retina, it is interpreted by the Human Visual System (HVS) to make up what we ultimately perceive as vision. Visible light cover a small part of the electromagnetic radiation spectrum: between 380 (violet) to 780 (red) nanometres. Colour is a perceived characteristic of light: as light is reflected off an object, hits the eye and is then processed by the HVS. Illumination is the particular use of light to achieve a practical or aesthetic effect. Studying the use of colour, light and illumination can reveal insight into the past (Brown et al. 1997; Devlin and Chalmers 2001; Sundstedt et al. 2004; Happa et al. 2012).

In digital documentation of heritage, light can be captured to a certain degree of accuracy and precision which relies on empirical data acquisition technologies such as cameras and other light measurement equipment. In simulation however, we need to use a light model to describe behaviour of light to accurately model it. We can achieve so different degrees of accuracy. The more accurate and precise the model, the more correct the output of our simulation. The term '*modelling light*' is used here to describe properties and behaviour of light, in particular how light propagates from its source and throughout virtual scenes. This is often referred to as physically-based lighting.

Whether capturing or recreating historical light, we also need to consider historically-based information to be present. This must be based on evidence available today, as well as expert opinion and historical sources. Examples of historically-based input includes for instance a description of how a light source '*was used in the past*' as it can affect the illumination in the scene. Furthermore, all resources used (both technical and historical) and the decision-making process must be well documented, in a reproducible manner, otherwise the scientific merit of any output of that simulation will remain questionable.

The field of computer graphics has tackled the challenge of documenting and modelling light for decades, but it is only in the last 20 years that graphics has accelerated its uses to aid historical research (Happa et al. 2010b). The purpose of this chapter is to provide readers with an overview of how and why documenting and modelling uses of light is becoming increasingly important when documenting real-world heritage. The chapter describes how light in computer graphics is used to study illumination of heritage through in-situ documentation using High Dynamic Range (HDR) imaging and recreating illumination using physically-based rendering. Readers interested in this subject should also be aware of the existence of *Reflectance Transformaton Imaging* (RTI) (Malzbender et al. 2001; Happa et al. 2010b; Earl et al. 2010; Mudge et al. 2010): a set of imagine techniques aimed to help viewers interactively display objects under varying, user-defined lighting conditions to reveal surface details. The purpose of this chapter however is to examine tools that help facilitate examination of heritage related to study of illumination specifically, rather than using light as a tool to study historical objects.

2.2   High-Fidelity Rendering and Display of Heritage

High-fidelity rendering and display of cultural heritage involves the accurate physical and historical documentation (or modelling) of geometry, materials and light to the highest accuracy and precision possible with present day technologies and methods. This allows experts to confirm or disprove assumptions about the past with greater scientific confidence through simulation, and allows new hypotheses to transpire. It should be noted however, that it is only possible to claim any high-fidelity rendering to be scientific best-guesses as simulations or predictions, because it is not possible to prove that the output of these simulations represents the past entirely correctly.

Events in history contribute to changes in appearances of heritage. Structural alterations in the environment (e.g. objects being added or removed), ageing and weathering can alter the physical shape of an object, but also visibly alter the material's light interaction properties from chemical, mechanical and biological processes (Dorsey et al. 2008). Over time, the way light is used by people in the scene change as well. Understanding the relationship between geometry, materials and light in a scene helps build a foundation to investigating sites throughout history using simulations and documentation better.

2.2.1   Representing Geometry, Material and Light

To understand how light is modelled in virtual environments, it is necessary to understand what light can interact with. A distinction is made between two and three-dimensional spaces. Image space assumes 2D data—an array of pixels that make up an image, projected onto a computer display. These pixels can be regarded as 'samples' of a real or virtual scene, and these samples are what we intend to study. Real scenes can be documented using film or digital cameras. Virtual scenes however, are generally made up of three constituent components: geometry (shape), materials (surface appearance) and light (a distribution of electromagnetic radiation in the scene emanating from one or more light sources). Different types of geometry data structures can be used to mathematically describe shapes. The most commonly used data structure today is polygons. Each polygon is a planar (flat) surface that is defined by a series of boundary points known as vertices. Once all boundary points of a planar surface have been added (typically as a triangle), a surface can be coloured, see Fig. 2.1.

Fig. 2.1 A flat shaded 3D model example of the exterior and interior of Panagia Angeloktisti, a Byzantine church on Cyprus. Once the points have been defined (left), we can identify which make up the surfaces of objects in the scene (right)

Many connected polygons that share vertices can make up more complex objects (often referred to as a '*mesh*'). Objects appear more detailed if more polygons are used to represent the geometry. Once an object has been formed from a series of points and polygons defining their surfaces, it is necessary to determine the colour of the surface. Material modelling helps us achieve this. Materials describe two aspects of virtual objects surfaces: their intrinsic colour (informally: the colours of the surface "*as they are*" without affected by light, also known as the surface '*albedo*') and their light reflectance functions (Nicodemus et al. 1977) (i.e., how incoming light will interact with the surface from any incoming angle). Materials (colours and functions) are assigned to surfaces, often as a 2D image (known as a texture map) mapped onto the 3D surface.

Real-world light sources can be described as a function of shape, position, direction, colour (or wavelength), time, polarisation (as light is considered both a particle and a wave, waves oscillate with more than one orientation) and phase of light (waves also have amplitudes). However, modelling light in virtual scenes typically ignores the latter three components and simplifies the light model to *Geometric Optics* (Cook and Torrance 1982). In the geometric optics model, light is assumed to be travelling in straight lines (as rays), in a vacuum and one ray cannot interfere with another.

Light-transport simulation is the problem of evaluating how rays intersect with surfaces given a scene configuration, i.e. how geometry, materials and light sources are laid out. Light interacts with materials typically in one of three ways: *reflection* (e.g. opaque surface such as bricks or stone), *transmission* (e.g. glass or water) and *absorption*. The amount of light that is reflected, transmitted and absorbed depends on the reflectance function of the material. While geometric optics generally does not describe visible phenomena that may happen at a quantum or wave level, it is still capable of describing most visual phenomena possible to observe using most camera equipment today. In order to represent colours in images as they appear on screen, we make use of colour models (also known as colour spaces), such as *RGB* (here colours can be expressed as a combination of three colour primaries that are Red, Green and Blue) (Wyszecki and Stiles 1982).

2.2.2 Capturing Light

Researchers can use experimental archaeology techniques to recreate objects (that no longer exist) in the real world. In the case of light sources, it is undesirable to use authentic light sources (if they still exist), but it possible to recreate past light sources in the physical world (using the same ingredients and processes), capture the output of that light source digitally, and then use the samples to light a virtual scene. Examples include for instance:

- Roussos and Alan (2003) presented a reconstruction of a section in the Knossos palace, a Bronze Age archaeological site on Crete. Perceptually realistic and computationally efficient flickering of flames were simulated with his technique, although the approach is limited to small flames from candles.
- Devlin (2004) for instance recreated lighting conditions of Roman frescoes in Pompeii by using the same ingredients and processes to create light sources as the Romans in the physical world, then measured the colour profile of the flame using a spectroradiometre (a device used to measure the spectral power distribution of a sample) to study the Roman motivations for light in Roman frescoes and the visual perception of this blue colour under a variety of different light source conditions.
- Sundstedt et al. (2004), Rudolfova and Sundstedt (2004) presented colourful Egyptian hieroglyphics viewed under sesame-oil candle, highlighting that in such case (also used during ancient Egypt) the blue paint appears almost green. The interior was modelled to allow exploration and reconstruction of hieroglyphics under contemporary lighting as well for comparison. Properties of real sesame-oil lamps were measured for the reconstruction in a similar fashion to Devlin and Chalmers work.
- Moullou et al. (2012) investigated lighting conditions in antiquity houses to assess the photometric basis of studies focusing on ancient lighting. The authors demonstrate an experimental approach to learning about the photometric properties of ancient lamps placed in their appropriate positions. The authors deduced that appropriate positioning of light sources in ancient Greek houses would allow for enough light to read, even in nocturnal conditions.

Another technique that allows acquisition of dynamic range of light available in the real-world is called High Dynamic Range (HDR) Imaging (Debevec and Malik 1997). Once acquired, this light data (now captured at a higher precision) can be used to re-light or study heritage and their illumination based on real-world data capture (Hawkins et al. 2001; Debevec 2005; Happa et al. 2010a).

2.2.3 Modelling Light

When applying graphics to heritage, parameters of all scene objects (including light sources) carry some semantic meaning in their historical interpretation. The key challenge to using and studying light for historical study is that we fundamentally care about correctness in the simulation and reproduction of light (whereas in many other fields if it looks *"believable"* to most observers then it is satisfactory). For instance, the definition and placements of a light source carry no contextual meaning for general-purpose rendering (i.e., only the fact that the light source is defined properly matters, not necessarily its position). However, in studying history, the placement, its ingredients matter for historical interpretations.

Light is commonly modelled as a geometric object that emits colour with an intensity. The metrics used to express intensity and perceived colours and light are taken from the physical sciences, in particular *Radiometry*: the field that studies measurement of electromagnetic radiation, including visible light and *Photometry*: the field that studies measurement of electromagnetic radiation in terms of perceived brightness by the human eye (McCluney 2014). Before we can represent light sources in virtual environments, we are required to measure them in the real-world to better understand how the correct spectral radiance, or colour and power of light can be added to our virtual models of light. Light sources in virtual scenes can take any geometric shape. Common ways to represent light shapes follow below:

- **Ambient Light**: An ambient light source evenly illuminates the scene in all directions from all directions. This is typically done by simply multiplying all parts the scene with a constant value. This is not an accurate method to illuminate a virtual scene, but is often used in real-time virtual environments (such as video games) where performance of the lighting computation matters more than the correctness of the output. Its intent is to simulate background illumination that does not appear to be emitted from any particular source.
- **Point Light**: A point light source is a light source definite at a position in space that illuminates in all directions, often used to represent a light bulb. This approach is also not physically correct, but provides a good approximation to localised lighting.
- **Spotlight**: A spotlight is a projection of light (often as an inner and outer cone), where the inner cone has more intensity than the outer cone. This is the type of lighting which is commonly used on theatre stages.
- **Directional Light**: A directional light source illuminates the whole scene from a given direction. It is often used to represent distant light sources such as the sun. It is often modelled as not attenuating with distance.
- **Area Light**: An areas light source is a surface area that emits light. This is typically defined as a piece of geometry, such as a square. Multiple area light sources can be combined to form more complex light source objects.
- **Infinite Area Light**: An infinite area light source is a representation of the far distant scene, i.e. the backdrop of any scene whose geometry or materials do not affect the rest of the scene. This is often referred to as an environment map (a photograph surrounding the local scene). The technique used to light a scene from an environment map is often referred to as Image-Based Lighting (IBL) (Debevec 1998).

2.3   Rendering and Light

Once the scene has been modelled, we need to simulate how the light interacts with the scene to draw the pixels that form an image. This achieved by the rendering equations (Kajiya 1986). Here, the transport intensity of light, from one surface point to another, is defined as the sum of the emitted light and the total light intensity which is scattered in a direction from all other surface points. In heritage research that focus on correctness of images, we require physically-based rendering methods. Most of these can be categorised as being based on one of two techniques: Rasterisation or Ray Tracing (Akenine-Möller 2018; Pharr et al. 2016).

2.3.1   Rasterisation

Typically, rasterisation is used to achieve believable, real-time (more than 24 frames generated per second) rendering. However, many of rasterisation-related methods do not reliably produce predictive results (simulation satisfactory for scientific inquiry). Rasterisation renders images by projecting polygonal-based geometric primitives (often triangles) to the image (that viewers see) using a series of transformations. Rasterisation is the most popular rendering techniques used today due to its widespread support on modern dedicated graphics hardware and real-time performances. Modern computer graphics APIs such as OpenGL (Khronos Group 2019) and DirectX (Blythe 2006) provide functionalities for programmers to straightforwardly write simple real-time analytical light models using rasterisation (called shader), in which light on a surface is the sum of all its reflectance properties. While the use of shaders provides useful ways to approximate lighting to give believable results, they do not necessarily incorporate highly accurate physically-based lighting. In these cases, the shading of surfaces is simply calculated as sum of different terms, and then added to make up the final output of the appearance of an object surface. Simplified, this can be written as:

Shading of a point = ambient light + diffuse light + specular light + emission

Each term expresses the contribution of light onto the objects of the scene. The ambient term is (almost always) a constant value that represents some idea of background (ambient) lighting in the scene. The diffuse term describes how light is reflected in all directions equally. While completely diffuse reflections do not happen in reality, it is a straightforward approximation of representing matte objects such as building bricks, sand or carpets. The specular term describes how shiny a surface point should be. In rare cases, in which a material emits light, an "emit" term can be added.

2.3.2 Ray Tracing

Ray tracing methods (Whitted 1979) tend to focus on delivering physically accurate images, but often at increased computational costs to ensure images are indeed accurate. Ray tracing based approaches are often implemented for offline rendering (requiring more than one second to compute an image), and are used to synthesise images of highest possible fidelity.

Ray tracing methods for rendering was originally based on a ray casting method (see Appel 1968), which check whether a ray intersects a surface or not. Ray tracing image synthesis is normally done in the reverse order of how our eyes operate. Rays are shot from the eye and an image is formed based on the information accumulated from the various sample rays shot into the scene (Shirley and Morley 2008).

Ray tracing is made up of three main components: ray generation, ray intersection and shading. First, a ray is generated for each stage of the path the light has to take. Second, using a point-to-surface intersection test (ray casting), it is possible to determine the closest intersection point visible from a point in a direction. Third, through shading, the specific ray tracing algorithm implemented determines pixel colour based on information from the surface point in the prior intersection test (Fig. 2.2).

The original ray tracing approach simulates light propagation by recursively tracing rays into the virtual scene (i.e. keep sending rays to traverse the scene over and over again). At each intersection, a shadow ray is shot towards the light (shortest distance) to determine whether the intersection point is in shadow or not, see Fig. 2.2. Recursion of all steps in the scene allows for computation of light propagation. These steps are repeated and results are accumulated, and then averaged for as long as required to generate a satisfactory image. Path tracing is a well-known extension

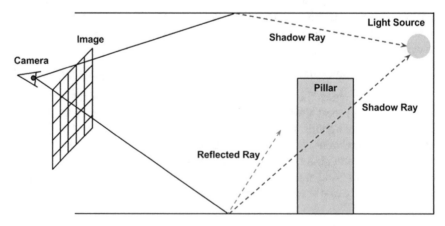

Fig. 2.2 Classical ray tracing example. Rays are shot into the scene and recursively traversed back to the light source. At each intersection point a shadow raw is cast to check if any objects exist between the ray-surface intersection and a light source

to ray tracing that is used for physically-based simulation by evaluating light-surface interactions as well. It was developed by Kajiya (1986), and is today often used as a benchmark to assess performance of new techniques.

2.4 High Dynamic Range Imaging

Visual documentation enables scholars to refer to particular sections or entire objects in greater detail than words can express. When a person is viewing a site not in-situ (e.g. in front of a computer monitor), key surface and subsurface information may be clipped if there is a high range of light; anything from 500:1 (standard non-LED LCD display today) to 1000:1 (LED-LCDs) to 200,000:1 (High Dynamic Range displays) and above. This *contrast ratio* expresses the relative range of the brightest colour (white) to that of the darkest colour (black) that the image or monitor is capable of producing.

Significantly wider ranges of light exist in the real world. Humans are capable of seeing a large range of light intensities ranging from daylight levels of around $10^8 \, cd/m^2$ to night light conditions of approximately $10^{-6} cd/m^2$. On the other hand, today we require capturing and displaying larger dynamic range then the one offered previously, i.e., wide colour gamut REC.2020 (Zhu et al. 2015), HDR+ 10-bit support for TV technology, compression technology for HDR content as JPEG XT (Artusi et al. 2016; Richter et al. 2016). However, still the captured and visualized bit-depth is often not enough for conveying the realistic experience of a human watching the same cultural artefacts in the real-world environment. In order to fully achieve this goal we need to capture this large dynamic range, referred to as HDR of *luminance*,[1] manipulate and visualize it for increasing the reproduction of level of realism in any image output. We can identify as main advantage of HDR imaging in the context of heritage documentation that the scene details, which may have relevance for its interpretation, can be seen in areas that are otherwise obfuscated by darkness, or clipped away in too bright sections. The added information may aid scholars extrapolate how illumination affects a building or object today, and help them discuss how illumination may have been different in the past.

Subtle phenomena such as slow-moving phenomena, such as participating media (e.g. sunbeams) may also be recorded using HDR still photography, as shown in Fig. 2.3. On the other hand, complex dynamic scenes, in which objects are moving fast needs to be recorded using HDR video acquisition solutions.

---

[1]The intensity of light emitted from a surface per unit area in a given direction.

Fig. 2.3 Participating media (sun beams) at the Red Monastery in Egypt. The figure shows multiple exposures, from low to high exposure. We see that on lower exposures, the camera does not capture the sunbeams. HDR imaging captures all these ranges and assemble them into a single photograph for future examination

2.4.1 Digital Camera Content Acquisition

In addition to a traditional photographic record, still images through digital photography can be edited to create texture maps for virtual 3D models. The advent of digital photography has pushed cameras to reach greater bit-depth and image resolutions. Today, high-quality digital cameras are available with sensors capable of capturing 12–16 bits per colour channel. However, lower-quality digital cameras exist that are equipped with less expensive, lower-performing hardware with precision limited to 10 bits or even lower. Moreover, in many application there is the need to acquire much large dynamic range then the one covered by 12–16 bits sensors.

In all these situations, only a small subset of the available dynamic range of the scene can be captured, resulting in overexposed and underexposed areas of the acquired image. To overcome this limitation, one can capture different portions of the dynamic range of the scene by varying the exposure time (multi-exposure) (Artusi et al. 2016, 2017). Starting from these images, we can reconstruct the HDR content of the originals scene, by first aligning each image to each other (registering), then estimating their camera response function, e.g., mapping input luminance values received by the camera sensor to pixel values. This is useful, because it will allows to estimate the physical quantities of the scene from the acquired images. The final step is to weight the contribution of each image at a given position to the final HDR sample value (Artusi et al. 2016, 2017). A common concern with the multi-exposure method is the misalignment of the images, either due to movements in the scene or by the camera itself (Orozco et al. 2016). Merging such images, without further processing, results in ghosting artefacts in the HDR output.

Video cameras allow for documentation of real-world objects from consecutive frames of images, and a minimum of 24 Frames-Per-Second (FPS) is necessary for the human eye to seamlessly interpret the images as natural motion. Video and single-image content both have advantages and disadvantages. Still photography allows for more control over the camera and its settings. Furthermore, planning needs to be an important part of the data acquisition pipeline. Most concepts from single image photography translate directly to video. The primary difference is the addition of temporal data. Motion blur due to fast motion can be interpreted correctly by the human eye in video. Temporal data makes video recording helpful in delivering a sense of spatial awareness of the environment, more than single photograph often can provide, especially if the camera moves in physical space (Happa et al. 2010a).

The addition of HDR video content is useful in historical study for several reasons. Firstly, the extended light range collected is valuable in the pursuit of understanding and recreating the past through experimental archaeology. Secondly, it allows for temporal data acquisition of light. This enables documentation and investigation of movable light sources in areas in deep shadow or intense sunlight, colour properties of artificial light sources as well as the interplay of light through participating media. This accurate data can be reused for virtual archaeology applications. Thirdly, video is a significantly faster approach to record data compared to traditional photography. Simplifying the data acquisition pipeline enables more measurements or video segments to be captured, in addition to reducing the potential of human error in data collection (Happa et al. 2010a).

2.4.2 HDR Content Visualization

The native visualization of HDR content is limited by the capabilities of the display device. Despite the fact that the current technology on the market can guarantee high contrast ratio, this is achieved by lowering the black level. However, the peak luminance remains limited, restricting the available dynamic range for bright images (Artusi et al. 2017). Even with enhanced contrast, many display panels offer only a limited precision of 8 or, at most, 10-bits per colour channel, and not all of them support a wide colour gamut.

Tone mapping is a process that compresses the dynamic range of an input signal to that available by the display while keeping the visualization convincing. Tone mappers can be roughly classified into global and local approaches. The former applies the same tone curve on all the image pixels. The latter takes the spatial position and its surrounding into account; with that, local operators can take advantage of known effects of the HVS such as local eye adaptation to the luminance. While the former is simple and efficient, it may fail to reproduce details in high contrast image regions. Although the latter can reproduce details in such regions better, it often comes at the cost of increased complexity and computational time; it may also introduce artefacts around edges (Artusi et al. 2017).

Typically tone mapping is focusing on one dimension, e.g., luminance, while colour is mainly mapped keeping the original colour ratio of the input HDR image. This generates two major drawbacks. First, appearance effects are often ignored, leading to images which may appear poorly or too saturated. Second, such a tone mapper may not guarantee that all the sample values of the tone mapped image are within the available colour gamut of the target display. Even though the output luminance may be reproducible by the display, the chrominance may fall out of the available gamut, resulting in clipping of extreme colours. This clipping may again introduce hue shifts. To improve the saturation of the tone mapped image, a simple solution is to introduce an adjustable parameter that allows the overall saturation of the tone mapped image to be controlled (Artusi et al. 2016).

To reduce hue and lightness shifts, one may work with perceptual uniform colour space to separate the colour appearance parameters such as saturation from hue and lightness. This will allow modifying the saturation of the tone mapped image to match the saturation of the input HDR image while hue and lightness of the tone mapped image will remain untouched (Artusi et al. 2018). Other approaches exploit the use of colour appearance models and extend the concept of gamut mapping to the HDR content (Sikudová et al. 2015). The former approach guarantees the matching of the colour appearance attributes between the input HDR and the tone mapped images. The latter ensures that all the tone mapped pixels are within the colour gamut of the display, minimising the hue and luminance distortion.

2.4.3 Image-Based Lighting (IBL)

The emergence of HDR has made it possible to extend the use of capturing HDR photographs to capture *radiance maps*, i.e. use HDR photographs as light sources for a scene. Such images are referred to as Light Probes or Environment Maps and their application is often referred to as Image-Based Lighting (IBL) (Debevec 1998). Instead of using synthetic light sources, it is possible to use sampled light values from HDR images mapped onto a sphere that acts as a sky dome to represent the distant illumination. This is useful in order to relight synthetic objects that occupy the same location as the light probe. There are several methods of capturing these HDR environment maps. Debevec (1998) details the use of a mirrored sphere. Stumpfel et al. (2004) discuss the capturing process of HDR hemispherical image of the sun and sky by using an SLR camera with a 180° fish-eye lens. In the commercial field, a few companies provide HDR cameras based on automatic multiple exposure capturing. The two main cameras are Spheron HDR VR camera (Spheron 2007) and Panoscan MK-3 (Panoscan 2002). For example, the Spheron HDR VR can capture up to 26 f-stops of dynamic range at 50 Megapixels resolution in 30 min (depending on illumination conditions). Light probe images can be represented in several formats, i.e., mirrored sphere format (Debevec 1998), the vertical cross cube format (Debevec 2006) and the latitude-longitude panoramic representation (Blinn and Newell 1976; Debevec 2006). The conversion between these different representations are easily done by using existing software such as HDRShop (2020).

The primary concern regarding lighting using light probe images is that a single light probe image is only valid for one point in space. Incident Light Fields allows for capture and rendering of synthetic objects with spatially varying illumination, see Unger (2009). In virtual archaeology, there are several applications of IBL.

It is possible to relight objects with illumination that exists within the site. If the aim is to estimate a light probe image that illuminates objects as they appeared in the past, it is necessary to recreate the distant scene to appear as it once did. This includes switching off modern light sources, remove recent additions to the scene and allow light to be projected in the scene as it would have in the past. Hawkins et al. (2001) extend the application of IBL by presenting a photometry-based approach to digitally document heritage artefacts. Each artefact is represented in terms of how it transforms light into images, this is also known as its Reflectance Field. The technique is data intensive and requires a light stage (Debevec et al. 2000) and thousands of photographs of the artefact.

2.5 Case Study: Panagia Angeloktisti

Panagia Angeloktisti (*"Our Lady Built by the Angels"* in Greek) is a Byzantine church located in Cyprus. Its origin can be traced back to the sixth century, erected on the ruins of a three-aisled, wooden roofed early Christian basilica (Foulias 2004), similar to the other churches in Cyprus (Stewart 2010). Its modern day appearance however, pertains largely from its twelfth century iteration. It has undergone many changes throughout history, most noticeably today are:

- A vaulted chapel from the twelfth century added on the north side of the church (now also containing wall-paintings from the fifteenth and sixteenth century).
- A Latin (Gothic) chapel added in 1302 on the south side of the church.
- Throughout the church's history a variety of wall paintings have been added and removed within its space.
- The removal of wall segments in the northern section, including a small tower.
- A modern Gothic-inspired bell tower that was added in the early 1900s only to be removed in 1955 as it was deemed inappropriate based on the history of the rest of the building, by the Antiquities Department of Cyprus. The interior has undergone a variety of changes related to additions of paintings and the placement of interior objects (Foulias 2004).

The church is still in use today. Tourists and visitors frequently enter the building to admire or pray inside the church. Few archaeological drawings of the church (using modern, high precision archaeological tools) exist today. Simple archaeological sketches were made available by Sotiriou (1935) and Foulias (2004), increasing the need for documentation and preservation.

To measure and model the physical wall geometry, a laser distance meter was used to acquire the dimensions for the 3D reconstruction stage of the project. This approach was chosen to minimise disrupting the everyday events at the church. Measurement tape was used for more accessible objects such as icons, chairs and ornaments found inside the church. Rulers and measurement tape were added to the photographs to allow distances to be documented. Altogether, data capture sessions lasted for seven days over the span of two-site visits (Happa et al. 2009).

All measurements were carefully mapped to digitised sketches and drawings of the church. Photographs were taken for texture mapping purposes, as well as for visual references during modelling the geometry of the scene, particularly with such few architectural drawings available. In total, a collection of approximately 10,000 images of the church were taken. They also aided in understanding how light changes in the interior of the church over the course of a day. The church's opening times were from 9am to 4pm however, which prevented interior data capture during sunrise and sunset.

All electrical light sources were switched off during data collection and candles were extinguished. Photographs were taken carefully avoiding shadows, specular highlights, caustics and colour bleeding using flash and non-flash photography, and a colour calibration chart to ensure appropriate texture maps could be taken. Large pieces of white cloth were used, where appropriate, to diffuse light surrounding icons that were in both shadow and light.

Two types of camera equipment were used for acquiring textures and HDR photographs; conventional digital cameras and a SpheroCam HDR (Spheron 2007) to capture outdoor environment maps. Due to inaccessibility to the roof of the church and no tall buildings in the nearby area all environment maps were acquired at approximately ten metres distance from the main southern entrance. Here, there was a significant enough distance to other large objects, yet it still physically close to the church, enabling us to capture the majority of the sky for relighting purposes during image acquisition. This approach is similar to Debevec's (Debevec 2005) IBL data capture of the Parthenon.

The church was manually reconstructed using a 3D object-modelling tool (Maya) after its modern-day appearance. The interior and exterior church were completed separately, and merged after completion of both versions. This was done as a means to ensure the model was proportional to scale to the rest of the scene. By combining two separate models into one allowed for erroneous data to be corrected in the merging stage. The main interior walls of the church (including arcs, pillars, floor, ceiling and semi-dome) were modelled first based on measurements and sketches. All metal materials were approximated using a Ward BRDF (Ward et al. 1992), while all matte materials were estimated to be diffuse. All subsequent objects were then positioned and modelled in relation to the main walls, measurements and photographs. Figures 2.4, 2.5 and 2.6 show the final output of Panagia Angeloktisti, most of which used IBL. In total 24 outdoor environment maps were taken over the course of 14 h from sunrise to sunset. Path tracing (Kajiya 1986) was used to render the scene (Happa et al. 2009).

As sky model we have used the Preetham's model (Preetham et al. 1999) with the following parameters: Month: 6, Day: 18, Hour: 12:00, Latitude: 34.48'N, Longitude: 33.36'E, Standard Meridian: 0.261, Turbidity (for Preetham's model): 1.0. IBL examples of Panagia Angeloktisti used light captured midday on 18th June 2008.

2.5.1 Discussion

Delivering images that are predictive as opposed to only believable is still challenging however. Even comparing the images side-by-side in Fig. 2.6, it is possible to

Fig. 2.4 Path tracing inside and outside Panagia Angeloktisti

Fig. 2.5 Daylight simulation. Left: 06:30. Middle: noon. Right: 19:30

Fig. 2.6 Top left: photograph. Top middle: Image-based Lighting (captured from site). Top right: Preetham Sky Model (Preetham et al. 1999). Bottom left: CIE clear sky model. Bottom right: Directional light source mimicking the sun

distinguish between each image from a photograph. A number of several practical challenges need to be overcome, these include:

- Ensuring straightforward and correct measurement of real-world sites.
- Appropriate uses of rendering algorithms.
- Improving correctness of realistic heritage visualization more generally.

Ensuring straightforward and correct measurement of real-world sites is perhaps the greatest challenge, particularly as correct measurement requires physical access, i.e. not only observational access (such as a photograph) but ability and permission to measure objects in more detail (which may lead to physically touching the objects). As new techniques and technologies develop, it is more likely that computational photography techniques will play a greater role in the future of virtual archaeology, particularly as these methods do not require objects to be touched, only that they are well-lit.

The uses of any rendering algorithm is an essential part in developing appropriate representations of scenes. If interactivity is the primary focus and not necessarily highest accuracy in light computation, real-time rendering approaches can be used to generate believable renditions of the past. However, if correct light computation be of most value, more physically-based approaches should be used to accurately compute the propagation of light in the scene. While outdoor images were straightforward to compute taking seconds, each interior image of the church took several hours each to compute on a 24-node quad core cluster of computers (from 2008), which makes for impractical times to generate images, even if they are physically-based.

The computer graphics community understands the strengths and weaknesses of existing rendering techniques, but only recently has the use of computer graphics become more frequently used to research past lighting through rendering, a detailed review was recently published by Happa et al. (2010a). Historians and archaeologists on the other hand have the knowledge to better understand the contexts and uses of these sites, and can make better judgement about image outputs. To date, efficient interdisciplinary collaboration between technical and non-technical experts has also been described as difficult to achieve (Moullou et al. 2012), and is said to be a contributing factor to why research on modelling light in virtual archaeology has not come further than it already has.

Many virtual archaeology researchers depend on existing implementations often found in commercial solutions. More often than not, third-party solutions are used to model and simulate light. While many of these solutions provide useful graphical user interfaces to simplify the development process, almost all of these were made with general-purpose high-fidelity rendering in mind, and not physical or historical accuracy. More importantly, most of these interfaces were not intended for scientific or historical research, but to deliver believable renditions that have some basis in physically-based methods. Commercial rendering solutions are problematic from a research perspective. This is because it is difficult to reproduce results that these solutions output. For instance, if the developer changes their software, it might not be possible to recreate the same image in the future. It is also near impossible for researchers reproduce simulation results without complete access to the mesh and all scene configurations that the other researcher made use of.

Any simulations that are produced using such rendering systems are not reproducible, and therefore not appropriate from a scientific researcher's standpoint. Users of these systems are not made explicitly aware of these underlying issues, and this is a significant problem to the research community as a whole. In the case of Panagia Angeloktisti, three different renderers were used to synthetise images during the project, including Maya's own renderer Mental Ray, Radiance (Ward 1994) and a heavily modified version of PBRT (Pharr et al. 2016).

2.6 Conclusion

This chapter has discussed the uses of documenting and modelling light in for historical research, including the uses of physically-based light and historically-based light. We examined how incorporating historical knowledge into virtual scenes is crucial for historical research. Historically-based input must be based on evidence available today, including expert opinion. Another crucial aspect of any investigation using computer graphics is that all decisions and processes involved must be well-documented, otherwise the value of any simulation output will suffer greatly. A case study with the use of physically-based and historically-based simulation was also presented.

Computer graphics and the topic of high-fidelity rendering in particular has tackled the problem of simulating light for a number of decades, but only in the recent decade have we identified how important modelling light can aid archaeological research. This chapter serves as an overview to how history research uses physically-based light simulations to study the past. Using physically-based and historically-based simulations still has a long way to go before becoming common practice in a scientifically rigorous and reproducible manner.

Acknowledgements Our thanks go to the Byzantine Art Gallery for providing permission for us to visit Panagia Angeloktisti, to the caretakers of the church and Andreas Foulias for his help on information regarding the church. Our thanks also go to the American Research Center in Egypt (ARCE) and Dr. Elizabeth Bolman for permission to visit the Red Monastery and organising the stay at the monastery. One of the images collected was Fig. 2.3.
Dr. Artusi work has been partially funded through the European Union's Horizon 2020 research and innovation programme under grant agreement No 739578 and the Government of the Republic of Cyprus through the Directorate General for European Programmes, Coordination and Development. Finally, the authors would also like to thank Prof. Alan Chalmers for supervising Jassim Happa during his PhD, coordinating visits to Panagia Angeloktisi, and for partly funding the visits to the site.

References

Akenine-Möller Tomas, Haines E, Hoffman N, Pesce A, Hillaire S (2018) Real-time rendering. AK Peters/CRC Press

Appel A (1968) Some techniques for shading machine renderings of solids. In: Proceedings of the spring joint computer conference, pp 37–45

Artusi A, Banterle F, Aydın TO, Panozzo D, Sorkine-Hornung O (2016) Image content retargeting: maintaining color, tone, and spatial consistency. AK Peters/CRC Press

Artusi A, Mantiuk RK, Richter T, Korshunov P, Hanhart P, Ebrahimi T, Agostinelli M (2016) JPEG XT: A compression standard for HDR and WCG images [standards in a nutshell]. IEEE Signal Process Mag 33(2):118–124

Artusi A, Pouli T, Banterle F, Akyüz AO (2018) Automatic saturation correction for dynamic range management algorithms. Signal Process: Image Commun 63:100–112

Artusi A, Richter T, Ebrahimi T, Mantiuk RK (2017) High dynamic range imaging technology [lecture notes]. IEEE Signal Process Mag 34(5):165–172

Badler NI, Badler VR (1978) Interaction with a color computer graphics system for archaeological sites. SIGGRAPH 12:217–221

Blinn JF, Newell ME (1976) Texture and reflection in computer generated images. Commun ACM 19(10):542–547

Blythe D (2006) The Direct3D 10 system. ACM Transactions on Graphics (TOG) 724–734

Brown DH, Chalmers A, MacNamara A (1997) Light and the culture of colour in medieval pottery. In: Method and theory in historical archaeology, pre-printed papers of the medieval europe brugge 1997 conference, vol 10, pp 145–147

Cook RL, Torrance KE (1982) A reflectance model for computer graphics. ACM Transactions on Graphics (TOG) 1(1):7–24

Debevec P (1998) Rendering synthetic objects into real scenes: bridging traditional and image-based graphics with global illumination and high dynamic range photography. In: SIGGRAPH '98: proceedings of the 25th annual conference on computer graphics and interactive techniques

Debevec P (2005) Making the parthenon. In: 6th international symposium on virtual reality, archaeology, and cultural heritage in pisa, Italy

Debevec P (2006) High resolution light probe gallery. http://gl.ict.usc.edu/Data/HighResProbes/

Debevec P, Hawkins T, Tchou C, Duiker HP, Sarokin W, Sagar M (2000) Acquiring the reflectance field of a human face. In: Proceedings of the 27th annual conference on computer graphics and interactive techniques. ACM, pp 145–156

Debevec P, Malik J (1997) Recovering high dynamic range radiance maps from photographs. In: SIGGRAPH '97: Proceedings of the 24th annual conference on computer graphics and interactive techniques, pp 369–378

Devlin K (2004) Perceptual fidelity for digital image display. PhD thesis, University of Bristol

Devlin K, Chalmers A (2001) Realistic visualisation of the pompeii frescoes. In: AFRIGRAPH 01 Conference on computer graphics, virtual reality, visualisation and interaction in Africa, pp 43–48

Dorsey J, Rushmeier H, Sillion F (2008) Digital modeling of material appearance. Morgan Kaufmann

Earl G, Martinez K, Malzbender T (2010) Archaeological applications of polynomial texture mapping: analysis, conservation and representation. J Archaeol Sci 37(8):2040–2050

Foulias AM (2004) The Church of our Lady Angeloktisti at Kiti, Nicosia

Happa J, Artusi A, Dubla P, Bashford-Rogers T, Debattista K, Hulusić V, Chalmers A (2009) The virtual reconstruction and daylight illumination of the panagia angeloktisti. In: VAST

Happa J, Artusi A, Czanner S, Chalmers A (2010a) High dynamic range video for cultural heritage documentation and experimental archaeology. In: Proceedings of the 11th international conference on virtual reality, archaeology and cultural heritage. Eurographics Association, pp 17–24

Happa J, Mudge M, Debattista K, Artusi A, Gonçalves A, Chalmers A (2010b) Illuminating the past: state of the art. Virtual Rity 14(3):155–182

Happa J, Bashford-Rogers T, Wilkie A, Artusi A, Debattista K, Chalmers A (2012) Cultural heritage predictive rendering. In: Computer graphics forum, Wiley Online Library

Hawkins T, Cohen J, Debevec P (2001) A photometric approach to digitizing cultural artifacts. In: VAST 2001: symposium on virtual reality, archeology, and cultural heritage, pp 333–342

HDRShop (2020) Example software to research HDRI. http://gl.ict.usc.edu/HDRShop/

Kajiya J (1986) The rendering equation. In: SIGGRAPH '86 Conference on computer graphics and interactive techniques, pp 143–150

Khronos Group (2019) OpenGL official website. https://www.opengl.org/

Malzbender T, Gelb D, Wolters H (2001) Polynomial texture maps. In: ACM SIGGRAPH '01, pp 519–528

McCluney WR (2014) Introduction to radiometry and photometry. Artech House

Moullou D, Madias EN, Doulos L, Bouroussis CA, Topalis FV (2012) Lighting in antiquity. In: Kostic M (ed) Balkan Light 2012, Proceedings of the fifth conference, Belgrade, pp 3–6

Mudge M, Schroer C, Earl G, Martinez K, Pagi H, Toler-Franklin C, Rusinkiewicz S, Palma G, Wachowiak M, Ashey M, Mathews N, Noble T, Dellepiane M (2010) Principles and practices of robust, photography-based digital imaging techniques for museums. In: 11th VAST international symposium on virtual reality, archaeology and cultural heritage

Nicodemus FE, Richmond JC, Hsai JJ (1977) Geometric considerations and nomenclature for reflectance, vol 160. U.S. Department of commerce, National bureau of standards report, National Bureau of Standards Washington, DC

Orozco RR, Loscos C, Martin I, Artusi A (2016) Multiview HDR video sequence generation. In: High dynamic range video. Elsevier, pp 121–138

Panoscan (2002) Panoscan MK-3, Company website. http://www.panoscan.com/

Pharr M, Jakob W, Humphreys G (2016) Physically based rendering: from theory to implementation. Morgan Kaufmann

Preetham AJ, Shirley P, Smits B (1999) A practical analytic model for daylight. In: SIGGRAPH '99: proceedings of the 26th annual conference on computer graphics and interactive techniques, pp 91–100

Reilly P (1991) Towards a virtual archaeology. In: Computer applications and quantitative methods in archaeology, pp 133–140

Richter T, Artusi A, Ebrahimi T (2016) JPEG XT: a new family of JPEG backward-compatible standards. IEEE MultiMedia 23(3):80–88 July

Roussos I, Chalmers A (2003) High fidelity lighting of knossos. In: VAST '03: symposium on virtual reality, archaeology and intelligent cultural heritage

Rudolfova I, Sundstedt V (2004) High fidelity rendering of the interior of an egyptian temple. In: CESCG

Shirley P, Morley RK (2008) Realistic ray tracing. AK Peters, Ltd

Sikudová E, Pouli T, Artusi A, Akyüz AO, Banterle F, Mazlumoglu ZM, Reinhard E (2015) A gamut-mapping framework for color-accurate reproduction of HDR images. IEEE Comput Graph Appl 36(4):78–90

Sotiriou G (1935) The Byzantine monuments of cyprus

Spheron (2007) HDR spherical camera, company website. http://www.spheron.com/

Stewart CA (2010) The first vaulted churches in cyprus. J Soc Arch Hist

Stumpfel J, Tchou C, Jones A, Hawkins T, Wenger A, Debevec P (2004) Direct HDR capture of the sun and sky. In: Proceedings of the 3rd international conference on computer graphics, virtual reality, visualisation and interaction in Africa. ACM, pp 145–149

Sundstedt V, Chalmers A, Martinez P (2004) High fidelity reconstruction of the ancient egyptian temple of kalabsha. In: AFRIGRAPH '04: proceedings of the 3rd international conference on computer graphics, virtual reality, visualisation and interaction in Africa, pp 107–113

Unger J (2009) Incident light fields. PhD thesis, Linköping University

Ward GJ (1994) The radiance lighting simulation and rendering system. In: SIGGRAPH '94: proceedings of the 21st annual conference on computer graphics and interactive techniques, pp 459–472

Ward GJ et al (1992) Measuring and modeling anisotropic reflection. Comput Graph 26(2):265–272

Whitted T (1979) An improved illumination model for shaded display. In: SIGGRAPH 79 computer graphics, vol 3. ACM, p 14

Wyszecki G, Stiles WS (1982) Color science, vol 8. Wiley, New York

Zhu R, Luo Z, Chen H, Dong Y, Wu ST (2015) Realizing rec. 2020 color gamut with quantum dot displays. Opt Express 23(18):23680–23693

Chapter 3
High Dynamic Range in Cultural Heritage Applications

Demetris Marnerides, Vedad Hulusic and Kurt Debattista

Abstract High dynamic range (HDR) technology enables the capture, storage, transmission and display of real-world lighting at a high precision as opposed to traditional low dynamic range (LDR) imaging. One of HDR's main features is its ability to reproduce very bright and very dark areas simultaneously. Dynamic range describes the span between these extrema in the brightness scale. HDR research investigates the generation, capturing, processing, transmission, storage and reproduction of HDR content. Cultural heritage represents our legacy that must be passed on to future generations. As it is increasingly threatened with deterioration, destruction and disappearance, its documentation, conservation and presentation is of high importance. Given the real-world dynamic range and the limitations of conventional capture and display technology, HDR imaging represents an invaluable tool for accurate documentation, virtual reconstruction and visualisation of cultural heritage. HDR is used by academics, museums, and media to visualise the appearance of sites in various periods in time. Physically-based 3D virtual reconstructions are used for studying existing or ruined cultural heritage environments. This in turn enables archaeologists to interpret the past and deduce new historical knowledge. In this chapter we present the HDR pipeline, along with its use for cultural heritage preservation, recreation and presentation.

D. Marnerides (✉) · K. Debattista
University of Warwick, Warwick Manufacturing Group, Coventry, UK
e-mail: Demetris.Marnerides@warwick.ac.uk

K. Debattista
e-mail: k.debattista@warwick.ac.uk

V. Hulusic
Faculty of Science and Technology, Bournemouth University, Poole, UK
e-mail: vhulusic@bournemouth.ac.uk

© Springer Nature Switzerland AG 2020
F. Liarokapis et al. (eds.), *Visual Computing for Cultural Heritage*, Springer Series on Cultural Computing, https://doi.org/10.1007/978-3-030-37191-3_3

3.1 Introduction

As defined by the UNESCO, cultural heritage (CH) is "the legacy of physical artefacts and intangible attributes of a group or society that are inherited from past generations, maintained in the present and bestowed for the benefit of future generations" (Unesco 2019). Typically, CH is divided into tangible and intangible heritage. The former consists of historic objects, buildings, places, monuments and other artefacts with a significant value for preservation. Their significance can be related to archaeology, architecture, design, science or technology of a culture. Intangible heritage consists of practices, knowledge, customs, oral traditions, skills, oral epics and similar cultural identities. This work mainly deals with tangible CH, mainly considering 3D objects and sites.

The protection and preservation of CH is of immense importance and demonstrates the recognition of the necessity of the past and its related artefacts and stories (Tanselle et al. 1998). While the main way of conservation, preservation and display of tangible heritage is still physical, allowing observing, exploring, studying and appreciating the artefacts, it is exceedingly expensive to maintain and safeguard these invaluable items from being damaged by tourist, the light when displaying them, and other human factors, such as wars and negligence, or natural disasters. Another limitation of physical exhibition is the accessibility limitation as the original artefact can be exhibited at only one physical location. One solution to these problems could be to use technology for digital documentation and presentation of CH. The whole pipeline is summarised in Fig. 3.1.

After the identification of the artefact or the site based on research on its cultural and historic significance, the first step would be to either collect all relevant data in case of non-existing objects or documentation of existing artefacts or sites. Based on the collected and/or acquired data, the digital representation of the 3D object can be generated. 3D digital representation of the artefact or the site then has to be stored in appropriate format or number of them, suitable for further usage in the last stage of the pipeline. Finally, the object is presented through interactive or non-interactive media, considering several additional elements as displayed in the last stage of the pipeline in Fig. 3.1.

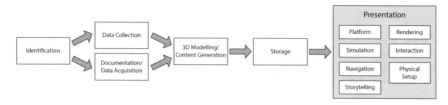

Fig. 3.1 3D virtual reconstruction pipeline

3.1.1   High-Fidelity in CH

For many years, computers and computer generated images have been used in archaeology for presentation, understanding and interpretation of ancient cultures. Computers are an integral part of every stage of the pipeline. However, the increase in hardware and software performance and decreased costs, do not inevitably lead to more accurate results. Therefore, in order to have truthful and reliable representations and virtual reconstructions, every step has to be undertaken carefully, including precise data acquisition, content generation, simulation of physical evidence from the site and presentation of the final artefact. One of the components that is often neglected or not given enough attention is the dynamic range of luminance in the original, real scene where the object or site is captured, and the virtual scene with a reconstructed artefact that is being displayed. Although, in some scenarios it might not make a significant effect on the representation, in others can lead to major shortcomings and eventually misguide the interpretation and understanding of the nature, purpose and appearance of the object or site.

3.2   High-Dynamic-Range

HDR imaging aims to capture, process and display the entire distribution of visible light of real or simulated scenes. Imaging has a long history of progress; it is suspected that the Shroud of Turin from the 13th century might be the first recorded photograph (Allen 1993). The 20th century saw an acceleration in the development of photography and imaging techniques, with advanced cameras, display monitors and the transitions to colour images and video.

3.2.1   Light and Luminance

Light is electromagnetic energy propagating in space as a wave and as discrete particles, photons. These waves/particles are associated with specific frequencies of oscillation, ν that correspond to specific wavelengths λ bound together with a constant, the speed of light in vacuum, c, such that $\lambda\nu = c$. A subset of all possible frequencies/wavelengths forms the visible part of the light spectrum from "violet" $\lambda \approx 400$ nm to "red" $\lambda \approx 700$ nm. Each photon is associated with an energy $E = h\nu$, where h is the Planck constant. While imaging in general deals with the whole spectrum of frequencies, some disciplines work with specific parts of the spectrum, for example astronomy uses radio imaging and certain areas in healthcare use X-ray imaging. HDR Imaging focuses on imaging of the visible spectrum.

To measure light distributions, two categories of quantities are considered, radiometric and photometric. Radiometric quantities measure light distributions with a

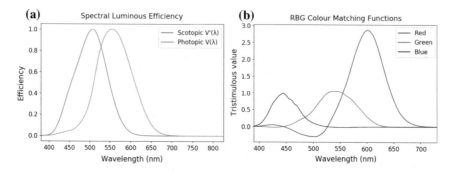

Fig. 3.2 **a** The photopic, $V(\lambda)$, and scotopic, $V'(\lambda)$, luminous efficiency functions. **b** The CIE RGB tristimulous colour matching functions

direct physical correspondence to the energy of the light, for example, radiant energy, Q_e, radiant flux, $\Phi_e = \partial_t Q_e$, and spectral flux, $\Phi_{e,\lambda} = \partial_\lambda \Phi_e$, which is radiant flux per wavelength. The subscript "e" is to denote these quantities as *energetic*.

An important radiometric quantity, radiance, L_e, measures the radiant flux, Φ_e emitted from a surface, A, through a solid angle, ω, along a specific direction, θ, relative to the surface normal and is defined as:

$$L_e = \frac{1}{\cos\theta} \frac{\partial^2 \Phi_e}{\partial A \partial \omega}. \tag{3.1}$$

Photometric quantities measure light power by taking into account the HVS and its response to different frequencies. These quantities are weighted versions of the radiometric quantities, for example, luminous energy, Q_v, luminous flux, $\Phi_v = \partial_t Q_v$, and spectral luminous flux (or power), $\Phi_{v,\lambda} = \partial_\lambda \Phi_v$, which is spectral flux per wavelength. Figure 3.2a shows the spectral luminous efficiency functions that are used to weigh the radiometric quantities. These functions correspond to the sensitivity of the HVS to particular frequencies in bright (photopic) and dark (scotopic) conditions.

Radiance as defined in Eq. 3.1 fully describes the light field distribution. However, a photometric quantity is preferred over a radiometric one in the case of imaging, since it is more representative of what the result looks like to the human observer. Luminance, L_v, is the photometric quantity that corresponds to radiance, weighing it according to a response function, typically the photopic luminosity function, $V(\lambda)$ from Fig. 3.2a and formally defined by the Commission internationale de l'éclairage (CIE) as:

$$L_v = k_m \int_0^\infty L_{e,\lambda} V(\lambda) \, d\lambda \tag{3.2}$$

where $L_{e,\lambda} = \partial_\lambda L_e$ is the spectral radiance and $k_m = 683.002 \, \text{lmW}^{-1}$ is the luminous efficacy of a 555 nm (ideal) source. Luminous efficacy measures how well a light source produces visible light. Luminance is measured in candelas per square meter

$(cd\,m^{-2})$. In HDR imaging, the main quantity of interest used is luminance and is denoted as L for ease of notation.

3.2.2 Colour

The HVS has two types of receptors, *cones*, which are sensitive to relatively high luminance levels (photopic vision: 10^{-2}–$10^{8}\,cd\,m^{-2}$), and *rods*, which are sensitive to lower luminance levels (scotopic vision: 10^{-6}–$10\,cd\,m^{-2}$) (Banterle et al. 2017). While rods are more abundant (10–20 times more), they are of only one type and thus can only produce images of one colour tone, interpreted as levels of grey by the human brain. This is why colour cannot be perceived in dark scenarios.

Cones are of three different types, each responding to different parts of the visible spectrum (with overlap). The combination of these three different signals is interpreted in the brain and perceived as colour. The CIE has defined the RGB colour-matching functions, $r(\bar{\lambda})$, $g(\bar{\lambda})$, $b(\bar{\lambda})$, based on the colour matching experiments of Wright and Guild, as shown in Fig. 3.2b.

From these functions, given a spectral power distribution, $S_{e,\lambda}(\lambda)$, the CIE RGB *colour space* can be calculated as follows:

$$(R, G, B) = \int_{380}^{830} I(\lambda)\,(r(\lambda), g(\lambda), b(\lambda))\,d\lambda \qquad (3.3)$$

Another important colour space is the CIE XYZ colour space which was defined using a different set of colour-matching curves such that the Y component matches the luminance of the pixel. Many other colour spaces, e.g. Adobe-RGB and sRGB (Reinhard et al. 2008), are based on or derived from the CIE XYZ colour space, which plays a central role in colour space transformations. The use of colour spaces is multifold, since they not only need to describe the light information, but they also, in many cases, need to correspond to other properties, for example display capabilities, hence the abundance of colour space standards. Most colour spaces can be mapped back to CIE XYZ and this is the main way that the luminance of an image can be computed.

3.2.3 Contrast and Dynamic Range

When describing a scene, be it real world, virtual or in an image, global or local differences in luminance can be expressed using contrast ratios. While these can be defined in multiple ways (Banterle et al. 2017), the most commonly used definitions are the direct ratio, C_r, Weber contrast, C_W, and Michelson contrast, C_M:

$$C_r = \frac{L_{max}}{L_{min}}, \quad C_W = \frac{L_{max} - L_{min}}{L_{min}}, \quad C_M = \frac{L_{max} - L_{min}}{L_{max} + L_{min}}. \qquad (3.4)$$

While contrast measures the relative intensity between the maximum and minimum luminance values, *dynamic range* can have slightly different meaning depending on the context. For example, in a real world scene with a (practically) continuous luminance distribution, the dynamic range of the scene is synonymous with the contrast ratio. It describes the extent of the luminance range. However, when the same scene is captured by a camera sensor, due to the imperfections and noise in the capturing process, it is more useful to describe the dynamic range of the captured content using the Peak Signal to Noise Ratio (PSNR):

$$\text{PSNR}_{capture} = 20 \log_{10} \left(\frac{L_{max}}{\sigma_{noise}} \right). \qquad (3.5)$$

where σ_{noise} is the standard deviation of the noise and L_{max} is the maximum captured luminance.

The dynamic range of a digitally stored image can be thought of as a measure of the global contrast ratio, in combination with the light information/entropy of the contents of the image, or alternatively, the minimum number of "grey" levels needed to describe that image. The more information in the scene, the more bits are required to encode it digitally.

3.3 High Dynamic Range Pipeline

There are multiple stages involved in the lifetime of an image. The first stage is the generation of the image content and its capture, followed by the storage or transmission of the captured scenes. The stored (or transmitted content) is then processed for display. Figure 3.3 shows an overview of this process. The rest of this section discusses these stages in more detail.

3.3.1 Capture

The two main types of content originate from real world scenes that are captured using camera sensors, or from virtual scenes captured by rendering, for example Path Tracing. While rendering can in theory be performed with arbitrary dynamic range and precision, capturing real world scenes with a camera is limited by the dynamic range and sensitivity of the camera sensor.

Camera sensor cells can only receive a certain amount of light before becoming saturated. This, combined with the acceptable noise level of the sensor signal, defines the maximum dynamic range the sensor can capture and can be described in terms of

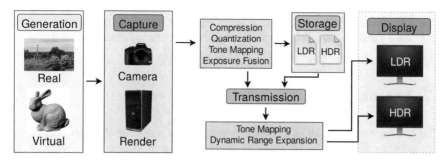

Fig. 3.3 The HDR pipeline, from generation to display. The capture, storage and display stages also have their own individual processes which change the generated information, for example Camera Response Functions (CRFs) and gamma encoding

the PSNR value from Eq. 3.5. If the sensor is exposed to incoming radiation, eventually all pixels will become saturated. The *exposure time* is adjusted to minimise the saturated cells. However, with low exposure times, dark parts of the scene might not get enough exposure time and thus become indistinguishable from sensor noise and are interpreted as black pixels. This sensor limitation means that it is in many cases impossible to capture the whole dynamic range of a scene with a single exposure.

The most popular way of capturing HDR content using current sensor technology is to take multiple exposures with varying exposure times and then combine them to form a single image (Reinhard et al. 2010), a process referred to as *exposure bracketing* followed by *exposure fusion*. Given N different exposures, I, with exposure times T, then the resulting image $\hat{I}$ can be computed using:

$$\hat{I} = \frac{1}{\sum_{i=1}^{N} w(I_i)} \sum_{i=1}^{N} \frac{1}{T_i} w(I_i) I_i \tag{3.6}$$

where w is a weighing function, providing higher weights for well-exposed mid-range values and less weight for noisy black-level and saturated pixel values. Equation 3.6 assumes that the camera responses are linear, which in most cases are not, and the non-linear Camera Response Function (CRF), f_{CRF}, must be taken into account, such that:

$$\hat{I} = \frac{1}{\sum_{i=1}^{N} w(I_i)} \sum_{i=1}^{N} \frac{1}{T_i} w(I_i) f_{\mathrm{CRF}}^{-1}(I_i). \tag{3.7}$$

Another assumption is the spatial correspondence of the pixels between exposures, which is often not true, since the camera might not be very stable during or between captures, or the scene might change due to motion. Misalignment due to camera shaking can be alleviated by aligning the images before merging (Ward 2003). Motion in the scene causes ghosting artefacts, which can be addressed using multiple methods (Tursun et al. 2015), for example patch matching, weighted filtering of intensity transfer functions, or weighted non-parametric models.

3.3.2 Storage

Captured or generated HDR images are usually stored in a digital form using floating point numbers. They are stored as linear RGB (not gamma corrected) but the luminance values are usually relative and do not correspond to the real world luminance values. One of the first formats introduced for storing HDR content was the Ward RGBE format (Ward 1991) (.hdr or .rad extension) which was initially used to store radiance values from rendered scenes. It uses 8 bits per channel, but introduces a fourth channel E for the exponent of the RGB values (which are assumed to be close, hence they share an exponent), effectively using 32 bits instead of 24 for each pixel. The format can also use the XYZE encoding. The compression used is run-length encoding, which uses a count-value strategy to represent repeated consecutive values (Reinhard et al. 2010).

A more recent HDR image format, the OpenEXR (.exr extension - EXtended Range), developed by Industrial Light & Magic (ILM), uses 16 bit half-float precision for each of the three channels but also supports 32 and 24 bit per channel encodings. This results in larger file sizes than the .hdr format but can represent content much more accurately. The EXR format uses the PIZ lossless wavelet compression (Reinhard et al. 2010). The JPEG-HDR encoding uses a tone mapped version of the original, along with a grey-scale ratio image to lossy compress the HDR image.

3.3.3 Display

The final stage of the HDR pipeline is the display of the captured or stored content. For the display of any type of content, be it LDR or HDR, there needs to be some adaptation, particularly of the dynamic range and contrast, such that an accurate and perceptually preferred viewing experience is achieved.

LDR Displays

LDR Content is linearised (if it was gamma encoded) and its colour space is adapted according to the display specifications. Its range is matched to that of the display, so there is no adaptation in terms of contrast or dynamic range. A gamma correction curve is applied, again depending on the specifications. Most displays are created with a specific colour space as a specification and vice versa. *HDR Content* needs to be altered to fit the dynamic range of the display. This requires for information to be removed from the HDR image. There are multiple ways to remove this information, each one resulting in a different viewing experience. These methods are called Tone Mapping Operators (TMOs) and are discussed in more detail in Sect. 3.4.

HDR Displays

LDR Content must be mapped to match the dynamic range of the screen via some EO. These are introduced and discussed in more detail in Sect. 3.5. *HDR Content* needs to have its dynamic range adapted to match that of the display, depending on the level of mismatch. This case is essentially the same as that of HDR content being displayed on an LDR display (just one with a wider range), since no display can match the (theoretical) real world lighting that HDR content can encode.

3.4   Tone Mapping

Tone mapping is the process of reducing the dynamic range of an image for display. Dynamic range reduction is performed by compressing, clipping or quantising the range or most commonly via a combination of the three. Multiple TMOs have been introduced, each one focusing on different aspects of the problem, but in general, these operators can be categorised as either global or local (Banterle et al. 2017). Global operators perform an operation on all pixels in the same fashion, whereas local operators adjust the operation given local context of the specific pixel neighbourhood. Local operators may depend on local properties, for example average contrast, or frequency aspects, for example if an edge exists (detail) or not.

There are multiple properties to consider when tone mapping an image, for example how global and local contrast is preserved, the average image brightness, as well as the tonal contrast between different colours. In the case of 8-bit precision, which is the most commonly used LDR format, the operation is defined as follows:

$$I_{\text{TM}} = f_{\text{TM}}(I_{\text{HDR}}), \text{ where } f_{\text{TM}} : \mathbb{R}^+ \to [0, 255] \tag{3.8}$$

where I_{HDR} is the HDR content, I_{TM} is the resulting tone mapped image and f_{TM} is the TMO. In most algorithms the image luminance, L_{HDR}, is first computed by taking the Y channel from the CIE XYZ colour space. The tone mapped single channel luminance, L_{LDR}, of the result is then computed, which is used to scale all three RGB input channels:

$$(R, G, B)_{\text{TM}} = \frac{L_{\text{LDR}}}{L_{\text{HDR}}^s} (R, G, B)_{\text{HDR}}^s \tag{3.9}$$

where $s \in (0, 1]$ is a factor affecting colour saturation. For display, or storage of the result, a gamma encoding is applied and the tone mapped image is quantised and clipped at the two ends $(0, 255)$.

$$I_{\text{LDR}} = \lfloor \text{clamp}(I_{\text{TM}}, 0, 255)^{\gamma} \rfloor \tag{3.10}$$

The simplest way to tone map is to use a linear function. This is a global operation and is equivalent to taking a single exposure from the HDR image, as a camera would from a real scene (assuming a linear CRF):

$$L_{\text{TM}} = e L_{\text{HDR}} \tag{3.11}$$

where the factor e adjusts the exposure level. When the number of well exposed (non clipped) pixels is maximised, then e is called automatic exposure. Debattista et al. (2015) propose the selection of e such that the information loss due to the clipping and quantisation of the HDR histogram is minimised, in which case e is termed the optimal exposure.

Drago et al. (2003) introduce a global adaptive logarithmic function which adjusts luminance in logarithmic space with the logarithm base adapted according to the luminance of the given pixel. Logarithmic spaces better correspond to the HVS sensitivity to brightness. The display adaptive operator by Mantiuk et al. (2008), takes into account the specific characteristics of the target display (e.g. LCD, OLED or e-paper) such that visible contrast distortions are minimised. An that takes into account the HVS is introduced by Reinhard and Devlin (2005), inspired by photoreceptor physiology. The resulting LDR image is computed by modelling the adaptation of cones to different levels of luminance.

Urbano et al. (2010) evaluate TMOs when applied for small screen devices, for example mobile phones. The psychophysical experiments performed show that the choice of TMO depends on the display type. They considered Liquid Crystal (LCD), Cathode Ray Tube (CRT) and Seven-Segment Displays (SSD). The different characteristics of the display type required different adjustment to the TMOs in order to get optimal performance.

HDR video is more difficult to tone map since there is an additional time correlation in effect. Tone mapping video sequences using a simple frame by frame approach frequently exhibit artefacts, for example brightness flickering (Boitard et al. 2014). Boitard et al. (2012) propose a post-processing step that also addresses object incoherency and brightness incoherency besides temporal flickering. Eilertsen et al. (2017) provide a comprehensive comparative review of video TMOs.

Tone mapping is a forward problem, whose solution varies depending on the constraints of the user, for example HVS response or display properties. Reconstructing HDR signals from LDR is the inverse version of this problem is discussed in the next section.

3.5 Dynamic Range Expansion

Expansion Operators (EOs), also known as inverse or reverse tone mapping operators, attempt to generate HDR content from LDR content. EOs can generally be expressed as:

$$\tilde{I}_{\mathrm{HDR}} = f_{\mathrm{EO}}(I_{\mathrm{LDR}}), \text{ where } f_{\mathrm{EO}} : [0, 255] \rightarrow \mathbb{R}^+ \tag{3.12}$$

where $\tilde{I}_{\mathrm{HDR}}$ is the expanded HDR content and f_{EO} is the EO. In this context, dynamic range expansion could be considered an ill-posed problem since there is no unique solution. The missing information that needs to be recovered could have been one of many valid forms, for example a single exposure image with over-exposed sky could have had clouds or clear blue skies.

A variety of methods have emerged that attempt to tackle the issue. Most non-learning based EOs follow some, or all of five steps (Banterle et al. 2017). First, the LDR image is linearised, via the removal of gamma correction and the application of inverse CRFs. Then the range of well-exposed, non-saturated areas is expanded via some function, locally or globally, depending on the algorithm. The expansion is computed on the linearised single-channel luminance, which is ultimately used to scale all three channels. At this point, as an additional step, some methods attempt to reconstruct badly-exposed areas as well. The final two steps attempt to reduce artefacts due to quantisation or compression, and apply colour-corrective algorithms that might be necessary due to partial saturation of one of the three RGB channels.

Global methods use a straightforward function to expand the content equally across all pixels. One of the first of such methods was the technique presented by Landis (2002) that expands content for displaying on an HDR display based on power functions. Akyüz et al. (2007) proposed a method that uses a linear transformation with a gamma correction to expand single exposure.

Local methods, similarly to the local tone mapping methods discussed in Sect. 3.4, use analytical functions that depend on local image neighbourhoods. These methods also use a locally dependent expand map.

One of the earliest local ITM methods introduced by Banterle et al. (2006), initially expands the range by applying the inverse of the PTR TMO (Reinhard et al. 2002), although any other invertible TMO could be used. A smooth low frequency expand map is generated by selecting a constellation of bright points and expanding them via density estimation (importance sampling). The resulting luminance is computed by interpolating between the expanded luminance, L_{ITM}, that was computed via the inverse TMO, and the LDR image luminance, L_{LDR}, as follows:

$$\tilde{L}_{\mathrm{HDR}} = E L_{\mathrm{ITM}} + (1 - E) L_{\mathrm{LDR}} \tag{3.13}$$

where E is the expand map. The role of the expand map is to avoid quantisation errors that would arise via inverse tone mapping only and also reconstruct content in over-exposed areas of the image.

Classification based methods such as by Meylan et al. (2006), Meylan (2006) and Didyk et al. (2008), operate on different parts of the image by classifying these parts accordingly, for example into diffuse and specular areas. The classification is performed via thresholding and filtering in the first method, or by a support vector machine classifier which is also corrected by a user in the second.

Eilertsen et al. (2017), use a deep Convolutional Neural Network (CNN) to predict values for saturated areas of badly exposed content, whereas non-saturated areas are linearised by applying an inverse camera response curve. Endo et al. (2017) also use a CNN model that predicts multiple exposures from a single exposure which are then used to generate an HDR image using standard merging algorithms. Marnerides et al. (2018) use a multi-branch CNN architecture to combine multiple scales of the image and predict HDR images directly from the LDR inputs in an end-to-end fashion.

3.6   Using HDR in CH Applications

HDR imaging holds an important role in CH research and is used not only for extending the luminance range during capture and display, but also for temporal light acquisition of movable light sources and participating media, and for light/sun simulations. The acquisition of HDR data, allows for more accurate documentation and recreation of tangible CH scenarios and understanding of how sites once looked and how they were used.

3.6.1   Documentation

One way to document CH is by using still and video cameras. This allows for capturing shape, colour and light of existing CH objects in their original or adjusted real world locations. Documenting objects or sites using traditional hardware with LDR capabilities might be insufficient. Therefore, either specialised HDR cameras or suitable iTMO should be utilised to preserve details in high-contrast scenes. This not only provides with greater accuracy and an extended luminance range (Jakubiec et al. 2016) but also allows for capturing specific light phenomena, such as caustics or participating media which might play an important role in the life of an artefact or historical site. Caustics are formed when light rays get reflected or refracted by a curved specular surface and then hit another surface. Typical examples are those formed through a glass of water or wine, through a water surface or of a metallic surface such as wedding ring. Due to a high luminance value of the concentrated light produced by this phenomenon, traditional LDR technology might not be able to adequately capture and reproduce this effect accurately.

While HDR could be very useful in overcoming such limitations, some artefacts might occur in dynamic scenes. In addition, intrinsically they are not suitable for

Fig. 3.4 Visible artefacts as a result of HDR bracketing used for a moving caustics (Happa 2010)

temporal data acquisition of light that might be important for documentation and investigation of light and colour properties of movable light sources and high-contrast environments. For example, we might want to simulate the day cycle of a historical site, or simply to capture the environment lit by a candle with some airflow around its flame causing it to move. Although the former could be achieved with a still HDR camera using a discrete sampling of a relatively slow moving light/environment, the latter could lead to ghosting or similar bending artefacts. For example, capturing dynamic caustics might result in ghosting effect when combining multiple LDR images with different exposures as shown in Fig. 3.4.

Rendering of caustics is still a challenging task as it is typically not suitable for a real-time simulations and requires manual tuning of the parameters. Although, significant improvements have been made, this is still an unresolved issue (Grittmann et al. 2018). Another important light phenomenon that is of significant importance in CH reconstruction and simulation is the participating media, typically in forms of a smoke, fog and dust particles (Gutierrez et al. 2008; Marco et al. 2019).

Another acquisition technique that might benefit from HDR is the reflectance transform imaging (RTI). This computational photographic method captures object's shape and colour from a single point of view but varying the light position and thus highlights and shadows on the surface in each image (Malzbender et al. 2001). This eventually enables the interactive relighting of the object from any direction and computational enhancements of its surface and colour features, thus better analysis, understanding and interpretation of the artefacts. Therefore, given the importance of the image details in this technique, capturing higher dynamic range for highly specular surfaces might be necessary for preserving reliable pixel values.

Relighting virtually reconstructed sites and objects using captured light information at the original site is an important aspect of virtual reconstruction of CH. In this case a 3D rendering technique termed Image Based Lighting (IBL) can be utilised (Debevec and Malik 2008; Debevec 2008). This technique comprises of omnidirectional real-world light capture, typically a dome or a sphere, and the projection of this information onto a scene geometry, for simulating the lighting in a virtual scene. Although the light probe can be generated at the same physical place, it cannot be captured in the original time, i.e. in the past, as for example in the reconstruction of the Parthenon by Debevec (2005). Nonetheless, these probes, typically called environment maps can be used instead of standard synthetic light sources to achieve more accurate representation of light for the given scene (Inanici 2010). In the CH context, it might be necessary to reconstruct the surrounding and distant objects and, at the same time, remove them from the captured light probe. In addition, all the light sources not belonging to the target time should be switched off. One of the main limitations of this method is the fact that each probe is captured at a single point in space, at a single point in time. This does not allow for recreating spatially and temporally varying lighting conditions. The solution for this would be a creation of a 4D HDR light field, typically called Incident Light Fields (ILFs) (Unger et al. 2008; Unger 2009). Alternatively, the sky can be modelled or simulated (Perez et al. 1993; Jensen et al. 2001; Satỳlmỳs et al. 2016). One of the most commonly used sets of generic sky models with conditions from completely clear to overcast is the one of the International Commission on Illumination (CIE) (CIE 2003).

3.6.2   Visualisation

When it comes to visualisation of CH material, the first thing that should be considered is whether it will be a passive or active experience. The former, can be rendered offline and requires no interaction or input from the user. It can be delivered with an extremely high level of detail utilising physically-based rendering techniques. The latter assumes certain level of user interaction and, although elements could be pre-rendered, relies on real-time rendering. Physically-based rendering is beyond the scope of this chapter, but the literature suggests that it is still not possible to deliver such imagery at very high resolutions and frame rates. The purpose of the (inter)active experiences is two-fold: for the research purposes by the experts, such as the documentation of the excavations or monitoring of the degradation of the artefacts; or for the enhancement and promotion of CH through virtual museums, serious games or other types of interactive presentations (Stanco and Tanasi 2011).

One of the best media for presentation of CH sites and artefacts are virtual museums (VM). Virtual museums are digital entities complementing, enhancing or augmenting the museum experience [v-must.net]. They are intrinsically immersive and interactive way of enhancing the understanding and connection with the past and present world around us. VMs can represent a digitised exhibition, section, department or a full physical museum, or can be an independent collection of artefacts acting as a separate, virtual entity. In addition, they can be multiplatform—standalone, mobile, web-based, VR/AR; have different physical setup and accessibility—running on site or remotely; and level of engagement—single or multi-user, game like experience (VaticanMuseum 2019; Louvre-Lens-Multimedia 2019; SGG 2019; NHM 2019). They could also be categorised based on various criteria: content, interaction technology, duration, communication, level of immersion, format, scope, sustainability (V-Must.net 2019).

One of the main goals of VMs is to communicate knowledge to a wide audience, whether they are general public, scholars or professionals. This is typically achieved or enhanced by using digital storytelling (Hulusic and Rizvic 2013; Pietroni et al. 2015; Selmanovic etg al. 2018). The stories can be about the artefacts or the site, contextualising them culturally, historically, geographically and through time, providing a wider picture of how they have been created, used, preserved, and changed over periods of time, thus augmenting the experience compared to a typical museum presentation.

3.6.2.1 Modes of Delivery

As discussed previously, dynamic range of the original scene could be of significant importance when capturing the environment. Similarly, it might be necessary to display that same range on the display. Therefore, different platform and types of display devices will be discussed.

The most conventional platform for CH application is desktop, either as a standalone or web-based system. In either case, the display hardware is a monitor that might support touch-screen interaction with the application. Although HDR seems to be widely present in current technology, from TVs, computer monitors and mobile phones, there is still a lot of debate in the scientific community what "true" HDR is. The first HDR display is considered to by Brightside's DR 37P HDR, Fig. 3.5(left).

The company has later been acquired by Dolby and the technology patented as Dolby Vision (Dolby 2016). This technology delivers more accurate, realistic colour and dynamic range compared to LDR technology and even its main rival HDR10 (Standard 2014) by using 12-bit per colour channel support, wide colour gamut (ITU-R 2015) with a peak brightness of 10000 nits. This technology allows much brighter and dimmer representations due to an LED-lit back panel, Fig. 3.5(right).

 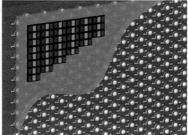

Fig. 3.5 Brightside DR 37P HDR display (left) and the LED array behind the LCD panel (right). Image courtesy of Brightside

At the same time, SIM2 has developed their own technology and released three display models HDR47E3, HDR47ES4MB and HDR47ES6MB with 2500, 4500 and 6000 nits peak brightness respectively (SIM2 2019). Nonetheless, this technology has still remained at the research and specialised domain, and could not truly penetrate the consumer market. This is partially due to the price of these units, but also lack of content and standardisation in the field. Instead, HDR10 technology, supporting 10-bit per channel, has been accepted as a de facto standard for HDR for the consumer market. There are many TV and computer screens supporting this "limited" HDR technology available at the moment. Although not as rich as "true" HDR, and introducing various artefacts, it is still a significant step forward from the conventional LDR technology which supports 8 bits per colour channel and has a narrower colour gamut (Rec. 709, BT 1886) (ITU-R 2015).

When it comes to mobile devices, the market is more focused on better appearance rather than truthfulness of real luminance reproduction. Similarly to TV, the most prevalent HDR standard on high-end mobile devices is HDR10. There are a few examples of support for Dolby Vision or HDR10+, which increases the dynamic range of HDR10, but they suffer from similar limitations as TV devices with this technology. Only recently the Ultra HD Alliance, made up of movie producers and technology companies, proposed a new standard called 'Ultra HD Premium' with two HDR definitions, one for LED screens with the range of 0.05–1000 nits, and one for OLED displays with the range of 0.0005–540 nits. However, in most cases of mobile HDR, the decoding is done by software, rather than hardware. While OLED technology is promising for the mobile display industry, there are still challenges to be addressed.

Virtual Reality (VR) and Augmented Reality (AR) technologies have recently advanced and might have significant impact on our lives in the future. These technologies allow to immerse into another "reality" either as an augmentation of the physical environment (AR) with additional synthetic content, or as a separate computer-generated environment with any type of real of fictional content and various modes of interaction. Unfortunately, VR/AR hardware slightly lacks behind the computer and mobile screen technology. Only very recently new head-mounted displays (HMDs) have been released with reasonably good resolutions, e.g. HTC Vive Pro with 2880×1600 pixels (1400×1600 pixels per eye). However, increasing the dynamic range on these devices is something that is not currently considered, and is possibly not something that we might expect in the very near future. Recent work by Goudé et al. (2019) proposes a TMO for 360° content viewed on HMDs that adjusts the content depending on the viewing angle, as well as a more globally consistent operator. Moving towards brighter screens in HMDs is not only a technological challenge but also raises many other considerations, such as health and safety, given the proximity of the displays to the eyes.

High dynamic range has proven a valuable and important tool for better representation and understanding of CH. If harnessed correctly with other stages throughout the pipeline it might create a great experience for both the general public and the academic community. Depending on the nature of the reconstruction and the system, different platforms could be considered. The fact that only desktop setups with dedicated display hardware can deliver "real" HDR experience is somewhat limiting. However, high-end mobile devices seem to be good alternatives for lower budgets and public displays. While VR and AR systems can make a significant user experience enhancement mainly through immersion and presence (Slater et al. 1996; Jung et al. 2016), there are still a few limiting factors with available HMDs, such as price, safety, comfort, setup and maintenance, and the display technology.

3.7 Conclusions

High Dynamic Range imaging can provide solutions for a variety of Cultural Heritage applications due to its ability to capture, process, store and reproduce the real world at high fidelity. Disciplines related to CH, such as archaeology and architecture, can benefit greatly from using HDR, for example by accurately reproducing artefacts and structures in virtual environments or by capturing and documenting current traditions, buildings and artefacts.

Implementing HDR pipelines is challenging, with each stage presenting new obstacles. Capturing HDR images an videos is an open problem, given the limitations of our sensors and software. Displaying HDR content presents another challenge due to the limited capabilities of actual light reproduction of current displays, requiring tone mapping. Historical content is predominantly LDR, requiring dynamic range expansion for converting it to LDR, which is a problem of substantial difficulty.

It would however be great if we could accurately reproduce the Parthenon and see it in its original state, as it was thousands of years ago, in some virtual environment. That is however extremely hard due to the limited documentation and data availability. Our current heritage, captured with HDR technology, will be better preserved and then reproduced by future generations, giving a more complete picture of history and tradition.

References

Akyüz AO, Fleming R, Riecke BE, Reinhard E, Bülthoff HH (2007) Do HDR displays support LDR content?: a psychophysical evaluation. ACM Trans Graph (TOG) 26(3):38
Allen NP (1993) Is the Shroud of Turin the first recorded photograph? S Afr J Art Hist 11:23–32
Banterle F, Artusi A, Debattista K, Chalmers A (2017) Advanced high dynamic range imaging, 2nd edn. AK Peters (CRC Press), Natick
Banterle F, Ledda P, Debattista K, Chalmers A (2006) Inverse tone mapping. In: Proceedings of GRAPHITE '06 p. 349. https://doi.org/10.1145/1174429.1174489
Boitard R, Bouatouch K, Cozot R, Thoreau D, Gruson A (2012) Temporal coherency for video tone mapping. In: Proceedings of the International society for optics and photonics applications of digital image processing XXXV, vol 8499, p 84990D
Boitard R, Cozot R, Thoreau D, Bouatouch K (2014) Survey of temporal brightness artifacts in video tone mapping. In: HDRi2014-Second international conference and SME workshop on HDR imaging, vol 9

CIE (2003) Spatial distribution of daylight - CIE standard general sky, Vienna (austria). CIE Publication No. S 011/E

Debattista K, Bashford-Rogers T, Selmanović E, Mukherjee R, Chalmers A (2015) Optimal exposure compression for high dynamic range content. Vis Comput 31(6–8):1089–1099

Debevec P (2008) Rendering synthetic objects into real scenes: bridging traditional and image-based graphics with global illumination and high dynamic range photography. In: ACM SIGGRAPH 2008 classes. ACM, New York, p 32

Debevec P, et al (2005) "Making" the parthenon. In: 6th International symposium on virtual reality, archaeology, and cultural heritage, vol 4

Debevec PE, Malik J (2008) Recovering high dynamic range radiance maps from photographs. In: ACM SIGGRAPH 2008 classes. ACM, New York, p 31

Didyk P, Mantiuk RK, Hein M, Seidel HP (2008) Enhancement of bright video features for HDR displays. Comput Graph Forum 27(4):1265–1274

Dolby (2016) Dolby vision: White paper

Drago F, Myszkowski K, Annen T, Chiba N (2003) Adaptive logarithmic mapping for displaying high contrast scenes. Comput Graph Forum 22(3):419–426. https://doi.org/10.1111/1467-8659.00689

Eilertsen G, Kronander J, Denes G, Mantiuk RK, Unger J (2017) HDR image reconstruction from a single exposure using deep CNNs. ACM Trans Graph (TOG) 36(6):178

Eilertsen G, Mantiuk RK, Unger J (2017) A comparative review of tone-mapping algorithms for high dynamic range video. Comput Graph Forum 36(2):565–592. https://doi.org/10.1111/cgf.13148

Endo Y, Kanamori Y, Mitani J (2017) Deep reverse tone mapping. ACM Trans Graph (TOG) 36(6):171–177

Goudé I, Cozot R, Banterle F (2019) Hmd-tmo: a tone mapping operator for 360° hdr images visualization for head mounted displays. In: Computer Graphics International Conference. Springer, Berlin, pp 216–227

Grittmann P, Pérard-Gayot A, Slusallek P, Křivánek J (2018) Efficient caustic rendering with lightweight photon mapping. In: Computer graphics forum, vol 37. Wiley, Berlin, pp 133–142

Gutierrez D, Sundstedt V, Gomez F, Chalmers A (2008) Modeling light scattering for virtual heritage. J Comput Cult Herit (JOCCH) 1(2):8

Happa J, Artusi A, Czanner S, Chalmers A (2010) High dynamic range video for cultural heritage documentation and experimental archaeology. In: Proceedings of the 11th International conference on virtual reality, archaeology and cultural heritage. Eurographics Association, pp 17–24

Hulusic V, Rizvic S (2013) Story guided virtual environments in educational applications. In: Transactions on edutainment IX. Springer, Berlin, pp 132–149

Inanici M (2010) Evalution of high dynamic range image-based sky models in lighting simulation. Leukos 7(2):69–84

ITU-R (2015) Parameter values for the hdtv standards for production and international programme exchange. ITU-R Recommendation BT.709-6

ITU-R: Parameter values for ultra-high definition television systems for production and international programme exchange. ITU-R Recommendation BT.2020-2 (2015)

Jakubiec JA, Van Den Wymelenberg K, Inanici M, Mahic A (2016) Improving the accuracy of measurements in daylit interior scenes using high dynamic range photography. In: Proceedings of the 32nd PLEA conference, Los Angeles, pp 11–13

Jensen HW, Durand F, Dorsey J, Stark MM, Shirley P, Premože S (2001) A physically-based night sky model. In: Proceedings of the 28th annual conference on computer graphics and interactive techniques. ACM, New York, pp 399–408

Jung T, tom Dieck MC, Lee H, Chung N (2016) Effects of virtual reality and augmented reality on visitor experiences in museum. In: Information and communication technologies in tourism 2016. Springer, Berlin, pp 621–635

Landis H (2002) Production-ready global illumination. https://www.spherevfx.com

Louvre-Lens-Multimedia (2019) https://www.louvrelens.fr/informations-pratiques/tarifs-abonnement/

Malzbender T, Gelb D, Wolters H (2001) Polynomial texture maps. In: Proceedings of the 28th annual conference on Computer graphics and interactive techniques. ACM, New York, pp 519–528

Mantiuk RK, Daly SJ, Kerofsky L (2008) Display adaptive tone mapping. ACM Trans Graph (TOG) 27(3):1. https://doi.org/10.1145/1360612.1360667

Marco J, Guillén I, Jarosz W, Gutierrez D, Jarabo A (2019) Progressive transient photon beams. Comput Graph Forum 38(6):19–30

Marnerides D, Bashford-Rogers T, Hatchett J, Debattista K (2018) ExpandNet: a deep convolutional neural network for high dynamic range expansion from low dynamic range content. Comput Graph Forum 37(2):37–49. https://doi.org/10.1111/cgf.13340

Meylan L (2006) Tone mapping for high dynamic range images. Technical report. EPFL, Lausanne

Meylan L, Daly SJ, Süsstrunk S (2006) The reproduction of specular highlights on high dynamic range displays. In: 14th Color imaging conference, pp 333–338. Scottsdale

NHM (2019) http://naturalhistory.si.edu/vt3/

Perez R, Seals R, Michalsky J (1993) All-weather model for sky luminance distribution-preliminary configuration and validation. Sol Energy 50(3):235–245

Pietroni E, Forlani M, Rufa C (2015) Livia's villa reloaded: an example of re-use and update of a pre-existing virtual museum, following a novel approach in storytelling inside virtual reality environments. In: 2015 Digital Heritage, vol 2. IEEE, Granada, pp 511–518

Reinhard E, Devlin K (2005) Dynamic range reduction inspired by photoreceptor physiology. IEEE Trans Vis Comput Graph 11(1):13–24

Reinhard E, Khan EA, Akyüz AO, Johnson G (2008) Color imaging: fundamentals and applications. AK Peters/CRC Press, Natick

Reinhard E, Stark M, Shirley P, Ferwerda J (2002) Photographic tone reproduction for digital images. ACM Trans Graph (TOG) 21(3):267–276. https://doi.org/10.1145/566654.566575

Reinhard E, Ward G, Pattanaik S, Debevec P (2010) High dynamic range imaging: acquisition, display and image-based lighting, 2nd edn. Elsevier, Amsterdam

Satÿlmÿs P, Bashford-Rogers T, Chalmers A, Debattista K (2016) A machine-learning-driven sky model. IEEE Comput Graph Appl 37(1):80–91

Selmanovic E, Rizvic S, Harvey C, Boskovic D, Hulusic V, Chahin M, Sljivo S (2018) VR video storytelling for intangible cultural heritage preservation. In: Sablatnig R, Wimmer M (eds.) Eurographics workshop on graphics and cultural heritage. The eurographics association. https://doi.org/10.2312/gch.20181341

SGG (2019) http://h.etf.unsa.ba/srp/

SIM2 (2019) http://hdr.sim2.it/productslist

Slater M, Linakis V, Usoh M, Kooper R (1996) Immersion, presence and performance in virtual environments: an experiment with tri-dimensional chess. In: Proceedings of the ACM symposium on virtual reality software and technology. ACM, New York, pp 163–172

Stanco F, Tanasi D (2011) Experiencing the past: computer graphics in archaeology. In: Digital imaging for cultural heritage, pp 1–37

Standard S (2014) High dynamic range electro-optical transfer function of mastering reference displays. SMPTE ST 2084:1–14

Tanselle GT, et al (1998) Literature and artifacts. Bibliographical Society of the University of Virginia, Charlottesville

Tursun OT, Akyüz AO, Erdem A, Erdem E (2015) The state of the art in HDR deghosting: a survey and evaluation. Comput Graph Forum 34(2):683–707. https://doi.org/10.1111/cgf.12593

UNESCO (2019) http://www.unesco.org

Unger J (2009) Incident light fields. Dissertation no. 1233, Linköping Studies in Science and Technology

Unger J, Gustavson S, Larsson P, Ynnerman A (2008) Free form incident light fields. Comput Graph Forum (Proceedings of EGSR 2008) 27(4):1293–1301

Urbano C, Magalhães L, Moura J, Bessa M, Marcos A, Chalmers A (2010) Tone mapping operators on small screen devices: an evaluation study. Comput Graph Forum 29(8):2469–2478. https:// doi.org/10.1111/j.1467-8659.2010.01758.x

V-Must.net (2019) http://v-must.net

VaticanMuseum (2019) http://www.museivaticani.va/content/museivaticani/en/collezioni/musei. html

Ward G (1991) Real pixels. In: Graphics gems II, pp 80–83

Ward G (2003) Fast, robust image registration for compositing high dynamic range photographs from hand-held exposures. J Graph Tools 8(2):17–30. https://doi.org/10.1080/10867651.2003. 10487583

Chapter 4
Procedural Modeling for Cultural Heritage

António Coelho, Augusto Sousa and Fernando Nunes Ferreira

Abstract Accurate 3D reconstruction and realistic visualization of cultural heritage allow experts to fine-tune their theories on the lost links in the history of civilization. Although the 3D reconstruction is a significant challenge, precisely because of the state of degradation over the years, it constitutes a crucial task for experts to study and interact with long disappeared settlements and structures. Furthermore, the public, in general, will be provided with the conditions to explore them in virtual environments, thus fostering cultural, social, and scientific participation. Highly accurate reconstruction is, nevertheless, a very complex task, where all stages of image synthesis must be carefully executed from highly detailed 3D models to obtain a faithful depiction of the object of interest. Meanwhile, the textual descriptions and geospatial data collected by archaeologists on-site may be used to overcome the absence of visual information. Still, this data will not suffice, in which case procedural modeling turns out to be essential to avoid a great deal of time and labor-consuming modeling processes. Procedural modeling tools automatically generate three-dimensional models through computational processes that extend the base information according to a specific algorithm. In order to avoid reprograming the procedural modeling systems, we use mathematical methods that operate on parametrical symbolic descriptions that, flexibly, can model different types of objects. The most used mathematical methods are fractal geometry and formal grammars, particularly L-systems and shape grammars. In this chapter, we will approach the current advances in the area of procedural modeling and how these tools can be used to generate 3D models of cultural heritage. We also explore the relevant dimension of time, extending the modeling tasks to 4D. These applications do not focus on very specific landmarks, like cathedrals or palaces, which require manual effort or image-based techniques to

A. Coelho (✉) · A. Sousa · F. N. Ferreira
Faculdade de Engenharia, Universidade do Porto (FEUP)/INESC TEC,
Rua Dr. Roberto Frias, Porto, Portugal
e-mail: acoelho@fe.up.pt

A. Sousa
e-mail: aas@fe.up.pt

F. N. Ferreira
e-mail: fnf@fe.up.pt

© Springer Nature Switzerland AG 2020
F. Liarokapis et al. (eds.), *Visual Computing for Cultural Heritage*, Springer Series on Cultural Computing, https://doi.org/10.1007/978-3-030-37191-3_4

capture the model with a high level of visual fidelity. Instead, we focus on modeling cities and their evolutions or the surroundings of these landmarks, that allow for an increased automation of the modeling process.

4.1   Introduction

Digital preservation of cultural heritage can be achieved through virtual environments, allowing the user to explore it with a great sense of immersion and presence. These virtual environments require a set of technologies but, mainly, a set of specific contents to provide a perceptually credible experience. For small environments, we normally need experts to do the modeling and animation. For extensive environments, we can use Procedural Modeling techniques to automate this process. One can define Procedural Modeling as the automatic generation of three-dimensional models through computational processes that extend the base information according to a particular algorithm. These algorithms implement sets of rules or are parametrical, often integrating randomness.

The procedural modeling emerges as a necessity to overcome difficulties inherent in the traditional modeling process, providing several advantages:

- Increased productivity, both by reducing costs through the use of smaller teams of specialists and by reducing the time associated with extensive modeling tasks.
- Higher iteration, through the possibility of automatically obtaining several solutions for a given problem (e.g., archeology) with a reduced additional effort. Also included is the ability to use new forms of expressiveness, enhancing the extension of this area to professionals without competencies in 3D modeling.
- Integration with diverse sources of information, through the conversion of the formats in which this information is defined and integrating it in the algorithmic processing. A typical example is the use of geographic information through integration with GIS (Geographic Information Systems).
- Information compression, making it possible to create smaller applications that dynamically manage three-dimensional models as they are needed (e.g., levels of a game). It is also possible to create "infinite worlds" that are generated in an unlimited way as the player progresses through the game.

The evolution of the area of procedural modeling has a consolidated basis in theories and mathematical models, which are described below, and has had a comprehensive evolution in the sense of trying to respond to the complexities inherent to urban environments. These models have given rise to several methods that allow the integrated modeling of virtual urban environments of any historical period.

4.2 Foundations

Procedural modeling techniques are based on a set of mathematical tools and methods to raise the level of flexibility of the process definition, avoiding the recurrent programming of the algorithms. The first works of procedural modeling were based on fractal geometry, particularly in the modeling of terrains, and on formal grammars, especially in the modeling of plants. We will take a closer look at the L-Systems, and later an approaching to the Shape Grammars, as the basis of the most current procedural modeling techniques.

4.2.1 Fractal Geometry

Fractal geometry is the branch of mathematics that studies the properties and behavior of fractals. It arose to describe situations that cannot be explained by the traditional definitions of Euclidean geometry. A fractal is a geometric object that can be fragmented into parts, and each of these parts has some similarity to the fragmented object. The term was defined by Benoît Mandelbrot, a French mathematician who discovered fractal geometry in the 1970s.

The fractals can be generated through several processes, from recursive functions to L-systems, which we will address in the next section.

4.2.2 L-systems

L-systems (Lindenmayer) appeared in 1968 in an article entitled "Mathematical models for cellular interaction in development" (Lindenmayer 1968). This article proposed a system for the modeling of the plant development process, based on a new class of production systems developed by Lindenmayer. The concept underlying the development of L-systems was the morphogenic theory of emergence in multicellular life (Taylor 1992). The concept of emergency reflects a development process in which a set of interacting units qualitatively acquires new properties that could not be deduced by simply overlapping their individual contributions. The strength of L-systems is thus the potential for data amplification (Smith 1984). From an initial set of simple data, it is possible to obtain a data set with much higher complexity.

4.2.2.1 Fundamental Concepts of L-systems

Formal grammars are a set of production rules in a formal language. The production rules describe how to create valid strings from the alphabet of the language and according to the syntax of the language.

Aristid Lindenmayer's approach to the morphological description of plants was based on a type of formal grammars, referred to as string-type rewriting systems, and used characters to describe the various constituent parts of plants. In this type of rewriting systems, production rules are used to operate strings belonging to a given alphabet. Starting from the initial character string and applying these rules iteratively along a sequence of steps, it is possible to model the essence of the modular development that occurs in plants. The concepts of rewriting and modular development are central to the definition of L-systems.

4.2.2.2   Graphic Interpretation of an L-system

According to the previous example, an L-system develops a certain axiom, producing a final character string that represents the definitive evolutionary state of a given organism or entity. At the level of Computer Graphics, this final modular chain will only have relevance if it can be translated into a graphic representation. The growth of the use of L-systems in this area was due to the work of Szilard and Quinton (Szilard and Quinton 1979), which demonstrates the applicability of the LOGO-style "turtle" language (Abelson and Disessa 1982) for the interpretation of L-systems.

4.2.3   Shape Grammars

A shape grammar is a type of production system that generates geometric shapes. This concept was defined by Stiny and Gips (1972) and consists of a set of rules that operate with shapes and a generation mechanism that selects and processes those rules. A shape rule defines how an existing shape can be transformed into another shape.

A shape is a limited arrangement of straight lines defined in a Cartesian coordinate system with real axes and an associated Euclidean metric. The points that make up the shapes can be associated with symbols, creating the so-called labeled shapes. A shape rule is similar to a production rule. The predecessor shape is replaced by the successor shape when the rule is applied (Stiny 1980).

A shape grammar consists of at least three shape rules: a start rule, at least one transformation rule, and a termination rule. The first rule is needed to start the shape generation process. The termination rule is required for the shape generation process to terminate. The simplest way to stop the process is by using a shape rule that removes the symbol. Shape rules can be applied in series (such as Chomsky's grammars) or parallel (like L-systems).

Shape grammars were originally presented for painting and sculpture but were studied in particular in architecture (computer-aided architectural design), as they provide a formalism for creating new designs. They thus present a high potential for procedural modeling of urban environments.

4.3   Procedural Modeling of Urban Environments

The first procedural modeling article that addressed the concept of urban environments in an integrated manner was published by (Parish and Muller 2001), and was developed based on L-Systems (Fig. 4.1). This was the seed that led to one of the commercial procedural modeling tools on the market: CityEngine.

The limitations of L-systems for modeling urban environments gave rise to the development of two innovative mathematical models. One of the developments was the integration of shape grammars, developing the Split Grammar (Wonka et al. 2003). The other approach was based on the integration of spatial contextualization, giving rise to Geospatial L-Systems (Coelho et al. 2007). Another more general approach, called Functional L-Systems (FL-Systems) (Marvie et al. 2005), was also developed for three-dimensional mesh modeling and was also used for procedural modeling of urban environments. A split grammar is a type of parametric grammar based on the concept of shape (Stiny 1980). The innovation of this new grammar lied in the set of production rules allowed, based on the concept of a split of geometric shapes and its parameterization. A parameter matching system lets you specify multiple high-level design goals and control randomness to ensure consistent output. However, another control grammar, a free context grammar, is required to deal with spatial distribution. The following figure shows the characteristics of split rules (split operation) (Fig. 4.2).

The need for a control grammar was a limitation of this approach and 3 years later comes a new contribution to overcoming it—Computer Generated Architecture (CGA) grammars (Müller et al. 2006). These grammars extend the concept of shape by adding a new entity—the scope—which is the bounding box of the shape, called CGA shape, associated with a local coordinate system (Fig. 4.3). This way, several spatial operations can be applied along the axes of the scope.

Fig. 4.1 Procedural modeling of urban environments with L-systems (Parish and Muller 2001)

Fig. 4.2 An example of a Split grammar. The "start" shape is splitted into 4 shapes that instanciate the elements of a façade element (Wonka et al. 2003)

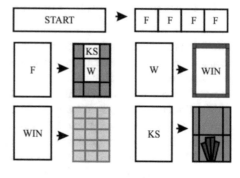

Fig. 4.3 Graphical representation of a CGA shape (Müller et al. 2006)

Geospatial L-systems (Coelho et al. 2007) were developed simultaneously, based on the concept of the geospatial string, which is a modular chain composed of geospatial modules. Geospatial modules are parametric modules associated with a geospatial object (Fig. 4.4). As an example, a geospatial module representing a road can be associated with the centerline, or a geospatial module representing a building can be associated with a polygon featuring its projection on the ground. Production rules that integrate spatial operators operate the geospatial string. These act on geospatial objects individually or as collections of these objects. As another example, a spatial operation of the intersection, between a particular module representing a building

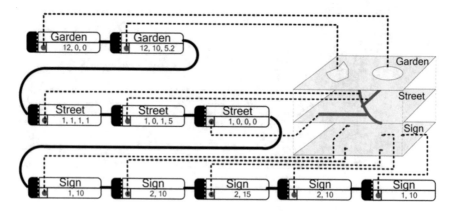

Fig. 4.4 Graphical representation of a geospatial string (Coelho et al. 2007)

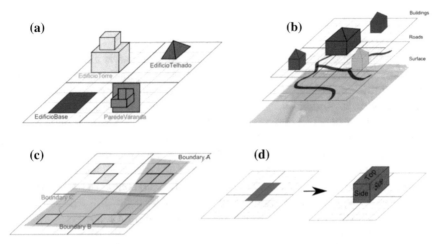

Fig. 4.5 Graphical representation of PG3DShape (**a**), PG3DLayer (**b**), PG3DBoundary (**c**) and PG3DTag (**d**) (Silva and Coelho 2011)

and a collection of objects representing the terrain, makes it possible to identify the altitude at which the base of that building is positioned.

This is an advantage over CGA grammars because they can only work spatial contextualization within the scope, whereas geospatial L-systems can perform geometric and topological operations on any spatial object and can incorporate the semantics of geographic information.

Geospatial L-systems provide greater flexibility for procedurally modeling of complex urban environments, while CGA grammars enable greater detail in building modeling. These characteristics led to the development of a new grammar called PG3D (Silva and Coelho 2011) which expands and integrates the concepts of CGA shape, through the definition of PG3DShape, with geospatial strings, through the concepts of PG3DLayer and PG3DBoundary. This grammar also adds greater semantic information handling capability with the concept of PG3DTag (Fig. 4.5). The PG3D grammar later gave rise to the Sceelix tool.

GIS information has great relevance for procedural modelling and also for cultural heritage, but it is necessary to standardize this information. Through the 3DWikiU project, it was possible to develop an urban ontology for the development of virtual environments that would allow direct interaction with this information (Martins et al. 2012). Thus, one of the first concepts of 3D GIS emerged, in which information is connected with 3D models and not just flat maps.

In the context of procedural modeling of urban environments, there have been several contributions that seek to respond to specific elements of these environments, which we will analyze in the following sections. A more complete literature review can be found in Smelik et al. (2014). But in Cultural heritage, there are distinct elements that require specific techniques.

Through the following sections, we will analyze such techniques.

4.3.1 Procedural Modeling of Terrains

Terrain modeling is the basis of any virtual environment and is the support for the other three-dimensional models. There are three main approaches to terrain modeling: using fractals, simulating physical erosion, and synthesizing terrain from point images or clouds. Another very often used fractal method is Perlin noise (1985). This method consists of creating an initial set of random values, which are then interpolated with coherent noise. You can compose multiple layers of noise together to create more natural terrain (Smelik et al. 2009). Several commercial tools already incorporate these techniques into terrain modeling. In order to enhance the realism of terrain models, the pioneering work of (Kelley et al. 1988) combines fractals with the simulation of the physical phenomena of erosion. Although, with realistic results, the computational cost is high. More recent works propose real-time approaches (Neidhold et al. 2005; Jacob 2004).

Due to the high level of randomness and lack of control, these methods have limitations to their effective use in specific scenarios, where the land has to be suitable for various urban uses. Stachniak and Stuerzlinger (2005) propose a method that uses constraints (in the form of image masks) in the terrain generation process. The algorithm searches for an acceptable set of deformation operations to apply to the ground so that a result is found that meets the specified constraints. Zhou et al. (2007) describes a technique that uses an example of terrain model as input and allows the user to draw desired features. Resources are extracted from the example and compared to the sketch and merged to generate the final result (Fig. 4.6). From Carpentier and Bidarra (2009) introduced the concept of procedural brushes so users can paint the elevation map directly in 3D.

One of the limitations of working with elevation maps is the impossibility of defining terrain with caves or other more complex morphological features. Figure 4.7 presents the results of the work of Peytavie et al. (2009) which through a more elaborate structure allows the modeling of different layers of materials, being able to model rocks, arches, overhangs and caves.

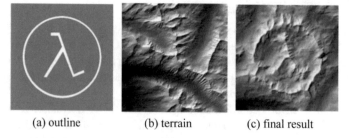

(a) outline   (b) terrain   (c) final result

Fig. 4.6 Terrain generation for example (Zhou et al. 2007)

Fig. 4.7 Modeling of complex orographic structures (Peytavie et al. 2009)

4.3.2 Procedural Modeling of Vegetation

As a culmination of their works under this line of research, Przemyslaw Prusinkiewicz and Aristid Lindenmayer published in 1990 the book "The Algorithmic Beauty of Plants" (Prusinkiewicz and Lindenmayer 1990). This book would become the reference for the application of L-systems in the area of Computer Graphics and on the modeling of plants, being the forerunner of the great advances that occurred during the 90s.

Some works were then developed in order to obtain increasingly realistic plant models. Hammel et al. (1995) presents a methodology for the creation of three-dimensional plant models, based on L-systems and incorporating biological data. It creates a qualitative model according to observations of plant growth and shape and then measures its fundamental characteristics. Starting from a statistical analysis of the-se data, it defines descriptive functions of plant growth.

Prusinkiewicz et al. (2001) presents a set of algorithms for plant modeling with a high level of visual realism. These algorithms take into account aspects considered fundamental by artists, such as posture, the gradual variation of characteristics, and progression of the design process from the general silhouette to the local details. These aspects are incorporated into the algorithms through positional information, which is defined as the position of the plant components along the axes of the supporting branches and stems. L-systems capture plant development over time and the simulation ends when the organism reaches a predefined terminal age, corresponding to a given number of derivation steps. The graphical interpretation of the obtained string is made through differential turtle geometry, allowing to obtain more realistic models of plants, contemplating more curvilinear configurations. Figure 4.8 shows two photographs of real plants and their three-dimensional models obtained using these algorithms.

The potential of realistic plant image synthesis for the film industry has motivated the development of complete natural ecosystem simulation work (Deussen et al. 1998) describes a system developed for realistic visualization of plant ecosystems. The modeling process begins with terrain modeling interactively, or from diverse

Fig. 4.8 Illustration of realistic models of two plants (Prusinkiewicz et al. 2001)

Fig. 4.9 Application examples of open L-systems (Deussen et al. 1998)

data sources such as GIS. Then the initial distribution of plant location is specified either explicitly (interactively or from actual data) or procedurally, and distributions are generated according to desired statistical properties. The ecosystem is further simulated using open L-systems in order to obtain a new specification of the distribution of plant locations according to the defined ecological model. The global ecosystem model is obtained by instantiating detailed three-dimensional plant models randomly selected from a set of similar specimens also generated by L-systems (Fig. 4.9).

Commercial plant modeling software solutions already can be used to produce vegetation for several applications.

4.3.3   Procedural Modeling of Road Networks

Road network modeling had emerged in the seminal article by Parish and Muller (2001) using L-systems. The approach is similar to plant development, from a global perspective. Starting with a street segment, new streets connected with it are derived, iteratively. However, to ensure road network connectivity, it is necessary to follow this first step by locally applying a set of constraints that corrects certain situations, avoiding node-free intersections and "dead ends". These grammars are called self-sensitive L-systems.

This type of approach fails to allow local control of the road network. To overcome this problem, a tensor fields based technique (Chen et al. 2008) has been developed to define the pattern of road network generation locally. This technique has the added advantage of being interactive, allowing the user to alter the road net-work by applying a "brush", changing the orientation of the tensors around that location (Fig. 4.10).

Defining the layout and later modeling the road network in a visually appealing way may not be sufficient for specific applications. In creating a virtual driving simulation environment, roads must comply with the rules set by Civil Engineering for their construction, and follow the particular geometry of the road design. Galin's work (Galin et al. 2010) presents an algorithm for generating roads, given two points, adapting to the characteristics of a given input scene. This is achieved by calculating the shortest path between these two points, minimizing a cost function that takes into account the slope of the terrain, rivers, lakes, forests, etc. In order to optimize the procedural modeling for driving simulators, the road construction rules can be mapped to the procedural modeling process, from route generation, according to user parameters, to the road profile creation (Campos et al. 2015) (see Fig. 4.11).

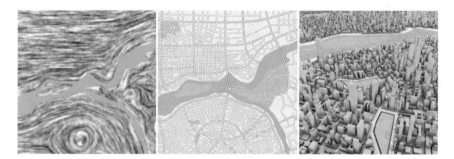

Fig. 4.10 Application of a tensor field for the generation of the road network (Chen et al. 2008)

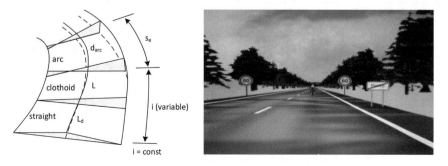

Fig. 4.11 Definition of the roads' geometry (Campos et al. 2015)

Fig. 4.12 Building extrusion with L-systems (Parish and Muller 2001)

This work obtains a dynamic behavior of the vehicles equivalent to the real response, besides achieving visually very realistic results.

4.3.4 Procedural Modeling of Buildings

The modeling of buildings and other man-maid structures, like walls and aqueducts, for example, is one of the most complex processes in Procedural Modeling. Nevertheless, one of the most relevant in the characterization of the urban environment and level of visual fidelity. L-systems were used in a first approach (Parish and Muller 2001) by creating the geometry of buildings through extrusions (Fig. 4.12).

For the detail of the facades, textures were applied. These textures were generated by composing a set of simpler textures, controlled by rectangular waves that interlace the vertical bands and floors of the buildings' facade (Fig. 4.13).

Geospatial L-Systems (Coelho et al. 2007) solve many of the problems of façade modeling, as spatial contextualization allows to determine the street-facing facade (where the door should be placed) or the facades that have neighboring buildings (and should not have windows or balconies), as well as splitting the facade into floors and vertical bands or positioning windows and balconies coherently.

The development of CGA grammars (Müller et al. 2006) aimed at detailed modeling of building facades. Although not capable of spatial contextualization like

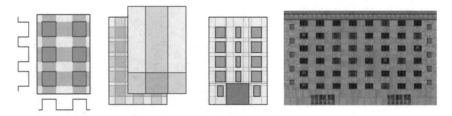

Fig. 4.13 Generation of facade textures (Parish and Muller 2001)

Fig. 4.14 Procedural modeling of buildings with a CGA grammar (Müller et al. 2006)

geospatial L-systems, it has a higher level of detail and flexibility in the development of individual buildings (Fig. 4.14).

In a different approach, called inverse procedural modeling, information is captured from actual façade images to reconstruct the production rules that model these facades (Müller et al. 2007). In a first step, it recognizes the structure of the facade (floors and vertical bands), following the process of identifying the constituent elements of that facade (windows, doors, and balconies) based on 3D models. In the third and last step, the production rules that generate this façade are created.

More complex facades, with ornaments, for example, require other procedural modeling processes such as the system developed by Finkenzeller (2008). The first step in the process requires the user to create a flat representation of the ground floor consisting of one or more convex polygons called the floor plan module (fpm). Upper floors are modeled on the lower floor, maintaining, removing, or dividing existing fpm. The system then generates a representation of the various facade elements. A wall is generated for each outer edge of fpm, which is vertically subdivided according to the chosen architectural style, creating partitions. Each partition, in turn, contains other structural elements and at most one door or window (Fig. 4.15).

The extensive architectural variability of the building facades led to the development of a more flexible solution, the Layered shape grammar (Jesus et al. 2016). This grammar extends CGA grammars with a set of additional operations that allow you to specify both the layers that make up a facade and the vector definition of 2D shapes. This methodology is thus capable of generating nontrivial layouts, going beyond the regular grid structure and transparently integrating more complex architectural elements such as arched windows and doors (Fig. 4.16).

Fig. 4.15 Detailed modeling of facades (Finkenzeller 2008)

Fig. 4.16 Composition of a facade (left) by planar normalization of the shapes of different layers (right) (Jesus et al. 2016)

4.4 Procedural Modeling of Cultural Heritage

There is a huge potential of using procedural modeling techniques for distinct applications in Cultural Heritage. Shape grammars have been used with success to model and visualize archeological sites, in 3D (Haegler et al. 2010) (Fig. 4.17).

Reconstructing archaeological sites is a non-precise task, as often there is not sufficient data for a accurate virtual environment. Procedural modeling thus allows to experiment with distinct variations according to the experts. Examples are the project Rome Reborn (Haegler et al. 2010) or the 3D model of a traditional settlement in the region of Central Zagori in Greece (Kitsakis et al. 2017).

But procedural modeling can be further used to model the past, the present and the future, i.e. the evolution and preview of a city, as the project focused on the changes that occurred on the Worlds' Fair site, in New York (Minner et al. 2017). In Cultural Heritage, 3D may be a limitation, as the dimension of time can be quite relevant. 4D systems incorporate this additional dimension, and can be used to: (a) reconstruct the diachronic evolution of a structure or environment that does not exist any longer; (b) reconstruct the diachronic evolution of a structure or environment based on the historical analysis of data acquired on physically accessible assets at the current or a previous time; (c) predict the diachronic evolution of a structure or environment into the future based on the historical analysis of data acquired on physically accessible assets at different times (Rodríguez-Gonzálvez et al. 2017). The usage of physically

Fig. 4.17 Images of project Rome Reborn (Haegler et al. 2010)

accessible assets at the current or a previous time can be used from a multitude of digital images and video available. Advances in the fields of Photogrammetry and Computer Vision have led to significant breakthroughs such as the Structure from Motion algorithm, which creates 3D models of objects using their 2D photographs (Kyriakakia et al. 2014). The use of input image data acquired through terrestrial laser scanning, as well as close range and airborne photogrammetry, can also be used for "precise" 3D models (Voulodimos et al. 2016).

Although accuracy is not always possible, when information is sparse, visual fidelity is essential, as the 3D models should present credible representations of the age of the object. As general procedural modeling tools are generic enough to model a broad scope of environments, special projects have focused on specific architectural rules. Besides Cartesian coordinate systems, by using cylindrical and spherical coordinate systems for generation of structures such as towers or domes, allowed for an easier modeling of castles and similar buildings (Edelsbrunner et al. 2017). Other studies focused on procedural modeling that make use of structural analysis methods, especially in its application to historic masonry buildings such as churches and cathedrals (Fita et al. 2017). Chinese roofs are also very characteristic and dependent on the age of the building. An approach based on a two-level semantic decomposition of the roof was developed according to the characteristics of ancient Chinese-style architecture (Li et al. 2017).

Culture has also influenced the architectural rules over time. Distinct projects have focused on these specificities: Classical Greek architecture (Piccoli 2016), ancient Chinese architecture of the Qing Dynasty (Liu 2018), the Ionic order of Greek and Ro-man temples (Konečný et al. 2016), Japanese ancient architectures [Kondo] and the 'Roman City Ruleset', a suite of procedural rules for creating 3D models of Roman and Hellenistic architecture in urban environments (Saldaña 2015).

Cultural heritage is approached by distinct professionals using a diversity of tools and formats. It is quite relevant that procedural modeling tools provide interoperable access to all the available sources of information. Geospatial L-systems already provided interoperable access to GIS information (Coelho et al. 2007) from the initial concept, and shape grammars evolved to integrate with the ArcGIS family, with the integration in the ESRI suite. Other projects have worked on using procedural modeling as a 3D GIS (Minner et al. 2017; Piccoli 2016). Another source of information for procedural modeling is the imagery of the sites and it is possible to produce environments that bring together unmanned aerial systems (UAS) imagery and procedural modelling. Not only is important to use available information but also to use the structure of that information to create the production rules—the semantics. Several works have approached semantic information in procedural modeling. PG3D was already developed to intrinsically introduce semantics and geospatial information (Silva and Coelho 2011). CityGML is a standard developed to integrate CAD and GIS information, and in Piccoli (2016) it was used to support the semantics of the project. Another relevant standard is BIM (Building Information Modeling) that integrates 3D information together with semantics, providing a good potential for the modeling processes (Murphy et al. 2017; Tobiáš 2016). Nevertheless, commercial tool integration is not easy and sometimes texture or semantic information (BIM) is hard to integrate (Minner et al. 2017).

Procedural Modeling can be of great value to Cultural Heritage, for 3D reconstruction and also the validation of distinct hypothesis (Richards-Rissetto and Plessing 2015). But it also allows for easier integration with game technology (Ma and Lien 2018) and even the development of digital games and virtual environments on cultural heritage (Konečný et al. 2016).

4.5 Conclusions and Future Challenges

Throughout this chapter, distinct methods, and even commercial tools have been introduced to enable procedural modeling of cultural heritage, in an integrated manner. When you want to get more detail on certain urban elements, you can re-sort to specific techniques.

Although the current state of the art of procedural modeling techniques can already overcome many of the challenges of urban environments, there are still some open problems:

- Inverse procedural modeling: Since many of the approaches presented use formal grammars, one of the challenges is to be able to extract production rules based on examples of existing cultural heritage. An approach to building facade modeling has already been developed (Müller et al. 2007).
- Grammars based on natural language: There are several texts, literary and historical documents, that describe cultural heritage. This line of research seeks to extract production rules based on these texts. Such an approach has already begun to be explored (Rodrigues et al. 2011).
- Visual languages: Defining mathematical language-based production rules in the procedural modeling process has the disadvantage that it is not intuitive, leading to long learning curves. Using visual languages makes the process more intuitive, particularly for architectural or design users. The work proposed by Lipp et al. (2008) presents a system where rule editing is done directly on the generated model, and there is no need to write production rules (Silva et al. 2015) presents a visual language based on procedural content graphs, which uses nodes to describe the procedures for creating, transforming, analyzing or filtering content, and the arcs to describe the flow between nodes. A recent work lays the groundwork for using sketch-based modeling to define production rules (Jesus et al. 2018).
- Semantic Information: On the one hand, semantic information present in many data sources (such as GIS) allows for greater expressiveness in procedural modeling processes by increasing process control by the user. On the other hand, the visual representation of 3D models is not always sufficient for all applications, such as digital games or driving simulators. In these cases, additional information is required for game mechanics, road signs, or vehicle trajectories. The integration of semantic information was previously addressed by Tutenel et al. (2011), having been expanded by Jesus et al. (2018, Silva et al. 2015, Campos et al. 2015).

References

Abelson H, Disessa A (1982) Turtle Geometry. Press, M.I.T

Campos C, Leitão JM, Coelho A (2015) Procedural generation of road paths for driving simulation. Int J Creat Interfaces Comput Graph 6(2):37–55

Chen G, Esch G, Wonka P, Müller P, Zhang E (2008) Interactive procedural street modeling. In: ACM SIGGRAPH 2008 papers on—SIGGRAPH '08, p 1. https://doi.org/10.1145/1399504.1360702

Coelho A, Bessa M, Sousa AA, Ferreira FN (2007) Expeditious modelling of virtual urban environments with geospatial L-systems. Comput Graph Forum 26(4):769–782. https://doi.org/10.1111/j.1467-8659.2007.01032.x

de Carpentier GJP, Bidarra R (2009) Interactive GPU-based procedural heightfield brushes. In: Proceedings of the fourth international conference on the foundations of digital games, pp 55. https://doi.org/10.1145/1536513.1536532

Deussen O, Hanrahan P, Lintermann B, Mech R, Pharr M, Prusinkiewicz P (1998) Realistic modeling and rendering of plant ecosystems. In: Proceedings of the 25th annual conference on computer graphics and interactive techniques (Siggraph '98), ACM, pp 275–286

Edelsbrunner J, Havemann S, Sourin A, Fellner DW (2017) Procedural modeling of architecture with round geometry. Comput Graph (Pergamon) 64:14–25. https://doi.org/10.1016/j.cag.2017.01.004

Finkenzeller D (2008) Detailed building facades. IEEE Comput Graph Appl 28(3):58–66. https://doi.org/10.1109/MCG.2008.50

Fita JL, Besuievsky G, Patow G (2017) Perspective on procedural modeling based on structural analysis. Virtual Archaeol Rev 8(16):44. https://doi.org/10.4995/var.2017.5765

Galin E, Peytavie A, Maréchal N, Guérin E (2010) Procedural generation of roads. Comput Graph Forum 29(2):429–438. https://doi.org/10.1111/j.1467-8659.2009.01612.x

Haegler S, Müller P, Van Gool L (2010) Procedural modeling for digital cultural heritage. EURASIP J Image Video Process 2009(1):1–11. https://doi.org/10.1155/2009/852392

Hammel M, Prusinkiewicz P, Remphrey W, Davidson C (1995) Simulating the development of Fraxinus pennsylvanica shoots using L-systems. In: Proceedings of the sixth western computer graphics symposium, pp 49–58. http://algorithmicbotany.org/papers/ash.ski95.pdf

Jacob O (2004) Realtime procedural terrain generation. J Dep Math Comput Sci, Imada Univ South Den

Jesus D, Coelho A, Sousa AA (2016) Layered shape grammars for procedural modelling of buildings. Vis Comput 32(6–8):933–943. https://doi.org/10.1007/s00371-016-1254-8

Jesus D, Patow G, Coelho A, Sousa AA (2018) Generalized selections for direct control in procedural buildings. Comput Graph (Pergamon) 72:106–121. https://doi.org/10.1016/j.cag.2018.02.003

Kelley, A. D., Malin, M. C., & Nielson, G. M. (1988). Terrain simulation using a model of stream erosion. In Proceedings of the 15th annual conference on computer graphics and interactive techniques—SIGGRAPH '88 (Vol. 22, pp. 263–268). ACM Press, New York, USA. https://doi.org/10.1145/54852.378519

Kitsakis D, Tsiliakou E, Labropoulos T, Dimopoulou E (2017) Procedural 3D modelling for traditional settlements. The case study of central zagori. In: International archives of the photogrammetry, remote sensing and spatial information sciences—ISPRS archives, vol 42, pp 369–376. https://doi.org/10.5194/isprs-archives-XLII-2-W3-369-2017

Konečný R, Syllaiou S, Liarokapis F (2016) Procedural modeling in archaeology: approximating ionic style columns for games. In: 2016 8th international conference on games and virtual worlds for serious applications, VS-games 2016, pp 1–8. IEEE. https://doi.org/10.1109/VS-GAMES.2016.7590358

Kyriakakia G, Doulamis A, Doulamis N, Ioannides M, Makantasis K, Protopapadakis E, Hadjiprocopis A, Wenzel K, Fritsch D, Klein M, Weinlinger G (2014) 4D reconstruction of tangible cultural heritage objects from web-retrieved images. Int J Herit Digital Era 3(2):431–451

Li L, Tang L, Zhu H, Zhang H, Yang F, Qin W (2017) Semantic 3D modeling based on CityGML for ancient Chinese-style architectural roofs of digital heritage. ISPRS Int J Geo-Inf 6(5):132. https://doi.org/10.3390/ijgi6050132

Lindenmayer A (1968). Mathematical models for cellular interactions in development I. Filaments with one-sided inputs. J Theor Biol 18(3):280–299. https://doi.org/10.1016/0022-5193(68)90079-9

Lipp M, Wonka P, Wimmer M (2008) Interactive visual editing of grammars for procedural architecture. In: ACM SIGGRAPH 2008 papers on–SIGGRAPH '08, p 1. https://doi.org/10.1145/1399504.1360701

Liu J (2018) Component-driven procedural modeling for ancient Chinese architecture of the Qing dynasty. Int J Arch Herit 12(2):280–307. https://doi.org/10.1080/15583058.2017.1410253

Ma YP, Lien HH (2018) Using game technology to enhance the interaction and visualization ability of 3DGIS historic site modeling. In: 1st IEEE international conference on knowledge innovation and invention, ICKII 2018, pp 66–69. IEEE. https://doi.org/10.1109/ICKII.2018.8569094

Martins T, Silva PB, Coelho A, Sousa AA (2012) An urban ontology to generate collaborative virtual environments for municipal planning and management. In: GRAPP 2012 IVAPP 2012—proceedings of the international conference on computer graphics theory and applications and international conference on information visualization theory and applications, pp 507–510. https://doi.org/10.5220/0003849705070510

Marvie JE, Perret J, Bouatouch K (2005) The FL-system: a functional L-system for procedural geometric modeling. Vis Comput. Springer Berlin Heidelberg. https://doi.org/10.1007/s00371-005-0289-z

Minner J, Chusid J, Shi X, Feng Y (2017) Visualizing the past, present, and future of New York City's 1964–5 World's fair site using 3D GIS and procedural modeling spatial analysis and mapping for strengthening rural-urban linkages to support rural economic development: the case of re-localized

Müller P, Wonka P, Haegler S (2006) Ulmer A, & Van Gool L: procedural modeling of buildings. ACM Trans Graph 25(3):614–623

Müller P, Zeng G, Wonka P, Van Gool L (2007) Image-based procedural modeling of facades. ACM Trans Graph 26:3

Murphy M, Corns A, Cahill J, Eliashvili K, Chenau A, Pybus C, Truong-Hong L (2017) Developing historic building information modelling guidelines and procedures for architectural heritage in Ireland. In: International archives of the photogrammetry, remote sensing and spatial information sciences—ISPRS archives, vol 42, pp 539–546. https://doi.org/10.5194/isprs-archives-XLII-2-W5-539-2017

Neidhold B, Wacker M, Deussen O (2005) Interactive physically based fluid and erosion simulation. In: Natural phenomena pp 25–32

Parish Y, Muller P (2001) Procedural modeling of cities. In: Proceedings of the 28th annual conference on computer graphics and interactive techniques (Siggraph '01). ACM, pp 301–308

Perlin K (1985) An image synthesizer. In: Proceedings of the 12th annual conference on computer graphics and interactive techniques—SIGGRAPH '85, vol 19, pp 287–296. https://doi.org/10.1145/325334.325247

Peytavie A, Galin E, Grosjean J, Merillou S (2009) Arches: a framework for modeling complex terrains. Comput Graph Forum 28(2):457–467. https://doi.org/10.1111/j.1467-8659.2009.01385.x

Piccoli C (2016) Enhancing GIS urban data with the 3rd dimension : a procedural modelling approach. In: CAA 2015 43rd annual conference on computer applications and quantitative methods in archaeology, pp 35–44

Prusinkiewicz P, Lindenmayer A (1990) The algorithmic beauty of plants. Springer

Prusinkiewicz P, Muendermann L, Radoslaw K, Lane B (2001) The use of positional information in the modeling of plants. In: Proceedings of the 28th annual conference on computer graphics and interactive techniques (Siggraph '01). ACM, pp 289–300

Richards-Rissetto H, Plessing R (2015) Procedural modeling for ancient Maya cityscapes: initial methodological challenges and solutions. In: 2015 digital heritage international congress, digital heritage, pp 85–88. https://doi.org/10.1109/DigitalHeritage.2015.7419458

Rodrigues R, Coelho A, Paulo Reis L (2011) Procedural modelling of monumental buildings from textual descriptions, pp 130–133. https://doi.org/10.5220/0002826401300133

Rodríguez-Gonzálvez P, Muñoz-Nieto AL, del Pozo S, Sanchez-Aparicio LJ, Gonzalez-Aguilera D, Micoli L, Barsanti S, Guidi G, Mills J, Fieber K, Haynes I, Hejmanowskae (2017) 4D reconstruction and visualization of cultural heritage: analyzing our legacy through time. Int Arch Photogramm Remote Sens Spat Inf Sci 42:609

Saldaña M (2015) An integrated approach to the procedural modeling of ancient cities and buildings. Digital Scholarsh HumIties 30(suppl 1):i148–i163. https://doi.org/10.1093/llc/fqv013

Silva PB, Coelho A (2011) Procedural modeling for realistic virtual worlds development. J Virtual Worlds Res 4(1). https://doi.org/10.4101/jvwr.v4i1.2109

Silva PB, Eisemann E, Bidarra R, Coelho A (2015) Procedural content graphs for urban modeling. Int J Comput Games Technol 2015:1–15. https://doi.org/10.1155/2015/808904

Smelik RM, Kraker KJ, Groenewegen SA, Tutenel T, Bidarra R (2009) A survey of procedural methods for terrain modelling. In: Proceedings of the Casa'09 workshop on 3D advanced media in gaming and simulation, pp 25–34

Smelik RM, Tutenel T, Bidarra R, Benes B (2014) A survey on procedural modelling for virtual worlds. Comput Graph Forum 33(6):31–50. https://doi.org/10.1111/cgf.12276

Smith AR (1984) Plants, fractals, and formal languages. ACM Siggraph Comput Graph 18(3):1–10. https://doi.org/10.1145/964965.808571

Stachniak S, Stuerzlinger W (2005) An algorithm for automated fractal terrain deformation. In: Proceedings of computer graphics and artificial intelligence, pp 64–76. https://doi.org/10.1.1.122.5463

Stiny G (1980) Introduction to shape and shape grammars. Environ Plan 7(3):343–351. https://doi.org/10.1068/b070343

Stiny G, Gips J (1972) Shape grammars and the generative specification of painting and sculpture, vol 71, North-Holland

Szilard A, Quinton R (1979) An interpretation for D0l systems by computer graphics. Sci Terrapin 4:8–13

Taylor CE (1992) "Fleshing out" Artificial life II. In: Langton CG, Taylor C, Farmer J, Rasmussen S (eds) Artificial life II, pp 25–38

Tobiáš P (2016) BIM, GIS and semantic models of cultural heritage buildings. Geoinf FCE CTU 15(2):27. https://doi.org/10.14311/gi.15.2.3

Tutenel T, Smelik RM, Lopes R, De Kraker KJ, Bidarra R (2011) Generating consistent buildings: a semantic approach for integrating procedural techniques. In: IEEE transactions on computational intelligence and AI in games, vol 3, pp 274–288. https://doi.org/10.1109/TCIAIG.2011.2162842

Voulodimos A, Doulamis N, Fritsch D, Makantasis K, Doulamis A, Klein M (2016) Four-dimensional reconstruction of cultural heritage sites based on photogrammetry and clustering. J Electron Imaging 26(1):011013

Wonka P, Wimmer M, Sillion F, Ribarsky W (2003) Instant architecture. ACM Trans Graph 22(3):669. https://doi.org/10.1145/882262.882324

Zhou H, Sun J, Turk G, Rehg JM (2007) Terrain synthesis from digital elevation models. IEEE Trans Vis Comput Graph 13(4):834–848. https://doi.org/10.1109/TVCG.2007.1027

Part II
Computer Vision and Photogrammetry

Chapter 5
Providing Access to Old Greek Documents Using Keyword Spotting Techniques

Anastasios L. Kesidis and Basilis Gatos

Abstract Keyword spotting is an alternative methodology for document indexing based on spotting words directly on images without the use of a character recognition system. In this paper, an overview of recent techniques and available databases for keyword spotting is presented focusing on the specific characteristics of old Greek machine-printed and handwritten documents. These documents are import treasures of cultural heritage and a valuable source of information for scholars. Indexing of such content is a very challenging task considering the additional problem of having many character classes as well as a variety of different diacritic mark combinations that may appear above or below Greek characters. All steps of a keyword spotting system are highlighted, namely, preprocessing for image binarization, enhancement and segmentation, feature representation, matching and word retrieval, in order to report the efficiency of current keyword spotting approaches when applied to old Greek documents.

5.1 Introduction

Historical documents existing in libraries and cultural institutions contain a vast amount of valuable information. Indexing of these documents is very important for quick and efficient access to valuable historical collections in order to assist scholars to search and study this valuable content. Optical character recognition (OCR) technology although is nowadays mature and widely used for indexing contemporary documents, it cannot be efficiently applied to historical documents which suffer from several problems such as document degradations (e.g., non-uniform illuminations,

A. L. Kesidis (✉)
Department of Surveying and Geoinformatics Engineering, University of West Attica, Agiou
Spyridonos St, 12243 Athens, Greece
e-mail: Kesidis@uniwa.gr

B. Gatos
Computational Intelligence Laboratory, National Center for Scientific Research "Demokritos",
Institute of Informatics and Telecommunications, Patriarchou Grigoriou St., Aghia Paraskevi,
15310 Athens, Greece

© Springer Nature Switzerland AG 2020
F. Liarokapis et al. (eds.), *Visual Computing for Cultural Heritage*, Springer Series
on Cultural Computing, https://doi.org/10.1007/978-3-030-37191-3_5

smears, shadows, bleeding through ink), low print quality, typesetting imperfections, writing style variations and complex layouts. Keyword spotting is an alternative solution to OCR exhibiting a growing interest for document indexing over the past decade (Giotis et al. 2017). While an OCR system analyzes different text regions in order to convert them to machine-readable text, a keyword spotting system searches whether a document image contains certain keywords without the need for correct segmentation and recognition.

In this paper, an overview of recent techniques and available databases for keyword spotting is presented regarding old Greek machine-printed and handwritten documents. Providing access to old Greek documents is a very challenging task considering the additional problem of having many character classes (usually more than 270). The Old Greek polytonic system includes a total of 28 different diacritic mark combinations that may appear above or below Greek characters. Although the proposed works for keyword spotting of old Greek documents may vary in methods and modules used for different system pipelines, some common steps can be distinguished. First, the document image is preprocessed in order to prepare an enhanced quality binary image, to correct orientation and skew, to remove noisy borders and frames and, finally, to segment the image at word level for the cases of the segmentation-based keyword spotting methods. Then, a suitable feature representation is used in order to achieve a common representation to describe both the query and the documents at a specific level (word, line or page). Finally, a matching is performed between the query and the document in order to achieve keyword retrieval. In some cases, user feedback and natural language processing techniques are also involved in order to improve the retrieval results.

In the following sections, all the above steps will be described along with the databases and protocols used for the evaluation of the performance of the available keyword spotting techniques for old Greek documents.

5.2 Preprocessing

Despite the variability in the proposed methodologies, the word spotting systems usually share a common pipeline regarding the several steps involved in the overall process. As a first step, the document images are preprocessed in order to extract as much as possible from the visual and structural information they contain. This section discusses the several preprocessing operations that may be applied.

5.2.1 Binarization and Enhancement

The original images are typically color or gray-scale images, thus, binarization refers to the conversion of such content to a binary image and is the starting step of most document image analysis systems. In Gatos et al. (2006), the foreground regions are roughly estimated by applying some kind of a low pass filter (e.g., a Wiener filter) while the background surface is estimated by interpolating neighboring background intensities. In order to produce the binary image, a thresholding process is involved that combines the estimating background with the original image. In Vasilopoulos and Kavallieratou (2013) an adaptive binarization is applied that uses the mean of the 9×9 neighborhood as a threshold for each pixel. Since historical document collections are usually characterized by very low quality, an image enhancement stage is also essential. Noise removal is a process typically applied so that the quality of the text regions is further improved by removing isolated pixels and filling possible breaks, gaps or holes.

5.2.2   Orientation and Skew Correction

Document pages may appear in both orientations, portrait and landscape and may suffer from high skew distortions due to the scanning process. Text orientation is determined by applying a horizontal/vertical smoothing, followed by a calculation procedure of vertical/horizontal black and white transitions (Yin 2001). Regarding the skew detection, the Hough transform can be involved while the binarized image is expressed as rectangular blocks (Perantonis et al. 1999).

5.2.3   Noisy Border and Frame Removal

The scanning process may result to documents framed by a solid or stripped black border. The segmentation process is facilitated by removing any potential frames around the text areas. Using projection profiles along with a connected component labeling process allows the removal of such borders (Stamatopoulos et al. 2007). Figure 5.1 depicts an example of preprocessing operations when applied to a colored historical document image. The resulting image is in binary form with the noisy borders and the surrounding frame removed.

5.2.4   Word Segmentation

The segmentation of the document image into words is the next most important step and its accuracy highly affects the overall performance of a word spotting system. A typical approach is to use the Run Length Smoothing Algorithm (RLSA) (Theodoridis and Koutroumbas 1997; Wahl et al. 1982), which examines the white runs existing in the horizontal and vertical directions. For each direction, white runs with length less than a threshold are eliminated. The threshold can be a system parameter or dynamically determined depending on the characteristics of the text,

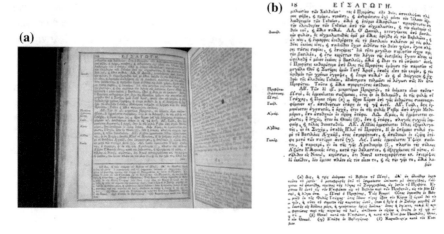

Fig. 5.1 **a** Original color document image and **b** the image after several preprocessing steps including binarization (Kesidis et al. 2011)

e.g., the average character height (Konidaris et al. 2007). For instance in Kesidis et al. (2011), the horizontal length threshold is experimentally defined as 50% of the average character height while the vertical length threshold is experimentally defined as 10% of the average character height. RLSA forces the characters of the same word to appear as a single connected component. Furthermore, constraints regarding the minimum expected word length can also be applied in order to eliminate stop-words. Figure 5.2 depicts the application of RLSA to the image of Fig. 5.1, resulting to a document image segmented into words.

Another word segmentation approach used for the word segmentation of historical and degraded machine-printed documents is based on projection profiles (Antonacopoulos and Karatzas 2005). The horizontal projection profile is calculated by summing the foreground pixels in every scan line followed by a smoothing procedure. Then, the local minima is calculated that defines the boundaries of the regions containing text lines. Using a similar process for every detected text line, the vertical projections are calculated in order to detect the document's words. Figure 5.3 gives an example of this approach. Often a combination of the last two word segmentation approaches is used. Specifically, both methods are independently applied and then, for each word, the bounding box that has a smaller distance to the query word is opted.

A semi-automated word segmentation process is used in Gatos et al. (2015). Initially, an automatic segmentation at several levels (text lines, words, characters) is provided by the method described in Gatos et al. (2014). At a next step, several users are involved to correct the segmentation results using the Aletheia framework (Clausner et al. 2011). An automatic transcript mapping procedure is also applied in order to assign the text information to the corresponding text line (Stamatopoulos et al. 2010). This procedure is further verified and corrected by human experts.

(a) 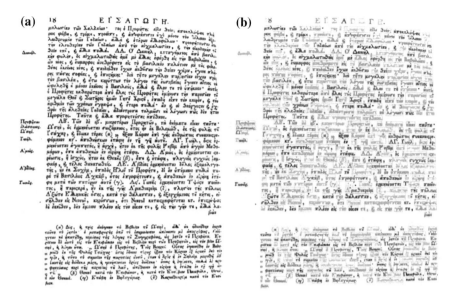 **(b)**

Fig. 5.2 Applying RLSA to the binarized image of Fig. 5.2. **a** The smoothed image and **b** the word segmentation results (Kesidis et al. 2011)

(a) 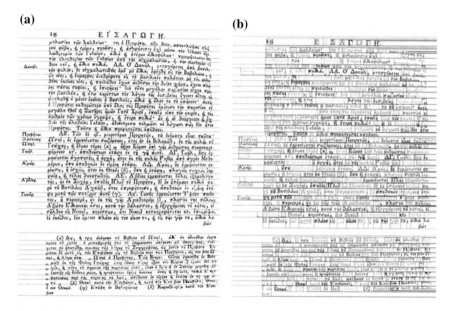 **(b)**

Fig. 5.3 Projection profiles when applied to the image of Fig. 5.1. **a** The text line segmentation results and **b** the word segmentation results (Kesidis et al. 2011)

5.2.5 Segmentation Free Approaches

Techniques based on word segmentation are particularly sensitive to possible segmentation errors, which undoubtedly will affect the word spotting process. This issue is even more apparent in degraded and handwritten documents. For this reason, several segmentation-free word-spotting techniques have emerged that are directly applied to whole document pages. In this context, the work in Vasilopoulos and Kavallieratou (2013) avoids segmentation and proposes a normalization pre-processing step in order to get rid of unnecessary details and smooth small differences in skew and scale. After the normalization, the query image is applied to every pixel of the image (left-upper corner) and is compared with the corresponding part of the image, using the Sum of Squared Differences matching algorithm. If the similarity is large enough the corresponding page is retrieved.

A segmentation-free approach is also followed in Konidaris et al. (2016). The absence of word segmentation is surpassed by the detection of candidate areas in the document image using a keypoint correspondence framework. Indeed, the Scale Invariant Feature Transform (SIFT) (Lowe 2004) is involved in order to find keypoint matches that are considered as indicators of candidate image areas probably corresponding to instances of the query word.

5.3 Feature Extraction and Word Retrieval

This section discusses some features extraction methodologies and how they are used in order to represent both documents and queries. Several matching approaches are also discussed in accordance with the similarity measures used to compare the query to the document corpus. Moreover, some additional processing steps are highlighted including user feedback which gains information from the original ranked results as well as linguistic approaches that incorporate natural language processing techniques in order to further enrich the retrieval results.

5.3.1 Methodologies

In Kesidis et al. (2011) and Konidaris et al. (2007) the word retrieval mechanism initializes by creating synthetic word data along with a robust hybrid feature extraction that supports meaningful representations of word images. Initially, a set of character templates is created. Specifically, for each character an image representative is defined and stored. The user provides the query word in ASCII format and the synthetic query word image is created by mapping each one of the ASCII letters to its corresponding character template. The query as well as all the segmented words of the document are described by features, which are used in order to measure the similarity between word images. The words are initially normalized in some prede-fined dimensions and then two types of features are calculated for each word. The first one divides the word image into a set of zones and calculates the density of the character pixels in each zone (Bokser 1992). The second type of features is based on word (upper/lower) profile projections. They are computed in each image column as the distance from the upper/lower boundary of the word image to the closest char-acter pixel (Rath and Manmatha 2003). There are 90 features based on zones and 60 features based on profile projections, leading to an overall of 150 features per word.

As an initial result, all the segmented words are ranked according to their simi-larity to the query. The similarity between the query and each one of the segmented words is calculated by their corresponding features using the L_1 distance metric, which has shown its effectiveness while providing low computational cost. The ini-tial ranking provides the words of the document that are similar to the synthetic keyword. These results might not present high accuracy because a synthetic key-word cannot a priori perform a perfect match with a real word image. Therefore, a user feedback mechanism is involved where the user selects one or more correct results from the initial ranked list. These are used as input query and a new matching process is initiated. The segmented words are re-ranked according to their similarity to the selected word(s), which, in this case, are not synthetic but real words of the document's corpus. The critical impact of the user feedback in the word spotting process lies upon this transition from synthetic to real data. Figure 5.4 illustrates the distinct steps of the system architecture proposed in Konidaris et al. (2007).

In Vasilopoulos and Kavallieratou (2013) a patch-based approach is followed in which a window corresponding to the normalized query image slides over the whole document. In each position, the Sum of Squared Differences is calculated in order to calculate the similarity of the query patch to the underlying document area. If the similarity is large enough (set to 85% in the aforementioned work), the corresponding point is considered as a true match.

A similarity measure is also proposed in Giotis et al. (2015) however applied in a features-level. Assuming that document images have already been binarized and segmented at word level, the first step of the proposed approach is to extract the con-tour from segmented word images using a thinning morphological operation. Each word is represented as a pairs of adjacent segments (PAS). Connecting segments over edge discontinuities increases the robustness of PAS features against interruptions along the word contour as well as short missing parts. Consequently, they can be easily detected across instances of the same word-class, in terms of finding a com-mon structure among similar instances. A dissimilarity based on PAS is proposed taking into account (i) the difference in the relative locations of the two PAS, (ii) the difference between their segment orientations and (iii) the difference in their segment lengths.

These scale invariant contour features are used for retrieving the location and scale of the candidate instance within the test image. For this purpose a non-rigid point matching algorithm is applied, which deforms the query word in order to capture the shape of the segmented words in the document. The authors also introduce a pruning criterion, which discards unlikely similar matches improving the average precision

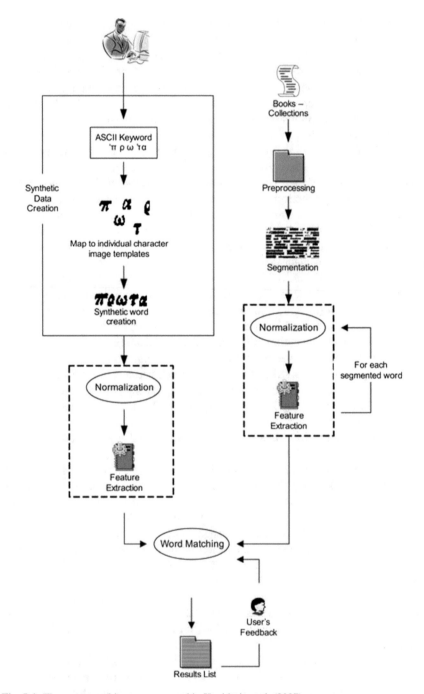

Fig. 5.4 The system architecture proposed in Konidaris et al. (2007)

of the system, with low risk of reducing its recall. It is based on the difference in the size of the descriptors between two words as well as the difference in their respective number of PAS. In this context, at least half of the total matches to be processed per query are avoided.

Scale invariance is highly concerned in the work of Konidaris et al. (2016) where a two steps methodology based on SIFT features is proposed. The purpose of the first step is to narrow down the search space, therefore, for every keypoint in the query keyword image, the nearest K points are found in the entire document page image without using any further segmentation information. These document key-points are candidate image areas that are matched against the query keyword image. The keypoint pairs are used in order to estimate the parameters of a transformation matrix. Using the RANSAC algorithm (Fishler and Bolles 1981) these parameters are robustly estimated even when the measurements contain outliers. Moreover, the inliers percent is used in the proposed method as an indicator of the goodness of fit.

An attribute-based model (PHOC) (Almazan et al. 2014) is adapted in Sfikas et al. (2015) for polytonic Greek documents. The basic framework to represent word images is the Fisher Vector description. For each word image, dense SIFT descriptors are extracted. A Gaussian mixture model (GMM) is trained using SIFT descriptors from all input images, and Fisher vectors are calculated for each image as a function of their SIFT description and the gradients of the GMM with respect to its parameters. This results to a fixed-length, highly discriminative representation, that can be seen as an augmented bag of visual words description that encodes higher order statistics. Three different ways were proposed to adapt PHOC for old (polytonic) Greek characters which correspond to three different transcription representations: (i) Atonic PHOC (A-PHOC), (ii) Polytonic Header PHOC (PH-PHOC) and (iii) Mixed Bin PHOC (MBPHOC). The difference of each one to the other is to the number and meaning of the bins used for the descriptor.

In the recent years, Convolutional Neural Networks (CNN) have shown an impressive applicability in several tasks including machine vision, classification etc. In Sfikas et al. (2016) a deep CNN, pretrained for a character classification task (Jaderberg et al. 2014) is used as a feature extractor. The pool of resulting convolutional features is aggregated to a single descriptor per word image. Aggregation is done by combining simple sum-pooling that has been recently demonstrated to be an appropriate encoding technique for convolutional features (Babenko and Lempitsky 2015). This simple aggregation model is combined with a zoning scheme, suitable for word images, to create the fixed-length word-level feature vector (Zoning-Aggregated Hypercolumns—ZAH). Figure 5.5 depicts the several steps for the creation of ZAH features.

5.3.2   Linguistic Approaches

Natural language processing techniques are powerful tools that can further enrich the retrieval results by query extension. They imply a morphological generation system,

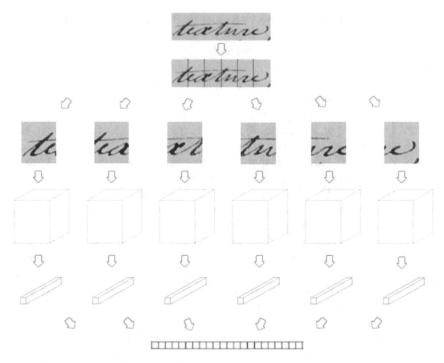

Fig. 5.5 Processing pipeline of ZAH features as proposed in Sfikas et al. (2016)

which provides users the ability to search documents by inserting a new keyword and selecting a pattern as a representative of the appropriate inflectional class. The work of Kesidis et al. (2011) proposes an extension to historical documents of work applied on Modern Greek morphological phenomena (Guillevic and Suen 1997; Ralli and Galiotou 2004) which allows the detection of inflected words of the document corpus based on the word stem and the related word-forms. Furthermore, access to the semantic content of the documents is facilitated by the implementation of a synonym dictionary (Turcato et al. 2000). Specifically, a ranking of the synonymy relations in terms of their weight in the religious—historical domain is performed in order to associate them with a score that estimates how often the relation is used in the specific domain. The system provides the user with options for both word synonym definition as well as for synonym retrieval according to a certain query word.

5.4   Evaluation

A word spotting system provides as a result a list of ranked words according to their similarity to a given query. In order to assess and compare the performance of the various methods it is beneficial to use common evaluation schemes. This refers to the dataset used for the evaluation as well as the evaluation protocols and measures. This section summarizes such evaluation aspects and also highlights the evaluation results provided by the several methods.

5.4.1   Datasets

In Kesidis et al. (2011) a corpus of 110 images is used in accordance to a query set of 32 keywords. The collection consists of digitized Greek documents printed during the seventeenth and eighteenth centuries. These texts contain a specific morphology, which reflects the evolution of the Greek language through the particular period containing word-forms from Ancient, Medieval and Modern Greek. For each keyword, the corresponding inflected word-forms are determined by the proposed morphological generator.

Vasilopoulos and Kavallieratou (2013) applied the segmentation-free approach in a collection of Greek document images of the Government Gazette of the Principality of Samos, that are kept at the General State Archives records (GSA) of Samos, Greece. For this dataset, ground truth results were extracted from 15 scanned images by a human reader. There are 10 queries corresponding to frequent as well as rarely occurring words with a variety of character lengths.

The Greek polytonic system was used from the late antiquity until recently (1982). It includes nine diacritic marks. Some of them are used pairwise resulting to 28 different diacritic mark combinations that may appear above or below Greek characters. A thorough and detailed work regarding Greek polytonic documents is given in Gatos et al. (2015). In this work, the GRPOLY-DB database is introduced which contains both machine-printed and handwritten documents. For instance, the GRPOLY-DB-Handwritten is a historical Greek text written by Sophia Trikoupi, during the 19th century. There are 46 pages of handwritten polytonic text containing 4939 words, which derive from the archives of the Hellenic Parliament library. A sample page is illustrated in Fig. 5.6a. It can be seen that the text is rather cursive accompanied by intra-writer variability among instances of the same word. Besides the polytonic documents, GRPOLY-DB database also provides human based annotation with detailed ground-truth information that can be used for training and evaluation of the four most common document image processing tasks, i.e., text line and word segmentation, text recognition, isolated character recognition and word spotting.

A dataset of 100 pages from a Greek historical machine-printed book of the Renaissance period is used for evaluation in Konidaris et al. (2016). A sample page is shown in Fig. 5.6b. The dataset is characterized by degradation problems that are typical in historical documents, namely, faded characters, bleed-through as well as curved text lines, ink fades, etc. A sample of 100 old Greek machine-printed document pages containing 27,702 words is also used in Konidaris et al. (2007). The query consists of 25 randomly selected keywords. When applying user feedback, the first 5% of the correct words in the results list are used.

(a)

(b)

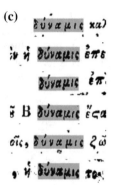

(c)

Fig. 5.6 **a** Sample page from GRPOLY-DB-Handwritten dataset (Gatos et al. 2015). **b** Sample from the Greek historical machine-printed book of the Renaissance period used in Konidaris et al. (2016). **c** Instances of word «δύναμις» in the dataset of Konidaris et al. (2016)

5.4.2 Protocols and Measures

In order to evaluate the accuracy of the word segmentation process, the overall ground truth regarding the word segmentation are determined in advance identifying all the instances of the keywords and the corresponding word-forms. The performance of each segmentation methodology is evaluated separately and then the evaluation takes into account the combination of both segmentation techniques. The word segmentation accuracy is calculated for all word instances that correspond to keywords and the corresponding inflected word-forms as defined in the ground truth. A word instance is considered as detected only if there is a significant overlap with an existing segmentation result (Wolf and Jolion 2006).

Often the ground truth consists not only of exact matches but also of partial matches containing the query keyword. For instance, in Konidaris et al. (2016) the query keyword may appear in the dataset either as an individual word or as part of a larger word. Finding if a query is part of a larger word does not involve any morphological rules or analysis into stems and affixes. Instead, the comparison is on a textual basis that simply tests if the query string is substring of a particular ground truth word.

For the evaluation of the word spotting results, the typical approach in the literature is to use metrics related to precision and recall. Precision is the fraction of retrieved words that are relevant to the query while recall refers to the fraction of relevant words that are successfully retrieved (Giotis et al. 2017). Based on these two metrics, the F-Measure, the R-Precision and the Mean Average Precision (MAP) are usually also calculated in order to facilitate the performance evaluation.

5.4.3 Evaluation Results

In Kesidis et al. (2011) each synthetic query keyword is compared against the corpus of segmented words and the 1st Tier, 2nd Tier and 1-NN retrieval statistics are recorded. The first two measure the recall value for the top K and 2 K closest matches, where K is the cardinality of the query class. The 1-NN indicates the case where the closest match belongs to the query class. The best result are given when the user selects three relevant instances and are 41%, 45% and 83% for the 1st Tier, 2nd Tier and 1-NN, respectively. Regarding the influence of the inflected word-forms, the experiments have shown a significant improvement in the overall performance. For instance, the increase in 1-NN accuracy climbs from 26% up to 75% when word-forms are involved.

The results in the segmentation-free approach of Vasilopoulos and Kavallieratou (2013) demonstrate an F-Measure ranging from 36% up to 97%. The authors denote that these results refer to the query word as is even though Greek is an inflectional language and for each noun, several similar word forms can be found (dative, genitive, accusative, etc.).

The GRPOLY-DB-Handwritten dataset is used in Giotis et al. (2015). The authors selected words whose occurrences appear more than five times and their length is greater than six characters. The query list provided by this criterion includes 21 distinct words along with their instances, yielding a total number of 141 queries. The MAP performance of the system is 60%, which outperforms other state-of-the-art methods.

In Konidaris et al. (2016) the evaluation is performed concerning a set of seven query keywords. Even though the documents are printed, there is a high visual variability across the instances of each keyword in the document corpus. For example, Fig. 5.6c depicts a few instances of a certain keyword that appear at different slopes, with variable inter-character spacing, light or heavily inked, etc. The method achieves a MAP near to 80%, which is better than other competitive methods. The authors provide also detailed MAP results per keyword length where the proposed method gives better results especially for keyword lengths between 5 and 11 characters, where the majority of the query keywords belongs.

Precision versus recall curves were used to demonstrate the experimental results in Konidaris et al. (2007). The evaluation demonstrated that (i) the hybrid scheme outperforms the single feature approaches, (ii) in all cases when the user feedback is applied, the precision/recall rates are improved by at least of 20%, (iii) combination of synthetic data creation and user feedback leads to improved performance in terms of precision and recall.

The GRPOLY-DB offers a rich collection of historical documents. The queries used for the experiments in Gatos et al. (2015) are cropped and binarized word images from the database. Evaluation is performed using a fixed set of queries for each dataset. The query descriptor is matched against all other descriptors in the dataset, and image distances that fall under a variable threshold are considered as true matches. Comparison between feature vectors is achieved using Dynamic Time Warping (DTW), which optimizes correspondence between matching feature components using dynamic programming (Rath and Manmatha 2003). For the purpose of evaluation, the average Precision is used as a metric on all possible thresholds. Mean average Precision (MAP) is then calculated as the mean over all query evaluation results. For the adaptive window features, MAP was recorded 61.35% while for the profile features using DTW it is 73.93%.

The experiments in Sfikas et al. (2015) regard polytonic Greek unconstrained handwritten word recognition. They are applied on the GRPOLY-DB database and are evaluated using the MAP. It is shown that including information about polytonic diacritics always gives better results. A-PHOC is the most naive adaptation of Almazan et al. (2014), and closest to the original PHOC descriptor in the sense that it uses bins for letters, digits and bigrams, completely disregarding polytonic diacritics. The PH-PHOC representation includes polytonic information using a short information header, which is low-cost and character-independent. PH-PHOC outperformed A-PHOC at the price of only a few extra variates added in the descriptor. The last proposal, MB-PHOC, includes feature vector variates that correspond to all valid combinations of letter and diacritic, and has been shown to be universally the most efficient choice, albeit with a high computational cost in the training phase.

The Zoning-Aggregated Hypercolumns technique proposed in Sfikas et al. (2016) is tested using a machine printed part of the GRPOLY-DB dataset (GRPOLY-DB-MachinePrinted-A). Querying with the proposed descriptor is performed by nearest-neighbour search in the (Euclidean) descriptor space. It is compared to Adaptive Zoning features (Gatos et al. 2011) and profiles combined with DTW (Lavrenko et al. 2004) providing superior results. Specifically, for ZAH, the MAP is 91.5% while for the Adaptive Zoning Features it is 81.9% and for the profile features using DTW it achieves 89.7%.

5.5   Conclusions

In this work, an overview of recent techniques and available databases for keyword spotting of old Greek machine-printed and handwritten documents is presented. All steps of a keyword spotting system, namely, preprocessing for image binarization, enhancement and segmentation, feature representation, matching and word retrieval, are presented in order to report on how current keyword spotting approaches for old Greek documents work. Table 5.1 summarizes the above discussion. Additionally, all databases and protocols used for the evaluation of the performance of the available

Table 5.1   Overview of key techniques applied at the various core steps of the word spotting pipeline

Publication	Preprocessing and word segmentation	Feature extraction and word retrieval	Dataset and evaluation
Konidaris et al. (2007)	Adaptive binarization (Gatos et al. 2006), Frame removal (Gatos et al. 2005) Segmentation by RLSA	Zones density (Bokser 1992), Projections of upper and lower profiles (Rath and Manmatha 2003) Synthetic keyword from ASCII equivalent. User feedback and re-ranking	100 old Greek machine printed document pages, 25 randomly selected query keywords Precision-recall curves
Kesidis et al. (2011)	Adaptive binarization (Gatos et al. 2006), Frame removal (Gatos et al. 2005), Text orientation (Yin 2001), Skew Detection (Perantonis et al. 1999), Noise removal (Stamatopoulos et al. 2007) Segmentation by RLSA	Zones density (Bokser 1992), Projections of upper and lower profiles (Rath and Manmatha 2003) Synthetic keyword from ASCII equaivalent. User feedback and re-ranking. Morphological generator + synonym dictionary	110 typewritten pages of 17th-18th century, 32 query keywords Precision-recall curves, 1st Tier, 2nd Tier and 1-NN
Vasilopoulos and Kavallieratou (2013)	Adaptive binarization, Morphological operations for normalization Segmentation-free	Query sliding over the whole document. Instance detection by SSD and thresholding	50 pages historical printed documents Precision, Recall, F-Measure
Gatos et al. (2015)	Adaptive binarization (Gatos et al. 2006) Text zones and lines (Gatos et al. 2014), Manual word segmentation + ground truth (Clausner et al. 2011)	Adaptive zoning features (Gatos et al. 2011), Projections of upper and lower profiles (Rath and Manmatha 2003) Comparison between feature vectors using dynamic time warping	GRPOLY-DB Mean Average Precision

(continued)

Table 5.1 (continued)

Publication	Preprocessing and word segmentation	Feature extraction and word retrieval	Dataset and evaluation
Giotis et al. (2015)	Adaptive binarization (Gatos et al. 2006) Segmentation provided by GRPOLY-DB	Contours by thinning morphological operation represented as pairs of adjacent segments (PAS) Shape-based similarity based on PAS	GRPOLY-DB 46 handwritten pages of 19th century, 141 queries Mean average precision
Sfikas et al. (2015)	Segmentation provided by GRPOLY-DB	SIFT features, Fisher vectors in attribute-based model (PHOC) (Almazan et al. 2014) Three extensions of PHOC (i) Atonic (A-PHOC), (ii) Polytonic Header (PH-PHOC) and (iii) Mixed Bin (MB-PHOC)	GRPOLY-DB Mean average precision
Konidaris et al. (2016)	Segmentation-free	SIFT features Keypoint correspondence for candidate area detection. Instance detection by RANSAC on fitted keypoint correspondence model	100 machine-printed pages of Renaissance period book, 7 query keywords Mean average precision
Sfikas et al. (2016)	Segmentation provided by GRPOLY-DB	CNN features, ZAH fixed-length word-level feature vector Nearest-neighbor search in the Euclidean descriptor space	GRPOLY-DB Mean average precision

key-word spotting techniques for old Greek documents are presented. Although several results using different databases and evaluation schemes have been presented, the publicly available old Greek database GRPOLY-DB has been recently introduced in order to offer a common environment for the evaluation of the keyword spotting task for old Greek documents. Regarding the core methodologies a continuing evolution of algorithms is recorded introducing segmentation-free approaches as well as sophisticated keypoint and shape-based features for word representation especially designed for work spotting purposes. Recently, CNN-based feature extraction and suitable encoding schemes have been also proposed, initiating a promising area of research where keyword spotting of old Greek documents is tackled in a deep learning framework.

References

Almazan J, Gordo A, Fornes A, Valveny E (2014) Word spotting and recognition with embedded attributes. IEEE TPAMI 36(12):2552–2566

Antonacopoulos A, Karatzas D (2005) Semantics-based content extraction in typewritten historical documents. In: Eighth international conference on document analysis and recognition, pp 48–53

Babenko A, Lempitsky V (2015) Aggregating local deep features for image retrieval. In: IEEE international conference on computer vision (ICCV), pp 1269–1277

Bokser M (1992) Omnidocument technologies. Proc. IEEE 80(7):1066–1078

Clausner C, Pletschacher S, Antonacopoulos A (2011) Aletheia—an advanced document layout and text ground-truthing system for production environments. In: 11th international conference on document analysis and recognition (ICDAR 2011), pp 48–52

Fischler MA, Bolles RC (1981) Random sample consensus: a paradigm for model fitting with applications to image analysis and automated cartography. Commun ACM 24(6):381–395

Gatos B, Konidaris T, Ntzios K, Pratikakis I, Perantonis SJ (2005) A segmentation free approach for keyword search in historical typewritten documents. In: 8th International conference on document analysis and recognition (ICDAR '05), pp 54–58

Gatos B, Pratikakis I, Perantonis SJ (2006) Adaptive degraded document image binarization. Pattern Recogn 39:317–327

Gatos B, Kesidis AL, Papandreou A (2011) Adaptive zoning features for character and word recognition. In: 11th international conference on document analysis and recognition (ICDAR '11), pp 1160–1164

Gatos B, Louloudis G, Stamatopoulos N (2014) Segmentation of historical handwritten documents into text zones and text lines. In: 14th international conference on frontiers in handwriting recognition (ICFHR '14), pp 464–469

Gatos B, Stamatopoulos N, Louloudis G, Sfikas G, Retsinas G, Papavassiliou V, Simistira F, Katsouros V (2015) GRPOLY-DB: an old Greek polytonic document image database. In: 2015 13th international conference on document analysis and recognition (ICDAR), pp 646–650

Giotis AP, Sfikas G, Nikou C, Gatos B (2015) Shape-based word spotting in handwritten document images. In: 2015 13th international conference on document analysis and recognition (ICDAR), pp 561–565

Giotis AP, Sfikas G, Gatos B, Nikou C (2017) A survey of document image word spotting techniques. Pattern Recogn 68:310–332

Guillevic D, Suen CY (1997) HMM word recognition engine. In: Fourth international conference on document analysis and recognition (ICDAR '97), pp 544–547

Jaderberg M, Vedaldi A, Zisserman A (2014) Deep features for text spotting. In: IEEE European conference on computer vision (ECCV), pp 512–528

Kesidis AL, Galiotou E, Gatos B, Pratikakis I (2011) A word spotting framework for historical machine-printed documents. Int J Doc Anal Recognit (IJDAR) 14(2):131–144

Konidaris T, Gatos B, Ntzios K, Pratikakis I, Theodoridis S, Perantonis SJ (2007) Keyword-guided word spotting in historical printed documents using synthetic data and user feedback. Int J Doc Anal Recognit (IJDAR). Special issue on historical documents 9(2–4):167–177

Konidaris T, Kesidis AL, Gatos B (2016) A segmentation-free word spotting method for historical printed documents. Pattern Anal Appl 19(4):963–976

Lavrenko V, Rath TM, Manmatha R (2004) Holistic word recognition for handwritten historical documents. In: Proceedings of the first international work-shop on document image analysis for libraries, pp 278–287

Lowe DG (2004) Distinctive image features from scale-invariant keypoints. Int J Comput Vision 60(2):91–110

Perantonis SJ, Gatos B, Papamarkos N (1999) Block decomposition and segmentation for fast Hough transform evaluation. Pattern Recogn 32(5):811–824

Ralli A, Galiotou E (2004) Greek compounds: a challenging case for the parsing techniques of PC-KIMMO v.2. Int J Comput Intell 1(2):152–162

Rath TM, Manmatha R (2003) Features for word spotting in historical documents. In: Proceedings of the 7th international conference on document analysis and recognition (ICDAR '03), pp 218–222

Sfikas G, Giotis AP, Louloudis G, Gatos B (2015) Using attributes for word spotting and recognition in polytonic Greek documents. In: 13th international conference on document analysis and recognition (ICDAR), pp 686–690

Sfikas G, Retsinas G, Gatos B (2016) Zoning aggregated hypercolumns for keyword spotting. In: 2016 15th international conference on frontiers in handwriting recognition (ICFHR), pp 283–288

Stamatopoulos N, Gatos B, Kesidis AL (2007) Automatic borders detection of camera document images. In: 2nd international workshop on camera-based document analysis and recognition (CBDAR '07). Curitiba, Brazil, pp 71–78

Stamatopoulos N, Louloudis G, Gatos B (2010) Efficient transcript mapping to ease the creation of document image segmentation ground truth with text-image alignment. In: 12th international conference on frontiers in handwriting recognition (ICFHR '10), pp 226–231

Theodoridis S, Koutroumbas K (1997) Pattern recognition. Academic Press, New York

Turcato D, Popowich F, Toole J, Fass D, Nicholson D, Tisher D (2000) Adapting a synonym database to specific domains. In: Klavans J, Gonzalo J (eds) Proceedings of the ACL workshop on recent advances in natural language processing and information retrieval, pp 1–11

Vasilopoulos N, Kavallieratou E (2013) A classification-free word-spotting system. In: Document recognition and retrieval XX, vol 8658. International Society for Optics and Photonics, p. 86580F

Wahl FM, Wong KY, Casey RG (1982) Block segmentation and text extraction in mixed text/image documents. Comput Graph Image Process 20:375–390

Wolf C, Jolion J (2006) Object count/area graphs for the evaluation of object detection and segmentation algorithms. Int J Doc Anal Recognit 8(4):280–296

Yin PY (2001) Skew detection and block classification of printed documents. Image Vis Comput 19:567–579

Chapter 6
Machine Learning for Intangible Cultural Heritage: A Review of Techniques on Dance Analysis

Ioannis Rallis, Athanasios Voulodimos, Nikolaos Bakalos, Eftychios Protopapadakis, Nikolaos Doulamis and Anastasios Doulamis

Abstract Performing arts and in particular dance is one of the most important domains of Intangible Cultural Heritage. However, preserving, documenting, analyzing and visually understanding choreographic patterns is a challenging task due to technical difficulties it involves. A choreography is a time-varying 3D process (4D) including dynamic co-interactions among different actors (dancers), emotional and style attributes, as well as supplementary ICH elements such as the music tempo, the rhythm, traditional costumes etc. Recent technological advancements have unleashed tremendous possibilities in capturing, documenting and storing Intangible Cultural Heritage content, which can now be generated at a greater volume and quality than ever before. The massive amounts of RGB-D and 3D skeleton data produced by video and motion capture devices. The huge number of different types of existing dances and variations dictate the need for organizing, archiving and analyzing dance-related cultural content in a tractable fashion and with lower computational and storage resource requirements. Motion capturing devices are programmable to extract humans' skeleton data in terms of 3D points each corresponding to a human joint. This information can be combined with computer graphics software toolkits for modelling, classification and summarization purposes. In this chapter, we present recent trends in choreographic representation in terms of modelling, summarization and choreographic pose recognition. We survey recent approaches employed for the extraction of representative primitives of choreographic sequences, the recognition of choreographic pose and dance movements, as well as for the analysis and semantic representation of choreographic patterns.

I. Rallis · A. Voulodimos · N. Bakalos · E. Protopapadakis · N. Doulamis · A. Doulamis (✉)
National Technical University of Athens, Athens, Greece
e-mail: adoulam@cs.ntua.gr

© Springer Nature Switzerland AG 2020
F. Liarokapis et al. (eds.), *Visual Computing for Cultural Heritage*, Springer Series on Cultural Computing, https://doi.org/10.1007/978-3-030-37191-3_6

6.1 Introduction

Cultural expression, in any form, includes fragile intangible live expressions and elements. Such expressions are built upon certain knowledge, skills and craftsmanship. These manifestations of human intelligence and creativeness constitute our Intangible Cultural Heritage (ICH), a basic factor of local cultural identity and a guaranty for sustainable development (Doulamis 2013; Voulodimos et al. 2016). UNESCO claims that ICH assets (e.g., music, dance, craft) are of equal importance to the tangible ones. Folk dances are important parts to ICH; they are directly connected to local culture and identity (Shay and Sellers-Young 2016; Doulamis et al. 2017). Recently, research approaches have been carried out for digitization (Hisatomi et al. 2011), modelling (Raptis et al. 2011), choreographic analysis (Rallis et al. 2017), posture classification (Protopapadakis et al. 2018), documentation (Aristidou et al. 2015a; Kapadia et al. 2013) and representation of folklore choreographies. In this context, research projects have been funded, such as i-TREASURES (Dimitropoulos 2014), TERPSICHORE,[1] Wholodance (Rizzo 2018), WebDANCE (Kavakli et al. 2004), AniAge[2] and projects with the purpose of capturing and modelling ICH.

A choreographic sequence is a time-varying 3D process (4D modeling), which contains dynamic co-interactions among different actors, emotional and style attributes, and supplementary elements, such as music tempo, and costumes. Dance analysis is an important research field in the cultural sector since it constitutes one of the components of Intangible Cultural Heritage (ICH) (Voulodimos et al. 2016). Nowadays, research focuses on the utilization of motion acquisition sensors, in an attempt to handle kinesiology issues. The extraction of skeleton data, in real-time, contains a significant amount of information (data and metadata), allowing for various choreography-based analytics. Analyzing choreographic sequences is a highly complicated task as it involves the inclusion and processing of many factors such as the dancer's emotions (Aristidou et al. 2015b), motion capturing systems calibration issues, the dancer's expressions (Aristidou and Chrysanthou 2013) and kinesiology differences. Moreover, folklore choreographies are very important not only for preserving ethnological aspects but is a different area in the kinesiology field encompassing the rhythm, the expression, specific postures and the folklore music.

The study of dance from a computational point of view has been enabled by the development of heterogeneous sensors, including visual cameras and motion capture devices, on the one hand, and the advancements in motion analysis fueled by the progress made in machine learning, as well as signal and image processing (Kico et al. 2018). Regarding the part of motion acquisition, characteristic examples of Motion Capture Systems are Kinect (Zhang 2012), Vicon, and OptiTrak (Wang et al. 2017), which can be seen as one of the most accurate motion schemes used to digitalize humans' movements (Chen et al. 2013; Zhou et al. 2013; Kico et al. 2018). Now, these systems are being rapidly incorporated as a critical component to many applications like gaming, 3D animation, education, engineering, rehabilitation and

---

[1]http://terpsichore-project.eu/.

[2]https://www.euh2020aniage.org/.

sports industry (Aristidou et al. 2015a; Kico et al. 2018). In addition, the visualization of the human body through joint identification and extraction of the dance movement based on motion capture and Labanotation (Choensawat et al. 2015; Rallis et al. 2018a; Wang et al. 2017; Kojima et al. 2009; Kico et al. 2018; Hajdin et al. 2019) opens new horizons in several fields such as kinesiology, neuroscience and computer graphics research.

Furthermore, Machine Learning (ML) learning techniques have progressed dramatically over the past decades from researched curiosity to a practical technology in many applications such as Computer Vision, Natural Language Processing, Bioinformatics, etc., succeeding to provide solutions to difficult research problems while also leading to a wide range of exciting applications. In the domain of ICH content, and particularly dance, Machine Learning provides many opportunities for analysis, classification, semantic annotation and emotional understanding of human choreographic movement. In this chapter, we will present a brief survey of the main approaches that have been proposed in the literature exploiting ML techniques to analyze choreographic time series. We will focus on three main pillars: the extraction the key choreographic primitives from a longer time series, i.e., *summarization*, the identification of key posture in dance movement, i.e., *dance pose recognition* of choreographic content, and the semantic representation and notation of dance movements through *Laban Movement Analysis*.

6.2   Dance Summarization

Content summarization is very useful application domain in the multimedia research community in general. Focusing on choreographic sequences, the automatic extraction of the choreographic elements is of significant interest, since such elements provide an abstract and compact representation of the semantic information encoded in the overall dance storyline. A large number of sensors capture the kinesiology of the dancers around the clock producing huge video sequences. Processing these videos is a time, energy, hardware and man power consuming progress. Due to the aforementioned parameters video summarization has an important role in this field enhancing the storage, browsing and retrieval of large collection of video data without losing important details of the captured subject.

One of the first approaches for extracting the most representative key frames from video programs introduced in Wolf (1996). After that, many approaches used kinesiological features for extraction the most representative frames. The approach in Chan et al. (2018) focuses on the decomposition of the dance movements into elementary motions. Placing this problem into a probabilistic framework, we propose to exploit Gaussian processes to accurately model the different components of the decomposition. The proposed framework relies on Gaussian processes allowing for a flexible representation, from extremely coarse to detailed, capturing the periodicities of the dance movement (Fig. 6.1).

Fig. 6.1 This illustration depicts the hierarchical sparse representational modelling for summarization purposes (Rallis et al. 2018b). This framework extracts the key representative frames of a choreographic sequence in an hierarchical manner

In Protopapadakis et al. (2017), the authors focus on segmentation and classification algorithms using depth images and videos of folkloric dances in order to identify key movements and gestures, compare them against database instances and determine the dance genres they represent, as well as to provide helpful metadata. A set of six traditional Greek dances consists the investigated data. A two-step process was adopted. At first, the most descriptive skeleton data were selected using a combination of density based and sparse modelling algorithms. Then, the representative data served as training set for a variety of classifiers. In Krüger et al. (2017), a segmentation method that can separate cyclic activities and their transitions for a number of data modalities is presented. This approach tackles the segmentation problem on a general level in terms of the choice of crucial parameters, e.g. the search radius and the feature offsets for stacking. The proposed feature bundling is a novel contribution and proves to be especially helpful for processing noisy data modalities such as EMG, accelerometer and Kinect motion capture. The authors used a five-point derivation to estimate the direction of movement in the bundling, but when faced with severe noise, one will need more robust methods. This will further reduce variance in the feature space, with few implications, as long as one does not try to synthesize new sequences from the feature space (Fig. 6.2).

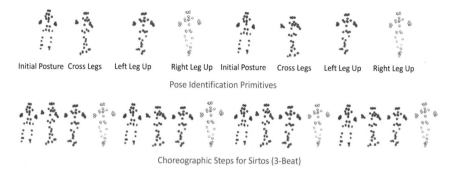

Initial Posture   Cross Legs   Left Leg Up   Right Leg Up   Initial Posture   Cross Legs   Left Leg Up   Right Leg Up

Pose Identification Primitives

Choreographic Steps for Sirtos (3-Beat)

Fig. 6.2   An example of the key primitives of a Greek folkloric dance (Sirtos)

Furthermore, the spatio-temporal summarization algorithm proposed in Rallis et al. (2018b) considers 3D motion captured data, instead of RGB information, represented by 3D joints that model human skeleton is introduced. In particular, the proposed approach, 3D joints are derived from the Vicon motion capture system. The advantage of directly handling 3D human skeleton points instead of raw depth data is that few data samples are involved in the processing of the dance sequences, making summarization far more efficient. The authors describe an hierarchical framework taking into consideration the Sparse Modeling Representative Selection algorithm (Elhamifar et al. 2012). The basic idea behind this approach is that every image frame of the choreographic sequence can be expressed as a linear combination of one or more representative samples.

A dynamic hierarchical layered structure to represent human anatomy is the core of the method proposed in Kahol et al. (2004), which uses low-level motion parameters to characterize motion in the various layers of this hierarchy, which correspond to different segments of the human body. This characterization is used with a naive Bayesian classifier to derive choreographer profiles from empirical data that are used to predict how particular choreographers segment gestures in other motion sequences. In contrast, the works of Voulodimos et al. (2018a, 2018b) propose two summarization approaches: a "time-independent" method based on k-means++ clustering algorithm for the extraction of prominent representative instances of a dance, and a physics-based technique that creates temporal summaries of the sequence at different levels of detail are presented. The main scope of the proposed framework is to extract the most representative instances of the dance, its key postures, or, differently put, its basic primitives, regardless of their order in the sequence. The authors define the selection of the most representative frames as an unsupervised clustering problem. Since a feature vector is assigned for each frame of a dance frame sequence, the vectors of all frames form a trajectory in a high dimensional feature space, which expresses their temporal variation. In the proposed work, the authors denote the magnitude of the second derivative of feature vectors for all frames within a sequence with respect to time as a curvature measure. The second derivative expresses the degree of acceleration or deceleration of an object that traces out the feature trajectory.

Summarization can also be useful in the context of fast searching of content in large motion databases, and for efficient motion analysis and synthesis. In Krüger et al. (2010), the authors demonstrate that identifying locally similar regions in human motion data can be practical even for huge databases, if medium-dimensional feature sets are used for kd-tree-based nearest-neighbor searches. Moreover, efficient approaches for local and global motion matching, which are applicable even to huge databases, have been presented. Moreover, the authors of Lee et al. (2002) present a framework that encompasses a connected set of avatar behaviors that can be created from extended, freeform sequences of motion, automatically organized for efficient search, and exploited for real-time avatar control using a variety of interface techniques. The motion is preprocessed to add variety and flexibility by creating connecting transitions where good matches in poses, velocities, and contact state of the character exist.

An approach for performance animation that employs video cameras and a small set of retro-reflective markers to create a low-cost, easy-to-use system that might someday be practical for home use is introduced in Chai and Hodgins (2005). The low-dimensional control signals from the user's performance are supplemented by a database of pre-recorded human motion. The system automatically learns a series of local models from a set of motion capture examples that are a close match to the marker locations captured by the cameras. A framework for synthesizing dance performance matched to input music, based on the emotional aspects of dance performance is proposed in Shiratori et al. (2006). This framework consists of a motion analysis, a music analysis, and a motion synthesis component based on the extracted features. In the analysis steps, motion and music feature vectors are acquired. Motion vectors are derived from motion rhythm and intensity, while music vectors are derived from musical rhythm, structure, and intensity.

On a different note, the work of Kitsikidis (2015) focuses on the use of game design elements for the transmission of Intangible Cultural Heritage (ICH) knowledge and, especially, for the learning of traditional dances. More specifically, the authors present a 3D game environment that employs an enjoyable natural human computer interface, which is based on the fusion of multiple depth sensors data in order to capture the body movements of the user/learner. Moreover, the proposed framework automatically assesses the users' performance by using a combination of Dynamic Time Warping (DTW) with Fuzzy Inference System (FIS) approach providing feedback in a form of a score as well as instructions from a virtual tutor in order to promote self-learning.

Finally, the authors of Ferguson et al. (2014) propose ways of comparing two similar dance performances, using the DTW algorithm. The DTW method is validated for use with dance performance motion tracking data by comparing its results with 'ground truth' results obtained from a comparison between videos of two motion tracked performances. The technique was extended to investigate two processes that affect movement timing-scaling (a fixed ratio alteration) and lapsing (caused by insertion or deletion of movement material). The authors applied the method to a comparison of dances performed with a musical soundtrack and without a musical soundtrack.

6.3 Laban Movement Analysis

Human movement analysis and recognition is an important field in computer vision area, and is of particular interest in the choreographic domain. Due to the fact that choreographic performances use complex kinesiology movements is necessary to define the notation of the body joints variations. Laban Movement Analysis (LMA) (ERIC—ED059225—The mastery of movement 1971) or Kinetography (Hutchinson et al. 1970) encodes the choreographic sequences of the body joints into dance notations. The Labanotation system encompasses symbols in order to recognize and to encode the human body movements defining a dance score as a music score respectively. Dance notation includes a set of scores, symbols and rules for encoding dance (or movement in general), in a similar way that music notation records music. Labanotation is recognized as one of the most widely used and accurate notation systems for recording dance highlights.

In Aristidou et al. (2015a), the authors present a framework based on the principles of Laban Movement Analysis (LMA) that aims to identify style qualities in dance motions. The proposed algorithm uses a feature space that aims to capture the four LMA components (Body, Effort, Shape, Space), and can be subsequently used for motion comparison and evaluation. The proposed framework is designed and implemented using a virtual reality simulator for teaching folk dances in which users can preview dance segments performed by a 3D avatar and repeat them (Fig. 6.3).

A mathematical framework that can automatically extract motion qualities, in terms of LMA entities, is presented in Aristidou and Chrysanthou (2013). The aforementioned approach aims to distinguish motions with different emotional states. The authors aim to appraise the significance of the proposed features in motion classification using Principal Component Analysis (PCA), where the weight of each feature in separating the performer's feeling is presented. A new classification space is introduced based, not only on the basic description of motion such as the posture, but

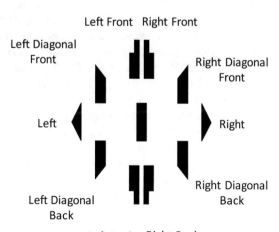

Fig. 6.3 The Laban system codes the variations of the human body joints into motion scores. The symbols are divided into the horizontal and vertical surface

on the motion qualitative and quantitative characteristics. PCA has been also used for dimensionality reduction, resulting in a less complex system; the reduced segments (principal components) are used as input to a Support Vector Machine (SVM) classifier, which decides about the segment with respect to emotion.

Moreover, in Ballas et al. (2017), LabanDance, a serious game for Labanotation is presented. The LabanDance is a real-time game using the Kinect sensor. The user is asked to perform a sequence of moves at a specific time as they are recorded in a score displayed on the screen. The game has two modes of operation. The first is addressed to users with little familiarity with Labanotation and is accompanied by a virtual trainer. In the second, the user is only required to perform the moves based on the score. The game includes four levels with hand, foot, jump, and a level with a combination of all moves. A different aspect of the use of LMA is presented in Hachimura et al. (2005), where the authors describe a framework in order to extract characteristic poses as well as highlight parts from data of dancing movement obtained by motion capturing technique. For this, the theory of LMA has been applied, and the physical feature values corresponding to the LMA components are defined. By observing the change over time of these feature values, body movements corresponding to the LMA components are extracted. In this approach, the authors focus on effort and shape components of LMA.

The similarities between various emotional states with regards to the arousal and valence of the Russell's circumplex model have also been investigated Aristidou et al. (2015b). A variety of features that encode, in addition to the raw geometry, stylistic characteristics of motion based on LMA is presented. Motion capture data from acted dance performances were used for training and classification purposes. The experimental results show that the proposed features can partially extract the LMA components, providing a representative space for indexing and classification of dance movements with regards to the emotion. In Bouchard and Badler (2007), an automatic motion capture segmentation method based on movement qualities derived from LMA is presented. LMA provides a good compromise between high-level semantic features, which are difficult to extract for general motions, and low-level kinematic features which, often yield unsophisticated segmentations. The LMA features are computed using a collection of neural networks trained with temporal variance in order to create a classifier that is more robust with regard to input boundaries.

Another work Zacharatos et al. (2013) proposes a set of body motion features, based on the Effort component of LMA, that are used to provide sets of classifiers for emotion recognition in a game scenario for four emotional states: concentration, meditation, excitement and frustration. Experimental results show that, the system is capable of successfully recognizing the four different emotional states at a very high rate. From the results achieved the authors conclude that Laban Movement Analysis is a valid and promising approach for emotion recognition from body movements due to the abstract level of Laban technique. Specifically this framework describes that two of Effort's component motion factors, Time and Space can result to high emotion recognition rates.

In the context of educational frameworks, a proposal for analysis and visualization of dance kinesiology based on Labanotation and embodied learning concepts is presented in Rallis et al. (2018a). The low-cost Kinect sensor is employed to extract skeletal data which are then processed and transformed geometrically. In the sequel, they are analyzed based on the Labanotation system to characterize the posture of the human limbs. Two modules have been developed. The first module serves for recording, analyzing and visualizing body movements. The second module is an application in which the user is required to perform with his upper limbs, a sequence of gestures given by the system in the form of Labanotation symbols. Dance notation consists of a set of symbols and rules for recording dance (or movement in general), in a similar way that music notation records music.

Lastly, a motion analysis framework based on LMA is described in Aristidou et al. (2018), which also accounts for stylistic variations of the movement is presented. Implemented in the context of Motion Graphs, it is used to eliminate potentially problematic transitions and synthesize style-coherent animation, without requiring prior labeling of the data. The effectiveness of the proposed method is demonstrated by synthesizing contemporary dance performances that include a variety of different emotional states. The constructed LMA-based Motion Graph (MG) by default satisfies posture correlation; in the proposed implementation, the authors select the transition with the highest LMA correlation. Although the MG algorithm may encourage transition to frames of other motions where body posture is highly similar, in contrast LMA MG selects those transitions that motion style is more coherent, despite body posture being less similar.

6.4   Pose Recognition and Dance Movement Classification

The particularities of dance motion make the already challenging computer vision problems of pose and action recognition even more interesting when explored in a choreographic context. In Protopapadakis et al. (2018), the authors scrutinized the effectiveness of a series of well-known classifiers (k Nearest Neighbors, Naïve Bayes, Discriminant Analysis, Classification Trees and Support Vector Machines) in dance recognition from skeleton data. In particular, the goal was to identify poses which are characteristic for each dance performed, based on information on body joints, acquired by a Kinect sensor. The datasets used include sequences from six folk dances and their variations. Multiple pose identification schemes are applied using temporal constraints, spatial information, and feature space distributions for the creation of an adequate training dataset. A similar approach for defining choreographic postures from data sequences is introduced in Bakalos et al. (2018). The selected classifiers are either probabilistic, linear or non-linear kernels.

A framework for body motion analysis in dance using multiple Kinect sensors is presented in Kitsikidis et al. (2018). The proposed method applies fusion to combine the skeletal tracking data of multiple sensors in order to solve occlusion and self-occlusion tracking problems and increase the robustness of skeletal tracking. Finally, body part postures are combined into body posture sequences and Hidden Conditional Random Fields (HCRF) classifier is used to recognize motion patterns. Furthermore, a Convolutional Neural Network-based approach for 3D human body pose estimation from single RGB images is presented in Mehta (2017), addressing the issue of limited generalizability of models trained solely on the starkly limited publicly available 3D pose data is proposed. Using only the existing 3D pose data and 2D pose data, the authors show state-of-the-art performance on established benchmarks through transfer of learned features, while also generalizing to in-the-wild scenes.

A combined approach, involving 3D spatial datasets, noise removal prepossessing and deep learning regression is presented in Kavouras et al. (2019) aiming at the estimation of rough skeleton data. The application scenario involved data sequences from Greek traditional dances. In particular, a visualization application interface was developed allowing the user to load the C3D sequences, edit the data and remove possible noise. The 3D points are selected on the use of a Convolutional Neural Network (CNN) model. Experimental results on real-life dances being captured by the Vicon motion capturing system are presented to show the great performance of the proposed scheme.

In Cao et al. (2016), the authors introduce a deep machine learning framework that exploits CNN representational capabilities to identify choreographic postures captured through the RGB channel of a Kinect II capturing device. To increase the performance, a background subtraction algorithm is utilized for preprocessing, so as to minimize the captured noise and only consider the kinesiological data. To enhance the classification performance, a background subtraction framework was utilized, while the CNN architecture was adapted to simulate a moving average behavior. The overall system can be used as an AI module for assessing the performance of users in a serious game for learning traditional dance choreographies. The main scope of the proposed architecture is to develop a pose identification tool for choreographic educational purposes in order to define automatically the appropriate dance postures from a video sequence (Fig. 6.4).

A method for classifying 3D dance motions especially selected from Korean POP (K-POP) dance performance is proposed in Kim et al. (2015). Compared to actions addressed in daily life and existing games, K-POP dance motions are much more dynamic and vary substantially according to the performers. To cope with the variation of the amplitude of pose, a practical pose descriptor based on relative rotations between two body joints in the spherical coordinate system is presented. As a method to measure similarity between two incomplete motion sequences, subsequence DTW algorithm is explored that supports partial matches.

On a different note, the authors of Kohn et al. (2012) present an algorithm for real-time body motion analysis for dance pattern recognition using a dynamic stereo vision sensor. Dynamic stereo vision sensors asynchronously generate events upon scene dynamics, so that motion activities are on-chip segmented by the sensor. Using this sensor body motion analysis and tracking can be efficiently performed. For dance pattern recognition, a machine learning method based on the Hidden Markov Model is used. On the other hand, in Tang et al. (2018), a music-oriented dance choreography synthesis method using a long short-term memory (LSTM)-autoencoder model to extract a mapping between acoustic and motion features is proposed. Moreover, the

Fig. 6.4 Transfer results. In each section the authors depict five consecutive frames. The top row depicts the source subject, the middle row depicts the normalized pose stick figure and the bottom row shows the model outputs of the target person (Chan et al. 2018)

authors improve the proposed model with temporal indexes and a masking method to achieve better performance.

A novel Spatio-Temporal Laban Feature descriptor (STLF) for dance style recognition based on Laban theory is proposed in Kohn et al. (2012). A novel feature descriptor for dance style recognition and test it on Indian Classical Dance (ICD) is presented. Using inspirations from Laban theory, the authors formulate its major entities and model seemingly trivial biological and psychological kinematics of body-motion into features. At another level, the authors of Wang et al. (2018) introduce a Bayesian Optimized Bi-directional Long Short Term Memory (LSTM) model, called BOBi-LSTM, that automatically estimates dancers' poses through 3D skeleton data processing. Bi-directionality models non-causal relationships occurred in a dance performance, in the sense that future dancer's steps depend on previous/current steps. Additionally, long-range dependence correlates choreographic primitives on a long time (memory) window. To model the aforementioned principles, the authors modify the conventional LSTM networks under a Bayesian Optimized framework in order to define the best network structure.

Chor-RNN (Crnkovic-Friis and Crnkovic-Friis 2016) is a recurrent neural network that is trained using a corpus of motion captured contemporary dance. The system can produce novel choreographic sequences in the choreographic style represented in the corpus. Using a deep recurrent neural network, it is capable of understanding and generating choreography style, syntax and to some extent semantics. Although it is currently limited to generating choreographies for a solo dancer there are a number of interesting paths to explore for future work. This includes the possibility of tracking multiple dancers and experimenting with variational autoencoders that would allow the automatic construction of a symbolic language for movement that goes beyond simple syntax.

A multimodal approach to recognize isolated complex human body movements, i.e., Salsa dance steps is proposed in Masurelle et al. (2013). The proposed framework exploits motion features extracted from 3D sub-trajectories of dancers' body-joints (deduced from Kinect depth-map sequences) using principal component analysis (PCA). These sub-trajectories are obtained thanks to a footstep impact detection module (from recordings of piezoelectric sensors installed on the dance floor). Two alternative classifiers are tested with the resulting PCA features, namely Gaussian mixture models and hidden Markov models (HMM).

Another interesting application is the transfer of motion between human subjects in different dance videos (Chan et al. 2018). Given a video of a source person and another of a target person, the main goal of this work is to generate a new video of the target person enacting the same choreography as the source. To address this task, the authors divide the proposed framework into three stages—pose detection, global pose normalization, and mapping from normalized pose stick figures to the target subject. In the pose detection stage the authors use a pretrained state of the art pose detector to create pose stick figures given frames from the source video. The global pose normalization stage accounts for differences between the source and target body shapes and locations within frame. Finally, the authors design a system to learn the mapping from the normalized pose stick figures to images of the target person with adversarial training. In order to extract pose keypoints for the body the authors adopt OpenPose (Cao et al. 2016). For the image translation stage, a framework proposed in the pix2pixHD (Wang et al. 2018) is provided. Additionally the authors adopt a single 70×70 Patch Generative Adversarial Networks (GAN) for the face discriminator (Isola et al. 2017).

Finally, the work of Barmpoutis et al. (2019) presents a method for action recognition using depth sensors and representing the skeleton time series sequences as higher-order sparse structure tensors to exploit the dependencies among skeleton joints and to overcome the limitations of methods that use joint coordinates as input signals. Moreover, the authors estimate their decompositions based on randomized subspace iteration that enables the computation of singular values and vectors of large sparse matrices with high accuracy. Specifically, the authors attempt to extract different feature representations containing spatio-temporal complementary information and extracting the mode-n singular values with regards to the correlations of skeleton joints. Then, the extracted features are combined using discriminant correlation analysis, and a neural network is used to recognize the action patterns. The experimental results presented use three widely used action datasets and confirm the great potential of the proposed action learning and recognition method.

6.5 Conclusion

The rapid developments in machine learning and computer vision technologies have enabled a variety of interesting applications in a vast range of domains, including human motion understanding. In this context, several steps have been made by the research community towards a multifaceted analysis of dance. The use of appropriately designed and fine-tuned machine learning models on data acquired by both visual sensors and motion capture devices has led to significant progress in the fields of choreography summarization, dance pose recognition, as well as further analysis of style and emotion, often using Laban Movement Analysis notation (a concise list of important milestones attained is given in Table 6.1). Despite the significant steps already made and, further research is needed towards a deeper understanding and analysis of dance and related elements, such as style, tradition and affect. The advancements of deep learning as well as the increasing accuracy and cost-effectiveness of visual and motion capture sensors are bound to play an important role to this direction in the following years.

Table 6.1 Important milestones in the history of the kinesiology analysis

Milestones/Contribution	Motion capturing systems	Contributor, year
Graphical editor for dance notation	Kinect	Kojima et al. (2009), 2002
Real-time control of three-dimensional avatars	VICON	Lee et al. (2002), 2002
Performance animation	Pulnix video cameras	Chai and Hodgins (2005), 2005
Dancing-to-music character animation	VICON	Shiratori et al. (2006), 2006
Real-time body motion analysis for dance pattern recognition (Hidden Markov Model)	Kinect	Chan et al. (2018), 2012
Analysis of dance movements using gaussian processes	Kinect	Liutkus et al. (2012), 2012
Multimodal classification of dance movements using motion trajectories and sound	Kinect	Masurelle et al. (2013), 2013
Hierarchical aligned cluster analysis (HACA) for temporal segmentation	VICON	Zhou et al. (2013), 2013
Motion indexing of different emotional states using LMA components (PCA, Laban, SVM)		Aristidou and Chrysanthou (2013), 2013
Dance analysis using multiple Kinect sensors	Kinect	Kitsikidis et al. (2018), 2014

(continued)

Table 6.1 (continued)

Milestones/Contribution	Motion capturing systems	Contributor, year
Dynamic dance warping	VICON	Ferguson et al. (2014), 2014
Emotion analysis and classification	VICON	Aristidou et al. (2015b), 2015
Classification of dance motions with depth cameras using subsequence dynamic time warping	Kinect	Kim et al. (2015), 2015
A game-like application for dance learning using a natural human computer interface	Kinect	Kitsikidis (2015), 2015
Folk dance evaluation using laban movement analysis	VICON	Aristidou et al. (2015a), 2015
Unsupervised temporal segmentation of motion data	Kinect	Krüger et al. (2017), 2017
Key postures identification	VICON	Rallis et al. (2017), 2017
CNN-based approach for 3D human body pose estimation	Monocular camera	Mehta (2017), 2017
Hierarchical sparse modeling representative selection	VICON	Rallis et al. (2018b), 2018
Physics-based keyframe selection for human motion summarization	VICON	Voulodimos et al. (2018), 2018
Style-based motion analysis for dance composition	VICON	Aristidou et al. (2018), 2018
An LSTM-autoencoder approach to music-oriented dance synthesis	VICON	Tang et al. (2018), 2018
Spatio-temporal laban feature descriptor (STLF) for dance style recognition		Dewan et al. (2018), 2018
Everybody dance now	n/a	Chan et al. (2018), 2018
Human action recognition through third-order tensor representation and spatio-temporal analysis		Barmpoutis et al. (2019), 2019

References

Aristidou A, Chrysanthou Y (2013) Motion indexing of different emotional states using LMA components. In: SIGGRAPH Asia 2013 technical briefs, New York, NY, USA, pp 21:1–21:4

Aristidou P, Stavrakis E, Charalambous P, Chrysanthou Y, Himona SL (2015a) Folk dance evaluation using laban movement analysis. J Comput Cult Herit 8(4):20:1–20:19

Aristidou A, Charalambous P, Chrysanthou Y (2015b) Emotion analysis and classification: understanding the performers' emotions using the LMA entities. Comput Graphics Forum 34(6):262–276 (2015)

Aristidou A, Stavrakis E, Papaefthimiou M, Papagiannakis G, Chrysanthou Y (2018) Style-based motion analysis for dance composition. Vis Comput 34(12):1725–1737

Bakalos N, Protopapadakis E, Doulamis A, Doulamis N (2018) Dance posture/steps classification using 3D joints from the kinect sensors. In: 2018 IEEE 16th international conference on dependable, autonomous and secure computing, 16th international conference on pervasive intelligence and computing, 4th international conference on big data intelligence and computing and cyber science and technology congress (DASC/PiCom/DataCom/CyberSciTech), pp 868–873

Ballas A, Santad T, Sookhanaphibarn K, Choensawat W (2017) Game-based system for learning labanotation using Microsoft Kinect. In: 2017 IEEE 6th global conference on consumer electronics (GCCE), pp 1–3

Barmpoutis P, Stathaki T, Camarinopoulos S (2019) Skeleton-based human action recognition through third-order tensor representation and spatio-temporal analysis. Inventions 4(1)

Bouchard D, Badler N (2007) Semantic segmentation of motion capture using laban movement analysis. In: Intelligent virtual agents, pp 37–44

Cao Z, Simon T, Wei S-E, Sheikh Y (2016) Realtime multi-person 2D pose estimation using part affinity fields. arXiv:1611.08050 [cs]

Chai J, Hodgins JK (2005) Performance animation from low-dimensional control signals. In: ACM SIGGRAPH 2005 papers. New York, NY, USA, pp 686–696

Chan C, Ginosar S, Zhou T, Efros AA (2018) Everybody dance now. arXiv:1808.07371 [cs]

Chen L, Wei H, Ferryman J (2013) A survey of human motion analysis using depth imagery. Pattern Recogn Lett 34(15):1995–2006

Choensawat W, Nakamura M, Hachimura K (2015) GenLaban: a tool for generating labanotation from motion capture data. Multimed Tools Appl 74(23):10823–10846

Crnkovic-Friis L, Crnkovic-Friis L (2016) Generative choreography using deep learning. arXiv: 1605.06921 [cs]

Dewan S, Agarwal S, Singh N (2018) Spatio-temporal laban features for dance style recognition. In: 2018 24th international conference on pattern recognition (ICPR), pp 2911–2916

Dimitropoulos K et al (2014) Capturing the intangible an introduction to the i-Treasures project. In: 2014 international conference on computer vision theory and applications (VISAPP), vol 2, pp 773–781

Doulamis A et al (2013) 4D reconstruction of the past. In: First international conference on remote sensing and geoinformation of the environment (RSCy2013), vol 8795, p 87950

Doulamis N, Doulamis A, Ioannidis C, Klein M, Ioannides M (2017) Modelling of static and moving objects: digitizing tangible and intangible cultural heritage. In: Mixed reality and gamification for cultural heritage, Springer, Cham, pp 567–589

Elhamifar E, Sapiro G, Vidal R (2012) See all by looking at a few: sparse modeling for finding representative objects. In: 2012 IEEE conference on computer vision and pattern recognition, pp 1600–1607

ERIC—ED059225—The mastery of movement 1971, July. https://eric.ed.gov/?id=ED059225. Accessed 11 July 2019

Ferguson S, Schubert E, Stevens CJ (2014) Dynamic dance warping: using dynamic time warping to compare dance movement performed under different conditions. In: Proceedings of the 2014 international workshop on movement and computing, New York, NY, USA, pp 94:94

Hachimura K, Takashina K, Yoshimura M (2005) Analysis and evaluation of dancing movement based on LMA. In: ROMAN 2005. IEEE international workshop on robot and human interactive communication, pp 294–299

Hajdin M, Kico I, Dolezal M, Chmelik J, Doulamis A, Liarokapis F (2019) Digitization and visualization of movements of slovak folk dances. In: The challenges of the digital transformation in education, pp 245–256

Hisatomi K, Katayama M, Tomiyama K, Iwadate Y (2011) 3D archive system for traditional performing arts. Int J Comput Vis 94(1):78–88

Hutchinson A, Hutchinson WA, Guest AH (1970) Labanotation: or, kinetography Laban: the system of analyzing and recording movement. Taylor & Francis

Isola P, Zhu J-Y, Zhou T, Efros AA (2017) Image-to-image translation with conditional adversarial networks. In: 2017 IEEE conference on computer vision and pattern recognition (CVPR), Honolulu, HI, pp 5967–5976

Kahol K, Tripathi P, Panchanathan S (2004) Automated gesture segmentation from dance sequences. In: Proceedings of 2004 sixth IEEE international conference on automatic face and gesture recognition, pp 883–888

Kapadia M, Chiang I, Thomas T, Badler NI, Kider JT Jr (2013) Efficient motion retrieval in large motion databases. In: Proceedings of the ACM SIGGRAPH symposium on interactive 3D graphics and games, New York, NY, USA, pp 19–28

Kavakli E, Bakogianni S, Damianakis A, Loumou M, Tsatsos D (2004) Traditional dance and E-learning: the WebDance learning environment

Kavouras I, Protopapadakis E, Doulamis A, Doulamis N (2019) Skeleton extraction of dance sequences from 3D points using convolutional neural networks based on a new developed C3D visualization interface. In: The challenges of the digital transformation in education, pp 267–279

Kico I, Grammalidis N, Christidis Y, Liarokapis F (2018) Digitization and visualization of folk dances in cultural heritage: a review. Inventions 3(4):72

Kim D, Jang M, Yoon Y, Kim J (2015) Classification of dance motions with depth cameras using subsequence dynamic time warping. In: 2015 8th international conference on signal processing, image processing and pattern recognition (SIP), pp 5–8

Kitsikidis A et al (2015) A game-like application for dance learning using a natural human computer interface. In: Universal access in human-computer interaction. Access to Learning, Health and Well-Being, pp 472–482

Kitsikidis A, Dimitropoulos K, Douka S, Grammalidis N (2018) Dance analysis using multiple Kinect sensors. In: 2014 international conference on computer vision theory and applications (VISAPP), vol 2, pp 789–795

Kohn B, Nowakowska A, Belbachir AN (2012) Real-time body motion analysis for dance pattern recognition. In: 2012 IEEE computer society conference on computer vision and pattern recognition workshops, pp 48–53

Kojima K, Hachimura K, Nakamura M (2009) LabanEditor: graphical editor for dance notation. In: 11th IEEE international workshop on robot and human interactive communication proceedings, pp 59–64

Krüger B, Tautges J, Weber A, Zinke A (2010) Fast local and global similarity searches in large motion capture databases. In: Proceedings of the 2010 ACM SIGGRAPH/eurographics symposium on computer animation, Goslar Germany, Germany, pp 1–10

Krüger B, Vögele A, Willig T, Yao A, Klein R, Weber A (2017) Efficient unsupervised temporal segmentation of motion data. IEEE Trans Multimed 19(4):797–812

Lee J, Chai J, Reitsma PSA, Hodgins JK, Pollard NS (2002) Interactive control of avatars animated with human motion data. In: Proceedings of the 29th annual conference on computer graphics and interactive techniques, New York, NY, USA, pp 491–500

Liutkus A, Dremeau A, Alexiadis D, Essid S, Daras P (2012) Analysis of dance movements using gaussian processes: extended abstract. In: Proceedings of the 20th ACM international conference on multimedia, New York, NY, USA, pp 1375–1376

Masurelle A, Essid S, Richard G (2013) Multimodal classification of dance movements using body joint trajectories and step sounds. In: 2013 14th international workshop on image analysis for multimedia interactive services (WIAMIS), pp 1–4

Mehta D et al (2017) Monocular 3D human pose estimation in the wild using improved CNN supervision. In: 2017 international conference on 3D vision (3DV), pp 506–516

Protopapadakis E, Grammatikopoulou A, Doulamis A, Grammalidis N (2017) Folk dance pattern recognition over depth images acquired via kinect sensor. ISPRS-Int Arch Photogramm Remote Sens Spat Inf Sci 587–593

Protopapadakis E, Voulodimos A, Doulamis A, Camarinopoulos S, Doulamis N, Miaoulis G (2018) Dance pose identification from motion capture data: a comparison of classifiers. Technologies 6(1):31

Rallis I, Georgoulas I, Doulamis N, Voulodimos A, Terzopoulos P (2017) Extraction of key postures from 3D human motion data for choreography summarization. In: 2017 9th international conference on virtual worlds and games for serious applications (VS-Games), pp 94–101

Rallis I, Langis A, Georgoulas I, Voulodimos A, Doulamis N, Doulamis A (2018a) An embodied learning game using kinect and labanotation for analysis and visualization of dance kinesiology. In: 2018 10th international conference on virtual worlds and games for serious applications (VS-Games), pp 1–8

Rallis I, Doulamis N, Doulamis A, Voulodimos A, Vescoukis V (2018b) Spatio-temporal summarization of dance choreographies. Comput Graph 73:88–101

Raptis M, Kirovski D, Hoppe H (2011) Real-time classification of dance gestures from skeleton animation. In: Proceedings of the 2011 ACM SIGGRAPH/eurographics symposium on computer animation, New York, NY, USA, pp 147–156

Rizzo A et al (2018) WhoLoDancE: whole-body interaction learning for dance education

Shay A, Sellers-Young B (2016) The Oxford handbook of dance and ethnicity. Oxford University Press

Shiratori T, Nakazawa A, Ikeuchi K (2006) Dancing-to-music character animation. Comput Graph Forum 25(3):449–458

Tang T, Jia J, Mao H (2018) Dance with melody: an LSTM-autoencoder approach to music-oriented dance synthesis. In: Proceedings of the 26th ACM international conference on multimedia, New York, NY, USA, pp 1598–1606

Voulodimos A, Doulamis N, Fritsch D, Makantasis K, Doulamis A, Klein M (2016) Four-dimensional reconstruction of cultural heritage sites based on photogrammetry and clustering. J Electron Imaging 26:011013

Voulodimos A, Rallis I, Doulamis N (2018a) Physics-based keyframe selection for human motion summarization. Multimed Tools Appl

Voulodimos A, Doulamis N, Doulamis A, Rallis I (2018b) Kinematics-based extraction of salient 3D human motion data for summarization of choreographic sequences. In: 2018 24th international conference on pattern recognition (ICPR), pp 3013–3018

Wang J, Miao Z, Guo H, Zhou Z, Wu H (2017) Using automatic generation of Labanotation to protect folk dance. JEI 26(1):011028

Wang T-C, Liu M-Y, Zhu J-Y, Tao A, Kautz J, Catanzaro B (2018) High-resolution image synthesis and semantic manipulation with conditional GANs. In: 2018 IEEE/CVF conference on computer vision and pattern recognition, Salt Lake City, UT, USA, pp 8798–8807

Wolf W (1996) Key frame selection by motion analysis. In: 1996 IEEE international conference on acoustics, speech, and signal processing conference proceedings, vol 2, pp 1228–1231

Zacharatos H, Gatzoulis C, Chrysanthou Y, Aristidou A (2013) Emotion recognition for exergames using laban movement analysis. In: Proceedings of motion on games, New York, NY, USA, pp 39:61–39:66

Zhang Z (2012) Microsoft kinect sensor and its effect. IEEE Multimed 19(2):4–10

Zhou F, Torre FD, Hodgins JK (2013) Hierarchical aligned cluster analysis for temporal clustering of human motion. IEEE Trans Pattern Anal Mach Intell 35(3):582–596

Chapter 7
Classification and Detection of Symbols in Ancient Papyri

Alexandros Haliassos, Panagiotis Barmpoutis, Tania Stathaki, Stephen Quirke and Anthony Constantinides

Abstract The advent of powerful image processing and machine learning tools has generated opportunities for more automated and efficient paleography. In this work, methods were developed to automate aspects of the transcription process of ancient papyri. First, a technique is proposed that employs color thresholding and contouring for the automatic extraction of symbols from papyri photographs. Second, two symbol classifiers are considered: a support vector machine that intakes Histogram of Oriented Gradients features, and a convolutional neural network. Finally, a novel system is described based on the sliding window approach that limits the number of windows to be considered and uses a combination of a support vector machine and a convolutional neural network to benefit from both accurate and fast detections. The performance of these methods was evaluated on a set of papyri photographs from the Petrie Museum of Egyptian Archaeology.

7.1 Introduction

The study of historical manuscripts brings about insights into the lives and cultures of ancient humans. Until recently, it has been solely the job of Egyptologists to investigate the writings transcribed on papyrus, a material derived from a plant that resembles thick paper. Their work includes the transcription and contextualization of the text, making connections between different documents, and building up the knowledge base pertaining to these ancient civilizations. The digital age has created opportunities for fruitful collaboration between archaeologists and engineers to aid in the transcription, interpretation, restoration, and preservation of ancient symbols on papyri. For example, image processing and computer vision can be applied to the reassembly of fragmentary documents, avoiding physical contact with the papyri and hence increasing their preservability; they can also be used to identify groups of

A. Haliassos (✉) · P. Barmpoutis · T. Stathaki · A. Constantinides
Department of Electrical and Electronic Engineering, Imperial College London, London, UK
e-mail: alexandros.haliassos14@imperial.ac.uk

S. Quirke
Institute of Archaeology, University College London, London, UK

© Springer Nature Switzerland AG 2020
F. Liarokapis et al. (eds.), *Visual Computing for Cultural Heritage*, Springer Series on Cultural Computing, https://doi.org/10.1007/978-3-030-37191-3_7

121

documents with similar handwriting, to study the evolution of signs over time, or to compare scripts from different periods.

Although related research has been conducted, for example on the transcription of ancient texts using genetic sequence alignment algorithms (Williams et al. 2014a), writer identification of ancient scripts (Panagopoulos et al. 2008; Bar-Yosef et al. 2007; Helli and Moghaddam 2008; Papaodysseus et al. 2014), digital image restoration of papyri (Sparavigna 2009; Labaune et al. 2010; Knox et al. 2008), and virtual reconstruction of fragmented documents at the Fraunhofer Institute (fraunhofer.de 2019), work on the identification of ancient symbols using image classification and object detection techniques is largely lacking. The aim of this work was to design and implement such techniques to help Egyptologists achieve faster and more accurate transcriptions of ancient texts, in an attempt to further bridge the gap between computer vision and paleography. This chapter heavily draws from results outlined in Alexandros Haliassos' master's thesis (Haliassos 2019) and focuses on symbol extraction, classification, and detection.

The data used are photographs of Lahun (also known as Kahun) papyri. These writings were discovered in 1889 by Flinders Petrie and are currently kept at the Petrie Museum of Egyptian Archaeology in London (see an example of a papyrus in Fig. 7.1). They are dated to 1850–1700 BC (late Middle Bronze Age), and their main themes revolve around accounting, law, religion, mathematics and medicine (ucl.ac.uk 2002). Given the age of these documents, the symbols are often heavily distorted, noisy, and/or occluded, posing a significant challenge to both humans and machines in identifying them.

The work presented in this chapter addresses this issue. With respect to symbol extraction, a method is proposed that identifies the presence of symbols in a papyrus photograph and automatically crops rectangular patches corresponding to those symbols. The primary motivation for this method is to ease the process of organizing a labelled dataset for classification and detection. Classification is demonstrated via

Fig. 7.1 Photograph of a clearly written Lahun papyrus with religious content (copyright UCL)

two methods: a support vector machine (SVM) (Cortes and Vapnik 1995) fed with Histogram of Oriented Gradients (HOG) (Dalal and Triggs 2005) features, and a convolutional neural network (CNN) (LeCun et al. 2015; Voulodimos et al. 2018; Guo et al. 2016). The labelled dataset consists of three symbol types, in order to demonstrate these multi-class classification methods on a manageable subset of the symbols, with the understanding that the same techniques can be applied to an extended dataset in future work. The detection of symbols, i.e., the process of locating and classifying them in a papyrus photograph, was tackled with a sliding-window approach that addresses its well-known computational issues by estimating the parameter space of detection window aspect ratios and sizes needed to be considered. A significant reduction in detection time is achieved by rejecting images with low variance and then using a cascade of a binary SVM and CNN for classification.

The chapter is structured as follows. Section 7.2 presents the procedure for symbol extraction. Section 7.3 discusses the implementation and results relating to the classification models. Section 7.4 is dedicated to the proposed detection system, and finally Sect. 7.5 concludes with limitations and future work.

7.2 Symbol Extraction

The aim of the symbol extraction method is to automate to some extent the laborious process of cropping images of symbols from papyrus photographs, which is necessary for the creation of a dataset for training classification models. In Sect. 7.4 we discuss another application of this method, that is, the estimation of the typical size of the symbols in a given photograph. Figure 7.2 illustrates the operation of the method on a papyrus fragment. The first step is to binarize the color images, such that all pixels belonging to the symbols are white and those belonging to the background are black. We exploit the fact that, unlike the background pixels, the symbols have been drawn in black, indicating that the symbols and background are clearly separable in the RGB space.

Given a papyrus photograph, it is first blurred with a Gaussian spatial filter kernel of size 3×3 to smoothen the contours and reduce noise. A further increase of the filter's kernel size removes more noise at the risk of fusing adjacent symbols and thus impeding successful extraction. To threshold the image, a suitable range of RGB values must be specified. Given an RGB pixel $\mathbf{f}$ (each component ranges from 0 to 255) and lower and upper thresholds $\mathbf{T}_L$, $\mathbf{T}_U$ we can obtain a binary pixel as follows:

$$g = \begin{cases} 1, & \mathbf{T}_L \leq \mathbf{f} \leq \mathbf{T}_U \\ 0, & \text{otherwise} \end{cases} \tag{7.1}$$

where the inequality should be interpreted elementwise. There is an apparent trade-off: if the range is too small, then some of the symbols will be lost; on the other hand, if it is too large, then unwanted structures will appear in the resulting binary image.

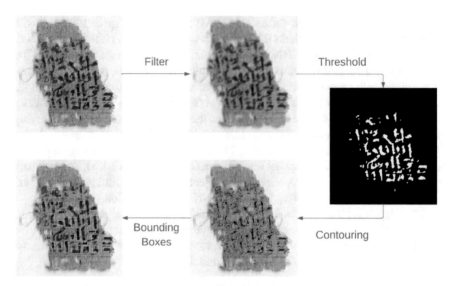

Fig. 7.2 Illustration of the symbol extraction method

Suitable lower and upper thresholds that work across a wide range of papyri were found to be $\mathbf{T}_L = [0\ 0\ 0]^T$ and $\mathbf{T}_U = [100\ 100\ 100]^T$.

The contours of the symbols are extracted using a border following algorithm (Suzuki 1985), and then bounding boxes are constructed that enclose the contours. By imposing minimum and maximum area values on the bounding boxes as well as lower and upper bounds on the aspect ratio of the rectangles, spurious structures (remnants of the binarization process) are rejected. Note that the bounds must be loose to accommodate all types of symbols across all papyri photographs.

7.2.1 Results of the Automatic Symbol Extraction Method

The method was applied to 10 test papyri images with varying degrees of distortion. The corresponding number of true positive (TP), false positive (FP), and false negative (FN) detections are 395, 95, and 139, respectively, implying precision and recall values of 0.81 and 0.74, respectively. Note that precision p and recall r are given by $p = \frac{TP}{TP+FP}$ and $r = \frac{TP}{TP+FN}$. The method is unable to correctly extract symbols when a symbol's boundary is not connected (either because of wear of the papyrus or because the form of the symbol class consists of more than one connected component) or when adjacent symbols are fused (e.g., cursive handwriting).

Fig. 7.3 Block diagram depicting HOG's operation (without gamma normalization step)

7.3   Classification of Papyri Symbols

In this section, two machine learning classifiers are described that recognize symbols belonging to three target classes. The first is a linear SVM that uses HOG features, and the second is a CNN. The input to the classifier is an image of a symbol, which must be provided by the user.

7.3.1   Background Theory

7.3.1.1   Histogram of Oriented Gradients

HOG features can be obtained as follows (see Fig. 7.3). The image is first filtered for horizontal and vertical edge detection (e.g., using Sobel operators), and the magnitude and orientation of the image gradient are obtained. The image is subsequently divided into cells, the optimal size of which depends on the image. A histogram for each cell is created, where the bins correspond to the gradient orientation, and the count (vote) depends on its magnitude. To reduce sensitivity to lighting variations, the vectors obtained from a concatenation of the histograms for a block of cells are normalized in a sliding-window fashion. Finally, the feature vector for the entire image is set to the concatenation of the normalized histograms.

7.3.1.2   Linear Support Vector Machine

In the case of images, the input to a linear SVM is usually a feature vector that distinctively and concisely characterizes a specific image. A linear SVM model is trained on a dataset to obtain a decision boundary (hyperplane) that separates the images into classes. It chooses the boundary with maximum distance (margin) to its closest data points, called support vectors, while potentially allowing for margin violations. Given the weights $\mathbf{w}$ and a bias term b describing the decision boundary, and an instance $\mathbf{x}$, we assign the label

$$\hat{y} = \begin{cases} 1, & \text{if } \mathbf{w}^T\mathbf{x} + b > 0 \\ 0, & \text{otherwise} \end{cases} \tag{7.2}$$

The goal of the SVM classifier is to find $\mathbf{w}$ and b such that the margin is maximized subject to constraints relating to margin violations.

Even though SVMs are inherently binary classifiers, it is possible to use them for multi-class classification. In the one-versus-all approach, a binary classifier is trained for each symbol class and the class that gives the highest decision output score is selected. Alternatively, in the one-versus-one method, a binary classifier is trained for every pair of symbols, and the class that has the most "wins" is chosen, requiring $N(N-1)/2$ binary classifiers for N classes.

7.3.1.3 Convolutional Neural Networks

CNNs are the deep learning models frequently used for tasks involving images, as they exploit the correlations between neighboring pixels. The neurons act locally, and their weights are usually shared. Moreover, they are invariant to translation, a desirable property for object identification. Intuitively, the shallow layers of the network can be thought of as exhibiting low level details whereas the deep layers tend to model high-level patterns of an image.

The input to a CNN is a 4-D array (tensor) with the dimensions corresponding to the number of images, width and height of the image, and number of channels. At each layer of the network, filters are convolved with the images in the preceding layer to produce so-called feature maps. The stride of the filter is the step made by the sliding window during the convolution. For example, if the stride is 2×2, then the resulting feature map is downsampled by a factor of four. Furthermore, the feature maps are passed through an activation function to model non-linearities. A typical activation function is the ReLu, which is efficient to compute and is given by

$$\phi(x) = \begin{cases} x, & \text{if } x > 0 \\ 0, & \text{otherwise} \end{cases} \tag{7.3}$$

The last layer of the network is fully-connected. Its activation function is typically softmax for multi-class classification tasks, analogous to the sigmoid in the binary classification case. The output of softmax can be expressed as

$$\hat{y}_k = \frac{e^{x_k}}{\sum_{i=1}^{K} e^{x_i}}, \quad k = 1, \ldots, K \tag{7.4}$$

where K is the number of classes. The prediction $\hat{y}_k$ can be viewed as the probability of the image belonging to class k. The corresponding loss to be minimized by the backpropagation algorithm (Werbos 1990) is the categorical cross-entropy loss, defined as

$$l(\hat{y}_c) = -\log_2(\hat{y}_c) \tag{7.5}$$

where $\hat{y}_c$ denotes the model prediction corresponding to the true label. This loss heavily penalizes confident and wrong predictions.

7.3.2   Dataset

In order to create the dataset for symbol classification, the images were cropped with the help of the automatic symbol extractor, and each data point was verified manually to ensure data veracity. The transcriptions from the cursive script into the underlying hieroglyphs, as published in the *UCL Lahun Papyri* series by Stephen Quirke and Mark Collier (Collier and Quirke 2002; Quirke and Collier 2004, 2006), were utilized to label the data.

Three common symbol classes have been considered here belonging to the "unilit-erals," a group of symbols that denote the individual phonemes of the language. 806 symbols were extracted for the first class, 872 for the second, and 809 for the third. The size of each image was converted to 32×32 by normalizing the larger dimension and zero padding the other dimension (see Fig. 7.4).

The data were split into a training and a test set in an 8:2 ratio. Regarding model selection, five-fold cross-validation was employed for the linear SVM models, whereas for the CNNs, 20% of the training set was sampled for validation due to training speed considerations.

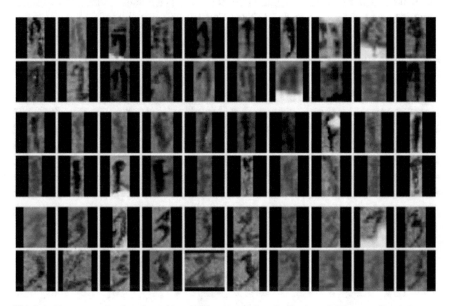

Fig. 7.4 Twenty randomly selected images from each class in the dataset. Top two rows belong to Class 1, middle two rows to Class 2, and bottom two rows to Class 3

7.3.3   HOG Features with Linear SVM

The linear SVM is a suitable classifier for when the data are approximately linearly separable in the feature space and/or when speed of prediction is a primary concern. To classify the symbols, the images are converted to grayscale format and HOG features are extracted, which are subsequently fed to the SVM classifier, employing a one-versus-all approach in our case. A coarse grid search followed by a finer search around the best points were performed to yield the optimal HOG hyperparameters (e.g., cell size, number of histogram bins, etc.) and box constraint for the SVM, which is related to the strictness of the classifier in separating the data points.

7.3.4   Convolutional Neural Network Classifier

A CNN has in general a significantly higher representational capacity than a linear SVM (even when the latter is coupled with HOG features). The model employed for this work is based on an architecture (Deotte 2019) that achieves the state-of-the-art accuracy score of 99.75% on MNIST (LeCun 1998).

7.3.4.1   CNN Architecture

The architecture is depicted in Fig. 7.5. There are two blocks of layers, both consisting of three convolutional layers, each followed by batch normalization (Ioffe and Szegedy 2015). At the end of each block, dropout (Srivastava et al. 2014) is used with drop probability of 0.5. The first two convolutional layers in each block use a kernel size of 3×3, whereas the third convolutional layer's kernel size is 5×5 with a stride of 2. The first block has 32 feature maps for each layer and the second 64. All activation functions (except just before the loss) are ReLu, and the weights are

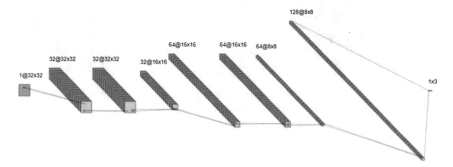

Fig. 7.5 CNN architecture used for symbol classification. All layers (except the last) are convolutional with every third connection having a stride of 2×2. Generated using open-source software at LeNail (2019)

initialized with He normal (He et al. 2015). After the two aforementioned blocks, a convolutional layer with kernel size 4 × 4 and 128 feature maps follows, as well as batch normalization, reshaping to 1-D vector, dropout (with drop probability again 0.5), and an output layer with softmax activation function. These parameters were found using a randomized grid search.

7.3.4.2   Training the Model

The classifier was trained on Google Colaboratory's Tesla K80 GPU (2496 CUDA cores, compute capabilities version 3.7, 12 GB GDDR5 VRAM) with categorical cross-entropy as the loss function, a batch size of 32, and early stopping. Data augmentation was utilized to artificially enlarge the dataset by applying transformations to the images, such as rotations (range of $[-15°, 15°]$), blurring (maximum kernel size of 3×3), and changes in contrast and brightness (see Fig. 7.6 for some examples). The following optimizers were compared on the validation set: stochastic gradient descent (SGD) with Nesterov momentum (Sutskever et al. 2013) (initial rate of 0.01 and momentum of 0.9), AdaGrad (Duchi et al. 2011), RMSProp (Tieleman and Hinton 2012), and Adam (Kingma and Ba 2014). As can be seen in Fig. 7.7, Adam performed slightly better than SGD.

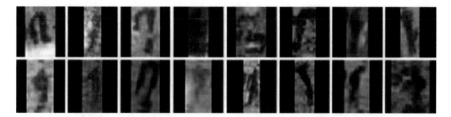

Fig. 7.6 Examples of augmented images of symbols

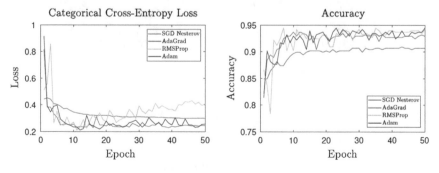

Fig. 7.7 Comparison of optimizers on the validation categorical cross-entropy (left) and validation accuracy (right)

7.3.5 Results of Symbol Classification Methods

The confusion matrices for the SVM and CNN models (on the test set) are given in Fig. 7.8. The macro precision, recall, and F1 measures can be directly computed from the matrix. These are defined as

$$\text{precision} = \frac{\sum_{i=0}^{N-1} \frac{TP_i}{TP_i + FP_i}}{N} \tag{7.6}$$

$$\text{recall} = \frac{\sum_{i=0}^{N-1} \frac{TP_i}{TP_i + FN_i}}{N} \tag{7.7}$$

$$F_1 = \frac{2}{\frac{1}{\text{precision}} + \frac{1}{\text{recall}}} \tag{7.8}$$

where TP_i, FP_i, and FN_i denote respectively the true positives, false positives, and false negatives in class i, and N is the number of classes; the scores are given in Table 7.1. Note that in this case, accuracy is a sufficient measure of performance since the three classes are almost balanced. As expected, the CNN classifier outperforms the SVM in terms of accuracy, precision, and recall. It is also important to point out, however, the difference in prediction time for the classifiers. To this end, 8,000 images were fed to the models, and the prediction time per image was recorded: the linear SVM was found to be faster than the CNN models by around a factor of 30.

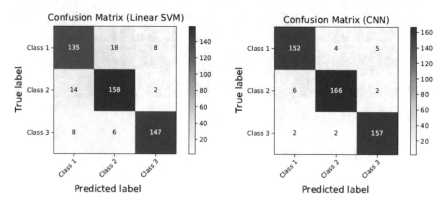

Fig. 7.8 Confusion matrices for linear SVM (left) and CNN (right)

Table 7.1 Comparison of linear SVM and CNN for symbol classification

Model	Accuracy	Precision	Recall	F1	Time per image (ms)
Linear SVM	0.8871	0.8881	0.8865	0.8873	0.065
CNN	0.9577	0.9575	0.9578	0.9576	2.091

7.4   Detection of Papyri Symbols

This section presents a system for symbol detection, which introduces further automation to the transcription process than the classification approaches discussed in Sect. 7.3, as it does not require the user to specify a symbol to be identified. Instead, it involves scanning the papyrus image using windows of varying aspect ratios and areas before image classification. The block diagram in Fig. 7.9 shows its main components.

7.4.1   Scanning the Papyrus Image

The initial stage of the symbol detector proposed here involves using multiple sliding windows to scan the image for potential instances of the three target classes, since the symbols appear in different shapes and sizes. This approach can be extremely computationally intensive, especially if a CNN classifier is used; thus, it is crucial to limit the windows considered in an informed way.

7.4.1.1   Limiting Aspect Ratios Using Lloyd-Max

It is possible to determine reasonable values for the aspect ratios using the training images that make up the dataset. For instance, most drawn symbols have aspect ratios greater than one (they are "tall"). To more precisely pin down their distributions, a histogram employing 37 bins was constructed from the images in the training set (see left plot of Fig. 7.10). It is evident from the figure that most of the aspect ratios lie between one and three. Choosing equally spaced values in this range would ignore the fact that ratios close to two are more likely to correspond to symbols in the target classes. We are more likely to increase the accuracy of the model if we choose more window aspect ratios near the mean and less close to the extrema of the histogram. To this end, the Lloyd-Max algorithm (Lloyd 1982) from the area of signal quantization is imported.

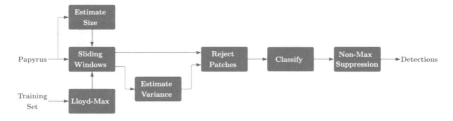

Fig. 7.9 Block diagram for proposed symbol detection method

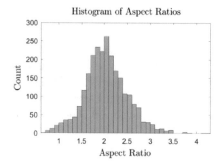 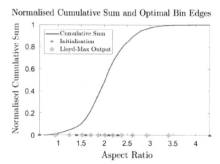

Fig. 7.10 Histogram of aspect ratios computed from the training set (left) as well as the normalized cumulative sum with indicated Lloyd-Max initialization and output (right)

Now, we derive the Lloyd-Max quantizer. Given a signal x with a certain PDF $p(x)$ it is possible to find the edges of the quantization bins a_k for $k = 0, 1, \ldots, n$ and the quantization levels x_l for $l = 1, 2, \ldots, n$ such that the mean quantization error

$$E = \sum_{i=1}^{n} \int_{a_{i-1}}^{a_i} p(x)(x_i - x)^2 dx \qquad (7.9)$$

is minimized. We set the derivative of the error to 0:

$$\frac{\partial E}{\partial x_l} = 2 \int_{a_{l-1}}^{a_l} p(x)(x_l - x)^2 dx = 0 \qquad (7.10)$$

$$\Rightarrow x_l = \frac{\int_{a_{l-1}}^{a_l} x p(x) dx}{\int_{a_{l-1}}^{a_l} p(x) dx} \qquad (7.11)$$

To find an expression for a_k in terms of x_k and x_{k+1}, notice that if x falls just to the right of a_k, then x_{k+1} will be chosen, and if it falls just to the left of a_k, then it will be quantized to x_k. If the quantization output given x is denoted by $Q(x)$, the square error is given by

$$q^2(x) = \begin{cases} (x - x_k)^2, & \text{if } Q(x) = x_k \\ (x - x_{k+1})^2, & \text{if } Q(x) = x_{k+1} \end{cases} \qquad (7.12)$$

Hence, x_k should only be chosen if

$$(x - x_k)^2 \leq (x - x_{k+1})^2 \qquad (7.13)$$

$$\Leftrightarrow x^2 - 2xx_k + x_k^2 \leq x^2 - 2xx_{k+1} + x_{k+1}^2 \qquad (7.14)$$

$$\Leftrightarrow x \le \frac{x_{k+1} + x_k}{2} \qquad (7.15)$$

This implies that the bin edges are given by

$$a_k = \frac{x_{k+1} + x_k}{2} \qquad (7.16)$$

Having Eqs. 7.11 and 7.16, we iteratively find the two sequences a_k and x_l. To ensure successful convergence of the Lloyd-Max algorithm, appropriate initialization of the bin edges is required. One possibility is to divide the histogram into n bins such that the signal falls into any of the bins with equal estimated probability. The values of the initialization in the case of $n = 10$ as well as the corresponding output of the Lloyd-Max algorithm are shown for the histogram of aspect ratios on the right plot of Fig. 7.10. The algorithm succeeds at providing us with a list of aspect ratios concentrated around the frequently occurring values.

7.4.1.2   Limiting Areas of the Windows

Unlike the aspect ratio, the area of the window highly depends on the specific photograph of a papyrus. Furthermore, within a specific papyrus we do not expect the size of the symbols to vary too greatly. These two observations lead to the conclusion that the considered areas should be tailored to the papyrus at hand and not on statistics computed over the entire training set.

We employ the method of automatic symbol extraction presented in Sect. 7.2 to give a robust estimate of the average size of the symbols in a given papyrus. To do so, the arithmetic mean μ of the areas of the output bounding boxes is computed. Despite the errors arising from distinct symbols being connected (resulting in an overestimate) or a symbol being characterized by breaks (leading to an underestimate) these errors are to a large extent "averaged out." A vector of n factors **k** can be specified with elements above and below one, such that the areas chosen are given by μ**k**.

7.4.2   Handling the "None of the Above" Class

To identify true negative detections, i.e., patches not belonging to one of the three target classes, it is possible to either use a threshold on the confidence score or train the classifiers with a "none of the above" class. The former approach did not work well in practice, partly because CNNs tend to be overconfident in their predictions (Guo et al. 2017); this subsection focuses, instead, on the latter.

The model had to be trained with instances that adequately capture the intra-variability of the class: the patches could belong to the papyrus paper without any drawn symbols, the surface on which the paper lies, the various symbols apart from the three considered, etc.

A key question arises when considering the creation of this class: what should be the proportion of images belonging to this class? One choice is to crop approximately the same number of images as have been cropped for each of the three target classes; this would result in an approximately balanced dataset. The disadvantage is that the variability of the "none of the above" class is high and limiting the corresponding data instances may unnecessarily prevent the classifier from learning the boundaries between this class and the rest. On the other hand, increasing the proportion of this class arbitrarily creates a highly imbalanced dataset, which can bias the network towards this class.

Even though the prior probability of a given image patch to be extraneous is relatively high, it is simpler and less time-consuming for humans to reject false positive detections than to manually scan the papyrus to find the false negative ones. This suggests that biasing the network towards negative detections is inappropriate for our application. To both utilize a large number of "none of the above" images and to reduce the false negative detections, a heavily imbalanced dataset was created, but this was counteracted by specifying for each class the weight that an example from that class carries in the training process. By properly choosing these weights, the misclassification of instances from the under-represented classes affect the loss function more strongly than from the over-represented class, thus effectively balancing the dataset.

7.4.3 Classifying the Patches

The images gathered from the scans of the papyrus are classified either into one of the target classes or into the "none of the above" class. If and only if a patch is in one of the three target classes, then a bounding box is placed around the location of the symbol, the color of the box depending on the detected class.

7.4.3.1 Speeding up Detection Using Local Variance

In order to reduce the number of image patches to be classified, we reject the patches with a variance below a given threshold, as these are likely to correspond to the background. This simple method manages to reduce the number of images substantially, since a large proportion of a papyrus photograph consists of nearly constant background regions. For instance, see Fig. 7.11, where the number of images to be classified was reduced by a factor of around 2.5 when a threshold of 1,000 was used. Of course, an excessively high threshold risks rejecting possible target symbols.

Fig. 7.11 Papyrus image (left) and remaining windows after applying variance thresholding (right)

7.4.3.2   Classifying with Binary SVM and CNN

Although the problem of distinguishing the symbol classes is non-trivial, the task of separating the symbols from the background is substantially simpler, and it is one that a linear SVM (with HOG features) is expected to solve with high accuracy. As such, after variance thresholding, the background patches are further filtered by identifying them with a binary, linear SVM; the CNN is then fed the heavily reduced set of candidate images (these are the difficult images to classify) and outputs predictions for the target classes (see Fig. 7.12). It is important to note that the macro F1 score, given in Eq. 7.8, was employed for model selection, as it eliminates the effects of the

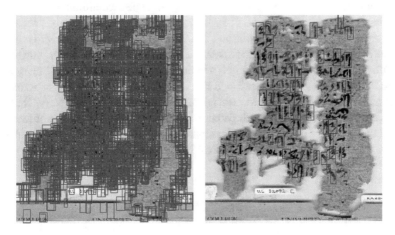

Fig. 7.12 Remaining bounding boxes after binary, linear SVM predictions (left) and symbol detection using CNN on remaining bounding boxes (right)

imbalance that the "none of the above class" introduces by assigning equal weights to each class and by favoring similar precision and recall values across all four classes.

7.4.3.3 Non-maximum Suppression

Because the algorithm scans the image multiple times, it is almost certain that more than one of the patches corresponding to the same symbol will be identified. The non-maximum suppression algorithm addresses this by retaining only the detection with the highest confidence score (as given by the softmax layer in a CNN). To this end, the Intersection Over Union (IoU) measure is employed, defined as $IoU = Area(A_1 \cap A_2)/Area(A_1 \cup A_2)$, where A_1 and A_2 denote two bounding boxes. We discard all bounding boxes that overlap with the box associated with the highest confidence score and which have an IoU value larger than a user-specified number (in Fig. 7.12 this number is 0.1).

7.4.4 Results of Symbol Detection System

The proposed system, which combines a binary SVM and a CNN, is compared with purely SVM- and CNN-based classifiers on 10 test papyri using the mean average precision (mAP) metric, where the precision-recall (PR) points are interpolated as in the (updated) PASCAL VOC challenge (Everingham et al. 2010). Five window aspect ratios and five sizes (i.e., 25 scans) were used. The average detection time of each method was measured on the test papyri. The PR curves for each class and method are given in Fig. 7.13, and the average precision (AP) for each class, mAP, and detection time are presented in Table 7.2. As expected, although the speed of detection is favorable, the linear SVM detector is not expressive enough to accurately detect and distinguish the symbols, and this is clearly reflected in the relatively poor AP scores for all classes. The CNN detector is approximately 17 times slower than the SVM but exhibits a two-fold improvement in mAP. Introducing the binary SVM before the CNN classification reduced the detection time for the test papyrus by a factor of four and did not compromise the mAP. It is noteworthy that the AP for Class 1 is significantly larger than for the other two classes, because the form of the Class 1 symbols is largely unique to the class, whereas symbols from Classes 2 and 3 are often extremely similar to symbols from other classes.

7.5 Conclusions, Limitations, and Future Directions

This chapter investigated computer vision techniques to aid Egyptologists in the identification of symbols in ancient papyri. For the creation or extension of a dataset containing such symbols, a user can benefit from significant savings in time by first

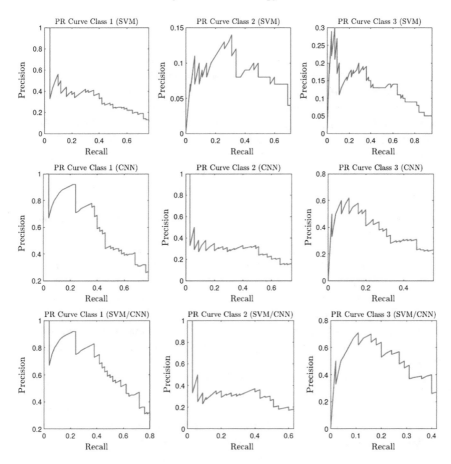

Fig. 7.13 PR curves for the different classification approaches used for detection and for each class

Table 7.2 Comparison of classifiers for the detection method on AP, mAP, and detection time per papyrus image

Method	AP Class 1	AP Class 2	AP Class 3	mAP	Time (s)
Linear SVM (HOG)	0.2839	0.0792	0.1450	0.1694	3.8
CNN	0.5084	0.2450	0.2368	0.3301	63.2
Linear SVM and CNN	0.5620	0.2265	0.2411	0.3432	15.5

automatically cropping the symbols using the proposed symbol extractor and then manually finding false positives and false negatives. The deep learning techniques have been demonstrated to be well-suited for classification, despite the distorted nature of the symbols. Furthermore, the same dataset used in classification can be employed for detection via a sliding window approach. Computational efficiency is achieved by estimating reasonable values for the areas and sizes of the windows, and by using a variance thresholder as well as a cascaded system of a linear SVM and a CNN.

An obvious limitation of this research is the relatively small number of symbol classes used. An efficient approach would be to crowdsource the task of extending the dataset, as in Williams et al. (2014b). As the number of classes increases, the inter-variability of the classes reduces; to improve the accuracy of classification in that case, transfer learning with a VGG (Simonyan and Zisserman 2014) or ResNet (He et al. 2016) network may be beneficial.

The mAP (for detection) is expected to substantially increase as the dataset is extended in the future, since not only will the system be able to detect more symbol classes, but the symbol detection method is also expected to further improve in terms of detecting the current target classes. This is because the dataset will contain more examples from similar symbol classes and will thus be more able to distinguish among them.

This research does not take into account that the class of a symbol in the cursive handwritten script is often heavily dependent on preceding or succeeding symbols. To further improve the system, it is possible to model the conditional probabilities of the occurrence of symbols given their neighbors. In order to classify a symbol, both the probability that each symbol could have arisen from each of the classes can be estimated, as well as the conditional probability of this class given the class of, for example, the previous symbol. A language model could prove useful in modelling these probability distributions.

Finally, it would be interesting to perform a comparison between the approach for detection presented in this work and the state-of-the-art, more general object detection techniques, such as Faster R-CNN (Ren et al. 2015), YOLO (Redmon et al. 2016), and SSD (Liu et al. 2016). For this comparison to be made, a labelled dataset for the three symbols considered here must be created which comprises the papyri images with ground truth bounding boxes around the symbols.

References

Bar-Yosef I, Beckman I, Kedem K, Dinstein I (2007) Binarization, character extraction, and writer identification of historical Hebrew calligraphy documents. IJDAR 9(2–4):89–99

Collier M, Quirke S (2002) The UCL Lahun Papyri: letters. Archaeopress

Cortes C, Vapnik V (1995) Support-vector networks. Mach Learn 20(3):273–297

Dalal N, Triggs B (2005) Histograms of oriented gradients for human detection. In: International conference on computer vision and pattern recognition (CVPR'05), vol 1. IEEE Computer Society, pp 886–893

Deotte C (2019) 25 Million Images! [0.99757] MNIST I Kaggle. [online] Kaggle.com. https://www.kaggle.com/cdeotte/25-million-images-0–99757-mnist. Accessed 2 Jan 2019

Duchi J, Hazan E, Singer Y (2011) Adaptive subgradient methods for online learning and stochastic optimization. J Mach Learn Res 12:2121–2159

Everingham M, Van Gool L, Williams CK, Winn J, Zisserman A (2010) The pascal visual object classes (voc) challenge. Int J Comput Vis 88(2):303–338

fraunhofer.de (2019) Reconstructing and restoring medieval manuscripts. [online] https://www.
    fraunhofer.de/en/research/current-research/preserving-cultural-heritage/reconstructing-and-
    restoring-medieval-manuscripts.html. Accessed 8 Oct 2019
Guo Y, Liu Y, Oerlemans A, Lao S, Wu S, Lew MS (2016) Deep learning for visual understanding:
    a review. Neurocomputing 187:27–48
Guo C, Pleiss G, Sun Y, Weinberger KQ (2017) On calibration of modern neural networks. In:
    Proceedings of the 34th international conference on machine learning, vol 70, pp 1321–1330.
    JMLR.org
Haliassos A (2019) Identification of symbols in Ancient Papyri. MEng thesis, Imperial College,
    London
He K, Zhang X, Ren S, Sun J (2015) Delving deep into rectifiers: surpassing human-level per-
    formance on imagenet classification. In: Proceedings of the IEEE international conference on
    computer vision, pp 1026–1034
He K, Zhang X, Ren S, Sun J (2016) Deep residual learning for image recognition. In: Proceedings
    of the IEEE conference on computer vision and pattern recognition, pp 770–778
Helli B, Moghaddam ME (2008) A text-independent Persian writer identification system using LCS
    based classifier. In: 2008 IEEE international symposium on signal processing and information
    technology. IEEE, pp 203–206
Ioffe S, Szegedy C (2015) Batch normalization: accelerating deep network training by reducing
    internal covariate shift. arXiv:1502.03167
Kingma DP, Ba J (2014) Adam: a method for stochastic optimization. arXiv:1412.6980
Knox KT, Easton RL, Christens-Barry W (2008) Image restoration of damaged or erased
    manuscripts. In: 2008 16th European signal processing conference. IEEE, pp 1–5
Labaune J, Jackson JB, Pages-Camagna S, Duling IN, Menu M, Mourou GA (2010) Papyrus imaging
    with terahertz time domain spectroscopy. Appl Phys A 100(3):607–612
LeCun Y (1998) The MNIST database of handwritten digits. http://yann.lecun.com/exdb/mnist/
LeCun Y, Bengio Y, Hinton G (2015) Deep learning. Nature 521(7553):436
LeNail A (2019) NN-SVG: publication-ready neural network architecture schematics. J Open
    Source Softw 4:33
Liu W, Anguelov D, Erhan D, Szegedy C, Reed S, Fu CY, Berg AC (2016) Ssd: single shot multibox
    detector. In: European conference on computer vision. Springer, Cham, pp 21–37
Lloyd S (1982) Least squares quantization in PCM. IEEE Trans Inf Theory 28(2):129–137
Panagopoulos M, Papaodysseus C, Rousopoulos P, Dafi D, Tracy S (2008) Automatic writer iden-
    tification of ancient Greek inscriptions. IEEE Trans Pattern Anal Mach Intell 31(8):1404–1414
Papaodysseus C, Rousopoulos P, Giannopoulos F, Zannos S, Arabadjis D, Panagopoulos M, Kalfa
    E, Blackwell C, Tracy S (2014) Identifying the writer of ancient inscriptions and Byzantine
    codices. A novel approach. Comput Vis Image Underst 121:57–73
Quirke SGJ, Collier M (2004) The UCL Lahun Papyri: religious, literary, legal, mathematical and
    medical. British Archaeological Reports, pp 1–160
Quirke S, Collier M (2006) The UCL Lahun Papyri: accounts. British Archaeological Reports
Redmon J, Divvala S, Girshick R, Farhadi A (2016) You only look once: unified, real-time object
    detection. In: Proceedings of the IEEE conference on computer vision and pattern recognition,
    pp 779–788
Ren S, He K, Girshick R, Sun J (2015) Faster r-cnn: towards real-time object detection with region
    proposal networks. In: Advances in neural information processing systems, pp 91–99
Simonyan K, Zisserman A (2014) Very deep convolutional networks for large-scale image
    recognition. arXiv:1409.1556
Sparavigna A (2009) Digital restoration of ancient papyri. arXiv:0903.5045
Srivastava N, Hinton G, Krizhevsky A, Sutskever I, Salakhutdinov R (2014) Dropout: a simple way
    to prevent neural networks from overfitting. J Mach Learn Res 15(1):1929–1958
Sutskever I, Martens J, Dahl G, Hinton G (2013) On the importance of initialization and momentum
    in deep learning. In: International conference on machine learning, pp 1139–1147

Suzuki S (1985) Topological structural analysis of digitized binary images by border following. Comput Vis Graph Image Process 30(1):32–46

Tieleman T, Hinton G (2012) Lecture 6.5-rmsprop: divide the gradient by a running average of its recent magnitude. COURSERA: Neural Netw Mach Learn 4(2):26–31

ucl.ac.uk (2002) Lahun Papyri. [online] https://www.ucl.ac.uk/museums-static/digitalegypt//lahun/papyri.html. Accessed 2 Nov 2018

Voulodimos A, Doulamis N, Doulamis A, Protopapadakis E (2018) Deep learning for computer vision: a brief review. Comput Intell Neurosci

Werbos PJ (1990) Backpropagation through time: what it does and how to do it. Proc IEEE 78(10):1550–1560

Williams AC, Carroll HD, Wallin JF, Brusuelas J, Fortson L, Lamblin AF, Yu H (2014a) Identification of ancient greek papyrus fragments using genetic sequence alignment algorithms. In: 2014 IEEE 10th international conference on e-science, vol 2, pp 5–10. IEEE

Williams AC, Wallin JF, Yu H, Perale M, Carroll HD, Lamblin AF, Fortson L, Obbink D, Lintott CJ, Brusuelas JH (2014b) A computational pipeline for crowdsourced transcriptions of Ancient Greek papyrus fragments. In: 2014 IEEE international conference on Big Data (Big Data). IEEE, pp 100–105

Chapter 8
Image-Based Underwater 3D Reconstruction for Cultural Heritage: From Image Collection to 3D. Critical Steps and Considerations

Dimitrios Skarlatos and Panagiotis Agrafiotis

Abstract Underwater Cultural Heritage (CH) sites are widely spread; from ruins in coastlines up to shipwrecks in deep. The documentation and preservation of this heritage is an obligation of the mankind, dictated also by the international treaties like the Convention on the Protection of the Underwater Cultural Heritage which fosters the use of "non-destructive techniques and survey methods in preference over the recovery of objects". However, submerged CH lacks in protection and monitoring in regards to the land CH and nowadays recording and documenting, for digital preservation as well as dissemination through VR to wide public, is of most importance. At the same time, it is most difficult to document it, due to inherent restrictions posed by the environment. In order to create high detailed textured 3D models, optical sensors and photogrammetric techniques seems to be the best solution. This chapter discusses critical aspects of all phases of image based underwater 3D reconstruction process, from data acquisition and data preparation using colour restoration and colour enhancement algorithms to Structure from Motion (SfM) and Multi-View Stereo (MVS) techniques to produce an accurate, precise and complete 3D model for a number of applications.

Dimitrios Skarlatos and Panagiotis Agrafiotis contributed equally to the work.

D. Skarlatos (✉) · P. Agrafiotis
Lab of Photogrammetric Vision, Civil Engineering and Geomatics Department, Cyprus University of Technology, 2-8 Saripolou str., 3036 Limassol, Cyprus
e-mail: dimitrios.skarlatos@cut.ac.cy

P. Agrafiotis
e-mail: panagiotis.agrafioti@cut.ac.cy; pagraf@central.ntua.gr

P. Agrafiotis
Department of Topography, School of Rural and Surveying Engineering, National Technical University of Athens, Zografou Campus, 9 Heroon Polytechniou str., 15780 Athens, Greece

© Springer Nature Switzerland AG 2020
F. Liarokapis et al. (eds.), *Visual Computing for Cultural Heritage*, Springer Series on Cultural Computing, https://doi.org/10.1007/978-3-030-37191-3_8

8.1 Introduction

Image-based underwater 3D reconstruction is a key tool for 3D record, map and model submerged heritage providing the 3D relief and the valuable visual information together. In this context, they represent an effective tool for research, documentation, monitoring and more recently public diffusion and awareness of UCH assets, through for example, virtual reality headsets, serious games, etc. (Skarlatos et al. 2016; Bruno et al. 2016; Liarokapis et al. 2017). They can serve also as a tool for the assessment of the state of preservation of the submerged heritage and its threats, natural or manmade. Depending on the archaeological needs and on the environmental conditions such as depth or water turbidity, sensors, techniques and methods may need to be used differently or may even be not suitable at all (Menna et al. 2018a).

Despite the relative low cost of the image-based methods in relation to others, they present a major drawback; optical properties and illumination conditions of water severely affect underwater imagery and data acquisition process. Colours are lost as the depth increases, resulting in a green-blue image effect due to light absorption, which mainly influences red wavelength. Therefore, red channel histogram has fewer values compared to green and blue. Water also absorbs light energy and scatters optical rays creating blurred images, reducing the exploitable visibility to a few meters.

Moreover, refraction causes additional issues on the processing of the underwater imagery. In the literature, two different approaches are reported for dealing with the refraction effect, when the camera is completely submerged; the first one is based on the geometric interpretation for light propagation through various media (e.g., air—housing device—water) and the other on the application of suitable corrections, in order to compensate for the refraction. Some researchers use a pinhole camera for the estimation of the refraction parameters, while others calibrate the cameras with the help of an object of known dimensions, which is put underwater in situ (Georgopoulos and Agrafiotis 2012). Nowadays, self-calibration is widely applied for the camera-housing system, as it is assumed that refraction effects are compensated by the interior orientation parameters (Skarlatos et al. 2019).

In this chapter, a brief reference to the state of the art in underwater 3D reconstruction of CH is followed by an analysis of the implications caused by the underwater environment to the Structure from Motion and Dense Image Matching techniques. Camera calibration, underwater network establishment and data acquisition issues are also discussed. Moreover, the need and use of image processing techniques in the underwater 3D reconstruction along with best practices, is discussed.

8.2 State of the Art in Underwater Image-Based 3D Reconstruction for Cultural Heritage

Underwater photogrammetry for seabed mapping has a long history, with initial systematic experiments dating back to the sixties (Rebikoff 1966). With its versatility, low cost equipment and lately the high degree of automation as its main advantages, became the most widely used technique in underwater CH 3D reconstruction nowadays, with first report of underwater Structure from Motion application reported in Skarlatos et al. (2010). Since shallow and deep waters impose different constraints, which influence the recording process, there are plenty applications reported in literature about underwater Cultural Heritage 3D reconstruction. In Menna et al. (2018a) a wide overview of the state of the art on the field is being reported. However, in the following paragraphs, some of the more interesting and recent works found in the literature are presented in respect to the data acquisition methodology; divers or robotics platforms.

8.2.1 Diver Based Data for Underwater 3D Reconstruction

An early report mapping amphorae discovered in a sunken ship off the shore of Syria can be found in Murai et al. (1988), where a digital orthophoto mosaic was generated. During the years that followed, sensors and cameras technology advancement together with the affordable waterproof housings and the availability of educational and low-cost commercial software for close range photogrammetry facilitated the spread of the image-based underwater 3D reconstruction.

During the recent years, a large number of published studies reports applications of photogrammetry and computer vision for underwater CH documentation for depths within the limits of most recreational diving certifications. Bruno et al. (2013), report over the documentation of an archaeological site in the Baiae underwater park, during experimental conservation operations. McCarthy and Benjamin (2014) discuss the 3D results from trials in Scotland and Denmark at depths of up to 30 m. Yamafune et al. (2017) present a methodology to record and reconstruct the wooden structures of a 19th century shipwreck in southern Brazil and of a 16th century shipwreck in Croatia. In Zhukovsky et al. (2013) a case study of application of photogrammetric techniques for archaeological field documentation record in course of underwater excavations of the Phanagorian shipwreck is reported. In Balletti et al. (2016) a survey and 3D representation of two Roman shipwrecks using integrated surveying techniques for documentation of underwater sites is described. In Skarlatos et al. (2012) and Demesticha et al. (2014) one of the first systematic approaches on the continuous 3D documentation of an underwater CH asset during the excavation process is reported. The site studied there is the classical shipwreck of Mazotos lying at 45 m depth, thus beyond recreational diving certifications.

More recently, Abdelaziz and Elsayed (2019) documented the archaeological site of the lighthouse of Alexandria situated at a varying depth of 2–9 m. Until 2016, only 7200 m^2 of the 13,000 m^2 of the submerged site, were covered. Bruno et al. (2019) presented an interesting approach for studying and monitoring the preservation state of an underwater archaeological site, by combining the quantitative measurements coming from optical and acoustic surveys with the study of biological colonization and bio-erosion phenomena affecting ancient artefacts. In Costa (2019) some methods for underwater documentation were presented and their advantages and disadvantages reported. Authors in Derenne et al. (2019) reported on the complementarity between in situ studies and photogrammetry by presenting the feedback from a roman shipwreck in Caesarea, Israel.

Most of the aforementioned approaches use the commercially available software application Agisoft Photoscan©. There are few reports in the literature using open source software for such applications (Skarlatos et al. 2010, 2012; Bruno et al. 2015) where, for the reconstruction process, the Bundler software (Snavely et al. 2008a) was used to orient the images and retrieve the camera calibration parameters. The successive DIM step was then performed using the PMVS (Patch-based Multi-View Stereo) software (Furukawa and Ponce 2010). For documenting a semi-submerged archaeological structure, Menna et al. (2018b) adopted a photogrammetric method, initially developed for marine engineering applications. In this method, two separate photogrammetric surveys are carried out, one in air above the water level and one underwater. Then, through several special rigid targets, that are partially immersed, rigid transformations are computed to combine the two separate surveys in a unique reference system.

8.2.2 Autonomous Underwater Vehicle (AUV) and Remotely Operated Vehicle (ROV) Based Data for Image-Based Underwater 3D Reconstruction

Image data acquisition carried out by scuba divers impose depth limit and several safety related constraints; limited bottom time and nitrogen narcosis (deeper than 30 m) may lead to several consecutive dives by several divers for the same data acquisition campaign, thus increasing risks and complicating logistics. To overcome the aforementioned shortcomings, robotic platforms like AUVs and ROVs have been adopted, especially in cases where larger areas must be covered or access is dangerous and depth prohibiting. However, while in shallow waters the use of these platforms may be an option over divers, exceeding the recreational diving limits on depth and limiting bottom time, reduces choices. Provided that the ROV and AUV systems can perform data acquisition needed for image-based 3D reconstruction purposes, they seem to be a safe choice to reduce or completely abandon use of divers, especially in depths more than 30 m where the use of artificial lighting is necessary. However, when it comes to real world applications, small ROVs are difficult to handle, especially in areas with strong currents, they are prone to water leaks and have limited operational time while larger and more reliable ROVs are expensive, requiring specialized boats and personnel for their operation, thus increasing the cost.

Captured data by these systems in image-based 3D reconstruction applications for CH consist mainly of optical data, but other sensors may also be on board, especially when larger ROVs and AUVs are employed. Typically, the imagery taken from an AUV or ROV system is acquired by following the principles of aerial photogrammetry. Captured data are processed using an SfM and MVS pipeline (Johnson-Roberson et al. 2010; Mahon et al. 2008; Ludvigsen et al. 2006; Bryson et al. 2013). Additionally to the SfM MVS processing, the extracted feature points are matched and tracked into overlapping stereo-image pairs. This resulting information is then integrated with additional navigation sensor data such as a depth sensor, a velocity sensor and data from the Inertial Navigation System (INS) in order to implement a SLAM algorithm and compute the trajectory of the platform. This estimated trajectory and the 3D points resulting from the SfM-MVS processing are then used to reconstruct a global feature map of the underwater scene. This step is of high importance when it comes to submerged CH mapping since it enables the AUV or ROV pilot to be aware of the area covered and thus the completeness of the delivered 3D reconstruction.

In the literature, many studies describe similar approaches. Johnson-Roberson et al. (2017) adopted an AUV and a diver-controlled stereo imaging platform (for very shallow water) in order to document the submerged Bronze Age city at Pavlopetri, Greece. Bingham et al. (2010) developed techniques for large-area 3D reconstruction of a 4th c. B.C. shipwreck site off the Greek island of Chios in the north eastern Aegean Sea using an UAV. Mahon et al. (2008) presented a vision-based underwater mapping system for archaeological use in the same area. Another interesting approach is presented by Bosch et al. (2015) where an omnidirectional underwater camera mounted on an AUV was used for a mapping a shipwreck. In Drap et al. (2015) an approach based on photogrammetry for surveying the Roman shipwreck Cap Bénat 4, at a depth of 328 m using an ROV is presented. The Visual Odometry technique presented there provides real time results, sufficient for piloting the ROV from the surface vessel and ensures a millimetric precision on the final 3D results. Finally, in the work presented in Roman et al. (2010), bathymetric maps of underwater archaeological sites in water depths between 50 and 400 m and different turbidity conditions were generated using an ROV equipped with optical cameras, laser and a multibeam sonar. Expected results over the comparison of the three different sensors indicated that in every case the laser and multibeam results were consistent while in stereo imaging the point density was highly dependent on scene texture, which is high turbidity environments may render photogrammetric approaches useless.

The aforementioned studies highlight that underwater image-based 3D reconstruction is a tool that has been accepted and applied by many disciplines and experts. Even though this facilitates faster mapping of submerged cultural heritage, with impressive results, implementation of those techniques by non-experts or ignoring the difficulties addressed in this chapter, underlies the danger of producing non-accurate and unreliable results.

8.3 Implications to Bundle Adjustment and Structure from Motion

Any given set of images of a specific object, captured from different viewpoints, must undergo bundle adjustment as part of the 3D reconstruction process. This task can be described as the simultaneous estimation of camera positions so that the bundles of rays from the images intersect in 3D spaces, both in common points and in control points, i.e., points with known coordinates in the reference system of choice. At any given photogrammetric project, the Bundle Adjustment (BA) is the critical task where all gross and systematic errors are to be detected, estimated and finally eliminated at a great extent. Remaining systematic errors will affect the final results, particularly the 3D reconstruction, in an unpredictable way. Moreover, these errors will remain undetectable, unless check points are utilised, as a mean to quantify the remaining errors. Camera's interior orientation is a potential systematic error source and as such, BA can be employed to resolve camera's (or cameras') geometry. This process is known as self-calibration.

Despite that BA was a well-established process in photogrammetry, the last decade this process is being replaced from Structure from Motion (SfM), which is a more generic process than BA and in fact includes robust BA as the last step. However, it differs significantly from conventional photogrammetry, where a priori knowledge for camera used, initial approximations of camera stations, and a set of control points is required. In fact, camera geometry and camera positions and orientation are solved automatically without the need to specify any a priori knowledge. These are estimated simultaneously using a highly redundant, iterative bundle adjustment procedure, based on a database of features automatically extracted from a set of multiple overlapping images (Snavely et al. 2008b). The SfM approach is most suited to sets of images with a high degree of overlap that capture full three-dimensional structure of the scene viewed from many different positions, or as the name suggests, images derived from a moving sensor (Westoby et al. 2012).

In essence SfM is more generic, as it includes both the automated task of feature points detection, descriptions and matching, followed by robust SBA (Lourakis and Argyros 2009). Several variations exist, each one with its own characteristics, strengths and weaknesses (Snavely et al. 2006). The most critical task of the process is feature detection, description and matching, as blunders are unavoidable in this phase. Poor detection and matching might lead to incomplete alignment, erroneous alignment of few images or total failure of the alignment. In all cases, some blunders will remain to the final solution, even after robust SBA and will affect final 3D reconstruction. It is advised that these errors are manually, or semi automatically selected and removed during the alignment phase.

In a similar way, underwater 3D reconstruction employing SfM, enjoys speed, ease of use and versatility but suffers the same limitations and shortcomings. In fact, due to particularities of the environment, there are several reasons for the SfM to fail.

Many problems have been reported that tend to be particularly profound in the underwater environment, posing either hard limitations or shortcomings, which if properly addressed may be overcome. Shortcomings may be divided in two categories; environmental and computational, with the former ones need to be addressed during the acquisition phase and the latter ones being able to address during processing.

Environmental shortcomings affect acquisition process, including control point network establishment, stability and coordinate system definition. The deeper the site the more the shortcomings. Depth, increases the colour absorption, decreases light, reduces bottom time and enhances nitrogen narcosis effects. All these problems must be dealt during the acquisition phase, with proper planning and dive logistics. Some problems, such as camera calibration, colour aberration, vignetting etc., can be dealt at some extend with dome lens housings and prime camera lenses. Remaining environmental problems effects, may also be dealt computationally, provided they are not severe.

8.3.1 Camera Calibration

The obvious consideration on underwater photogrammetry is camera calibration, which although a trivial task in air, underwater implementation is not. Two media photogrammetry is governed by law's of physics, and therefore, collinearity equation may be modified and used for underwater camera calibration. Several authors have investigated the influence of flat or dome port in underwater photogrammetry, both in terms of geometry, and colour (Menna et al. 2018b; Shortis 2019; Sedlazeck and Koch 2012). The use of dome port, in theory completely removes refraction if the projection centre is positioned at the centre of the dome (Sedlazeck and Koch 2012), but in general case, this is very difficult to achieve unless the camera and housing are being manufactured as a uniform body. Deviations below 1 cm from the concision of the two centres might be ignored, or absorbed by the central and tangential distortion parameters of the camera calibration model (Kunz and Singh 2008). In case the camera is misaligned to the dome or a flat port is being used, the conventional distortion model will not suffice and a full physical model must be adopted (Sedlazeck and Koch 2012) such as in Treibitz et al. (2008) or Constantinou et al. (2014), taking into consideration the glass thickness. Other researchers perform calibration on air and then compile parameters in underwater environment (Lavest et al. 2000).

Chromatic aberration (Fig. 8.1), is severe in underwater environment and may result in several pixels deformation (Menna et al. 2018b). Although it seems as an irrelevant radiometric problem, it can affect image geometric properties during both calibration and 3D reconstruction, in several ways. For example, calibration channel (colour) and 3D reconstruction channel (colour), should be compatible (the same), otherwise deformations will occur. Therefore, good practice on underwater SfM, is selecting a channel to work with, both during alignment and 3D reconstruction phase, while for texturing the full colour images maybe used, instead of the single channel ones. Post processing to amend chromatic aberration could be applied but analysis

Fig. 8.1 Samples of underwater chromatic vignetting (left) and chromatic aberration in detail (right), where the colour shift of a white line is demonstrated

of the actual image-point correction due to refraction shows that for close-range imaging, the actual aberration is depth dependent, and three dimensional problem (Sedlazeck and Koch 2012; Shortis 2015; Telem and Filin 2010).

Light absorption and vignetting affects are also significant, especially in wide angle lenses, but the they are bounded to radiometry without any geometric extension. Using underwater strobes is effective in small distances, and even then, the effect is not uniform (Fig. 8.1). Light absorption also affects clarity and crispness of images, hence deteriorating the performance of feature detectors. Backscattering, caused by floating particles and false strobe positioning, render photos useless by feature detectors (Fig. 8.2). Hence, these effects might influence texturing or orthoimage production. Underwater photography is a difficult task, governed by many issues, and must be mastered before performing photogrammetric documentation of a cultural site.

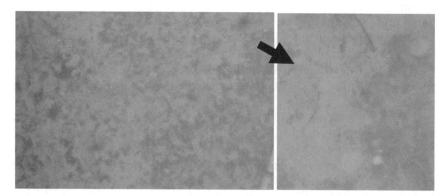

Fig. 8.2 Typical sample of backscattering effect, if lights are not positioned correctly. Such mild effects can be processed correctly from SfM, but when more profound, the results are unexpected

8.3.2   *Network of Control Points Establishment and Solving*

Georeferencing of CH sites is a standard process in land sites, but underwater is a difficult task at depths more than 3 m. Up to such depths, use of large poles allows surfacing of GPS receiver and correct geolocalization of a rather limited number of points, as the process is time consuming. In larger depths, use of buoys is not recommended as currents and waves do not allow vertical lines to the surface. Available systems for exact geolocalization of underwater sites, such as long baseline acoustic positioning system, may provide accuracy of up to few centimetres, but the cost of the system is so high that cannot be sustainable, only for archaeological purposes. Most sites are documented in local reference systems, as establishing a reference system is necessary if site is to be revisited for monitoring or due to multiple excavation periods.

Even so, establishing an underwater network of control points, is not a trivial task. Selecting position of control points (design), fixation of control points, measurement acquisition, become difficult to perform, the deeper the site is (Skarlatos et al. 2019). Limited bottom time, low visibility and poor communication underwater are challenging conditions, which render many land practices completely useless. The prevailing measuring methods in underwater CH documentation are tape measurements and photogrammetry, with the latter having a true advantage in terms of acquisition speed (Skarlatos et al. 2019), as a whole site may be measured within a single dive, where tape measurements require several dives, complicating dive logistics and overall planning of the expedition.

Even so, computational aspects on solving the network should also be considered, since vertical reference in not given, like in land CH sites. Buoys suffer from currents and cannot provide true vertical reference, inverted hoses with air inside, may transfer depth from point to point and provide relative depth differences, but not absolute depth, and dive computers are accurate to 10 cm and very unreliable as reading differs from day to day and from brand to brand. By using photogrammetry and a free network bundle adjustment, one may take advantage and relate several dive computer depth readings into a single solution and therefore provide vertical reference to a site. In a similar way when using only tape measurements for trilateration adjustment, depth readings remain unrelated measurements as the inherent unreliable vertical solution of trilateration, cannot take advantage of them in a holistic adjustment solution. In (Skarlatos et al. 2019) authors, based on realistic assumptions, demonstrated that when using photogrammetric measurements for free network adjustment, to assign coordinates in the control points, the average σXY error is 0.02 m and the average σZ error, is 0.02 m. Similar values, when using trilateration and tape measurements, are σXY 0.06 m and the average σZ error, is 0.64 m. Nevertheless, they point out that different assumptions over network might change results, although photogrammetric measurements will always be more precise.

8.4 Colour Processing of Underwater Images

Despite the relative low cost of the image-based methods in relation to others, they present a major drawback in underwater environment; optical properties and illumination conditions of water severely affect underwater imagery. Colours are lost as the depth increases, resulting in a green-blue image due to light absorption, which affects mainly red wavelength. Therefore, red channel histogram has fewer values compared to green and blue. Water also absorbs light energy and scatters optical rays creating blurred images.

8.4.1 Caustics Effect

Even though the above phenomena affect RGB imagery in every depth, when it comes to shallow waters (less than 10 m depth), caustics, the complex physical phenomena resulting from the projection of light rays being reflected or refracted by a curved surface (Fig. 8.3), seems to be the main factor degrading image quality for all passive optical sensors (Agrafiotis et al. 2018a). Unlike deep water photogrammetric approaches, where midday might be the best time for data capturing due to brighter illumination conditions, when it comes to shallow waters, the object to be surveyed needs strong artificial illumination, or images taken under overcast conditions, or with the sun low on the horizon, in order to avoid lighting artefacts on the seabed (Agrafiotis et al. 2018a).

If not avoided during the acquisition phase, caustics and illumination effects will affect image matching algorithms and are the main cause for dissimilarities in the generated textures and orthoimages, if these are the final results. In addition, caustics effects throw off most of the image matching algorithms, leading to less accurate matches (Agrafiotis et al. 2018a).

In the literature, only a few techniques have been proposed for the removal of caustics from images and video in the context of image enhancement. Trabes and Jordan (2015) propose a technique which involves tuning a filter for sunlight-deflickering of dynamically changing underwater scenes. A different approach was proposed in Gracias et al. (2008) where a mathematical solution was presented involving the calculation of the temporal median between images within a sequence. The same authors later extend their work in Shihavuddin et al. (2012) and propose an online sunflicker removal method which treats caustics as a dynamic texture. As reported in the paper this only works if the seabed or bottom surface is flat. In Schechner and Karpel (2004) authors propose a method based on analysing by a non-linear algorithm a number of consecutive frames in order to preserve consistent image components while filtering out fluctuations. Finally, Forbes et al. (2018) proposed a solution based on two small and easily trainable CNNs (Convolutional Neural Networks). This proposed solution was evaluated in terms of keypoint detection, image matching and 3D reconstruction performance in Agrafiotis et al. (2018a).

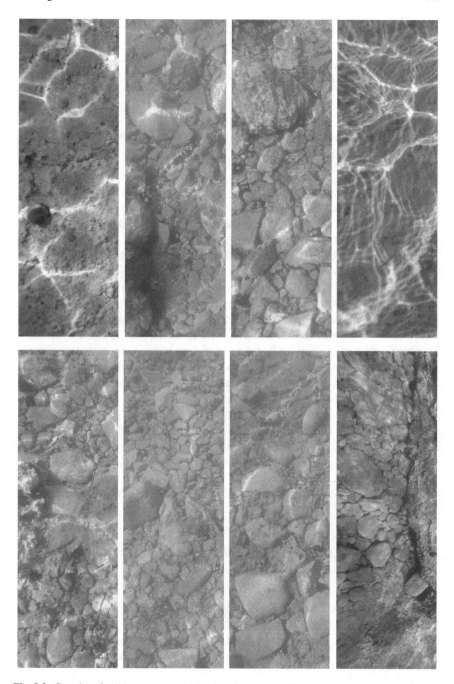

Fig. 8.3 Caustics of various patterns and density are present in the underwater imagery on shallow depths

Despite the innovative and complex aforementioned techniques, addressing caustic effect removal with procedural methods requires that strong assumptions are made on the many varying parameters involved e.g., scene rigidity, camera motion, etc. (Agrafiotis et al. 2018a).

8.4.2 Underwater Image Restoration and Underwater Image Enhancement

During the last decades, the acquisition of correct or at least realistic as possible underwater colour imagery became a very challenging, as well as promising, research field which affects the image-based 3D reconstruction and mapping techniques (Agrafiotis et al. 2017). To address these issues, two different approaches for underwater image processing are implemented according to their description in literature. The first one is image restoration. It is a strict method that is attempting to restore true colours and correct the image using suitable models, which parameterize adverse effects, such as contrast degradation and backscattering, using image formation process and environmental factors, with respect to depth (Hou et al. 2007; Treibitz and Schechner 2009; Akkaynak and Treibitz 2018; Berman et al. 2018; Akkaynak and Treibitz 2019). The second one uses image enhancement techniques that are based on qualitative criteria, such as contrast and histogram matching (Ghani and Isa 2014; Mangeruga et al. 2018). Image enhancement techniques do not consider the image formation process and do not require environmental factors to be known a priori (Agrafiotis et al. 2017, 2018b). In both approaches, recent advances in machine and deep learning facilitated the implementation of new improved techniques (Li et al. 2019) for underwater image processing however, due to the lack of sufficient and effective training data, the performance of deep learning-based underwater image enhancement algorithms do not match in many cases the success of recent deep learning-based high-level and low-level vision problems (Li et al. 2019).

8.4.3 Pre-processing or Post-processing the Underwater Imagery

Having developed various underwater image colour restoration and colour enhancement techniques, experts in underwater image-based 3D reconstruction faced the challenge of exploiting them and integrate them into the reconstruction steps. This integration is usually tackled with two different approaches; the first one focuses on the enhancement of the original underwater imagery before the 3D reconstruction in order to restore the underwater images and potentially improve the quality of the generated 3D point cloud. This approach in some cases of non-turbid water (Agrafiotis et al. 2017, 2018b) proved to be unnecessary and time-consuming, while in high-turbidity water it seems to have been effective enough (Mahiddine et al. 2012). The second approach suggests that, in good visibility conditions, the colour correction of the produced textures or orthoimages is sufficient and time efficient (Agrafiotis et al. 2017, 2018b).

Recently, a combination of the above was proposed in Mangeruga et al. (2018). There, an investigation as to whether and how the pre-processing of the underwater imagery using five implemented image enhancement algorithms affects the 3D reconstruction using automated SfM-MVS software is performed. This work follows and completes the work of presented in Agrafiotis et al. (2017, 2018b).

Specifically, each one of the presented algorithms in this article is evaluated according to its performance in improving the results of the 3D reconstruction using specific metrics over the reconstructed scenes of the five different datasets of submerged Cultural Heritage. To this end underwater imagery ensuring different environmental conditions (i.e., turbidity etc.), depth, and complexity was used. Results suggest that the 3D reconstructions were not significantly improved by the applied methods, probably the minor improvement obtainable with the LAB colour enhancement algorithm (Bianco et al. 2015) could not justify the effort to pre-process hundreds or thousands of images are required for larger models.

In the case of an underwater 3D reconstruction, the tool presented in Mangeruga et al. (2018) can be employed to try different combinations of methods and quickly verify if the reconstruction process can be improved somehow. However, as can be observed in Fig. 8.4, if no artificial light is present from a depth and below, images cannot be improved due to severe lack of the red channel, and most of the image enhancement methods fail.

A strategy that is suggested is to pre-process the images with the LAB (Bianco et al. 2015) method trying to produce a more accurate and dense 3D reconstruction and, afterwards, to enhance the original images with another method such as ACE (Getreuer 2012) to achieve a textured model more faithful to reality. Employing this tool for the enhancement of the underwater images ensures to minimize the pre-processing effort and enables the underwater community to quickly verify the performance of the different methods on their own datasets.

8.5 Conclusions

This chapter discussed critical aspects of all phases of image-based underwater 3D reconstruction process, from data acquisition and data preparation using image processing techniques to Structure from Motion (SfM) and Multi-View Stereo (MVS) techniques to produce an accurate, precise and complete 3D representation of the submerged heritage for a number of applications. It is straightforward that image-based 3D modelling of CH underwater sites offers the best performance to cost ratio. It is affordable, easy and fast, while offers excellent 3D spatial resolution and important visual information. However, it heavily depends on visibility, which renders the

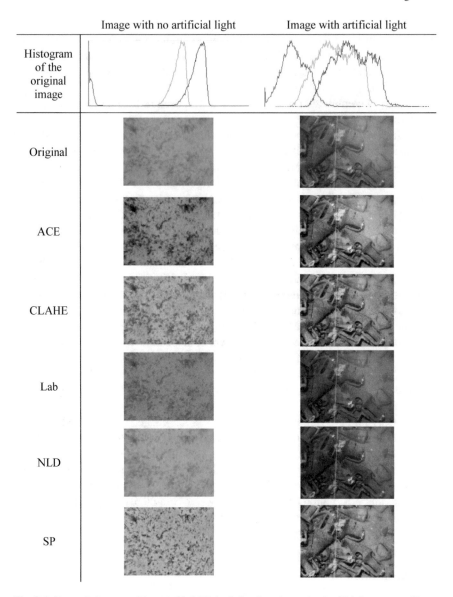

Fig. 8.4 Example images without artificial light (left column) at a depth of 34.5 m captured by an ROV and with artificial light (right column) at a depth of 45 m (*Credits* Photogrammetric Vision Lab. of Cyprus University of Technology for the left column and MARELab, University of Cyprus, for the images of the right column)

method inadequate for turbid waters. Quality of final results depend on many factors and are highly variable, depending on environmental conditions and data acquisition experience. The most important of these parameters is the camera to object distance reducing the field of view of a single image, minimizing the distance from the object and rendering full object coverage a challenge for any diver or ROV operator. Therefore, current bottleneck of what seems a flawless 3D reconstruction and texturing technique for VR applications, are illumination problems colour variations, processing power imitations, experience over data acquisition and reference system definition.

Acknowledgements Part of the work presented here conducted in the context of the iMARECUL-TURE project (Advanced VR, iMmersive Serious Games and Augmented REality asnTools to Raise Awareness and Access to European Underwater CULTURal heritagE, Digital Heritage) that has received funding from the European Union's Horizon 2020 research and innovation programme under grant agreement No 727153. Authors would like also to thank M.A.RE Lab from University of Cyprus and the lead archaeologist Prof. S. Demesticha for providing data from several underwater sites, and moreover challenging the authors to overcome problems and shortcomings of the 3D documentation process in underwater CH.

References

Abdelaziz M, Elsayed M (2019) Underwater photogrammetry digital surface model (DSM) of the submerged site of the ancient lighthouse near Qaitbay Fort in Alexandria, Egypt. Int Arch Photogramm Remote Sens Spatial Inf Sci XLII-2/W10:1–8. https://doi.org/10.5194/isprs-archives-XLII-2-W10-1-2019

Agrafiotis P, Drakonakis GI, Georgopoulos A, Skarlatos D (2017) The effect of underwater imagery radiometry on 3D reconstruction and orthoimagery. Int Arch Photogramm Remote Sens Spatial Inf Sci XLII-2/W3:25–31. https://doi.org/10.5194/isprs-archives-XLII-2-W3-25-2017, 2017

Agrafiotis P, Skarlatos D, Forbes T, Poullis C, Skamantzari M, Georgopoulos A (2018a) Underwater photogrammetry in very shallow waters: main challenges and caustics effect removal. Int Arch Photogramm Remote Sens Spatial Inf Sci XLII-2:15–22. https://doi.org/10.5194/isprs-archives-XLII-2-15-2018, 2018

Agrafiotis P, Drakonakis GI, Skarlatos D, Georgopoulos A (2018b) Underwater image enhancement before three-dimensional (3D) reconstruction and orthoimage production steps: is it worth. In: Remondino F, Georgopoulos A, González-Aguilera D, Agrafiotis P (eds) Latest developments in reality-based 3d surveying and modelling

Akkaynak D, Treibitz T (2018) A revised underwater image formation model. In: Proceedings of the IEEE conference on computer vision and pattern recognition, pp 6723–6732

Akkaynak D, Treibitz T (2019) Sea-thru: a method for removing water from underwater images. In: Proceedings of the IEEE conference on computer vision and pattern recognition, pp 1682–1691

Balletti C, Beltrame C, Costa E, Guerra F, Vernier P (2016) 3D reconstruction of marble shipwreck cargoes based on underwater multi-image photogrammetry. Digit Appl Archaeol Cult Herit 3(1):1–8

Berman D, Treibitz T, Avidan S (2018) Single image dehazing using haze-lines. IEEE Trans Pattern Anal Mach Intell

Bianco G, Muzzupappa M, Bruno F, Garcia R, Neumann L (2015) A new color correction method for underwater imaging. Int Arch Photogramm Remote Sens Spatial Inf Sci XL-5/W5:25–32. https://doi.org/10.5194/isprsarchives-XL-5-W5-25-2015

Bingham B, Foley B, Singh H, Camilli R, Delaporta K, Eustice R, … Sakellariou D (2010) Robotic tools for deep water archaeology: surveying an ancient shipwreck with an autonomous underwater vehicle. J Field Robot 27(6):702–717

Bosch J, Ridao P, Ribas D, Gracias N (2015) Creating 360 underwater virtual tours using an omnidirectional camera integrated in an AUV. In: OCEANS 2015-Genova. IEEE, pp 1–7

Bruno F, Gallo A, De Filippo F, Muzzupappa M, Petriaggi BD, Caputo P (2013) 3D documentation and monitoring of the experimental cleaning operations in the underwater archaeological site of Baia (Italy). In: 2013 digital heritage international congress (DigitalHeritage), vol 1. IEEE, pp 105–112

Bruno F, Lagudi A, Gallo A, Muzzupappa M, Davidde Petriaggi B, Passaro S (2015) 3D documentation of archeological remains in the Underwater Park of Baiae. Int Arch Photogramm Remote Sens Spatial Inf Sci XL-5/W5:41–46. https://doi.org/10.5194/isprsarchives-XL-5-W5-41-2015

Bruno F, Lagudi A, Muzzupappa M, Lupia M, Cario G, Barbieri L, … Saggiomo R (2016) Project VISAS: virtual and augmented exploitation of submerged archaeological sites-overview and first results. Mar Technol Soc J 50(4):119–129

Bruno F, Lagudi A, Collina M, Medaglia S, Davidde Petriaggi B, Petriaggi R, Ricci S, Sacco Perasso C (2019) Documentation and monitoring of underwater archaeological sites using 3D imaging techniques: the case study of the "Nymphaeum of Punta Epitaffio" (Baiae, Naples). Int Arch Photogramm. Remote Sens Spatial Inf Sci XLII-2/W10:53–59. https://doi.org/10.5194/isprs-archives-XLII-2-W10-53-2019

Bryson M, Johnson-Roberson M, Pizarro O, Williams SB (2013) Colour-consistent structure-from-motion models using underwater imagery. Robot: Sci Syst VIII:33

Constantinou C, Loizou S, Georgiades G, Potyagaylo S, Skarlatos D (2014) Adaptive calibration of an underwater robot vision system based on hemispherical optics. Oceanic Engineering Society—IEEE AUV 2014, Autonomous Underwater Vehicles 2014, 6–9 Oct., Oxford, Mississippi, US

Costa E (2019) The progress of survey techniques in underwater sites: the case study of Cape Stoba Shipwreck. Int Arch Photogramm Remote Sens Spatial Inf Sci XLII-2/W10:69–75. https://doi.org/10.5194/isprs-archives-XLII-2-W10-69-2019

Demesticha S, Skarlatos D, Neophytou A (2014) The 4th-century BC shipwreck at Mazotos, Cyprus: new techniques and methodologies in the 3D mapping of shipwreck excavations. J Field Archaeol 39(2):134–150. https://doi.org/10.1179/0093469014Z.00000000077

Derenne B, Nantet E, Verly G, Boone M (2019) Complementarity between *in situ* studies and photogrammetry: methodological feedback from a Roman Shipwreck in Caesarea, Israel. Int Arch Photogramm Remote Sens Spatial Inf Sci XLII-2/W10:77–83. https://doi.org/10.5194/isprs-archives-XLII-2-W10-77-2019

Drap P, Seinturier J, Hijazi B, Merad D, Boi JM, Chemisky B, … Long L (2015) The ROV 3D project: deep-sea underwater survey using photogrammetry: applications for underwater archaeology. J Comput Cult Herit (JOCCH) 8(4):21

Forbes T, Goldsmith M, Mudur S, Poullis C (2018) DeepCaustics: classification and removal of caustics from underwater imagery. IEEE J Ocean Eng

Furukawa Y, Ponce J (2010) Accurate, dense, and robust multi-view stereopsis. IEEE Trans Pattern Anal Mach Intell 32(8):1362–1376

Georgopoulos A, Agrafiotis P (2012) Documentation of a submerged monument using improved two media techniques. In: 18th international conference on virtual systems and multimedia, Milan, pp 173–180. https://doi.org/10.1109/vsmm.2012.6365922

Getreuer P (2012) Automatic color enhancement (ACE) and its fast implementation. Image Process Line 2:266–277

Ghani ASA, Isa NAM (2014) Underwater image quality enhancement through composition of dual-intensity images and Rayleigh-stretching. SpringerPlus 3(1):757

Gracias N, Negahdaripour S, Neumann L, Prados R, Garcia R (2008) A motion compensated filtering approach to remove sunlight flicker in shallow water images. In: OCEANS 2008. IEEE, pp 1–7

Hou W, Weidemann AD, Gray DJ, Fournier GR (2007) Imagery-derived modulation transfer function and its applications for underwater imaging. In: Optical engineering + applications. International Society for Optics and Photonics, pp 669622

Johnson-Roberson M, Pizarro O, Williams SB, Mahon I (2010) Generation and visualization of large-scale three-dimensional reconstructions from underwater robotic surveys. J Field Robot 27(1):21–51

Johnson-Roberson M, Bryson M, Friedman A, Pizarro O, Troni G, Ozog P, Henderson JC (2017) High-resolution underwater robotic vision-based mapping and three-dimensional reconstruction for archaeology. J Field Robot 34(4):625–643

Kunz C, Singh H (2008) Hemispherical refraction and camera calibration in underwater vision. In: OCEANS, pp 1–7

Lavest JM, Rives J, Lapreste JT (2000) Underwater camera calibration. In: ECCV '00: proceedings of the 6th European conference on computer vision-Part II, pp 654–668

Li C, Guo C, Ren W, Cong R, Hou J, Kwong S, Tao D (2019) An underwater image enhancement benchmark dataset and beyond. arXiv:1901.05495

Liarokapis F, Kouřil P, Agrafiotis P, Demesticha S, Chmelík J, Skarlatos D (2017) 3D modelling and mapping for virtual exploration of underwater archaeology assets. Int Arch Photogramm Remote Sens Spatial Inf Sci XLII-2/W3:425–431. https://doi.org/10.5194/isprs-archives-XLII-2-W3-425-2017

Lourakis MIA, Argyros AA (2009) Sparse bundle adjustment. ACM Trans Math Softw 36(1):1–30. https://doi.org/10.1145/1486525.1486527

Ludvigsen M, Eustice R, Singh H (2006) Photogrammetric models for marine archaeology. In: OCEANS 2006. IEEE, pp 1–6

Mahiddine A, Seinturier J, Boï DPJ, Drap P, Merad D, Long L (2012) Underwater image preprocessing for automated photogrammetry in high turbidity water: an application on the Arles-Rhone XIII roman wreck in the Rhodano river, France. In: Proceedings of the 2012 18th international conference on virtual systems and multimedia, Milan, Italy, 2–5 September 2012, pp 189–194

Mahon I, Williams SB, Pizarro O, Johnson-Roberson M (2008) Efficient view-based SLAM using visual loop closures. IEEE Trans Rob 24(5):1002–1014

Mangeruga M, Cozza M, Bruno F (2018a) Evaluation of underwater image enhancement algorithms under different environmental conditions. J Mar Sci Eng 6(1):10

Mangeruga M, Bruno F, Cozza M, Agrafiotis P, Skarlatos D (2018b) Guidelines for underwater image enhancement based on benchmarking of different methods. Remote Sens 10(10):1652

McCarthy J, Benjamin J (2014) Multi-image photogrammetry for underwater archaeological site recording: an accessible, diver-based approach. J Marit Archaeol 9(1):95–114

Menna F, Agrafiotis P, Georgopoulos A (2018a) State of the art and applications in archaeological underwater 3D recording and mapping. J Cult Herit 33:231–248

Menna F, Nocerino E, Remondino F (2018b) Photogrammetric modelling of submerged structures: influence of underwater environment and lens ports on three-dimensional (3D) measurements. In: Latest developments in reality-based 3D surveying and modelling. MDPI Basel, Switzerland, pp 279–303

Murai S, Kakiuchi H, Hano K, Tsuboi K, Tanabe S (1988) Computer generated mosaic of underwater photographs of ancient amphorae, Offshore the Syria. Int Arch Photogramm Remote Sens Spat Info Sci XXVII (Part B5)

Rebikoff DI (1966) Mosaic and strip scanning photogrammetry of large areas underwater regardless of transparency limitations. In: Underwater photo optics I, vol 7. International Society for Optics and Photonics, pp 105–115

Roman C, Inglis G, Rutter J (2010) Application of structured light imaging for highresolution mapping of underwater archaeological sites. In: OCEANS 2010 IEEE-Sydney. IEEE, pp 1–9

Schechner YY, Karpel N (2004) Attenuating natural flicker patterns. In: OCEANS '04. MTTS/IEEE TECHNO-OCEAN '04, vol 3. IEEE, pp 1262–1268

Sedlazeck A, Koch R (2012) Perspective and non-perspective camera models in underwater imaging—overview and error analysis. In: Dellaert F, Frahm J-M, Pollefeys M, Leal-Taix L, Rosenhahn

B (eds) Book perspective and non-perspective camera models in underwater imaging—overview and error analysis. Springer Berlin Heidelberg, pp 212–242

Shihavuddin ASM, Gracias N, Garcia R (2012) Online sunflicker removal using dynamic texture prediction. In: VISAPP, vol 1, pp 161–167

Shortis M (2015) Calibration techniques for accurate measurements by underwater cameras. Sensors 15(12):30810–30826

Shortis M (2019) Camera calibration techniques for accurate measurement underwater. In: McCarthy JK, Benjamin J, Winton T, van Duivenvoorde W (eds) 3D Recording and interpretation for maritime archaeology. Springer International Publishing, pp 11–27

Skarlatos D, Agapiou A, Rova M (2010) Photogrammetric support on an underwater archaeological excavation site: the Mazotos shipwreck case. In: 3rd international conference dedicated on digital heritage, Euromed 2010, Digital Heritage, 8–11 November, Lemesos. EuroMed2010, Arcaeolingua, pp 14–20

Skarlatos D, Demestiha S, Kiparissi S (2012) An 'open' method for 3D modelling and mapping in underwater archaeological sites. Int J Herit Digit Era 1(1):1–24

Skarlatos D, Agrafiotis P, Balogh T, Bruno F, Castro F, Petriaggi BD, … Kikillos F (2016) Project iMARECULTURE: advanced VR, iMmersive serious games and augmented REality as tools to raise awareness and access to European underwater CULTURal heritagE. In: Euro-mediterranean conference. Springer, Cham, pp 805–813

Skarlatos D, Menna F, Nocerino E, Agrafiotis P (2019) Precision potential of underwater networks for archaeological excavation through trilateration and photogrammetry. Int Arch Photogramm Remote Sens Spatial Inf Sci XLII-2/W10:175–180. https://doi.org/10.5194/isprs-archives-XLII-2-W10-175-2019

Snavely N, Seitz SM, Szeliski R (2006) Photo tourism. ACM SIGGRAPH 2006 papers on—SIGGRAPH '06. https://doi.org/10.1145/1179352.1141964

Snavely N, Seitz SM, Szeliski R (2008a) Modeling the world from internet photo collections. Int J Comput Vision 80(2):189–210

Snavely N, Garg R, Seitz SM, Szeliski R (2008b) Finding paths through the world's photos. ACM SIGGRAPH 2008 papers on—SIGGRAPH '08. https://doi.org/10.1145/1399504.1360614

Telem G, Filin S (2010) Photogrammetric modeling of underwater environments. ISPRS J Photogramm Remote Sens 65(5):433–444

Trabes E, Jordan MA (2015) Self-tuning of a sunlight-deflickering filter for moving scenes underwater. 2015 XVI workshop on information processing and control (RPIC). IEEE

Treibitz T, Schechner YY (2009) Active polarization descattering. IEEE Trans Pattern Anal Mach Intell 31(3):385–399

Treibitz T, Schechner Y, Singh H (2008) Flat refractive geometry. In: Proceedings of IEEE conference on computer vision and pattern recognition CVPR 2008, pp 1–8

Westoby M, Brasington J, Glasser N, Hambrey M, Reynolds J (2012) 'Structure-from-Motion' photogrammetry: a low-cost, effective tool for geoscience applications. Geomorphology 179:300–314. https://doi.org/10.1016/j.geomorph.2012.08.021

Yamafune K, Torres R, Castro F (2017) Multi-image photogrammetry to record and reconstruct underwater shipwreck sites. J Archaeol Method Theory 24(3):703–725

Zhukovsky MO, Kuznetsov VD, Olkhovsky SV (2013) Photogrammetric techniques for 3-D underwater record of the antique time ship from Phanagoria. Int Arch Photogramm Remote Sens Spat Inf Sci 40:717–721

Part III
Extended Reality

Chapter 9
Virtual Reality Reconstruction Applications Standards for Maps, Artefacts, Archaeological Sites and Monuments

Anastasios G. Bakaoukas

Abstract Virtual Reality (abbreviated VR), although far from being a new concept in computer science, is increasingly considered nowadays as the digital media technology that can most directly linked with Archaeology and Archaeological Reconstruction (with the term "reconstruction" in this context being officially agreed on meaning the "re-building of a monument to its state at a time of its history chosen for that particular representation"). The potential along with the many degrees of freedom offered by this branch of technology in the sector recently led experts to even start talking about the dawn of the hyper-tourist era. The ever increasing amount of research in the area, as well as the number of actual archaeological sites that have been reconstructed in a VR environment to the present, appear to support both directly and indirectly such a strong statement. It is not an exaggeration to say that archaeological research is now dependent on VR more than ever before. Also, many of these applications include a pedagogical aspect in their design that makes them ideal educational platforms for students in archaeology and professionals in the area alike.

9.1 Introduction

Only a couple of decades back, at the beginning of the new millennium, VR was still considered to be a piece of technology that only future generations could hope to have at their disposal as a fully-fledged technological achievement. Although VR technology had by then already gone into its forth decade of development (officially VR history started with the release of the "Sensorama" VR device in 1962), the time when the average user would be able to interact with VR equipment on a daily basis at the convenience of his home was seemingly lying very far away in the future.

Now, almost two decades later, and VR equipment at least for some branches of the computer games development sector, is considered as standard equipment. The

A. G. Bakaoukas (✉)
Computing & Immersive Technologies Department, Faculty of Arts, Science & Technology, University of Northampton, University Drive, Northampton NN1 5PH, UK
e-mail: Anastasios.Bakaoukas@northampton.ac.uk

© Springer Nature Switzerland AG 2020
F. Liarokapis et al. (eds.), *Visual Computing for Cultural Heritage*, Springer Series on Cultural Computing, https://doi.org/10.1007/978-3-030-37191-3_9

161

average user can buy at an affordable price not only a reliable VR headset and controllers, but even a VR Development Kit to start creating custom-made VR-enabled applications (HTC Vive, Sony PlaystationVR, Oculus Rift and Samsung Gear VR). The available with VR equipment software (computer games and/or pedagogical software) has reached an availability considered before unimaginable and the prediction is that the global VR market concerning both developmental branches (hardware and software) will continue to grow exponentially for years to come (https://www.grandviewresearch.com/industry-analysis/virtual-reality-vr-market).

But what is VR? The truth is that there is no official definition of the term to include all aspects of this technological achievement. A generally accepted description (if not definition) for VR relevant to our discussion in this chapter could be: "every computer-generated environment of the kind that when a user is finding himself surrounded by feels like having transported into a new and fully interactive one, along with the involvement of created signals capable of deceiving the user's three of five senses (i.e. Sight, Hearing, and to some extent, Touch), when at the same time electronic devices respond to the user's input by accordingly adjusting the environment is surrounded by, is a VR environment".

In this respect and at a very early stage had become apparent that three types of applications were more than every other suited to VR technology. That is, Computer Games (including Serious Games), various types of Simulations and, Environment Reconstructions (including Architectural). Reconstruction of Maps, Artefacts, Archaeological Sites and Monuments, falls naturally into the last category (the first officially recorded use of VR in a heritage application was in 1994. The system was designed by engineer Colin Johnson and was featured in a conference held by the British Museum in November 1994. The first applications running on this system provided an interactive "walk-through" of a three-dimensional reconstruction of Dudley Castle in England as it was in 1550 (Higgins et al. 1591)).

Because reconstruction is very often confused with restoration and vice versa, needs to be made clear at this point that in the context of what we are about to discuss in this chapter, restoration is the procedure through which, starting with an original model and by means of manual interventions, we are trying to reinstate what has been destroyed, in an attempt to bring back the model to its original status. Reconstruction, on the other hand, is the procedure through which, when we are not in possession of an original model (because so little of it remains) we set to build it almost from the beginning, taking into account only some original remaining parts of it (https://mw17.mwconf.org/paper/virtual-reality-and-archaeological-reconstruction-be-there-be-back-then-ullastret3d-and-vr-experience-in-htc-vive-and-immersive-room/).

9.2 Interdisciplinary Teams in VR Reconstruction Applications

As an old saying goes: "the whole is greater than the sum of its parts". In respect to the subject we are investigating in this chapter, we cannot but emphasise on how perfectly encapsulates the workings within an interdisciplinary team. That is, the very team structure that becomes the most key element when comes to recreating Maps, Artefacts, Archaeological Sites and Monuments in a 3D VR environment. Largely, this is because the very nature of the projects falling into the category we examine here calls for the involvement of a group of people who are trained on the use of diverse tools and among whom there is an organised division of labour around a common problem (Nancarrow et al. 2013; Beacham et al. 2006; Vassilios et al. 2001).

Mentioning here only the most key of the specialists involved in every recreational procedure of this nature, we need to naturally start from mentioning the Archaeologists; the very people that are expected to supply all the fundamental information. The Designers will take up the task of initially assembling this piece of information in such a way as to can be used from a computer science perspective. After that stage has been completed, the role of the Programmers in the team becomes important in the sense that these are the people who in the end will be entrusted with the translation of all the archaeological data and initial design work into a complete 3D model by using suitable computer games development software matched by some suitable VR hardware.

Building on each other's experience and work, each member of the team progresses the overall project from stage to stage so the final result achieved is as faithful as humanly possible to the archaeological data available.

As expected, such an approach comes with its challenges. Having several professionals, holding their expertise in different disciplines, gathered together and assigned a common task cannot by itself guaranty that everything is going to flow smoothly and they will necessarily function to the best of their abilities. It is not without reason that how to effectively work as part of an interdisciplinary team has become nowadays a major focus in the whole educational system.

9.3 User's Perception of a VR Environment

From the user's point of view, free movement in all directions; the ability to closely interact with surrounding objects and the overall environment in a highly realistic way; to wander the streets and enter a building; to take a closer look in order to come to appreciate artistic detail and the feeling that "you are actually there", are only a few key elements out of a list of attractions relating to VR technology. Users can now more than ever experience in full what an archaeological site was like, grasp more than the basics of its architecture, and get to appreciate how people used to live there as well.

A cracking combination of applications at an irresistible level of quality matched by fast hardware, make VR admittedly one of the most exciting branches of today's technology. VR applications really possess the ability to absorb a user's senses and irrespective of where looking, in a fully enabled 3D environment, to completely enclose him in an unbelievably realistic but imaginary world. That is, to achieve a transition from a completely real world to a completely virtual one. The transition from reality to the virtual domain is taking place through computational means, and the transition from the virtual to the reality domain is taking place through realism.

Of course, all the above are not to imply by any means that we do not have an even brighter future laying before us. State-of-the-art VR hardware designed in the future, possibly including a fully integrated brain-computer interface system, will prove to be one of these crucial factors of improvement that will take the technology of this kind to the next stage.

9.4   A Virtual Reality Reconstruction Methodology

Of an outmost importance, in every field of science, is undeniably the methodology followed in order to obtain scientifically sound results. For projects in the field we are concerned with in this chapter, methodology is the procedure or set of procedures that outline the way in which stages unfold as part of the VR reconstruction process of Maps, Artefacts, Archaeological Sites and Monuments.

While in several other cases, as scientists working on a topic directly relevant to our field of expertise, we can use standard methodologies that have been tested for their validity under a number of different circumstances, archaeological VR reconstruction provides an additional challenge in the sense that being a rather new discipline lacks standards. This remains as true despite collective attempts to fill-in the gap in recent years, since effectively archaeological virtual reality standards have not been revised since 2009/2012 (Beacham et al. 2006; Denard 2012) or even since 2000 in many sectors (Pletinckx et al. 2000).

In this section we will attempt to outline a procedure with the potential to formulate a standardised VR reconstruction methodology and demonstrate the multidisciplinary, open, interactive and transparent approach that such a methodology incorporates within its structure so can be considered suitable for the purpose (Barcelo 2000). The methodology unfolds in four stages that truly have suggested themselves while participating in development teams in the field as well as after reflecting on other peoples' experiences.

9.4.1   Typical Steps in a VR Reconstruction Process

Let us first concern ourselves with the predictable steps involved in a typical VR reconstruction project. This will enable us next to start sketching out the stages of a universal VR reconstruction methodology in the following sub-sections.

As already mentioned, the undeniable key element of every VR reconstruction project is a well-structured multidisciplinary team. The actual specialities in the team depend, in the general case, massively every time on the very nature of the topic investigated. In the specific context of the field that we are focusing on in this chapter someone could catalogue potential specialities needed as: archaeologists, anthropologists, hydrogeologists, architects, engineers, naval architecture specialists, programmers, designers and artists. Also, the addition of some external partners may prove necessary on the fly as the project unfolds, depending on individual challenges and difficulties arising either occasionally and/or on a calculated manner. In general, whatever the initial outline of the team involved, for every VR reconstruction project there are four fundamental layers requiring population by specialised people in the team, (a) *realistic snapshot of the past*, (b) *linking archaeological information and VR capabilities*, (c) *analysis and design procedures* and, (d) *archaeological/VR tools* (Fig. 9.1).

The case is that, as with every technical project, the fundamental commitment of a VR reconstruction project must be to quality. Quality, in this context, is reflected on the need to achieve in the end an as *realistic snapshot of the past* as it is possible at the time of reconstruction. This constitutes the foundation layer upon which the other layers in the scheme rest.

Fig. 9.1 The four fundamental layers involved in every VR reconstruction project

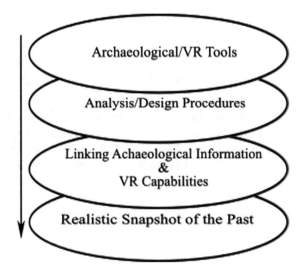

Archaeological/VR Tools

Analysis/Design Procedures

Linking Archaeological Information
&
VR Capabilities

Realistic Snapshot of the Past

Directly supported upon the commitment to a realistic recreation of a snapshot of the past—namely, the next layer up—is the need for effectively *linking archaeological information and VR capabilities*. A major factor at this layer constitutes the realisation that not absolutely everything can be accommodated within a VR application, or, in equal terms, the realisation that not absolutely everything is convenient to be accommodated within a VR application. Admittedly, it is a fact that nowadays mentality has been shifted towards the consideration that today's computing machines come with unparalleled capabilities and an abundance of resources. While this turns out to be relatively true, still we are lying very far away from that point where we will be able as developers to create a virtual environment at the maximum humanly possible level of detail. Compromising with what we have available and making happen the absolute best that can be achieved by using existing resources has been the bread-and-butter of developers ever since the dawn of computing.

Before any application based on gathered data can be developed, the *analysis and design procedures* must have first been completed. In this third layer up, the emphasis is on achieving the best possible translation of the row data available so appropriate design procedures based on this translation can be enabled. By large the analysis and design procedures determine the overall success of the task at hand.

The possibility of one's goal achieved by inappropriate, or even half-appropriate, tools is admittedly minute in the VR reconstruction world. An ideal combination of both automated and semi-automated *archaeological/VR tools* will in principle lead to practising a safe and error-proof procedure in gathering and prototyping data, respectively.

So, by considering what discussed so far, and taking a top-down approach, we can summarise by saying that the first challenge a VR reconstruction project team is to be faced with is the selection of the appropriate tools.

9.4.2   Stage 1: Selecting an Archaeological Site and Tools for Collecting Archaeological Data

Has been acknowledged since the early days that a good practise to follow in choosing an archaeological site for reconstruction is to consider, at a first filtering stage, those available that come (from a scientific point of view) from a well-known historical period. At a second filtering stage, to consider those offering best chances for a good VR reconstruction that will be based on a very specific moment in history. A sequence of events can then added around the main reconstruction, for which we may possess only partial knowledge. The actual requirement here is for the user to be informed of the fact that these additional events are including archaeological recreation based not on solid facts throughout but, rather, on previously scattered historical information later reassembled and interpolated.

Archaeologists are primarily based for their judgement of the past on excavation reports, historical research, iconography and/or historical landscaping. Also, nowadays, ever more increasingly, they are based on geophysical scanning as well. Assisting to these techniques are secondary ones like: hydrography, anthropology and physical reconstruction. Not all of them can offer reliable information in all cases, and for this reason a very objective assessment of the information provided by each is first required.

The next step constitutes the correlation phase, which focuses on comparing information. That is, during correlation, the archaeologist attempts to identify what collected and documented information can be considered as reliable, what possible further processing of the information is required, what can be expected from the information, what constraints exist in relation to the information, and what validation criteria are required in order to come to sound conclusions based on those pieces of information that have been labelled as reliable.

It is also a common practice, at this stage, for the team to require the construction of the so called "preliminary comparative/experimental models". Usually, such kind of models are not based entirely on archaeologically proven facts and their only purpose is to provide a first idea (like a first draft) of what line the VR reconstruction is to follow later. Despite of what effort put into the construction of such models no one in the team is expected to rely on them for drawing final conclusions. In the best of cases, such models will be subjected to many revisions, if not at some point discarded all together.

The undeniable tool(s) of the last twenty years in archaeological VR reconstruction is the latest generation of archaeological geophysical survey methods. Among them two are the most widely used and praised for the quality of the results produced. These are the Ground-Penetrating Radar (GPR) method and the Electrical Resistivity Tomography (ERT) method. Very often in practice GPR and ERT (Fig. 9.2) are the only geophysical methods considered, primarily because of their fundamentally non-invasive nature as methods and secondarily because of the directly transferable to a 3D mapping results they offer.

Of course none of the two techniques is to be taken as the absolute optimum for the purpose; since they are both prone to errors and cases where they have failed to yield useful results have been reported. As field archaeologists very well know, many lessons about applying geophysical survey methods have come to be learned from sporadic success and failure, as well as from the realisation that conditions at some archaeological sites may not permit for the application of geophysical survey methods at all.

Much more recently, two additional methods have been added to those mentioned above with very promising results; these are the Digital Camera Imagery (DCI) and the Laser Scanning (LS) methods. In particular, the Laser Scanning method is an immensely convenient one when it comes to VR reconstruction because of its ability to directly capture 3D images of an archaeological site that can almost immediately fed into a 3D imagery processing tool. Very often, especially in artefact reconstruction related projects, the Laser Scanning method is paired with 3D printing.

From our discussion about archaeological and technical field methods, must have become apparent that the archaeological site selection and the geomorphological identification of the structure of the site, are two phases in the overall methodology

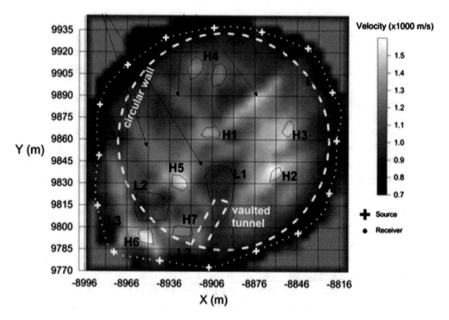

Fig. 9.2 Plan view map of Electrical Resistivity Tomography (ERT) survey results from the Amphipolis Tomb in Macedonia, Greece

the significance of which is hard to overestimate. The end goal here is primarily to locate an archaeological site within its geographical/geophysical context. With this achieved, the VR reconstruction will in succession succeed in localising the archaeological site at a realistic terrain assisting enormously that way in users' perception of the reality of the historical period the particular reconstruction falls within.

Usually considered of secondary importance, but nevertheless deserving attention at the initial stages of every VR reconstruction related project, is the issue of considering what kind of vegetation would have possibly existed at the time. Realistically, reconstructing the terrain of an archaeological site is one thing, but being able to populate this very terrain with the appropriate grass, bushes, plants and trees, is completely another.

As an extension to the above requirement also comes the necessity for accounting for the human-made transformation to the vegetation layer arising from the creation of access routes, agricultural exploitation and extraction of mineral resources related activities. No civilisation has ever been in existence that curried out its activities in a totally environmental friendly way. All civilisations, one way or another, caused a documentable effect on the environment inhabited. For some particular archaeological sites an accurate, to the extent that this is feasible, reproduction of the effect of human activities on the environment may be of substantial importance in projecting a fully-fledged picture of the period reconstructed to the user.

9.4.3 Stage 2: Reconstructing the Archaeological Site

As soon as the archaeological data have been assembled; then assessed and validated from a scientific point of view, the categorisation of them thematically leads to a first-impression creation of the archaeological site itself.

Usually, the reconstruction is firstly based on recreating the peripheral to the main structures, along with the creation of models and textures. The civil infrastructure can follow, by considering streets, walls, trenches, pathways, bridges, etc. to assist primarily in creating the 2D outline of main buildings and other constructions, so can later the 3D volumes of them can be determined.

At a final stage, the creation of all the movable elements of the reconstruction can be considered. Furniture, and various other artefacts, can be based on actual excavated items or items prototyped after textual descriptions.

At the purely technical sector, 3D models of land and buildings can be constructed from 3D maps, leading to the creation of geometrical meshes that then can be used to represent the objects within a game engine. Also, 3D outlines and vectorised drawings exported to a 3D format have been very successfully used in the past for reconstructing landscapes and architectural features.

The point at which we need to pay particular attention at is in relation to the methodology followed for constructing the virtual models. Many practitioners in the area agree, and personal experience has verified, that the best policy is for someone to continuously check the models for scientific accuracy. This means that thorough checks need to be carried out even at primitive stages when the models only exist as meshes and extended throughout the entire process. By following this simple methodology can be made sure that when the need arises to introduce any essential corrections to the models these corrections will have an effect only on the points of interest, and not on the entire model or even on the textures created much later. Needless to say, this will eventually lead to a highly recursive procedure that will have to be faithfully repeated for every single model in our VR reconstruction.

9.4.4 Stage 3: Tools for Reconstructing Archaeological Sites, Maps, Artefacts, and Monuments

Software packages like "Cinema4D", "Blender", "Maya" and "3D Studio Max" can be used for recreating landscapes and architectural features alike, while both "Unity3D" and "Unreal Engine 4" game engines have to offer an integrated, straight forward to use, and very powerful landscape creation component.

When all models (i.e. for the terrain, the vegetation, the pathways, the lakes and/or rivers, the buildings and the artefacts) are ready, they can be imported into a game engine for the final assembly of them to provide a photorealistic quality overview on how the overall creation looks like. Easy and straight forward assembly of models in a fully enabled 3D environment and photorealistic quality, though, are not the only attractions for using a game engine for the purpose. All modern game engines meeting professional standards like "Unity3D" and "Unreal Engine 4" can directly export projects for application on a variety of platforms, including all VR platforms (i.e. Multiscreen Projection, Virtual Reality Headsets, etc.).

The traditional (and still recommended by many practitioners in the field) way of navigating through the VR reconstructed world is by means of using the VR Headset and the Touch Controllers. The by default set functionality of these two devices is for the headset to translate user's head movement into a change in the field of vision (the measurement per unit is in degrees) and for the touch controllers to translate user's hands movement into a corresponding virtual hands movement (the measurement per unit is in pixels). These two main functionalities are complemented by a secondary one found on the touch controllers and provided by means of an analogue stick (full 360° spinning capability around the central vertical axis) that can be used for "walking" around in an area (the measurement per units is in degrees and pixels).

Although this standard functionality will offer all a developer needs in most of the cases and is the optimum solution for third-person scenarios, had from a very early stage become apparent to the author that by sticking to this functionality someone limits the sense of realism in first-person applications like VR reconstruction applications fundamentally are.

Simply stated, in our everyday lives we pensive our environment in first-person and we are not using an analogue stick to walk ourselves around the environment we inhabit. Thinking about possibilities in improving on this, the author devised an alternative navigational method as part of a VR reconstruction project undertaken at the University of Northampton, UK in collaboration with the Caroline Chisholm School, Northampton, UK (the project was funded by a partnership grant from The Royal Society, partnership grants summer 2017, PG\170067).

The core software for the project was written around the VRTK Virtual Reality Toolkit (https://vrtoolkit.readme.io), an extension software package written for the "Unity3D" game engine. For the implementation, the standardised primary role of the navigation devices, VR Headset and Touch Controllers, was maintained, with a variation introduced at the way the walk-through functionality was achieved. Instead of using the analogue stick for the purpose, the A-button on the right-hand touch controller was given a Boolean functionality. When released (equivalent to state "false"), the control devices function under their primary functionality (Standard Mode of operation) with no walk-through. When pressed (equivalent to state "true"), head movement is combined with walk-though functionality (Walk-through Mode of operation). In this second case, the user experiences a situation where head movement changes the visual field while at the same time experiences walking towards the direction indicated by the visual field line of sight. Walk-through Mode of operation is achieved by a series of decisions hard-wired in the code and implemented on the basis of the human visual field pattern (Fig. 9.3).

In this context, when the user's head is detected to be in the area of the right-hand-side or the left-hand-side monocular visual field, the user experiences a full 90° turn in respect to the vertical meridian of the visual field towards the corresponding direction, along with walking movement towards the far point indicated by the direct

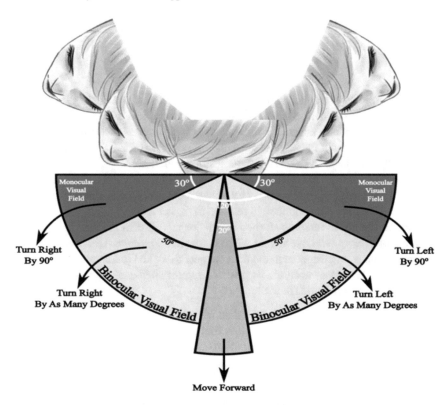

Fig. 9.3 The human visual field pattern. With the A-button on the right-hand touch controller pressed (equivalent to Boolean state "true"), head movement is combined with walk-though functionality (Walk-through Mode of operation)

horizontal line of sight. When the user's head is kept within the area of the central 20° of the visual field, the user experiences a straight-a-head type of walk-through movement towards the far point indicated by the direct horizontal line of sight with an at the same time 0° turn in respect to the vertical meridian of the visual field. Finally, the user's head found within the area of either one of the binocular visual fields results to as many degrees turn towards the corresponding direction.

As an extension to this the author is now working on developing a navigational system that will include along with the standard VR equipment an eye-tracking device and a Brain-Computer Interface (BCI) device. With positive results already achieved, when the system is ready, the hope is, to be able to introduce another degree of freedom in the hyper-realistic experience offered to the user when engaging with a VR application. That is, the feeling of an absolute transition for the user to the virtually reconstructed world casually achievable and independent of application characteristics (Dohan and Mu 2019).

9.4.5 Stage 4: Data Acquisition or "The Battle for Realism" in VR Reconstruction Applications

By attempting someone to discuss the problem of realism standards in VR reconstruction applications, namely, how realism can be achieved, what are its limitations, etc. needs necessarily to also discuss, in direct relation to this, the problem of obtaining those detailed data necessary for achieving the highly realistic reconstruction. This problem, throughout the years since the introduction of data-based science, has acquired the special name "The Data Acquisition Problem".

The significance of this problem becomes apparent when we come to understand that the representational quality of every model recreated is mirroring the quality of the original detailed data obtained in relation to that model.

With all the above mentioned, the importance of real data to base on the representation of every model taking part in the reconstruction, cannot be overestimated. In general, many practitioners in the field suggest that three fundamental steps need to be taken when an as accurate as possible representation of objects in a digital reconstruction is required. These are:

1. To make every effort possible to obtain realistic high quality images.
2. To post-process these realistic images for maximum quality.
3. To superimpose all obtained information (as discussed in the previous section) on the real images to maintain close contact with reality for those models requiring the intervention of human creativity to fill-in possible gaps.

Throughout the previous decade obtaining realistic images of objects' appearance and converting them into useful row data was a process that was requiring manual handling, the employment of stereo-photogrammetry surveying, 3D laser-scanners, or any combination of the three. Particularly the laser-scanner technique, since its first introduction in the field, with its ability to provide the spatial coordination of the surface points of the objects of interest had been proved a really invaluable tool. Nevertheless, as invaluable as it might have been proved, there is a well-known drawback associated with the technique. Using a laser-scanner in a massive scale (and ignoring at this point the relatively high cost involved), automatically means the generation of a huge amount of data, the distribution of which over the web or their use in web-based applications is problematic; particularly when there is a need to deal with large objects possessing many parts that require to be detailed.

Nowadays, a new technique has come to substitute for this practice that takes advantage of the capabilities and the many degrees of freedom offered by the Small Unmanned Aircrafts (SUA) (those flying devices we are accustomed of collectively calling "Drones"). Although drones have been identified as particularly suitable in bridging ground-based surveys and expensive air-borne remote sensing, can also handle situations where general landscape and individual buildings or other structures have to be investigated stretching the spectrum of potential applications from landscapes, to excavations, to monuments, to buildings and many more.

In reality, the application of a drone-based technique combines the best of many worlds with its capability to offer higher resolution 3D data (processed by a photogrammetric software application), in a shorter period of time and at a significantly lower cost than the majority of the other well-known techniques including Air-borne Laser Scanners (LiDARs—Light Detection And Ranging) when applied using a full size aircraft.

Relatively recently (2016), has been reported (https://www.mola.org.uk/blog/drone-mounted-lasers-see-between-leaves) that a combination of a drone and laser-scanner (Drone-mounted Laser-scanner) achieved excellent results at a site of interest that was initially considered of presenting unsurpassed difficulties. The difficulty factor was mainly due to the site being completely covered by trees. By using very effectively the main characteristic of this new technique, which comes as a result of a combination of extremely rapid in succession and very dense laser pulses used, the involved technicians managed to get enough laser beams to reach through to the ground that made for enough points of reference. While, at the same time, many millions more of laser beams were bounced off the leaf canopy. In the end all the reference points gathered were used to create a model of the surface, which could then be further examined and processed.

Despite the level of modernisation data acquisition techniques are currently experiencing, the goal of any modelling process remains fundamentally the same. That is, to create a high resolution, as accurate as possible, representation of the site of interest. The answer to this problem is to proceed in an uneven manner, starting from the creation of a large scale unrectified model including a superposition of all the acquired data, before specific details for which even more data will be needed are introduced. It is at this very stage that acquired data that initially had produced components of the model that seemed valid when treated individually may prove as producing a completely different visual result when viewed in the context of the big picture.

The whole of the data acquisition problem can be viewed collectively, as have been treated in our discussion so far, or even as individual entities that can be summarised as below:

- The data required for the 3D geometry models.
- The data required for the photorealistic rendering of models' surfaces (i.e. light, textures, etc.).
- The data required for allowing the creation of interactive surfaces for the user to interact with.
- The data required for allowing for realistic movement in the VR environment.
- The data required for accurate reproduction of both models and VR environment in the case of other display means than a simple computer screen.

The final aspect in our discussion about the data acquisition problem is that of Data Integration. From what discussed above must have become apparent that in extremely rare situations only we will be faced with the relatively straight forward problem of having to deal with data that have been gathered using only one data acquisition method. In the grand majority of cases we will need to integrate data that have been acquired using a variety of methods.

The solution exercised for a good number of years now to address this problem requires the gradual addition of data, as acquired, directly into a Data Integrated Environment that is implemented and maintained as a single platform. The most characteristic example of such an approach is the Integrated Archaeological Database System (IADB) developed and used by the Scottish Urban Archaeological Trust (SUAT) (Rains 1995). Since then, any major or minor database system build for the purpose comprises in one or the other way the following elements making up the prototype structure of this original database:

- *Section 1*: Data related to the creation of the VR environment.
- *Section 2*: Data related to the creation of the models (wireframes).
- *Section 3*: Data related to the application of textures on the VR environment.
- *Section 4*: Data related to the application of textures on the models.
- *Section 5*: Data related to the various relationships between the environment and the models.
- *Section 6*: Data related to specific links between environment and models.
- *Section 7*: Data related to photorealistic digital images (textures) used for creation of duplicates or variations in case of procedurally generated extensions to the original design of the VR environment.

Retrieving of the data takes place by means of using a Structured Query Language (SQL) to query the database. Then the results of those queries can be further processed before used for rendering the actual VR environment and the models.

Because of this need for further processing the preference here is to store data leading to baked textures in order to avoid employing the multi-pass rendering technique. Despite the fact that this practice may lead to a requirement for higher storage capacity, still is considered much more preferable because of the ability to combine material decals with illumination texturing.

9.5   Conclusion

This chapter is the result of an attempt to create a basis for the formulation of a precise recreational and data acquisition methodology for VR reconstruction projects, emphasising on good practises that have been tested in a number of related to the field projects.

Particular emphasis paid on the degrees of freedom offered by today's technology in relation to archaeological site investigation, data gathering, data analysis and reconstruction. The distinction was also made between VR reconstruction for visualisation purposes and VR reconstruction for conducting research purposes.

Applications in the area of VR reconstruction have now opened up possibilities for standardisation in both reconstruction practises and applications' quality since the advantages offered by virtual models have become more than evident. Current research in the area of integrating Brain-Computer Interface and Eye-Tracking technology with the standard VR input devices and controllers suggests that in near future the applications spectrum for VR will become even more broad, with user experience reaching unparalleled levels of realism.

Of course, in relation to the above mentioned, we will need to fully appreciate at some point the fact that such a developmental route will potentially demand the involvement of scientists from other branches than the usual, and especially that of psychologists and sociologists, to mention just the two most obvious, in order to assess the potential psychosocial impact of VR reconstruction applications.

References

Barcelo J (2000) Visualizing what might be. An introduction to virtual reality in archaeology. In: Barcelo JA, Forte M, Sanders D (eds) Virtual reality in archaeology. Archeo Press, pp 9–36

Beacham R, Denard H, Niccolucci F (2006) The London Charter—for the computer-based visualisation of cultural heritage. The E-volution of ICTechnology In Cultural Heritage, Papers from the Joint Event CIPA/VAST/EG/EuroMed Event. http://www.londoncharter.org

Denard H (2012) A new introduction to The London Charter. In: Bentkowska-Kafel A, Baker D, Denard H (eds) Paradata and transparency in virtual heritage digital research in the arts and humanities series, Ashgate. http://www.londoncharter.org

Dohan M, Mu M (2019) Understanding user attention in VR using gaze controlled games. In: TVX '19 proceedings of the 2019 ACM international conference on interactive experiences for TV and online video, June 05–07, Salford (Manchester), UK, pp 167–173. ISBN: 978-1-4503-6017-3. https://doi.org/10.1145/3317697.3325118

Doulamis A et al (2015) 5D Modelling: an efficient approach for creating spatiotemporal predictive 3D maps of large-scale cultural resources. ISPRS Ann Photogramm Remote Sens Spat Inf Sci 2

Higgins T, Main P, Lang J, British Museum (eds) (1996) Imaging the past: electronic imaging and computer graphics in museums and archaeology. Volume 114 of British Museum London: Occasional paper Issue 114 of Occasional paper, British Museum. ISSN: 0142-4815. ISBN: 0861591143 – 9780861591145

https://vrtoolkit.readme.io

https://www.mola.org.uk/blog/drone-mounted-lasers-see-between-leaves

Ioannides M et al (2013) Online 4D reconstruction using multi-images available under open access. ISPRS Ann Photogramm Remote Sens Spatial Inf Sci II-5W 1:169–174

Konečný R, Sylaiou S, Liarokapis F (2016) Procedural modeling in archaeology—approximating ionic style columns for games. In: Proceedings of the 8th international conference on virtual worlds and games for serious applications (VS-Games 2016), 7–9 Sept 2016. IEEE Computer Society, Barcelona, Spain, pp 1–8

Kyriakaki G et al (2014) 4D reconstruction of tangible cultural heritage objects from web-retrieved images. Int J Herit Digit Era 3(2):431–451

Nancarrow S, Booth A, Ariss S, Smith T, Enderby P, Roots A (2013) Ten principles of good interdisciplinary team work. Hum Resour Health 11. https://doi.org/10.1186/1478-4491-11-19

Noghani J, Liarokapis F, Anderson E (2010) Procedural generation of urban environments through space and time. In: Proceedings of the 31st annual conference of the European Association for computer graphics (Eurographics 2010), Poster Session, Norrkoping, Sweden, 4–7 May, 2010

Noghani J, Anderson E, Liarokapis F (2012) Towards a Vitruvian shape grammar for procedurally generating classical Roman architecture. In: Proceedings of the 13th international symposium on virtual reality, archaeology and cultural heritage VAST 2012, short and project papers, Eurographics, Brighton, UK, 19–21 November 2012, pp 41–44

Papaioannou G, Gaitatzes A, Christopoulos D (2003) Enhancing virtual reality walkthroughs of archaeological sites. In: 4th international symposium on virtual reality, archaeology and intelligent cultural heritage. The Eurographics Association

Pletinckx D, Callebaut D, Killebrew AE, Silberman NA (2000) Virtual-reality heritage presentation at Ename. IEEE MultiMedia 7(2):45–48. https://doi.org/10.1109/93.848427

Pollefeys M, Proesmans M, Koch R, Vergauwen M, Van Gool L (1998) Acquisition of detailed models for virtual reality. In: Virtual reality in archaeology, vol 843, BAR International Series, CAA. Archaeopress, Publishers of British Archaeological Reports, pp 71–77

Rains MJ (1995) Towards a computerised desktop: the integrated archaeological database system. In: Huggett J, Ryan N (eds), pp 207–10

Saggio G, Borra D (2011) Augmented reality for restoration/reconstruction of artefacts with artistic or historical value. In Book: Augmented reality—some emerging application areas. https://doi.org/10.5772/27066

Slavova Y, Mu M (2018) A comparative study of the learning outcomes and experience of VR in education. In: IEEE conference on virtual reality and 3D user interfaces (VR)—conference paper. https://doi.org/10.1109/vr.2018.8446486

Vassilios V, John K, Manolis T, Michael G, Luis A, Didier S, Tim G, Ioannis TC, Renzo C, Nikos I (2001) Archeoguide: first results of an augmented reality, mobile computing system in cultural heritage sites. In: Proceedings of the 2001 conference on virtual reality, archaeology and cultural heritage, Glyfada, Greece. ACM

Virtual reality (VR) market analysis by device, by technology, by component, by application, by region, and segment forecasts, 2018–2025. Report ID: GVR-1-68038-831-2, May 2017. https://www.grandviewresearch.com/industry-analysis/virtual-reality-vr-market

Virtual reality and archaeological reconstruction: be there, back then, MW17: MW 2017, Published February 2017, Consulted May 2019. https://mw17.mwconf.org/paper/virtual-reality-and-archaeological-reconstruction-be-there-be-back-then-ullastret3d-and-vr-experience-in-htc-vive-and-immersive-room/

Vlahakis V, Ioannidis M, Karigiannis J, Tsotros M, Gounaris M, Stricker D, Gleue T, Daehne P, Almeida L (2002) Archeoguide: an AR guide for archaeological sites. Comput Graph Appl IEEE 22:52–60

White M, Mourkoussis N, Darcy J, Petridis P, Liarokapis F, Lister PF, Walczak K, Wojciechowski R, Cellary W, Chmielewski J, Stawniak M, Wiza W, Patel M, Stevenson J, Manley J, Giorgini F, Sayd P, Gaspard F (2004) ARCO—an architecture for digitization, management and presentation of virtual exhibitions. In: Proceedings of the 22nd international conference on computer graphics (CGI'2004), June 16–19. IEEE Computer Society, Hersonissos, Crete, pp 622–625

Chapter 10
Using Augmented Reality, Gaming Technologies, and Transmedial Storytelling to Develop and Co-design Local Cultural Heritage Experiences

Lissa Holloway-Attaway and Lars Vipsjö

Abstract As technologies are integrated in museum and cultural heritage contexts, digital heritage design increasingly depends on innovative, embodied and experimental storytelling features focused on users. These developments create opportunities to incorporate gaming technologies that may include immersive, affective mixed reality (MR) systems with narrative innovation at the core. To support such engagements, researchers in the Division of Game Development at the University of Skövde have developed a number of projects, educational programs, interdisciplinary research practices and collaborations. In our chapter we will foreground the KLUB project, a sub-project in the *KASTiS* project (in English, the "Cultural Heritage and Game Technologies in Skaraborg" project), a funded regional development initiative in western Sweden focused on engaging citizens in local cultural heritage at a number of municipalities. KLUB uses transmedial storytelling techniques and gaming elements within an Augmented Reality enhanced children's book series and related media (board games, locative experiences) that have been co-designed with a number of stakeholders to tell and play the local micro-histories of the Skaraborg region in Sweden. We contextualize our research in humanistic interventions and practices for co-designing transmedial game/stories and outline some of our related intra-disciplinary activities and impacts in research.

10.1 Humanistic Frameworks for Cultural Heritage Storytelling

As digital technologies have become more integrated (and expected) in museum and cultural heritage contexts over the past decade, research and scholarship on the evolving nature of the new digital museum has emerged. Much of this research has

L. Holloway-Attaway (✉) · L. Vipsjö
University of Skövde, Skövde, Sweden
e-mail: lissa.holloway-attaway@his.se

L. Vipsjö
e-mail: lars.vipsjo@his.se

© Springer Nature Switzerland AG 2020
F. Liarokapis et al. (eds.), *Visual Computing for Cultural Heritage*, Springer Series on Cultural Computing, https://doi.org/10.1007/978-3-030-37191-3_10

centered on the increasingly distributed and pervasive nature of heritage spaces that have overflowed the traditional, contained exhibition spaces and architectures of museums. Nina Simon, in the Participatory Museum (2010) argues that visitors must become *cultural participants* in their museum experiences, not *passive consumers*. This requires that museums must become *audience-centered institutions* where visitors are able to "construct their own meanings" and use their voices to "inform and invigorate both project design but public-facing programs (Simon 2010, "Preface"). Drawing inspiration from social media and from other digital venues that support user-generated content, she outlines in detail the ways a museum may become more engaging by their ability to *connect, create, and share* their content (Simon 2010, "Preface"). For a decade, Museum Studies scholar Ross Parry has also identified a shift in the culture and cultural spaces of museum, in particular under the pressure of digital influences which he claims have activated "a tipping point in the adoption of new media in the museum" as we recognize digital technology as normative, not revolutionary (Parry 2013, p. 24). Extending Parry and Simon's research, many others have reflected on the impact of digital tools and technologies and technologies in museum spaces that have reformed key relationships between museums and museum visitors. These include networking contexts participation/interactivity between visitors and museum professionals (curators, pedagogues, exhibition designers), as well as the role of authenticity, public education and evaluation and assessment (Din and Hecht 2007; Parry 2010, 2013). Collectively they reinforce the significance of the shift from the museum visitor to the museum/heritage user and lay a foundation for considering how interactive gaming opportunities may support this transformation.

10.2 Humanistic Frameworks for Cultural Heritage Storytelling

As digital museums increasingly overtake non-digital spaces, the possibilities to transform visitor interactivity with museum assets have exponentially increased. Opportunities to integrate multiplayer gaming technologies, serious games and immersive mixed reality (MR) systems that create recursive relationships between physical and virtual spaces are also now standard in many heritage sites (Liarokapis et al. 2017; Sylaiou et al. 2017; Skarlatos et al. 2006; White et al. 2004a, b, c). This current phase has been described by Parry as *postdigital*—meaning that the integration of digital technology has become so pervasive throughout museum and heritage institutions, that using the phrase 'digital museum' and/or asking for museums to discuss their 'digital strategies' has become almost as redundant (and ultimately meaningless) as phrases like 'paper museum' or developing a 'paper strategy' for museum communication (Parry 2013). Parry's concept of the digital in contemporary museums is based on his extensive research with multiple national museums in the UK through semi-structured interviews with key personnel. In his conclusions, he characterizes digital tools and the experiences they afford as now normative and naturalized. For Parry, there is a clear advantage to developers and designers of digital tools and experiences to support this postdigital perspective, one that surpasses the rhetoric of revolutionary digital change from the late 20th century first initiated through Internet technologies. Currently the postdigital viewpoint creates a kind of generative critical distance that brings focus away from tools and technologies, and/or digitally enhancing the artifact 'body' and instead, it focuses attention on the body and experience of the visitor. This shift toward embodiment allows for new approaches in research, development, curation design, and pedagogy (Holloway-Attaway and Rouse 2018). It also provides a solid base form which to explore how heritage experiences may be examined in terms of narrative complexity in story-games (games that to engage users, particularly in light of the performative and affective functions enabled through play and gaming.

Games, Mixed Reality technologies (MR), critical co-design, and participatory approaches have particular advantages to offer cultural heritage and museum contexts, particularly to those who choose to foreground story-based experiences. *Story-Games* (that is games that incorporate play as embodied forms of reading and writing in interactive virtual/material worlds) are particularly suited to such dense, hybrid encounters (Holloway-Attaway 2018). Similar to postdigital museum developments, games for both entertainment purposes and beyond (in Serious Games and Game-Based Learning tools, for example) have long been established as participatory, performative, storytelling spaces with potential for socio-cultural impact (Flanagan 2013; Sicart 2011; Bogost 2010). Several extended studies summarize the state of the use of digital gaming technologies in the heritage and museum fields. Anderson et al. (2010) review the hardware, software, and graphics pipeline techniques in use across museums, heritage sites, and they also highlight the connections to the commercial games sector who create playable content inspired by historical content. Reviewing games (primarily from the 2009-era), this research outlines the important connections for interaction between historical facts and gaming. Additionally it outlines how interactivity between historical subject-matter and ludic tools to explore the subjects are enabled. Given the time period of the study, this research mainly focuses on massive multiplayer online game spaces and open sandbox worlds, such as Second Life, but it also includes commercial 'historical' games (war games primarily). The researchers argue there is a growing critical interest in creating interactive game stories around history to support user engagement and that the genre is well-suited this purpose. A more recent study by Mortara et al. (2014) surveys a wide sample (51 projects in all) of contemporary serious games designed for cultural heritage. They see the sample as indicative of a general trend and interest in creating games for heritage. This study also provides a foundational taxonomy for understanding the aims of games for heritage across the following three broad categories: (1) cultural awareness; (2) historical reconstruction; and (3) heritage awareness. Additionally, Mortara et al. call for the development of new educations to better serve industry interests and needs in related fields. This subject is further reinforced and developed in the context of a need to design new research educational programs for 'postdigital curators,' a designation for those who work specifically to create digital game narrative experiences for heritage and who represent a unique emerging niche in game development educations (Rouse and Holloway-Attaway 2018).

In addition to supporting approaches to ludic and playful design with games technologies, MR offers deep connections between physical and digital artifacts and spaces, providing affective and polysemic experiences that can support developers,' curators' and historians' desires to tell complex and connected stories for museum and heritage site visitors. However, much of the current work in MR is still very focused on technical development and user testing for MR and, thus, fails to consider the complexity of the user (who is not an unbiased or neutral participant or observer) and the potential layered context(s) for play (which may be multiple and diverse). In contrast, at the core of the research by Rouse et al. (2015) presented as a foundation for a special section on Understanding MR in *Digital Creativity,* the authors argue that much of the research predating their own study is in fact far too focused on the technical dimensions of work (specifically with graphical computing models) within AR/VR/MR without a clear enough focus on creating a humanistic framework for analysis and development and on the experiential dimensions of such applications for specific, rather than generalized, users (Rouse et al. 2015, p. 177). Moving beyond the oft-cited framework for understanding the defining linear 'spectrum' engaged by AR (as a core part of MR) offered by Milgram and Kishino (1994, see Fig. 10.1), and by those after who provided modifications of it (Billinghurst et al. 2015; Rekimoto and Nagao 1995; Mann 2002; Smart et al. 2007) Rouse et al. seek to deepen an understanding of the relationship between users, mediating technologies/virtual domains, and the physical world, designating such experiences as MR^x to signify the experiential qualities apart from traditional/technical definitions of MR. Their approach is interdisciplinary, drawing from media studies, performance studies, and design studies and highlighting three corresponding lenses through which to see the work: *esthetic, performative,* and *social.* Each of these lenses and disciplines indicate that designing *experiences* for users is far more complex than designing *technologies* for them. The artistic, dynamic, and socio-cultural dimensions must be integrated and explored and transmedial storytelling (and particularly story-games) support this quest to move beyond technical development.

We work to engage this experiential approach to interdisciplinary complexity focused on storytelling via story-games in postdigital heritage, combining and

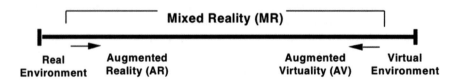

Reality-Virtuality (RV) Continuum

Fig. 10.1 MR linear spectrum of MR from Milgram and Kishino (1994)

extending it with Simon's call (2010) to involve visitors' own voices in new ways within museum experiences. We argue transmedial and game-based approaches to storytelling with MR technologies for cultural heritage enable these layered dynamics. Additionally we work from research and development through implementation to engage visitors and other stakeholders in the design and delivery process to help re-center attention on the heritage visitor's body, voice, and agency, shifting emphasis away from technical tools/systems alone designed to (hyper-) focus attention on objects and artifacts (as with laser scanning, photogrammetry, topography and GIS data, for example) but that may be inattentive to the storytelling frameworks. Additionally, the locative aspects of the experiences we create are key, and we work to enhance, emphasize, and individualize the multiple places/spaces users encounter. Following, again, Rouse et al. in their claims for the importance of recognizing location and location awareness as not only a defining technical affordance in MR experiences, but "fundamental to the experience, either esthetically or culturally," we feature this principle as core to many heritage experiences that are meant to engage visitors (Rouse et al. 2015, p. 179). We believe focusing museum and heritage site experience design on the body and perception of the visitor can enable the creation of performative, liminal, and affective experiences that actively transform space into place, providing deep kinesthetic, or even *polyaesthetic* responses, those particular to digital experiences and that foreground multiple sensory awareness from users (Engberg and Bolter 2015). We may extend this into theories of affect, broadly defined by Gregg and Seigworth as a state between cognitive knowing and embodied feeling, experienced as a visceral state of forces that emerges in encounters when one feels suspended somehow amongst bodies and worlds (technical and material), inside and outside of one's self (Gregg and Seigworth 2010, p. 1). For Gregg and Seigworth, such suspension invites co-participation and extends sensations of relatedness, and in our work we invite such relationality into our design and development process. Work within recent Digital Humanities scholarship that finds the power of narrative performativity in texts released through digital interventions but that are beyond pure human control (as with data visualization, AI, and biomedia) are also central to our design (Foster 2013; Drucker 2009, 2013; Gold 2013). In *Feed-Forward*, Hansen (2015) goes further and claims that our sensory capacities are being deeply transformed through digital media and users and developers are now reconfigured as complex elements entangled within media, no longer in control of their responses or choices: "human experience is currently undergoing a fundamental transformation caused by the complex entanglement of humans within networks of media technologies" (Hansen 2015, p. 4). Although we do not purport to be entirely *out of control* in our design process, we do work to create multiple sites for input and responsiveness in our co-design process, and we work to create media with multiple sensory affordances, following Hansen, that we believe resonant effectively (and affectively) with digital cultural heritage experiences seen as part of an elemental network of agents and forces.

Detailed and evocative examples of these elements are discussed by a number of MR researchers and application developers with specific reference to heritage and provide an inspirational foundation for further reflection in our story-game design

(Barba et al. 2010; Rouse 2015; Vosinakis et al. 2016). In Barba et al., for example, MR experiences as seen on a smartphone are represented as a form of a dynamic ecosystem, and the user is represented as a *living* component in the network through three key humanistic transformations: vision becomes perception, space become place, and technologies become capabilities (Barba et al. 2010, p. 931). Moving from an understanding of vision as a functional ability *to see*, to one of *perception* (a more complex embodied, affective, sensory, cognitive state) offers new humanistic challenges as we consider the user more profoundly. We believe all of these networked components may certainly be afforded through our forms of AR-enhanced, transmedial storytelling, particularly when involving location sensitive media. Traditionally a desirable deep connection with site (in the movement from space to place) is often of core importance for exhibit design at cultural heritage locations and is used to help visitors *imagine* a location in the past, future, or outside the visitors direct, material reach. Increasingly a major desire of exhibit design and curation at these sites is to transform visitors' experience of space (as abstract, impersonal) into one of place, (imbued with value, personal). Drawing parallels to research in cultural geography, as discussed by early pre-digital MR researchers like Tuan (1977), curators and exhibit designers may incorporate these concepts in ways directly relevant to museum design. For Tuan *space* is understood as a kind of meta-volume one moves through, a generic container defined by parameters and designated boundaries, whereas *place* and *place-making* are indicated by more individualized and specialized interests of specific persons. Place is delineated by *explorer interests* and as such, necessitates a reflective *pause* (Tuan 1977, p. 6). The pause is necessary for critical distance to develop, and for learning and deepening of sensory experience to occur. This reflective re-centering, focused on the individual body of the visitor and his/her movement through immersive space offers a new interdisciplinary perspective to traditional architectural and museum design scholarship on the movement of the visitor through space, and works beyond the designation of a perceptual field or of an 'isovist' perspective, as with architectural engineering designs to be enacted independently by a single, undistinguished visitor (Benedikt 1979; Choi 1997; Wineman and Peponis 2009).

Other related work in Design Research (Bardzell and Bardzell 2013) and in Human-Computer Interaction (Irani et al. 2010) as well as in Media Studies (Engberg and Bolter 2015) further illustrate the need for layered, interdisciplinary reflection when considering MR in heritage contexts. Taken collectively, they support the three primary lenses identified by Rouse et al. for MR media critique and design: *esthetic*, *performative*, and *social*. The Bardzells carefully unpack the concept of *criticality* in design as highly complex, ranging from theoretical work to artistic design and application. Irani et al. argue for a shift from the traditional user profiling, ideation, and iteration (processes that tend to overlook experiential domains) to a different method focused on *exploiting*, *engagement*, *articulation* and *translation* as core needs, particularly to innovate postcolonial perspectives that don't suppress potential alternative expressions. Engberg (2017) extends this work to describe a design process centered on the concept of *care*, particularly as historical digital narratives work to retell narratives from the perspective of *the other*. Citing her own work creating mobile AR experiences for re-telling Danish colonial pasts in Copenhagen, she describes a framing principle of care-taking relevant to heritage experiences, particularly for difficult or sensitive subject matters (race, slavery, immigration). Here in the design process one must not re-inscribe violence and erasures previously done to colonized subjects whose stories may not have been represented through insensitive MR design, excluding narrative/user complexity. Such *careful* design is more than just an acknowledgement of the need for 'telling' new (old) stories through digital means; it offers a foundational process to begin healing imperialist wounds by using a "postcolonial computing approach" open to alternative processes for inclusion and hyper-sensitive to the sites, locations, and persons for whom the heritage experience are designed.

Reflecting on the postdigital state of museums and heritage sites, and the range of technologies and alternative, layered techniques available to designers, it becomes clear, then, that simply presenting a system or technology to display and present historical facts is not enough to create a meaningful, experiential connection for many visitors to a heritage site. Unlike a museum, certain sites such as battlefields, prehistorical burial grounds, prisons, and even concentration camps may be particularly opaque, certainly affectively, to the visitor without deep narrative context. However, our research shows that MR transmedial performative interventions can be enacted to transform the space into a place with more lasting resonance. Strategies, methods, and techniques from such interventions can also enliven design within the museum gallery space. Game design techniques, MR technologies, and critically infused approaches are now implemented at heritage sites and museums across the world, and we are investigating the methods and resources needed to develop and design them.

10.3   Context for Research and Development: University Research and Regional Development in the KASTiS Project

As a central point for research in the interdisciplinary field of digital critical heritage, particularly on games and interactive play-focused story-game development, the University of Skövde offers a solid foundation. The University (and the Division of Game Development in the School of Informatics, in particular) has developed a very successful International framework for research across a range of intersecting fields (art, literary studies, cognitive science, computer science, experience design) to support research and development in digital games for heritage, as well as in related fields such as Serious Games, User Experience Design and Human-Computer Interaction. Since 1997 games research has been a focus of the University and computer games development research has evolved over decades of experience to integrate with the changing responses to technical development in socio-cultural formations.

Currently through activities in the Sweden Game Arena (SGA), a regionally funded consortium among local businesses, game developers, and the university, the game research combines technical and humanist expertise with theoretical and practical activities for maximum social outreach. These range from work and workshops with cultural stakeholders (politicians, schools, local studios) to explore gender diversity and other inclusive game development strategies, to hosting an annual game research and development conference (Sweden Game Conference) focused on key themes (such as Politics, Inclusiveness, and Sustainability) that regularly draws up to one thousand participants and International visitors and speakers. The SGA also has a game incubator program to support developing independent game studios.

The University games education has over 600 students enrolled (at both graduate and undergraduate levels) and 45+ researchers in 7 different computer games development programs (ranging from programming, to arts, writing, design and sound/music). It is not only the largest game education in Northern Europe, but it is unique in its clear commitment to exploring socio-cultural and humanistic formations and contexts for media development. Such research is primarily supported through the Media, Technology and Culture (MTEC) research group, as well as in other dedicated research fields outside of the "games for entertainment" sector. This includes works in Serious Games, Games User Experience, and in Digital Narratives for Cultural Heritage. The newly established MTEC Games User Lab (2019), also provides an integrated context and venue for development and research. The University games education and research lab focuses to a large extent on user and player experience, and it is very human-centric and socio-culturally focused in its analysis of outcomes, while at the same time innovative in its practical and applied technical development activities. These include integration with sites such as museums, art galleries, schools, hospitals, and military associations. As such it has been a solid 'laboratory' to deepen exploration in critical heritage and critical heritage pedagogy, but also explore collaborative and co-design partnerships with museums and heritage based organizations.

With original funding from 2015 to 2018 (KASTiS 1.0) and continued funding from 2019 to 2021 (KASTiS 2.0), the KLUB project ("KLUB," or "Kira and Luppe's Bestiary") is an on-going digital cultural heritage transmedial storytelling project focused on telling the local heritage and history of the Skaraborg region in Western Sweden though digital platforms and related networks. KLUB (discussed in more detail in the following section) is included as a sub-project within the larger KASTiS Project (in English the "Cultural Heritage and Game Technologies in Skaraborg" project) and is funded through the region's municipal authority (Skaraborgs Kommunlförbund) with additional funding through several participating organizations in the region and co-financing from the University of Skövde (primarily within the MTEC Research Group). The KASTiS projects have been aimed at strengthening the sub-regional cultural infrastructure and are deeply connected to promoting issues of sustainable growth, innovation, and renewal within 'experience' industries (heritage, tourism, for example). A central method to achieve this has been in technology co-development projects (as with KLUB) but also to create a sustainable hub that can host and coordinate seminars and other public events for disseminating knowledge about how digital gaming technology may be used in sustainable ways to support visitor targeting and cultural heritage mediation throughout the Skaraborg sub-region. In this way the development tools have been carefully workshopped, communicated, and explored within a network of related stakeholders in and out of the region, nationally and internationally. KASTiS has, thus, grown over time, connecting and linking organizations strategically so that its initial core focus has exponentially expanded and dynamically transformed as well. As such, both KLUB and KASTiS are exemplary models for illustrating how digital development must be seen in a living nexus, or an ecosystem of influence. With the continuation of the project through additional funding in its second phase (KASTiS 2.0, 2019–21), the region showed strong support for our model and for the outputs achieved. In particular it recognized KLUB as a positive demonstrator for achieving the overarching goals of the region's funding program: to connect all 14 municipalities through the strengthening of a (digital) cultural infrastructure based on narrative innovation.

At the start of the project in August 2015, seven municipalities were explicitly involved as financiers together with Skaraborg's municipal association and the University of Skövde. Afterwards seven more municipalities became involved and all 14 are currently involved in the continuing 2.0 demonstrators in development for the project. All are focused on visitor integration at multiple sites and venues through digital narrative development (with games and story-games at the center) for heritage and other related fields (tourism, for example). With the aim of supporting sustainable knowledge development within the sub-region's visitor 'experience' industry, natural resources and environments, and cultural heritage institutions, KASTiS 1.0 initially planned to develop and study demonstrators in three *narrative technical platforms*: the first platform was intended to work in an interconnected way to contextualize historical stories around visitor destinations; the second was to primarily focus on creating site-specific and location-based cultural heritage experiences; and the third platform was intended to be inside museums and other manned places. The municipalities contributed financially to individual projects, mainly in the form of staff hours and with the use of their premises for exhibition and experience development. But direct financing of projects has also occurred, including external ones to the original funding profile. Through the Project Leader (Lars Vipsjö) and Research Leader (Lissa Holloway-Attaway) there were many opportunities to connect more people from the University in the form of staff, researchers and teachers, but also many students at the graduate and undergraduate levels. This is as an important and strongly positive pedagogical outcome of the project, not least through the large number of students (more than 50) who have participated in the work and it secures our goal to create dynamic networks for exchange.

Important to note is that even before the initial KASTiS funding, a solid foundation was in place to support the project goals, illustrating the importance of the depth and breadth of socio-cultural resources ideally needed to develop sustainable heritage projects beyond technical implementation. For example, the basis for the development of the regional collaborations and for the knowledge network and three narrative platforms identified in KASTiS 1.0 were already evident in several completed MTEC research projects and from experiences in a number of previously implemented collaborative projects in the cultural heritage and the gaming technology sector. Examples include: The Hunt for the Lost Gold Reserve—an MR adventure trip at Karlsborg Fortress (2011) and the digital tablet application Elin's Mysterium (2013) a place-based game aimed at children to build heritage experiences in the city space (supported by Skövdes kulturmiljöprogram). Several other museum exhibitions based on local history and social themes were jointly produced with local museums that went on to tour nationally in major museums Pedagogical initiatives were also in place. Prior to KASTiS, and several undergraduate and graduate Masters thesis projects from our Games Education were also carried out by students in collaboration with cultural heritage stakeholders and with faculty supervisors from the university. Both students and faculty gained expertise in the fields during the course of the educational developments. KASTiS operations have allowed us, then, formally to gather and collect these kinds of projects under a common theme and aim, and as such, knowledge exchange among the many actors in our network of influence has been further intensified.

Networking organized by the University and the MTEC Games faculty was also carried out for several years prior to KASTiS in the sub-region Skaraborg and also in the larger Västra Götaland Region. For example, part of the work on the dissemination of knowledge between cultural heritage actors, business and academia, was via a cultural heritage and gaming technology open seminar that pre-dated the funding period and was repeated annually between 2012 and 2014. Intended as a form of information gathering about work in an emerging field, it helped to create a sort of informal expert-group and to share resources and ideas about how to move forward and in some cases allowed for collaboration opportunities with new projects. During the KASTiS project, this seminar has continued and was most recently implemented in October 2018 for the seventh consecutive year. In addition, in December 2014, a workshop/feasibility study was conducted with representatives from the cultural heritage area and the business community within the municipalities of Skaraborg at Gothia Science Park in Skövde. The aim was to explore if there were already existing resources for common ideas about specific collaboration projects and to as far as possible direct the KASTiS 2.0 application to fulfill these needs. After the start of the project, the knowledge and collaboration work was established during the first two project years through contacts with representatives from the participating municipalities, primarily with their cultural and tourist managers. But in the network formation, contacts were also made with other stakeholders, such as the regional resource unit Västarvet, focused on general heritage work in the region. Further contacts were established with companies within gaming and app. development and with cultural heritage services for technical development. Collectively these activities formed a webbed structure for reaching out to many relevant communities, while building expertise in digital cultural heritage for humanistic exploration.

10.4   KLUB: Transmedial Storytelling and Co-design Practices for/with Stakeholder Engagement

As stated above, KLUB is a sub-project within a larger heritage grant project, KASTiS, the goal of which is to explore multiple technical narrative platforms for interaction with heritage and citizens to increase engagement via a mobile AR-enhanced children's book series (14 books so far in 2019) and other media experiences. The intended readers/users of the KLUB stories and app. are primarily youth, but ideally also, their families who read/travel together to visit heritage locales referenced by the stories and interact with them via the mobile application. The book is also intended to increase reading interest in general for the young people who explore all the KLUB features, so an embedded educational component is included in the aim. From the beginning KLUB was designed as a blended narrative (books, AR, locative elements) that would use traditional storytelling media (generally books) and digital media (a mobile AR application), but with the possibility to include live action events and related exhibitions, along with 'unknown' other media, to be determined in the scope of the work. The choice of media reflected the desire to be as inclusive as possible, capturing digital and non-digital users, so creating inter-generational resonance and cooperation). But also the goal was to appeal to the multiple stakeholders we hoped to engage through out the development period that included, for example, local school and libraries with a goal toward education and literacy, as well as to encourage community engagement. Libraries have long been known as sites for interactive 'reading' activities that might include, for example, live performance and related playful pedagogical activities out in the community. Also as digital literature for children (and to some extent their parents) was still new to many of these actors, and as the budget to support the use of computer devices was small, there was initial wariness about using a complex technical delivery system. In some cases, as we discovered in earlier work with the Skövde Library on the *Elins Mysterium* project—a locative, tablet-based AR experience for children to be carried out in the city center in waking proximity to the library—even having reliable access to tablets was difficult for users, for the library to find and maintain, and for developers to continually support with needed bug fixes and upgrades. So our challenges were to create narrative depth, with technical simplicity, along with co-creative input from our users and stakeholders to better understand the difference.

The inclusion of co-design as a core principle for development is strongly influenced by movements in the last 10 years in Design Research that reconsider the role of designers, users, and stakeholders as significant for influencing options for development at the earliest stages of design production. In their comprehensive review of past and current design practices, particularly for making prototypes, Sanders and Stappers (2014) define the process of *cooperative making* as key to understanding how a tool or artifact will function. That is they encourage hands-on development of objects together with a team of related experts, both in and out of design fields. This design process is particularly *forward-thinking*, and they point toward an iterative process ideal for *future* designing, for considering not what is good for the now, but what is flexible, open and inspirational for future ways of living. From this work we identify also many of the artifact and objects we build in KLUB as prototypes and as learning tools for the growing network of objects that are/have been recruited (Jaye-manne et al. 2015) during the two phases of KASTiS development. Because we not only value the stakeholders' opinions, but want their *buy-in* (socially and sometimes, monetarily) for the artifacts we deliver and the experiences we co-create, for us it was important to develop with an understanding that we were engaged in *serial prototyping* of sorts. With 14 books to develop in the first KLUB series and an undetermined set of books and related game-stories in the second phase, we were continually in process with a shifting set of participants. We prepared for that form the beginning. Although each book might be published in a particular phase, each previous book served as a tool for developing the future others. The mobile AR KLUB application was also built with the idea of creating a growing database of figures and information in the Bestiary, and although it was released with the first KLUB book to the public, it has been continually updated and enhanced.

As of mid-2019, 14 books have been published, one for each village or town in the region. More are being developed with KLUB characters for the KASTiS 2.0 project, but also for spinoff characters that may be featured in related work, or that may be used based on the KLUB model for entirely different content. For example, work is in development now to create characters that will also work in AR-enhanced books, locative media (as with KLUB) but also for web-based delivery for children, that is focused specifically on environmental and scientific issues connected to local geological formations within the Table Mountain Geopark. This is also a proposed location for a UNESCO world heritage site, and KLUB researchers are developing the application for this designation in collaboration with the Geopark. In KLUB, the local histories and cultures of each of the municipalities is captured through a frame narrative structure in a series of books dedicated to each major town and village in the region In each book characters are iteratively introduced in the books, but also in related media (such as in board games, interactive exhibitions, LARPS and local fairs). The multiple story forms and figures are *told* through a traditional printed children's book series (distributed through local libraries, book fairs, and at museums), but also through an AR mobile application created with local developers and downloadable for free from Google Play and the App Store. The mobile application allows characters from the books and other media to *come to life* in 2D and 3D animation and in visual sketches scanned from trigger images in the books and media. (See Fig. 10.2). Sometimes visuals are enhanced with added music and sound or complemented, as with the LARPs (Live Action Role Play) with live figures who are recreated, or who are invented entirely, for interactive performance.

To incorporate digitality and multimodality, the stories are designed to include many possible dimensions, without increasing technical complexity. The mobile AR characters are re-contextualized in a database format (after being scanned from the books), and this allows users to receive additional content about each, telling more of their folkloric history and adding more story elements to enhance their histories. Even the database is *storified* as it is characterized in the narrative context as a Bestiary, a reference to allegorical catalogue texts from the Middle Ages that

Fig. 10.2   3D animation (*L*) and 2D sketch (*R*) from KLUB books available in AR app

incorporated both real and fantasy figures and were often based on animals or other mythical creatures. The reference to the Bestiary, as well as the use of decorated initials as trigger images for scanned characters, reference also older forms of print texts, such as illuminated manuscripts, where text and images were easily blended. In this way, even the print texts are trans-historical, and have the multimodal advantage not only of traditional children's books (that is they tell via picture-stories), but of older forms that encouraged multiple literacies with moral or ethical dimensions at the core. Medieval manuscripts utilized graphical content to bring Biblical stories to life, for example, through images to convey morality stories to a generally illiterate public. The moralistic features of the original Bestiaries are reimagined in a tale about generosity and empathy enacted by the main characters as they work to *free* the creatures in the book from an evil master who dominates them. Other multimodal and transmedial features include a related KLUB board game (with possible AR capabilities) in development with students and faculty, based on the Bestiary figures and set in the Skaraborg region including themes and quests related to historical regional assets and artifacts, folktale figures, and to local geographical features. (See Fig. 10.3.) Additionally, on site in specified locations identified in the stories, users can encounter more digital characters by locating and scanning figures on signage and by reading more about them there. Thus, the KLUB series also allows

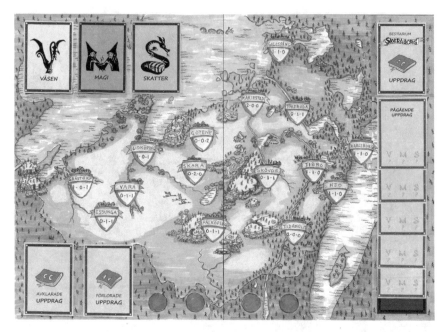

Fig. 10.3 KLUB gameboard prototype showing regional landscape backdrop and features

physical/virtual interaction with heritage sites in the Skaraborg region—including at an Iron Age stone graveyard, at Viking burial grounds, and even at important local architectural structures (ship-making and paper-making factories and old churches, for example). Even environmental features are used as settings for the books to bring attention to hyper-local legends of the landscapes and to maximize the use the locative affordances of MR experiential design.

As indicated by the name of the series ("KLUB," or "**K**ira and **L**uppe's **B**estiary"), the book series focuses on the protagonists Kira (a girl-Vampire) and Luppe (a boy-Werewolf, or shape-shifter, as he prefers to be called). Together they rescue mythical creatures that are being forced to perform in a circus by an evil Ringmaster, who is himself a mountain troll. Kira and Luppe chase the evil Ringmaster and his circus figures across the region, as they perform from town to town. They are aided in their quest by a Troll Researcher named Lovis whom they encounter in the first book. The first book is set in Skara at a well-known actual library, realistically rendered in the book so as to be recognized by young readers and engage their interest. Assisted by Lovis' knowledge about all of the regional mythic figures, Kira and Luppe also attempt to recapture a book containing Lovis' information and research about all the figures that she has gathered, but that the Ringmaster has stolen. To get it back, they move throughout the region, chasing him and his circus of enslaved creatures and consulting periodically with Lovis. The series includes a host of trolls gnomes, giantesses, and fairy-tale figures populated by Scandinavian and Nordic folktales, as well as drawn from local oral histories and legends in the small villages and towns of

Skaraborg. Some are hyper-localized, as with Kåffan, a character in the book about Mariestad, a small town on Lake Vänern. Kåffan is a kind of female lake creature very specific to that one lake, in that one city, and she is retold through folktales from that specific area. Such a creature is representative of many more in each of the books that the writers, illustrators, and developers learned of during an iterative process of co-design and development with a range of experts. As such knowledge about the content for each book in the KLUB series was gathered by the writers and illustrators (mostly students and faculty), by local developers, and through strategic interactions between all of them and the cultural experts: from archeologists, to anthropologists, pedagogues, local historians and storytellers. The characters Kira and Luppe appear in all of the books, and new characters are added as the narrative progresses across all of the books, customized to each location and historical setting. Kira and Luppe themselves were designed strategically to offer both a balanced gendered perspective (using both a girl and a boy protagonist) but also in their character traits which defy gender stereotypes in their interactions.

The focus on the graphical dimensions of the KLUB books are key and much of the work is carried out by designers who work in computer game graphics in 2D, 3D and Animation who design images not only specific for each form of media, but also with an awareness of their interactive capabilities and to include iterative dimensions (to consider how the same character might work in a colorful animation versus a 2D black and white sketch, for example). In a work such as KLUB, where reader/users are encouraged to find and activate (*bring to life*) the decorated initials associated with characters and creatures in the books, the design is such that users are not merely animating the figures as a form of replication in the AR, repeating what they find in the books. The graphical images are intended to offer 'something more' and are constructed to surprise the reader or to encourage more exploration, either in the Bestiary or on the signage on site, and/or as they are included as pop-up overlays on the physical environment in other ways. To that end, many of the AR representations depict alternative 3D and 2D versions of the characters seen in the books. Some have animations associated with them (they wave or twitch) and some show 2D sketches depicting other graphical styles, more scientific-looking ones, or more reminiscent of drawings from a technical text. Some might even suggest a drawing is *in process*, a sketch form, and thereby illustrate its dynamic and continually transformative nature. In installations based on KLUB (of which there have been many at local museums), even more characters are created to be scanned from figures on the walls, such as in a gallery space, or integrated with historical artifacts. These graphics are designed to be more suitable for an exhibition experience, rather than for the ones found in the books. As such, children and other visitors can continually renew their association with the creatures and stories. (See Fig. 10.4.)

This kind of graphical and iterative development is at the heart of the story-game form, which suggests elements are always in play and not intended to be realistically defined, rather they are created to be interacted with in multiple instances. Such story-game elements are not defined by their finished, technical and/or clearly polished, aesthetic properties. In fact, in many of the books, the graphical styles, based on the illustrators' desire or expertise, may also transform to a degree and the characters may

Fig. 10.4 Images of AR characters on site at Falbygdens Museum KLUB installation

appear older, younger, with more or less detail and a different color palette. They are not meant to *translate* in and across book content, purely from one to the other, and as such, they don't assume a user needs only to see or recognize the character *once*. Instead, the user is assumed to have more embodied perceptual and even affectual responses via the differing graphical components, and the goal is to 'surprise' the user and stimulate more visceral reactions through deliberate change. This has proved an effective choice, and one needs only to watch the users of the AR application, often and usually children, to see their delight and curiosity for more exploration when they 'discover' the AR figures on their phones or tablets after activating the trigger images. In this way, we see them as engaged in the kind of *postdigital aesthetics of recruitment* that Jayemanne et al. outline when they suggest the power of playable digital objects is to entice users on to more, and then even more exploration, and to engage a host of related objects into a networked experience (Jayemanne et al. 2015). The creation of a *storified* framework, connected to the carefully graphically composed media, is a key factor in evoking this aesthetic and affective response.

The complex and vital materials keep their representational values in process, moving not only across graphical and visual forms, but also across time registers and in space. This is a design strategy to keep re-telling the stories in varied ways, from past to present, and to connect to places that *come to life* through interaction. Across the whole of the KLUB book series many different legends, histories, and landscapes are invoked and mixed together. Readers/users are encouraged to discover them in multiple ways, through imagination, but also, as indicated above, through their own physical exploration of historical sites in proximity to their towns, which they might not otherwise have noticed if not called out in the books and incorporated in the stories. In many heritage locations within the Skaraborg Region, with ancient petroglyphs, megaliths and rune stone sites, for example, the historical locations are unmarked. Especially to a child, but also to many adults, the locations may seem quite innocuous and even invisible if viewed from the road or on a stroll through a landscape. They are often surprised to find them 'in their own backyards.' Of course many other archeological sites and geological formations have been fully annotated and referenced for the public, through careful scientific investigation, and they are more formally documented and incorporated into museum and heritage locations. KLUB purposefully draws from both of these sources and encourages investigation of all types, illustrating history can be formally discovered, but is open for further investigation through a range of sensory affordances and perceptual density.

In the *Lindormen* book for example, set in Tidan, the author, Patrik Erlandsson, uses a time-traveling theme as a way to exploit both the real and historical elements he chooses to incorporate. Working to render a form of narrative (not technical) complexity, a story framework was developed to incorporate knowledge about the historical past in both legend (Nordic Saga) and in the physical features of the land-scape. This required working with both literary anthropologists and archeologists. In this book, the main protagonists Kira and Luppe travel back in time (ca. 400–600 AD) with the help of two talking Ravens, Hugin and Munin. Well-known figures in Norse Mythology from the migration period, at least), these figures might be known to many Swedish children, but (re-) set in their local town or region, they offer pow-erful elements for surprise and discovery and function as powerful narrative focal points. In the story, Kira and Luppe follow instructions from the Ravens to travel back in time, and in the past, they confront King Råne, another well-known mytho-logical figure in Sweden. Discovering King Råne through the help of the Ravens, and entering a magic portal found at the site of a mysterious gathering of Rune stones, called the Stone Ship (an actual location found outside of the village of Tidan), they work to dig up King Råne's treasure with the help of a magic water serpent, the "Lin-dorm," for whom the book is named. Because some of these characters and settings are known from broad Nordic myths and some from hyper-local legends, and still others are discovered in previous books in the series, the reader/users move among many planes and registers of reality, imagination, and polysensual engagement. They also move from reading activities to physical activity and playful exploration of their environment. And for children, this also means they must discover meaning along with parents or other adults (who sometimes need to transport them by car to remote locations), thus encouraging intra-generational collaborative exploration. The over-all locative designs assure also there is more to discover on site. In the case of the Stone Ship, for example, reader/users can not only activate AR figures from the dec-orated initials in the book connected to the site, but when they travel to the actual locations, more history is available on signs and plaques. (See Fig. 10.5.) In other locations too, additional AR trigger images, recognizable from the books are also found in situ, and they can be activated through the AR application. When figures are animated, different content (textual and graphical) from what they find in the books is then also revealed. This way the story operates in a configuration of performative interventions, and it encourages many modes of activation to keep the content in process.

The KLUB project has increased in scope during the work. The transmedial approach has made it possible to study narrative functions and techniques that can prepare the potential visitor for a visit to a cultural heritage site and to enhance the experience on site. But through the complex narrative layers, the adventure does not need to end after a singular visit or experience. There are more stories to read, more

Fig. 10.5 King Råne AR figure on site at stone ship, triggered from KLUB signage

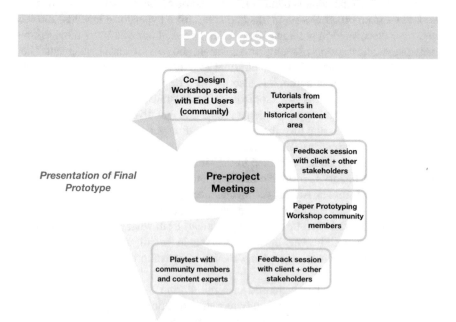

Fig. 10.6 Co-design process developed by Rouse (2019)

places to visit, and more stories to collect. At the same time, KLUB is intended as a stable tool for educators (in schools and museums), to use according to their own interests and interests. Thus although books are developed by game development students, it is important that they have happened together with museum educators, children's librarians and cultural secretaries. With each new book and each experience, a series of workshops and visits have been implemented with a core expert team from interdisciplinary fields to represent the interests of heritage, technical development, games education, and any other designated areas deemed necessary to the storytelling. (Sometimes an archeological expert might be needs, for example, or a geologist.) Content for each book is discussed and shared though group discussions with experts and carefully vetted for historical accuracy, but also for narrative strength and innovation. That is conversations are formalized on the story forms first, and then the technical decisions are made after. Given the relative simplicity of the AR tools with the stories and the generally repetitive nature of the technology use from book to book, this is possible. Having an open and flexible format, as in a serial prototype discussed above, in place from the first book, has been key. Even though some variation is possible to new media (board games, for example, or LARPS) with the story frame and basic platform for development in place, the rest follows. With a story-first perspective, many workshops and discussions, then, begin with sharing powerpoint mockups of the book pages, showing both graphical content and textual content, and they are worked on together as a team. From black and white sketches to basic storylines the books are completed in a series of study visits and workshops. In this way the key actors at the municipalities have been invested in the process and can share their ideas through co-creative and future thinking making.

10.5 Reflections and Lessons Learned

With interactive narrative complexity, simplified technical development, educational cultural heritage, and collaborative design at the core of KASTiS and of KLUB, our work was conceived as interdisciplinary, experimental, and multi-institutional. Our goal was to include technical developers and cultural stakeholders (libraries, art galleries, heritage experts and influencers, schools, and politicians), as well as students and faculty who might use it. It has been a highly successful (as indicated by our prolonged funding), but it has served too as a learning experience from the very challenging development process with a focus on narrative innovation and co-design. Because of the relatively compressed timeline of the project in KASTiS 1.0 (three years) and given the need for so many outputs (multiple books, digital media content, user workshops, community engagement activities, public relations), the content has generally followed our goals, but some of our processes require a more robust and strategic framework. Working with multiple authors, artists, programmers, and heritage experts, means that many of the elements in KASTiS 2.0 will be more strategically implemented, and we are currently working to refine a methodological approach for prototype building identified by one of our new faculty, Senior Lecturer

Fig. 10.7 *Here's Life* interactive mobile AR map with visitors at the Läckö Nature Center

Rebecca Rouse, who has much experience with co-design interventions with cultural stakeholders for creating cultural mobile AR applications and other playable digital experiences. Based on Rouse's model, we will work to integrate our own co-design practices from workshops with end users, meetings with experts, paper prototyping, and play-testing and build the system into a practical project course in our new Masters curriculum. With such a systematic method in place, we hope both to refine our process, but also allow for more assessment and evaluation along the way (Fig. 10.6).

Although external technical developers were hired for much of the AR development, students too were recruited from both undergraduate and graduate games educations (technical and artistic) and invited, for example, to work on components in teams, or individually, and for research in their thesis and other project work. However, given their levels of expertise or time constrictions, students may not have had sufficient time to follow through on projects and see them to completion. Some authors and artists collaborated over long terms and worked together at length on a single book, but others had more limited involvement, since there was no one course or level from which could encapsulate their work. Some students worked on components even after graduation, because of personal interests or for part of their own portfolio development. Although we see this as 'admirable' on the students' part it is not necessarily a sustainable, strategic, and some might argue moral way, to recruit resources and it may even signal wrong information to our partners who may not see the full value of student work (bur even future developers' work) in terms of monetary compensation. We continue to refine this process, and we hope with the growing network we are also more skilled at attracting available funds to fully pay the students or former students for their participation. And despite having a one-year

Master's program specifically focused on Digital Heritage (called "Digital Narration: Cultural Heritage and Game Technologies"), students were often only able to participate on KASTiS and KLUB projects for a single semester. Sometimes this meant that the scope and scale of the work was beyond what they could realistically complete. Further, their ability to comprehend the many interdisciplinary facets of digital heritage co-creation and the need to thin deeply about users from the affective and performative dimensions we desire was impeded given the short time frame for their education. Nonetheless, KLUB has provided a solid forum from which to investigate how one might begin to develop other related work and to understand what kinds of skill sets or needs are required, particularly in the field of interactive digital cultural heritage (Fig. 10.7).

Although many KLUB team-meetings were held over the development time, often the progress was impeded by the schedules and interests of the external (to the university) cultural partners and with what they were able to assist with given a number of constraints (from time to topic knowledge). Many factors originally conceived as central to the project (such as a focus on education and literacy) were difficult to navigate, sustain and fully implement as the partners in schools were eager to help, but had limited time and resources to fully instruct developers and help iterate content. The project garnered much interest from libraries that hosted workshops for students to gain interest by experimenting with AR, for example. And they served as central sites for other community activities, and this was a valuable association given our aims. The project too was very well-supported by museum and heritage experts who were often very open to cooperation and were interested in learning form us as well. And yet it was sometimes difficult to coordinate and assess their input in proper iterative evaluation. In a project such as ours, questions of historical accuracy, literacy, incorporation of folkloric traditions, and digital narrative innovation, in combination with user testing for technical devices and implementation on location were, and are, still challenging and somewhat overwhelming for all. Despite much success, then in KASTiS 1.0, in the second phase, we hope to reinforce the aims by developing an appropriate curricula to support our design challenges. Fortunately, in response to this project and to the others that have come before and since, the University of Skövde has approved a transition in the Games Division to move to a two-year model for the Cultural Heritage Masters program. We are now then currently in development for 2021 for an International Masters tentatively titled "Games, Stories, Aesthetics." It is funded by a strategic initiative by the University Vice Chancellor, and is conceived of as a way to train new *experts* in digital cultural heritage story-games through connection to co-design partners. The program will include interdisciplinary faculty (for example from media and literary arts, computer science, user experience design, and game design) with an aim to integrate critical humanities, computer science, and technical development for heritage together in one program. It will coordinate with an extend our current one year Masters in Digital Narrative for Cultural Heritage but also with our one-year Masters in Serious Games, and possibly even with a new Masters program also in development for 2020 on Game User Experience. We hope the changes will assure faculty and students can work in long-term and ongoing partnerships with core museums and community partners to build a sustainable knowledge foundation and a network for critical co-design practices focused on experiential design for users.

Additionally we hope to refine our seminar culture around heritage. Despite our goal to include local actors and heritage actors in building our knowledge base through seminars, we discovered that it was difficult to get a large number of participants from the municipalities to come to these themed seminars held at the university. We tended to attract only the same members over time, and often they could not stay for the full two-day seminar. Although it was helpful to share work, we recognized the need to grow and diversify our network to get the maximum input in the many kinds of collaboratively built projects that were possible, but also to find ways to develop, share, and refine our design methods and our critical vocabularies. In short, we need to create a deeper synergy to understand how the discrete knowledge fields might connect (from heritage to game development, but also from the cultural sector to the academic and to technical fields). The main challenge, then, to include municipal experts and technology developers has seemed to be the difficulties for staff to be away from the daily activities of their jobs. In view of this, the KASTiS seminar implementation was changed to include more local work seminars on site at each municipality where the municipal stakeholders were needed to develop specific demonstrators and where we could more easily bring local developers. For these seminar meetings, we included, then, students (as part of course work, but also as paid partners when relevant), along with experts from technology companies to collaboratively discuss content, design, and even ultimately to test the prototypes with parts of the public. We also arranged study trips to various museums outside the Skaraborg sub-region where students and researchers came together to learn about the museums' goals and to understand the specific mission of each institution. (Especially in small local museums, it is important to understand their regional mission as it can be highly specialized as with our partners in Falbygden's Museum in Falköping where the focus is on prehistorical megalith gravesites common to the area—and featured in one of the KLUB books in consultation with archeological experts at the museum.) These meetings served both as inspiration and to create contacts, but also to share expertise in the cultural heritage area and in understanding the kinds of research questions that engaged faculty (transmediality, narrative forms specific to mobile or locative media, non-human narration). We found that although it is not always necessary for heritage experts and technologists to understand fully the research behind the development initiatives, it was helpful to share for example reasons why a book form, a mobile application, or a board game might need to be designed differently to support different narrative tasks or engage different kinds of users. Following the suggestions of Helguera (2011), in his reflections on working with socially engaged art practices, we continually work to find ways to understand our vocabularies and processes across disciplinary fields. In view of our own reflections, the seminar implementation in late 1.0 and in 2.0 has already changed to include local work seminars at each municipality with core municipal actors included more easily on site and a focus on creating shared critical vocabularies.

In addition to local seminars, KASTiS has also participated in several network meetings with museum teachers in Skaraborg and we plan to include this more fully in our next stages too, especially with our new two-year Masters program where there will be more time to share knowledge and pedagogical strategies. Given the diversity of the educators in our evolving network, we face many challenges to cross over other knowledge thresholds. For example, in the past we have included educators from shipbuilding museums (at Forsvik), from other industrial museums with highly specialized interests (paper manufacturing, glass blowing), at Viking history museums, and museums dedicated to creating sustainable actions for preserving and educating the public about natural environments, such as at the Vänermuseum and Naturum (Nature Center) in the Lidköping city center and by Läckö Castle, both located on Lake Vänern, the largest lake in Northern Europe, with a very delicate and threatened ecosystem. We have had success, and we have models from which to learn. At Naturum, for example, we helped collaboratively design with experts, students, and a local developer, a mobile application (*Here's Life*) and locative game to learn about UNESCO's 17 sustainable goals for Agenda 2030 and about the specific flora and fauna in the area. (See "Spin-off Section" below for more details about this project.) One result of this long-term seminar series and our localized work with pedagogues, heritage experts and technologists is that KASTiS has helped profile Skaraborg and the University of Skövde, as an innovative and sustainable *cultural knowledge center* (as opposed to a technical games developer) in the field of digital storytelling and heritage mediation. As such, KASTiS demonstrators have been presented in scientific contexts at multiple seminars and conferences at other colleges or universities in Sweden, but also throughout Scandinavia, Europe, the US, Canada, and Australia. Digitization and sustainable communication of cultural heritage is a topical subject that during the project period gained an increasing interest in society, but also at the University as a whole that embraced *digitization for sustainable development* as the central research aim from 2016 onward. Our work fit neatly in this goal and is showcased as an example at the University.

Illustrating the intra-disciplinary focus our research affords, KASTiS researchers have also been invited to present the projects in Sweden at a number of smaller and larger seminars and conferences organized by a range of institutions, from museums and universities, but also to International academic conferences with diverse disciplinary interests, ranging from: Geography and GeoMedia themes (at the Royal Geographical Society Conference '19 in London and the Geomedia Research Group Conference '19 in Karlstad, Sweden), to Interactive Digital Narrative Conferences (ICIDS '17 and '18, for example in Portugal Ireland), and Digital Literature and Digital Humanities conferences and seminars (ELO '18 in Montreal, Canada, the Digital Nordic Humanities in Helsinki, Finland and the British Library Digital Curator Seminar Series in '18 and '19 in London). Furthermore, the work has been highlighted in Digital Heritage conferences and publications (at the Advances in Digital Workshop at Madeira, Portugal in 2017 and the Digital Heritage Congress and Expo in San Francisco, USA in 2018). And as a final opportunity for dissemination of knowledge in KASTiS 1.0, a seminar was held during the last month of the project, organized by the University of Skövde during an important Swedish national political forum, at

Almadalen's Week in Visby, Gotland, where annually all the Swedish political parties come together to discuss key issues. It is an important and highly visible forum and the inclusion of KASTiS project Leader Lars Vipsjö in a panel called "Will Nature and Cultural Heritage Be More Alive If Digital?" along with local politicians, business managers, heritage experts, and computer game industry professional demonstrates the intra-disciplinary and socio-cultural impacts of the work.

10.6   Spin-off Effects and Related Story-Games

KLUB is the largest single coherent demonstrator within KASTiS, and it has already formed the basis for other projects that show is possible to work with the primary goals focused on developing innovative transmedial storytelling techniques for heritage. We have classified the primary dimensions of story-games for heritage and defined them according to the following criteria:

- contextualised and interwoven
- usable on cultural heritage sites and in unmanned destinations sites
- integrated in parts of museums or other types of manned visitor destination

Three development projects in particular demonstrate that our aims are transferrable to other similar creation. That is: (1) the application *Here's Life*, with the associated map and game to be played at Naturum (The Nature Center) outside the Läckö Castle; (2) the museum game *Ebba and Ture*, at the glass factory museum in Limmared and at Målerås glassworks; (3) the *Skogsmulleriket* game at Åsbotorpsjön on Billingen, a local table mountain with recreational facilities just outside of Skövde. In all three cases, the local application developers have been Solutions Skövde, and a number of computer game students have also participated in the production. In the AR KLUB app., no actual gaming mechanics have yet been implemented (but they are to come in KASTiS 2.0). However in the three examples above, gaming implementation and connection to local visitor destinations is much more fully developed and forms the basis for future work.

In the exhibition *Here's Life*, for example, the map designed for visitor interaction includes an AR game based on UNESCO's Agenda 2030, and it was developed because of UNESCO's appointment of Mariestad, Götene and Lidköping (all in the Skaraborg Region) as examples of model areas in the world for sustainable development. In *Here's Life* at the exhibition site in the Nature Center, a player finds examples of, and takes part in, the UN's global goals via access of trigger images on the extra large map designed to be playable. And in the related 'superpower' game (playable on a nature trail in the forest outside the Castle Läckö on the shores of Lake Vänern), the player learns more about different plants and animals and about how out ecosystems and biodiversity work. At the same time, players get answers to define which kind of animal they are most similar to and to see how their natural animal 'superpower' can help to make the planet a desirable place to live—now and in the future.

In the game *Ebba and Ture* designed for the Glasets Hus Museum in Limmared and at Målerås glassworks, Ebba and Ture are the two protagonists who need help producing a new glass vase for an exhibition in Stockholm, because the factory's 'nasty' cat has broken the old one. Through an adventure trip told through a game told inside the museum and with several mini-games to complete, the children learn through playing how to make glass based on past traditions (ca. 100 years ago). This project is an excellent example of how gaming technology is used to interactively relate stories about industrial and working life history. The same basic model can be used to create games that interactively describe other forms of industrial history production. Text and image material from the initial mobile game was reused for a book in the same format as the KLUB series.

In the mobile *Skogsmulle* app., there are also story-game elements, and the narrative is focused on helping a character called Skogsmulle find the tail that he has misplaced in the surrounding woods. (See Fig. 10.8.) When the children meet Mulle's friends at their respective huts during the search, they get various assignments that have to do with natural science. The mobile game was itself based on what has been a live performance for children often held on location in the woods, or in visits to schools. Its digital format allowed the stories to be resituated for the new mobile form, and the development process provided a valuable framework for considering how blended MR experiences may be designed in future iterations.

Fig. 10.8 Images from the Skogsmulle mobile game app

These three game applications have been developed within the framework of KLUB's brand and illustrate once again the flexibility of both the storytelling framework, but also the technical platform. The transmedial KLUB narrative can be at once both site-specific and interwoven with other elements It may be developed locally but also included in a larger regional or sub-regional context. KLUB and the other three examples are aimed specifically at children, but the model can be used advantageously for other target groups and with completely different themes than nature and cultural heritage. In KASTiS 2.0 the model will be then expanded to include for example immigrant communities, environmental issues, and media development for users other than youth and children. We will then continue to adapt and grow our dynamic model for humanistic intervention in digital story-games for heritage.

References

Anderson EF, McLoughlin L, Liarokapis F, Peters C, Petridis P, de Freitas S (2010) Developing serious games for cultural heritage: a state-of-the-art review. Virtual Real 14(4):255–275

Barba E, Rouse R, Bolter JD, MacIntyre B (2010) Thinking inside the box: meaning-making in handheld AR experiences. In: 2010 Proceedings of the ninth IEEE international symposium on mixed and augmented reality, pp 19–26

Bardzell J, Bardzell S (2013) What is 'critical' about critical design? In: CHI'13 April 27–May 2, 2013, Paris, France

Benedikt ML (1979) To take hold of space: isovists and isovist fields. Environ Plan B 6:47–65

Billinghurst M, Clark A, Lee G (2015) A survey of augmented reality. Found Trends Hum-Comput Interact 8(2–3):73–272

Bogost I (2010) Persuasive games: the expressive power of videogames. MIT Press, Cambridge

Choi YK (1997) The morphology of exploration and encounter in museum layouts. In: Complex buildings: the proceedings of the first international symposium on space syntax, vol 1, pp 1–10

Din H, Hecht P (eds) (2007) The digital museum: a think guide. American Association of Museums, Washington DC

Drucker J (2009) SpecLab: digital aesthetics and projects in speculative computing. University of Chicago Press, Chicago

Drucker J (2013) Humanistic theory and digital scholarship. In: Gold MK (ed) Debates in the digital humanities. University of Minnesota Press, Minneapolis, pp 85–92

Engberg M (2017) Augmented and mixed reality design for contested and challenging histories. In: MW17: museums and the web, Cleveland, Ohio, 19–22 April 2017

Engberg M, Bolter JD (2015) MR^x and the aesthetics of locative writing. Digit Creat 26(3–4):82–192

Flanagan M (2013) Critical play: radical game design. MIT Press, Cambridge

Foster I (2013) How computation changes research. In: Bartscherer T, Coover R (eds) Switching codes: thinking through digital technology in the humanities and the arts. University of Chicago Press, Chicago

Gold M (ed) (2013) Debates in the digital humanities. University of Minnesota Press, Minneapolis

Gregg M, Seigworth G (eds) (2010) The affect theory reader. Duke University Press, Durham

Hansen MBN (2015) Feed-forward: on the future of twenty-first-century media. University of Minnesota Press, Minneapolis

Helguera P (2011) Education for socially engaged art: a materials and techniques handbook. Jorge Pinto Books, New York

Holloway-Attaway L (2018) KLUB: transformative culture/trans*medial practice/postdigital play: exploring augmented reality children's books, local cultural heritage and intra-active design. In:

Rouse R, Dionisio M (eds) Looking forward, looking back: interactive digital storytelling and hybrid art-scholarship approaches. Carnegie Mellon ETC Press, Pittsburgh

Holloway-Attaway L, Rouse R (2018) Designing postdigital curators: establishing an interdisciplinary games and mixed reality heritage network. In: Ioannides M, Martins J, Zarnic R, Lim V (eds) Advances in digital heritage. Springer Publishing, New York

Irani L, Vertesi J, Dourish P, Philip K, Grinter R (2010) Postcolonial computing: a lens on design and development. In: CHI 2010, Atlanta, Georgia, April 10–15 2010

Jayemmane D, Nansen B, Apperly TH (2015) Postdigital play and the aesthetics of recruitment. In. Proceedings of Digra 2015: diversity of play: games, cultures, identities

Liarokapis, F, Petridis, P, Andrews, D, de Freitas, S (2017) Multimodal serious games technologies for cultural heritage, mixed reality and gamification for cultural heritage (V) Springer International Publishing, 371–392

Mann S (2002) Mediated reality with implementations for everyday life. Presence Connect, August, 6. http://wearcam.org/presence-connect/. Accessed 15 July 2019

Michela Mortara, Chiara Eva Catalano, Francesco Bellotti, Giusy Fiucci, Minica Houry-Panchetti, Panagiotis Petridis (2014) Learning cultural heritage by serious games. Journal of Cultural Heritage 15(3):318–325

Milgram P, Kishino F (1994) A taxonomy of mixed reality visual displays. Proc Trans Inf Syst 77:1–28

Rekimoto J, Nagao K (1995) The world through the computer: computer augmented interaction with real world environments. In: Proceedings of the 8th annual ACM symposium on user interface and software technology (UIST'95), New York, NY, pp 27–36

Rouse R (2015) MRx as a performative and theatrical stage. Digit Creat 26(3–4):193–206

Rouse R (2019) AR design for hidden histories: community engagement, co-design, and interdisciplinary collaboration (talk). In: Digital humanities conference 2019: complexities, Utrecht, Nl, July 9–12 2019

Rouse R, Holloway-Attaway L (2018) Re-engineering computational curricula with postdigital heritage, critical humanities, and community engagement. In: IEEE DigitalHERITAGE 2018: 3rd international congress + expo, San Francisco, October 2018

Rouse R, Engberg M, JafariNaimi N, Bolter JD (eds) (2015) Special section: understanding mixed reality. Digit Creat 26(3–4):175–227

Sanders EBN, Stappers J (2014) Probes, toolkits, and prototypes: three approaches to making in codesign. CoDesign 2014:5–15

Sicart M (2011) The ethics of computer games. MIT Press, Cambridge

Simon N (2010) The participatory museum. Museum 2.0, Santa Cruz, CA

Skarlatos D, Agrafiotis P, Balogh T, Bruno F, Castro F, Davidde Petriaggi B, Demesticha S, Doulamis A, Drap P, Georgopoulos A, Kikillos F, Kyriakidis P, Liarokapis F, Poullis C, Rizvic S (2006) Project iMARECULTURE: Advanced VR, iMmersive Serious Games and Augmented REality as Tools to Raise Awareness and Access to European Underwater CULTURal heritagE, Digital Heritage. In: Progress in cultural heritage: documentation, preservation, and protection, volume 10058 of the series lecture notes in computer science, pp 805–813

Smart J, Cascio J, Paffendorf J (2007) Metaverse roadmap: pathways to the 3D web: overview. http://metaverseroadmap.org/overview/. Accessed 15 July 2019

Sylaiou S, Mania K, Paliokas I, Pujol-Tost L, Kilintzis V, Liarokapis F (2017) Exploring the educational impact of diverse technologies in online virtual museums. Int J Arts Technol (IJART) Inderscience Publishers 10(1):58–84

Parry, R (ed) (2010) Museums in a Digital Age. Routledge, London and New York

Tuan F (1977) Space and place: the perspective of experience. University of Minnesota Press, Minneapolis

Vosinakis S, Koutsabasis, Makris D, Sagia E (2016) A kinesthetic approach to digital heritage using leap motion: the cycladic sculpture application. In: Proceedings of the IEEE games and virtual worlds for serious applications (VS-Games) conference

White M, Mourkoussis N, Darcy J, Petridis P, Liarokapis F, Lister PF, Walczak K, Wojciechowski R, Cellary W, Chmielewski J, Stawniak M, Wiza W, Patel M, Stevenson J, Manley J, Giorgini F, Sayd P, Gaspard F (2004a) ARCO-an architecture for digitization, management and presentation of virtual exhibitions. In: Proceedings of the 22nd international conference on computer graphics (CGI' 2004), 16–19 June 2004. IEEE Computer Society, Hersonissos, Crete

White M, Liarokapis F, Mourkoussis N, Basu A, Darcy J, Petridis P, Sifniotis, M, Lister PF (2004b) ARCOlite—an XML based system for building and presenting virtual museums using Web3D and augmented reality. In: Proceedings of theory and practice of computer graphics 2004, Eurographics UK Chapter, 8–10 June 2004. IEEE Computer Society, University of Bournemouth

White M, Liarokapis F, Mourkoussis N, Basu A, Darcy J, Petridis P, Lister PF (2004c) A lightweight XML driven architecture for the presentation of virtual cultural exhibitions (ARCOLite), Proceedings. In: Guimaraes N, Isaias P (eds) IADIS international conference of applied computing 2004, March 23–26 2004. IADIS Press, Lisbon

Wineman JD, Peponis J (2009) Constructing spatial meaning: spatial affordances in museum design. Environ Behav

Chapter 11
Tackling Problems of Marker-Based Augmented Reality Under Water

Jan Čejka and Fotis Liarokapis

Abstract Underwater sites are a harsh environment for augmented reality applications. Divers must battle poor visibility conditions, difficult navigation, and hard manipulation with devices under water. This chapter focuses on the problem of localizing a device under water using markers. It discusses various filters that enhance and improve underwater images and their impact on marker-based tracking. Then, it presents different combinations of ten image-improving algorithms and four marker-detecting algorithms and tests their performance in real situations. All solutions are designed to run real-time on mobile devices to provide a solid basis for augmented reality. The usability of this solution is evaluated on locations in the Mediterranean Sea. Results show that image improving algorithms with carefully chosen parameters can reduce the problems with underwater visibility and enhance the detection of markers. The best results are obtained with marker detecting algorithms specifically designed for marine environments.

11.1 Introduction

Cultural heritage sites and artifacts are spread all around the world, and people search for them to learn more about their history and lives. Today, they are not limited only to observe these objects in their current state and read about their story, but thanks to modern technologies like augmented reality (AR), they can see these objects as virtual models superimposed into the real world to see how they fit into the scene and how they interact with their surroundings. These technologies can show even missing parts of settlements or whole buildings (Vlahakis et al. 2002; Panou et al. 2018).

Historical artifacts are not only on land, but many of them hide under water. These artifacts include wrecks of ancient ships transporting goods between cities or seaside settlements that submerged over the last thousands of years. Unfortunately, underwater sites are not only harder to access for people that wish to see the artifacts, but they

J. Čejka (✉) · F. Liarokapis
Faculty of Informatics, Masaryk University, Botanická 68a, 60200 Brno, Czech Republic
e-mail: xcejka2@fi.muni.cz

© Springer Nature Switzerland AG 2020
F. Liarokapis et al. (eds.), *Visual Computing for Cultural Heritage*, Springer Series on Cultural Computing, https://doi.org/10.1007/978-3-030-37191-3_11

also impose many problems for technology to work. Localization techniques based on GPS, Wi-Fi, or Bluetooth technology do not work as their signal is absorbed very quickly. AR and other computer vision solutions that require visual input struggle with problems like low contrast of images, sensor noise caused by recording images in low light, occlusions caused by small particles and fish floating in water, unnatural colors due to uneven absorption of light, and low visibility limited due to turbidity.

The idea of using AR under water is not new (Gallagher 1999); however, solutions are limited mostly on the clear water of swimming pools (Bellarbi et al. 2013; Oppermann et al. 2013, 2016). In marine areas, AR solutions use acoustic beacons to replace the visual input (Bruno et al. 2016a, b), but they are limited only to show a map and textual information about the area since they are not able to track precise position of the diver required to superimpose virtual objects accurately. The impact of low visibility conditions on algorithms of computer vision was tested in laboratory conditions (Cesar et al. 2015) and as a part of an evaluation of a single image improving algorithm (Ancuti and Codruta 2014; Gao et al. 2016), but such evaluation did not focus on marine environments.

This chapter describes solutions used for improving marker-based tracking for project iMareCULTURE (Skarlatos et al. 2016) and is based on the results of Žuži et al. (2018) and Čejka et al. (2018, 2019). These works focus on post-processing images taken under water to increase their quality to improve the detection of markers for AR. It is divided into three parts. First, it evaluates nine algorithms for improving images to assess their performance for enhancing the quality of images before detecting markers for AR. Second, it chooses the most promising solutions and performs a more in-depth analysis of various sea environments. The final part inspects which components of marker detecting algorithms are affected in low visibility conditions and presents results of a cultural heritage use case scenario.

11.2   Performance of Image-Enhancing Algorithms

Underwater visibility is affected by many factors like turbidity or a presence of small organisms (Čejka et al. 2018). These factors are hard to separate to explore their impact individually. For this reason, all algorithms in this chapter are evaluated using data recorded in sea environments. This section presents a brief analysis of nine solutions to get an initial insight into the performance of image-enhancing algorithms. It records a video with markers placed under water, processes it offline, and comparing the number of detected markers. The most promising solutions are chosen and studied in more detail in the following sections.

The test was conducted with a video with two divers holding a board with markers (see Fig. 11.1). A camera operated by another diver is moving closer to them to decrease the impact of low underwater visibility conditions when the distance to the markers gets smaller. The video is recorded using a GoPro camera with a resolution of 1920 × 1080, in the Mediterranean Sea near Athens in depths ranging from 5 to 7 m. At the beginning of the video, the size of the smaller markers is roughly 20

Fig. 11.1 Two divers holding sheets with markers for initial assessment of image-improving algorithms

pixels to assess the influence of turbidity on the detection of small distant markers. The larger marker is approximately 85 pixels at the beginning of the video, which focuses more on the problem of turbidity if the size of the marker is just a minor issue.

ARUco library (Garrido-Jurado et al. 2014) is used to detect markers in images. This library is open-source, kept up-to-date, robust to different lighting conditions, runs in real time, and provides excellent results in a reasonable time (Cesar et al. 2015). Its implementation is a part of OpenCV 3.2.0. It detects markers in gray-scale images, so before the detection, all images are converted to YUV color space. This color space was chosen because it many mobile devices natively support it. The colors are converted before or after enhancing original images, depending on the enhancing algorithm.

The boards contained seven markers. To identify individual markers, ARUco uses a binary matrix of six rows and six columns to create a code with 36 bits. Thanks to this, it can correct up to six incorrectly detected bits. Six markers were printed on an A4 paper, formed in a grid of two rows and three columns. Each marker measured approximately seven centimeters with one centimeter of white space between them, and the seventh marker was printed larger with a size of approximately 15 cm on a separate paper. This setup allows evaluating the performance of two potential settings: single-marker tracking (in which one marker represents one object), and multi-marker tracking (where multiple markers represent one object). Regardless, the detection of each marker of this multi marker was evaluated separately to obtain more accurate results. It is worth mentioning that the markers were plasticized to 'survive' in underwater environments.

The video was processed offline on a standard PC with processor Intel Core i5 760, 8 GB of operating memory, and operating system Windows 10. Each frame was treated separately, first increasing its quality by applying image-improving algorithms, and then detecting markers.

11.2.1   Tested Image Enhancing Algorithms

This section evaluates nine image-improving algorithms: two algorithms designed to improve the colors of underwater images (fusion based on the work of Ancuti et al. (2012), and bright channel prior based on the work of Gao et al. (2016)), three algorithms for denoising (Gaussian filter, median filter, and bilateral filter), three algorithms for increasing contrast (histogram equalization, contrast limited adaptive histogram equalization, and white balancing), and one algorithm for image sharpening (deblurring), see Fig. 11.2. The algorithms were implemented in MATLAB, OpenCV 3.2.0, and C++. To assess them, different parameters were explored to find

Fig. 11.2 Image enhancing algorithms. Top row from left to right: original image, fusion, bright channel prior, Gaussian filter, median filter; bottom row from left to right: bilateral filter, histogram equalization, contrast limited adaptive histogram equalization, white balancing, deblurring

out how they affect tracking accuracy. Algorithms based on neural networks (Guo et al. 2016; Voulodimos et al. 2018) were not considered in this experiment, as they require a large amount of data for training.

11.2.1.1 Fusion

The fusion algorithm is based on the work of Ancuti et al. (2012). It restores the colors and enhances the contrast of images taken under water by deriving two improved versions of the input image, and combines them using a multi-scale fusion process with a weight function computed from each image.

The restoration process is simplified by using general image-improving techniques instead of choosing a more sophisticated method based on the physical properties of the scene. It obtains the first enhanced version of the input image by using a white balancing algorithm that corrects the shift of colors caused by various illuminations of the scene. This algorithm is based on the Gray-World approach (Buchsbaum 1980), which was found as the most appropriate method for underwater images. The second enhanced version of the input image is aiming at reducing noise and improving the contrast of the underwater image by applying the bilateral filter on the color-corrected image created in the previous step. The contrast is further enhanced by using a local adaptive histogram equalization method.

Fusion of the derived images is controlled by local contrast weights derived from the luminance of the images, and saliency weight to highlight the objects with higher importance. The final image is created by blending the two derived input images by their normalized weight values. The implementation was done in Matlab, where most of the filters and operations are available directly, using its Image Processing Toolbox.

11.2.1.2 Bright Channel Prior

Bright channel prior (BCP) is a technique developed by Gao et al. (2016), which is based on a method of He et al. (2011) to dehaze images taken on land affected by fog. He et al. observes that the intensity of one color channel is very low in images taken on land with no fog. However, this assumption fails to work for images taken under water, since uneven absorption of light shifts the colors. The red color is absorbed more quickly, which results in underwater scenes being green or blue due to very low intensities of the red color channel. Because of this, Gao et al. defines the bright channel image as follows:

$$J^{bcp} = \max_{y \in \Omega(x)} \left(\max_{c \in \{r,g,b\}} I^{new}(y) \right) \tag{11.1}$$

where $\Omega(x)$ denotes a window neighborhood centered at pixel x and I^{new} is the input image with the original red color channel and inverted green and blue channels.

Intensities of all color channels of this bright channel image are close to one for pixels without the haze and lower for pixels affected by the fog and turbidity.

To estimate atmospheric light defining the color distortion of the image, Gao et al. takes one percent of darkest pixels, and a pixel with the least variance is selected. Transmittance is then derived from the bright channel image and estimated atmospheric light by the following equation:

$$t^c(x) = \frac{\left(J^{bcp}(x) - A^c\right)}{1 - A^c} \tag{11.2}$$

where c denotes red, green, and blue color channels, $t^{c(x)}$ denotes the transmittance of this channel, and A^c denotes the value of atmospheric light. The final transmittance is obtained by averaging values across all color channels, which is then processed with a guide filter (He et al. 2013) to remove halos. The final haze-free image is restored by formula:

$$J(x) = \frac{I(x) - A}{t(x)} + A \tag{11.3}$$

where J is the haze-free image, $I(x)$ is the degraded underwater image, A is the previously estimated atmospheric light, and $t(x)$ is the transmittance of the scene. BCP algorithm was implemented in Matlab using Image Processing Toolkit.

11.2.1.3   Gaussian Filter

Gaussian filter is a standard filter for reducing noise in images. It is defined as:

$$I^{out}(x) = \frac{1}{W} \sum_{x_i \in \Omega} I^{in}(x_i) G_{space}(|x_i - x|) \tag{11.4}$$

with normalizing factor:

$$W = \sum_{x_i \in \Omega} G_{space}(|x_i - x|) \tag{11.5}$$

where G_{space} is a Gaussian function with parameter σ_{space}. Gaussian filter is a linear filter that sums neighbor pixels using weights based on their mutual distance in image space. It decreases the number of edges found by edge detecting algorithms, and thus improves the image for marker detection. Gaussian filtering was applied on the Y channel of our images after their conversion to YUV color space.

11.2.1.4 Median Filter

Median filter is another standard filter reducing noise in images and can be defined as:

$$I^{out}(x) = median_{x_i \in \Omega}\left(I^{in}(x_i)\right) \tag{11.6}$$

The median filter is used for removing noise in an image like the Gaussian filter, but unlike it, it provides excellent results when removing impulse noise. Median filtering was applied on the Y channel after the images are converted to YUV color space.

11.2.1.5 Bilateral Filter

Bilateral filter is a variation of the Gaussian filter, but unlike this filter, it preserves edges while simultaneously removing noise in smooth areas. It is defined as:

$$I^{out}(x) = \frac{1}{W} \sum_{x_i \in \Omega} I^{in}(x_i) G_{space}(|x_i - x|) G_{color}(|I(x_i) - I(x)|) \tag{11.7}$$

with normalizing factor:

$$W = \sum_{x_i \in \Omega} G_{space}(|x_i - x|) G_{color}(|I(x_i) - I(x)|) \tag{11.8}$$

where G_{space} is a Gaussian function with parameter σ_{space}, and G_{color} is a Gaussian function with parameter σ_{color}. It sums the weighted intensities of neighbor pixels like the Gaussian filter, but unlike it, the weights do not depend only on the spatial distance of the weighted pixels in image space, but also on the difference between intensities of these pixels in color space, allowing the filter to decrease the amount of blurring over edges. The implementation of the bilateral filter is based on the work of Tomasi and Manduchi (1998) and is applied to the Y channel after the input image is converted to the YUV color space.

11.2.1.6 Histogram Equalization

Histogram equalization technique is a method that maps intensities of pixels of the original image to different values to balance the histogram of the filtered image. This test uses an ordinary histogram equalization implementation from OpenCV. It is applied on the Y channel after the images are converted to YUV color space.

11.2.1.7   Contrast Limited Adaptive Histogram Equalization

Contrast limited adaptive histogram equalization (CLAHE) (Pizer et al. 1987) is an adaptation of histogram equalization, which works with a histogram of a small window around each pixel and reduces the contrast of output image by clipping the highest values of the histogram. CLAHE is applied to the Y channel after the images are converted to the YUV color space. CLAHE has a single parameter (clip limit), which influences the number of values clipped in the histogram.

11.2.1.8   White Balancing

The white balancing algorithm changes the colors of the input image to render white objects correctly under different illuminations like the sun or clouded sky. In this test, we used an algorithm presented by Limare et al. (2011):

foreach *color channel* **do**

    compute histogram of this channel;
    channel$_{min}$ ← *black*-th percentile of values in histogram;
    channel$_{max}$ ← *white*-th percentile of values in histogram;
    linearly transform all intensities so that *channel$_{min}$* = 0 and *channel$_{max}$* = 255;

end

    The main advantages of this method include speed and simplicity. The restored image may not represent the colors of objects accurately, but this is not a problem since the image is just processed by the marker detection algorithm and not presented to the viewer. The algorithm is applied to all channels of the RGB image before it is converted to the YUV space for marker detection.

11.2.1.9   Deblurring

The last filter used is a deblurring filter (or unsharp mask filter (Krasula et al. 2017)), which emphasizes high frequencies in the input image by subtracting its low frequencies from itself as shown below:

$$I_{out} = (1 + w) \cdot I_{in} - w \cdot Gaussian\left(I_{in}, \sigma_{space}\right) \tag{11.9}$$

where w represents the weight of subtracted low frequencies, and *Gaussian* $\left(I_{in}, \sigma_{space}\right)$ is a Gaussian filter with standard deviation σ_{space} applied to the input image I_{in}. This method was implemented and applied on the Y channel after the image was transformed into the YUV color space.

11.2.2 Results of Enhancing Underwater Images

Each technique was tested with different values of their parameters. We counted the number of newly found markers, which were detected in the enhanced video and not detected in the original video, and the number of lost markers, which were detected in the original video and not in the enhanced video. All image-enhancing algorithms were also compared between each other, counting the number of detected markers in images processed with one algorithm and not detected in images processed with another algorithm. The following tables show only the results of the best parameters for each algorithm that obtain the highest number of newly detected markers while keeping the number of lost markers as low as possible. The following parameters were selected:

- Gaussian filter, $\sigma_{space} = 0.4$;
- Median filter, window size $= 3$;
- Bilateral filter, $\sigma_{color} = 2.0$ and $\sigma_{space} = 4.0$;
- CLAHE, clip limit 2;
- White balancing, *black/white* percentile 2/98;
- Deblurring, $\sigma_{space} = 2.8$ and weight $= 1.9$.

The evaluation of the results is shown in Table 11.1 and demonstrates that the white balancing algorithm provides the best outcome, followed by deblurring, then CLAHE, and BCP. Other algorithms produced similar or worse results than with the original image. Also, it is worth noting that the Gaussian filter parameter σ_{space} is very low, which indicates that a high amount of blur worsens the results.

The performance of the algorithms depends on the chosen parameters. Improper parameters for CLAHE and white balancing algorithms make the results of detection worse than when detecting markers in the original images. Also note that the best results are obtained with very low values of parameters. For example, in the case of deblurring, sufficiently good results are available even with small values.

This test did not focus on measuring the time to process the images, only to see that real-time algorithms CLAHE, white balancing, and deblurring outperformed more sophisticated BCP. It showed that even a simple real-time algorithm can improve the detection of markers under water.

11.2.3 Summary of Algorithms Enhancing Underwater Images

We see that no algorithm would be strictly better than other algorithms. Many algorithms improved the detection of markers, but in all cases, some markers in the original image were lost. Also, sophisticated offline solutions are not necessarily better than general real-time solutions. This test shows that the most promising algorithms are algorithms that improve the sharpness of the image (deblurring), colors

Table 11.1 Results of various image improving algorithms. BCP, CLAHE, white balancing, and deblurring show a significant increase in the number of detected markers when compared to the original image

Algorithm	Found markers	Number of found markers that were not found by following algorithms									
		Original image	Fusion	BCP	Gaussian filter	Median filter	Bilateral filter	Hist. equalization	CLAHE	White balancing	Deblurring
Original image	4811	0	231	35	57	312	30	625	43	28	20
Fusion	4611	31	0	16	26	152	27	457	17	9	8
BCP	**5097**	321	502	0	336	592	309	876	91	83	71
Gaussian filter	4795	41	210	34	0	298	48	612	40	24	19
Median filter	4515	16	56	10	18	0	13	395	13	7	7
Bilateral filter	4818	37	234	30	71	316	0	628	35	29	20
Histogram equalization	4238	52	84	17	55	118	48	0	20	14	12
CLAHE	**5120**	352	526	114	365	618	337	902	0	75	58
White balancing	**5264**	481	662	250	493	756	475	1040	219	0	116
Deblurring	**5249**	458	646	223	473	741	451	1023	187	101	0

of the image (white balancing), and its contrast (CLAHE). The following sections inspect these algorithms into more depth with more videos and more marker detecting algorithms.

11.3   Methodology of the Second Test

The second test focuses on the image-enhancing algorithms that gave the best results in the first test and analyses them in other underwater environments. Also, it adds the results of an improved version of which balancing algorithm, marker-based underwater white balancing (MBUWWB) (Čejka et al. 2018) that is better adapted to underwater conditions. Additionally, it compares the results with AprilTag (Wang and Olson 2016), a marker detecting algorithm that provides better results than ARUco at a higher detection time, as shown by Cesar et al. (2015).

11.3.1   Testing Sites

Three additional sets of videos were tested to the total number of four, including the video from the previous experiment, see Table 11.2.

The first set of videos is the video tested in the previous section. As already noted, it was taken in a depth of approximately 7–9 m in a moderately turbid environment with a GoPro camera with a resolution of 1920 × 1080. We refer to this set as Environment 1. The video was recorded using MPEG-4 compression and decoded into RGB frames. The camera starts far from the markers and moves slowly towards the markers.

The second set of videos consists of videos taken in depth of 5–6 m in a highly turbid environment using iPad Pro 9.7-inch with a resolution of 1920 × 1080. We refer to this set as Environment 2. These videos were recorded using MPEG-2 compression and decoded into RGB frames. In these videos, the camera starts at very large distances, where the markers are not distinguishable due to the turbidity, and ends at distances of tens of centimeters.

The third set of videos consists of ten videos taken in the depth of 20–22 m in a moderately turbid environment with a GARMIN VIRB XE camera with a resolution of 1920 × 1440. We refer to this set as Environment 3. These videos were recorded using MPEG-4 compression and decoded into RGB frames. This set of videos contains not only videos with the camera moving towards the markers, but also videos with markers recorded from multiple directions and distances.

The fourth set of videos consists of eight videos taken in the depth of 7–9 m in a moderately turbid environment with an NVIDIA SHIELD tablet. We refer to this set as Environment 4. Two of these videos were recorded with a resolution of 1920 × 1080 using MPEG-4 compression and decoded into RGB frames. The rest was recorded with a resolution of 1280 × 720 and stored without using any compression

Table 11.2 Four different testing sites

Environment 1	Environment 2
Moderate turbidity	High turbidity
Depth 5–7 m	Depth 5–6 m
GoPro camera	iPad Pro 9.7
1920 × 1080	1920 × 1080
MPEG-4	MPEG-2
29.97 fps, 31 s	30 fps, 85 s

Environment 3	Environment 4
Moderate turbidity	Low turbidity
Depth 20–22 m	Depth 7–9 m
GARMIN VIRB XE	NVIDIA SHIELD
1920 × 1440	1920 × 1080
MPEG-4	MPEG-4
24 fps, 160 s	30 fps, 81 s

as YUV frames. As with the third set of videos, this set of videos also contains not only videos with the camera moving towards the markers but also videos with markers recorded from multiple directions and distances.

11.3.2 Tested Algorithms

In addition to the best algorithms tested in the previous test, CLAHE, deblurring, and white balancing, this section also contains the results of a fourth algorithm, marker-based underwater white balancing (MBUWWB), that is adapted for marker-based tracking under water (Čejka et al. 2018). This algorithm solves an intrinsic part of white balancing algorithms, which is finding the colors that are subsequently mapped to the white and black in the filtered image. The white balancing algorithm defined in the previous section chooses these colors as a percentile of values in the input image histogram. MBUWWB assumes that the marker is black and white, and instead of computing the histogram of the whole image, it calculates the histogram only of the part of the image which contains markers.

In this experiment, MBUWWB is applied to all channels of RGB image, and afterward, the improved is converted into YUV space, similarly as with the simple white balancing. The images stored in YUV format are also converted to RGB before MBUWWB processes them.

11.3.3   Results in Various Environments

Image enhancing algorithms and marker detection algorithms were compared in two aspects: the total number of detected markers, and performance in different visibility conditions.

Table 11.3 illustrates a summed number of all markers found by ARUco in every set of enhanced videos. It demonstrates that all tested algorithms improve the detection of markers in strongly turbid environments. In moderately turbid environments, visibility is better, so the improvement in detection is not very apparent.

The behavior of the CLAHE algorithm is hard to predict. Using CLAHE can lead to an improvement in the detection of markers (Environment 1, Environment 2), but it can also decrease the number of detected markers (Environment 3, Environment 4). The result is also highly dependent on the value of the clip limit. On the other hand, deblurring, white balancing, and MBUWWB provide more stable results. The

Table 11.3 Total number of markers detected with ARUco in tested sets of videos enhanced by tested algorithms

	Environment 1	Environment 2	Environment 3	Environment 4
Original video	5338	512	5847	9925
CLAHE, clip limit 2	**5670**	3904	**5405**	**8227**
CLAHE, clip limit 4	5541	4916	4801	7276
CLAHE, clip limit 6	5399	**5010**	4190	7057
Deblurring, weight 1	5696	1852	6033	10105
Deblurring, weight 4	**5804**	**4622**	**6050**	**10,372**
White bal., perc. 0/100	5557	3603	**6053**	**9988**
White bal., perc. 3/97	**5668**	**5159**	5950	9558
MBUWWB, perc. 0/100	5781	5842	**6094**	10026
MBUWWB, perc. 3/97	**5787**	**6351**	6069	**10,085**

results of deblurring clearly show that using value 4 for subtraction weight w leads to a higher number of detected markers.

The results also illustrate that MBUWWB provided better overall results than the original white balancing, although the difference is much lower in moderately turbid environments. Careful choice of percentile affects the performance of both these algorithms, especially in highly turbid environments. This difference is more visible in the case of the white balancing algorithm, while in the case of MBUWWB, percentile 3/97 provided better or nearly the same results when compared to percentile 0/100.

The results for AprilTag are in Table 11.4. Unlike ARUco, the AprilTag algorithm is much more robust to environments with strong turbidity (similar results were observed by Cesar et al. (2015)). The detection provides already excellent results in the original video, and the improvement obtained by enhancing the image is not very large if any. The best results in individual sets were obtained by CLAHE with clip parameter 2 (Environment 1) and deblurring (Environment 3 and Environment 4). However, these two algorithms provided much worse results on other videos.

Unlike the results of ARUco, these results show that the proper choice of subtraction weight w in deblurring algorithm is not easy. It shows that in environments Environment 1 and Environment 2, weight 1 leads to a higher number of detected markers than weight 4, but in environments Environment 3 and Environment 4, the result is opposite.

The results also show that WB and MBUWWB were not improving the detection, but they are also not making it worse. This is true only with percentile 0; the results when using percentile 3 were always worse.

The camera moves towards and away from the markers in some videos of all sets. With decreasing distance, the marker gradually emerges from the turbid, which allows us to evaluate the behavior of image-enhancing algorithms in different levels of marker visibility.

Table 11.4 Total number of markers detected with AprilTag in tested sets of videos enhanced by tested algorithms

	Environment 1	Environment 2	Environment 3	Environment 4
Original video	**5925**	6884	5775	9141
CLAHE, clip limit 2	5868	**7032**	5552	8119
CLAHE, clip limit 4	5667	6679	4974	6655
CLAHE, clip limit 6	5381	6186	4362	6326
Deblurring, weight 1	5850	6652	5781	9351
Deblurring, weight 4	5474	5542	**5847**	**9526**
White bal., perc. 0/100	5922	6873	5648	9091
White bal., perc. 3/97	5479	6476	5597	8769
MBUWWB, perc. 0/100	**5925**	**6914**	5705	9067
MBUWWB, perc. 3/97	5887	6695	5697	8925

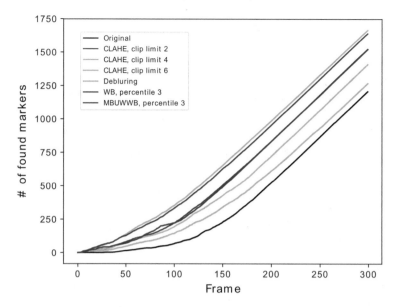

Fig. 11.3 Number of markers detected by ARUco in a video from environment 2

We focused on the ARUco detector and the video from Environment 1 and plotted the progress of the number of detected markers in time, see Fig. 11.3. In the video, markers start partially in turbid, and as the camera moves towards them, it reaches very soon the distance where all the markers are visible.

This experiment shows that all image enhancing algorithms improves the detection of the markers in worse visibility conditions (first frames of the video), with deblurring giving the best results, only slightly better than MBUWWB. Since approximately the 150th frame, the visibility is excellent for all algorithms to find all markers.

11.3.4 Summary of Algorithms Performing in Various Environments

Results indicate an additional image-enhancing step improves the detection of markers. However, the proper choice of the algorithm and its parameters is heavily dependent on the environment and the marker-detecting algorithm. If the marker-detecting algorithm is robust, there is no need to improve the input image. Its "enhancement" may make the results even worse, but robust algorithms run very slowly. In the final section of this chapter, we will focus on the ARUco marker detector to find which parts are affected by bad visibility conditions.

11.4   Underwater Marker-Detecting Algorithms

The last part of this chapter is focused on the structure of the ARUco marker-detecting algorithm to identify components that are affected by underwater conditions. It also presents the results of a cultural heritage use case scenario from Baiae, Italy.

11.4.1   Structure of Marker-Detecting Algorithm ARUco

The ARUco detector runs fast and reliably recognize markers. First, it thresholds the input image using an adaptive thresholding algorithm, then it finds all contours to detect marker-like shapes, and filters out non-square polygons. Then, it reprojects them to remove perspective distortion, obtains the inner binary marker code, and compares it with a dictionary to eliminate errors. Finally, it computes the relative position of the marker using its corners.

Čejka et al. in (2019) investigates which parts of ARUco are influenced by image improving algorithms. They find that the most vulnerable part is the initial thresholding. Figure 11.4 shows that when an underwater image is thresholded by ARUco, the border often breaks, and the marker is not recognized as a square-like object. Changing the parameters of the thresholding avoids this issue, but this increases the number of small contours, which increases the processing time. All four image-improving algorithms in previous sections increased the contrast of the image, which led to a similar result as changing the parameters of thresholding, but the number of false contours was lower. For this reason, they did not increase the detection time very much.

Čejka et al. (2019) presents an improved version of ARUco called UWARUco that is adapted to underwater environments. This algorithm creates a mask to remove image parts that contain no contour and applies it to an image thresholded with proper parameters. This approach provides results that are comparable with robust marker detecting algorithms, but their algorithm runs faster.

11.4.2   Use Case: Presenting Submerged Ancient Buildings with AR

The last part of this chapter focuses on using marker-based AR to present virtual structures to divers that dive in Baiae in Italy at locations of ancient villas. The focus of the testing was limited to one building, Villa a Protiro, with a unique mosaic in one of the rooms. With the improved approach, divers were able to perceive a 3D reconstruction of Villa a Protiro in AR. The test used nine markers from the ARUco DICT_6X6_50 dictionary, forming a grid of 3×3 markers. The size of each marker

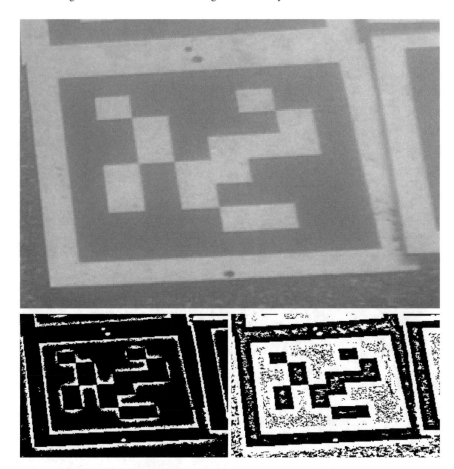

Fig. 11.4 Top: input image taken under water; lower-left: thresholded by ARUco, notice a broken contour; lower-right: the contour is solid with better parameters of ARUco, but the image contains a lot of noise

was 19 cm, and the space between markers was approximately 5 cm. The setup and the application are illustrated in Fig. 11.5.

Solutions for AR were tested with a video recorded with Samsung S8 in FullHD resolution. Table 11.5 presents the results taken from (Čejka et al. 2019). We see that both solutions that improve the detection of markers, ARUco with MBUWWB and UWARUco, provide better results than original ARUco. ARUco3 (Romero-Ramirez et al. 2018) is a newer version of ARUco that is optimized for speed and is less robust to the underwater environment, which is visible in the results. Robust AprilTag detects a high number of markers without the necessity of improving images, but its computation time is very high.

Fig. 11.5 Top: nine markers placed at the location of a room with mosaic of Villa a Protiro in Baiae, Italy. Bottom: a virtual model superimposed in augmented reality at the place of these markers

Table 11.5 Number of detected markers and computation time for various augmented reality solutions

	ARUco	ARUco with MBUWWB	UWARUco	ARUco3	AprilTag
# of markers	14,457	19,398	20,145	12,589	20,082
Time (ms)	75.747	45.239	62.872	2.368	323.005

11.5 Conclusion

This chapter targeted applications that use AR to present additional information about cultural heritage sites and described problems with detecting markers in marine underwater environments. First, it presented a comparison of general solutions that improve images affected by bad visibility conditions under water. It showed that there is no solution strictly better than other solution and that more elaborated algorithms designed for underwater images do not always provide better results than general solutions. Then, the chapter focused on the most promising solutions in multiple underwater environments. Here, the results showed that the image-improving step improved the detection of markers if the parameters of the image improving algorithm were correctly set. Finally, it investigated the impact of underwater visibility conditions on a single marker detecting algorithm. It showed that a properly adapted algorithm outperformed general algorithms combined with image enhancing algorithms.

The problem of detecting markers still contains many opened issues. The results heavily depend the visual conditions of the environment, unfortunately, there is no classification of factors of underwater visual conditions affecting algorithms of computer vision. For this reason, image-enhancing and marker-detecting algorithms must be selected according to the conditions at a specific site and cannot be chosen automatically and online.

Additionally, the evaluation of image-enhancing algorithms can be extended by evaluating their impact on the results of marker-less tracking and marker-less recognition of underwater objects. Although these algorithms recognize objects similarly as marker-based techniques, issues that are specific to underwater conditions may arise and present additional obstacles.

References

Ancuti C, Codruta A (2014) Effective contrast-based dehazing for robust image matching. IEEE Geosci Remote Sens Lett 11:1871–1875

Ancuti C, Ancuti CO, Haber T, Bekaert P (2012) Enhancing underwater images and videos by fusion. In: Proceedings of the 2012 IEEE conference on computer vision and pattern recognition (CVPR), pp 81–88

Bellarbi A, Domingues C, Otmane S, Benbelkacem S, Dinis A (2013) Augmented reality for underwater activities with the use of the DOLPHYN. In: 10th IEEE international conference on networking, sensing and control (ICNSC), pp 409–412

Bruno F, Lagudi A, Barbieri L, Muzzupappa M, Ritacco G, Cozza A, Cozza M, Peluso R, Lupia M, Cario G (2016a) Virtual and augmented reality tools to improve the exploitation of underwater archaeological sites by diver and non-diver tourists. In: 6th international conference on digital heritage. Progress in cultural heritage: documentation, preservation, and protection, EuroMed, pp 269–280

Bruno F, Lagudi A, Muzzupappa M, Lupia M, Cario G, Barbieri L, Passaro S, Saggiomo R (2016b) Project VISAS: virtual and augmented exploitation of submerged archaeological site—overview and first results. Mar Technol Soc J 50:119–129

Buchsbaum G (1980) A spatial processor model for object colour perception. J Frankl Inst 1–26

Čejka J, Žuži M, Agrafiotis P, Skarlatos D, Bruno F, Liarokapis F (2018) Improving marker-based tracking for augmented reality in underwater environments. In: Proceedings of the Eurographics workshop on graphics and cultural heritage, pp 21–30

Čejka J, Bruno F, Skarlatos D, Liarokapis F (2019) Detecting square markers in underwater environments. Remote Sens 11(4)

Cesar DBdS, Gaudig C, Fritsche M, Reis MAd, Kirchner F (2015) An evaluation of artificial fiducial markers in underwater environments. In: Proceedings of OCEANS, pp 1–6

Gallagher D (1999) Development of miniature, head-mounted, virtual image displays for navy divers. In: Proceedings of OCEANS '99, vol 3, pp 1098–1104

Gao Y, Li H, Wen S (2016) Restoration and enhancement of underwater images based on bright channel prior. Math Probl Eng 1–15

Garrido-Jurado S, Salinas R, Madrid-Cuevas F, Marín-Jiménez M (2014) Automatic generation and detection of highly reliable fiducial markers under occlusion. Pattern Recognit 47:2280–2292

Guo Y, Liu Y, Oerlemans A, Lao S, Wu S, Lew MS (2016) Deep learning for visual understanding: a review. Neurocomputing 27–48

He K, Sun J, Tang X (2011) Single image haze removal using dark channel prior. IEEE Trans Pattern Anal Mach Intell 33(12):2341–2353

He K, Sun J, Tang X (2013) Guided image filtering. IEEE Trans Pattern Anal Mach Intell 35:1397–1409

Krasula L, Callet P, Fliegel K, Klíma M (2017) Quality assessment of sharpened images: challenges, methodology, and objective metrics. IEEE Trans Image Process 26:1496–1508

Limare N, Lisani J, Morel J, Petro A, Sbert C (2011) Simplest color balance. Image Process Line

Oppermann L, Blum L, Lee J-Y, Seo J-H (2013) AREEF multi-player underwater augmented reality experience. In: 2013 IEEE international games innovation conference (IGIC), pp 199–202

Oppermann L, Blum L, Shekow M (2016) Playing on AREEF: evaluation of an underwater augmented reality game for kids. In: Proceedings of the 18th international conference on human-computer interaction with mobile devices and services, pp 330–340

Panou C, Ragia L, Dimelli D, Mania K (2018) An architecture for mobile outdoors augmented reality for cultural heritage. ISPRS Int J Geo-Inf 7(12)

Pizer S, Amburn E, Austin J, Cromartie R, Geselowitz A, Greer T, Romeny B, Zimmerman J (1987) Adaptive histogram equalization and its variations. Comput Vis Graph Image Process 39:355–368

Romero-Ramirez F, Salinas RM, Medina-Carnicer R (2018) Speeded up detection of squared fiducial markers. Image Vis Comput 38–47

Skarlatos D, Agrafiotis P, Balogh T, Bruno F, Castro F, Petriaggi B, Demesticha S, Doulamis A, Drap P, Georgopoulos A, Kikillos F, Kyriakidis P, Liarokapis F, Poullis C, Rizvic S (2016) Project iMARECULTURE: advanced VR, iMmersive serious games and Augmented REality as tools to raise awareness and access to european underwater CULTURal heritagE. In: Proceedings of digital heritage. progress in cultural heritage, pp 805–813

Tomasi C, Manduchi R (1998) Bilateral filtering for gray and color images. In: International conference on computer vision, pp 839–846

Vlahakis V, Ioannidis N, Karigiannis J, Tsotros M, Gounaris M, Stricker D, Gleue T, Daehne P, Almeida L (2002) archeoguide: an augmented reality guide for archaeological sites. IEEE Comput Graph Appl 22:52–60

Voulodimos A, Doulamis N, Doulamis A, Protopapadakis E (2018) Deep learning for computer vision: a brief review. Comput Intell Neurosci 1–13

Wang J, Olson E (2016) AprilTag 2: efficient and robust fiducial detection. In: Proceedings of the IEEE/RSJ international conference on intelligent robots and systems (IROS)

Žuži M, Čejka J, Bruno F, Skarlatos D, Liarokapis F (2018) Impact of dehazing on underwater marker detection for augmented reality. Front Robot AI 5:1–13

Chapter 12
A True AR Authoring Tool for Interactive Virtual Museums

Efstratios Geronikolakis, Paul Zikas, Steve Kateros, Nick Lydatakis, Stelios Georgiou, Mike Kentros and George Papagiannakis

Abstract In this work, a new and innovative way of spatial computing that appeared recently in the bibliography called True Augmented Reality (AR), is employed in cultural heritage preservation. This innovation could be adapted by the Virtual Museums of the future to enhance the quality of experience. It emphasises, the fact that a visitor will not be able to tell, at a first glance, if the artefact that he/she is looking at is real or not and it is expected to draw the visitors' interest. True AR is not limited to artefacts but extends even to buildings or life-sized character simulations of statues. It provides the best visual quality possible so that the users will not be able to tell the real objects from the augmented ones. Such applications can be beneficial for future museums, as with True AR, 3D models of various exhibits, monuments, statues,

E. Geronikolakis (✉) · P. Zikas · S. Kateros · N. Lydatakis · S. Georgiou · M. Kentros · G. Papagiannakis
Foundation for Research and Technology Hellas, 100 N. Plastira Street, 70013 Heraklion, Greece
e-mail: stratos@oramavr.com

P. Zikas
e-mail: paul@oramavr.com

S. Kateros
e-mail: steve@oramavr.com

N. Lydatakis
e-mail: nick@oramavr.com

S. Georgiou
e-mail: stelios@oramavr.com

M. Kentros
e-mail: mike@oramavr.com

G. Papagiannakis
e-mail: george.papagiannakis@oramavr.com

G. Papagiannakis
Computer Science Department, University of Crete, Voutes Campus, 70013 Heraklion, Greece

E. Geronikolakis · P. Zikas · S. Kateros · N. Lydatakis · S. Georgiou · M. Kentros · G. Papagiannakis
ORamaVR, 100 N. Plastira Street, 70013 Heraklion, Greece

© Springer Nature Switzerland AG 2020
F. Liarokapis et al. (eds.), *Visual Computing for Cultural Heritage*, Springer Series on Cultural Computing, https://doi.org/10.1007/978-3-030-37191-3_12

characters and buildings can be reconstructed and presented to the visitors in a realistic and innovative way. We also propose our Virtual Reality Sample application, a True AR playground featuring basic components and tools for generating interactive Virtual Museum applications, alongside a 3D reconstructed character (the priest of Asinou church) facilitating the storyteller of the augmented experience.

12.1 Introduction

Augmented Reality has revolutionized many fields in the industry, from medical planning, to educational and training tools. It enhances the physical world with holographic assets, extending the possibilities of new learning and educational systems. Specifically, in the field of Digital Cultural Heritage, the rendering quality needs to be as high as possible to properly illuminate the artifacts, buildings or even characters, highlighting their natural beauty.

In this project, we followed a holistic approach generating True AR experiences by documenting both tangible and intangible heritage. To develop the holographic application, we exploited our M.A.G.E.S platform (Papagiannakis et al. 2018) as the core system architecture. This platform started as a tool to recreate psychomotor scenarios in VR for surgeons to master their skills but quickly expanded into other sectors like emergency scenarios, training courses and mechanical solutions. With this project, we aim to expand the capabilities of our system to support Cultural Heritage applications for educational purposes (Sylaiou et al. 2017). Our system generates realistic, gamified and interactive applications though Rapid Prototyping and Visual Scripting methodologies, forming an SDK for development of educational projects. By detecting the main restrictions that AR and HoloLens has, we took appropriate actions to transfer this work to AR, in order for the two versions to be as "close" as possible. The fact that someone is able to see objects or characters in AR and interact with them using their hands, increases the realism of AR (since a highly important element of realism is interaction as well, apart from the appearance of the characters, illumination etc.), thus getting us closer to our goal, which is True AR.

12.2 Previous Work

12.2.1 The M.A.G.E.S Platform

In this project, we exploited our award winning M.A.G.E.S. platform to generate a gamified AR scenario as an example of a holographic Virtual Museum (White et al. 2004). This system can generate a fail-safe, realistic environment for surgeons to practice on VR scenarios, extending their skills in an affordable and portable solution. The key component of M.A.G.E.S platform lies on the customizable SDK

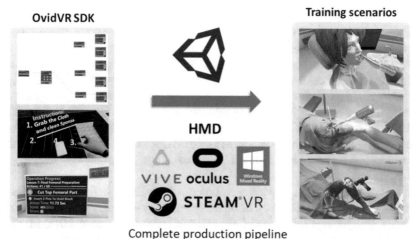

Fig. 12.1 The M.A.G.E.S. flow diagram

platform able to generate educational training scenarios and immersive experiences with minimal adaptations and code-free due to the **Visual Scripting** and **Rapid Prototyping** mechanics (Fig. 12.1).

The Visual Scripting component offers a node-based interface to generate VR behaviors and interactive tasks following a consistent educational pipeline. Utilizing this authoring tool, we developed a variety of medical training simulations, among them Total Knee and Hip Arthroplasties, a Dental Implant placement, an Endotracheal Intubation surgery and emergency medical scenarios (car-motorbike evacuation, trauma operations).

Rapid Prototyping of training scenarios reflects the classification methods to extract and break down complex educational pipelines into reusable and flexible building blocks. After documenting fundamental interaction tasks (insertion of objects/tools into highlighted areas, use of tools to complete an action, removal of objects using other tools etc.) we integrated those features into the M.A.G.E.S. platform forming a library of prototyped VR Actions in a user-friendly format, capable to generate more complex scenarios. Inspired from software design patters, we developed new VR design patterns, following interactive principles to replicate natural behaviors from real life into the VR world.

12.2.2   Holographic Virtual Museums

Since the advancement of holographic technology, AR headsets are evolving including interactive features like gesture and voice recognition, as well as improvements on resolution and FOV. In addition, untethered AR headsets paved the way for mobile experiences without the need of external processing power from a PC. Such embedded systems, facilitate great tools to represent virtual museums (Liarokapis et al. 2004) due to their lack of cables and enhanced interactive capabilities. Virtual Museums are institutional centers in the service of society, open to the public for acquiring and exhibiting the tangible and intangible heritage of humanity for the purposes of education, study and enjoyment. In addition, True Augmented Reality has recently been defined to be a modification of the user's perception of their surroundings that cannot be detected by the user (Sandor et al. 2015) due to their realism. Virtual characters and objects should blend with their surroundings, achieving the "suspension of disbelief".

In recent years, many approaches on holographic cultural heritage applications emerged, each one focusing on a different aspect of representing the holographic exhibits within the real environment. A published survey (Jung et al. 2016) investigated the impact of Virtual and Augmented reality on the overall visitor experience in museums, highlighting the social presence of AR environments. Papaeftymiou et al. (2018) presented a comparison of the latest methods for rapid reconstruction of real humans using as input RGB and RGB-D images. They also introduce a complete pipeline to produce highly realistic reconstructions of virtual characters and digital asserts suitable for VR and AR applications. Another project (Geronikolakis et al. 2018) discussed the development of a cross/augmented reality application for the Industrial Museum and Cultural Center in the region of Thessaloniki, Greece, to promote the preservation of CH in the area of Central Macedonia. The presented Mixed Reality application, integrates ARKit and ARCore to implement portal-based AR virtual museum along with a gamified tour guidance and exploration of the museum's interior. The storytelling factor of the application is dominant, focusing on the history of the museum, previous expeditions and its impact to the society of Thessaloniki in micro and macro level. Storytelling, Presence and Gamification are three very important fields that should be taken into account, when creating an MR application for cultural heritage. Papagiannakis et al. (2018) presented a comparison of existing MR methods for virtual museums and pointed out the importance of these three fields for applications that contribute to the preservation of cultural heritage (Ioannides 2018). Moreover, in (Ioannides et al. 2017) fundamental elements for MR applications alongside examples are presented.

Another recent example (Zikas et al. 2016) presented two Mixed Reality Serious Games in VR and AR comparing the two technologies over their capabilities and design principles. Both applications showcased the ancient palace of Knossos in Minoan Crete, Greece through interactive mini games and a virtual/holographic tour of the archeological site using Meta AR glasses. Abate et al. (2018) successfully published an AR application for visualizing restored ancient artifacts based on algorithm that addresses geometric constraints of fragments to rebuild the object from the available parts.

12.2.3   Platforms for Gamified Content Creation

Authoring tools and other content creation platforms emerged in recent years to fulfill the need for interactive MR applications. BricklAyeR (Stefanidi et al. 2019) is a collaborative platform designed for users with limited programming skills that allows the creation of Intelligent Environments through a building-block interface. ExProtoVAR (Pfeiffer-Leßmann and Pfeiffer 2018) is a lightweight tool to create interactive virtual prototypes of AR applications designed for non-programmers lacking experience with AR interfaces. RadEd (Xiberta and Boada 2016) features a new web-based teaching framework with an integrated smart editor to create case-based exercises for image interaction, such as taking measurements, attaching labels and select specific parts of the image. It facilitates a framework as an additional tool in complex training courses like radiology. ARTIST (Kotis 2019) is a platform which provides methods and tools for real-time interaction between human and non-human characters to generate reusable, low cost and optimized MR experiences. Its aim is to develop a code-free system for the deployment and implementation of MR content, while using semantically data from heterogeneous resources. The mentioned solutions provide developing environments to generate MR experiences, however they lack of advanced authoring tools and educational curriculum to support advanced educational—training scenarios.

12.3   Mixed Reality Sample App Application

Our Sample app is a MR application, in which users are presented with basic examples of all the functionalities that our SDK supports. It is considered to be a playground for MR. We consider it as a room, where the users can experiment with the basic mechanics of our SDK, try them, and even create their own using our tools. In addition, these mechanics can be applied to other scenes as well, as they are not bound only on the specific application. The users can experience simple examples of different mechanics interacting with many objects in the scene (pick them up, hold them, even throw them), thanks to our "interactable item" utility that our SDK provides. They can use this functionality to possible objects that they will create, in order to interact with them and be able to move them around the scene with their virtual hands.

Another interesting mechanic that our SDK contains, is the virtual hands. They are automatically set up to follow and respond correctly to different kinds of controllers (Oculus, Vive, Mixed Reality, etc.). Users can easily set these hands to interact with objects of their choice. The hands are animated to perform the appropriate gesture that someone would perform in real life when the corresponding controller button is pressed. This functionality increases the realism and thus the feeling of presence in the scene.

An Inverse Kinematic (IK) object, a lamp, can be found in our MR scene, on the table. The users are free to interact with it, like any other movable objects in the scene and note how the IK mechanic works on the lamp (the base of the lamp moves with respect to the top of the lamp and vice versa), adding a great value of realism. In addition, users can use the presented IK mechanism to objects of their choice, including not only "lifeless" objects but virtual characters as well.

The Sample app application, offers a variety of interactive tasks (Actions). There is a variety of Actions where users can experiment with. Based on these Actions, users are able to create their own custom actions in the same or a new project simply by importing the SDK to their new project. Moreover, it provides the users with some basic tools (scalpel, mallet, scissors), which are in the scene during the whole operation and can be used to perform different kinds of actions. Based on these tools the users can even create their own tools to accomplish possible new actions that they will generate, according to their needs.

For the completion of some actions, (insertion of objects into specific positions) extra information is needed to inform user how to proceed and execute this interactive task. This is done with another feature that our SDK provides, which is the *holograms*. They can be easily set up and can be used to indicate the correct position and rotation of an object during an "insert action", or the movement that the users have to do with an object in order to complete a "use action" successfully. The types of actions mentioned here are described later in this work.

A strong feature of our SDK is the UIs and the aidlines that it provides. Users can easily create their own UIs, based on our prototypes as well adding advanced functionalities to occur after pressing a UI button. The UIs are fully supported and interact with the virtual hands. The aidlines are mainly used to guide inexperienced users into tricky tasks. They include arrows, which can point to the preferred direction, followed by a message to inform the users of what they need to do. A typical example would be the aidline pointing to a tool and a message telling the users to pick up the specific tool and use it in a proper way.

In Fig. 12.2, a basic example of the "Insert Action" for Sponza can be seen. The class inherits the InsertAction interface and implements the Initialize method, which is called at the beginning of the action. The method SetInsertPrefab, instantiates the interactable 3D model of Sponza in the scene and sets its final position to be the one indicated by the SponzaFinal prefab in this case. SetHoloObject generates a hologram (of the Sponza model, in this example) to the position where the interactable model should be set. Finally, the SetAidLine method generates the aidline prefab, the name of which is passed as an argument that becomes visible in the scene. Based on this prototype, the users can create their own actions from any 3D models, prefabs, holograms, aidlines etc.

Our UIs also offer another great feature. They can be used as notifications, providing helpful information to the users, as warnings, to inform them that they are possibly doing (or already did) something wrong (which may have not severe consequences but it is advisable to avoid it) and as errors to let them know that their actions caused a severe/critical error. With only a few lines of code, the users can generate whichever type of UI notification they prefer alongside a message.

```
/// <summary>
/// Example of Insert Action
/// </summary>
public class AssembleSponzaPartOfAction : InsertAction
{
    /// <summary>
    /// Initialize method overrides base.Initialize() and sets the prefab user will insert
    /// </summary>
    public override void Initialize()
    {
        //Set Prefab to insert
        //First Argument: Interactable prefab
        //Second Argument: Final prefab
        //Third Argument: Hologram
        SetInsertPrefab("Lesson0/Stage1/Action0/SponzaInteractable", "Lesson0/Stage1/Action0/SponzaFinal");
        SetHoloObject("Lesson0/Stage1/Action0/Hologram/HologramSponzaFinal");
        SetAidLine("AidLine_Decision");


        base.Initialize();
    }
}
```

Fig. 12.2   A basic example of an "insert action"

Our Sample app application also supports a multiplayer collaborative environment. Many users (up to 7+) can join a virtual room, in order to collaborate with each other and complete actions together. To support a large number of participants in the virtual environment, we implemented our custom Conformal Geometric Algebra (CGA) GPU interpolation engine to reduce the data transfer on the network. Furthermore, thanks to dual quaternions, we accomplish smoother translations and rotations for our virtual objects. Since these functionalities are a part of our SDK, any user will be able to use them to create their online sessions of their application, without encountering many difficulties.

The application described in this work, is an AR version of this playground, the main objective of which is to help developers get started with the basic components of our SDK.

12.4   Integrate AR Features into M.A.G.E.S. Platform

The M.A.G.E.S. platform was designed for VR environments, thus integrating AR support as a part of the SDK was a challenging task. Virtual Reality reflects a fully digital environment to enhance immersion and embodiment, presenting a different reality through the virtual environment. On the other hand, Augmented Reality blends the virtual and the real world through the selective rendering of holographic assets. It is important to pay attention to the augmentations we add on top of the real environment, in order for them to blend well with their surroundings, obey the laws of gravity and match the environmental illumination. As it seems, AR and VR have not much in common. They present the digital content following different principles and design patterns. The figure below illustrates a screenshot from the VR application featuring the interaction with the North Gate of the palace of Knossos (Fig. 12.3).

Fig. 12.3 Interacting with the north gate of Knossos Palace

Our goal is to transform our platform into a cross-reality SDK capable to integrate multiple technologies (AR/VR/MR) within the same system. In the following sections we will discuss how we integrated AR support into a platform designed for VR.

12.4.1 The Modular Device Controller

The initial challenge is to design the system to manage and select the deployed device. We want our application to be cross-platform, able to generate executables for different devices and operating systems. M.A.G.E.S was built on Unity3D game engine to enable this feature. Unity may support exporting to different platforms but we have to change specific application-wise parameters and design principles to truly support this mechanic. Our goal was to develop a modular platform capable to support different realities without any parametrization from the developer's side, thus we had to integrate the AR support to the core engine of our system.

Our architecture contains different components to support multiple devices and technologies. We manage the deployed devices through the device controller module, which implements the callbacks for different buttons, analog sticks and gestures. As an example, we integrated SteamVR into our device controller module to support all the compatible VR headsets like Oculus, HTC VIVE, Microsoft Mixed Reality and many more. However, HoloLens does not support SteamVR, instead they offer HoloToolKit as the native API to manage the device. To integrate HoloLens into our platform, we implemented the HoloLens controller, a module which derives

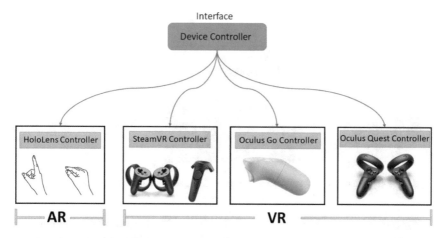

Fig. 12.4 The device controller implementation diagram featuring the AR controller (left) and the VR controllers (right)

from the generic device controller and manages the callbacks from the HoloLens controller. However, HoloLens does not have a physical controller. Instead, users interact with the holographic environment using hand gestures. For this reason, we implemented HoloLens controller to support all the gestures and interactions from Holo-ToolKit. The diagram below illustrates our modular device controller architecture which supports input from various headsets and technologies (Fig. 12.4).

This implementation offers great flexibility over the platform enabling the project to run in different devices with minimal changes. To utilize the modular device controller, right before building the executable, we need to select the device in which we are deploying the application. Device controller is represented as a component in the Unity3D editor, thus we can select the deployed device from a convenient drop down menu we designed for this reason.

12.4.2 Interaction with Holographic Objects

The M.A.G.E.S. platform gives user the ability to interact with the 3D objects and the virtual environment through the interaction module we integrated. To support runtime interaction with the virtual objects, we integrated NewtonVR physics system as the main engine to handle the manipulation of 3D assets. The interaction physics engine of NewtonVR is velocity based, which means that interaction is not relied on parenting objects to user's hand but the objects are connected to the hands according to their current velocity. This approach gives the sensation of a more natural movement than the parenting mechanism. NewtonVR has a port for Unity engine with an active community and a significant number of successful VR applications.

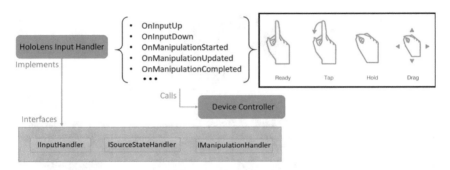

Fig. 12.5 Diagram of the interaction module with additions to support HoloLens gestures

Our interaction module is closely related to the device controller to support different headsets and devices. To integrate HoloLens platform into ours, we had to integrate the interaction system of HoloToolKit with NewtonVR. Currently, the most common way to interact with holographic objects through HoloLens is by using the pinch gesture to grab a hologram and change its position within the virtual environment. This method utilizes a simple parenting mechanic to grab the object just by switching the parenting of the object to be the user's hand position. This mechanic is simple, but offers limited functionality and poor user experience. To improve the parenting grab mechanic and to unify the interaction mechanic in our platform, we integrated the HoloLens gesture grabbing system to the NewtonVR system, that we already support in our platform. The diagram below illustrates the interaction module which manages the input from HoloLens to send feedback to the platform (Fig. 12.5).

Our methodology was to create an intermediate module between the device controller and the HoloToolKit. This module is the HoloLens Input Handler. It implements three interfaces from HoloToolKit to link the inputs from HoloLens gestures and vocal controllers directly to our platform. For example, OnInputUp method is called when user is rising his pointer, indicating the first stage of tapping gesture. When HoloLens Input Handler recognizes this gesture, it automatically calls the appropriate Device Controller method to signal our platform that the gesture was performed.

12.4.3 Port an AR Application to a VR System

At this point, we implemented the interaction module to handle the virtual assets with natural gestures. The next step is to reconstruct the augmented environment, where the user will interact with. The Sample App application (Fig. 12.6) was designed for a VR environment, thus the visualization of the 3D assets and the virtual room is fully digital. However, in AR applications, the rendered environment blends with the virtual and the real world since the augmentations do not cover the entire Field of View, but they are placed in key locations respecting physical objects.

Fig. 12.6 The VR version of our sample application

In more detail, to design the AR application, we have to keep only a small amount of digital assets and delete the majority of them to make room for the real environment. For this reason, we kept only the wooden table from the sample app room along with the interactable items and the priest of Asinou. In addition, to improve the realism of the holographic assets, we integrated a shadow plane under each object to replicate a real time shadow. This technique is simple enough but enhances the depth of field including an additional layer of illumination.

Another module we need to consider when changing the deployed medium (AR/VR) is the camera object, which represents the used HMD. For this reason, we integrated the HoloLens camera from the HoloToolKit into our system to support both cameras and technologies. In this way, developers can set the camera with a single click without the need to import any additional packages or libraries transforming sample app into a plug and play system.

12.5 An Interactive AR Cultural Heritage Application

In this work, an innovative way of supporting AR in the VR version of our cultural heritage application is presented, in which the construction and the restoration of archaeological sites is simulated. This application combines education with entertainment featuring a serious game experience. The users, who complete this simulated procedure will learn about the buildings from within the archaeological sites, since they experienced their reconstruction/restoration. This is very important for the preservation of cultural heritage, because in case such an application is installed in the museum, the users will more likely want to visit the museum again, in order to try the application once more retaining more knowledge from their additional visit(s). For this reason, we enhanced the application with gamification elements (Liarokapis et al. 2017) making the experience more appealing.

In this application, the construction of Knossos and the restoration of Sponza are simulated (Fig. 12.7), but it can also be extended to support more monuments in the future. In terms of Knossos, users can pick up the indicated parts of Knossos (for which holographic representations are used to guide the users to the correct parts) and place them in the correct positions, again indicated by the use of holographic representations. In terms of Sponza, users have to restore the building of Sponza, by placing it in the annotated position and then executing the appropriate actions to restore the damaged building to perfect condition. If the user makes an error, it is indicated in the application by applying temporarily red color to the area of the error. All the actions that are referenced above, must be executed in a specific order, in order to complete the training scenario.

The featured types of actions in this application are described below:

- **Insert Action**: The user has to pick up an object and place it in the position indicated by the corresponding hologram.
- **Remove Action**: The user has to pick up the flashing object and move it away from its current position.
- **Tool Action**: The user has to execute a specific tool-driven action (cutting with scissors or scalpel, for instance).
- **Use Action**: The user has to execute an action using an object that is not a registered tool in our SDK (wiping over a surface with a cloth, for instance).

Fig. 12.7 Main application. Restoration of Knossos (right) or Sponza (left)

Quizzes are also a part of the application. When starting the application, users are asked "Where is Sponza located?" and they have to choose one of the three proposed countries (each represented by its flag) by gazing at it and performing the tap gesture. Once the users choose an answer, both a visual (red/green color) as well as an audio feedback is given to them indicating whether they chose the correct answer or not (Fig. 12.8).

The application also features a life-sized priest, from the Asinou church, which is located in Cyprus. The priest stands behind the table all the time, watching the users executing the actions. Also, on the table in front of the priest, there is a miniature version of the Asinou church. The users can pick it up and inspect it by gazing at it and using the pinch gesture (Fig. 12.9). Once the church is picked up, the priest

Fig. 12.8 The user (top right) answering the question by performing the "tap" gesture

Fig. 12.9 The user moving an object using the "pinch" gesture

Fig. 12.10 The priest telling
history of the Asinou church
(model on the table)

notices it and starts speaking, informing users about the history of the church. As he
speaks, the priest moves his arms and his body posture in general, to emphasize the
important information in his sayings (Fig. 12.10).

The priest mentioned above, is the real priest of the Asinou church. In fact, he
was reconstructed by scanning the real priest with the occipital structure sensor, a
sensor that connects to an iPad and is able to scan real 3D geometry (Papaeftymiou
et al. 2018). After the scanning procedure, the model of the priest was improved with
additional editing software (both in terms of geometry as well as texturing) to come
correct scanning faults.

This application contributes a lot to the preservation of cultural heritage. Specifically, it provides the users with the chance to build or restore an archaeological
monument themselves. By allowing the users to be actively involved to the recon-
struction/restoration of the archaeological monuments, they gain even more knowledge by the end of the day as the application becomes more interesting and appealing
(Fig. 12.11).

The installation of gamified applications like this to museums, will lead to even
greater attraction of people of younger age to museums. Nowadays, younger people
believe that a visit to a museum is tiresome and only a few of them actually want
to visit a museum. This is mostly because they do not have something, with which
they will be able to interact. By offering interaction through immersive applications,
the knowledge that museums offer will spread more quickly to younger ages, which
will make it easier to preserve cultural heritage across generations.

Fig. 12.11 The user restoring the site by performing the action that the hologram indicates

12.6 Conclusions and Future Work

In this work, we presented a first integration of AR features in our SDK. By using the HoloToolKit for HoloLens and implementing an input handler for it that "communicated" with our Device Controller, we were able to use the gestures supported by HoloLens, in order to interact with different objects in our application. The main content of this application is the restoration of archaeological sites, in which the users can restore or reconstruct Sponza and Knossos respectively, by using gestures, which are mapped to the respective buttons of the controllers that were used in the VR mode. It is a great approach for the preservation of cultural heritage, since it provides the ability to be used in the real monuments, since the users are able to see the real world as well. By allowing, for instance, the visitors of the Knossos archaeological site to use this application on the site itself, during their visit, it will make their experience more interesting and fun, something that will increase the chance that they will visit Knossos again (in this specific example), or that they will recommend this site to others.

We also presented a 3D reconstructed virtual character for storytelling. This character tells the story of a monument (Asinou church in Cyprus), by using appropriate lips and body animations to make the interaction more realistic. This character, the priest, was reconstructed out of the real priest of the Asinou church. The fact that a virtual person exists in the application and can interact with the users, is an element that increases the feeling of presence and the realism of AR, bringing us one step closer to True AR.

During our work, we faced some limitations regarding the hardware of the holographic device. HoloLens has a rather small field of view, which does not allow the users to see the entire virtual scene, something not present in VR or in real life. Instead they are able to see the virtual scene through a small window (about 35°), which repels them from fully immersing into the virtual experience. Another limitation is the processing power, as it is significantly lower than a desktop computer, in which the VR version of this application was running flawlessly. As a result, a scene that contains a large number of 3D objects (with complex geometry) may cause frame drops in HoloLens. Thus, it would be useful to create an algorithm/plugin in the future, which will be able to revise the complex geometry of a 3D object/model automatically, that it will be able to run in devices with less processing power. Lastly, we encountered a challenge during the port of actions that required tools, which respectively needed a specific button to be pressed in order for them to be used, i.e. scissors. A possible solution for this limitation is discussed later in this section.

There are many interesting and useful goals to be considered in the future. Since it is the first time that our application is transferred to AR, the walls, ceiling and floor that were surrounding the virtual room are removed, as they did not contribute in realizing the main concept and features of AR. For the future, it is worth considering a mechanism, which will be able to detect and do this automatically. By choosing, for instance, whether the project/scene is considered to be in AR or not, or by marking the objects of the scene that we would like to remain in the AR mode, the same version of the application will be able to run correctly both in AR and VR. Also, another feature that we would like to add, is a plugin, which will set up the scene automatically (setting up all the necessary objects for the reality that interests us at the moment). The programmer will only have to choose whether this is an AR project or not and the operating system that the project will run on, in order for it to set up all the required objects for the specific platform. This feature will be a meaningful addition to our SDK, as it will allow us to quickly build any project to whichever reality we want, without setting it "by hand".

Also, another important feature that we would like to add to the AR version is the online multiplayer part. In our SDK, more than one users can join the virtual room, in order to cooperate and reconstruct the building at the same time, by helping each other or with the guidance of an expert. That feature is missing from our AR version, and it is of high priority to support it in AR as well. Apart from the online cooperation of the users from anywhere in the globe, we would also like to try mixed online sessions with users that are using the VR version of the application and users using the AR version. The users in VR will be able to roam the room and execute the actions with AR users. This cross-reality online session is a great novelty both in the field of VR/AR, as well as cultural heritage preservation.

In the future we aim to conduct a qualitative evaluation survey to examine and document the capabilities of our system in real use. Our evaluation process will be based on Qualitative Evaluation Checklist (https://wmich.edu/sites/default/files/attachments/u350/2018/qual-eval-patton.pdf) as this model reflects better our system functionalities and usage.

Finally, we aim to extend our SDK for HoloLens, in order to use voice commands, which are supported by HoloToolKit. Currently, the actions can be completed only by performing pinch and tap gestures. As HoloLens does not have any controllers, it is difficult to simulate the action where the users hold a tool with the grip button and press the trigger button to activate it at the same time. By supporting voice commands, the users will be able to hold a tool with their hand and say, for instance, a word like "use", in order to use the tool. The support of voice commands is not limited only to this, but can be more general, like giving the users the ability to execute the actions with their voice, or even more interestingly to start a conversation with the priest through dialogue-based interaction, asking him questions about the church, in order for him to provide the answers.

A video of this work is available here: https://www.dropbox.com/s/eqzpsp0xbspzhik/TrueAR.mp4?dl=0.

References

Abate A, Barra S, Galeotafiore G, Díaz C, Aura E, Sánchez M, Mas X, Vendrell Vidal E (2018) An augmented reality mobile app for museums: virtual restoration of a plate of glass. In: Proceedings of 7th international conference, EuroMed 2018, Nicosia, Cyprus, 29 Oct–3 Nov 2018, Part I. https://doi.org/10.1007/978-3-030-01762-0_47

Geronikolakis E, Tsioumas M, Bertrand S, Loupas A, Zikas P, Papagiannakis G (2018) New cross/augmented reality experiences for the virtual museums of the future. In: Proceedings of digital heritage. Progress in cultural heritage: documentation, preservation, and protection. Springer International Publishing, pp 518—527

Ioannides M et al (eds) (2018) Digital heritage. Progress in cultural heritage: documentation, preservation, and protection. In: Proceedings of 7th international conference, EuroMed 2018, Nicosia, Cyprus, 29 Oct–3 Nov 2018, vol 11196. Springer

Ioannides M, Magnenat-Thalmann N, Papagiannakis G (eds) (2017) Mixed reality and gamification for cultural heritage. Springer-Nature. https://doi.org/10.1007/978-3-319-49607-8

Jung T, Tom Dieck MC, Lee H, Chung N (2016) Effects of virtual reality and augmented reality on visitor experiences in museum. https://doi.org/10.1007/978-3-319-28231-2_45

Kotis K (2019) ARTIST—a reAl-time low-effoRt mulTi-entity Interaction System for creaTing reusable and optimized MR experiences. Res Ideas Outcomes 5:e36464. https://doi.org/10.3897/rio.5.e36464

Liarokapis F, Petridis P, Andrews D, de Freitas S (2017) Multimodal serious games technologies for cultural heritage, mixed reality and gamification for cultural heritage. Part V. Springer International Publishing, pp 371–392

Liarokapis F, Sylaiou S, Basu A, Mourkoussis N, White M, Lister PF (2004) An interactive visualisation interface for virtual museums. In: Proceedings of the 5th international symposium on virtual reality, archaeology and cultural heritage, Eurographics Association, Brussels, Belgium, 6–10 Dec, pp 47–56

Papaeftymiou M, Kanakis EM, Geronikolakis E, Nochos A, Zikas P, Papagiannakis G (2018) Rapid reconstruction and simulation of real characters in mixed reality environments. Digital cultural heritage. Lecture notes in computer science, vol 10605, pp 267–276

Papagiannakis G, Geronikolakis E, Pateraki M, Bendicho VM, Tsioumas M, Sylaiou S, Liarokapis F, Grammatikopoulou A, Dimitropoulos K, Grammalidis N, Partarakis N, Margetis G, Drossis G, Vassiliadi M, Chalmers A, Stephanidis C, Thalmann N (2018) Mixed reality gamified presence and storytelling for virtual museums

Papagiannakis G, Lydatakis N, Kateros S, Georgiou S, Zikas P (2018) Transforming medical education and training with VR using M.A.G.E.S. In: Proceedings of SIGGRAPH Asia 2018 posters, SA '18, New York, NY, USA. ACM, pp 83:1–83:2

Pfeiffer-Leßmann N, Pfeiffer T (2018) ExProtoVAR: a lightweight tool for experience-focused prototyping of augmented reality applications using virtual reality. https://doi.org/10.1007/978-3-319-92279-9_42

Qualitative Evaluation Checklist. https://wmich.edu/sites/default/files/attachments/u350/2018/qual-eval-patton.pdf. Accessed 12 Oct 2019

Sandor C, Fuchs M, Cassinelli A, Li H, Newcombe R, Yamamoto G, Feiner S (2015) Breaking the barriers to true augmented reality

Stefanidi E, Arampatzis D, Leonidis A, Papagiannakis G (2019) BricklAyeR: a platform for building rules for AmI environments in AR. https://doi.org/10.1007/978-3-030-22514-8_39

Sylaiou S, Mania K, Paliokas I, Pujol-Tost L, Kilintzis V, Liarokapis F (2017) Exploring the educational impact of diverse technologies in online virtual museums. Int J Arts Technol (IJART) 10(1):58–84 Inderscience Publishers

White M, Mourkoussis N, Darcy J, Petridis P, Liarokapis F, Lister PF, Walczak K, Wojciechowski R, Cellary W, Chmielewski J, Stawniak M, Wiza W, Patel M, Stevenson J, Manley J, Giorgini F, Sayd P, Gaspard F (2004) ARCO-an architecture for digitization, management and presentation of virtual exhibitions. In: Proceedings of the 22nd international conference on computer graphics (CGI'2004), Hersonissos, Crete, 16–19 June, pp 622–625. IEEE Computer Society

Xiberta P, Boada I (2016) A new e-learning platform for radiology education (RadEd). Comput Methods Programs Biomed 126:63–75. https://doi.org/10.1016/j.cmpb.2015.12.022. ISSN 0169-2607

Zikas P, Bachlitzanakis V, Papaefthymiou M, Kateros S, Georgiou S, Lydatakis N, Papagiannakis G (2016) Mixed reality serious games for smart education. In: European conference on games based learning 2016, ECGBL'16

Part IV
Serious Games

Chapter 13
Transforming Heritage Crafts to Engaging Digital Experiences

Nikolaos Partarakis, Xenophon Zabulis, Margherita Antona and Constantine Stephanidis

Abstract **Heritage Crafts** (HCs) involve craft artefacts, materials, and tools and encompass craftsmanship as a form of Intangible Cultural Heritage. Intangible HC dimensions include dexterity, know-how, and skilled use of tools, as well as identity and traditions of the communities in which craftsmanship is, or was, practiced. HCs are part of history and have impact upon the economy of the areas in which they flourish. Despite their **cultural significance**, efforts towards HC digital representation and presentation are scattered. In this chapter, as a first step towards the **Representation** and **Presentation** of Heritage Crafts as cultural heritage (CH), pertinent requirements and needed technological components are investigated. **Representation** is expected to capture the wide spectrum of knowledge that a HC covers, from objects and their making, to hand gestures and tool uses that define craft motor skills, to the societal value, economic impact, and historical significance of HCs. **Presentation** is expected to address the need of exploiting **Representation** to conserve cultural resources, contribute to their accurate interpretation, provide essential and authentic experiences, as well as stimulate revenues of cultural resources through thematic tourism. This chapter lays the foundations and envisions the further development and formalisation of a suitable approach to HC representation and presentation in the form of a generic protocol that together with the appropriate technological tools can be applied to any HC instance.

N. Partarakis · X. Zabulis · M. Antona · C. Stephanidis (✉)
Institute of Computer Science, Foundation for Research and Technology – Hellas (FORTH),
100 N. Plastira Str., 70013 Heraklion, Crete, Greece
e-mail: cs@ics.forth.gr

N. Partarakis
e-mail: partarak@ics.forth.gr

X. Zabulis
e-mail: zabulis@ics.forth.gr

M. Antona
e-mail: antona@ics.forth.gr

C. Stephanidis
Computer Science Department, University of Crete, Heraklion, Crete, Greece

© Springer Nature Switzerland AG 2020
F. Liarokapis et al. (eds.), *Visual Computing for Cultural Heritage*, Springer Series on Cultural Computing, https://doi.org/10.1007/978-3-030-37191-3_13

13.1 Introduction

Cultural Heritage (CH) is the legacy of physical artefacts and intangible attributes of a group or society that are inherited from past generations, maintained in the present and bestowed for the benefit of future generations. Such physical artefacts are items of Tangible CH (TCH) and include buildings, historic places, monuments and artefacts, as well as objects significant to the archaeology, architecture, science or technology of a specific culture (Kalay et al. 2007).

Intangible CH (ICH) regards the practices, representations, expressions, knowledge, skills—as well as the instruments, objects, artefacts and cultural spaces—that communities, groups, and individuals recognize as part of their CH. ICH is transmitted from generation to generation, and is constantly recreated by communities and groups in response to their environment and their interaction with nature and history. ICH provides a sense of identity and continuity, thus promoting respect for cultural diversity and human creativity (UNESCO 2003b). Thus, in contrast to TCH, ICH requires its practice by human participants, in order to exist, or otherwise, be preserved.

ICH includes oral traditions, performing arts, social practices, knowledge and practices concerning nature and the universe, as well as the knowledge and skills to produce traditional crafts (UNESCO 2003b). Crafts are defined as "an occupation or trade requiring manual dexterity or artistic skill" (Meriam-Webster on Craft). Crafts are characterised by a certain type of making, in which objects are created by hand through the skilled use of tools (Donkin 2001), to make or repair objects of functional use (Jennings 2012) and not solely of ornamental value. Nevertheless, very often, craft and artistic creation are related and craft products may be also works of art (Markowitz 1994). Often, a craft is medium specific or characterised by a type of product, as well as the handicraft or technologies required for its making (Metcalf 1993). Craftsmanship differs from industrial production as "the quality of the result is not predetermined, but depends on the judgement, dexterity and care which the maker exercised" (Pye 1968). In this chapter, we call Heritage Crafts (HCs) the crafts that are of significance to Cultural Heritage. A baseline towards the definition of HC is "practices which employ manual dexterity and skill, and an understanding of traditional materials, designs and techniques" (Jennings 2012).

In this chapter, we also aim to describe the requirements towards a systematic approach for HC representation and presentation. Moreover, we aim at defining additional requirements that stem from using such representation to:

1. Contribute to CH with technically appropriate and scientifically correct representations for craft preservation, as well as captivating and accurate narratives for CH audiences.
2. Stimulate revenues to fund craft preservation. Global trends in valorisation of CH indicate that the digital representation of CH is recommended[1] and of significance to support the economic resource yielded through heritage and thematic tourism.

---

[1]UNWTO Annual Report 2017: https://www.e-unwto.org/doi/pdf/10.18111/9789284419807.

3. Provide engaging educational tools, as well as attract interest to craft practice, thus increasing motivation for craft conservation. Part of the demotivation of younger generation towards the practice of HC is the lack of certification. Using a craft representation can provide the basis of certifying authenticity and traditional making of a product.

Prior to reviewing the state of the art and proposing requirements towards craft representation and presentation, we make more specific the scope of craft. Crafts include materials, tools, and products, while also knowledge, dexterous skill, know-how, traditions, as well as the sense of identity belonging to the communities in which they are, or were, practiced. Crafts of significance to CH, such as traditional crafts, are called **Heritage Crafts** (HCs). HC preservation is nowadays particularly urgent, as "several are threatened with extinction, due to the declining numbers of practitioners and apprentices" (UNESCO 2003b) (UNESCO), which is caused by lack of interest in younger generations, lack of authenticity certification, and urbanization (UNESCO 2003b).

Craftsmanship has been interwoven with mythology, religion and folklore of communities. Like any form of ICH, HCs are performed by persons. As such, they include historic, geographical, artistic, traditional, economic, and religious dimensions. HCs have a cross-border nature and are objects of cultural exchange. They are part of the history, the economic life and progress of the communities in which they have flourished.

Craft communities and guilds have been relevant to state and religious politics in the past, and avail a historic understanding of the formation of common origins of modern societies, cities, and nations since the Renaissance. They are also relevant to the distribution of wealth, the formation of social classes and, thereby, social and political changes.

Craftsmanship has contributed very significantly to change and progress in the history of humanity, from the first making of tools, to their mechanisation and automation that led to the Industrial Revolution, to the Arts and Crafts movement that retained art in usable items, to contemporary industrial design. The significance, the materials, the tools and practice of crafts, varies over time. The study of HCs can provide essential knowledge in historical, societal and economic topics, and the significance of HCs can only be understood against these contexts, which have a strong interdisciplinary nature.

13.2 State-of-the-Art in Craft Representation and Presentation

HCs cover a broad spectrum of tangible and intangible dimensions, whose representation requires the contribution of multiple scientific disciplines. Correspondingly, multiple dimensions related to multiple types of tangible and intangible content which, in turn, may require different ways of presentation or may concern different audiences.

13.2.1 Historical Research on the Practice of HCs

Existing works on the description of specific craft instances include literature studies, documentaries, and inscriptions (Hecht 1989; Geijer 1979). A wide range of textual HC descriptions are available online from the UNESCO's World Heritage Portal.[2] UNESCO identified the need of testimonies in the "Living Human Treasures" programme, which encourages official recognition to talented tradition bearers and practitioners. Accordingly, UNESCO has been recording and archiving intangible forms of cultural expressions, including HCs.[3]

Efforts towards appropriate treatment of preservation and curation of HC knowledge have emerged, through the collaboration of a wide range of experts by UNESCO, providing a theoretic basis towards the representation of ICH (UNESCO 2003b). Tangible and intangible craft dimensions have been outlined in Donkin (2001).

International projects underpin the need for documentation and preservation of craft knowledge. The Erasmus+ EU programme "Discovering Traditional Crafts across Europe" aims to such traditional crafts, some of which are slowly disappearing from today's societies. Several national projects have been funded in China through the "Chinese Craft Project" that targets promotion and preservation of Chinese ICH. Folk art preservation has the focus of national projects in Italy (Barra 2012).

13.2.2 Digitization of TCH

Progress during the last two decades in standardizing TCH digitization has provided guidelines on how to digitize printed matter and 3D objects, as well as monuments of cultural heritage. Guidelines regarding file management, digital preservation, online publication, and IPR management have been elaborated,[4] as well as by online heritage repositories, such as Europeana (Aloia et al. 2011).

The most common digitisation modality is **photographic documentation**. It is relevant to the digitisation of 2D (i.e. documents, paintings) or 3D items (i.e. materials, man-made objects). Good practice and strategic guidelines have been compiled as a result of digitisation projects (ETH-Bibliothek 2016; Brosseau et al. 2006; CARLI Digital Collections Users' Group 2016). The development of technologies for the **3D digitisation** of artefacts and monuments has allowed the representation and documentation of geometrical and structural information. Several modalities have been developed, each of which addresses different circumstances and requirements and records different characteristics of the scanned physical object including scanning techniques, authenticity, realism, complexity, documentation, lightweight web deployable scans, etc. (Arnold and Geser 2008; Scopigno et al. 2011; Pratikakis et al. 2018; Kasnesis et al. 2019; Vico 2018; D'Andrea et al. 2012). Furthermore

---

[2]https://whc.unesco.org/en/list/.

[3]https://unesdoc.unesco.org/archives.

[4]http://www.minervaeurope.org/.

research efforts have resulted to digitisation guidelines to assist new digitisation efforts (3D-ICONS 2014). Besides digital preservation, the significance of accurate digitisation is important to the conservation of TCH.

13.2.3 Digitization of CH Activities

Digitisation of ICH has included human activities as well as the capture of semantic concepts and contextual knowledge (e.g. historical, religious, economic, and social). **Human motion** is a key component of many forms of ICH such as dances, crafts, and rituals. Human motion has been the target of ICH digitisation with research efforts targeting singing, dancing,[5] theatrical performances[6] traditional crafts, etc. (Dimitropoulos et al. 2014; Camurri et al. 2016; Giannoulakis et al. 2018; Dimitropoulos 2018; Doulamis Anastasios et al. 2017). The context of crafts binds together the intangible dimension of human motion, skill and design, with tangible objects such as tools, materials and artefacts. Digitisation of human motion has been achieved by a number of methods. Two main method categories are **Motion Capture** (or MoCap), which requires human subjects wear technological items (Brigante et al. 2011), such as markersor sensors, and **Visual Tracking** methods, which do not impose such requirement. MoCap technologies measure the movement of subjects in 3D. Two main technologies are used: optical and inertial measurement. The results encapsulate human motion in 3D with great detail and provide a complete representation of the recorded motion. Visual Tracking methods use visual sensors to record human subjects (Cao et al. 2017). Motion is estimated in 3D by processing of the visual stream. The cost of the unobtrusive nature of these methods is the confrontation with the problem of treating visual occlusions and the inference of subject motion missing from the acquired images, due to these occlusions. Visual tracking is of particular importance for documentation of CH, because it means that a 3D representation of motion can be obtained from documentaries and archive footage.

Intangible heritage also includes **audio assets** such as testimonies, songs, and music. International digitisation projects have provided guidelines and standard for audio recordings and their digital preservation (IFLA/UNESCO 1999; Bradley 2006; UNESCO 2003a, 2016; Bradley et al. 2007).

13.2.4 Representation of Contextual and Semantic Knowledge

The representation of semantic knowledge is important as it can capture both abstract and contextual information (e.g. historic, social, economic and political context).

---

[5]http://www.modul-dance.eu/wp-content/uploads/2015/02/Modul-dance-book.pdf.
[6]https://www.europeantheatrelab.eu/.

One of the most important efforts towards knowledge representation in CH provided an approach towards making knowledge sharable between communities of people, culture, languages and computers through an open platform for mining facts (Vossen et al. 2010). In the same context, representation of collections of heterogeneous data (Carmel et al. 2012) and the provision of ways to access and to preserve cultural and scientific resources (Giaretta 2008; Doulamis 2017) remains crucial.

As sources of such knowledge include records and historical documents, relevant efforts include the conversion from digitised conventional and historic documents to text. In this context, the use of tools for the digitisation of historical documents (scans) into textual information, through state-of-the-art OCR (Neudecker and Tzadok 2010), is considered important. Furthermore, tools and approaches for the indexing, search and full transcription of information from historical handwritten document images were developed in (Sánchez et al. 2013) and are available through a web portal for structured crowdsourcing transcription projects.

From an ICT perspective, the use of ontologies for describing and classifying objects is now a well-established practice in the CH sector. The Getty vocabulary databases, maintained by the Getty Vocabulary Program, provide a solid basis that is a de facto standard in the area.[7] These databases are thesauri compliant with the ISO standard for thesaurus construction. They comprise: the Art & Architecture Thesaurus (AAT), the Union List of Artist Names (ULAN) and the Getty Thesaurus for Geographic Names (TGN). The AAT, in particular, contains more than thirty thousand concepts, including terms, descriptions, bibliographic citations and other information relating to art. The AAT is organized as a hierarchy with seven levels, called facets, in which a term may have more than one broader term. The Getty Research Institute has also developed a metadata schema, called the Categories for the Description of Works of Art (CDWA), for describing art works. CDWA includes 381 categories and sub-categories, a small subset of which are considered core, in the sense that they represent the minimum information necessary to identify and describe a work. Complementary to CDWA, the Conceptual Reference Model (CRM) of the International Committee for Documentation of the International Council of Museums (ICOM-CIDOC) has emerged as a conceptual basis for reconciling different metadata schemas.[8] CRM provides definitions and a formal structure for describing the implicit and explicit concepts and relationships used in cultural heritage documentation. CRM is an ISO standard (21127:2006) that has been integrated with the Functional Requirements for Bibliographic Records (FRBR) and the Europeana Data Model,[9] which plays the role of upper ontology for integrating metadata schemes of libraries, archives and museums.

---

[7]http://www.getty.edu/research/tools/vocabularies/index.html.

[8]http://www.cidoc-crm.org/.

[9]http://pro.europeana.eu/web/guest/edm-documentation.

13.2.5 Knowledge Based Narratives

The emergence of rich methods for the representation of contextual and semantic knowledge calls for new approaches to the presentation of such knowledge in various contexts and for various purposes, such as education and training. Narratives can be used to construct explanations and make sense of the world (Mulholland and Collins 2002). In this chapter, narratives are referred to as particular ways in which stories can be told. A story can be considered as a conceptual space representing events, people and objects that may be presented in alternative ways, to create different effects and to target different user categories (Brooks 1996).

Computational narratology (Mani 2012) studies narratives from a computation perspective. In the Artificial Intelligence field, computational narratology refers to story generation systems, i.e. computer applications that create a symbolic (written, spoken, or visual) presentation of a story, typically based on a story grammar. Recently, ontologies were used to generate narratives. For example, MAKEBE-LIEVE (Liu and Singh 2002) uses common sense knowledge, selected from the ontology of the Open Mind Commonsense Knowledge Base (Singh 2002), to generate short stories from an initial one given by the user. ProtoPropp (Gervás et al. 2005) uses an ontology of explicitly relevant knowledge and the Case-Based Reasoning method over a defined set of tales. In FABULIST (Riedl and Young 2010), the user supplies a description of an initial state of the world and a specific goal, and the system identifies the best sequence of actions to reach the goal. **The concept of event is a core element of narratology theory and of narrative**. People conventionally refer to an event as an occurrence taking place at a certain time at a specific location. Various models have been developed for representing events on the Semantic Web, e.g. Event Ontology (Raimond and Abdallah 2007), Linking Open Descriptions of Events (LODE) (Shaw et al. 2009), and the F-Model (Scherp et al. 2009). More general models for semantic data organization are CIDOC-CRM (Doerr 2003), the ABC ontology (Lagoze and Hunter 2006), and the Europeana Data Model (Doerr et al. 2010). Narratives have been recently proposed to enhance the information contents and functionality of Digital Libraries, with special emphasis on information discovery and exploration. For example, in Lopez de Lacalle (2012), a system is proposed that acts as an interactive personalized tour guide through existing digital library collections. In the same context, in (Wolff et al. 2012) a system is proposed that allows describing stories that span museum objects while (van den Akker et al. 2012) developed methods and techniques to support the narrative understanding of objects in VMs collections.

13.2.6 Presentation of CH Through Digital Experiences

Telling stories through immersive cultural experiences provides the feeling of being inside the story (Stogner 2011). Although the reader of a book often has the feeling of being immersed in the story, new technology offers additional potential as the reader can explore a virtual world, perhaps from the viewpoint of one of the characters in the story (Mulholland and Collins 2002). Furthermore, immersive experiences provide a "sense of place" and a "sense of time" contributing to the creation of memories that bind the audience to the story. Examples of engaging storytelling experiences include (a) exploring collections by creating conceptual paths, linking the items (Clough et al. 2011); (b) exploring digital collections as part of coherent narratives, which included the knowledge structures that connect them and give them meaning (De Polo 2011); and (c) exploring collections through interactive stories for visitors of cultural sites, authored by curators (Pujol et al. 2012).

In this section a short overview of immersive technologies currently exploited in the presentation CH content is provided.

13.2.6.1   Interactive Technologies

Cultural Heritage Institutions seek new ways to attract and engage new visitors. One of the ways to obtain competitive advantage is the investment and implementation of interactive experiences on site (Tscheu and Buhalis 2016). Over the years, several technologies have emerged each of which provides different forms of interaction and different level of immersion, but also poses different requirements in terms of space, setup and deployment. In this sub-section, the most prominent of these technologies are presented.

Virtual Reality (VR): An example of a high immersion VR environment for CH is Kivotos, a VR environment that uses the CAVE® system, in a room of 3 m by 3 m, where the walls and the floor act as projection screens and in which visitors take off on a journey thanks to stereoscopic 3D glasses.[10]

Augmented Reality (AR): AR exhibition offers more advantages to museum visitors as virtual information is overlaid upon video frames captured by a camera, giving users the impression that the virtual cultural artworks actually exist in the real environment. AR has been experimentally applied to make it possible to visualize incomplete or broken real objects as they were in their original state by superimposition of the missing parts (Liarokapis and White 2005). The ARCO system (ARCO 2013; White et al. 2004) provides customized tools for virtual museum environments, ranging from the digitization of museum collections to the tangible visualization of both museum galleries and artworks.

Mixed reality (MR): MR relies on a combination of VR, AR and the real environment. According to Milgram and Kishino's virtuality-continuum, real world and virtual world objects are presented together on a single display (e.g. the screen of a mobile phone) (Milgram and Kishino 1994) that displays the visual representation of both the real and the virtual space (Hughes et al. 2005). An example of the use of MR techniques in a museum environment is the Situating Hybrid Assemblies in Public Environments (SHAPE) project (Hall et al. 2001) that uses hybrid reality technology

---

[10]Foundation of the Hellenic World: http://www.ime.gr.

to enhance users' social experience and learning in museum and other exhibition environments, with regard to cultural artworks and to their related contexts.

X-Reality: AR, VR and MR applications when coexisting in a physical context are referred to as X-Reality (Extended Reality) or XR applications (Fast-Berglund et al. 2018). The use of such technologies has the potential to enrich the information of cultural heritage artefacts and museum exhibits and turn passive visitors into active participants engaged in an interactive and immersive blend of physical and virtual as if it was a single unified "world" (Margetis et al. 2019).

13.2.6.2 Storytellers

Virtual characters can be well suited as museum storytellers, due to their inherent ability to simulate verbal as well as nonverbal communicative behaviour (Jung et al. 2011). This type of interface is made possible through multimodal dialog systems, which extend common speech dialog systems with additional modalities similarly to human-human interaction (Jung et al. 2011). The visual representation of a character including its perceivable behaviour, from a decoding perspective, such as facial expressions and gestures, belongs to the domain of computer graphics and likewise implicates many open issues concerning natural communication. However, employing virtual characters as personal and believable dialog partners in multi-modal dialogs entails several challenges, because this requires not only a reliable and consistent motion and dialog behaviour, but also nonverbal communication and affective components. Over the last decade, there has been a considerable amount of success in creating interactive, conversational, virtual agents, including Ada and Grace, a pair of virtual Museum guides at the Boston Museum of Science (Swartout et al. 2010), the INOTS and ELITE training systems at the Naval Station in Newport and Fort Benning (Campbell et al. 2011), and the SimSensei system designed for healthcare support (DeVault et al. 2014). There is also some precedence for the use of virtual agents in facilitating anti-bullying education, such as the FearNot! application developed by Aylett et al. (2007).

13.3 Requirements of Heritage Craft Representation and Presentation

In this chapter, as a first step towards the **Representation** and **Preservation** of HCs, pertinent requirements are investigated. These high level requirements have been solidified through an extensive literature review and an iterative requirements elicitation process, based on multiple collection methods, as outlined below.

Brainstorming, where mixed groups of ICT experts (interactive technologies, semantic knowledge representation, storytelling, narratives authoring) and domain experts (HCs professionals, museum personnel, curators) participate in order to define the basic steps towards craft representation and presentation.

Focus groups with experts. These groups target a single technology or single step to elaborate technical requirements.

Scenario building, following a co-design process where experts and end users are formulating scenarios of use. These sessions focus on how perceivably users wish to interact and experience HCs.

13.3.1 Representation

Representation is required to capture the wide spectrum of knowledge that HC cover, from objects and their making, to hand gestures and tool uses that define craft motor skills, to societal value, economic impact, and historical significance of HCs.

13.3.1.1 Collection of Digital Assets for HC Documentation

HC **Representation** involves the definition of information regarding both the tangible and intangible dimensions of HCs. Indicatively, tangible dimensions regard materials, artefacts and tools. Intangible information regards the way of making, the skills required, the teaching process, as well as personal creativity. Intangible information would furthermore answer questions about religious or political dimensions, the role of guilds, and the impact of the HC on local communities and society. As HCs have an economic dimension, such information should provide answers to questions about the origin of materials, the cost of the products and the ways these products are sold (e.g. local craft stores, festivals), trade and export of products, and impact on economy, culture, and the lives of people. Archives, documentaries, literature, and linked data repositories are important and can be enriched with artefact reconstructions. Contributions from human resources and LHTs should also be collected through workshops, collaborative and participatory activities with craft practitioners, testimonies and demonstrations.

Technical requirements: Digital assets identification, identification of Linked Data Repositories, digitization of new content using existing asset digitization technologies (scanning, 3D reconstruction, photography, etc.) and implementation of basic asset storage facilities prior to knowledge representation.

13.3.1.2 Basic Knowledge Representation

Basic knowledge representation regards the gathering, annotation and documentation of content from heterogeneous sources, such as 3D digitisation, motion capture, textual, records, documents, etc. This requires the definition of a Crafts Ontology (CrO) that includes a vocabulary of terms to be used upon data entry. Information will be comprised of existing digital assets or new digitisations, such as in the case of expert motion capture. The CrO should represent tangible and intangible knowledge of the HC. Entries should contain knowledge about tangible aspects, human motion representation, processes as sequences of motions, and intangible aspects extracted from sources such as records, descriptions and testimonies. An authoring interface for annotating and inputting the digital assets into the HC repository can assist this phase.

Technical requirements: Definition of a crafts ontology (CrO), usage of advanced digitization technologies (e.g. Motion Capture) and implementation of the appropriate authoring tools to provide access to scholars, researchers and communities to the CrO.

13.3.1.3 Semantic Representation of Knowledge

The basic knowledge representation is not sufficient. Establishing semantic links between the digital assets and contextual information (e.g. historic, social, economic and political context) is required in order to instantiate the model of a HC into a HC representation. Information should be encoded using the HC vocabulary and should conform to the CrO. The Semantic representation of Knowledge can benefit from a collaborative or participatory approach in authoring descriptions and HC attributes, ensuring that complementary stakeholder perspectives are included in the HC representation. The outcome of these activities would comprises the digital representation of the HC.

Technical requirements: The CrO and vocabulary should be extended and or modified to address new representation requirements. Pertinent tools should enable: (i) authoring semantic descriptions, (ii) establishing links between model entities, and (iii) connect digital assets.

13.3.1.4 Definition of Semantic Narratives

The rationalisation of the vast amount of information around a HC should be assisted by the formal semantic representation and linkage of content. This should result in fundamental text based narratives for the following reasons: (a) rationalisation will lead to links between threads and shreds of history; (b) rationalisation can lead to the emergence of new links that can form storylines; and (c) rationalisation will help the creation of a well-defined and thus ease to manage knowledge base. The first step for authoring semantic narratives is the definition of text based narratives to act as a baseline of information for their technical implementation in the semantic model. Then the **authoring of semantic narratives** should be aided by narrative generation tools that capitalize on the achieved HC representation. Narratives should contain links to digital assets and multimedia (i.e. motion-driven narratives, documentaries, 3D digitisations) in order to create engaging storylines and bind stories with traditions, items, testimonies, etc.

Technical requirements: A narrative authoring environment that is based on the HC representation and assists the authoring of comprehension and motion-driven narratives, which include links to CrO entities and instances. Possibly this environment could be an extension of the authoring tools.

13.3.2 Presentation

Presentation addresses the need of exploiting the representation described above to preserve cultural resources, contribute to their accurate interpretation, provide essential and authentic fruition experiences, as well as stimulate revenues of cultural resources through thematic tourism.

13.3.2.1 Informational Applications

HC representation and narratives could be availed through the authoring tools providing access to general and scientific audiences. Both access types could support appropriate querying and browsing capabilities on the HC representation. Research access could expose query mechanisms for digital assets and semantic information. Composite queries could also be available, such as ones targeting the monitoring contextual information in time, or comparative assessment of HCs.

Access to HC communities, makers, tourists and the general public could be available through a portal view of the repository and HC representation. Online applications for practitioners and HC communities could provide an opportunity for virtual promotional exhibitions, documentation of product authenticity, and collaboration with local tourism industries. Such a platform could also host virtual exhibitions authored by curators. All represented content, digital assets, authored narratives, and educational experiences could be customized for on-line access and provided through the platform.

Technical requirements: a portal view of the authoring tools for providing access to communities to HC knowledge advanced querying mechanisms, co-designed applications for practitioners.

13.3.2.2 Storytelling Applications

Storytelling applications can acquire content from the produced narratives and the HC representation to provide multifaceted presentations of HCs. These presentations can provide comprehensive views of HCs and be enriched with digital assets. Contextualized and personalised versions of these narrations are authored to tell the story from multiple perspectives (e.g. geographic, technological and contextualize the economic and societal impact and its evolution along the course of time. Presentations can also be personalized according to user context and multiple profiles (e.g. practitioner, customer). Storytelling can be availed through mobile platforms and a virtual character playing the role of an interactive narrator and, also, through the authoring environment. AR can augment real exhibits showing illustrated annotations upon digital assets (e.g. human motion and tool handling upon documentaries or practitioner recordings).

Technical requirements: Storytelling components utilize narratives to create HC presentations and stories. Storytelling may be implemented through augmentations of the craft workspace with virtual characters acting as guides, VR environments that provide immersive storytelling experiences, dissemination through online virtual storytelling applications, etc.

13.3.2.3 Educational Applications

Educational applications could target HC skill-learning and introductory experiences to HCs. First-person acquaintance applications to basic skills can be implemented through MR, which could allow the manipulation of virtual and real objects and tools. The educational scenario could be mediated by an interactive virtual character playing the role of the craft master, while the visitor assumes the apprentice role. A version of the educational applications could be adapted for access through the online authoring environment.

Potential applications include demonstrations of skills and processes, powered by intuitive visualizations of practitioner movements and techniques, as well as illustrated and animated instructions. The craft master uses instructions and motion-driven narratives to explain the task to the user (apprentice), who needs to exercise. User hands are tracked and gesture recognition is utilized to produce actions in the virtual world. Hand-tracking and gesture recognitions can be registered, and compared with recordings from LHTs or documentaries. The craft master may optionally provide feedback and advice on the performance of the technique. Depending on the application, HC, and user context, accurate achievement of dexterity may be optional; e.g. may not require accurate mimic master dexterity and may utilise approximate gestures, or simply required issuing of appropriate commands that implement a crafting process.

Technical requirements: Augmentation of expert motion and summative visualisations for educational purposes. MR applications that host educational experiences and allow users to learn and replicate basic craft movements. Real-time motion tracking monitors user skills. Motion registration visualizes and compares user motion with digitised functional testimonies. The authoring tools are facilitated as a means of providing access to educational material such as tutorials, step by step guides, books, etc.

13.4   Discussion and Future Work

This chapter has presented the significance of HC as CH and the urgent need for HC representation, preservation and conservation. HCs are related to the origins of modern societies, their history, and culture, have economic and societal impact, as well as, impact on gender roles. HCs have a paramount cultural value and offer a thematic thesaurus of stories and narratives of which general audiences can relate to. As such, they exhibit potential for valorisation due to the captivating content of stories, memories, and meaning that a representation of HCs can offer. Although technically many of the basic ingredients to achieve such a representation do exist they remain unconnected.

Preservation of HCs calls for a systematic process of their **representation** and **presentation**. To this end, this chapter has defined the basic requirements. This remains a work in progress with the envisioned outcome to be formalised in the near future in the form of a protocol. This representation should: (a) cover tangible and intangible HC dimensions; (b) adhere to digitisation standards for CH documentation; (c) formally represent knowledge and semantics; (d) aid the capture characteristic craft qualities; (e) provide computational ways to create narratives for HC documentation and preservation; and (f) contribute to the design and implementation of applications that: (i) aid CH professionals in digital curation and CH research; (ii) support HC educators in the transmission of HC knowledge, and (ii) provide stimulation for revenues of cultural resources through thematic tourism.

Limitations of the proposed approach relate to the extent that technology can be used to represent and present intangible dimensions of HCs. Such a dimension lacking is the type of "felt" or sensory knowledge based on the sensory perception of practitioners. This is the practitioner's interpretation of his/her own qualia,[11] to perceive the materials and her makings. Examples are the haptic sensation of a material (i.e. plaster dampness of the potter, or roughness of a textile), the sensations of heat and smell (i.e., in the glassmaking process), or the colour of an object, which are exploited by a skilled practitioner.

Another limitation is the representation and assessment of artistic content embedded in craft products. Although the representation of the artistic dimensions can be further elaborated in multiple ways by including e.g. the principles of composition in art (unity, balance, movement, rhythm, etc.) there will always be a difficulty on representing and therefore presenting how someone can become an artist and therefore produce new art.

Acknowledgements This chapter reports research work conducted in the context of the EU Horizon 2020 research and innovation programme under grant agreement No. 822336 (Mingei).

---

[11] Qualia are subjective, conscious experiences or "the ways things seem to us" (Dennett 1988).

References

3D-ICONS (2014) Guidelines & case studies. 3D-ICONS is a project funded under the European Commission's ICT Policy Support Programme, project no. 297194

Aloia N, Concordia C, Meghini C (2011) Europeana v1. 0. In: Italian research conference on digital libraries. Springer, Berlin, Heidelberg, pp 127–129

ARCO (Augmented Representation of Cultural Objects) consortium (2003). http://www.arco-web.org

Arnold D, Geser G (2008) EPOCH research agenda for the applications of ICT to cultural heritage. EPOCH project

Aylett R, Vala M, Sequeira P, Paiva A (2007) FearNot!—an emergent narrative approach to virtual dramas for anti-bullying education. Lecture Notes Comput Sci 4871:202–205. https://doi.org/10.1007/978-3-540-77039-8_19

Barra G (2012) Chinese craft project, Politecnico Di Milano, M.Sc. thesis

Bradley K (2006) Risks associated with the use of recordable CDs and DVDs as reliable storage media in archival collections: strategies and alternatives

Bradley K, Lei J, Blackall C (2007) Memory of the world: towards an open source repository and preservation system. In: Conference: meeting of the international advisory committee of the memory of the world programme, Pretoria, South Africa

Brigante C, Abbate N, Basile A, Faulisi A, Sessa S (2011) Towards miniaturization of a MEMS-based wearable motion capture system. IEEE Trans Ind Electron 58(8):3234–3241

Brooks KM (1996) Do story agents use rocking chairs? The theory and implementation of one model for computational narrative. In: ACM Mutlimedia '96, Boston, MA

Brosseau K, Choquette M, Renaud L (2006) Digitization standards for the Canadian Museum of Civilization Corporation. Version 1.1

Campbell JC, Hays MJ, Core M, Birth M, Bosack M, Clark RE (2011) Interpersonal and leadership skills: using virtual humans to teach new officers. In: Proceedings of interservice/industry training, simulation, and education conference (I/ITSEC). IITSEC

Camurri A, Canepa C, Ferrari N, Mancini M, Niewiadomski R, Piana S, Volpe G, Matos J-M, Palacio P, Romero M (2016) A system to support the learning of movement qualities in dance: a case study on dynamic symmetry. In: BodySenseUX workshop, held in conjunction with UBICOMP

Cao Z, Simon T, Wei S, Sheikh Y (2017) Realtime multi-person 2D pose estimation using part affinity fields. In: Proceedings of CVPR

CARLI Digital Collections Users' Group (2016) Guidelines for the creation of digital collections. Consortium of Academic and Research Libraries at the University of Illinois

Carmel D, Zwerdling N, Yogev S (2012) Entity oriented search and exploration for cultural heritage collections: the EU cultura project. In: Proceedings of the 21st international conference on world wide web, pp 227–230. ACM

Clough P, Ford N, Stevenson M (2011) Personalizing access to cultural heritage collections using pathways. In: International workshop on personalized access to cultural heritage

D'Andrea A, Niccolucci F, Bassett S, Fernie K (2012) 3D-ICONS: world heritage sites for Europeana: Making complex 3D models available to everyone. In: 2012 18th international conference on virtual systems and multimedia. IEEE, pp 517–520

De Polo A (2011) Digital environment for cultural interfaces: promoting heritage education and research. In: Proceedings of museums and the web 2011. Arch Mus Inform. Toronto

Dennett D (1988) Quining Qualia. In: Marcel A, Bisiach E (eds) Consciousness in modern science, Oxford University Press. In: Lycan W (ed) (1990) Mind and cognition: a reader. MIT Press (Reprinted). In: Goldman (ed) (1993) Readings in philosophy and cognitive science. MIT Press

DeVault D, Artstein R, Benn G, Dey T, Fast E, Gainer A, Georgila K, Gratch J, Hartholt A, Lhommet M, Lucas G, Marsella S, Morbini F, Nazarian A, Scherer S, Stratou G, Suri A, Traum D, Wood R, Xu Y, Rizzo A, Morency L-P (2014) SimSensei Kiosk: a virtual human interviewer for healthcare decision support. In: Proceedings of the 2014 international conference on autonomous agents and multi-agent systems. IEEE, pp 1061–1068

Dimitropoulos K et al (2018) A multimodal approach for the safeguarding and transmission of intangible cultural heritage: the case of i-Treasures. IEEE Intell Syst 33(6):3–16

Dimitropoulos K, Manitsaris S, Tsalakanidou F, Nikolopoulos S, Denby B, Al Kork S, Tilmanne J et al (2014) Capturing the intangible an introduction to the i-Treasures project. In: 2014 international conference on computer vision theory and applications (VISAPP), vol 2. IEEE, pp 773–781

Doerr M (2003) The CIDOC conceptual reference model: an ontological approach to semantic interoperability of metadata. AI Mag 24(3):75–92

Doerr M, Gradmann S, Hennicke S, Isaac A, Meghini C, van de Sompel H (2010) The Europeana data model (EDM). In: World library and information congress: 76th IFLA general conference and assembly, pp 10–15

Donkin L (2001) Crafts and conservation. Synthesis report for ICCROM

Doulamis Anastasios D et al (2017) Transforming intangible folkloric performing arts into tangible choreographic digital objects: the terpsichore approach. In: Proceedings of VISIGRAPP (5: VISAPP)

Doulamis N et al (2017) Modelling of static and moving objects: digitizing tangible and intangible cultural heritage. Mixed reality and gamification for cultural heritage. Springer, Cham, pp 567–589

ETH-Bibliothek (2016) Best practices digitization (Version 1.1, 2016)

Fast-Berglund Å, Gong L, Li D (2018) Testing and validating extended reality (xR) technologies in manufacturing. Procedia Manuf 25:31–38. https://doi.org/10.1016/j.promfg.2018.06.054

Fernie K, Griffiths J, Archer P, Chandrinos K, de Polo A, Stevenson M, Lopez de Lacalle, O et al (2012) PATHS: personalising access to cultural heritage spaces. In: 2012 18th international conference on virtual systems and multimedia (VSMM). IEEE, pp 469–474

Geijer A (1979) A history of textile art. Pasold Research Fund, p 141

Gervás P, Dìaz-Agudo B, Peinado F, Hervás R (2005) Story plot generation based on cbr. Knowl Based Syst 18(4):235–242

Giannoulakis S, Tsapatsoulis N, Grammalidis N (2018) Metadata for intangible cultural heritage: the case of folk dances

Giaretta D (2008) The CASPAR approach to digital preservation. Int J Digit Curation 2(1)

Hall T, Ciolfi L, Fraser M, Benford S, Bowers J, Greenhalgh C, Hellstrom S, Izadi S, Schnadelbach H (2001) The visitor as virtual archaeologist: using mixed reality technology to enhance education and social interaction in the museum. In: Spencer S (ed) Proceedings of the VAST 2001 conference, Greece, Nov 2001. ACM Press, New York

Hecht A (1989) The art of the loom. British Museum Publ

Hughes CE, Stapleton CB, Hughes DE, Smith E (2005) Mixed reality in education, entertainment and training: an interdisciplinary approach. IEEE Comput Graph Appl 26(6):24–30

IFLA/UNESCO (1999) Survey on digitisation and preservation. Emerald Group Publishing Limited

Jennings H (2012) Towards a definition of heritage craft, creative & cultural skills

Jung Y, Kuijper A, Fellner DW, Kipp M, Miksatko J, Gratch J, Thalmann D (2011a) Believable virtual characters in human-computer dialogs. Eurographics (STARs) 2011:75–100

Jung Y, Kuijper A, Fellner D et al (2011) Believable virtual characters in human-computer dialogs. Eurographics 2011—state of the art report, pp 75–100

Kalay Y, Kvan T, Affleck J (eds) (2007) New heritage: new media and cultural heritage. Routledge

Kasnesis P, Kogias DG, Toumanidis L, Xevgenis MG, Patrikakis CZ, Giunta G, Calsi GL (2019) An IoE architecture for the preservation of the cultural heritage: the STORM use case. In: Harnessing the internet of everything (IoE) for accelerated innovation opportunities. IGI Global, pp 193–214

Lagoze C, Hunter J (2006) The ABC ontology and model. J Digit Inf 2(2)

Liarokapis F, White M (2005) Augmented reality techniques for museum environments. Mediterranean J Comput Netw 1(2):90–96

Liu H, Singh P (2002) Makebelieve: using commonsense knowledge to generate stories. In: Proceedings of AAAI/IAAI, pp 957–958

Mani I (2012) Computational modeling of narrative. Synth Lect Hum Lang Technol 5(3):142

Margetis G, Papagiannakis G, Stephanidis C (2019) Realistic natural interaction with virtual statues in X-reality environments. Int Arch Photogramm Remote Sens Spat Inf Sci 42(2/W11)

Markowitz S (1994) The distinction between art and craft. J Aesthetic Educ 28(1):55–70

Metcalf B (1993) Replacing the myth of modernism. American Craft

Milgram P, Kishino F (1994) A taxonomy of mixed reality visual displays. IEICE Trans Inf Syst. Special issue on Net- worked Reality E77-D (12):1321–1329

Minerva Project Editorial Board (Minerva Project 2003–11). Last revision 2005-09-12. www.minervaeurope.org/structure/nrg/documents/charterparma.htm

Mulholland P, Collins T (2002) Using digital narratives to support the collaborative learning and exploration of cultural heritage. In: Proceedings of 13th international workshop on database and expert systems applications. IEEE, pp 527–531

Neudecker C, Tzadok A (2010) User collaboration for improving access to historical texts. Lib Q 20(1)

Pratikakis I, Savelonas MA, Mavridis P, Papaioannou G, Sfikas K, Arnaoutoglou F, Rieke-Zapp D (2018) Predictive digitisation of cultural heritage objects. Multimed Tools Appl 77(10):12991–13021

Pujol L, Roussou M, Poulou S, Balet O, Vayanou M, Ioannidis Y (2012) Personalizing interactive digital storytelling in archaeological museums: the CHESS project. In: 40th annual conference of computer applications and quantitative methods in archaeology. Amsterdam University Press

Pye D (1968) The nature and art of workmanship. Cambridge University Press, Cambridge

Raimond Y, Abdallah S (2007) The event ontology. Technical report

Riedl MO, Young RM (2010) Narrative planning: balancing plot and character. J Artif Intell Res 39(1):217–268

Sánchez JA, Mühlberger G, Gatos B, Schofield P, Depuydt K, Davis RM, de Does J et al (2013) TranScriptorium: a European project on handwritten text recognition. In: Proceedings of the 2013 ACM symposium on document engineering. ACM, pp 227–228

Scherp A, Franz T, Saathoff C, Staab S (2009) F—a model of events based on the foundational ontology DOLCE+DnS ultralight. In: Proceedings of the fifth international conference on knowledge capture. ACM, pp 137–144

Scopigno R, Callieri M, Cignoni P, Corsini M, Dellepiane M, Ponchio F, Ranzuglia G (2011) 3D models for cultural heritage: beyond plain visualization. Computer 7:48–55

Shaw R, Troncy R, Hardman L (2009) Lode: linking open descriptions of events. In: The semantic web. Springer, pp 153–167

Singh P et al (2002) The public acquisition of commonsense knowledge. In: Proceedings of AAAI spring symposium: acquiring (and Using) linguistic (and World) knowledge for information access

Stogner MB (2011) The Immersive cultural museum experience–creating context and story with new media technology. Int J Incl Mus 3(3)

Swartout W, Traum D, Artstein R, Noren D, Debevec P, Bronnenkant K, Williams J, Leuski A, Narayanan S, Piepol D, Lane HC, Morie J, Aggarwal P, Liewer M, Chiang J-Y, Gerten J, Chu S, White K (2010) Virtual museum guides demonstration. In: Proceedings of the 2010 IEEE spoken language technology workshop. IEEE. https://doi.org/10.1109/JPROC.2012.2236291

Tscheu F, Buhalis D (2016) Augmented reality at cultural heritage sites. In: Information and communication technologies in tourism. Springer, Cham, pp 607–619

UNESCO (2003a) National Library of Australia. Guidelines for the preservation of digital heritage. CI.2003/WS/3

UNESCO (2003b) Text of the convention for the safeguarding of the intangible cultural heritage

UNESCO (2016) Digitization and online accessibility of cultural content and digital preservation, Latvia

van den Akker C, van Erp M, Aroyo L, Segers R, Van der Meij L, Legêne S, Schreiber G (2012) Understanding objects in online museum collections by means of narratives. In: Proceedings of the third workshop on computational models of narrative (CMN'12)

Vico L (2018). Authenticity and realism: virtual vs physical restoration. McDonald Institute

Vossen P, Rigau G, Agirre E, Soroa A, Monachini M, Bartolini R (2010) KYOTO: an open platform for mining facts. In: Proceedings of the 6th workshop on ontologies and lexical resources, pp 1–10

White M, Mourkoussis N, Darcy J, Petridis P, Liarokapis F, Lister PF, Walczak K, Wolciechowski R, Cellary W, Chmielewski J, Stawniak M, Wiza W, Patel M, Stevenson J, Manley J, Giorgini F, Sayd P, Gaspard F (2004) ARCO—an architecture for digitization, management and presentation of virtual exhibitions. In: Proceedings of the CGI' 2004 conference, Hersonissos, Crete, June 2004, Los Alamitos, California. IEEE Computer Society, pp 622–625

Wolff A, Mulholland P, Collins T (2012) Storyspace: a story-driven approach for creating museum narratives. In: Proceedings of the 23rd ACM conference on hypertext and social media. ACM, pp 89–98

Chapter 14
Everyone Is not a Gamer! Developing Cultural Heritage Experiences for Diverse Audiences

Ulf Wilhelmsson and Per Backlund

Abstract Serious games and gamification have been proposed as approaches to solve problems in various areas by utilizing game technologies, game design components and even fully fledged games. However, when games are applied in a context outside the gaming sphere where users are not used to game interfaces and game culture, this may cause problems. In the case of cultural heritage applications this may create confusion or even put people off if they don't understand what to do to take part in the experience. This chapter contributes a synthesized retrospective overview of three successive research and development projects conducted at the University of Skövde since 2007 and will present theoretical frameworks, conceptual studies, and production models for cultural heritage experiences for diverse audiences. In particular, we present a detailed case of a cultural heritage site which has been enhanced by game design concepts and visualizations to provide a richer experience for visitors. The chapter will also show the importance of user experience testing as an integral part of the production cycle in order to ensure a pleasant and understandable visit for visitors with different backgrounds and experiences of video games.

14.1 Introduction

Imagine yourself and a stranger standing in front of something that resembles a giant green metallic painted telephone handle with a television screen containing strange objects facing you. There are buttons and levers marked with words such as "Thrust" and you are unable to connect these words to any meaningful context. You leave this object, Computer Space (Nutting Associates 1971), in total confusion. Now, picture yourself and the stranger in front of a large brown wooden cabinet. A television screen facing you shows a line in the middle, two smaller lines on each side of the screen and on each side of the middle line the number "0". There are two wheels at the front of the cabinet, one to the left and one to the right. Above the left one are the words "Player One" written and to the right "Player Two". There is a metal plate

U. Wilhelmsson (✉) · P. Backlund
University of Skövde, Skövde, Sweden
e-mail: ulf.wilhelmsson@his.se

© Springer Nature Switzerland AG 2020
F. Liarokapis et al. (eds.), *Visual Computing for Cultural Heritage*, Springer Series on Cultural Computing, https://doi.org/10.1007/978-3-030-37191-3_14

on the cabinet saying "Deposit quarter. Ball will serve automatically. Avoid missing ball for high score." You follow the instruction and insert a quarter in a little slot that is also present. Voila! You and the stranger just began playing PONG! (Atari 1972).

This chapter provides a retrospective overview of research and development projects utilizing game technology and game mechanics in various areas were the end user not necessarily is accustomed to play computer mediated games. As such, this chapter will provide valuable insights in serious games design and development at large, evaluation methods tailored to suit such game projects and not least provide insights in games for cultural heritage experiences. The main knowledge contribution of this chapter is a tried and tested approach for developing game based solutions for cultural heritage experiences for non-gamer audiences. The approach we propose is prototype driven and iterative and often utilizes story driven game design with portions of fiction (or fictionalized facts). Furthermore, it also takes usability and user acceptance into account while balancing engaging cultural heritage experiences and correctness with respect to fact based old museum style exhibits. We strongly advocate the importance of play context as an important design factor when developing games for non-gamers.

We will explore three projects: SIDH (Backlund et al. 2007); Elinor (Backlund et al. 2013) and The Search for the lost Gold Reserve (Wilhelmsson et al. 2014). The first two are not in the domain of cultural heritage, but are nevertheless relevant as they provide insights and methods that are beneficiary when developing games for diverse audiences with low or no prior gaming experience or possibly not even an interest in playing games. Designing games for anyone that is not a gamer is not an easy task, and this is likely what you do when you design a game based cultural heritage experience. Even tough digital games are widespread and game culture is growing, the audience for cultural heritage experiences is a diverse group of people. It's therefore not certain that a specific audience at a specific location even knows each other before they meet at this location. It is also likely that the members of the audience will not meet again. These are challenges that need to be addressed in the production cycle of a game based cultural heritage experience. Furthermore, as someone that manages a cultural heritage, such as museum curators, tourist offices etc. you will probably also want to know how well facts and stories about the objects, locations, people who once lived here etc. are absorbed by the audience and if the audience would recommend others to also pay you a visit. That is: what are the benefits of using a game based approach as part of a cultural heritage experience compared to other tried and tested approaches?

14.2 Background

As part of a new paradigm of learning (de Freitas and Liarokapis 2011) games designed for the purpose to inform an audience of a specific cultural heritage, such as the history of an old military fortress, pose a number of interesting challenges. First of all why choose a game as the vehicle for this? Why not an exhibition of artifacts, small texts that explain the role of the artifacts in a historical perspective, maybe add a guided tour in which the guide informs the audience of different aspects of the cultural heritage? Maybe a book would be a better choice, providing in depth discussions, facts and visual illustrations. On the other hand within what is called New Museology there is a shift in focus from exhibits to experiences (Sylaiou et al. 2017; Alvarez Diaz et al. 2015) and games might actually be a good platform in making cultural heritage accessible, providing in depth knowledge by allowing the player to interact with materials of different kinds within the game environment. Games have the benefit of being highly interactable (Wilhelmsson 2001, 2006, 2007, 2008) and are also inherently multi modal (Liarokapis et al. 2017). Objects might be provided to the player in digital form, allowing an active use and exploration of them. Fact based scenarios may be played rather than read. What could be fatal to do in real life can be quite harmless, but still physically challenging when played out in a digital game. It could obviously be fatal if visitors play with real fire inside a fortress filled with barrels of gunpowder. But in a game, the real environment can be intertwined with the simulated environment of the game. You can use a real fortress and let the game be played out with digital artifacts and assets within that very location and hence make use of an actual location's history and historic value as part of the game set up. All of the above probably holds for any interactable visualization and might be more or less within the current state of the art (Anderson et al. 2010). However, we strongly believe that the game design aspect adds other values. One thing that is often held forward as an important feature of serious games is that they increase learning motivation (c.f. de Freitas et al. 2010). But what are the features that help achieving this? In the following sections we will explore this through the lens of three different projects.

14.3 Developing Serious Games

In this section, we present two serious game projects from which both technical solutions and test methods have been applied within The Search for the lost Gold Reserve to a greater or lesser extent: SIDH (Backlund et al. 2007) and Elinor (Backlund et al. 2013).

SIDH is a game based firefighting simulator in which the objective is to apply search methods to save victims in smoke filled indoor environments. It was construed to facilitate as an alternative to real world simulation of such training exercises for the Swedish Rescue Services Agency. The SIDH project provided the player with an overall context and a specific role as a firefighter. Since this role within the game was the same as the player's professional role this was easily achieved. SIDH utilized several game design features to achieve its goals, to create motivation and interest for individual training and also the additional learning goals to be conveyed by the game. The learning objectives in the game were all grounded in the curriculum for the Swedish firefighter training program. The more "game like" features of SIDH included a traditional level structure of the assignments i.e. the tasks to be performed gets increasingly more difficult as the game progress. There were sixteen different scenarios including the introductory tutorial. By using a basic narrative style in the SIDH project, the mission of the player was introduced and the result of a game session could be evaluated from a list of objectives addressed by the player. The introduction to the mission was done by a non-player character (NPC) in a short briefing and after a finished mission the player was given feedback from the NPC. The feedback given is best described as feedback on the task (Hattie and Timperley 2007). The game was set to auto advance to the next level if a mission was successfully performed. There was also a scoring system attached to the tasks and the scores were mapped to the real life variables that were the target for training. These were effective search patterns, i.e. to make sure that the whole premises were searched and no victims left behind. The mapping was not 1-1 but there were some deliberate connections between the real life tasks and the game tasks (Backlund et al. 2007).

The game was played wearing parts of a firefighter turn-out gear such as boots, breathing mask and coat for an enhanced realism and cognitive grounding in the experience. To further enhance this, a set of controls and a game environment to expose the player to physical and psychological stress factors in similitude to a real *Breathing Apparatus Entry* (BAE) were developed. The SIDH game was played inside a cave system consisting of four flat surface semitransparent walls measuring 1.6×1.2 m each (excluding the mounting legs of the screen which raised the screen to approximately 2 m in height) onto which the game graphics were projected from outside the cave. The system made use of 5:1 sound as well as the Savox radio unit mounted inside the breathing mask. The 5.1 system provided the sound effects and was placed outside the cave not to interfere with the visual impressions from the screens, and the Savox system provided an audio connection to the NPC instructor. This design made possible an efficient way to substitute the real world outside the cave with the simulated environment inside the cave for the duration of a game session. In order to expose the player to the physical strain of a real world simulation or a real world situation an accelerometer driven step plate that controlled the pace of movement in the game environment was developed. The higher the frequency of steps, the faster the player moved. To simulate the weight of a picked up victim, the step frequency needed to be increased to keep the pace. To choose the direction of movement, the player had a real fog fighter nozzle of substantial weight, connected by a piece of nylon string to a Gametrak control placed in center over the cave. To make it even more physically challenging and closer to a real rescue situation, the health level of the player would be improved if the player held a crouching position close to the floor which in turn makes its more physically challenging to move forward adding to a physically challenging game session. To add psychological stress, in some of the scenarios, the victims would start to scream hysterically. When a mission was unsuccessful, the feedback from the NPC instructor was harsh and unpleasant, adding yet another instance for psychological stress.

The system was evaluated with respect to self-reported learning. The results show that a majority of the participants stated that they learned something with respect to the learning objectives of the game. This is, of course, a positive result but there are several drawbacks with the evaluation. One is the reliance on self-reported learning.

This is a crude measure that does not say anything about real performance. There were however an increase of performance between simulator sessions but the mapping to real life performance is still to be determined. Furthermore, the mapping between game variables and real life variable is somewhat crude (Backlund et al. 2007). These issues were addressed in the Elinor project along with more deliberate game design and evaluation strategies.

The Elinor project (Backlund et al. 2013) which was an attempt to use game based motoric rehabilitation for stroke patients provided valuable insight in the complexity of the act of playing a digital game. In quite a few respects this project was the direct opposite of the SIDH project and its firefighting simulator. One key factor for the Elinor project was ease of use and easy of set up. Elinor showed that there a numerous steps that needs to be undertaken by the player even before actually playing a specific game. In order to address this complexity, it was decided that an easy to use standalone game station with a stripped down user interface was the preferred way to go. The fewer steps that the stroke patient needed to go through in order to start a session, the more likely they would actually use the system as intended. Generally, the design rational is to hide as much of the complexity as possible and to focus on understandable interaction with a very low entry-level. The Elinor system was shipped on a specifically designed console to ensure both ease of use and rehabilitation effect. Moreover, the interactions with the game were designed to support the rehabilitation goals. As an example, one rehabilitation goal was to activate the impaired arm. To support this goal the system was adapted to the user at set-up so that a participant with a left-side impairment would use the left hand for navigation as well as being more challenged on the left hand side during play sessions.

The Elinor games were designed using two different approaches. One was to base the game on a physical movement (suggested as a good movements for rehabilitation purposes by the medical experts) and then try to map it to gameplay. This approach is exemplified by a bicycle game. The other approach was to explore classic games that the developers themselves enjoyed and then analyse if they could be given a suitable interaction model based on the specific controls of the console. This approach is exemplified with a puzzle bobble game. In the evaluation it was apparent that the latter type of games were the ones that were by far the most appreciated. The evaluation model in the Elinor project was more elaborated and included a process of pre-tests, continuous evaluation and post-tests. There were several challenges that had to be addressed in the evaluation process, some of which will be touched upon in this chapter: testing in authentic context; specific characteristics of the target group and the mapping between game variables and the serious goal of the project.

Whereas the SIDH project made use of a complex system of interacting parts such as several computers, projectors, the large cave structure and the fact that participants/players needed to dress up in firefighting equipment and also go to a specific location to play the game, the Elinor system is a small box brought to the home of the participant. As such these two games are at the opposite ends of a continuum on which at the one end we find very complex installations and at the other very simple ones. However, they share some important features: (1) both are targeted towards, potentially, inexperienced players, and (2) both utilize an easy access and high playa-bility philosophy. These features are essential to the envisioned usage situations for the two solutions. In the case of SIDH, one target was to encourage spontaneous training outside the regular teaching activities and in the case of Elinor home-based rehabilitation was at the core of the project. This fact introduces additional chal-lenges in that whatever solution that is developed needs to be possible to use with minimal instruction and overhead for starting as well as being robust and reliable. We have addressed such issues of practical usefulness of serious games in several of our projects and it has turned out to be an important aspect of evaluation. In par-ticular, the evaluation of Elinor targeted aspects of unsupervised use in real usage contexts. The evaluation took place during five weeks in the homes of the partici-pants (Backlund et al. 2013). This was considered important since the home context was central to the whole concept. Naturally, the rehabilitation effect was central to evaluation and it was measured by means of variables from the domain of stroke rehabilitation as defined by physio therapists and occupational therapists. However, from a game developer perspective, we were also interested in whether the games we had designed were appreciated by the players. This information was captured in several different ways: qualitative measures such as play experience were collected in interviews and quantitative measures such as play time for different games were collected via a logging system. The latter gave information about overall play time and what games were played the most. This is important information since play time under voluntary conditions is likely to be a good measure of engagement. Voluntary play is a key feature here since such information could not have been captured under any other evaluation conditions than the real usage context. Hence, we advocate the importance of play context as factor to take into account for serious games. We define play context as the specific located situation in which the game is actually meant to be played and experienced.

14.4 Case Study of the Search for the Lost Gold Reserve

The Search for the lost Gold Reserve is a partly fiction, partly fact based, trans-media adventure tour inside a 19th century military fortress in south west Sweden (Wilhelmsson et al. 2014). The tour last approximately one hour and is played out at a number of locations (henceforth rooms) in the fortress. Visitors will walk or run between these rooms during the progression of the tour. This project was initiated by Karlsborgs Turism AB, a municipally owned company, which approached the University of Skövde early in 2010. They wanted a major facelift and overhaul of a by then 20 year old and heavily outdated guided tour of the fortress.

The idea proposed to the project group was to make a standalone game, played on PCs hosted in a small room inside the fortress. It came out rather different, with 18 specially built game stations, to great extent based upon the step plate controller developed within the SIDH project as well as the server-client approach and the use of back projection of the game graphics. The reasons for this were quite simple. The

SIDH and Elinor projects respectively had shown the quite obvious: not everyone is a gamer. To just put a number of computers in a room and invite visitors to play a game they have never seen before is a challenge indeed, even though the target group for the game initially was children with prior gaming experience. However, since the adventure tour not only included children but their guardians there was an interesting problem to be solved: What should the guardians do while the children played the game? Should they pause participating in the adventure tour and stand beside the children and look at them playing the game? No. Designing a good cultural heritage experience is the craft of including the majority of the visitors in the experience and find ways to overcome obstacles that hinders such an inclusion.

To better understand the play context and the design choices made some background information concerning the actual cultural heritage site in question is necessary. This is especially important since the evaluation of the digital game developed in this project clearly showed that the location and context of play had a protruding effect whether or not the game was appreciated and found interesting and fun by visitors. The fortress was originally built as part of a military strategy in order to host the Swedish government and serve as a deposit for the Central Bank of Sweden's gold reserve in case of war. This served as the historical backdrop and scenario. The area of the fortress is approximately 140,000 m^2 and it is surrounded by a 5000 m long wall. The fortress could hold up to 8000 troops, store 100.000 guns and a battery of well over 200 canons. Even though still an active military facility, it has become a tourist attraction and a cultural heritage site of importance.

When the project started the old adventure tour used outdated technology that did not contribute to an immersive experience but had one feature that the project group saw should be incorporated in the new adventure tour. It included a movie that provided the initial scenario and context for the following experience.

14.4.1 Overall Design of the Adventure Tour

As a vehicle for creating suspense and interest for the fortress the project group wanted to focus on the fact that glimmering gold was supposed to be held within its walls in case of war. So a fictional story of grand theft was outlined in which a villain have the gold stolen and tucked away deep inside the fortress. There was also a need of having two children, one girl and one boy, as the heroes of the story, in order to create a basis for the visitors' empathy and willingness to participate in the adventure to find the gold and defeat the villain. Equal representation of the heroes' gender was a top priority. The project group wanted to increase the immersion of the player through a multiple sensory design. The intention was also to diminish the borders between the game environment and visitors. To achieve this the narrative was distributed in three media. The adventure starts with a 3D movie with live actors that sets the scene, introduces the main characters and the conflict between the protagonists and the antagonist. It then turns into a role playing game, in the widest meaning of such, by the entrance into the cinema of one of the protagonists from the movie who is then transformed into a live actor functioning as a game master. It may be either the girl or the boy that enters the room. This was done for practical reasons for recruiting actors. The actor is wearing the same clothes as the hero in the movie and use a similar verbatim to be easily recognized by the visitors. The actor also points out that the villain knows that the visitors have witnessed the events of the movie and that therefore they must flee not to become his next victims. At the end of the adventure the computer game works as an integrated part in which the villain is caught by one of the heroes with help from the visitors playing the game. That is, in the computer game one of the heroes are part of the game as an NPC. The game can be started in two different modes depending on the gender of the live actor. If the game master is male, the NPC will be a female and vice versa. The intention was to create a frame for the adventure that filtered out the ordinary world and substitute a fictional one but at the same time make use of the fact that the adventure is played out at that very specific location. This can also be understood as an interaction membrane (Goffman 1961) in which rules of irrelevance and rules of realizable resources are in play. According to Goffman any given social situation is surrounded by an interaction membrane that constitutes the rules to be followed inside the membrane. When playing a game certain objects might also get specific meanings added to them. A piece of wood can be the Queen in chess, a piece of paper with a black symbol could be the Ace of spades etc. These latter are realizable resources of specific meaning in a game. There might also occur events that are irrelevant to the game such as a chess player accidentally tipping a piece over with her sleeve (Goffman 1961). In an adventure tour taking place in a military fortress there are many objects that need to be categorized as irrelevant to withhold the experience of being part of an adventure rather than the real world. To frame the experience inside a narrative was the strategy chosen to help the visitor to be immersed psychologically by means of the suspension of disbelief.

As a basis for this story driven design lays what is known as The Heroes Journey (Campbell 1949/1993; Vogler 2007). The objective was to create an involving and fun experience by applying and interconnect the aforementioned media formats, a 3D movie, a role playing game and a computer game. Involvement and fun are the results of emotional responses from external stimuli, thus in the overall design of a mediated narrative and, in particular, in the game design.

Based on the physical environment that the fortress offers in the form of a number of specific and distributed rooms, historical archives and oral tradition stories about people who once actually lived in Karlsborg and that had connections to the fortification, the outlines of the framing story was drawn up. A fight between good and evil forces at both macro and micro level came to be the foundation. Sweden is about to go to war (macro level), the gold reserve is moved to Karlsborg's fortress which is still under construction, and the gold is stolen by an evil villain that also happens to be a sergeant in the Swedish army (micro level). Following a very long tradition of storytelling and for the purpose of rapidly introducing the main characters and plot of the adventure, the project group made the characters stereotypical. Stereotypes have the benefits of being easily identified and for this project it was considered necessary to use stereotypes, not least since the narrative and hence the characters were to be distributed via three different media and needed to be rapidly identified by the visitors regardless of the media as such. The protagonists, the two heroes, are siblings of unknown heritage, they are protected by the commander of the fortress and are part of his household. They wear plain clothes that are easy to discern from other characters. The antagonist, Sgt. Ståhlhammar was modeled as a mean and brutal man. Firstly, he is a man of a certain power as he is an officer in the army. This feature gives him access to the gold and a possibility to move around the fortress freely. It also provide him with a uniform that works as a contrast to the protagonists' clothes. Secondly, he is slightly disfigured in his face by a scar across his left eye giving him a sinister expression. In the narrative of the adventure tour this disfiguration is explained by a story of how he got drunk one night from drinking beer and falling on his own sword. Thirdly, he acts with cruelty and brutality, both physically and verbally, towards others when introduced to the participants in the introductory 3D-movie.

As a functional model for engaging the visitors in the adventure tour, the project group drew on the powers embedded in a dramatic narrative structure since this has been proven to work well to involve audiences during at least the past two millennia. Dramatic structures are heavily based on conflict and a situation of change put forth to the audience by the careful plotting of events of the story to create tension. As Ryan points out "The preferred narrative structure of the adventure game is the archetypal plot of the quest of the hero, as described by Vladimir Propp and Joseph Campbell." (Ryan 2004 p. 351).

The narrative of The Search for the lost Gold reserve was divided into three media: a 3D movie, the physical environment based role playing game (in a broad meaning of role playing) and a computer game. These media combined with the interaction between game master and visitors provides the playground for the overall experience. The content of the dramatic storyline was carefully distributed over the three media from a functional perspective. From the outset of the preproduction phase, each media form was evaluated with respect to its primary functional aspects: what part of the content would suit each media best? A movie allow rapid presentation of the plot and characters and may shorten or prolong time through editing the sequences. It also provide varied framing of the events and can freely move from one location to another. It does not however support interaction in the sense of the visitors changing the content of the movie. The role playing on the other hand allows the visitors to interact with the game maser but also allow a scripted chain of events to occur in a pre-specified order. It also allow for a varied framing of the events since the visitors will move from one room to another during the adventure. It does not allow for much of time editing in the specific case of the adventure in question, but may in essence provide this feature since nothing hinders the game master to make a statement such as "now we have waited here for three hours" while in fact it has been just two minutes. The computer game allow interaction, varied framing and time editing.

However, structure is not to be considered as the only important aspect of storytelling.

Since face-to-face interaction constantly renegotiates the role of the participants, every listener is, at least in principle, a potential storyteller. [...] face-to-face storytelling is more than purely mental experience of language based on syntax and semantics; it is also a corporeal performance in which meaning is created through gestures, facial expression and intonation. (Ryan 2004, pp 41–44)

The game master use face-to-face communication with the participants from the very onset of co-presence, after entering and sharing the same actual environment. There is a script designed to portion out the plot throughout the adventure but from time to time it is both possible and sometimes necessary for the game master to adhere to improvisation depending on the reaction and behavior of the participants. In that respect, even though there is a script, meant to be followed to keep up the suspension of disbelief, large parts of the adventure is based on oral storytelling as described by Ong (1982/2002).

These are the stages of the hero's journey (Vogler 2007; Campbell 1949/1993) as played out in the adventure tour. Italics summarize what Vogler writes on the subject.

1. *Birth: Fabulous circumstances surrounding conception, birth, and childhood establish the hero's pedigree, and often constitute their own monomyth cycle.* The two heroic children are presented as orphans in the 3D-movie, and that they are regarded as part of the local high commander's household and hence can move around freely inside the fortress.

2. *Call to Adventure: The hero is called to adventure by some external event or messenger. The Hero may accept the call willingly or reluctantly.* In the movie the protagonist are called to adventure first by seeing gold bars dropped from a chest and later by watching Sgt. Ståhlhammar order the assassination of "The Rat", the man who has helped Ståhlhammar steal the gold and who has drawn a map to the hiding place. The next step of them being drawn into the following events is that they are spotted by Ståhlhammar at the site of the Rat's assassination and hence are forced to escape. Then, they interfere with Ståhlhammar's plan to steal the gold by trying to retrieve the map, of which they only get one half, and Ståhhammar the second half. From that point, the heroes have no choice but to fully enter the adventure.

3. *Helpers/Amulet: During the early stages of the journey, the hero will often receive aid from a protective figure. This supernatural helper can take a wide variety of forms, such as a wizard, and old man, a dwarf, a crone, or a fairy godmother. The helper commonly gives the hero a protective amulet or weapon for the journey.* A supernatural helper, the ghost of the main architect behind the fortification, Baltzar von Platen, helps the group and provides clues how to solve the first test in his old office. He is made co-present by his voice and a painting and he puts forth a number of riddles that the participants need to solve. He may therefore be comprehended as an acousmêtre, (Chion 1994). Later the character Bulta Maja, based on a real person from the 19th century, gives the group more clues. She is not supernatural per se, but is renowned for making a very strong beer called Bult (Bolt). She is reminiscent of a good witch. Her co-presence in the adventure is only through her voice i.e. she is also an acusmêtre (Chion 1994).

4. *Crossing the Threshold: The hero must undergo some sort of ordeal in order to pass from the everyday world into the world of adventure. In the tour there are*

several stages of entering into the adventure world. First the participants will enter the cinema which serves as a first step to leave the ordinary world and provide an alternative fictional world. The movie's main purpose is to provide the background for the fortification, the current situation in the adventure world and introduce the conflict and the main characters, i.e. the heroes and the villain. As the movie ends, one of the heroes (which here then turns into the game master of the role playing game) enters the cinema and urges the group to follow into the physical adventure world of the fortress itself. The first part takes place outdoors inside of the fortress where the game master recapitulate the most important parts of the plot, briefly hints at that the fortress is still under construction and therefore it is dangerous to enter the buildings and most importantly add a number of characteristics of Sgt. Ståhlhammar making him yet more evil and sinister. The game master and the helpers then enter von Platen's office inside the fortress and encounter the first test, a puzzle game with back lit tiles on the floor of the office. Just when the puzzle is solved there is an explosion at the far end of a long dark tunnel and the voice of Sgt. Ståhlhammar is heard screaming at the group and hurrying his henchmen to catch them. The group must now flee from the office into a 400 m long tunnel in which the sound of the chasers is heard, creating a sense of hurry and present danger.

5. *Tests: The hero travels through the dream-like world of adventure where he must undergo a series of tests. These trials are often violent encounters with monsters, sorcerers, warriors, or forces of nature. Each successful test further proves the hero's ability and advances the journey toward its climax.* The secluded environment inside the fortress is not like the ordinary world of the visitors. There is a ghost, strange sounds and dreamlike qualities to the environment.

6. *Helpers: The hero is often accompanied on the journey by a helper who assists in the series of tests and generally serves as a loyal companion. Alternately, the hero may encounter a supernatural helper in the world of adventure who fulfills this function.* The hero in the adventure is the game master. The participants are the helpers as are the ghost of Balzar von Platen and Bulta Maja.

7. *Climax/The Final Battle: This is the critical moment in the hero's journey in which there is often a final battle with a monster, wizard, or warrior which facilitates the particular resolution of the adventure.* The final battle takes place in the computer game and in the physical environment. In the last playable room of the game, Sgt. Ståhlhammar is captured and immobilized. In the physical environment, this is also manifested by the physical locking of a door to his office while his voice is heard cursing the heroes.

8. *Flight: After accomplishing the mission, the hero must return to the threshold of adventure and prepare for a return to the everyday world. If the hero has angered the opposing forces by stealing the elixir or killing a powerful monster, the return may take the form of a hasty flight. If the hero has been given the elixir freely, the flight may be a benign stage of the journey.* At the last phase of the adventure the group finds the gold in the hidden treasure vault. This vault however, begins to collapse and the group must flee and avoid getting killed under the rocks and gravels. The collapse of the gold room is a combination

of wall projections, rumbling sound effects and smoke machines to provide a strong sense of the building collapsing around the visitors.

9. *Return: The hero again crosses the threshold of adventure and returns to the everyday world of daylight. The return can for instance be the emergence from a cave or forest.* After fleeing from the collapsing gold room the group exits the adventure through a narrow corridor leading to the ordinary world outside the adventure. At this stage they begin to leave the adventure world and reenter the ordinary world of everyday life.

10. *Elixir: The object, knowledge, or blessing that the hero acquired during the adventure is now put to use in the everyday world.* The group does not get any gold bars with them but they do, in the final battle against Sgt. Sthålhammar, manage to steal a letter in which he admits to be the one that has stolen the gold. They also leave with the knowledge of the exact location of the stolen gold that hero will provide to the general of the fortress. The heroes role in society is strengthened, the gold is located and the villain is trapped and exposed as whom he really is which is part of the restorative process of the stolen gold situation at both the micro level and the macro level. The gold reserve is needed to fund the upcoming war and without it the war might be lost.

11. *Home: The hero comes back from this mysterious adventure with the power to bestow boons on his fellow man.* The group leaves the hero before this part but can feel comfortable that the hero will use the knowledge to return the gold to the government.

14.4.2 Design of the Game and the Game Stations

There were some specific challenges that needed to be resolved, especially that the computer game was to be central part of the overall narrative dramatic structure and would incorporate a scene in which the villain is caught but still should not contain any graphical violence directed towards him due to the young age of the initial target group i.e. 7–14 year.

Since the adventure tour is a commercial tourist attraction, there was a need to make the groups participating quite large to get a feasible economic turn over. One way of addressing this was to rather than aim for a single player experience, make a cooperative game where two players solve the tasks of the game together and making it possible for up to 36 concurrent participants. This approach was also more challenging from a game design perspective. For example, it is not certain that the two players know each other before entering the adventure. The game had to be extremely easy to understand from the user experience perspective and be quite self-explanatory concerning the game play and game mechanics. The learning curve of controlling the game had to be almost flat as in the games made for the Elinor project. The players will possibly only play the game once since it is a location based game installation and the only opportunity to play the game is to participate in the adventure tour.

14.4.2.1 The Game Station's Controls and Spherical Back Projection

To keep the visitors in play mode, inside the magic circle (Salen and Zimmerman 2003) and keep the interaction membrane (Goffman 1961) between the adventure and the ordinary world intact much thought and effort was put in the construction of the game stations hardware solutions. Even though players of a game might be quite good at filtering out things by applying rules of irrelevance (Goffman 1961) while playing, it certainly is valuable to help them in this process by avoiding to add realizable resources that simply does not fit the given context. Adding a digital game to an adventure set in the midst 19th century definitely demands some careful consideration in order not to collapse the membrane between the adventure and the ordinary world why no computers could be visible and also made impossible the use of ordinary computer screens. These objects simply did not fit in the context. At the same time, the project group wanted the computer game to really stand out and be one of the highlights of the tour both with respect to its integration in the adventure as well as by its hardware appearance when first encountered. Simply put the game needed to have a "WOW!" factor. In order to achieve this the game stations lent their basic technological platform from the SIDH and Elinor projects with the addition of a spherical back projection canvas, a jDome. Both the SIDH and Elinor projects made use of Gametrak controllers to play the game and facilitate player agency within the game environment. The Gametrak use a nylon string to turn potentiometers inside the unit generating the control data and hence would support this idea of putting physical strain on the visitor to play the game. Since prior experienced using this control had shown them to work well and provide a not so common but interesting interface it was decided to include them. Another reason for this was the ambition to preserve the energy level of the visitors, having been running around in crammed dark tunnels etc. prior to entering the game room and let them play a game that demanded a lot of physical activity. Controlling the game with the Gametrak control means that the player needs to move not only his or her fingers and hands but rather the whole arm. Game evaluations showed that the spacing of the control strings running from the Gametrak would cause players' arms or even heads colliding during game play, why the Gametraks were sawn in two parts and mounted further apart in the housing of the step plate. It took several iterations the find the correct spacing between them as did the construction and location of the ferrule guiding the string from the Gametrak to its handle to avoid breaking the string when pulling the handle. From the SIDH project the idea of using a pressure sensitive step plate as part of the control system was included. It was redesigned to admit rough handling and visitors jumping on it. The wear in the step plate used in this context will of course be higher than in the firefighting simulator due not least to the substantially increased number of players using it on a daily basis. Electro magnets that were connected to the sound output of the game were also added. The low bass frequencies of the sound was sent to the electro magnets (basically solenoids) and sent shockwaves into the very surface structure of the step plate. This in turn generated a sense of "the floor is rumbling under my feet effect" which was suitable not least when things explode in the game.

As the project group did want to keep the visitors in play mode much thought was put into how to display the game graphics to this end. Placing an ordinary computer screen would break the magic circle (Salen and Zimmerman 2003), or put the rules of irrelevance (Goffman 1961) in relation to the interaction membrane established during the tour in a critical state in which the real world would impose its force on the fictional world inside the adventure. jDome is a back projection system in which the image is projected onto a half sphere measuring 1.5 m in diameter. Its visual appearance is quite extraordinary and it does not resemble an ordinary rectangular screen. To play a game using the jDome, the player needs to be very close to or even inside the half sphere which produce an immersive effect. Since the jDome's original foldable construction was weak, wobbly and had an appearance that did not suit the historical setting of the adventure walk, it was replaced by building a sturdy wood frame holding the screen placing the step plate right in front of it. This structure fitted the overall setting and visual experience of the adventure tour as such much better. Projecting 2D images onto a half sphere is a challenge and several iterations were necessary to solve this. First of all, the space for the game station had limitations in distance between the jDome and the projector which led to that the projector beam did not fill the half sphere satisfactory in the horizontal plane and the centre of the image became distorted due to the difference in distance between centre and edge of the half sphere. Mirrors were tried to solve this, as had been done in the SIDH project (Backlund et al. 2007) prolonging and widening the beam. This attempt did only move the problem from the horizontal plane to its vertical plane since a problem with the structure holding the half sphere over shadowing the sphere occurred. Two projectors splitting the image between them with a Warpalizer software was also tried which solved the problem reasonable well but was deemed to be too expensive since 18 game stations should be installed which of course means that this solution would require 36 projectors. It would also be problematic to keep two projects aligned over time. The final decision was to use only one projector per station, use the Warpalizer software to handle the distortion, and to accept that the image did not reach to the edge of the sphere.

14.4.2.2   The Game Play

Several iterations of the game were evaluated at the lab before it was brought on location for further on site evaluations. Initially the evaluations focused on the user experience and the basic mechanics of the game. The game had to be simple enough to be playable with a minimum of instructions not to break the suspension of disbelief or the established interaction membrane of the adventure.

The overall narrative of the adventure should move from a cinematic experience via a role play and make its way into a computer game. The game consists of three playable rooms that expands some of the events of the introductory 3D-movie. That is, themes from the movie are carried over to a different medium. The first playable room is an underground gunpowder storage. The room is filled with barrels of gunpowder and a fire that starts in the movie, have now reached this room. The players need to extinguish the fire as well as they can and at the end of this sequence the back wall of the room will be demolished by a large

The second room is an outdoors environment in which large amounts of rats are running away from the fire in somewhat smoke-filled streets. The players' task in this room is to collect gold coins that some of the rats have in their mouths. This part of the game requires the two players at each game station to co-ordinate their movements so that one of them catches a rat and the other one sweeps the coin out of the rat's mouth. The last room is a return to Baltzar von Platen's office which is the first indoor room of the adventure and hence a place the adventure already have visited. Here the task is to create a chaos by stepping rapidly on the step plate so that Sgt. Ståhlhammar cannot enter the room. At the end of the sequence Sgt. Ståhlhammar eventually enters the room, the players manage to steal his half of the map leading to the gold and even lock him up inside the room. They also steal a letter in which he reveals himself as the one who has stolen the gold.

14.4.3 Game Evaluation

The game was evaluated through observations and focus group interviews during the spring of 2013 (Wilhelmsson et al. 2014). The evaluation of the computer game involving the target group started with the Beta 1 version and was carried out within the lab environment at the University of Skövde. This initial evaluation was arranged to get a first indication of the players' overall first impression of the game completely out of its actual context of play. The lab environment allowed for a quite controlled evaluation and data collection based on only one prototype installation of the game technology. A school class of 13 year old pupils played the game and were interviewed in focus groups after the play sessions. They also wrote a short essay that in their own words described their experience of playing the game. The data collected through these methods indicated that the game was perceived as interesting but not very exciting. That is, they found the game installation, the step plate, the controllers and the jDome screen, as such to be innovative but that the game play was not as exciting. This evaluation also showed that the game system was robust and stable from a technical perspective apart from some deficiencies that were known prior to the evaluation. When the same group of pupils were invited to evaluate the game within its context, inside a damp, dark and cold underground room at the fortress and integrated as just one part of an overall narrative adventure design, they found the game play to be really exciting and engaged fully with the game. Some of the participants wanted to do the adventure once again to get another chance to play the game when they have reached the end of the tour. The final version of the game has to date been further evaluated on location and within its context. This data consist of 160 visitor questionnaires (age 12–62 yrs.), video recordings of players interacting with the game and their co-players and recorded interviews. The data indicates that visitors overall are generally content with the computer game as such and the average rate on a 4-point Likert scale is 3.46 (n = 160). The primary target group, age 10–13, are the most content giving it an average rate of. 3.72 (n = 62) on the 4-point Likert scale. The least content, average 3.18 are male visitors age 16–60 (n = 50). However, the game is primarily not to be understood apart from its role and the context of the adventure tour as a whole. On the contrary, the point of making the game in the first place, was to use it as an integral and important part of the narrative structure and make it meaningful within that very context. The data show that the overall rating is actually a little higher, 0.01, when understood as part of the adventure tour. (n = 160, avg 3.47). The primary target group (age 10–13) are the ones that are most content giving an average rate of 3.81 (n = 62) which is 0.06 higher compared to the game as such. The least content are again the male visitors (n = 22) that give an average rate of 3.05 which is 0.13 lower compared to the game as such. However, a rating above 3 could in any case be considered as a good overall rating for the game in both cases. The result of the evaluation indicates that the game as part of the adventure tour serves its purpose and enhances the visitors' experience of the cultural heritage site in question. The overall narrative enhances the gaming experience and the performance of the game master has an important impact on the computer game experience.

14.5   Summary and Concluding Remarks

This chapter has focused on the importance of making games for a non-gamer audience accessible and interesting to play. The main knowledge contribution of the chapter is a tried and tested approach for developing game based solutions for cultural heritage experiences for non-gamer audiences. The approach is prototype driven and iterative and often utilizes story driven game design with portions of fiction. Furthermore, it also takes usability and user acceptance into account while balancing engaging cultural heritage experiences and correctness with respect to fact based old museum style exhibits.

This chapter has presented three successive serious game projects. We have shown how methods and technological solutions have been transferred from one project to another and emphasized the importance of evaluating games for non-gamers within their play context. The first project, SIDH, described how hardware and software solutions for a firefighting simulator was developed. A step plate control developed for this project played a crucial role for The Search for the lost Gold Reserve as did the iterative prototype driven overall design process.

The second project, Elinor, in which a specially designed portable game unit and a number of games for the purpose of rehabilitation of stroke patients was developed showed the importance of simplifying both the hardware and software with respect to the target group. Some of the hardware and software solutions from this project provided a tried and tested foundation for the cultural heritage experience game The Search for the lost Gold Reserve. SIDH and Elinor respectively also provided important insights on how to work with non-gamers in user experience testing. The Search for the lost Gold Reserve in which a computer game and a game station was construed to form an integral part of an adventure tour using the technology from both SIDH and Elinor in a modified form. The aim of the project was to diminish the border between the game environment and the game player by combining three different platforms within the frame of an adventure tour: a 3D movie, a role playing game lead by a game master and a computer game. Initial evaluations of the computer game performed in the lab at the university were a bit discouraging while evaluations made on the actual location, in the play context clearly showed that it made the mark. Evaluation a game within its play context is crucial and a key factor for succeeding in designing games for non-gamer audiences.

There are numerous factors to keep in mind in this kind of game development. We can divide the process of storytelling and game design into several different stages.

1. Pre-production: During pre-production a focus on the overall goals for the project is in focus, decisions concerning which media should be used to manifest the game etc. are to be made at this stage
2. Production: The actual production of all the assets needed for the final product are construed, tested, evaluated in iterative processes.
3. Distribution: How to deliver the game experience to its audience. In the case studies in this chapter there are basically two different ways used: in the case of SIDH and The search for the Lost Gold Reserve the players need to visit the actual location where the game is installed to play the game. The context of play is decided by the game designers and the facilitator of the game experience. In the case of Elinor, the game is brought home to the player, either by the player or by another party that is not necessarily equal to the designer or the facilitator.
4. Consumption: the act of playing, the consumption phase will differ due to the context in which the game is played.

Ease of use for the player versus ease of use for the game provider is one of the crucial points. The SIDH project and the game installation for the adventure tour are both complex installations that needs a certain amount of system service. In the case of the adventure tour, there are lots and lots of interacting parts that all needs to be up and running concurrently for the game experience to work as intended. As described above, several components of The Search for the lost Gold Reserve were used in and/or originated from our previous projects. The step plate was developed in-house for the SIDH project and then applied in the fortress adventure. This means that their usability and usefulness were already tested but in other contexts. However, the usage context in the fortress adventure was much more challenging, not least with respect to the significantly higher number of users as this is an open installation at a cultural heritage site. At the end of the day, the best game in a cultural heritage experience context is the game that is actually played despite that everyone is not a gamer.

References

Alvareż Díaz M-G, Wilhelmsson U, Lebram M, Toftedahl M (2015) Your answer will make an impression. VS-Games 2015. In: 7th international conference on games and virtual worlds for serious applications, Skövde, vol 1–4. IEEE Computer Society

Anderson EF, McLoughlin L, Liarokapis F, Peters C, Petridis P, de Freitas S (2010) Developing serious games for cultural heritage: a state-of-the-art review. Virtual Real 14(4):255–275 Springer

Atari (1972) Pong [arcade game]

Backlund P, Engström H, Hammar C, Johannesson M (2007) SIDH: a game based firefighter training simulation. In: Proceedings of the 11th international conference information visualization (IV '07). IEEE Computer Society, pp 899–907

Backlund P, Alklind Taylor A-S, Engström H, Johannesson M, Lebram M, Slijper A, Stibrant Sunnerhagen K (2013) Games on prescription!: evaluation of the Elinor console for home-based stroke rehabilitation. In: Transactions on edutainment IX, pp 49–64

Campbell J (1993) The hero with a thousand faces. Fontana, London

Chion M (1994) Audio vision—sound on screen (Trans. C. Gorbman.) Columbia University Press, New York

de Freitas S, Liarokapis F (2011) Serious games: a new paradigm for education? Serious games and edutainment applications. In: Ma M, Oikonomou A, Jain LC (eds) Springer, pp 9–23

de Freitas S, Rebolledo-Mendez G, Liarokapis F, Magoulas G, Poulovassilis A (2010) Learning as immersive experiences: using the four-dimensional framework for designing and evaluating immersive learning experiences in a virtual world. Br J Educ Technol 41(1):69–85. Blackwell Publishing

Goffman E (1961) Encounters: two studies in the sociology of interaction. Bobbs-Merrill, Oxford, England

Hattie J, Timperley H (2007) The power of feedback. Rev Educ Res 77(1):81–112

Liarokapis F, Petridis P, Andrews D, de Freitas S (2017) Multimodal serious games technologies for cultural heritage. Mixed reality and gamification for cultural heritage. Part V. Springer International Publishing, pp 371–392

Nutting Associates (1971) Computer space [arcade game]

Ong W (1982/2002) Orality and literacy: the technologization of the word, 2nd edn. Routledge, New York

Ryan M-L (2004) Narrative across media. University of Nebraska Press

Salen K, Zimmerman E (2003) Rules of play: game design fundamentals. The MIT Press, Cambridge

Sylaiou S, Mania K, Paliokas I, Pujol-Tost L, Kilintzis V, Liarokapis F (2017) Exploring the educational impact of diverse technologies in online virtual museums. Int J Arts Technol (IJART) 10(1):58–84 Inderscience Publishers

Vogler C (2007) The writer's journey: mythic structure for writers. Michael Wiese Productions

Wilhelmsson U (2001) Enacting the point of being. Computer games, interaction and film theory: affordances and constraints, metaphorical concepts and experientialist cognition observed through the environment in computer games. Doctoral dissertation. University of Copenhagen, Copenhagen

Wilhelmsson U (2006) What is a game ego: or how the embodied mind plays a role in computer game environments. In: Pivec M (ed) Affective and emotional aspects of human-computer interaction: game-based and innovative learning approaches. IOS Press, Amsterdam, Berlin, Oxford, Tokyo, Washington, DC, pp 45–58

Wilhelmsson U (2007) What is a computer/video game experience? In: Hernwall P (ed) The virtual: designing digital experience. A conference 2006. M3 4, pp 34–50

Wilhelmsson U (2008) Game ego presence in video and computer games. In: Leino O, Wirman H, Fernandez A (eds) Extended experiences. Lapland University Press, Rovaneimi, pp 58–72

Wilhelmsson U, Marcus Toftedahl M, Susi T, Niklas Torstensson N, Sjölin A, Tuori P (2014) A computer game for an enhanced visitor experience: integration of reality and fiction. In: Proceeding of game and entertainment technologies conference 2014. IADIS Press, pp 149–156

Ulf Wilhelmsson is associate professor in media, aesthetics and narration at the University of Skövde, Sweden. He has been working in serious games projects within cultural heritage, raised online risk awareness for young children and inclusive game design. He is a member of the research group Media, Technology and Culture at the School of Informatics, University of Skövde, Sweden.

Per Backlund is a professor of Informatics at University of Skövde in Sweden. He has been working in several national and international projects on serious games since 2005. His main research interests are in the development and evaluation of serious games and their practical application and usefulness. He is a member of the Interaction Lab research groups at the School of Informatics, University of Skövde, Sweden.

Chapter 15
Beyond Virtual Museums: Adopting Serious Games and Extended Reality (XR) for User-Centred Cultural Experiences

Stella Doukianou, Damon Daylamani-Zad and Ioannis Paraskevopoulos

Abstract Since museums, heritage sites and archives are important for the preservation of our cultural heritage; recently there has been an attempt to promote better absorption of cultural knowledge by involving the learners in the process.

15.1 Introduction

Since museums, heritage sites and archives are important for the preservation of our cultural heritage; recently there has been an attempt to promote better absorption of cultural knowledge by involving the learners in the process. This new tendency along with the digitalisation of the learning environment has sparked the creation of Virtual Museums (VMs). According to Schweinbenz (1998), VM is considered a set of digital objects built in a variety of media, which due to its capacity to provide access and connection between users and objects, goes beyond the traditional methods of interacting with the visitors. A VM provides different levels, perspectives and depth of information about a specific topic: it provides a variety of multimedia from visual information to audio and digital data that have not been filtered out through traditional methods of presenting them (Hoptman 1992).

As VMs have become the new paradigm in museology, a step has been taken further to shift from a 'collection-driven museum' to a more 'audience driven' and user centred approach. A user centred approach that relates to a particular visitor group and answers to their interests. The possibilities of outreaching these groups and reinforce such an approach to VM can be achieved through the rapid advances

S. Doukianou (✉) · D. Daylamani-Zad
School of Computing and Mathematical Sciences, University of Greenwich, Park Row, London, UK
e-mail: s.doukianou@greenwich.ac.uk

D. Daylamani-Zad
e-mail: d.d.zad@greenwich.ac.uk

I. Paraskevopoulos
Intelligent Systems Expertise Center, Altran Italy, Corso Sempione, 66A, 20154 Milan, Italy
e-mail: ioannis.paraskevopoulos@altran.it

© Springer Nature Switzerland AG 2020
F. Liarokapis et al. (eds.), *Visual Computing for Cultural Heritage*, Springer Series on Cultural Computing, https://doi.org/10.1007/978-3-030-37191-3_15

283

in digital technologies in recent years from new media (Augmented Reality) to high-speed networks, such as the longed for 5G cellular network evolution (Brusaporci et al. 2018). The possibilities to reach out to new age visitors with different demands and expectations can be offered not only by telecommunication services but also by innovative and engaging methods that other mediums, such as serious games, can provide. Such technologies are easily employed using engaging AR interfaces that immerse and fascinate audiences and create the space for both synchronous and asynchronous cases, where visitors can be either offsite or onsite. All of these can be achieved by delivering the content through existing telecommunication networks and low cost smartphones; a recipe for ubiquitous propagation and dissemination of culture related content to the masses.

Furthermore, serious games have long been used to support cultural heritage purposes. The popularity of video games among young individuals has made serious games an ideal medium to engage them. Serious games can occur in a variety of forms of mobile applications, simple web-based solutions or in the shape of more complicated applications that combine digital and physical interactions, all of which can be used for different cultural heritage applications. In combination with multimodal interfaces, serious games aim to engage the user and let him explore in their space and time. However, as the field matures, several studies aim to assess the effectiveness of their use regarding the overall museum experience, virtual or otherwise (Roussou and Katifori 2018). There are several challenges that need to be addressed for the design and deployment of such technologies, including lack of one-size-fits-all implementations that restricts the personalisation of the experience and limits user control. Therefore, there is a danger that inept attempts can lead to impractical or ineffective experiences that instead of exploiting the potential of the medium might deprecate its value. Nevertheless, innovation in this area maintains presence in museums as well as providing compelling experience which has to be strongly connected to the synergy between expertise knowledge in the field and the role of these new technologies (Papagiannakis et al. 2018).

This chapter presents firstly a critique the state-of-the-art on mixed reality technologies and serious games that can be used along with them which aim to bring the user to the centre of cultural heritage experiences, exposing the opportunities and challenges. This chapter will start by presenting the state-of-the-art in mixed reality technologies for VMs, then presents the attempts using serious games both past and present. It will continue by discussing the challenges and issues identified in cases studies and then builds on the practical implications to direct the future developments in the area to achieve a sustainable user centred approach in cultural heritage. Finally, we will conclude by discussing the future directions and the potential next steps.

15.2   Virtual Museums: Bringing the User to the Centre

According to Sylaiou et al. (2009), there are three types of VMs that can be divided between brochure museums, content and learning museums. The brochure museum that is information heavy, mainly used as a marketing tool to motivate the audience to visit the museum. The content museum that offers information related to the collections in the museum and is object oriented. The latter, the learning museum is the one offering information in a more context oriented way so that it can be accessed by a variety of visitors from different age groups, background and knowledge level. These learning museums are usually connected to other information, which aim to motivate the visitors' interest. The ultimately goal of these museums is to create a personal relationship with the museum so the visitor would visit again.

Despite the digital opportunities and the deep understanding of the user needs and expectations, developments in the VM area have not progressed extensively, with a few examples diverging from this model. According to recent studies, online museum collections are the least popular features on a museum's website, (Haynes and Zambonini 2007; Fantoni et al. 2012; Fernandes 2018). Several museum experts have related that to limited interest by the visitors in viewing objects through a computer screen. While this might be true for a segment of the population, there are also studies which argue that the low popularity of the online museums is due to their poor user experience (MacDonald 2015). These studies suggest that some VMs have not considered whether the visitor would repeat the visiting and some have completely ignored visitors' personal agency and the post-visit user experience (Perry et al. 2017). In this sense, these VMs can be viewed as outdated tools with questionable relevance for the visitor.

The need to nurture a connection between the visitor and the museum has turned the focus towards the design of the user experience in a VM. User experience has become an integral part of the cultural institution's approach to attract visitors. Museums have a need to embrace a more holistic approach, targeting to connect with the visitor in a personal and emotional level. The digital era played an important role in shaping these experiences and creating VMs that go beyond the typical learning experience only by providing access to different layers of interaction, which can be either personalised, synchronous, asynchronous, or even plain and monotonous.

The more recent innovative examples of VMs, which focus on visitors engagement by employing different methods of interactivity, mostly experiment with storytelling, personalisation, adaptation and social media activity (Perry et al. 2017). A four-year European funded project V-Must (Virtual Museum Transnational Network, 2011–2015) looked at different VM projects across Europe and beyond resulted in proposing a framework for "responsive museums". The term refers to the aim of museums to explore different kinds of interactions that engage the visitors (Hazan and Hermon 2015) the framework presented guidelines for implementation that includes, among others, interactivity, personalisation, coherent content and narrative. In this sense, the VM can be stretched beyond the traditional institutionalised tools and connect with visitors in a measurably emotional and interactive way. To achieve this, an employment of 'new' and 'older' paradigm tools can provide new level of engagement beyond the standard expectations of VMs, such interacting with basic images and videos similar to any information based website. These tools, which often involve game mechanics and immersive technologies, allow visitors to person-alise their experience, relate to the content, actively re-use it and also participate by contributing their part to the narrative.

Therefore, VMs in fact open up new directions with the user-driven scenarios for the museums themselves but also for the perseverance of cultural experience. They offer the opportunity to the visitor to interact with both physical and non-physical museum with contemporary ways making use of emerging tools. The next section reviews the state-of-the-art in cases of using Serious Games in place or accompanying VMs to a more participatory experience. Then we move forward by discussing other technologies that bring forward the user experience by adding different layers of depth in the process.

15.3   XR and Virtual Museums: Working Towards Immersive Experiences

Extended Reality Technologies (Fast-Berglund et al. 2018) as a term is now including a spectrum defined by AR, VR, MxR which are technologies that are aimed at creating immersive experiences. Such technologies and approach have a long history in cultural heritage, virtual museums and tourism.

ARCO (Wojciechowski et al. 2004) was one of the earliest architectures that used AR and VR for virtual representations of virtual museums. The system developed in this project used a sophisticated pipeline to build and manage VR and AR exhi-bitions based on 3D models of the artefacts. The system showed very interesting and successful results when used to provide exhibitions (Walczak et al. 2006). How-ever the AR and VR hardware has come a long way since. The focus of the system was always on the artefacts, as evident in the interfaces provided, however recent approaches clearly show that a non-user centred approach will not provide the same log-term results.

Haynes (2018) proposes the development of Veholders (Virtual Environment for Holdings and Online Digital Educational Repositories) as community projects, where related artefacts, objects and collections are assembled together in order to create blended environment to improve visitor experience and immersion. The research suggests that using AR on smartphones allows visitors to take an active role in the curation and creation of exhibits, changing the role from passive consumers to a blend of consumer and active contributor.

An important aspect that requires investigation is the acceptance and perspective of the users when using new technologies such as AR and VR. Different groups of population have differing willingness, requirements, perspectives and abilities that should be considered (Southall et al. 2019). Museums are a core part of the culture and tourism industries which attracts visitors from various age groups, cultural and financial backgrounds, and physical abilities. A recent study (tom Dieck et al. 2019) has conducted interviews with elderly tourists at a cultural heritage tourist attraction in the UK, examining the impact of VR on their experience. The results demonstrated an overall positive attitude towards the use of technology in this context and suggested strong intentions to revisit due to the experience of VR.

A recent study (Hammady and Ma 2019) has looked at utilising MxR through Microsoft HoloLens in order to create Virtual Museum Guides. They identify that the use of MxR was highly popular with visitors and genuine physical guides that take advantage of the real world by enhancing it with information and guidance has a positive immersive effect on visitors. However, they identify several issues with the device. The main issue that is addressed by the research is the narrow field of view on the device. They design a Spatial UI to tackle this problem and demonstrate that suitable interaction and UI design can improve the user experience. Other issues identified includes instability of spatial mapping in the current hardware, bulkiness of the current devices which can hinder long-term use and engagement, and finally concerns over the real-time rendering which could lead to lags and delays.

The current state-of-the-art XR has clear benefits for attracting visitors and encouraging revisits. However they also identify various issues and shortcomings which relate to the hardware, software and designing an experience that would be immersive and encourage long-term use and further visits without losing its novelty.

15.4 Serious Games and Virtual Museums: Past and Present Case Studies

The use of SGs in cultural heritage has been demonstrated and tested with promising results with regards to the learning outcomes. However, the state of the art in SGs can be reviewed and given the emphasis in regards to a variety of contexts. For example, the use of SGs in museums, the outcome measures, the learning experience, the gaming technology or the increase in museum visits. There is also a substantial part of the literature reviewing the integration of learn and fun in SGs used in cultural heritage (Andersen et al. 2011; Bellotti et al. 2012; Mortara et al. 2014; Holloway-Attaway and Rouse 2018). The main issue in presenting the state-of-the art in SGs is the lack of a standardisation in evaluation methods among the different case study prototypes which makes it difficult to compare all of them and discuss challenges or advantages (Paliokas and Sylaiou 2016). This chapter that discusses the use of SGs to bring users to the centre and create experiences that are unique, personalised and flexible. This section will review the techniques used by specific case studies to develop VMs and SGs that focus on the user.

Establishing a connection between people and museums, is a goal that often museums struggle to achieve. As it has been recommended by the International council of Museums (International council of Museums (ICOM) 2019), the museums are not just institutions where visitors are educated but also places for enjoyment. To achieve this, among many other ways, is to allow people to rediscover the museums on personal and emotional level. SGs can spark curiosity by embedding rewards in the whole narrative experience. In other words, SGs can create the narrative that is missing from the museums that unfolds a story while people are playing. These kind of SGs can be of great use for museums because storytelling is an important communication tool for cultural experiences.

A SG that was created as part of a cultural exhibition experience, themed "The Building Works of Saint NEgratia: The pantheon under the republic" is the game Solis' Curse (Neto et al. 2011). This game belongs to the category of the virtual museum, mainly due to the different scenes in the game which are digital representations of the cultural heritage sites. The main purpose of this game was to assess the knowledge of the visitors that was acquired during the exhibition visit. Apart from that though, this SG provided a different way of interacting with the exhibition as it offered speech interaction with an embodied agent that navigates the user through the 'game' and assist him to complete the tasks. This embodied Conversational Agent (ECA) has been developed with a personality to invoke feelings of empathy towards specific audiences to communicate effectively the cultural values and to determine the importance of maintaining them. As, Mortara et al. (2014) have suggested empathy with a game character can be valuable for understanding historical events or different cultures and historical behaviour or problems. Even though the visitor is not physically a player in a game, as it would consume too much time for the player to explore the scene and missing the information conveyed by the agent, the narrator accompanies the player between rooms that depict the exhibition. This interactive dialogue not only allows the user to engage in a personal way with the exhibition but also gives the opportunity to participate with an active role, feeling that he is part of the unfolding story. Additionally, this SG allows for an asynchronous visit to the exhibition so that the visitor can engage with the game even when not in the site which provides access to a variety of visitor groups. As Sylaiou et al. (2017) confirmed from an evaluation study involving online museums resources that can enhance participants leaning outcomes, VMs in the form of interactive experiences apart from effective engaging methods, are also efficient methods of learning due to the edutainment dimension connected to game-like experiences (Doulamis et al. 2011).

Another game that used embodied conversational agents as companions to children during the time spent at an art museum is the "Monsters Eat Art" (Rehm et al. 2014; Rehm and Jensen 2015). The 'monster' of the game serves as the narrator that guides the children through a treasure hunt at the art museum but at the same time is also passing information about the artworks to the children. Treasure hunts in museums have been criticised as it motivates visitors to see the cultural space as a bunch of disconnected artefacts and not as part of a narrative, which would have a deeper cultural meaning (Klopfer et al. 2005). Similarly, a treasure hunt embedded in a serious game for museum environments focusing in younger generations demonstrated successfully the potential of education using serious games in museum (Doulamis et al. 2011). Additionally, as was shown at the study conducted at the Boston Museum of Science where the "Mystery at the Museum "game was used by family members to gather information in a problem solving activity, participants felt that they had a participatory role in the museum experience which added value to their visit (Klopfer et al. 2005). Treasure hunts as part of a pedagogical approach has enacted quite well with children in the older years even without the digital means that exist today (Elliott 1926). In the experiment, where 57 children participate, it was shown that children engaged more with the artefacts when they played a digital tablet version of the game rather than a paper based version. The results also showed a higher retention rate for the details of the artworks.

An example of using digital technology and serious game methodology to enhance visitors experience in the museums is the "Undercroft Game" which was developed along with another mobile application for Herbert Museum and Art Gallery to enrich visitors' experience (Petridis et al. 2013). The purpose of the game was to offer further insights on the daily activities of the monks of Coventry's original Benedictine monastery. The game also tried to increase the younger audience's interest towards cultural knowledge. It is a simple puzzle game where the player has to interact with various non-player characters uncovering clues to solve the puzzles. The evaluation of the enjoy-ability of the game, even though was conducted with a small sample size (five users), showed potential in using the game to learn and understand more about the history of Priory Undercrofts. This example reinforces the digitisation of VMs but not just in the rigid context of a Virtual exhibition of artefacts but rather an interactive way of bringing the user in the centre of the learning experience.

Whilst users employed digital technology to access the game, it does not allow engagement for ongoing long-term experiences. As Benford et al. (2009) have pointed, new techniques need to be employed to support visitors for episodes of engagement. Apart from the bespoke interface that currently most museum tools rely on, there is a need for orchestrating tools than can automatically (or semi-automatically) create the interfaces based on the specification of an experience.

Despite the tools like SGs and embodied conversational agents, narrative is the most usual approach as a method to communicate through the selection and display of the artefacts. Similarly, museums have tried to embed the storytelling aspect in the VMs. However, most of the times it remains descriptive or scholarly prose (Perry et al. 2017). In most cases of SGs or narratives in VMs the meaning is communicated in didactic fashion, not connected with emotions and morals that have proven to motivate large audiences (Vagnone and Ryan 2016). An ongoing project to engage visitors emotionally by designing a VM that focuses not just on the story but which supports interaction among the visitors and the objects themselves is EMOTIVE (Katifori et al. 2019). This is an EU funded (HORIZON 2020) project that aims to integrate activities, which take place pre-during and post-visit and involves interactions with tangible and intangible objects. This project tried to cater the patterns of visitors while in cultural sites or museums and sees them more as visitors in social experiences. The approach employed is user-cantered both in the design but also in the evaluation phases and customises the experiences using customer profiles that allow creating personal views of the visitors as social agents. In terms of the technology, there is a mix of 3D/2D spaces that were integrated without though focusing a lot on the technology itself but rather in the emotional part of the experience. The preliminary results were promising, potentially opening new doors in involving multi-disciplinary work to approach and orchestrate new interfaces that will engage visitors and initiate meaningful cultural experiences.

Digital storytelling for cultural applications is not new in museums virtual or not. For example, the PEACH Project automatically creates video clips on visitor's device and it is using a life-like character to present the information (Damiano et al. 2008). In a similar manner with game mechanics, in Ghosts in the Garden (Poole 2018), visitors use a device to view the "ghosts" of characters based on real people in a historical garden in Bath, UK. Finally, CHESS project (Katifori et al. 2014), which was also EU funded, was looking to develop stories that were interactive, personalised and adaptive. Using game mechanics and storytelling techniques the main aim was to motivate visitors to find personal and meaningful connections with the objects.

15.5   Current Challenges and Opportunities in the Industry

The proliferation of Extended Reality Technologies (Fast-Berglund et al. 2018) included to the spectrum defined by AR, VR, MxR enables for immersive experiences in the area of cultural heritage, education and also tourism. Opportunities arise to develop more emotional and impactful experiences relevant to heritage, tradition, culture, and history of a place or folk with the use of such advanced immersive technologies. The next generation of XR apps will have to build on and as described in Sects. 15.3 and 15.4.

This means that they would have to appeal to a wider audience, thus at a more personalised level (Bohnert and Zukerman 2014), as well as the penetration to markets and end users that lack the technological elements that these technologies might require for financial reasons. For one, inasmuch as AR can be seen as a cutting edge technology, one could argue that is not so widely accessible only judging by the short length of compatible devices across available major AR SDKs (Vuforia,[1] ARCore,[2] ARKit,[3] Wikitude[4]). Same applies for VR with expensive headsets not widely accessible to user groups potentially defined as target groups for immersive heritage related apps. Content delivery on those platforms can be proven a challenge and it limits, in technological terms, the extent to which one can reach out to users. Add to that the costs of app and content development and maintenance and the proliferation of such products to mainstream solutions is bound to be limited. A recent study for museums and technology in the USA reveals that 35.5% of visitors think that the museums in their proximity never exhibit new technologies (Stage 2 Studios 2018) with another 20.5 answering "rarely" and 37.2% answering "sometimes"; only 6.8% of the population finds that their museums exhibit new technologies. This is an

---

[1]https://developer.vuforia.com/.

[2]https://developers.google.com/ar/.

[3]https://developer.apple.com/augmented-reality/.

[4]https://www.wikitude.com/.

indication that the average museum visitor does not interact with these technologies for various reasons. One of which is lack of simple and easy to use apps that can be directly installed on their mobile phones.

This latter assumption of using the visitor's own device to run the museum app to serve the content in one XR modality is limited by the performance of the device and its compatibility with various SDKs. Hence, there is a need to overcome this issue and realise a platform agnostic solution that could be ubiquitous in terms of compatibility.

The evolution of telecommunication infrastructures and the longed for fifth generation of mobile cellular networks (5G) that encompasses also Multiaccess Edge Computing (MEC) can provide a consequential solution to this problem. Having provisioned a MEC server close to the user (edge) provides an immense capability of computational performance that is characterised by low distance to the user, thus low latency, and also the opportunity to design system architectures that would enable the balance of computational need lopsided to the network instead of the end user's device. In other words, the need for computational intensity can now be moved to the Cloud, releasing the pressure from the mobile device, thus enabling content to be accessible to many more users and not limited to those with compatible devices. Processes such as rendering of 3D models, lighting and visual effects can be allocated to the MEC and streamed with low latency to the mobile device. This fact solves another significant issue apart from the need for expensive and high end mobile devices for XR experiences. Recent announcements from technological giants such as Google (Stadia[5]), Microsoft (xCloud[6]) and Apple (Arcade[7]) for relevant gaming platforms with remote rendering for ubiquitous access and with any kind of device demonstrate that 5G will be the enabling arbiter to define the future of Virtual Worlds, being entertaining games or educational applications such as VMs.

Content creation is another blocking point for the proliferation of such experiences. Content availability is scarce across mainly micro-enterprises (freelancing) and availability of quality content is not yet centralised (Tan and Rahaman 2009; Pacheco Estefan et al. 2014; European Commission 2019). Although mainstream commercial solutions exist as per repositories of 3D models, characters and animations, these are mainly focused on gaming (ref to Unity marketplace, mixamo, turbosquid) and there is a huge gap in content relevant to historical sites and with some confidence level of historical accuracy. A solution such as EUROPEANA[8] (Isaac and Haslhofer 2013) that has been around since 2008 does not yet contain a large amount of content relevant to XR, for example culturally relevant 3D models of objects and personalities. Combined with the previous point about centralising the rendering on the network (MEC) and streaming the content to the user, one can realise that such approach opens the way to educational, cultural, heritage related, emotionally engaging applications that will disseminate history, traditions, culture

---

[5]https://stadia.dev/.

[6]https://blogs.microsoft.com/blog/2018/10/08/project-xcloud-gaming-with-you-at-the-center/.

[7]https://www.apple.com/uk/apple-arcade/.

[8]https://www.europeana.eu/portal/en.

and will engage and penetrate to a wider audience beyond the conventional museum user.

Furthermore, such heavily graphical based applications can be separated from the museum as a location and can work in any kind of environment. Especially where there is emotional value connected to the geolocation. For example, a 3D model of Colossus of Rhodes, or more recent example of statues smashed by ISIS in Mosul, Iraq, projected in an XR application within the boundaries of a museum will create much less impact than the same 3D model presented in the actual place it is thought to have been located. Same for points of interest that now do not exist for a variety of reasons (war, decay, natural disasters); XR can help recreate their virtual equivalents and preserve the emotional value connected to the place itself (Dumiak 2018; IEEE 2018).

Finally, to further increase the engagement of the user with the medium and content one should utilise well established mechanisms for such engagement, which is no other than games. Gamifying the use, other than the experience itself is a way to make users come back to the medium, engage them with the content and retain the knowledge objective (Huynh et al. 2016). XR apps for cultural heritage are a perfect application of gamification with geo-localisation in the lines of the very successful Pokemon Go game made by Nintendo (Sicart 2017). So apart from designing Serious Games relevant to VMs that would contain a game objective and utilise game mechanics to engage the user within unique sessions (gameplay), one can design an overarching framework to engage with gamification of XR apps. Building on the impact factor brought by the use of new technologies like AR, VR, MxR, the gamification element will provide the retention factor for the customer to return to the platform and further engage, explore, play, learn and have an emotionally engaging experience.

15.6 Discussion: A Conceptual Framework

Considering current industry trends and the state-of-the-art in using XR and serious games in VMs and greater cultural heritage field, it is possible to identify great potential but also important challenges. This paper summarises the discussions into a three layered framework. These three layers are; Users, Technology and Content. Each of these layers presents unique challenges for the future of VMs. The discussion so far has presented previous approaches and also possible opportunities provided by the trends and advances in the technology and user-centric development. This section will discuss these in further detail.

Table 15.1 presents the summary of the challenges and the approaches and possible opportunities which could tackle them in our framework. As mentioned previously there are three layers of challenges identified in this framework. These layers are inter-related and the challenges in each would be dependent on other challenges in other layers, for example access to technology impacts user acceptance and user

Table 15.1 Challenges and approaches in using XR and SGs for future user-centric VMs

Layer	Challenge	Approaches/Opportunities
Users	Acceptance	Personalisation XR
	Awareness	Serious games and gamification XR 5G
	Software usability	Serious games and gamification UX design
	Engagement	Serious games and gamification XR
Technology	Access to technology	Accessible devices 5G Centralised rendering
	Device performance	5G Centralised rendering
	Software performance	5G Centralised rendering
Content	Creation	Community sourcing Centralised rendering Open libraries
	Delivery	5G Centralised rendering
	Localisation	Geo-tagged content Community sourcing

engagement. Similarly, the approaches and solutions could impact multiple challenges, especially in a user-centred approach. The complex dynamic relations of the framework have been conceptualised in Fig. 15.1.

The challenges in the *User* layer are focused on the behaviour and preferences of the users towards cultural experiences. This layer is the core of a user-centred approach and impacts on all other aspects of the intended experience. The challenges in this layer are categorised into four topics.

User acceptance: This challenge focuses on personalising the experience of the user in order to create a memorable yet repeatable experience tailored to the needs and preferences of the user. As mentioned before visitors have different needs, expectations and abilities. Personalisation of the experience becomes a key factor in the success of any experience. Research shows that personalisation in games (both serious games and entertainment games) increases user acceptance and user engagement, even leading to better performance in achieving the goal of the game (Daylamani-Zad et al. 2016, 2018).

User Awareness: As previously mentioned, the uses need to be aware of the available services such as XR apps that can be acquired or the devices available at the museum. But this challenge goes beyond this simple awareness of facilities.

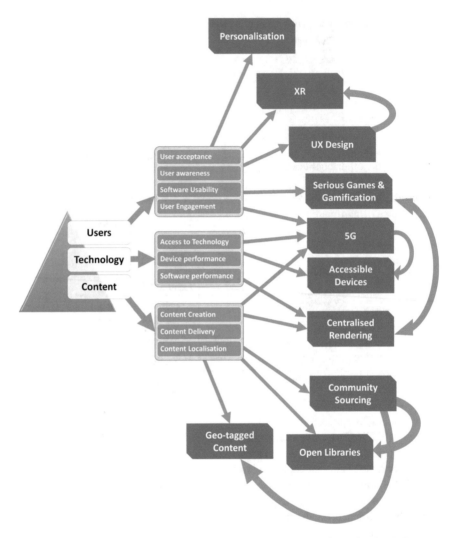

Fig. 15.1 Conceptual framework of challenges, approaches, opportunities and their relations

The visitors should also be aware of the artefacts and the collections on exhibit in order to have a meaningful experience. Immersive experiences created using XR and also serious games that guide the visitor through the exhibit, allow the users to have an enhanced experience designed beforehand for maximum experience. Such experiences of course would need to be personalised to the each visitor type and might have different goals and paths for different types of visitors.

Software Usability: This challenges is concerned with creating an experience that is tailored to the users. Such software must be designed and developed with the users in mind. Suitable UX design greatly contributes to the success of an experience and has a direct impact on the acceptance of XR technology and the immersion of users in the VM.

User Engagement: The focus of this challenge is to engage visitors in the experience and get them involved and feel part of the experience. Serious games have shown clear positive impact in increasing engagement. There is also strong evidence that immersive experiences using XR technologies also contribute to increasing user engagement. They also show evidence of revisits because of the immersive experience that they create for the visitors. It is important to highlight that increased user engagement has a positive impact towards a number of approaches that would address other challenges. For example increased engagement would benefit community sourcing, geo-tagging content and content creation,

The challenges in the *Technology* layer relate to the issues regarding access and performance of hardware and software used. These are more technology dependant yet the challenges are related to creating a better experience for the users and reaching a wider range of users.

Access to Technology: As mentioned earlier, XR devices and SDKs are still not widely accessible to all users. Not all visitors would able or willing to install apps on their personal devices and finally not all users have devices that can perform well enough to support XR immersive experiences. Fortunately, the devices are becoming more accessible and affordable. The tech giants are producing more powerful and affordable devices. More importantly with the emergence of 5G technology, centralised rendering and fast content delivery will be soon possible even to devices that might not be suitable for the current state of XR technology. High speed streaming of pre-rendered content would allow even devices on the low-end of the performance spectrum to support immersive XR experiences.

Device Performance: This challenge related to the ability of current personal and professional devices for creating immersive XR experiences. Similar to the challenge of access, the devices are improving and becoming more wide-spread whilst centralised rendering and fast delivery through 5G would compensate for many of the current issues such as lags and incompatibilities. However there are other issues in the category such as limited FOVs which are already being addressed both by software developers and hardware manufacturers.

Software Performance: This challenge related to the compatibility and performance of XR apps. Similar to the previous points in this layer centralised rendering and fast delivery through 5G would be soon able to overcome many of the obstacles in this area.

The challenges in the *Content* layer relate to the issues regarding creation, delivery and localisation of suitable content for immersive XR cultural experiences. There are three challenges in this layer.

Content Creation: This challenge relates to the ever present challenge of content generation for XR experiences. This challenge becomes much more important in the cultural heritage domain as the content cannot be as easily sourced as other domains. The content has to be based on existing artefacts, descriptions and remnants. The challenge is further deepened in this domain as the content would also need to be updated as new discoveries could either change them or make them entirely inaccurate and obsolete. As mentioned earlier there are open libraries that actively seek to create more content. However a great approach to this problem could lie in community sourcing. By including users and visitors in the content creation process, not only more content is generated but also the visitors and users would be taking a more active role, leading to more engagement. Centralised rendering which would be possible through 5G technology would also be another factor here as content available on closed or licensed libraries could be used on a much more affordable basis.

Content Delivery: This challenge is concerned with the delivery of XR content to users. The content in XR apps, which includes 3D models, textures, materials, audio, video and text, can create large downloads. These can be preloaded to museum devices or be downloaded on demand by users as they progress through the experience. However, both scenarios would require large download bandwidths, low latency and rendering at the point of delivery. As per the previous challenges, centralised rendering and content streaming via 5G technology can be a great solution for addressing this challenge.

Content Localisation: This challenge is concerned with the localisation of content for cultural heritage experiences. From virtual and actual museums to real-life locations such as monuments and important locations, the localisation of XR experiences is of outmost importance. The users should be able to receive all relevant content to their physical/requested location. This can only be achieved with increased geo-tagged content. Creating geo tags for existing content is also a great challenge here which could be addressed through community sourcing and incorporation of user generated content. An intricate detail in this challenge is content that might be related to multiple locations, complicating the setup of current libraries. Knowledge graphs and graph databases have shown great potential in addressing such challenges (Tseng et al. 2013; Amirian et al. 2015).

15.7 Conclusion

In this chapter, a review of state-of-the-art for using XR technologies and Serious Games in Cultural heritage and virtual museums was presented. The presented work was discussed in detail and analysed based on their approach to a user-centred design of solutions for VMs. The discussion was followed by identifying the current trends and challenges in the industry, highlighting potential opportunities and approaches currently focused-on in the industry. The results of these discussions were then summarised into a framework with three layers; Users, Technology and Content. The framework conceptualises the challenges, approaches and opportunities currently available towards creating immersive serious games in XR to enhance cultural heritage experiences through increasing user engagement and encouraging visitors to get involved, contribute and revisit. This framework is designed from 'lessons learned' that derive from state-of-the-art and past projects. It is expected to be used as a tool to inform design and ideation. In practise, designers can use this framework as a guide to create experiences which focus more on the user, exploit effectively the resources on hardware and software, to provide a compelling museum experience that has the user's needs and preferences at its core. Nonetheless, there are some limitations to the work presented here, as this framework is not an exhaustive audit of all the VM related projects that exist but rather a synthesis of findings from research projects that have applied key concepts of storytelling, narrative, mixed reality technologies and serious games. Finally, besides the mentioned concepts, others such as social interactions play important roles in the formation of an inclusive museum experience. Analysis in this area could extend the framework in the future supported by further empirical validation and evidence.

References

Amirian P, Basiri A, Gales G et al (2015) The next generation of navigational services using Open-StreetMap data: the integration of augmented reality and graph databases. In: OpenStreetMap in GIScience. Springer, pp 211–228

Andersen S, Ertaç S, Gneezy U et al (2011) Stakes matter in ultimatum games. Am Econ Assoc 101:3427–3439. https://doi.org/10.1257/aer.101.7.3427

Bellotti F, Berta R, De Gloria A et al (2012) A serious game model for cultural heritage. J Comput Cult Herit 5:17

Benford S, Giannachi G, Koleva B, Rodden T (2009) From interaction to trajectories: designing coherent journeys through user experiences. In: Proceedings of the SIGCHI conference on human factors in computing systems. ACM, pp 709–718

Bohnert F, Zukerman I (2014) Personalised viewing-time prediction in museums. User Model User-adapt Interact 24:263–314

Brusaporci S, Graziosi F, Franchi F, Maiezza P (2018) Remediating the historical city. Ubiquitous augmented reality for cultural heritage enhancement. In: International and interdisciplinary conference on digital environments for education, arts and heritage. Springer, pp 305–313

Damiano R, Gena C, Lombardo V et al (2008) A stroll with Carletto: adaptation in drama-based tours with virtual characters. User Model User-Adapt Interact 18:417–453

Daylamani-Zad D, Agius H, Angelides MC (2018) Reflective agents for personalisation in collaborative games. Artif Intell Rev 1–46. https://doi.org/10.1007/s10462-018-9665-8

Daylamani-Zad D, Angelides MCMC, Agius H (2016) Lu-Lu: a framework for collaborative decision making games. Decis Support Syst 85:49–61. https://doi.org/10.1016/j.dss.2016.02.011

Doulamis A, Liarokapis F, Petridis P, Miaoulis G (2011) Serious games for cultural applications. Intelligent computer graphics 2011. Springer, Athens, Greece, pp 97–115

Dumiak M (2018) Ancient sculptures return to Mosul as digitally reconstructed replicas. IEEE Spectr

Elliott H (1926) The educational work of the museum. Metrop Museum Art Bull 21:202–217

European Commission (2019) Europe 2020 strategy. Digital Single Market

Fantoni SF, Stein R, Bowman G (2012) Exploring the relationship between visitor motivation and engagement in online museum audiences. In: Trant J, Bearman D (eds) Museums and the web. Archives & museum informatics, Toronto

Fast-Berglund Å, Gong L, Li D (2018) Testing and validating extended reality (xR) technologies in manufacturing. Procedia Manuf 25:31–38. https://doi.org/10.1016/j.promfg.2018.06.054

Fernandes AB (2018) "But will there be visitors?" Public outreach efforts using social media and online presence at the Côa Valley Museum and Archaeological Park (Portugal). Internet Archaeol 47

Hammady R, Ma M (2019) Designing spatial UI as a solution of the narrow FOV of Microsoft HoloLens: prototype of virtual museum guide. In: Augmented reality and virtual reality. Springer, pp 217–231

Haynes J, Zambonini D (2007) Why are they doing that!? How users interact with museum web sites. In: Trant J, Bearman D (eds) Museums and the web. Archives & museum informatics, Toronto

Haynes R (2018) Eye of the Veholder: AR extending and blending of museum objects and virtual collections. In: Jung T, tom Dieck MC (eds) Augmented reality and virtual reality: empowering human, place and business. Springer International Publishing, Cham, pp 79–91

Hazan S, Hermon S (2015) On defining the Virtual Museum. A VMUST research project

Holloway-Attaway L, Rouse R (2018) Designing postdigital curators: establishing an interdisciplinary games and mixed reality cultural heritage network. In: Advances in digital cultural heritage. Springer, pp 162–173

Hoptman G (1992) The virtual museum and related epistemological concerns. In: Barrett (ed) Sociomedia-multimedia, hypermedia, soc constr knowledge, E 141–159

Huynh D, Zuo L, Iida H (2016) Analyzing gamification of "Duolingo" with focus on its course structure. In: International conference on games and learning alliance. Springer, pp 268–277

IEEE (2018) Preserving history in 3D. IEEE Transm

International Council of Museums (ICOM) (2019) Creating the new museum definition

Isaac A, Haslhofer B (2013) Europeana linked open data–data. europeana. eu. Semant Web 4:291–297

Katifori A, Karvounis M, Kourtis V et al (2014) CHESS: personalized storytelling experiences in museums. In: International conference on interactive digital storytelling. Springer, pp 232–235

Katifori A, Roussou M, Perry S et al (2019) The EMOTIVE project-emotive virtual cultural experiences through personalized storytelling. CIRA@ EuroMed 2018:11–20

Klopfer E, Perry J, Squire K et al (2005) Mystery at the museum: a collaborative game for museum education. In: Proceedings of the 2005 conference on computer support for collaborative learning: learning 2005: the next 10 years! International Society of the Learning Sciences, pp 316–320

MacDonald C (2015) Assessing the user experience (UX) of online museum collections: perspectives from design and museum professionals. In: Museums and the web

Mortara M, Catalano CE, Bellotti F et al (2014) Learning cultural heritage by serious games. J Cult Herit 15:318–325

Neto JN, Silva R, Neto JP et al (2011) Solis' curse—a cultural heritage game using voice interaction with a virtual agent. In: 2011 third international conference on games and virtual worlds for serious applications. IEEE, pp 164–167

Pacheco Estefan D, Wierenga S, Omedas P et al (2014) Spatializing experience: a framework for the geolocalization, visualization and exploration of historical data using VR/AR technologies. In: Proceedings of the 2014 virtual reality international conference (VRIC 2014); 9–11 Apr 2014, Laval, France. ACM, New York. Article no. 1. ACM Association for Computer Machinery

Paliokas I, Sylaiou S (2016) The use of serious games in museum visits and exhibitions: a systematic mapping study. In: 2016 8th international conference on games and virtual worlds for serious applications (VS-GAMES). IEEE, pp 1–8

Papagiannakis G, Geronikolakis E, Pateraki M et al (2018) Mixed reality, gamified presence, and storytelling for virtual museums. Encycl Comput Graph Games 1–13

Perry S, Roussou M, Economou M et al (2017) Moving beyond the virtual museum: engaging visitors emotionally. In: 2017 23rd international conference on virtual system & multimedia (VSMM). IEEE, pp 1–8

Petridis P, Dunwell I, Liarokapis F et al (2013) The herbert virtual museum. J Electr Comput Eng 2013:16

Poole S (2018) Ghosts in the garden: locative gameplay and historical interpretation from below. Int J Herit Stud 24:300–314

Rehm M, Jensen ML (2015) Accessing cultural artifacts through digital companions: the effects on children's engagement. In: 2015 international conference on culture and computing (Culture Computing). IEEE, pp 72–79

Rehm M, Jensen ML, Wøldike NP et al (2014) Smart cities for smart children. In: Smart city learning

Roussou M, Katifori A (2018) Flow, staging, wayfinding, personalization: Evaluating user experience with mobile museum narratives. Multimodal Technol Interact 2:32

Schweibenz W (1998) The "Virtual Museum": new perspectives for museums to present objects and information using the internet as a knowledge base and communication system. ISI 34:185–200

Sicart M (2017) Reality has always been augmented: play and the promises of Pokémon GO. Mob Media Commun 5:30–33

Southall H, Marmion M, Davies A (2019) Adapting Jake Knapp's design sprint approach for AR/VR applications in digital heritage. In: tom Dieck MC, Jung T (eds) Augmented reality and virtual reality: the power of AR and VR for business. Springer International Publishing, Cham, pp 59–70

Stage 2 Studios (2018) 2018 museums & tech survey and report

Sylaiou S, Liarokapis F, Kotsakis K, Patias P (2009) Virtual museums, a survey on methods and tools. J Cult Herit 10:520–528

Sylaiou S, Mania K, Paliokas I et al (2017) Exploring the educational impact of diverse technologies in online virtual museums. Int J Arts Technol 10:58–84

Tan B-K, Rahaman H (2009) Virtual heritage: reality and criticism. In: CAAD futures. Les Presses de l'Université de Montréal, pp 143–156

tom Dieck MC, Jung T, Michopoulou E (2019) Experiencing virtual reality in heritage attractions: perceptions of elderly users. In: tom Dieck MC, Jung T (eds) Augmented reality and virtual reality: the power of AR and VR for business. Springer International Publishing, Cham, pp 89–98

Tseng E, Cahill M, Murarka NI, Jolley C (2013) Recommendations based on geolocation

Vagnone FD, Ryan DE (2016) Anarchist's guide to historic house museums. Routledge

Walczak K, Cellary W, White M (2006) Virtual museum exhibitions. Computer (Long Beach Calif) 39:93–95

Wojciechowski R, Walczak K, White M, Cellary W (2004) Building virtual and augmented reality museum exhibitions. In: Proceedings of the ninth international conference on 3D web technology. ACM, pp 135–144

Chapter 16
Fostering Engagement with Cultural Heritage Through Immersive VR and Gamification

Stuart O'Connor, Simon Colreavy-Donnelly and Ian Dunwell

Abstract Digital games provide a recognised means of engagement and education when addressing challenges in educating and immersing individuals in their own heritages, and those of other cultures. Similarly, gamification techniques, commonly expressed as the addition of game elements to an existing process, have been successfully applied to augment existing resources and programmes. The many examples of gamification or serious games focusing on cultural heritage also highlight the potential benefits of using these principles for the purposes of supporting preservation and learning. In this chapter, we present I-Ulysses, a virtual-reality game designed to engage based around the notable work Ulysses by Irish author James Joyce. The rationale for the selection of Ulysses as a basis for the game's content and design was two-fold; firstly because of its cultural impact within Ireland, and secondly as its content appeared well-suited to exploration as a virtual reality experience. Facets of gamification are explored in I-Ulysses through key mechanics, including a focus towards virtual worlds and crowd intelligence based on real-world data, to highlight how these principles can be employed for cultural heritage preservation and knowledge transfer. Through feedback obtained from focus groups interacting with I-Ulysses, it can be seen that the gamified mechanics presented through the lens of virtual reality provide an informative and educational guide to Ulysses that would engage and appeal to a wide audience.

S. O'Connor (✉) · S. Colreavy-Donnelly
De Montfort University, Gateway House, Leicester LE1 9BH, UK
e-mail: stuart.oconnor@dmu.ac.uk

S. Colreavy-Donnelly
e-mail: simon.colreavy-donnelly@dmu.ac.uk

I. Dunwell
Coventry University, Priory St, Coventry CV1 5FB, UK
e-mail: aa6537@coventry.ac.uk

© Springer Nature Switzerland AG 2020
F. Liarokapis et al. (eds.), *Visual Computing for Cultural Heritage*, Springer Series on Cultural Computing, https://doi.org/10.1007/978-3-030-37191-3_16

16.1 Introduction

A holistic definition of cultural heritage includes both tangible and intangible societal attributes (Unesco definition of cultural heritage 2019; Doulamis et al. 2017).
Many digital tools focus towards the tangible, either virtually recreating historical
sites, or providing remote access to archives and virtual museums (Styliani et al.
2009; Sylaiou et al. 2017). Games, similarly, have often focused on the educational
aspects of tangible heritage, seeking to convey historical facts in an engaging fashion,
whether through mobile apps, desktop games, and more recently virtual or augmented
reality (Liarokapis et al. 2017; Boboc et al. 2017; Schofield et al. 2018). Games also
exist addressing intangible attributes, which encompass practices, representations,
expressions, knowledge, and skills passed down through generations. Projects such
as e-Vita sought to allow older generations to communicate their lived experiences to
youths through the form of digital games, taking these stories and adapting them to
game-based narratives (Pappa et al. 2011). However, given the age-based aspects of
the digital divide (Peters 2013), it can easily be argued games are challenging, rather
than solving, the issue of intergenerational transfer of cultural heritage. Nonetheless,
storytelling is recognised as an established and vital means of conveying intangible
heritage, either intergenerationally or cross-culturally (Rizvic 2014). Methods range
from narratives of historical events, often told from a nuanced, individual perspective,
though to fairy tales or fictions which often convey the moral principles of a culture.
Whilst game-based learning need not require a narrative in all cases, its addition can,
contextually, provide a powerful scaffold for engagement and immersion.

In the background of this chapter, existing work relating both serious and entertainment games to cultural heritage applications is explored. A particular emphasis
is given to storytelling, and how games can provide an immersive backdrop against
which a story can be told, and, perhaps more significantly, how they can provide a
means of non-linear storytelling in which the player becomes an active participant in
the narrative. Furthermore, by adopting procedural techniques for both foreground
and background content, this non-linearity can become less of a choice of fixed
paths, and rather an immersive and open-ended 'sandbox' experience. This leads to
our cases in I-Ulysses, demonstrating the translation of a novel to a VR experience,
and its facilitation through gamification.

16.2 Background

Gamification has been applied to cultural heritage in various forms throughout the
years (Anderson et al. 2010). It is therefore important to consider the process of
gamification and how it has been applied within the medium. This leads to identification in terms of design principles and the potential benefits for implementing such
mechanics for cultural heritage. The applications of gamification however are varied, with some resultant games being purposed towards entertainment, while others

focus on more serious pursuits, including preservation and education. By considering these all these elements, it serves to highlight how gamification can be a powerful tool towards engagement for specific purposes such as immersive VR experiences.

16.2.1 Video Games

Historical contexts and monuments have proved a rich source of inspiration for entertainment games, with examples such as Creative Assembly's Total War series, or Ubisoft's Assassin's Creed (Assassins Creed: Unity. [PS3 DVD] 2014). The latter gained recent media attention following the partial destruction of Notre Dame, as Ubisoft made one title which includes a detailed 3D replica of the cathedral free-to-play. This provides an interesting example of games providing a degree of digital preservation, and more generally how tangible heritage is being increasingly pre-served in digital form outside of deliberate acts of preservation. Understandably, though, such games focus on entertaining the player, at the cost of historical accuracy, be this in terms of geography, language, culture, or mechanics. In such contexts, whilst they may facilitate and enable awareness, and engagement, detailed and accurate knowledge transfer is hard to assess or infer.

Entertainment games may have a closer connection to the intangible heritage present in many fairy tales, in that they often contain narratives with a strong moral undertone yet are set in a fictional environment. This can be as simple as 'good vs evil', though, of course, nuances in culture can still be ascertained in terms of how protagonists and antagonists are portrayed. Game-based storytelling has also evolved: firstly towards non-linearity, and secondly towards moral ambiguity (Christiansen 2017). The former enables the player to shape their experience through the choices they make; the latter increases engagement with these choices by making them more complex than simply doing the 'good' or 'bad' thing, and instead encouraging them to apply their own judgement to moral dilemmas. This progression is partly a consequence of the maturation of games as a creative medium, but also reflects the increasing capacity of underlying technology to create richer, dynamic content.

Whilst objectives may differ, a wide range of entertainment game technologies have already brought benefits to cultural heritage. Not only do modern game engines such as Unity or Unreal expedite development; higher-level technologies often also have relevant applications. These include the use of tools for structuring narratives and objectives, which can often be straightforwardly repurposed to educational contexts, but also tools for procedural generation and the production of immersive environments. A key area of focus for this chapter is the use of crowd simulation to add plausibility and depth to environments, facilitating a transition from a static environment towards a more dynamic recreation of a setting. Implementing crowd simulations in a learning context requires consideration of the levels of interactivity required (Panzoli et al. 2010), which can range from a crowd service as a component of an immersive backdrop, though to explicit roles for crowds and characters as interactive agents.

The case study described in this chapter uses entertainment game technology to recreate a multi-linear narrative from Joyce' (2011). Before introducing this case alongside the role of crowd simulation in such a context, the next section considers, primarily from a pedagogical design standpoint, the specific use of 'serious' games when addressing the transfer of tangible and intangible heritage artefacts.

16.2.2   Serious Games

One could assume the role of 'serious' games when compared with entertainment games is to shift focus and emphasis towards accuracy and pedagogy; though a risk exists in compromising engagement, which is often the primary rationale for the use of game-based learning (O'Connor et al. 2017). Existing examples of serious games in the area of cultural heritage often use fictional narratives, with tropes such as time-travel commonly applied as in the case of the Time Explorer game (Raptis et al. 2016). This is a common compromise due to the difficulty and expense involved with high-fidelity recreation, as well as the impossibility of creating a ubiquitously correct version of a historical setting. Whilst the games industry tends to delineate between pre-production and production in larger-scale projects, the smaller scale of most serious gaming ventures also means the cyclic approach effectively locks the game into pre-production as a prototype, rather than delivering a finished product. In a research sense, this affords opportunities to flexibly investigate and understand efficacy, however, engagement can also be difficult to assess using prototypical 'unpolished' products, given the frequent expectations of gamers towards high quality player experiences and fidelity.

Frameworks for the design, development, and evaluation of serious games in cultural heritage, such as that of Andreoli et al. (2017), tend to emphasise interactive models that provide a cyclic basis for concept design, development, and evaluation. Whilst valid, these pose some inherent risks: in practical terms, finite resources and time-frames can limit iteration, and it is important to consider iteration as an approach with drawbacks as well as benefits, rather than purely as a conceptual ideal. Particular risks include the dilution of resources across multiple iterations, at the cost of fidelity in the end-product, and difficulty efficiently feeding back evaluation outcomes into pragmatic redesigns. This is particularly an issue for serious games as compared to entertainment games, as the simpler question of 'is it fun?', is typically compounded with transdisciplinary questions such as 'is it historically accurate?', 'is it pedagogically effective?', and 'does it engage the target audience?'.

A consideration with respect to fidelity is its complex relationship to learning outcomes. For simulator-based learning, a common assumption is that increased fidelity benefits learning outcomes. Fidelity itself is often separated into different subcategories (McMahan and Herrera 2016), for example visual fidelity, in terms of how realistically a scene is rendered, through to interactive fidelity, in terms of how objects and processes operate and interact. This subcategorisation is useful when considering different facets of learning and engagement: a recreation of an ancient monument may benefit from high levels of visual fidelity, whereas a simulation of an interpersonal interaction or historical process can benefit more from interactive fidelity. Identifying where fidelity is non-critical can prove more valuable than identifying critical cases, not only because it allows resources to be focused appropriately, but also because it grants levity to the designer when seeking to provide an engaging experience.

Holistic consideration of fidelity beyond required learning outcomes is also worthy of consideration. When seeking to engage a target audience, consideration of their context of play is also essential. Target demographics that already engage widely with entertainment games can bring accompanying higher expectations of fidelity, and attempting to engage such groups in their leisure time is particularly risky in terms of successful reach. Often, the solution lies in the use of games as part of more structured or blended learning solutions, ameliorating the need to stimulate intrinsic motivation. However, as technology matures, it is increasingly feasible to provide high-fidelity recreations of sites and characters within the pragmatic constraints of a typical game-based learning project. In the next section, the i-Ulysses project is introduced, which sought to capitalise on these technologies to provide a gamified approach to learning cultural heritage within a virtual environment.

16.3   I-Ulysses

The I-Ulysses: Poetry in Motion project focused on development of a virtual-reality game, using the process of gamification to engage players with cultural heritage. Joyce's (1969) is a culturally significant novel that takes place in the busy streets of Dublin circa 1904. The novel introduces spatial and auditory metaphors as core mechanics, with crowd psychology and behaviour utilised as narrative elements. I-Ulysses investigates the value of gamification and pedagogy to that end and for potential use in educating and preserving cultural heritage as an immersive experience. The project referenced the concepts of Derryberry, Salen and Zimmerman on meaningful play and serious learning in games; Dondlinger's work on virtual learning environments; Ellis' work on educational game design; and Norman's The Design of Everyday Things (Derryberry 2004; Salen et al. 2004; Willis 2006; Dondlinger 2007; Norman 2013).

At its core, I-Ulysses adapts the Ulysses novel into a spatial virtual environment. Here the spatial and auditory aspects of the virtual environment are connected to specific audio-spatial events from the book, following the same method of employing sound cues as employed by Joyce in Ulysses. The main objectives of the project were:

- To educate players in the narrative and storytelling techniques of a classic literary work using an immersive virtual reality experience.
- To facilitate this learning, in an integrated, multi-modal manner that reflects key aspects of the specific novels structure.

- To enable players to consult contextual information about a book in a real-time context on a mobile platform, whilst traversing around the virtual environment it takes place in.
- To create an interplay between the themes of a book, the historical and physical environment it takes place in and the current virtual environment that the player inhabits.

I-Ulysses was designed to be as close in relation to the novel as possible with its story presentation and core mechanics. In this regard, it follows a multi-linear story pattern through its virtual environment and the objectives contained therein. There are several bonus characters or stories that vary throughout the virtual environment depending on player choices (Bloom, Kernan, Blazes Boylan, The Secretary etc.). These characters stories can be accessed as bonus missions upon completing the final level, which takes place in the Martello Tower. The Martello Tower is like the central hub of the game; the means by which the other sections of the story are connected together and can be accessed from any direction in the level structure, so-to-speak. It should be noted that the story of the game is based on the 'Wandering Rocks' chapter of the book, but it interlinks events that take place throughout its story. Each back-story, or bonus level, comes with text taken from the relevant chapter. This presence may be an image, a sound or something that Joyce directly hints at in the text. These sections of the book take place on the busy streets of Dublin during the day and so the representation of crowd behaviour and psycho-dynamics is an aspect of the experience.

In addition to the directional prompts, the game incentivises the player to pursue specific goals, but does not constrain them to certain choices. The environment transitions from the city, to back stories in the Tower, Kildare, and The Chapel, and then reverts to the relevant 'Wandering Rocks' section of the city. The stream-of-consciousness of each character in the book is represented by the players character being able to float around the scene in an unrestricted first-person perspective, rather than the more confined space of the city. When the player clicks on the text menu they are returned to the broader environment, which has been changed by their interaction in the back-story level, and is encouraged to look for other interaction events, which again reveal further dimensions of the story. In the flow chart below one set of connections and interaction outcomes, and the paths needed to unlock them, is represented (Fig. 16.1).

Interactive elements within the environment help to provide a new means of understanding Ulysses. Within the environment certain events, such as back-stories and thought bubbles, appear at different times, depending on the choice of objectives that each character attempts to complete. This is illustrated with the time-keeping function of the clock, used to suggest that certain elements of the active environment can alter depending on player choices. In the city-version of the environment, the camera also changes its depth of field and moves closer or further away from the player depending on which character they are using, indicating that several different points of view on the environment are possible simultaneously. The thought bubble enables the player to see what the character is thinking based on the objectives and

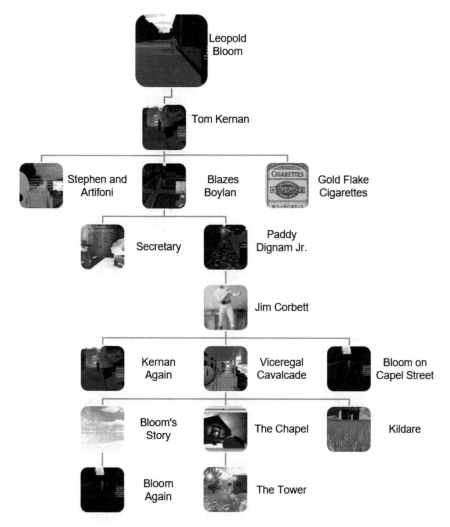

Fig. 16.1 Story nodes highlighting the path of interaction and connections between key events

back stories which they have completed. An alternate viewport appears in the bottom right hand corner of the screen showing other characters paths. These features sought to more fully realise the interactive potential of the virtual reality and explore means by which interior monologue and multi-linear storytelling techniques of Ulysses could be transferred to an interactive experience.

The setting also sought to enforce the player's sense of objective, since certain choices are result in visible changes to the environment and affect what level they progress to, whilst others will not. This assumes the player will be more engaged with the environment, as they observe the relationship between their actions and consequences. The technique also sought to provoke interest in learning about the network that underpins the character's relationships. As shown above (Fig. 16.1), completing interactions in a particular order will change the outward environment and the possibility for new interaction events to occur within specific missions. The environment emulates these effects in real-time, so that choices shape the player's understandings of time and the overall structure of the environment. In this way the player sees their own actions held in sharp relief against the other character's stories and the behaviour of the larger crowd on that day.

This real-time effect foregrounds the objectives of the environment; it focuses specifically on what drives or motivates the player in the environment and what mechanisms are being used to direct their attention. The real-time effect also focuses on how to make the player aware of the fact that they are being directed towards discrete learning goals, having both a specific and general goal. The objective-based environment is themed around Joyce's use of key sound events and so the environment uses certain cues or tropes from Joyce's work, namely representing how sound cues interact with the interior monologue and multi-linear storytelling techniques. Use of songs mentioned in Joyce's work and advertising motifs help to establish the Victorian setting of the environment (such as the Gold Leaf Cigarettes advertisement for example), by establishing it within the time period using references from Ulysses.

As described in this section, I-Ulysses is a closely linked narrative embedded within a virtual environment. Establishing a sense of presence in this environment, whilst also creating an environment capable of supporting exploratory learning, required a degree of adaptivity and depth in the design. One particular need was to recreate an urban environment immersively; in particular, it was desirable to use crowds and crowd simulation. In the next section, we discuss an approach to crowd simulation in the Unity engine, as used for the I-Ulysses project, and describe its implementation to create plausible crowd behaviours based on human perception.

16.4   Inhabited Virtual Dublin

Producing realistic crowds to inhabit virtual locations consists of various challenges, due in part to the interlinked components that comprise a system for simulating emergent crowd behaviour (Lerner et al. 2007; Thalmann and Musse 2012). Contributing is the fact that a distinction can be made between crowds employed for serious applications (Almeida et al. 2013) and those geared more towards entertainment purposes (Cournoyer and Fortier 2015). Crowds for serious applications are often modelled using crowd data (Zhao et al. 2018) and have a limited amount of human interaction, being built towards specialised purposes. In contrast, virtual crowds utilised for entertainment are typically have a user-centered focus, wherein user interaction and perception are highly important considerations (Pagulayan et al. 2002). A clear example can be seen looking at crowds applied as interactive elements in video games, with developers stressing the importance of believability or perceived realism (Bernard et al. 2008). Serious games on the other hand, such as I-Ulysses, need to offer a middle ground between a serious focus and entertainment. I-Ulysses in particular, incorporates both elements from the real-world in the form of the novel and crowd data, as well as a design paradigm based in gamification and pedagogy to support engagement and learning.

For the development of the crowds, an adapted three-stage methodology was employed, covering analysis, synthesis, and perception. These stages, in more detail, are: (1) analysis of real-world instances of crowd behaviour; (2) synthesis of crowd behaviour into a simulation; and (3) perceptual evaluation of the resultant crowd behaviour. Related research has shown that conducting these three tasks is a necessity for producing a robust study that contains a model, which is 'grounded in reality' (Peters and Ennis 2009; O'Connor et al. 2015). By consulting crowd data to build the scenario and parameters it ensures this real-world grounding exists for the model and can be preserved.

For analysis, Temple Bar in the center of Dublin was selected due to its place within the Ulysses novel and the importance of dense crowds as a narrative mechanic. Temple Bar being pedestrianised and highly trafficked provides a source of high-density crowd data that can be applied to various locations within the virtual environment. In addition, by selecting typical pedestrianised streets, which are a prominent type of location utilised in both video games and serious applications, results can be applicable to a wide range of future endeavours. Other important factors for the selection of the location include; being a central location in a major city, with a viable perspective on the pedestrian lanes, having limited boundaries comparable to the size of the space, and being viable for reconstruction.

Crowd footage was acquired at peak times during clear weather from live web camera feeds that were a part of the EarthCam network (2017). A manual annotation was tailored towards the crowd configuration. In this process, an annotator manually adds semantically relevant descriptors. Generally, the annotation should be as simple and efficient as possible, only considering relevant factors (Peters and Ennis 2009). This of particular importance when considering video footage, where different frames need to be analysed. Two variables of interest for I-Ulysses were group frequency, referring to the number of different groups that are present within the given scene, and group density, referring to the number of individuals in these groups. By annotating the groups using the mark-up method, values for these two variables are tagged and calculated at each key frame (Fig. 16.2).

The I-Ulysses virtual environment, objects, and mechanics were developed within the Unity game engine. Using the functionality of 'prefabs', a generic feature that allows a developer to group game objects together into packages that can be quickly instantiated in the game environment, development could be quickly accelerated as collections of assets could be packaged and modified for all instances simultaneously. This functionality enables a convenient hypostasis effect referred to as inheritance, where the designer can implement changes to a specific asset or can make changes backwards compatible to all instances of an asset.

For synthesis of crowds, an agent-based system was implemented to give their form of intelligence. Typically, an agent approach will include a form of decision making, pathfinding and steering, which allows agents to perceive, think, and act, to a limited extent. For the purposes of I-Ulysses, a focal point was given to group frequency and group density, so it was important to limit the behavioural variability

Fig. 16.2 A key frame from the Temple Bar crowd footage, showing an example of the annotation process whereby groups are tagged. The colour of the annotation denotes density of the group

of the agents for perceptual evaluation, as implementing more complex algorithms that consider more factors such as social forces, would potentially lead to emergent behaviour influencing results and detracting from the established narrative of Ulysses. As such, the sophistication of the agent system was kept suitably limited with the steering behaviours and overall group controller.

To limit emergent behaviour, a steering force based approached was utilised in a similar fashion Reynolds (1987). This consisted of multiple steering behaviours to act as the main behavioural control system for the agents. Several key steering behaviours are initialised for each agent in a defined group:

- Cohesion: Determines how closely each member of the group sticks together.
- Alignment: Determines how closely the group follows in formation.
- Separation: Determines how far agents in the group can move apart from each other.
- Separation from other groups: Determines how the group as a whole move to avoid colliding with other groups.
- Path-following: Determines the predefined paths groups follow within the virtual environment to reach their intended destination. Through a corrective force pointing down the path, agents are able to respond dynamically and then navigate back onto course.

These rules consist of two key variables, a weight to determine how much impact a specific rule has in relation to the other rules, and a radius to determine the size of the local neighbourhood considered for that rule. The key differences to the Boids model are the additional rules and weighting factor, which prevents agents from exhibiting the flocking behaviour and instead become autonomous pedestrians in their select groups. To compliment this, a group controller allowed for the initialisation of the desired number of groups and their density (Fig. 16.3), defined at runtime by an area calculated and visualised through a connected spline. Individual agents are selected

Fig. 16.3 Dublin, Temple Bar crowd simulation showing low density on the top and high density on the bottom

from a large quantity of agent prefabs setup within a pool. In this manner, the majority of agents visible are unique so obviously repeated models are minimised within the scene. Each agent has a number of key variables, including a minimum and maximum speed, a specific size represented as a radius, a maximum force value and a mass. These variables are kept constant, as the focal point is towards group frequency and density for I-Ulysses and subsequent perceptual evaluation.

For perception, psychophysical evaluation was conducted using stimuli recorded from runtime in a virtual recreation of the temple bar area as seen in the initial crowd footage (Fig. 16.3). A total of seventy-eight participants (69 males; 9 females) (4 aged 13–18; 57 aged 19–25; 12 aged 26–35; 5 aged 36–50) registered responses through the online platform, for each of the experiment's twelve trials relating to the Dublin, Temple Bar location. The six group frequency trials were presented first, followed by the six group density trials. On each trial, participants were shown both the original and simulated video clips for a duration of 10-seconds. They were asked how realistic do you find the groups in the simulated video and then told to give a percentage before moving on the next trial. For each trial within a set, a different intensity was presented (10, 30, 50, 70, 90 and 100%), with 50% intensity being the value extracted from the crowd data for that variable and the others being calculated from that. A lower intensity means less groups or fewer agents within each group, depending on the variable being examined, with a higher intensity signifying an opposite effect.

For group frequency in Temple Bar, the highest average response of 0.71 was for 70% intensity, equating to a value of 22 groups. For group density in Temple Bar, the highest average response of 0.88 was for 50% intensity, equating to a value of 2.3 agents per group. These results highlight what was perceived as being most realistic in terms of composition and are complimented through identification of absolute thresholds, which determine the point at which the composition stops being perceived as realistic. The absolute thresholds for group frequency in Temple Bar were identified as 35% intensity and 95% intensity, which links to a frequency of 12 and 31. In addition, the absolute thresholds for group density in Temple Bar were identified as 33% intensity and 81% intensity, which links to a density of 1.5 and 3.7.

These results highlight some important considerations for I-Ulysses, in particular when examining a comparison between the crowd data and these perceptual results. It can be seen that perception of a realistic crowd is within a close range to the 50% extracted from the crowd data, with optimum density at 50% and optimum frequency at a single increment of 70%. Additionally, there is flexibility in terms of the thresholds, with the upper threshold for frequency as high as 95%. This shows that participants were determining a larger number of agents within the scene to be within the realms of realism, where as reducing the number proved more problematic, with the lower threshold for density only as low as 33%. By establishing these thresholds, the frequency and density of the crowds can be potentially increased to give a more immersive experience closer to Joyce's intentions with Ulysses, while keeping the crowds of realistic composition to ensure integrity is not comprised.

As previously noted for I-Ulysses, by employing serious elements with an emphasis towards accuracy and pedagogy, a risk exists in compromising engagement and it is therefore important to balance the mechanics for this type of application. In the next section, we discuss this balance through the lens of a story focused cross-section adapted for I-Ulysses and describe its reception for the purposes of engagement with cultural heritage.

16.5 Story Cross-Section

What follows is a specific example of a story cross-section, adapted from the book. In the following example, the player is introduced to some of the first instances of the interior monologue in the environment. The interior monologue is the mechanism by which Joyce shows us the inner-world and thoughts of the character. In the first segment we learn that Blazes Boylan is placing a bet on Sceptre, the Horse that was favourite to win the Ascot Cup in 1904. It is later revealed that Bloom had accidentally given a tip 'Throwaway' (when he told a friend to throwaway the newspaper, advertising the race), which was the name of the horse that actually went on to win the Cup, in 1904. Bloom walks past places in the environment that are mentioned in the dialogue (Fig. 16.4). It is at this point that the player transitions between Boylan and Bloom, as playable characters.

This arc creates an important link between events from the book, because it is an example of Joyce's use of multiple points of view, or opinions, on the same events and characters. As the player progresses they gain insights from Boylan's secretary about his character, references to his gambling problems, with relevant dialogue and narration, cutting, like a film, to the description of the outside world, in the following sections. The concepts discussed in this cross-section form a part of the instructional mode of a 'blended learning' framework, wherein a tutor can read this section of the book, draw attention to the key techniques and then visually demonstrate this through having a student play the game. The benefit of having an interactive virtual model is that its use emphasizes the participatory learning dimensions of the blended learning framework. Additionally, I-Ulysses is designed to function independently as a virtual environment that a player can interact with and learn about Joyce's work from. This means that the operational aspects of the environment require a different set of developmental criteria from what would be involved in developing an educational website, an E-Book or a Digital Companion.

The I-Ulysses environment has a virtual design emphasis (Fig. 16.5), unlike the Digital Companion and E-Book formats. By engaging with the virtual environment, the player learns about the book through the design elements of the environment itself. The virtual scenarios were based on the author's interaction with students and tutors, who have taught Joyce and were informed by several user-test samples and focus groups that concentrate on improving the interface by having it tested, as much as possible. In total there were seven samples; a total of eighteen students of English from National University of Ireland Galway, thirty students from the University of Vienna, nine students from the School of Computer Science, in Trinity College Dublin and members of the public on several occasions, at the James Joyce Centre

Fig. 16.4 An example story arc where Bloom walks past key locations in the environment that are discussed in the dialogue

Fig. 16.5 Virtual
environments showing
Georgian-era Dublin Castle
and Christ Church

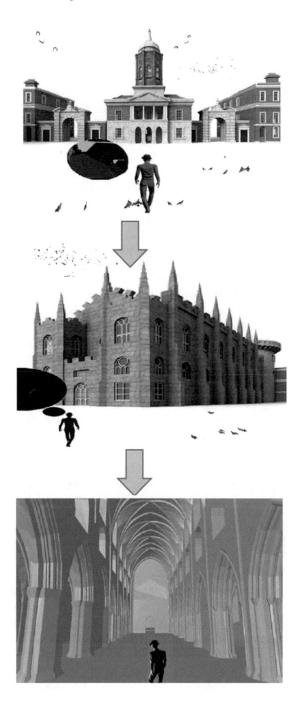

in Dublin, Ireland. The first sample at the James Joyce Centre consisted of seven participants: they were Joyce enthusiasts, a journalist writing for a national newspaper and students at University College Dublin, studying Joyce. The subsequent samples consisted of seven and five participants respectively, all of whom were members of the general public with no extensive knowledge of Joyce. Each sample played the game and filled out a questionnaire, detailing areas that they felt needed improving.

It was noted that the main objective of the virtual environment would be to facilitate the player's understandings of the innovative storytelling techniques that Joyce employed in Ulysses. This list of learning outcomes was derived by compiling each of the unique storytelling devices employed by Joyce and dividing them into three broad effects or modes: the interior monologue (or thought bubble), the multi-linear storytelling technique and the use of back stories. The responses of the attendees from the focus groups created a re-evaluation of the initial stated learning outcomes, referred to now as learning objectives. By interacting with the environment, the players from the groups were better able to:

- Note the difference between interior monologue segments from Ulysses, the dialogue and the environment in a visualised, aural context.
- Discern the character's motives, in an educational context.
- Explore the back stories of each character in a way that connected their shared experiences to the wider environment of the city.
- Discover more about the cultural world of Joyce's Ulysses and Joyce's main works, in an educational context.
- Describe a multi-linear perspective on the events of the chapter, rather than focusing on a single story-facet at one time in one place.
- Describe the events of 'Wandering Rocks' in a way that emphasised the space, setting, use of sound effects and the interconnectedness of key events and characters from the book.
- Evaluate how Joyce used sound to connect events across different spatial, geographical and temporal locations in the city.

The respondent samples stated that being able to see the difference between the character's imagination and reality, while having corresponding thought bubbles to delineate these elements of the experience, made the experience more engaging and informative in the context of seeing the technique represented from the book in a virtual format.

The respondents also argued that they felt the use of the map and the presentation of the city provided a good overview of the space of the book and the character interactions occurring in it. The consensus was that the environment, from a graphical point of view, made an effective use of the urban environment and that it felt as if the player was walking around the actual space of Dublin. A respondent from the Vienna test noted that the ability to see the streets of Dublin in a visualised context, while also exploring the narrative of the book, made the experience of using the environment more engaging and was comparable to a walking guided tour of the area.

One of the primary areas of difficulty was assessing and operationalising the data extracted from the focus groups. In many cases the types of data gathered were not formatted for a statistical evaluation; rather than exploring the mean data, information and insight gathered was more anecdotal than procedural. As Sandoval, McKenny and Reeves argue, a virtual reality format lends itself to novel forms of education-design; but because the subject matter of the I-Ulysses project is esoteric, specifically in relation to Joyce's work, it is more difficult to assess the output in a scalable format like Conjecture Mapping.

Where the mapping format and education-design theories were useful, however, was in providing the template for an 'Iterative' design process, whereby the process and practice underwent significant revision, which integrated a discourse involving both the content of Joyce's work and the employment of virtual reality technologies. This is ultimately why I-Ulysses benefited from having explored commercial and technological underpinnings, in the EI-commercialisation study and academic placement, because they provided an opportunity to test the design-hypothesis and 'High-Level Conjecture' in a real-world setting.

Without this data and the data gained from the focus groups, the project could potentially have focused solely upon a single facet of the design-hypothesis at a given time. Where the I-Ulysses sought to break new ground was in offering the potential for the design-process to be externalised into the format of the learning environment; incorporating both the Joyce-focused and technology-focused aspects simultaneously. This externalisation provided another layer of engagement that reflects the type of continuous and recursive engagement that readers traditionally have with Ulysses.

The virtual reality setting is a means to draw a player into Joyce's work and involve them in the learning environment, with a distinct set of goals and criteria for progress. The main drawback of this approach, is attempting to find a 'best fit' for the game objectives of the environment and the literary nature of the work. In terms of the manner in which user-testing scenarios and focus groups were conducted, there was a fairly broach pitching of backgrounds and specialisms, however, ideally more user-testing scenarios and focus groups could have been conducted, to that end. Often times, the specialisms of literature and interactive digital media do not easily cross over and so it is not easy to find candidates intersecting with these areas. However, since the project was undertaken, general interest, awareness of digital technology, location-based augmented and virtual reality projects (Pokémon Go) has increased immensely among the younger generations, and so such a market would prospectively exist for the project now, in a way that was not the case when it was initially devised.

There are also potential areas for improving I-Ulysses; in terms of design emphasis and methodological focus, the primary objective of the project was to establish a functional interface for the implementation of 3D game assets that would resemble and reflect key elements of the content of Ulysses. However, there are other areas that could be focused on, in a more developed format. One such area is the use of sophisticated rendering technology to reproduce an architecturally authentic 'Georgian-era' Dublin, for the benefit of tourism and cultural heritage.

Fig. 16.6 Map of the key elements that the player can instantiate

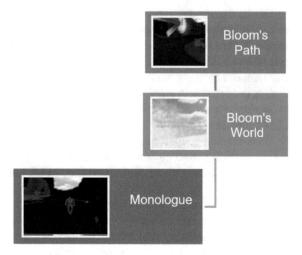

Another area that was explored was the granularity of the game-assets employed in its development; the manipulation of its pre-existing hierarchy, whereby the system could be updated in real-time and instantiate instances of player avatars or 'thought-bubbles', reflecting their own educational design-architecture and the student's engagement with the content. In the formats indicated below (Fig. 16.6), it would be possible for the tutor to update modules for player avatar appearance; what the thought bubbles would show and to re-format aspects of the environments design and realisation, reflecting an ongoing discourse.

The data employed in this hierarchy would allow such to occur in an online server-based context, thus expanding the horizons of I-Ulysses into something more closely resembling an online community, or an archive or repository of digital knowledge maintained by its subscribers. This educational-design architecture maps key features of the educational-design curriculums proposed by Sandoval, McKenny and Reeves; positioning them in a live, practical context, which could conceivably connect with other online resources.

16.6 Conclusions

The main objective of I-Ulysses was to explore new ways for players to engage with the cultural heritage and learn about aspects of Joyce's work through an immersive VR experience. Key elements of Joyce's storytelling techniques were adapted and made conceptually easier for players to understand, balancing the accuracy and pedagogy of the serious elements with gamification. The virtual environment formed the crux of the various mechanics, with player agency at the forefront as they navigate through circa 1904 Dublin to interact with the works of Joyce and discover narrative connections. The virtual environment was supported through an exploration towards simulating realistic crowds within Dublin, to capture the tone from the novel whilst retaining perceptual plausibility. This served to highlight the importance of taking player perception into account and the utilisation of perceptual thresholds when developing a cross-purpose application, such as a serious game. Thus, the virtual environment is aimed to be educational in teaching Joyce and Ulysses, but it is also intended to be entertaining to support player immersion and engagement with cultural heritage materials.

Feedback from the user tests indicated that the I-Ulysses delivered in providing an informative, educational guide to Ulysses that would appeal to a range of players, from academics and casual readers of the book. The most important aspect to emphasise, however, is that while it represents a guide to the book, it is also primarily a virtual reality experience. The choice of a virtual reality model has the distinct advantages of separating physical space and narrative, enabling the player to interrogate the differences between historical, narrative space and physical space. One of the main objectives of the project was to provide the player with a virtual model that adapts the techniques that writers employ. The I-Ulysses environment remodels and remediates these techniques into a multi-linear, 3D game experience. The project researched the areas of overlap between games, virtual reality and literature. In this regard, it could form an effective template for adapting different kinds of literary narratives into virtual reality formats. The practical work done for I-Ulysses in Unity was about demonstrating how to do this most effectively, with an efficient use of resources to target a wide range of platforms, including those with limited specifications such as mobile devices.

Acknowledgements Research on the I-Ulysses project was undertaken as part of the Digital Arts Humanities program between 2011 and 2015. An industrial/academic placement also took place in the third year, with the Computer Graphics Department (GV-2) at Trinity College Dublin, with Professor John Dingliana. During this placement, the author was given access to assets in Ogre from the Inside Joycean Dublin Project, a sister-project, and was tasked with gamifying them. The project was involved in a commercialisation spinout fast track (CFTD-1), with Enterprise Ireland's Kevin Burke, in the third year, and the involvement of the Inagh Valley Trust.

References

Almeida JE, Rosseti RJ, Coelho AL (2013) Crowd simulation modeling applied to emergency and evacuation simulations using multi-agent systems. arXiv preprint arXiv:1303.4692
Anderson EF, McLoughlin L, Liarokapis F, Peters C, Petridis P, De Freitas S (2010) Developing serious games for cultural heritage: a state-of-the-art review. Virtual Reality 14(4):255–275
Andreoli R, Corolla A, Faggiano A, Malandrino D, Pirozzi D, Ranaldi M, Santangelo G, Scarano V (2017) A framework to design, develop, and evaluate immersive and collaborative serious games in cultural heritage. J Comput Cult Herit 11(1):4:1–4:22. https://doi.org/10.1145/3064644
Assassins Creed: Unity (2014) [PS3 DVD]
Bernard S, Therien J, Malone C, Beeson S, Gubman A, Pardo R (2008) Taming the mob: creating believable crowds in assassin's creed. In: Game developers conference, San Francisco, CA, 18–22 Feb

Boboc RG, Gîrbacia F, Duguleană M, Tavčar A (2017) A handheld augmented reality to revive a demolished reformed church from Braşov. In: Proceedings of the virtual reality international conference—Laval virtual 2017, VRIC '17. ACM, New York, NY, USA, pp 18:1–18:4. https://doi.org/10.1145/3110292.3110311

Christiansen P (2017) Designing ethical systems for videogames. In: Proceedings of the 12th international conference on the foundations of digital games, FDG '17. ACM, New York, pp 21:1–21:7. https://doi.org/10.1145/3102071.3102088

Cournoyer F, Fortier A (2015) Massive crowd on assassin's creed unity: Ai recycling. In: Game developers conference, San Francisco, CA, Mar 2–6

Derryberry A (2004) Serious games: online games for learning. http://www.adobe.com/resources/elearning/pdfs/serious-games-wp.pdf. Accessed 25 July 2012

Dondlinger MJ (2007) Educational video game design: a review of the literature. J Appl Educ Technol 4(1):21–31

Doulamis AD, Voulodimos A, Doulamis ND, Soile S, Lampropoulos A (2017) Transforming intangible folkloric performing arts into tangible choreographic digital objects: the terpsichore approach. In: VISIGRAPP (5: VISAPP), pp 451–460

Earthcam network (2017) Available online: http://www.earthcam.com/. Accessed on 25 April 2017

Joyce J (2011) Ulysses. Simon & Brown

Joyce J (1969) Ulysses. Bodley Head, London

Lerner A, Chrysanthou Y, Lischinski D (2007) Crowds by example. In: Computer graphics Forum, vol 26. Wiley Online Library, pp 655–664

Liarokapis F, Petridis P, Andrews D, de Freitas S (2017) Multimodal serious games technologies for cultural heritage. In: Mixed reality and gamification for cultural heritage. Springer, pp 371–392

McMahan RP, Herrera NS (2016) Affect: altered-fidelity framework for enhancing cognition and training. Front ICT 3:29. https://doi.org/10.3389/fict.2016.00029

Norman D (2013) The design of everyday things: Revised and expanded edition. Basic Books

O'Connor S, Doukianou S, Awad M, Dixon R, O'Neill D, Dunwell I (2017) Developing gamified elements to influence positive behavioural change towards organisational energy efficiency. In: European conference on games based learning. Academic Conferences International Limited, pp 488–497

O'Connor S, Liarokapis F, Jayne C (2015) Perceived realism of crowd behaviour with social forces. In: Information visualisation (iV), 2015 19th international conference on. IEEE, pp 494–499

Pagulayan RJ, Keeker K, Wixon D, Romero RL, Fuller T (2002) User-centered design in games. CRC Press Boca Raton, FL

Panzoli D, Peters C, Dunwell I, Sanchez S, Petridis P, Protopsaltis A, Scesa V, de Freitas S (2010) Levels of interaction: a user-guided experience in large-scale virtual environments. In: Proceedings of the 2010 second international conference on games and virtual worlds for serious applications, VS-GAMES '10. IEEE Computer Society, Washington, DC, USA, pp 87–90. https://doi.org/10.1109/VS-GAMES.2010.27

Pappa D, Dunwell I, Protopsaltis A, Pannese L, Hetzner S, de Freitas S, Rebolledo-Mendez G (2011) Game-based learning for knowledge sharing and transfer: the e-VITA approach for intergenerational learning. IGI Global, pp 974–1003. https://doi.org/10.4018/978-1-60960-495-0.ch045

Peters C, Ennis C (2009) Modeling groups of plausible virtual pedestrians. IEEE Comput Graph Appl 4:54–63

Peters A, Winschiers-Theophilus H, Mennecke B (2013) Bridging the digital divide through facebook friendships: a cross-cultural study. In: Proceedings of the 2013 conference on computer supported cooperative work companion, CSCW '13. ACM, New York, NY, pp 249–254. https://doi.org/10.1145/2441955.2442014

Raptis GE, Fidas CA, Avouris NM (2016) Do field dependence-independence differences of game players affect performance and behaviour in cultural heritage games? In: Proceedings of the 2016 annual symposium on computer-human interaction in play, CHI PLAY '16. ACM, New York, NY, pp 38–43. https://doi.org/10.1145/2967934.2968107

Reynolds CW (1987) Flocks, herds and schools: a distributed behavioral model. In: ACM Siggraph computer graphics, vol 21. ACM, pp 25–34

Rizvic S (2014) Story guided virtual cultural heritage applications. J Interact Human 2

Salen K, Tekinbaş KS, Zimmerman E (2004) Rules of play: game design fundamentals. MIT press

Schofield G, Beale G, Beale N, Fell M, Hadley D, Hook J, Murphy D, Richards J, Thresh L (2018) Viking vr: designing a virtual reality experience for a museum. In: Proceedings of the 2018 designing interactive systems conference, DIS '18. ACM, New York, NY, pp 805–815. https://doi.org/10.1145/3196709.3196714

Styliani S, Fotis L, Kostas K, Petros P (2009) Virtual museums, a survey and some issues for consideration. J Cult Heritage 10(4):520–528

Sylaiou S, Mania K, Paliokas I, Pujol-Tost L, Killintzis V, Liarokapis F (2017) Exploring the educational impact of diverse technologies in online virtual museums. Int J Arts Technol 10(1):58–84

Thalmann D, Musse SR (2012) Crowd Simulation, 2 edn, State-of-the-Art. Springer, pp 9–30

Unesco Definition of Cultural Heritage (2019) http://www.unesco.org/new/en/culture/themes/illicit-trafficking-of-cultural-property/unesco-database-of-national-cultural-heritage-laws/frequently-asked-questions/definition-of-the-cultural-heritage/. Accessed 17 June 2019

Willis J (2006) Research-based strategies to ignite student learning: insights from a neurologist and classroom teacher

Zhao M, Cai W, Turner SJ (2018) Clust: simulating realistic crowd behaviour by mining pattern from crowd videos. In: Computer graphics forum, vol 37. Wiley Online Library, pp 184–201

Part V
Storytelling

Chapter 17
Exploring the Potential of Visually-Rich Animated Digital Storytelling for Cultural Heritage

The Mobile Experience of the Athens University History Museum

Akrivi Katifori, Fay Tsitou, Myrsini Pichou, Vassilis Kourtis, Evangelos Papoulias, Yannis Ioannidis and Maria Roussou

Abstract Digital storytelling in cultural heritage has been recognized as an effective technique for communicating heritage interpretation to the public. This chapter reports on the iterative design, development, and evaluation of a mobile digital storytelling experience for the Athens University History Museum. The experience combines a visually rich, illustrated and animated story of a fictional character, an aspiring young student of the University in 1840, with informational content about the museum's exhibits. The chapter discusses the insights gained from the composition and integration of the visual form, the design of the story and overall experience, and the evaluation of its impact on visitors, focusing both on the technology and the story perspective. It includes insights for the effective design of digital storytelling experiences, identifying also challenges and needs for future work in the field.

17.1 Introduction

Traditionally, museum labels and other textual information used to be the most popular interpretation means in cultural heritage settings. However, museums today have turned into "highly interpretative landscapes" MacLeod (2012) and the combination of various forms of narratives has become a common practice in contemporary exhibition design. Particularly, in the last decade digital storytelling has been recognized as an effective technique for heritage interpretation and communication (Staiff 2014, p. 24) and mobile guides offering different forms of digital narratives are often

A. Katifori (✉) · V. Kourtis · Y. Ioannidis · M. Roussou
Department of Informatics and Telecommunications, National and Kapodistrian University of Athens, Athens, Greece
e-mail: vivi@di.uoa.gr

F. Tsitou · M. Pichou · E. Papoulias
History Museum, National and Kapodistrian University of Athens, Athens, Greece

© Springer Nature Switzerland AG 2020
F. Liarokapis et al. (eds.), *Visual Computing for Cultural Heritage*, Springer Series on Cultural Computing, https://doi.org/10.1007/978-3-030-37191-3_17

employed to enhance the visitor experience (Bedford 2001; Twiss-Garrity et al. 2008; Pujol et al. 2013; Selmanovic et al. 2018).

As the borders between informative narratives and storytelling are not very well defined in this field, the definition of digital storytelling has been "overextended" to include, in some cases, even multimedia guides (Katifori et al. 2018) where narrative has been used narrowly, mostly as descriptive, scholarly prose (Brittain and Clack 2007).

The CHESS project explored digital storytelling as a means to shift focus from the traditional set of exhibit-centric, information-loaded descriptions, to story-centric narrations with references to the exhibits (Katifori et al. 2014; Roussou and Katifori 2018; Vayanou et al. 2014). It adopted a drama-based storytelling approach, combined with exploratory and interactive activities like games and augmented reality presentations of cultural artefacts. The visitor is guided around the site, museum or open archaeological site, through a mobile application which delivers a story with a coherent plot. The exhibits and points of interest in the site are presented through the perspective of their role in the story and their significance for the main characters. At each point, additional information is available for these relevant exhibits and points of interest, as per the visitor's request.

The evaluation of the digital storytelling experiences created in the context of CHESS (Roussou and Katifori 2018) led to interesting conclusions and guidelines concerning the complex interactions between the visitor, the space, the exhibits and the app (Katifori et al. 2018). How to balance information about the site with engaging storytelling? How to ensure the visitor's attention is not absorbed fully by the screen? To further explore the insights collected by our experience in CHESS, we decided to apply them in a digital storytelling experience created for the History Museum of the University of Athens, Greece.

Taking into account the Museum context and needs, we designed and created a visually rich storytelling-based guided tour app with the objective to enhance the visitor experience in the museum. The app, titled "What should I study", highlights the history of the first years of the establishment of the National and Kapodristrian University of Athens, which took place in 1837, in the building where the Museum is now housed. The visitor experiences the museum through the eyes of a young man of that time, Emmanouil.

In this work we present the results of our experimentation with digital storytelling for cultural heritage in a real life setting. In the next section we provide more details about the museum itself and its needs in relation to a digital app. Then we briefly present the technological solution employed to implement the app, before focusing on the story design and the stages of the interdisciplinary team work it involved. The evaluation of the app and its results are discussed in the following sections along with general conclusions about the experience and design process.

17.2   The Site

The History Museum of the National and Kapodistrian University of Athens (from now on University of Athens) is housed in a building (Fig. 17.1) in the historical and touristic Plaka area of Athens, Greece, on the foot of the Acropolis. The building has more than 300 years of history and it is one of the few buildings in Athens dating before the Pre-Ottonian era. It is where the University of Athens was first housed at its establishment in 1837 and operated there until 1841. The museum was founded in this building in 1987, when the University celebrated its 150 years.

The museum is an original example of a University Museum in Greece which is, at the same time, a historical site. Its exhibits highlight the history of Athens University life and of its diverse scientific fields. In parallel, they narrate the influence of the institution to the cultural and political life of the country throughout the years (see also Papoulias and Kapsimalis 2016).

The permanent exhibition is housed in the first and second floor of the building and includes university professor portraits, books, photos, rare scientific instruments and other heirlooms of the University from its foundation to about the mid 20th century.

Administratively, the museum plays a strategic and pivotal role at the Athens University Museum Network which consists of 15 museums and a Historical Archive. It falls under the Department of Museums and Historical Archive of the Directorate

Fig. 17.1   The building of the Museum, underneath the Acropolis. Phot.: K. Xenikakis. © National and Kapodistrian University of Athens

of Public and International Relations governed directly by the administrative bodies of the University. The fact that the museum does not belong to any School, underlines a key point of the vision of its foundation: to serve as a medium of communication and interaction between the university community and the wider public and as a vehicle to promote the University's heritage (Kitta et al. 2018).

Since its inauguration in 1987, on a regular basis, the museum hosts or organizes a variety of cultural and scientific events (temporary exhibitions, theatrical performances, talks, symposiums, conferences, etc.) addressed not only to members of University communities but also to the wider public.

A significant part of the museum visitors are school students who visit the museum with their class. The museum is also visited by families, adults and many tourists throughout the whole year as well as the audience and participants of the parallel events that it hosts.

17.3   Experience Production and Delivery

The "What should I study" digital storytelling experience was created with the Narralive Storyboard Editor (Fig. 17.2), our web based authoring tool for interactive digital storytelling experiences (Katifori et al. 2019a). After creating an experience in the authoring tool, it can be exported as a Narralive mobile application (Fig. 17.2). The combination of these Narralive tools enable the creation and the delivery of a series of screens containing various media, along with menus that act as branching points in the overall narrative, enabling visitors to adjust their tour to their current needs.

Fig. 17.2 The Narralive tools: Storyboard Editor (left) and Mobile Application (right), as they were used for the creation and delivery of the "What should I study" experience

The storytelling experience is available for download in the Google Play Store in Greek[1] and English[2].

17.4 The Story: Concept and Design Choices

In order to explore a guided mobile digital storytelling approach in the Museum, we designed a 45 min to one hour experience for mobile devices.

The main challenge we had to face was to design a museum experience based on a coherent, intriguing narrative for an audience of the 21st century, while highlighting the importance of the university establishment about two hundred years ago. As already mentioned, the historical context of the site is part of the big narrative of the Greek history. It coincides with the time when the Modern Greek State was founded (1830), just a few years after the successful outcome of the Greek War of Independence against the Ottoman Empire.

In order to highlight this important historical period, we decided to use it as the background canvas of our story. There, we incorporated selected museum exhibits and placed our main character, preoccupied with a problem with which even a contemporary audience could identify.

The story starts with our fictional main character, Emmanouil, a young man in Athens of 1840, facing an important and crucial dilemma of his age, that of deciding what career to pursue: Is he to follow the path his father decided for him, become a pharmacist like him and inherit the family business? Or instead, try to obtain the approval of his father, attend Law School, following his own dreams to become an important figure like his role model, the first governor of the Modern Greek State, Ioannis Kapodistrias (1776–1831)? The visitor follows Emmanouil (Fig. 17.3) on his day of registration at the University and his attempt to make a decision and find a way to pursue his dream. The introduction of a character in crisis aims at the emotional engagement of the visitor, which enhances learning and understanding (Rizvic et al. 2017).

Through the app, the visitors are guided to explore selected exhibits of the Museum, the majority of which are objects relevant to the first years of the operation of the University. The information for the exhibits as well as any navigational cues are provided through a narrator personified by the Owl, one of the university emblems (Fig. 17.4c).

The main part of the story takes place at the first building of the University of Athens which now houses the Museum. The visitor's navigation inside the museum advances in parallel with the animation which shows Emmanouil in the same building but in 1840, attempting to find a solution to his problem, while also interacting with the fictional and historical characters he meets there.

---

[1] https://play.google.com/store/apps/details?id=gr.narralive.hmua.emmanouil.

[2] https://play.google.com/store/apps/details?id=gr.narralive.hmua.emmanouil_en.

Fig. 17.3 **a** Young Emmanouil, the main character of the story, **b** older Emmanouil, reminiscing about his time at the University

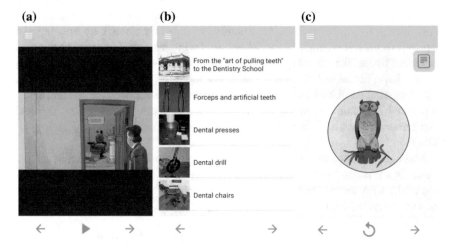

Fig. 17.4 **a** Emmanouil in front of the room with Dentistry instruments, **b** menu with information available for different exhibits related to Dentistry, and **c** the Owl giving information on one of the exhibits—the narration is available in text format by using the button in the upper right corner

The visitor assumes the role of a new student that Emmanouil is asked to guide around the building, when they go to the Secretary for their enrollment at the same time. So in this sense, the visitor is given a first person perspective within the story, being guided by Emmanouil both in the digital and physical world.

At certain points of the story, Emmanouil appears in old age (Fig. 17.3b), reminiscing briefly on the events of the time the story unfolds or referring to events that had not yet taken place at the time of the younger Emmanouil.

The remainder of the section discusses our main design choices about the experience and elaborates as to the reasons they were made.

17.4.1 Why Fictional Storytelling?

The story of Emmanouil aspired to become the main ingredient of a recipe to create a memorable museum experience taking advantage of the powerful tool of storytelling, as Fraser and Coulson argue: "story patterns give us the tools to meet the unknown, their familiar frameworks offering ways to mitigate surprise or peculiarity" (Fraser and Coulson 2012, p. 224).

The concept of the young Emmanouil (Fig. 17.3a) resulted from the objective to create a character that is closer to our targeted visitor persona, that of a young student. Emmanouil, as a young man of a historical period that now seems distant and different to contemporary life, surprisingly has concerns and thoughts about his future that are not so different from those of a young person of his age today. In this sense, this character, familiar and different at the same time, is designed to engage the younger audience, while also appeal to older visitors who will most probably have experienced a similar dilemma earlier in their life.

We interweaved fictional dramatic elements to highlight our protagonist's story, however, at the same time we attempted to increase the degree of verisimilitude and to maintain historical authenticity. Emmanouil's story is fictional, however it is not unrealistic for this specific historical period, and this is also the case for the rest of the fictional characters he encounters, including his father, other students and the Secretary. Emmanouil also interacts with historical figures, university professors and scientists of that time. This interaction is carefully designed so that it matches these characters' recorded personality. An example is the professor of Botany and amateur poet, Theodoros Orphanides (1817–1886), who surprises Emmanouil while passing by and reciting a poem to himself (Fig. 17.6a).

Furthermore, developing a fictional character as the protagonist of our storytelling and mixing the story with real elements and carefully dramatized written testimonies enabled us to advance the action and overcome complex authenticity issues (see also Tsitou 2012 pp. 188–195). We employed a fictional narrative, but one still aligned with universally accepted facts (dates, historical events, etc.) and related archival material. For example, design elements made possible by the interactive nature of the medium enabled us to address effectively gender issues while introducing the user to the protagonist. Within the story's male-dominated setting, it would be unrealistic to introduce a female student, let alone a female academic. As an alternative, we decided to introduce the gender issues of that time, indirectly, by asking the users to select how they wish to "follow" our main character, Emmanouil, i.e. taking the role of a male or a female co-student. Accordingly, we either explain the reasons why it is not possible to continue the story as a female co-student, or let the user continue as a male co-student, explaining the privileges in education of young men of the time. In both cases, we also communicate information about the history of women in education and explain that the first woman was in fact accepted in the Athens University about fifty years after its foundation.

17.4.2 Why Guided?

We opted for a linear, guided approach in storytelling, as we considered that this would ensure the coherency of the story (one hero, one day, one plot) in relation to the coherency of a full-length museum experience.

We should note here that offering the visitor a tour around the whole building was one of the main prerequisites of the project, since the exhibits linked to our storytelling period are dispersed in all the galleries of the museum. While the visitors move therefore from one gallery to the next, they are motivated to focus on specific objects and historical figures until the resolution of the story. Then they can re-visit specific galleries at their own pace and have a closer look at any exhibits that may have caught their attention.

Although the main story plot itself is linear, the experience as a whole can be considered as a branching narrative as in several points the user is given choices on the informational content offered, in the form of menus in the device. An example is presented in Fig. 17.4b.

Lastly, from the early design stages of the project, we all agreed that our aim was not to focus on testing the visitors' knowledge, neither to reward them for the right answers in quizzes. In other words, we did not intend to interrupt the visitor's "flow" experience by using "external rewards" (see also Csikszentmihalyi and Hermanson 2007). In this sense, we considered that adding gamification elements in our app might further complicate the museum experience and hinder the visitor's motivation for learning in this mixed setting (digital and physical).

Overall, it was clear to us also that the decision to avoid creating a complete free choice experience based on a deconstructed story, would be contrary to the preferences of some of our visitors. Nevertheless, we were also aware that this would attract others with different tastes and paces.

17.4.3 Why Visual?

Employing a sketch and comic artist and storyteller, a graduate of the School of Art of the Aristotle University of Thessaloniki, we provided him with the script (text and dialogues) and basic guidelines on storyboard, direction, set design and visitor's navigation to transfer the main story plot into an illustrated digital comic book, with some animation elements.

We took advantage of the visual economy of these illustrations to communicate instantly and efficiently the historical context and other information content in multiple ways.

Taking into account that, the location of our story coincides with the visitor's physical location, we decided to capitalize on this aspect by enhancing our story with carefully designed architectural elements and the perspective of the space.

Also, the visual representation of the internal of the building intended to facilitate the visitor's navigation inside the visual representation building, enhancing the Owl's navigation instructions.

Additionally, the visual representation of the story aimed at making the exhibits come to life in their natural setting and thus highlight their use. In the same way, historical figures appear to the visitor not as exhibited, in the form of two dimensional still portraits, but are rather brought to life through the animated images and sound.

In Fig. 17.5a, Emmanouil at the introduction of the story is being scolded by his father about his aspirations to become a lawyer, while he is working in the pharmacy.

(a)   **(b)**

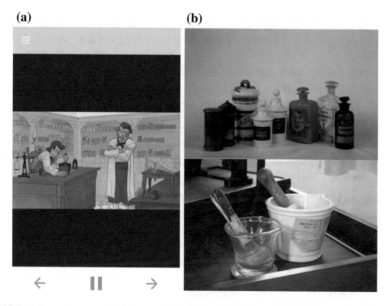

Fig. 17.5 a The pharmacy of Emmanouil's father, as it is illustrated for the needs of the story. **b** Pharmaceutical instruments and vials as they are exhibited in the museum

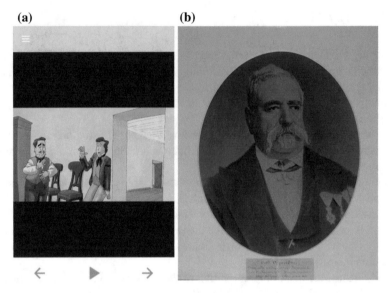

Fig. 17.6 **a** Emmanouil meets the student, poet and later professor Orphanides in the story world of the experience. **b** Professor Orphanides's photo as exhibited in the Museum

He is using a mortar (a hard bowl) to crash substances and on the pharmacy shelves we can see several vials and other pharmaceutical instruments now exhibited in the museum (Fig. 17.5b).

Similarly, professor Orphanides, whose photo is exhibited in the Museum (Fig. 17.6b), appears in the story's illustrations at the time when he was still a student (Fig. 17.6a).

To conclude, our main incentive for investing on a strong visual element for the story plot was to engage the visitor in an alternative museum experience, indirectly promoting historical contextualization of the museum exhibition.

17.4.4 Balancing the Site and the App

One of our main concerns even from the conceptualization stage of the story was not to neglect the visiting aspect of the experience in favor of the visitor's needs as a mobile device user, i.e. not to focus solely on the usability and experience aspects of the app, isolated by the space and artifacts. In previous work (Katifori et al. 2018), we have discussed the absorbing power of the screen in mobile digital storytelling applications. The visitors when given a device that offers multimedia content tend to focus more on the screen than on the physical space and exhibition. In some cases we have even observed visitors standing before an exhibit in the physical world and focusing their attention on its photo available on screen. This effect seems to be even more powerful in younger visitors who are even more comfortable with the use of mobile devices than adults. Taking into account this observation, we compensated for the absorbing power of the screen with specific design elements.

Firstly, we made a conscious decision to design differently for the story plot and the informational content. As already discussed, the story plot where the story of Emmanouil is presented, proceeds with multimedia elements and powerful visuals. Colour sketches and animations are used to present to the visitor a vivid image of the space as it was then and the people of that time.

On the other hand, when the visitor is to be presented with information about the exhibits by the Owl, the narrator's voice is only combined with an image of the Owl on screen (Fig. 17.4c) while the visitors are in most cases specifically instructed to look at specific interesting details of the exhibits, turning their attention away from the screen and to the physical world of the exhibition. This design decision not to show on screen images of the exhibits is consistent throughout the whole app with one exception, the case of the University seal, a small object with writing that is difficult to discern on the physical item. In this case, the image can significantly enhance the experience of the object, allowing the visitor to observe its details on screen.

An initial concern of the design team was that this lack of strong exhibit imagery on screen would hinder navigation. However, initial testing confirmed that the users had no problem locating the exhibits if properly instructed with audio cues on how to find them. Small icons of the objects were also added in the menus in the cases where the user would have the possibility to select amongst several objects of interest (see for example Fig. 17.4b).

17.4.5 Separating Information from the Story Plot

An early design decision for our storytelling app has been to keep, to the extent where that was possible, a clear separation between the story world and the physical world of the exhibition. While the plot advances, the main character refers to the historical context or to the use of some of the exhibits. This reference functions as a "hook" for the visitors, intending to spark their interest on the additional information introduced by the Owl narrator. In most cases, this information links to the selected exhibits.

The visitor is given then the opportunity to find out more about these objects or continue with the main story plot. In some cases, the information about the objects is structured in more than one level of details, allowing those who wish to, to delve even deeper into the relevant information. In this way, all information is offered to the visitors upon demand, according to their own preferences and attitudes, personality and ability to concentrate on that particular point in time.

This approach serves a double purpose. Firstly, the storytelling is unburdened by the need to constantly inject information that should be delivered to the users of the app by the characters. Secondly, the experience becomes up to a point adaptable to the visitor profile leading to a more personalized approach. As our previous work

(Katifori et al. 2019b) confirms, the visitors' personality traits indeed play a role on their preferences and abilities to consume content, in terms of, for example, attention span. In this sense, offering to the user control of how much content to consume at each point can improve engagement.

17.5 Evaluation Process

The digital storytelling app went through iterations of formative evaluation, assessing different aspects of the app, including the technical implementation and the content, before reaching its final version. This version has been evaluated through a two phase process which involved a total of 43 visitors (30 adults and 13 teenagers) experiencing the app in real life conditions.

	Adults	Teenagers	Total
Invited participants	18	10	28
Museum visitors	12	3	15
Total number of visitors			43

In the first evaluation phase, invited visitors of the museum were asked to test the app and then provide their feedback through a semi-structured interview and focus group session. After minor improvements to the content, following this evaluation, we proceeded with the second evaluation phase during a normal working day for the museum where visitors were asked at the entrance if they would like to use the app during their visit.

In both cases the main objectives of the evaluation revolved around the following main hypotheses:

- H1. The digital storytelling app promoted visitor engagement
- H2. The digital storytelling app promoted learning and deeper reflection on the historical context and exhibits

Our design choices for the app presented in the previous section are examined from the perspective of these two hypotheses, assessing to what degree these choices contributed or hindered the visitor experience.

The rest of this section summarizes our main organized evaluation activities. For the long term evaluation of the app we have included a user feedback form at the end of the app once the story ends.

Fig. 17.7 Evaluation with individual visitors and pairs of visitors using one device

17.5.1 Evaluation with Invited Visitors

In this phase, the app was tested by 28 visitors in total, including 18 adults, between ages 27–50 and 10 teenagers, 14–15 years old. The users presented a diverse background and attitude towards cultural institutions, ranging from museum enthusiasts to visitors that professed that they are usually "dragged" by friends and/or family to visit a museum.

The visitors were invited to participate by the evaluators and to come at the museum at a specific date and time. They were given the app and asked to use it to visit the museum at their own pace. During their visit, they were discreetly observed by the evaluators. Once they finished, they were interviewed individually and then participated in bigger groups of 3–4 persons in a focus group discussion.

The interview and focus group followed the structure of a questionnaire created with the purpose to record the user perspective on various aspects of the experience, including the story plot and its presentation, the informational content, the user experience of the App and the general approach itself (Fig. 17.7).

17.5.2 Evaluation with Museum Visitors

Our next step for the app evaluation was to introduce it to museum visitors during a normal working day of the museum. 15 visitors experienced the app. These included:

- A retired couple who mentioned that they have visited the museum several times in the past
- A group of students visiting with their professor
- 2 small groups of tourists
- 1 family
- 2 individual visitors

The visitors upon their entrance in the museum were greeted by the evaluators stationed in the Narralive app booth. They were explained that this is an experimental digital storytelling guided tour app and they could try it if they'd like. To ensure that the visitors felt as comfortable as possible during the visit, they were not observed by the evaluators. When they returned the devices to the booth, they were asked, if they wished to, to provide their opinion on the app.

17.6 Evaluation Findings

The evaluation findings confirm our two hypotheses: The storytelling app did in fact promote engagement, historical contextualization and learning, fostering a deeper reflection on the historical period and relevant social issues.

A clear indication of visitor engagement is the perceived sense of the length of the story. When asked about the duration of the story all users felt that it was appropriate and not too long. Seven of them even mentioned that they would have liked it to be longer, with more details on the informational content.

In the remainder of this section we present more details on our evaluation findings, from the perspective of our five main design choices presented in the previous section.

17.6.1 A Fictional Story

Interestingly, the approach of using a fictional story seemed to work more effectively for the less interested and "museum-motivated" visitors. As one of the visitors commented "Emmanouil kept me company and guided me to the most interesting aspects of the museum." And another: "I would like to visit museums only with this type of app. Otherwise, I am too bored."

Presenting the building and artefacts through the eyes of a young man of that period positively promoted perspective taking as it helped the visitors see that historical period through a new light. This engagement and reflection can be discerned in comments like "I had never imagined that people of that time, with so little resources could accomplish so much in science." Or "Unbelievable, at that period we almost did not have a country but we did have a University!".

It was interesting that even an older couple, repeated visitors of the museum, mentioned that the storytelling helped them "see the museum through a new light and truly realize its value, for the first time!".

There were however specific users that commented that they would have liked the story to be based solely on real and not fictional characters.

17.6.2 A Guided Experience

Our approach was to create a guided, linear experience, directing the visitor to go through all the museum galleries, and focusing on specific exhibits in each one. This approach seemed to be effective with most visitors, who considered Emmanouil as a companion and guide.

On the other hand, some of the visitors felt that strictly following the story was restrictive. They expressed the need to be able to find out more about the rest of the exhibits in a gallery, those not included in the storytelling experience. These users addressed the issue by pausing the app to look at the exhibits that caught their interest and then continuing when done.

17.6.3 The Visual Elements

The majority of the interviewed users really enjoyed the animation presenting the story. 17 confirmed that it helped them "travel in time" and "make the past more tangible" and 14 considered it "an original way to learn the history of the University" Only one found the animation "childish" and a second one "boring".

Some users also commented that a more visual approach would also be effective for the representation of processes to demonstrate the use of specific exhibits like the scientific instruments.

17.6.4 The Balance Between the Museum and the App

Presenting the exhibits mostly through audio, using the Owl narrator, seemed to be a successful design approach in making the visitors focus on the physical artefacts. As they were guided by the Owl to look and explore them, the visitors had a chance to connect with them.

However, some visitors did comment on the "absorbing" power of the mobile device in relation to space. They felt that they experienced the space more through the animations and less by physically being there. Realizing that the building itself is in fact a historical monument, they would have liked to focus more on features of the building, suggesting that possibly this disconnect would be resolved by the app explicitly directing them to do so at points.

Navigation in space, although given only through audio instructions, slight hints in the animation and small exhibit icons, was sufficient. Almost all users were able to navigate from one point of interest to the next and locate the exhibits.

Some users however proposed that the objects that form part of the storytelling experience could be marked with a specific notation.

17.6.5   Story Versus Information

As already mentioned, the perspectives of the user as far as the balance between informational content and story plot are concerned, varied. Some of the users were able to spend time in the museum and enjoy it only because of the story whereas there were some that felt that they would easily replace the story with more informational content. Some even expressed the need for a strictly informational approach: "The owl was the best, I really loved it! Go owl!" However, they also explained that they liked the way the information was offered, through interesting facts and anecdotal stories, often enriched by quotes of the historical figures.

Most users commented positively on the optional informational content offered and the possibility to skip it if it was not interesting enough. In this sense the users did not feel bored or pressured.

17.7   Discussion and Future Directions of Research

In this section we discuss bilateral findings collected during the evaluation on additional functionality for the app that could enhance the user experience.

17.7.1   "Keep It for Later" Option

Some of the users who expressed the need for more informational content on exhibits not included in the story, proposed the use of a "keep it for later" option. This option would allow the visitor to select interesting exhibits in an "inventory" thus being able to review them later, maybe after the visit.

QR or NFC codes were also proposed as a means to "collect" informational content for interesting exhibits for later review.

17.7.2   Collaboration—Social Interaction

Several users expressed the wish to experience the story with their friends, while visiting the museum. As they would very rarely visit alone, they would have liked to interact with their company at some points during the story, to be able to discuss parts or decide how to proceed.

To explore this approach, we offered in some cases one mobile device to two users who could hear the audio through their own headphones with the use of audio splitters. This preliminary test did in fact confirmed that the app was effective to enhance visitor engagement through the interaction between the users and thus re-enforced the need for a group version of the experience.

Taking this notion a step further and taking into account that a large part of the museum audience is school groups, it would be an interesting direction to investigate how to transform this individual storytelling experience into a group one, to be shared collectively by larger groups of visitors.

17.7.3 Digital Storytelling as a Virtual Experience

An interesting finding that came out of demonstrating the digital storytelling experience in exhibitions and events is that with an adequate representation of the museum space the story could also work off-site, as a virtual museum experience. This is a direction we plan to investigate so as to make the storytelling app available to visitors who would not have access to the Museum.

17.8 Insights for Good Practice

Our story had to be developed around a historical site, original exhibits and historical figures deriving mainly from a specific period. The prerequisite for this was to prepare a well-documented scenario (using archival material and written testimonies), where we mixed fictional with historical figures and thus attempted to overcome the authenticity issues.

In this project, we argue that any interpretation, even the so-called "objective" museum narrative, cannot be but a subjective interpretation of history (see also Nichols 1991). With this knowledge, we attempted to approach "authenticity" in its broader scope and considered each visitor's personal "authentic" museum experience and their motivation to "authentically" identify with our main character, equally significant to the content information and messages we aimed to transfer.

From the very beginning, we recognized the value of finding the right balance between the museum space, the artefacts and the app, in order to provide a meaningful experience inside the museum, instead of an attractive application for a distant visitor. For this, in all stages we did not forget to "wear the shoes" of an imaginary visitor and also worked hard on finding the right balance between a complex dramaturgy and mise-en-scène in a digital as well as in the physical setting.

We also tried to learn and use a common language to communicate with collaborators from diverse disciplines and backgrounds (IT experts, museum practitioners, artists, script-writers). We realized that the successful outcome of such an endeavour can only be the result of open-mindedness, mutual understanding, respect, flexibility, as well as a lot of time spent to learn together within the emerging community of practice of digital museum-storytelling making. In the long run, accepting this fact saved us time, enhanced communication and understanding among us all, and made our narrative richer and more visitor-friendly.

From the very beginning, we all agreed on the power of the visual language, the dramaturgical means and of the connotative potential of the text. We incorporated selectively codes and techniques of all of the above in our story. We tried to transfer content information through images, symbols, metaphors, short dialogues. We also used the flash forward technique, by presenting our hero in an older age. Thus, we facilitated the transfer of significant content information while staying consistent with the plot.

Previous experience of the computer scientists of the team in similar projects guided the project team and was more than valuable. In addition, communication and understanding were further facilitated by the museum staff which has a background in the arts (museum theatre/puppetry, theatre design) and acted as cultural brokers among the museum and its external collaborators.

Multi-disciplinary efforts in the museum sector can only be successful through effective communication and mutual respect from the early stages of the project.

17.9 Conclusions

In this work we present our findings and insights from the design, development and evaluation of a mobile digital storytelling experience for the Athens University History Museum.

Our evaluation, both structured and "in the wild" confirms the strength of this approach to promote engagement, learning and deeper reflection, even in visitors with no particular interest on the specific period and themes. The storytelling app functioned as an incentive to delve deeper into a pivotal historical period for Greece, seen through the eyes of a fictional but convincing young man of that time. This familiar and relatable character played the role of companion and guide, and the perspective he offered helped visitors foster a deeper understanding and connection with the exhibits and history. The visual elements, designed to support the story plot and bring to life exhibited objects and historical figures, were positively evaluated and contributed significantly to the aforementioned engagement.

The variety of opinions of the users on their preferences in terms of favorite exhibits and themes, as well as the level of detail of information offered confirms that visitor profiles should be taken into account when designing such an app.

Furthermore, the concrete need of the visitors to interact with each other while visiting in small or big groups, hints at the need to create a second version of the app which will include group activities.

As a result of a multi-disciplinary collaboration, this work highlights the need to establish effective communication channels and a common language between all stakeholders involved in the creation process.

Having established a concrete methodology for the development of such a digital storytelling approach, which has been validated through our evaluation activities, one of the questions we will investigate is the feasibility of the application of such approaches in the museum sector. We need to examine the different perspectives of putting in practice such an app, including its dissemination and its possible potential to attract new audiences to the Museum.

Our immediate objective is to promote the app further so as to gather more feedback from visitors "in the wild" in the context also of the aforementioned issues. So far it has been promoted through the Museum social media and website and it has been demonstrated in various events to gather feedback by cultural heritage experts and visitors, including the 17th UNIVERSEUM Annual Meeting in Amsterdam in 2016 and in a Symposium organized by the Museum in the context of the ICOM International Museum Day entitled "Hyperconnected Museums, New approaches, new publics". The application has also been demonstrated in several science fairs open to the public, including the Researcher's Night Event and the Athens Science Festival.

Further targeted promotion of the app is needed, however, to reach its intended audiences and gauge their response and feedback. Will the visitors be convinced to use the app? And will the promotion of the app be successful in attracting more people in the museum?

Digital storytelling has been examined in research and it has been demonstrated that it has clear advantages for an enhanced visitor experience. However, its application in practice has not yet been sufficiently studied in real life contexts, to include issues of dissemination and exploitation of such applications, who are in fact costly to design and produce. This uncertain market perspective remains still an open issue and a concrete limitation for establishing this approach in the museum sector.

Acknowledgements This work has been partly funded by EMOTIVE. EMOTIVE has received funding from the Horizon 2020 EU Framework Programme for Research and innovation under grant agreement no. 727188.

References

Athens University History Museum: www.historymuseum.uoa.gr

Bedford L (2001) Storytelling: the real work of museums. Curator: Museum J 44(1):27–34. https://doi.org/10.1111/j.2151-6952.2001.tb00027.x

Brittain M, Clack T (2007) Introduction. In: Clack T, Brittain M (eds) Archaeology and the Media. Left Coast Press, Walnut Creek, pp 11–66

Csikszentmihalyi M, Hermanson K (2007) Intrinsic motivation in museums: why does one want to learn?". In: Hooper-Greenhill Helen (ed) The educational role of the museum. Routledge, London, pp 146–160

Fraser A, Coulson H (2012) Incomplete stories. In MacLeod S et al (eds) Museum making. Narratives, architectures, exhibitions. Routledge, Oxon, pp 223–233

Katifori A, Karvounis M, Kourtis V, Kyriakidi M, Roussou M, Tsangaris M, Vayanou M, Ioannidis Y, Balet O, Prados T, Keil J, Engelke T, Pujol L (2014) CHESS: personalized storytelling experiences in museums. In: Mitchell A, Fernández-Vara C, Thue D (eds) Interactive storytelling. ICIDS 2014. Lecture notes in computer science, vol 8832, pp 232–235. https://doi.org/10.1007/978-3-319-12337-0_28

Katifori A, Karvounis M, Kourtis V, Perry S, Roussou M, Ioannidis Y (2018) Applying interactive storytelling in cultural heritage: opportunities, challenges and lessons learned. In: 11th international conference on interactive digital storytelling. ICIDS 2018, Dublin, Ireland, 5–8 Dec 2018

Katifori A, Kourtis V, Vrettakis E, Lougiakis C, Karvounis M, Ioannidis Y (2019a) Narralive tools technical, report. https://drive.google.com/open?id=1UjJRNP6CfOh_lQd4bPcrh3wgNEVZEwGN

Katifori A, Vayanou N, Antoniou A, Ioannidis IP, Ioannidis Y (2019b) Big five and cultural experiences: impact from design to evaluation. In: Proceedings of the 10th ACM workshop on personalized access to cultural heritage (PATCH 2019). ACM Press, New York, NY

Kitta E, Pichou M, Savvani E, Tsitou F (2018) The Athens University history museum: a platform for the University Community and the wider audience. In: Mouliou M, Soubiran S, Talas S, Wittje R (eds) Turning inside out European University heritage: collections, audiences, stakeholders, Proceedings of the 16th annual UNIVERSEUM meeting, Athens. National and Kapodistrian University of Athens Press, pp 67–76. https://en.uoa.gr/fileadmin/user_upload/PDF-files/anakoinwseis/ekdoseis/2205_universeum-teliko-screen.pdf

MacLeod S et al (ed) (2012) Museum making. Narratives, architectures, exhibitions. Routledge, Oxon

Nichols B (1991) Representing reality: issues and concepts in documentary. Indiana University Press, Bloomington and Indianapolis

Papoulias E, Kapsimallis K (2016) The perspective of a network of museums of the National and Kapodistrian University of Athens. In: Erbay F, Erbay M (eds) Değişen Üniversite Müzeleri, pp 94–101

Pujol L, Roussou M, Poulou S, Balet O, Vayanou M, Ioannidis Y (2013) Personalizing interactive digital storytelling in archaeological museums: the CHESS project. In: Earl G, Sly T, Chrysanthi A, Murrieta-Flores P, Papadopoulos C, Romanowska I, Wheatley D (eds) Archaeology in the digital era. Papers from the 40th annual conference of computer applications and quantitative methods in archaeology (CAA). Amsterdam University Press, Southampton, UK, 26–29 March 2012. Retrieved from http://dare.uva.nl/cgi/arno/show.cgi?fid=545855

Rizvic S, Djapo N, Alispahic F, Hadzihalilovic B, Cengic FF, Imamovic A, Boskovic D (2017) Guidelines for interactive digital storytelling presentations of cultural heritage. In: 2017 9th international conference on virtual worlds and games for serious applications, VS-Games 2017—Proceedings, pp 253–259. https://doi.org/10.1109/VS-GAMES.2017.8056610

Roussou M, Katifori A (2018) Flow, staging, wayfinding, personalization: evaluating user experience with mobile museum narratives. Multimodal Technol Interact 2(2):32. http://www.mdpi.com/2414-4088/2/2/32/pdf

Selmanovic E, Rizvic S, Harvey C, Boskovic D, Hulusic V, Chahin M, Sljivo S (2018) VR video storytelling for intangible cultural heritage preservation (November). https://doi.org/10.2312/gch.20181341

Staiff R (2014) Re-imagining heritage interpretation: enchanted the past-future. Routledge, London

Tsitou F (2012) Authenticity/reliability and other issues involved in big institutions commission. In: Puppetry in museum interpretation and communication. PhD thesis, Royal Holloway University of London, pp 188–195

Twiss-Garrity BA, Fisher M, Sastre A (2008) The art of storytelling: enriching art museum exhibits and education through visitor narratives. In: Trant J, Bearman D (eds) Museums and the Web 2008. Archives & Museum Informatics, Montreal, Quebec, Canada

Vayanou M, Katifori A, Karvounis M, Kourtis V, Kyriakidi M, Roussou M, Tsangaris M, Ioannidis Y, Balet O, Prados T, Keil J, Engelke T, Pujol L (2014) Authoring personalized interactive museum stories. In: Mitchell A, Fernández-Vara C, Thue D (eds) Interactive storytelling. ICIDS 2014. Lecture notes in computer science, vol 8832. Springer, Cham

Chapter 18
Digital Storytelling

Selma Rizvic, Vensada Okanovic and Dusanka Boskovic

Abstract In modern era digital technologies are intensively used for presentation of tangible and intangible cultural heritage. High fidelity 3D reconstructions of cultural monuments and sites, virtual presentations of dances, crafts and traditions offer the users time travel to the past. However, all these digital assets need to incorporate the information on the context of presented cultural heritage objects, as well as related events and characters. This is implemented through digital storytelling. Interactive digital stories become parts of museum exhibitions, virtual and augmented reality applications and, of course, serious games. This chapter will present an overview of techniques and implementations of digital storytelling and its incorporation into virtual cultural heritage presentations. It will discuss challenges of adjusting classical storytelling methods and tools to virtual environments and VR videos, telling stories which users will find educational and entertaining at the same time, stories fitting into VR and AR navigation and complementing the 3D geometry with emotional and emphatic content. Novel interactive digital storytelling methods presented in this chapter will revolutionize the visual language and offer new media expressionism for the future.

18.1 Interactive Digital Storytelling

Since the beginning of mankind people have communicated through storytelling. All over the history the concept has remained the same, but the tools and methods have changed with time. People started writing down their stories, recording at first the sound of their voices and finally recording audio video clips nowadays called

S. Rizvic (✉) · V. Okanovic · D. Boskovic
Faculty of Elecrical Engineering, University of Sarajevo, Zmaja od Bosne bb, 71000 Sarajevo, Bosnia and Herzegovina
e-mail: srizvic@etf.unsa.ba

V. Okanovic
e-mail: vokanovic@etf.unsa.ba

D. Boskovic
e-mail: boskovic@etf.unsa.ba

© Springer Nature Switzerland AG 2020
F. Liarokapis et al. (eds.), *Visual Computing for Cultural Heritage*, Springer Series on Cultural Computing, https://doi.org/10.1007/978-3-030-37191-3_18

movies. Digital technologies enhanced the ways of presenting stories and digital storytelling was born. As a consequence, digital storytelling can be defined as the narrative entertainment that reaches the audience via digital technology and media (Handler-Miller 2014). Handler Miller defines digital storytelling as the use of digital media platforms and interactivity for narrative purposes, either for fictional or for non-fiction stories (Handler-Miller 2014). Interactive digital storytelling (IDS) enables the user to influence the flow and sometimes even the content of the story. Various IDS methods compete in level of user immersion and aim to teach the viewers about the topic in an engaging and attractive way. The quality of user experience is the main success factor of IDS applications. We will measure it through the **edutainment value** (a combination of education and entertainment).

The use of IDS for cultural heritage (CH) presentation is becoming very popular. Virtual Reality, Augmented Reality, Mixed Reality and all kinds of combinations of digital technologies are more effective in conveying heritage information if accompanied with storytelling (Rizvić 2017). The visitors of museums and CH sites are interested to find out "the story behind" the cultural monuments and get acquainted with the characters and events from their history.

18.2   Related Projects

California State University Chico class generated a five part definition of digital stories, according to which, for assessment purposes, they should: include a compelling narration of a story; provide a meaningful context for understanding the story being told; use images to capture and/or expand upon emotions found in the narrative; employ music and other sound effects to reinforce ideas; invite thoughtful reflection from their audience(s) (Alexander 2011). This definition introduces some key words for our research: narration, images, music, emotions. It shows that only multidisciplinary teams can combine all these notions into an interactive application.

All authors in the literature agree that the foundation for successful IDS applications is the skillful use of general storytelling principles defined through history in all kinds of media. Aristotles seven golden rules (plot, character, theme, dialog, music, decor, spectacle) are easily recognized in engaging and immersive interactive digital stories (Aristotle, Poetics).

Hero's journey is another storytelling structure which is or could be used in IDS. It is a pattern of narrative identified by the American scholar Joseph Campbell that appears in drama, storytelling, myth, religious ritual, and psychological development (Campbell 1949). It describes the typical adventure of the archetype known as The Hero, the person who goes out and achieves great deeds on behalf of the group, tribe, or civilization. The proposed structure consists of 12 stages, starting with introduction of Hero's world, describing the call for adventure and following him through different obstacles until the desired goal is fulfilled. This structure is better suited for adventure movies and novels then for documentary narrative, but some elements could be applied.

As the focus of our research is IDS in virtual cultural heritage applications and serious games, we present here some examples of such projects and discuss their advantages and drawbacks.

Etruscanning 3D project (Pietroni et al. 2013) is an IDS application created to present findings from Etruscan Regolini-Galassi tomb through an interesting combination of storytelling with 3D environment of the tomb and interactive models of artefacts found there. The user stands in front of the screen where the virtual environment of the tomb is projected and interacts with the application using gesture-based interaction interface with Kinect motion sensor. This project is a great example how to use storytelling to convey to the user the history and importance of archaeological findings. However, gesture-based interface limits its usability to a museum setup.

Admotum application created within the Keys to Rome exhibition on Roman culture during the rule of Emperor Augustus, is a serious game engaging the user in the quest for objects from 4 involved museums (Pagano et al. 2015). The exhibition was held in 2014 at the same time in Rome, Alexandria, Amsterdam and Sarajevo, with goal to present different parts of Roman Empire in that historical period through a combination of museum collections and digital content. Admotum application was designed as a treasure hunt, where the users explore first the virtual environments of Roman objects from their location, and, upon finding all objects, they can unlock virtual environments from remaining three locations and look for their objects. Storytelling plays significant role in this application, as every virtual reconstruction and particular objects are described through narrations of virtual characters. However, the users are so engaged with a not simple gesture-based navigation, that most of them do not pay much attention to stories they hear.

Importance of interactive digital storytelling for presentation of cultural heritage has been recognized by the European Commission by issuing several calls for proposals in this area. EMOTIVE project (http://emotiveproject.eu) is already offering valuable contributions through production of prototype tools and applications capable of generating immersive, personalized digital narrative experiences for museum and heritage site visitors. However, in our research we are not focused on personalization of user experience as much as on level of perception of conveyed information and edutainment value of the presented content. We strongly believe that users need to see all available material, otherwise the production costs are not justified.

One of the most important challenges for IDS presentations is the narrative paradox. It is the conflict between pre-authored narrative structures—especially plot—and the freedom a virtual environment (VE) offers to a user in physical movement and interaction, integral to a feeling of physical presence and immersion (Schoenau-Fog 2015). In this chapter we will describe several our solutions, coming to the introduction of a motivation factor which will inspire the users to watch all the story structure elements.

In our quest for narrative paradox problem solution, we encountered several works arguing in favor of emergent narratives (Louchart and Aylett 2003; Aylett 1999; Temte and Schoenau-Fog 2012), as stories that emerge from the interaction between players and the systems that govern gameplay. In Temte and Schoenau-Fog (2012) the authors propose a solution in form of modelling the narrative as multiple threads, woven together to create a braid, thus managing the narrative paradox by separating logical cohesion within threads from thematic cohesion across the whole braid. However, this solution refers to adaptive documentaries, while our applications aims to combine storytelling with interactive virtual reality.

Most of the literature related to narrative paradox solutions, while discussing alternate reality and role playing games suggests implosive stories, present in alternate reality games (ARGs), which allow to understand the problem of action and narration in interactive fiction and can help design more engaging spaces and environments (Gouveia 2009). The described experiences are of great value in serious games for cultural heritage.

Among interactive storytelling cultural heritage presentations there is the "Heart of stone" project (Dvorko 2015), containing interactive documentary which immerses the user in the culture and traditions of the Khakas people, (Mulholland et al. 2013) providing intelligent assistance to story construction in museum story-telling, (Vayanou et al. 2014) explaining how multimodal serious games can create immersion to enhance the visitor's experience, and finally a very valuable CHESS project (http://www.chessexperience.eu/) which attempted to integrate interdisciplinary research in personalization and adaptivity, digital storytelling, interaction methodologies and narrative-oriented mobile and mixed reality technologies with a theoretical basis in museology, cognitive and learning sciences.

IDS in recent years also takes a form of VR storytelling, where 360 video is used as a storytelling tool. Russia's Museum (2017), in partnership with Russian video production company Videofabrika, has created a novel VR experience for visitors, called The Hermitage VR Experience. It is a 19 min movie in 360 format, where the narrator tells stories about the Hermitage palace, recreating some events from its past using actors in historical costumes. Here the user cannot choose the order of the stories, but it is still a new format in historical pedagogy offering an interactive and immersive experience.

18.3 Storytelling Methods

Recent developments in media communications imposed a need to develop new methods of IDS, corresponding with Internet media culture. Nowadays the attention span of information consumers is getting shorter. People do not read, but rather choose audiovisual information on demand. Still, they lack time to dedicate to watching, so the videos need to be short and informative. The only way to convey a significant amount of information is to structure it in the same way as Internet pages are structured—using hypertext.

Sarajevo Graphics Group has been researching and developing new storytelling methods in this direction and evaluating them through user experience. In the following sections we will describe that process and results we obtained from the users.

In (Handler-Miller 2014) Miller states that digital storytelling techniques can make a dry or difficult subject more alive and engaging to the viewers. In order to further improve the classical concept, Glassner defined interactive storytelling as a two-way experience (http://public.cyi.ac.cy/scrollsdemo), where "the audience member actually affects the story itself". Manovich also introduced the possibility for the audience to change the story and offered the concept of an interactive narrative as "a sum of multiple trajectories through a database" (Manovich 2002).

One of the most common concepts of hyperlinked story structures is the hyper-video. It was first demonstrated by the Interactive Cinema Group at the MIT Media Lab. Elastic Charles (Brøndmo 1989) was a hypermedia journal developed between 1988 and 1989, in which micons (video footnotes) were placed inside a video, indicating links to other content. Following the Storyspace project, a hypertext writing environment, the HyperCafe, an award-winning interactive film, places the viewer inside a virtual caffee. It is a video environment where stories unfold around the viewer (Sawhney et al. 1996). After these first works, and a rather long period of stagnation, many different methods of hyper-video implementations started to appear in 2010s, most of them for use in advertising and marketing. However, hyperlinked storytelling has been also used in virtual cultural heritage applications, e.g. Human Sanctuary (http://public.cyi.ac.cy/scrollsdemo) and Keys to Rome exhibition (Rizvic et al. 2014) among others.

A deeper analysis of the state-of-the-art would show that there are many hyper-video techniques and interactive digital storytelling methods, but there is not a universal standard for storytelling presentation, such as hypertext standard for text presentation. Besides, the invention of hypertext has changed the way we perceive text. Browsing web sites is now a part of our lives and most of us have no patience to read in continuity a text longer than a few sentences. In Nielsen (1997) the author asks "How users read on the web?" and answers: "They don't. People rarely read Web pages word by word; instead, they scan the page, picking out individual words and sentences." This attitude has grown so much that it transfers into other media, such as movies. Therefore, there is a need to introduce a step change of traditional storytelling concepts by the development of a new interactive digital storytelling method, hyper-storytelling, that exploits the potential of digital media in presenting the information in virtual environments and serious games.

Sarajevo Graphics Group implemented various IDS methods in virtual reconstructions of disappeared or damaged cultural heritage and in virtual museum applications. From interactive video virtual tours (Kraljic 2008), we went on with the concept of "a story guided virtual museum', implemented in the Sarajevo Survival Tools project (Rizvić et al. 2012). The digital story provides the user with the historical context of the siege of Sarajevo 1992–1996, guiding him/her through the virtual museum of objects created by the citizens during that time. The virtual exhibition is divided in thematic clusters connected by stories. In Šljivo (2012) we introduced and evaluated through user studies the concept of audio guided virtual museum. The user evaluation showed that visitors were so focused on the story that they did not notice that movement through 3D environment was not enabled, but they could move only through clicking on hotspots in the pre-rendered images. In the computer animation of the "zikr" ritual in Isa bey's tekke (Huseinović and Turčinhodžić 2013), the animated virtual environment was exported to Unity 3D and adjusted to place the user in the middle of the animation. The user observes the Dervish ritual going on around him/her and has a possibility to explore in more detail the highlighted elements.

The next step in IDS methods development was implemented in the Isa bey's endowment project. It united the interior animation of "zikr" ritual with the exterior virtual environment consisting of the tekke, the accommodation complex, soup kitchen and water mills. The main story about the endowment and sub stories about particular objects are realized in form of audio stories in corresponding areas Rizvic et al. (2014). Once the user starts the interactive environment, the main story starts; if the user is detected inside one of these activation areas, a trigger is launched to pause the main story and start the sub-story of the activated area.

Another IDS method is based on interconnecting the video file of the main story with sub-stories and the interactive 3D model of the Tašlihan object using Unity hyperlinks. In the application (Rizvic and Prazina 2015), the main story represents a summary of the information about the object, its history and related events and characters. It consists of 7 thematic clusters. After each thematic cluster the user can activate a link to a sub-story, which describes in more detail a topic mentioned in the main story. In (http://h.etf.unsa.ba/sarajevocharter/) we showed that the storytelling is more engaging and immersive if there is a character telling the story. Therefore in this project the story is told by Murat Bey, the first associate of Gazi Husref bey, who sponsored the construction of Tašlihan, the largest accommodation complex in Bosnian province of the Ottoman Empire.

1. Sarajevo Charter Guidelines

In the process of developing a new method for interactive digital storytelling, hyper-storytelling, we engaged experts from computer science, visual arts, film directing, literature, psychology, communicology and human computer interaction. They have analyzed a sample interactive digital storytelling application, the 4D presentation of White Bastion fortress (Rizvic et al. 2016) and offered their insights and recommendations to be embedded in the new methodology (Rizvic et al. 2017). These recommendations are published as Sarajevo Charter for IDS (http://h.etf.unsa.ba/sarajevocharter/) and consist of the following guidelines:

- engage professionals for all content creation fields
- all content has to have unique visual identity
- use multimedia and virtual reality
- divide content in sub stories which can be watched independently
- stories should be short, dynamic and informative
- use characters to communicate emotion and raise edutainment value
- introduce motivation factor to solve the narrative paradox
- create IDS application to be platform independent

According to these guidelines, the hyper storytelling IDS application development consists of preproduction, production and post production stages. This is a common workflow for digital production process (Kerlow 2009), but we extended it with a number of elements particular for IDS. In preproduction the producer, director and visual artist should agree upon the scenario and visual styling of the application. All production planning activities (actors casting, location scouting, team members selection, budget planning) are performed in this stage. The production will be performed according to the scenario and storyboard, the main results of this stage. Production stage includes all assets creation (music, illustrations, footage, computer animations, 3D models), web design and design of interactive virtual environments. In postproduction stage all results of the previous stage are put together through editing and implemented online.

2. Kyrenia Case Study

The first virtual CH application we developed according to the Sarajevo Charter Guidelines was the Kyrenia shipwreck virtual presentation Rizvic et al. (2017). The goal of this application was to introduce the general public with a ship that sank around 288 B.C. near Kyrenia, Cyprus. Its remains were found in 1967 by a Cypriot diver looking for sponges. A major salvage operation has been conducted. Remains of the ship were conserved using special chemical procedures. Studying them, the archaeologists discovered the details from ship's past, life on board and other interesting elements of seafaring in Mediterranean during that historic period (Katzev 2005; Demesticha 2013). Several replicas of the ship were created, one of them exhibited in Thalassa Museum at Cyprus.

Kyrenia IDS aims to introduce Internet users with this ship, as an important cultural heritage object, through a set of short stories. After watching all stories the user is granted an opportunity to virtually embark the ship, browsing the interactive virtual environment based on its 3D model. Two actors are engaged as narrators in the stories. Motivation factor for users to see all stories is the possibility to browse the interactive model of the ship.

Stories are divided in two groups: technical and artistic. Technical stories introduce the viewers with the technical characteristics of the ship, the cargo transported by the ship and the routes where it might have sailed. Artistic stories are about the following topics: sailors' beliefs and superstitions, life on board the ship and assumptions how it sunk. Artistic stories are designed as a combination of footage recorded in natural locations and animations of illustrator's drawings (Fig. 18.1a, c), while technical stories are a combination of the actor recorded on the green screen and blueprints of the ship and its particular parts, seafaring routes and objects found in the shipwreck (Fig. 18.1b).

After the users have seen all stories, the virtual environment opens and they are placed inside the 3D model of the ship. They can explore it and sail it around the virtual seascape. The main design elements of the project are illustrations based on motives from Greek vases. They are used for animations in artistic stories and as the background image for the web site (Fig. 18.1a, d). After the illustrator has set up the visual style of the project, the rest of production consisted of composing original music, location and green screen footage recording, UI/UX design and backgrounds animation.

(a)   **(b)**   **(c)**

(d)   **(e)**

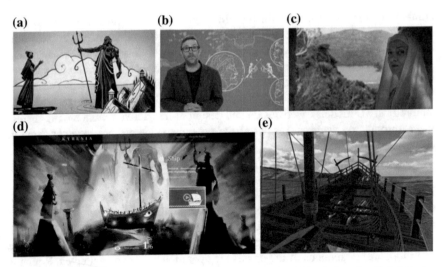

Fig. 18.1 Kyrenia hyper-storytelling application screen shots: **a** illustrations for digital stories, **b** actor superimposed upon the animated background, **c** captain's wife telling a story, **d** kyrenia project's home page, **e** interactive virtual environment of the ship

Interactive virtual environment of the reconstructed ship was created in Unity 3D (Fig. 18.1e). The 3ds max model of the ship was imported into Unity 3D and added the realistic skybox with lighting, water and terrain. For the user we have designed two types of interactions with the ship: drive the ship in virtual environment from the third person perspective, or walk on the ship and examine the model in detail from the first person perspective. The virtual environment was exported to Unity WebGL Player and incorporated into Kyrenia web site.

In post-production we put together all elements prepared in production stage. They were also combined into an intro video to be played at the beginning of the user visit. The intro has a role to kindle users' interest in the content, informing them that they can embark the virtual model of the ship only if they see all six stories. They can follow their progress through a counter of watched stories at the bottom of the home screen (Fig. 18.1d).

Kyrenia interactive digital storytelling application (http://h.etf.unsa.ba/kyrenia) was created by 20 people from different professional backgrounds. We believe this is the only way to create a successful IDS product and obtain maximum user satisfaction.

3. VR Storytelling

The most immersive form of storytelling is VR storytelling. The user is placed inside a virtual environment (360 video or virtual scene) with the opportunity to explore it looking around and/or moving while following the story. This form of storytelling is very challenging. The first issue is the already mentioned narrative paradox. The second issue is how to stage the scene in order not to make the users miss a part of the plot. We created several applications using this form of storytelling. Our experience is that directing VR storytelling is similar to directing a theater play. The rules of film language grammar do not apply any more, as the users can look all around. Therefore we need different tools to attract their attention, such as in the theater where the audience is in the middle of the stage.

18.3.1 Baiae Case Study

The first case study where we experimented with VR storytelling is Baia Dry visit application. This application has been created within the H2020 727153 iMARECULTURE project. The goal of this project is to present the underwater cultural heritage to the general public using VR and AR technologies. Three test underwater archaeological sites have been selected for the project: Baiae in Italy, Mazotos in Cyprus and Xlendi in Malta. While the last two are shipwreck sites, the first one contains remains of a city that was a luxurious resort for Roman Emperors and aristocracy. In the late antiquity, Baiae began to sink into the water as a result of bradyseism and now a large part of the city is almost completely submerged. The remains of villas, streets and statues are still preserved 7 m under the sea and can be seen only by diving. The Dry visit application will enable the users to virtually dive using the Head Mounted Display and experience the underwater environment. Additionally, they will be able to activate the villa virtual reconstruction and follow the story happening there. That story we created using VR storytelling Rizvic et al. (2019).

The story was created according to the Sarajevo Charter guidelines. It is about a Roman aristocrat who wants to buy a statue from a sculptor and decorate his garden. The storytelling, conceived and written by Barbara Davidde Petriaggi and Roberto Petriaggi, consists of 6 parts: the intro story (360° video of Baiae remains on land with a voice-over introducing the viewer with the city and its historical significance), the sculptor's workshop where all characters introduce themselves (the sculptor, his apprentice, the aristocrat, and the slave), the street with shops (where the sculptor tells his apprentice how beautiful is Baiae), the villa entrance, the room with mosaics where the slave announces the visitors to the aristocrat, the atrium (the sculptor is introducing his apprentice with the villa) and the discussion of the sculptor and the aristocrat about the statue design and price. The screenshots of stories are shown in Fig. 18.2.

The stories are implemented as VR videos either recorded with 360 camera (intro story) or composited from backgrounds obtained as 360 renders from 3D scenes and actors recorded against the green screen background. The storytelling is incorporated in a Unity 3D project and triggered by click on points of interest inside the underwater simulation.

The user experience evaluation has shown that the use of actors in VR storytelling contributes to the quality of user experience and evokes positive level of immersion in virtual cultural heritage applications. User scores for edutainment were even higher,

Fig. 18.2 The screenshots from Baiae VR storytelling

and we can conclude that personalizing historical roles presents a novel and entertaining way for users to learn about historical sites and ancient societies. Users' feedback brings to our attention an important feature for the future work: the ability to pause the story and explore the 360° environment and rewind the narrative to some point of interest. The interactivity could be extended to include a search for a specific object or to help the user to learn some important fact (Rizvic et al. 2019).

18.3.2 Mostar Bridge Diving VR

The Old bridge in Mostar is a UNESCO heritage site in Bosnia and Herzegovina (Fig. 18.3). Apart from the tangible heritage of the bridge and its surroundings, there is also a tradition of bridge diving more then 300 years old. We created a virtual presentation of the Bridge and diving tradition using VR storytelling.

The application consists of an intro story presenting briefly the content available to the users. After the intro, the users find themselves inside a 360 video of the place

Fig. 18.3 The Old bridge in Mostar, Bosnia and Herzegovina

Fig. 18.4 Mostar Bridge diving simulation

below the bridge (Fig. 18.3) and are offered a choice of stories about the history of the Bridge, its architecture, its destruction during the war and reconstruction after the war and the interview with the bridge diving champion.

After watching the stories, they are requested to take a quiz, implemented in a virtual model of the room aside the Bridge, and answer a few questions from the stories. This ensures that they will pay attention to the stories and learn something about the Bridge. If they pass the quiz, they can perform the virtual jump from the Bridge, which represents the motivational factor according to the Sarajevo Charter guidelines. The simulation of the jump is implemented in Unity 3D, as well as the whole application (Fig. 18.4). The stories are 360 videos with narrator's voice-over.

The user experience evaluation of this application has shown very interesting results. The users who are afraid of height are equally afraid to use the VR. In the first version of the application we had a very poor quality of the 3D environment of the Bridge, but no user have noticed that. The user study highlighted several recommendations due to the observed shortcomings in some components of the aggregated system. The study also demonstrated the correlation between the virtual and the real world environments and the emotions that are conveyed through either. This indicates the transfer of context and the experience of the community involved with the intangible heritage, as one of the key elements of preservation (Selmanovic et al. 2018).

18.3.3 Sarajevo War Tunnel VR

Sarajevo was under the siege of the Serb paramilitary forces and the former Yugoslav Army from 1992 to 1996. It was the longest siege in the modern history. The city was without food, water, heating and electricity and under the constant shelling and sniper fire. In 1993 the city exhausted all reserves of food, weapons and medical

Fig. 18.5 A screenshot from the VR story about the tunnel

supplies. The Bosnian authorities decided to build a tunnel under the airport runway and connect the city with the free territory outside. Today only 20 m of the Tunnel is open for visitors within the Museum (Fig. 18.5). It is impossible to experience what Sarajevo citizens who passed through the Tunnel were feeling. Or it was, until the Sarajevo Tunnel VR project.

We created a VR simulation of the Tunnel crossing accompanied with the stories about the siege and a quiz for the users. The application consists of 3 virtual environments (VE), recorded with 360 camera and imported into Unity 3D as backgrounds. Over them we placed the links to the stories in the first VE, the quiz in the second VE and the links to additional stories told by the Museum curator and some documentary videos from the war times in the third one.

The VR simulation of the Tunnel is started after the users pass the quiz. The simulation contains 3 challenges: the maximum height of the Tunnel was 160 cm, so the user has to bend in order not to bump his/her head; the Tunnel was usually full of water; and at some point a person appears from the opposite direction, so the user needs to move aside and make space (Jajcanin et al. 2019).

This project is still in progress, so we have not performed a proper user experience evaluation. The initial one however has showed very good results. The users appreciate the opportunity to experience something that is not possible to experience in reality. They feel immersion in the virtual environment of the Tunnel and similar emotions as those who passed it during the war. They also appreciate the storytelling as a way to learn about the historical context and the life in Sarajevo during the siege.

18.3.4 The First BH VR Movie

With support of the BH Ministry of Civil Affairs and as research within the COST CA COST Action CA16213 New Exploratory Phase in Research on East European Cultures of Dissent (NEP4DISSENT), we created the first BH VR film entitled

Fig. 18.6 Gameplay video of a movie used for the premiere

"Nine dissidents". The film tells a still forbidden story about Bosniak writers who were prosecuted during the socialist regime in Yugoslavia for their dissent with the communist party. Six of them were arrested after the WWII and accused for collaboration with fascists, although they just held some public functions or were publishing their works unrelated with politics during the war. The last three were prosecuted in 1970s and 1980s because they expressed dissent with the party officials regarding literature. Their lives were destroyed, they lost their jobs, majority of them served prison sentences and they were completely banned from the society, to be never mentioned in any bibliographies or learned about in schools.

The film "Nine Dissidents" (https://youtu.be/w3vKIQ2NFW0) is telling this story in a satirical way. It is happening in an improvised courtroom where the solicitor of revision is trying to convince the judge and jury (still very communist) to rehabilitate those writers, while the solicitor of history is trying to prevent him together with the jury (Fig. 18.6).

The movie was recorded using Garmin VIRB 360 camera. The directing needed to be done in advance through consultations with the actors, as we had to reduce the number of cuts in order to accommodate better quality of user experience through Head Mounted Displays. Our experience shows that the users may feel uncomfortability or even motion sickness due to higher number of cuts within the movie. The cuts were performed using fade out—fade in transition for the same reasons. The audio was recorded by four Shure FP15 wireless microphones and produced in ambix output format for postproduction.

The premiere was a technical challenge itself, we had only one VR setup, so we decided to show a gameplay video of a person watching the movie in VR (Fig. 18.6). That way we had several layers of directing: the inherent directing within the movie, the directing of a viewer person and the final directing while editing together the video of the person watching the movie and the screen capture of what that person sees through the VR device.

18.4 Web Technologies Used in IDS Applications

For the purpose of user-friendly web presentation of virtual cultural heritage we have used a few different web technologies in our applications.

In the Keys to Rome exhibition the interactive digital storytelling was used to present the reconstructed Roman remains from Rome, Amsterdam, Alexandria and Sarajevo in combination with physical museum exhibits. In this application we used the Unity 3D game engine to connect the hyperlinked stories and combine them with interactive virtual models.

Our Tašlihan application was created in Maya and exported to Unity 3D, where textures and illumination were adjusted and optimized for online use. The geometry of the model is based on the scientific work of archaeologists and historians who excavated the remains of the object. Unity 3D has been chosen as we needed to introduce interactivity into a video. In our previous projects we used Flash, but presently it is not supported by all platforms.

In the process of White bastion application development, in order to present the White Bastion through history, we consulted the archaeologist who was leading the excavations on the site. He identified six 3D models of the object to be created, some of them different from each other by the addition of interior objects, and exterior extensions. The modeling process was started by building the terrain. In order to create precise terrain model the Digital Elevation Model over Balkans area from the GMES RDA project (http://www.eea.europa.eu/data-and-maps/data/eu-dems) was used. This geotiff map was then imported in Global Mapper—GIS application for reading and conversion of different kinds of spatial datasets. Sarajevo area terrain was extracted from the map and exported as 3D VRML file which was then used in Cinema 4D as the precise Sarajevo terrain model. 3D models of White bastion are created in Cinema 4D, while Adobe Photoshop is used for creating and adjusting the textures. Six final 3D models correspond to six different construction phases, the first one, from the medieval period, looking completely different from the last one from Austro-Hungarian period. In the 4D presentation of White Bastion fortress we have used Unity Web Player (http://unity3d.com/webplayer) with which we have had the most success in the other projects. 3D models of White bastion, created in Cinema 4D, were exported as FBX file used in Unity Web Player. From Unity Web Player we have built the web presentation of the models without any difficulties.

In the White Bastion project there is a web page for each of the digitalized archaeological findings. The web page's layout is made of two three js scenes; in the first scene 3D model of the excavated object is presented and in the second scene the reconstruction of the object is displayed. In the initial version of the project the objects can be viewed from all sides using the mouse for movement and rotation. In the new version the Leap Motion interaction is added. Thus, we have used a novel solution for natural interaction with small 3D objects in virtual environments, using Leap motion as a sensor and WebGL for presenting virtual hand and 3D objects. In the quantitative user experience analysis of this solution the participants noticed that the Leap Motion interaction has precision and reliability issues in comparison with the traditional mouse interaction.

We have also developed a web based service oriented mobile solution for interactive digital storytelling with 3D models and videos. The concept is implemented on a case study of White Bastion. For this solution we have used jMonkeyEngine. It is a free integrated development environment for developing 3D applications for multiple platforms. The application uses jMonkeyEngine libraries imported in Android studio (https://developer.android.com/studio/index.html). The Android device needs to support OpenGL ES 2.0 for the application to work. It offers a list of available 3D objects which will be downloaded and displayed on a mobile device. The complete solution is based on free and open source technologies, which are available to everyone. As a development environment for Android application, Android studio is used, which is free for download from the official page (https://developer.android.com/studio/index.html). Although there are many popular development environments like Eclipse, Corona, IntelliJ or Xamarin Studio, we have chosen Android studio because it is designed particularly for Android development with support for Windows, Mac OS X and Linux. In order to develop and run Java applications, it is required to configure Java Development kit (JDK), as for any other case where Java programming language is used. Android studio relies on Gradle, open source build automation system, which is used for simple management of dependencies used in this solution.

In the Kyrenia hyper storytelling application, the interactive virtual environment of the reconstructed ship was created in Unity 3D. The 3ds max model of the ship was imported into Unity 3D and added the realistic skybox with lighting, water and terrain. The user was offered to drive the ship in virtual environment from the third person perspective, or walk on the ship and examine the model in detail from the first person perspective. The virtual environment was exported to Unity WebGL Player and incorporated into Kyrenia web site.

In the Sarajevo war tunnel application the 3D model was made in Blender and Physically-Based Rendering (PBR) was used to make materials and texture files for a more realistic approach. After the model creation and the preparation of materials, the next step was importing the model into a Unity application. Every object has its own collider, so there are no flaws and possibilities for unrealistic movement. Also, some objects may be picked up. When it comes to lightning, blinking point lights were used, in order to achieve realism and represent possible situations at the time when the tunnel was still active. All of the scripts used in this project were written in C#. The application was then adjusted to use HTC Vive Head Mounted Display.

18.5 User Experience Evaluation

In the area of multimedia applications both for education (Karolcík et al. 2015) and digital heritage presentation (Bolchini and Garzotto 2007) the authors notice lack of evaluation tools. Methods for evaluation of multimedia applications commence with identification of attributes to be measured (Karolcík et al. 2015), often referred to as heuristics (Bolchini and Garzotto 2007), and are classified in groups or dimensions of evaluation. Developing an evaluation framework for multimedia cultural heritage applications is a challenging process due to involvement of multidisciplinary dimensions including: interaction and design for multimedia applications, pedagogy and cognitive theory, heuristics involving history, archeology, arts, and etc.

Approaches in evaluating user experience (UX) for IDS differ by the primary goal of the study: finding flaws and helping developers to improve the interaction (Lazar et al. 2010) or acquiring standardized data for systematic testing of research hypotheses (Vermeulen et al. 2010). The common feature of these different evaluation goals is informative feedback to designers and developers, with substantial qualitative component. Additional objective was to evaluate importance of the VR technology for the user experience.

Qualitative studies are essential in understanding user behaviors and evaluating the situational use of technology, especially to address interaction when delivering novel designs and understanding user needs for future designs (Blanford 2013). In designing our qualitative evaluation studies, we followed renowned guidelines and established criteria (Creswell 2008; Flick 2009), but also had to balance attainment of the study objectives with the challenge of the available resources (Blanford 2013). We have opted for the qualitative approach for the initial evaluation of the Mostar Bridge Diving VR (Selmanovic et al. 2018) and similarly for the Sarajevo War Tunnel (Jajcanin et al. 2019).

An example of a quantitative evaluation can be found in our evaluations for Kyrenia (Rizvic et al. 2017; http://h.etf.unsa.ba/kyrenia) and Baiae (Rizvic et al. . 2019) case studies, and follow-up studies for the Mostar Bridge Diving VR. The quantitative questionnaires were organized in different sub-scales, where each sub-scale was represented by balanced number of items. We have tried to follow similar approach in designing questionnaires in order to provide a standardized measurement tool for user experience. Evaluating a IDS application is linked to measuring good experience and its important feature: immersion, and in addition, involves measurement of another important factor combining education and entertainment: edutainment.

18.5.1 Qualitative Evaluations: Old Bridge Mostar

There are not many case studies for user experience evaluation of intangible cultural heritage applications, and for the evaluation of the user experience in the case study of preserving the Mostar bridge diving tradition we have opted for qualitative approach. Our primary objective was not limited to the assessment of the VR application, but also to identify strengths and limitations of our approach in order to improve interaction and subsequent quality attributes such as immersion and edutainment. The study was designed to evaluate user needs and behaviors, compare their interaction with respect to different levels of preconditioning, and explore the link between effort and performance.

In the study we combined semi-structured interviews and contextual observations, and subsequent basic content analysis, as presented in Selmanovic et al. (2018). The experiment was conducted at the University of Sarajevo, Birmingham City University and the University of Bournemouth. Participants were recruited by invitation. Evaluation sessions were conducted individually, lasting for around 35 min on average. Since presentations of digital heritage are intended for a broad audience, we have invited users representing different groups. Prior to engaging with the VR application, participants were informed about the experiment procedure and tasks. Participants were advised to freely express their satisfaction or dis-satisfaction, and to elaborate upon their experience when answering the questions. Interviewers were observing the users during the experiment and noted any significant interaction issues, user specific path through the digital narrative, and knowledge quiz success. Immediately after experiencing the VR application, the users were asked a list of semi-structured questions, beginning with a direct question on the user experience and followed by a request to provide a rationale.

Questions were aimed to assess gestural interaction accomplishments and to summarize experience as perceived by the users. In order to obtain quantitative assessment on how appropriate a 3D approach is for documenting intangible cultural heritage, we have designed an additional web-based questionnaire. The questions were organized into two themes, one addressing the sensation of presence and the other, 3D experience.

The younger participants showed a readiness to explore, to point and try at-a-distance interaction, without fear of making mistakes. This type of user behavior is welcomed, but demands additional interaction improvements: preventing accidental selections, which happened in several cases. More senior participants expressed reluctance to explore the VR interaction paradigm freely, often waiting for narrative or other prompting. Few participants were assuming a passive role and only after being instructed, expressed a more active attitude. Embedded user behavior monitoring would be beneficial and should trigger written or narrative guidelines and instructions, when needed. We have identified improvements to navigation: dynamic scaling of control buttons to encompass whole floating menu items and zooming in menu items, especially quiz questions and answers when these are the focus of interaction.

There were several reports of navigational difficulty within the VR simulation where some of the users needed either additional instructions or assistance from the interviewer in order to climb the ladder. We have observed that it is important to provide control of the application by natural gestures and movements, but also it is good to enable controller based interaction as well. The latter is important to accommodate different user types and also to compensate for space and equipment restrictions, such as HMD cable length. It is important to note that for all user types the overall perceived performance and user satisfaction is linked to their emotional state. This emotional state is influenced by the quality of their gesture interaction and user skill, but mostly by the unique experience of 360° digital stories and the VR diving simulation. Important conclusion is that the perceived satisfaction with the navigation is not correlated to the needed level of assistance.

By extrapolating from the participant interview transcripts, the key themes linked to the experience of virtual diving are: height, fear, jump, excitement, nauseous, and realistic. These are the themes mentioned in texts covering real diving competitions. This suggests that current technologies such as VR can facilitate an empathetic connection with the community and preservation of intangible heritage. The identified themes are relevant for designing a novel evaluation instrument to measure immersion and edutainment. The most frequent themes have been identified as: fear, jump, height, and real. These themes were observed with frequencies from the interview transcripts.

18.5.2 Quantitative Evaluations: Baiae

Quantitative evaluations of IDS we have conducted involved data collection by user surveys designed as structured questionnaires. The studies were conducted in the research lab at our University and evaluators were able to observe the participants while engaged in VR interactive digital story. The quantitative analyses were often supported with the documented observations.

Baiae case study was developed with a primary hypothesis that the use of actors in VR storytelling adds to the quality of user experience and improves the immersion and edutainment attributes for virtual cultural heritage applications. Research question was "How the use of actors in the VR storytelling affects user experience related to the immersion and edutainment value of virtual cultural heritage applications?" The participants were recruited by invitation, balancing number of representatives of different user groups, regarding their age, professional interests and the role in the education. Participants were informed about the experiment procedure, their tasks and instructed to freely express their satisfaction or dissatisfaction. Immediately after engaging with the Baiae VR digital stories the users answered questions summarizing their perceived experience.

Evaluators were observing the users during the experiment and noted user behavior, movements, objects of attention and possible undesirable effect of using the VR equipment. The questionnaire contained the following sections: demographics data, user experience evaluation with Likert scale items organized in 3 sub-scales measuring immersion, edutainment and ease of use, and the concluding section: user feedback and knowledge question measuring effectiveness of the educational part. It is significant to note that among the items with the highest score per sub-scale we can mention the following: "I7—Live actors make the VR story more personal and vivid", "I had fun watching the actors and viewing the Baiae surrounding."

The following items in the edutainment sub-scale: "I would like to use a similar VR story to learn about destroyed historical sites," and "The VR stories like Baiae can generate learning content and help the transmission and preservation of knowledge," were assessed with the highest score both by students and teachers. For us this was a significant improvement since in our previous research we have identified the difference in how students and teachers assess the benefits of bringing cultural heritage in the classroom using the VR (Rizvic et al. 2019).

The achieved results were supporting our hypotheses, the VR digital stories involving actors resulted in achieving a high level of user immersion. User satisfaction with the edutainment was even higher, and we concluded that personalizing historical roles presented a novel and entertaining way for users to learn about historical sites and ancient societies.

Approaches in data analyses and presentations of the results, including interpretations, were selected according to the specific evaluation study. For pilot studies aimed to identify strengths and weaknesses of the IDS application as in the case of the Kyrenia pilot study (Rizvic et al. 2017) distribution of responses were instrumental in identifying areas for improvement, distribution metrics as Net Promoter Score were used as a bases for the benchmark as presented in the case study of the White Bastion (Boskovic et al. 2017), or responses were interpreted to prove research hypotheses as in the Baiae case study (Rizvic et al. 2019).

References

Alexander B (2011) The new digital storytelling: creating narratives with new media. Praeger Publishers, Westport, CT, USA

Aylett R (1999) Narrative in virtual environments â˘A¸S towards emergent narrative. In: AAAI fall symposium on narrative intelligence, pp 83–86

Aristotle, Poetics, 384 to 322 B.C

A Human Sanctuary Project, Cyprus Institute. http://public.cyi.ac.cy/scrollsdemo

Android Studio. (https://developer.android.com/studio/index.html)

Blanford A (2013) Semi-structured qualitative studies. In: Soegaard M, Dam RF (eds) The encyclopedia of human-computer interaction, 2nd edn. The Interaction Design Foundation, Aarhus, Denmark. http://www:interaction-design:org/encyclopedia/semi-structured_qualitative_studies:html

Bolchini D, Garzotto F (2007) Quality of web usability evaluation methods: an empirical study on MiLE+. In: Web information systems engineering–WISE 2007 workshops. Springer Berlin/Heidelberg, pp 481–492

Boskovic D, Rizvic S, Okanovic V, Sljivo S, Sinanovic N (2017) Measuring immersion and edutainment in multimedia cultural heritage applications. In: 26th international conference on information, communication and automation technologies—ICAT 2017, Sarajevo, Bosnia and Herzegovina

Brøndmo G (1989) Davenport, creating and viewing the elastic Charles—hypermedia journal. Chapter 5—Hypertext: state of the ART, pp 43–51

Campbell J (1949) The hero with a thousand faces, 1st edn

Creswell JW (2008) Research design: qualitative, quantitative, and mixed methods approaches, 3 edn. Sage Publications Ltd.

Demesticha S (2013) Harbours, navigation and trade. In: Pilides DPN (ed) Ancient cyprus: cultures in dialogue. Exhibition, pp 80–83

Chess cultural heritage experiences through socio-personal interactions and storytelling. http://www.chessexperience.eu/

Dvorko R (2015) Digital storytelling for cultural heritage presenting. In: EVA 2017 electronic imaging the visual arts international conference, pp 68–70

Emotive storytelling for cultural heritage. http://emotiveproject.eu

Flick U (2009) An introduction to qualitative research/Uwe Flick, 4th edn. SAGE Los Angeles, London

Glassner A (2004) Interactive storytelling. A. K. Peters

Gouveia P (2009) Narrative paradox and the design of alternate reality games (args) and blogs. In: 2009 international IEEE consumer electronics society's games innovations conference, pp 231–238

GMES RDA project (EU-DEM). http://www.eea.europa.eu/data-and-maps/data/eu-dems

Handler-Miller C (2014) Digital storytelling: a creator's guide to interactive entertainment. Elsevier/Focal Press

Huseinović M, Turčinhodžić R (2013) Interactive animated storytelling in presenting intangible cultural heritage. In: Central European seminar on computer graphics, Bratislava, Slovakia

Jajcanin A, Chahin TA, Ivkovic-Kihic I (2019) Sarajevo war tunnel VR experience. In: Proceedings of the central European seminar on computer graphics 2019, Smolenice, Slovakia

Karolcík S, Cipková E, Hrusecký R, Veselský M (2015) The comprehensive evaluation of electronic learning tools and educational software. CEELTES Inform Educ 14(2):243–264

Katzev S (2005) Resurrecting an ancient greek ship: Kyrenia, Cyprus, beneath the seven seas. Bass, (Ed.), Thames Hudson Ltd, London, pp. 72–81

Kerlow IE (2009) The art of 3-D computer animation and effects. Wiley

Kraljic N (2008) Interactive video virtual tours. In: Proceedings of CESCG 2008

Kyrenia interactive digital story. http://h.etf.unsa.ba/kyrenia

Lazar J, Feng JH, Hochheiser H (2010) Research, methods in human-computer interaction. Wiley Publishing

Louchart S, Aylett R (2003) Solving the narrative paradox in VEs—Lessons from RPGs. Springer Berlin Heidelberg

Manovich L (2002) The language of new media, 1st edn. MIT Press pbk, Cambridge, Mass

Mulholland P, Wolff A, Zdrahal Z, Li N, Corneli J (2013) Constructing and connecting storylines to tell museum stories. Springer International Publishing, Cham, pp 121–124

Museum H (2017) VIDEOFABRIKA: The hermitage vr experience. http://www.inavateonthenet.net/case-studies/article/immersive-history-russia-s-hermitagemuseum-embraces-vr

Nielsen J (1997) How users read on the web? http://www.nngroup.com/articles/how-users-read-on-the-web/

Nine Dissidents movie. https://youtu.be/w3vKIQ2NFW0

Pagano A, Armone G, Sanctis ED (2015) Virtual museums and audience studies: the case of x201c; keys to rome x201d; exhibition. In: 2015 digital heritage, vol 1, pp 373–376

Pietroni E, Pagano A, Rufa C (2013) The etruscanning project: gesture based interaction and user experience in the virtual reconstruction of the regolini-galassi tomb. In: 2013 digital heritage international congress (DigitalHeritage), vol 2, pp 653–660

Rizvić S (2017) How to breathe life into cultural heritage 3D reconstructions. Eur Rev 25(1):39–50

Rizvic S, Prazina I (2015) Taslihan virtual reconstruction—interactive digital story or a serious game. In: Proceedings of IEEE 7th international conference on games and virtual worlds for serious applications (VS-Games), pp 1–2

Rizvic S, Pletinckx D, Pescarin S (2014) Keys to Rome—the next generation virtual museum event, South East European digitization conference SEEDI 2014, Belgrade, Serbia

Rizvic S, Sadzak A, El Zayat M, Žalik B, Rupnik B, Lukač N (2014) Interactive storytelling about Isa Bey endowment, review of the national center for digitization. Faculty of Mathematics, Belgrade. ISSN: 1820-0109, Issue: 25, pp 66–74

Rizvic S, Okanovic V, Prazina I, Sadzak A (2016) 4D virtual reconstruction of white bastion fortress. In: Proceedings of 14th eurographics workshop on graphics and cultural heritage, pp 79–82. ISBN 978-3-03868-011-6

Rizvic S, Djapo N, Alispahic F, Hadzihalilovic B, Fejzic-Cengic F, Imamovic A, Boskovic D, Okanovic V (2017) Guidelines for interactive digital storytelling presentations of cultural heritage. In: Proceedings of 9th international conference on virtual worlds and games for serious applications (VS-Games 2017), pp 1–7. ISBN 978-1-5090-5812-9

Rizvic S, Boskovic D, Okanovic V, Sljivo S (2017) Kyrenia—hyper storytelling pilot application. In: Proceedings of 15th eurographics workshop on graphics and cultural heritage 2017, pp 177–181

Rizvic S, Boskovic D, Bruno F, Davidde Petriaggi B, Sljivo S, Cozza M (2019a) Actors in VR storytelling. In: 11th international conference on virtual worlds and games for serious applications (VS-Games)

Rizvic S, Boskovic D, Okanovic V, Sljivo S, Zukic M (2019b) Interactive digital storytelling: bringing cultural heritage in a classroom. J Comput Educ 6(1):143–166

Rizvić S, Sadžak A, Hulusić V, Karahasanović A (2012) Interactive digital storytelling in the sarajevo survival tools virtual environment, SCCG 2012. ACM Digital Library

Sawhney N, Balcom D, Smith I (1996) HyperFace: narrative and aesthetic properties of hypervideo. In: Hypertext '96 proceedings, ACM, New York. pp 1–10

Schoenau-Fog H (2015) Adaptive storyworlds. Springer International Publishing, Cham, pp 58–65

Selmanovic E, Rizvic S, Harvey C, Boškovic D, Hulusic V, Chahin M, Šljivo S (2018) VR video storytelling for intangible cultural heritage preservation. In: Proceedings of 16th EUROGRAPHICS workshop on graphics and cultural heritage 2018

Šljivo S (2012) Audio guided virtual museums. In: Central European seminar on computer graphics, Bratislava, Slovakia

Sarajevo Charter for Interactive Digital Storytelling. http://h.etf.unsa.ba/sarajevocharter/

Temte BF, Schoenau-Fog H (2012) Coffee tables and cryo chambers: a comparison of user experience and diegetic time between traditional and virtual environment-based role playing game scenarios. Springer Berlin Heidelberg, Berlin, Heidelberg, pp 102–113

Vayanou M, Katifori A, Karvounis M, Kourtis V, Kyriakidi M, Roussou M, Tsangaris M, Ioannidis Y, Balet O, Prados T, Keil J, Engelke T, Pujol L (2014) Authoring personalized interactive museum stories. Springer International Publishing, Cham, pp 37–48

Vermeulen IE, Roth C, Vorderer P, Klimmt C (2010) Measuring user responses to interactive stories: towards a standardized assessment tool. Springer, Berlin Heidelberg, Berlin, Heidelberg, pp 38–43

Unity Web Player. (http://unity3d.com/webplayer)

Chapter 19
Storytelling in Virtual Museums: Engaging A Multitude of Voices

Stella Sylaiou and Panagiotis Dafiotis

Abstract This chapter explores the integration of affective storytelling in virtual museum (VM) experience. The use of Information and Communication Technologies (ICT) affects the way people create, communicate and learn, opens novel opportunities and provides new means for museums to create narratives, express their points and provide quality experiences. Museums' integration of new media, empowers people to construct their own understandings within an open-ended framework. ICT permeate cultural life, not only by introducing new forms of creative expression and meanings for art, but also by enriching, transforming and enhancing the museum experience. ICT in museums can empower curators to disseminate their ideas and facilitate understandings of the complexities regarding museum exhibits and thus develop aesthetic perception, sensitivities and creativity. In this chapter, the function and cultural significance of storytelling as such is addressed, before venturing into discussing digital storytelling vis-à-vis cultural heritage organizations' practices. Furthermore, the potential of digital storytelling as fulcrum for rethinking museums as affective spaces in-dialogue with their audiences is delineated.

19.1 Introduction

Museums are public and social spaces. Museums, since the advent of New Museology in the second half of 20th century, seek to adapt to a wider call for audiences' empowerment, involvement and acknowledgment of visitors' individuality. Postmodern theoretical approaches further entrenched distrust to master narratives (be them ideological, epistemological or otherwise) leading to a tendency to afford, celebrate and promulgate multiple viewpoints and voices. The inclusion of a multitude of voices, narratives, personal stories not only introduces a participatory twist to museums, but heralds a new paradigm in which museums become sites for shared

S. Sylaiou (✉) · P. Dafiotis
School of Visual and Applied Arts, Faculty of Fine Arts, Aristotle
University of Thessaloniki, Thessaloniki, Greece
e-mail: sylaiou@gmail.com

F. Liarokapis et al. (eds.), *Visual Computing for Cultural Heritage*, Springer Series
on Cultural Computing, https://doi.org/10.1007/978-3-030-37191-3_19

and dialogic meaning-making, rather than repositories of predetermined meanings to be relegated.

In the world of marketing, cultural organisations, such as museums, have realized that the brand and the brandname are not enough. Cultural consumers, museum visitors want stories. Life is about stories and people love stories. So, museums have become storytellers. They transformed their cultural products by attaching additional features, such as storytelling and digital storytelling, that combine educational and entertainment aspects, so as to make them more appealing and easier to understand. The museum exhibits are not important *per se*, but because of the stories they can tell, that trigger visitors' imagination and can thereby create unforgettable memories. These stories can reveal human presence behind the objects, make sense of museum exhibits by understanding an exhibit's function and meaning, and help visitors draw links between past and the present. Contemporary museum experience can be enhanced by providing tools for different visitor categories to help them create their own interpretations and share them with others.

The digitization of museums offers the possibility of a parallel virtual doppelganger of the original collections. However, this useful, yet limited in scope use of ICT, becomes sidelined, as the true potential of digital technologies in re-inventing museums' role becomes gradually realized. Virtual Museums (VMs) and emerging technologies, such as Virtual or Augmented Reality (VR/AR) have encouraged a transformation in terms of how museums connect to their audiences, how they engage them and what degree of agency they bestow to them. The countless possibilities ICT offer to cultural organizations have generated *lines of flight* into new methodological approaches favoring investment in affective, multimodal and immersive experiences, personalized interactivity and even co-authorship of the narratives framing their exhibitions. The passive museum, which presupposes and constructs a passive visitor, gives way to a new conceptualization of the user, since "the reader or critic shifts from the role of consumer to that of producer" (Eagleton 2008).

Storytelling is an age-old way to reproduce and pass on cultural content and norms dating back to the dawn of civilization. Religions undertook to promulgate their narratives, through language as well as visual means. Religion in 19th century Britain relegated to some extent the role of the moral and cultural arbiter to the newly emerged concept of museum, as mass industrialization led to a 'rationalization' of social discourses thereby creating a vacuum to be filled. The modernist era of grand narratives, as mentioned, receded, thus allowing for a *rhizomatic* symbiosis of a multitude of 'subjective' stories, intertwining to give a kaleidoscopic spectrum of personal voices, meanings, interpretations. Museums followed suit by introducing visitor-generated content, artists' interpretative interventions, and digital extensions into the domain of the virtual, which facilitate the circulation of affects, stories, ideas to an unprecedented degree. Interactive Digital Narratives, as cultural form, gathered pace and in the late 90s 'coalesced into a recognizable media practice' (Murray 2018) weaving themselves into the fabric of museums' digital resources. VMs utilize the potential of (interactive) storytelling through new tools, not as means to have their stories heard beyond their walls but all the more, in order to listen, incorporate and encourage the voices of their audiences to enter into a fruitful dialogue with them.

The following section presents the structure, stages and characteristics of multimodal digital storytelling, outlining practical, as well as theoretical considerations. This leads to an investigation of the underpinnings, implications and conundrums related with participatory, affective digital narratives as voices-in-dialogue within the context of institutional practices, which increasingly relegate agency to their visitors. The interrelation between personal narratives, interpretative meaning-making and the construction of knowledge is outlined. Lastly, a case is made for the value of fostering inclusive polyphonies, ambivalence and polysemy in VMs.

19.2 Terms

19.2.1 A Short Story of Storytelling

Storytelling is one of the oldest existing forms of art, it is about sharing a story linking people in time and it plays a central role in all cultures. The ancient drawings in the cave walls of Lascaux around 30,000 years ago, can be considered as one of the most ancient storyboards and show that people wanted to communicate and deliver stories to others. It is an act of communication of events or happenings, real or imaginary. A story can be a blend of legends, facts, myths, beliefs, feelings and emotions. In Homeric epics, Odyssey and Iliad heroes tell stories about their lives and at the same time they deliver historical events. Storytelling can also be considered as the oldest form of teaching and concurrently, the first and most essential form of human learning, since stories are more easily remembered than raw facts, because they contain an underlying structure and can catch the attention of the listener and be linked with prior experiences.

Storytelling is based on a story and define a story structure, a narrative. It is the production of a narrative that communicates experiences and it can use words, sounds, gestures and expressions. According to the National Storytelling Network 'Storytelling is the interactive art of using words and actions to reveal the elements and images of a story while encouraging the listener's imagination' (https://storynet.org/what-is-storytelling/). Storytelling is important for people, because it helps them to understand and organise their thoughts in a convincing way. Stories help visitors to understand and empathise, and museum to communicate its messages. There are three types of storytelling: "direct" storytelling (the museum tells about itself)—"indirect" storytelling (visitors tell about their experience); —"participatory" storytelling (virtuous mix of direct and indirect) (http://www.svegliamuseo.com/en/raccontare-il-museo-storytelling/). Museums can establish direct communication with the visitors, in which museum is the communicator and the visitor the receiver and *vice versa*, providing the visitor with the opportunity to actively participate in the story. Museum can have a conversation with the visitors, who can share their experiences and personal views.

Storytelling allows the democratization of knowledge and promotes the social integration, since the visitors can learn about their own heritage and reinforce the sense of belonging to a community and at the same time, learn about and understand cultural diversity and become acquainted to other ways of thinking. Technological advances that have emerged as areas of crucial interest, are making it possible to use sophisticated tools to generate VMs and deliver digital stories and information in a number of ways for experience emotions' enhancement, knowledge construction and meaning making (Sylaiou et al. 2020).

19.2.2 Digital Storytelling

During the 90s, the use of computers opened a new field called digital storytelling, a combination of the art of telling stories and digital multimedia. Digital Storytelling has been developed as a systematized methodology and widely spread, firstly by the Centre for Digital Storytelling (CDS) (https://www.storycenter.org) in Berkeley, California, founded in 1998. Moreover, the International Conference on Interactive Digital Storytelling (ICIDS) was created (http://icids.org/). According to the CDS, a digital story is a collection of audio, video, images, text, all put together to form a story on a screen that help individuals rediscover how to listen to each other and share first person stories and its goal is to inform or instruct on a particular topic (http://storycenter.org/about-us/).

The narrative of the museum exhibition involves interactive components and is linked with digital content, like images, sounds and videos, to produce a multimedia experience that allows the active participation of the museum visitor. Nowadays, ICT provide tools, such as digital storytelling, that deliver complex and interactive information in VMs, permitting onsite and online experiences and start conversation with the visitors. Museums can provide meaning to the ways that people interact with technology, use various content delivery methods, such as Web browsers, tablets, smartphones, provide interactive storytelling experiences not only for individuals, but also for groups and use multiple layers to present a story (Wyman et al. 2011).

Storytelling in VMs can describe relationships between exhibits and contribute to visitors' engagement via interactivity and the use of dramatic elements, as well as through the personalization of the information delivered, since the user can decide which parts of the story to explore. It is attractive and engaging to a variety of audiences, since stories can evoke emotion and contribute to learning. VMs are often considered as places of learning associated with the presentation of facts. However, they are also places, where curiosity is invoked through culturally rich and memorable museum experiences that can lead to deeper understanding and learning.

People that watch stories perceive themselves as participants: *scans of their brains show it, not as a spectator, but as a participant in the action* (https://www.museumnext.com/insight/digital_storytelling_in_museums/), a fact that sheds new light on the concepts of *mimesis, poiesis* and *praxis* (Ancient Greek: μίμησις, imitation; ποίησις, making; πράξις, doing, acting), philosophical terms used by Aristotle. Nicholas Davey (Macleod and Holdridge 2006) posits that 'If the roots of modern theory are traced back to the ancient Greek conception of *theoria* ($\theta\varepsilon\omega\rho\acute{\iota}\alpha$, contemplation) and *theoros* ($\theta\varepsilon\omega\rho\acute{o}\varsigma$, participant), a path to rearticulating theory as a mode of participation in practice is opened' [ibid., p. 23]. The importance of the *engaged participant* becomes foregrounded in this conceptualization of *theoros* and can inform the reimagining of VMs users' role, as active participants in negotiating meanings in museums.

19.3 Rethinking Museums Through Storytelling

As Saroj Ghose explains in 'Rethinking Museums: The Emerging Face of Storytelling' (http://www.maltwood.uvic.ca/cam/publications/other_publications/Text _of_Rethinking_Museums.pdf) the very concept of introducing storytelling in museums emanates from a paradigm shift according to which museums were reimagined as activity-oriented places and not as passive repositories of collections. He mentions the Deutsches Museum in Munich in the 1930s as probably the first example of a museum, which encouraged hands-on interactive approaches, thus introducing the museum that does things rather than has things. Ghose posits that technology functioned as catalyst in rethinking museums' role towards visitors' active participation, and the fact that Deutsches Museum was according to him a forerunner in this direction, relates to its technical orientation showcasing and promoting technological advancement, in terms of content and intent. Today, as Ghose notes, ubiquitous technological advances support the proliferation of such practices in cultural heritage organizations, which increasingly invest in storytelling as the benefits are 'manifold', ranging from making museums more attractive, effective and efficient by providing context and coherence to their collections: Storytelling presents 'a particular episode of history, partially with artefacts and largely through personal experience so that the episode is presented in its complete form' [ibid.].

Danks et al. (2007) explain that even in storytelling 'determined' by the museum, 'Digital technologies allow more sophisticated nonlinear stories; allowing visitors to interact with the story at different points in time'. They refer to the example of the ART-E-FACT project 'which introduced MR interactive storytelling with virtual characters, positioned next to real art pieces in an exhibition, discussing art, while prompting visitors for their opinions and questions (Spierling and Iurgel 2003). Danks et al. (2007) developed (and tested) the Interactive Storytelling Exhibition Project, which combined 'both interactive television storytelling and gaming technologies to immerse museum visitors with artefacts on exhibition, engaging the user into physical space using virtual stories'. Their imaginative approach engaged users who found the experience unanimously enjoyable, as well as informative and inspiring. Their game-based approach, which involved narratives throughout, is illustrated by their exclamation that in their project, game drives narrative and narrative drives game. This is in line with General Learning Outcomes (GLOs) that underpin the aims of museum education in the UK. GLOs emphasize, apart from the targets of skills, understanding and knowledge, aims related to emotion and enjoyment as equally important and indispensable for efficient meaning-making (Hooper-Greenhill 2004; Graham 2013; Falk and Dierking 2000). This fact draws attention to the importance of emotions as fulcrums for engaged learning especially in immersive museum experiences.

This shift towards storytelling brought about the question of what stories will be shared and whose voice will be prevalent. Wyman et al. (2011) note that 'The museum's approach to storytelling has evolved. What was once primarily a voice of authority speaking to the public through exhibition display and publications has dramatically turned, in many places, into a multifaceted experience that invites conversation and interaction with visitors.' Fisher et al. (2008) discuss the integration of visitor-contributed narratives into the narratives of art museums, within both curatorial and educational programs. They present the 'Art of *Storytelling* Project' in which the construction of narratives by visitors in relations to exhibits created strong bonds between the institutions and their users, as they felt that their trace has been inscribed in the corpus of the museum.

Hein's book (2006) with the telling title *Public Art: Thinking Museums Differently,* outlines a reconceptualization of the museum, according to which *concurrent stories* could emerge from visitors' interpretative or emotive accounts of their encounter with artworks. This paradigm shift could not only expand into VMs but, in them, could find a prime framework. Hein refers to Julian Spalding, former director of the Glasgow Museums and Art Galleries, who 'holds that museums should not tell one history, but rather facilitate many concurrent stories. In his book The Poetic Museum, he proposes that the museum be something like a self-generated poetry anthology, permissively equipped with stimulating artifactual props' [ibid., p. 110].

19.4 Interactive and Participatory Storytelling in VMs

19.4.1 Parts of Storytelling

Digital storytelling in VMs can be constructed similarly to a theatrical production. In his essay *Poetics* (c. 335 BCE), Aristotle writes that a story shall imitate a whole action with a beginning, a middle and an end, and the events shall follow each other (http://classics.mit.edu/Aristotle/poetics.mb.txt). The parts of a good storytelling, as outlined by him, like the *mythos* or plot ($\mu\tilde{\upsilon}\theta o\varsigma$, the imitation of the action, the storyline), the *character* ($\tilde{\eta}\theta o\varsigma$, the actors), the *thought*, the *diction* ($\lambda\acute{e}\xi\iota\varsigma$, the expression of the meaning in words), the *melody* ($\mu\epsilon\lambda o\pi o\iota\acute{\iota}\alpha$), the *spectacle* ($\check{o}\psi\iota\varsigma$), have been translated into some rules for storytelling in User Experience (https://www.interaction-design.org/literature/article/aristotle-on-storytelling-in-user-experience) that can also be used for the needs of a VM creation. Storytelling techniques have been also explored by (Freytag 1863), which introduces the standard model of the narrative plot (Callaway et al. 2012), the dramatic arc that is divided in:

exposition (with important background information to the audience), *rising action* (series of events that lead to build up the climax), *climax* (the turning point of the story), *falling action,* and *dénouement* (the resolution, the conclusion of the story with a sense of catharsis).

A more contemporary story structure as Atasoy and Martens note (2011) can be detected in Field's Paradigm, (Duarte 2010) a three-act structure, that is a simplified and compressed version of Freytag's five-act structure. Three-act structures consist of: Set-up, Confrontation, and Resolution. According to Field, what moves a beginning to the middle and the middle to an end are called plot points which are definitive moments where an event happens that changes the direction of the story (http://classics.mit.edu/Aristotle/poetics.mb.txt; https://www.interaction-design.org/literature/article/aristotle-on-storytelling-in-user -experience).

As Atasoy and Martens explain, (2011) Freeman, interpreted the three-act structure as an energy curve, called Aristotle's Plot Curve, that visually communicates the relationship between time (horizontally) and dramatic intensity (vertically).

Moreover, 'Glebas[1] took a step further and interpreted dramatic intensity as emotional involvement. In his interpretation, the vertical axis depicts how much the audience is involved or 'lost' in the story' (Atasoy and Martens 2011).

The Aristotle's formula comprising of seven elements is presented, in order to convey the subtle balance between structural elements as well as affective ones such as the emotional impact of melody. This illustrates the complex interdependence of sensuous, emotional, thematic and content-related aspects of a multimodal narrative.

19.4.2 Key Stages In Creating Multimodal Storytelling-Based Resources

Interacting with digital storytelling applications may lead to confusion and the need for some support in a museum space. All the more, engaging in digital storytelling as (co) producer of multimodal resources is a daunting task, exciting as may be, and for non-experts (e.g. museum casual visitors) there is need for step-by-step guidance (Bán and Nagy 2016). A rough outline of the steps involved in Digital Storytelling follows: The first step is to identify the scope, the main idea and the gist of a personal story, in a creative, open ended and brainstorm-like process. The story should be outlined bearing in mind, what it 'wants' to achieve.

A supporting context in the shape of a team of prospective storytellers with the guidance of an experienced professional as trainer is highly desirable if not necessary. The task of trainers in such case is complex (Bán and Nagy 2016). In the course of developing and dramatizing the stories, they may often have to address sensitive, difficult or psychologically taxing situations, and in the meantime, they also have to

---

[1] Glebas, F. Directing the story: professional storytelling and storyboarding techniques for live action and animation. Focal Press, 2008.

maintain group cohesion and coordinate processes of group dynamics. The merit of having support also relates to the organizational phase that follows later on, which involves a compilation of relevant resources (visual or other) and supporting the multimodal story with a clear workflow blueprint and time framework. The group can also be invaluable as a peer-review matrix, providing feedback that could inform the course of the storytelling foray.

Scripting is the first stage towards giving shape to the actual contents of a digital narrative; and is highly important—as is the case with the following storyboard phase that also addresses the visual/aural aspect and overall composition of different modes. Scripting, the creation of the account as text, fine-tunes the point of view, the register, purpose and affective potential of the story ironing out issues of pace, economy (i.e., creation of succinct and to the point narrations) and content.

As Bán and Nagy (2016) stipulate 'In the script it is best to think in simple, short sentences, taking care of using expressions and idioms characteristic of the storyteller and avoiding phrases which are strange to their personality. It is important for the storyteller to feel that at the end the story is their own'.

Boase 2013 presents a study focusing on the benefits of digital storytelling shedding light on the scope of favoring scripted narrative over spontaneous ones: 'Comparing the pros and cons of a free-spoken narrative to one that is scripted before being spoken, Nygren and Blom (2001) conclude that one of the positive experiences of using prepared narratives is that the 'empirical material is more structured, as well as more reflective, than the transcripts from interviews. The higher degree of reflection implies that the story is more 'understood' by the narrator. Thus, the material can be assumed to say much about the narrator's self-conception, something that is important for research on identity, life-stories etc.'

This outlining of scripted accounts' benefits, in effect conveys what these scripts should try to achieve in order to be successful: namely, a thoroughly elaborated outcome of reflexive procedure that is in fact an effort to work on one's notion of self. Understanding, organizing and presenting their own way of thinking/feeling is akin to a meta-process of reconstructing their world-views and sharing them. Boase (2013) refers to the philosopher Hannah Arendt, who posits that narratives are a fundamentally communicative form, because, as she sees it, a story 'amplifies the circle of selfhood into an enlarged mentality' and because all narrative is written with the anticipated communication with others in mind (Kearney 1998).

Storyboard gives shape to how diverse modalities will work together, how the (visual) structure will progress and become finalized offering a platform for amendments, testing solutions in an increasing level of fidelity to the final product.

The storyboard stage is in effect the design phase of the storytelling project. As such, it is fairly pertinent to artistic practice in the sense that orchestrating how different modalities will work together, as well as honing the aesthetic qualities of the multimodal narrative is in essence, an effort to balance content and form in order to achieve a meaningful and affective end product akin to a multimedia artwork. So, the next step after the 'scenario' is established in the form of scrip, is to illustrate and delineate, with the use of visuals, a storyboard. There are several templates that can be followed; however, they all converge to the same basic principle of aligning voiceover, i.e. parts of the account in written text with the respective imagery that will appear in the video, along with notation of probable effects, transitions and if applicable, the soundtrack or soundscape that accompanies the narration. A simple template can be described as follows: '*This is a simple two-column table, one column of which has the text divided according to a certain rhythm—usually sentence by sentence—paired with the appropriate photos in the other. The storyboard makes the proportion of pictures versus the text in the story visible*' (Bán and Nagy 2016).

The narrative is thus presented visually as well, following the elaboration on the written script. Storyboarding as a technique is extensively used in Human Computer Interaction design (Truong et al. 2006). Storyboards present the difficulty and challenge that the author's motivation, emotion and outlook in relation to an issue, subject or situation have to be clearly encapsulated and represented (Rubin and Chisnell 2008).

As is the case with every assemblage of modes, everything affects the potential to affect the senses and concomitantly the intellect, so the tonality of the voice (itself a mode which influences how the story is perceived or interpreted) the quality of recording, existence or lack of ambient noise/sound, all are part of the overall message conveyed. Moreover, this is the first proper technical stage and put in simple terms, 'Both the technical quality and the "subjective feel" of the recorded voice are crucial for the success of digital storytelling' (Bán and Nagy 2016). The same principle applies to the visuals that will be processed and edited.

At all stages, the quality of imagery, appropriateness and awareness of how image, sound (recorded narration of other), interrelate and become mutually enhancing is crucial. Pacing, the rhythm, moments of intensity and accentuations along with parts of subdued, subtle feel to them, silences even, play a major role in affecting how storytelling works. Use of adequate software is another consideration, as the affordances of each application should be taken into consideration before making pertinent choices, bearing in mind the characteristics that are desirable and apposite for the digital storytelling project at hand. Putting it all together and making it work, is a continual procedure of trying out possibilities, sharing them with others, in a reflexive cycle that leads to the final stage of how actually this is going to be shared, projected into the social domain, or into a cultural heritage context. The last stage brings about a need to consider issues of authorship, copyright and dissemination.

Furthermore, ethics come into the equation, especially when the story narrated involves others, touches upon sensitive issues, or is altogether the story of someone else either in the form of interview, or as an account about a non-present person. This is also a lateral indication of the differing ontologies of storytelling that pertain to the self, i.e. stories about oneself, or even story as the (construct of) self.

Moreover, differentiation in register and meaning accrues, when an account is akin to an interview, or is in a discursive format—in which case the account is co-authored. Such forms of storytelling entail an encounter with the 'other'. Nevertheless, dialogic approaches can be the optimal approach for a series of instances or situations.

Taking a step further, even critique of, or contemplation on the very concept of narrative form, as bearer of meaning or truth, may be the scope of digital storytelling. Vertical Features Remake (1978), a film by Peter Greenaway, can be an example (albeit an artwork), that nevertheless, addresses and to an extent explores the very conventions underpinning of narration and storytelling. As it hovers between reality and fiction, it offers an imaginative form of reflexive critique that mockingly mimics documentary filmic accounts.

19.5   Discussion of Theoretical Implications

19.5.1   Engaging Stories as an Enabling Factor for Meaning-Making

Sylaiou et al. (2017) in their study investigate the educational impact of diverse technologies in online VMs. In relation to the implications and value of narrative in the form e.g. of videos presenting first-person accounts in VMs, they explain that '…storytelling is inserted into the visitor's experience to offer a personal view and foster engagement'. Engagement is the key point and therefore pertinent research and approaches gravitate towards the inclusion of interactivity and all the more, co-authorship of the narratives that increasingly support (or even comprise) the contents of VMs. Glassner (2004) defined interactive storytelling as a two-way experience, where "the audience member actually affects the story itself". Riznic et al. (2012) explain the motives behind the use of digital storytelling with elements of interactivity in a compelling VM environment whose design and affective potential has been put to the test in their study: "Digital storytelling is narrative entertainment that reaches the audience via digital technology and media". Miller (2008) states that digital storytelling techniques can make a dry or difficult subject more alive and engaging to the viewers. This was exactly our aim when introducing digital storytelling in a VM application (ibid.).

Giaccardi (2006) presents in his study the VM of the Collective Memory of Lombardia (MUVI). MUVI relies principally on the public's contribution of stories, photographs, even spoken accounts recounted on a 'radio' platform especially designed to encourage storytelling. It is an early example of collective storytelling in VMs and employed a necessary processing and filtering process (often involving local volunteers) to digitize and foreground the most effective photographic documentation framing the participants' accounts for the preservation of the fleeting memories of Lombardia. According to Giaccardi (2006) MUVI 'shows how the collection and preservation of physical artifacts can be connected to expressions of social creativity by means of processes of participation and collective storytelling that are sustained and empowered by the convergence of different media and information technologies…MUVI is a "relational museum," that is, a museum that promotes knowledge not as a body of facts reliable at any time and any place, but as a more complex reality in which multiple narratives play an important role.'

As Giaccardi (2006) posits, virtuality in museums is not a facile process of digitally replicating artefacts, but a whole new opportunity to create frameworks that encourage engaged participation and relation, co-construction of meanings and interpretations, thereby bestowing agency to the bearers (and seekers) of a community's collective memory: 'Virtuality does not mean merely to reproduce preexisting objects, but also to actualize new ones. Virtuality can be used to invent new methods of producing meaning, and hence technologies capable of activating and sustaining emotional mechanisms, triggering new relationships, and engendering new knowledge' [ibid.].

19.5.2 Narratives and the Construction of Knowledge: A Troubled Relation

Bakhtin, a prominent author who exerts considerable influence on contemporary theorists, investigated narratives and introduced the concept of Chronotope. According to Bakhtin, fictional narratives are based on specific genre-dependent perception of a time-space continuum. Bakhtin's multifaceted research opens up a discussion on the extent to which (modern) history and other social sciences are structured in the image of fiction. That is, non-fictional discourses related to narratives e.g. history, art history, are constructed on a logic emanating from (and even resulting in) fiction. This seemingly innocuous affair means that sense of reality itself is conforming to fictional terms. A key objection to the fictional narratives typically based on the convention of 'decisive moments' is that they affect the perception of reality itself. Changes in 'real life' happen slowly, brew under the surface and are brought about, not as result of 'fateful moments' but as the effect of multiple factors interrelating in ways which are hard to map out. Stories can be inspiring, spectacular and emotive. However, the issue discussed here is how to avoid a distortion of the logic behind the evolution of situations so that it matches a sensationalist urge for fascination.

The suspension of disbelief that support every form of narrative (especially those involving visual communication) should by no means entail suspension of critical and contextual thinking. Conversely, addressing the complexity socio-cultural processes should not result to jettisoning the affective and engaging potential of the narratives. This is a challenge that, if answered properly, can offer informed, pleasurable and thought-provoking uses of narratives mediated by ICT.

A characteristic example of the emerging technological possibilities in the field is the work of Casillo et al. (2016) who present a study aiming at 'the realization of a dynamic storytelling engine that can allow the dynamic supply of narrative contents, not necessarily predetermined and pertinent to the needs and the dynamic behaviors of the users'. In their paper an array of related studies in digital storytelling outside the linear paradigm is also presented. As Casillo et al. (2016) explain, digital storytelling exists in many forms and encompasses multiple fields; in particular, there are the following typologies: linear, non-linear, adaptive, social/collaborative, mobile and game.

An indication of the richness of forms that storytelling can take, is the foregrounding of non-language-based ways of conveying a story: As Doulamis et al. (2017) note, 'during dancing performances, motion gestures are used to communicate a storyline'. In their paper they presented the concept of the Terpsichore project, in which technological means are proposed as ways to capture and render in 4D choreographies as elements of intangible heritage that can also tell a story.

The relationship between storytelling as somewhat subjective representation of meaning on the one hand and knowledge proper as an objectively constructed body of factual information or demonstrable skills, on the other, can be seen as a binary opposition. What eschews such a conceptualization is the fact that representation of meaning is what all symbolic systems, language withstanding, actually do: all forms of language-based knowing, scientific or otherwise, emanate from and are based on the intricacies of how representations of meaning are perceived, decoded and interpreted something which in turn, entails an element of subjectivity—especially evident in the field of humanities. This is not an effort to relativize meaning-making and knowing, but quite conversely, given the multitude of forms storytelling can take, language-based or even movement/gesture-based, at this point, the interrelation between knowledge and multimodal narration as representation of meaning, becomes the focal point. With reference to the relation between Intangible Cultural Heritage (ICH) that relates to forms of storytelling (language-based or not), and knowledge, the connection is twofold: ICH *encompasses knowledge* in its many forms, while the analysis, codification and the semantics of storytelling entail the need for the production of further knowledge in the field, particularly when digitization is involved, and all the more when non-language based representation of meaning is concerned—as is the case with folkloric choreographies which incorporate narrational aspects.

As Doulamis et al. (2017) who present their research, precisely in this field, note, citing UNESCO,[2] ICH content means "the practices, representations, expressions, *knowledge*, skills—as well as the instruments, objects, artefacts and cultural spaces associated therewith" (emphasis added). Moreover, they outline their elaborate process of capturing, modelling/rendering and most importantly deciphering in terms of semantic content the movements, gestures, trajectories involved in the choreographies which according to them pertain to storytelling, albeit through different modes:

> During dancing performances, motion gestures are used to communicate a storyline in an aesthetically pleasing manner. Although, humans automatically perceive and understand such gestures, from the point of view of computer science these gestures have to be analyzed under an appropriate framework with appropriate features, such as repetitive patterns, motion trajectories and motion inclusions, in order to extract their semantics. (Doulamis 2017)

Doulamis et al. developed such framework through Terpsichore project, and their relevance to the moot point of whether knowledge construction and symbolic representation through forms of storytelling are indeed inextricably related, is answered in

---

[2]UNESCO, Text of the Convention for the Safeguarding of the Intangible Cultural Heritage: Article 2—Definitions at https://ich.unesco.org/en/convention.

two ways: storytelling within, as well as without language encompasses knowledge. Most importantly, the effort to render such representations in digital form entails the necessary production of further knowledge in the field. Rendering these multi-modal narrative-related resources in ways that do not truncate their meanings, and in interoperable formats that allow for future interaction with them on pertinent online platforms/libraries (e.g. the EU digital library EUROPEANA), or in VMs, allows for re-interpretations and possibly as a next step, given that such operability is afforded in the future, input from other users.

19.5.3   Who Is Authorized to Tell the Stories? Towards a Polyphony-in-Dialogue

There is a major issue on cultural heritage organizations' *mode of address*: who is authorized to tell the stories, whose voice is legitimized i.e., who has the agency to speak. The institutional authority of the museum as the arbiter of what is deemed valid, significant and even true, is questioned within a developing discussion that foregrounds dialogic, participatory and inclusive approaches valorizing the multiple voices of the public. Technology, not as a panacea, but as an aid, renders the possibility of visitors' co-authoring of the narratives framing exhibitions, collections and artefacts, practically feasible, thus removing an obstacle which conveniently bolstered the exclusiveness of agency to institutions.

   The solution to the conundrum of how a narrative can include a multitude of voices, may be traced back to Bakhtin once again: Bakhtin introduced the notion of dialogism focusing on 'Polyphonic Novel' that according to Allen 'fights against any view of the world, which would valorize on 'official' point-of-view, one ideological position, and thus one discourse, above all others'. A Polyphonic narrative has 'no objective narratorial voice to guide us through the vast array of voices, interpretations, world-views, opinions and responses' (Allen 2000, p. 24). Bakhtin's theory of dialogism (Bakhtin 1990) and *heteroglossia* relate to the interplay of different aspects registers and aspects of language. The 'official', institutional language as the given, is referred to as Langue, while the living language the Parole. *Langue* as the closed system of language and *Parole*, as individual utterances, form a binary opposition dating back to Saussure. Langue is the conceptualization of language as a machine organised around a fixed syntax whilst *Parole* refers to how *Langue* is actualized, lived and used by people.

   Terry Eagleton argues that "Bakhtin shifted attention from the abstract system of langue to the concrete utterances of individuals in particular social contexts" and that "language was seen as inherently 'dialogic'…" (Eagleton 2008, p. 101). What Eagleton, a prominent 'public intellectual', underlines here, is that the language of institutions and the multitude of individual voices are inextricably interrelated. Language *is* a heteroglossia, a double-voiced dialogue between the established and the emerging voices. The importance for this paper here, is that a model based on the dialogue between institutional and visitors' voices can form the basis of storytelling in VMs.

Dissonance and mental conflict are not what dialogic is about; Kristeva in her explanation of Bakthin dialogism posits: *text belongs to both writing subject and addressee* (Kristeva 1980, p. 66). In her discussion on intertextuality she argues that "signifying practice is never simple and unified. It is the result of multiple origins or drives and hence, it does not produce a simple uniform meaning" (McAfee 2004, p. 26). Ambivalence and polysemy may be the result of this lack of uniform meaning; however, this is a welcomed outcome.

Gabriel and Connell (2010) present their study in the potential of Collaborative storytelling and quote Watson (2000) who pioneered 'ethnographic fiction science' (chiming with Djerassi's term 'science-in-fiction'). Watson investigates elements of storytelling in social sciences drawing 'legitimacy from Czarniawska's extended and persuasive arguments that virtually all theory of organizations, including that which is based on claims of literal truth, has a narrative character' (Gabriel and Connell 2010; Czarniawska 1999; Czarniawska 2004). What transpires here is that organizations construct truths in the way fiction is created.

Boase (2013) refers to the hermeneutical philosopher Paul Ricoeur also saw narrative-making as a process of socialisation, because by giving our story and receiving those of others, we 'renarrate' ourselves and increase our understanding of others (Kearney 1998). For Ricoeur, there is a parallel between narrative imagining and 'the practical wisdom of moral judgement' and building on Aristotle he believes that narrative is particularly well-suited to ethics because it deals with the singularity of human experience (Boase 2013; Kearney 1995).

Quesenbery and Brooks (2010) note that stories are not to be perceived as a form of broadcasting, in which case a given account is simply disseminated, but they should be seen mostly as conversations. Papagiannakis et al. (2018) suggest that Museums can act as primus inter pares (first among equals) and create a direct communication with the visitors, in which museum is the communicator and the visitor is the receiver and vice versa, providing the visitor the opportunity to actively participate in the story. Museums can have a conversation with the visitor, which can share her/his experiences and personal views. To this end, recent AR/VR commercial h/w technological advances enable the use of sophisticated tools to deliver VM stories and information in a number of ways for experience enhancement, knowledge construction, and meaning making (Sylaiou et al. 2020).

Moreover, in the same vain, Quesenbery and Brooks (2010) posit that 'Stories…are as much a part of the audience as of the storyteller. They come to life in the imaginations of the audience members, whether it is one person or hundreds of people' (Quesenbery and Brooks 2010, p. 24). In this respect stories function in the same way that artworks do: they are not meaningful per se, as unalterable hoardings of meaning, but conversely their value relates to their ability to actualize meaning-making at the level of the viewer or beholder. As Addison explains: *'the art work is not a repository of meaning but a site for meaning-making'* (Addison 1999, p. 36), this evidently applies to how storytelling, in its manifold modalities, operates, which in last analysis, oftentimes takes the form of an artwork proper.

Nicholas Addison is a prevalent theorist and practitioner in the field of Art and Design Education, and has done extensive research in the *volatile space* between art, semantics, meaning-making and learning. The relation between art education and digital storytelling might not be salient, or even obvious, but as new methodologies and technologies emerge, the two fields converge if not conflate, something that bear particular interest for the roles and uses VMs may acquire. Chung (2006) posits that:

> With Internet technologies, digital storytelling makes it possible for individuals to produce their own knowledge…In arts classrooms, the processes of making a digital story propel students to move beyond simply making art for its own sake, because for a story to make sense, it must entail certain contextual meanings to which the audience can relate. Incorporating digital storytelling into arts education is a powerful way to integrate school subjects, teach life issues, and create postmodern works of art that are inspiring to the digital generation.

The last sentence albeit not being the most pertinent to how digital storytelling relates to contextual inferences at the level of user thus fostering active engagement, it nevertheless underlines the confluence of art and digital multimodal narratives, as well as their relevance to the 'digital generation's' sensibilities—both issues bearing considerable importance in relation to how VMs could or should incorporate digital storytelling as dialogic platforms fostering bonds with audiences.

It is characteristic that multimodal storytelling forms the backbone of students' art sketchbooks a form of narrating though artistic/visual/textual means the process of forming/informing stances, influences and personal research in the visual arts. These influences come from the users' interaction with artworks oftentimes seen at VMs. Art sketchbooks are primarily used as means for reflexive meaning-making by advanced, arts-orientated secondary students, on the basis of which assessment on arts-related skills and understandings takes place, and are often showcased by their makers as online narratives through videos posted mostly on YouTube.

In these instances, a lengthy storytelling process recounting how these multimodal accounts progressed provides both an afterlife to these elaborate art sketchbooks (which themselves have narrative form), and another layer of narrational explanation/interpretation shared and open to feedback. To the extent that such assemblages relate to VMs' impact they could well become embedded into virtual/online museums as resources and instances of arts-based input that essentially falls under the definition of digital storytelling privileging the visual.

As Chung (2006) notes, citing Meadows (2003) digital stories can be described as "short, personal multimedia tales told from the heart." She then relates these multimodal accounts to the manifold benefits as well as to their societal aspect: 'The application of digital storytelling to arts education is an interdisciplinary and inquiry-based pedagogy with a hands-on project that integrates the arts, education, local communities, technology, and storytelling'. Addison, highlights that fact that besides the dialogic element pertaining to a wider community, such narratives in the form of art sketchbook which are often shown in video under the economy of a personal account, or could well morph into digitized multimodal storytelling proper, and even most importantly these also entail a formative dialogue with the maker's very self: The sketchbook/diary could be argued as a site for self-reflexivity, an opportunity for an aesthetic working on the self that enables the student to achieve 'the perfect supremacy of oneself over oneself' (Foucault 1992, p. 31), a process in which the critical and productive are blissfully indivisible (Addison 2007).

Most forms of digital storytelling relate to the authors' self, in an autobiographical manner. Nevertheless, revisiting one's (life) story is akin to reinventing one's self in a reflexive way. Writing or drawing the diary of the self, redefines and thereby enriches the self. This is inevitable as the self essentially is a diary, a form of self-written palimpsest. Freeman asserts that 'the self is indistinguishable from the life story it constructs for itself...' (Ellis and Bochner 2003, p. 220) after (Dafiotis 2011).

Lambert (2013), p. 127, in his book Digital Storytelling: Capturing Lives, Creating Communities draw attention to the Storytelling as reflective practice:

> *You become present, and step into a zone of awareness...Digital Storytelling is a form of reflective practice. This reanimation of the image artifact as part of the edit makes you feel as if you thinking about people, places, and objects in new ways. The plasticity of images, music, voice, the very playfulness of arranging and re-arranging meaning by visual sequence and juxtaposition, the entire process becomes regenerative for many people.*

What is suggested here is that art sketchbook, revisited as a (digital) form of storytelling, offers a new possibility for meaningful and apposite inclusion of such methods in VMs: In specific, encounters with artworks can be framed with digital storytelling, and become embedded in VMs and thereby be open to users' input and redefinition. These multimedia/multimodal responses could well weave into the fabric of the virtual exhibitions in an effort to create more responsive, inclusive and dialogic cultural online platforms that aim at making audiences, quite literally speaking, part of the story. The polyphony in dialogue envisaged in this paper in such case, does not only include the voices of many, but the many forms voices can take. That is to say foregrounding also the praxis and the artistic production in the form of multilayered, personal accounts 'from the heart'. These may tell the tale of how their makers engaged with artworks, which (re) shaped their practices as reflexive practitioners who may thereby inform and enrich the energies, dialogues as well as artworks that permeate online museums, as an additional arts-based possibility for audience engagement.

Another twist is being introduced by Kahl et al. (2017) and refers to the emerging possibility of engaging audiences by means of a narrative framework that goes across museums. In specific, based on a network of museums in the Rhine-Waal region of Germany and the Netherlands, they present their research on 'the concept of a continuation network, i.e. we are creating concepts, techniques and software to integrate several museums within a narrative and experience framework, where a satisfactory UX [User Experience] within a museum leads to the desire to continue the experience within another museum' [ibid.]. Motivation of young/adolescents to visit museums here is the key quest, but the use of storytelling that in effect create a space of dialogue amongst them, by connecting their narratives, in order to generate a keen interest in a commonly shared space of cultural organizations. So (virtual) museums that 'talk to' or have something to say to each other, apparently mobilize and encourage youngsters to go and listen, and moreover, given an appropriate framework as several researchers indicate, could well become part of this discursive space themselves. This appears to be a key element in order to sustain interest as users experience that is not restricted to a certain node/VM but rather pertains to a constellational network of institutions, sites, museums evidently creates space and appropriate conditions for a new digital generation to become involved and stay engaged.

19.6 Conclusions

This text calls for the inclusion of polyphony-in-dialogue between users and institutions, establishing a fruitful and engaging symbiosis beyond arbitrary authoritarian narrative constructs—in denial of their provenance from fiction. This polyphony might result in cacophony if not properly framed in theoretical as well as in methodological (practical/technological) terms. Digital storytelling interfaces might be designed for example in a layered manner, allowing for a workable, flexible and personalized manner. Thereby they can adapt to the profile of users and cater for different needs and degrees of visitors' interest, involvement and commitment. Difficult heritage artefacts, such as e.g. relics of 'liberatory' anti-colonial struggles in the London War Museum, could afford the voices of those involved from both sides. Thus, they can provoke thinking in a participatory and reflexive way, without simply juxtaposing conflicting outlooks.

As Zengin notes (2016), 'In Bakhtin's theory of dialogism, the central idea is that every word "is directly, blatantly, oriented toward a future answer-word: it provokes an answer, anticipates it and structures itself in the answer's direction" (Bakhtin 1990, p. 280)'. Texts, narratives, storytelling in VMs aim at engaging audiences, principally referring to artworks and artefacts. After all, this is what artworks especially in contemporary art do: they pose or even embody a question or an *aporia*, leaving the space for interpretation open to multiple voices: Today's public artists incline to replace answers with questions. They seek to advance debate and discussion. Their art is left open-ended and invites participation. Its orientation is toward process and change rather than material stability. Since its borders are indefinite, so is its authorship (Hein 2006, p. 76). The same could be the case with narratives and storytelling in VMs as Hein suggests [ibid.] as they incorporate the technological means for the materialization of open-ended platforms that encourage *dialogic* encounters with artworks mediated by, and resulting in storytelling. Storytelling in VMs can foreground these radical ambivalences and the meaning that 'never fully arrives' underlining and enriching dialogic interpretations beyond the explanatory paradigm, convenient as may be.

Last but not least Kuhn (1970) has shown that the production of systematic theoretical or 'scientific' knowledge always takes place and indeed requires a knowledge-producing community of some sort no matter how flexible and loosely structured it may be (Usher 2001, p. 51). The role this paper envisages for VM visitors is for them to become an empowered knowledge-producing community. Visitors can collaboratively construct narratives using VM storytelling platforms, partaking in equal terms in the production of their personal truths, akin to the way in which art produces them.

References

Addison N (1999) Who's afraid of signs and significations? defending semiotics in the secondary art and design curriculum. Int J Art Des Educ 18(1):33–38

Addison N (2007) Identity politics and the queering of art education: inclusion and the confessional route to salvation. Int J Art Des Educ 26(1):10–20

Allen G (2000) Intertextuality. Routledge, Taylor and Francis Group, London

Atasoy B, Martens J-B (2011) Crafting user experiences by incorporating dramaturgical techniques of storytelling. In: Procedings of the 2nd conference on creativity and innovation in design— DESIRE'11

Bakhtin MM (1990) The dialogic imagination, (Ed. Michael Holquist, Trans. Carly

Bán D, Nagy B (2016) IDig Stories, digital storytelling in practice, training manual for digital storytelling workshops. http://idigstories.eu/wp-content/uploads/2016/09/Digital_Storytelling_in_Practice.pdf

Boase C (2013) Digital storytelling for reflection and engagement: a study of the uses and potential of digital storytelling. https://gjamissen.files.wordpress.com/2013/05/boase_assessment.pdf

Callaway Ch, Stock O, Dekoven E, Noy K, Citron Y, Dobrin Y (2012) Mobile drama in an instrumented museum: inducing group conversation via coordinated narratives. New Rev Hypermedia Multimed 18(1–2):37–61

Casillo M, Colace F, De Santo M, Lemma S, Lombardi M, Pietrosanto A (2016) An ontological approach to digital storytelling. In: Proceedings of the 3rd multidisciplinary

Chung SK (2006) Digital storytelling in integrated arts education. Int J Arts Educ 4(1):33–50

Czarniawska B (1999) Writing management: organization theory as a literary genre. Oxford University Press, Oxford

Czarniawska B (2004) Narratives in social science research. Sage, London

Dafiotis P (2011) Art practice as a form of research in art education: towards a teaching artist practice. PhD thesis, Institute of Education, University of London

Danks M, Goodchild M, Rodriguez-Echavarria K, Arnold DB, Griffiths R (2007) Interactive storytelling and gaming environments for museums: the interactive storytelling exhibition project. In Hui K et al (eds) Technologies for e-learning and digital entertainment. Edutainment 2007. Lecture notes in computer science, vol 4469. Springer, Berlin

Doulamis A et al (2017) 'Transforming intangible folkloric performing arts into tangible choreographic digital objects: the terpsichore approach'. VISIGRAPP (5: VISAPP)

Duarte N (2010) Resonate: present visual stories that transform audiences. Wiley, Hoboken

Eagleton T (2008) Literary theory: an introduction. University of Minnesota Press, Minneapolis

Ellis C, Bochner AP (2003) Autoethnography, personal narrative, reflexivity, collecting and interpreting qualitative materials. Sage Publications, London

Falk JH, Dierking LD (2000) Learning from museums: visitor experiences and the making of meaning. Alta Mira Press, Walnut Creek, CA

Fisher M et al (2008) The art of storytelling: enriching art museum exhibits and education through visitor narratives. In: Trant J, Bearman D (eds) Museums and the Web 2008: Proceedings. Archives & Museum Informatics, Toronto

Foucault M (1992) The use of pleasure. the history of sexuality: 2, trans. R Hurley, Penguin, London

Freytag G (1863) Die Technik des Dramas. https://www.lernhelfer.de/sites/default/files/lexicon/pdf/BWS-DEU2-0032-03.pdf

Gabriel Y, Connell NAD (2010) Co-creating stories: Collaborative experiments in storytelling. Manag Learn 41(5):507–523

Giaccardi E (2006) Collective storytelling and social creativity in the virtual museum: a case study. Des Issues 22(3):29–41

Glassner A (2004) Interactive storytelling. A.K. Peters, Natick

Graham J (2013) Evidencing the impact of the GLOs 2008–13. http://www2.le.ac.uk/departments/museumstudies/rcmg/publications/Evidencing%20the%20impact%20of%20the%20GLOs%20report.pdf. Accessed 10 Jan 2015

Hein H (2006) Public art: thinking museums differently. Rowman & Littlefield Publishers Inc, Lanham, MD

Hooper-Greenhill E (2004) Measuring learning outcomes in museums, archives and libraries: the learning impact research project (LIRP). Int J Herit Stud 10(2):151–174

Kahl T, Iurgel I, Zimmer F, Bakker R, van Turnhout K (2017) RheijnLand.Xperiences—A storytelling framework for cross-museum experiences. Lecture notes in computer science, pp 3–11

Kearney R (1995) The hermeneutics of action. Sage, London

Kearney R (1998) Poetics of imagining: modern and postmodern. Fordham University, New York

Kristeva J (1980) Desire in language: a semiotic approach to literature and art. (Ed. Leon S. Roudiez, Transl. Thomas Gora, Alice Jardine and Leon S. Roudiez). Columbia University Press, New York

Kuhn TS (1970) The structure of scientific revolutions. University of Chicago Press, Chicago

Lambert J (2013) Digital storytelling: capturing lives, creating community. Routledge, New York

Macleod K, Holdridge L (eds) (2006) Thinking through art: reflections on art as research. Routledge, New York

McAfee N (2004) Julia Kristeva. Routledge, New York

Meadows D (2003) Digital storytelling: research-based practice in new media. Vis Commun 2(2):189–193

Miller C (2008) Digital storytelling. Elsevier, Amsterdam

Murray JH (2018) Research into interactive narrative: a kaleidoscopic view. In: Rouse R et al (eds) Proceedings of the Interactive storytelling: 11th International conference on interactive digital storytelling, ICIDS 2018, Dublin, Ireland, 5–8 Dec 2018

Nygren L, Blom B (2001) Analysis of short reflective narratives: a method for the study of knowledge in social workers' actions. Qual Res 1(3):369–384

Papagiannakis G, Geronikolakis E, Pateraki M, López–Menchero VM, Tsioumas M, Sylaiou S, Liarokapis F, Grammatikopoulou A, Dimitropoulos K, Grammalidis N, Huebner N, Dhemre N, Partarakis N, Margetis G, Drossis G, Vassiliadi M, Chalmers A, Stephanidis C, Magnenat-Thalmann N (2018) Mixed reality gamified presence and storytelling for virtual museums, encyclopedia of computer graphics and games. Springer, Berlin, pp 1–13

Quesenbery W, Brooks K (2010) Storytelling for user experience: crafting stories for better design. Rosenfeld Media, New York

Rizvic S, Sadzak A, Hulusic V, Karahasanovic A (2012) Interactive digital storytelling in the sarajevo survival tools virtual environment. In: Proceedings of the 28th spring conference on computer graphics—SCCG'12

Rubin J, Chisnell D (2008) Handbook of usability testing, 1st edn. Wiley Pub, Indianapolis, IN

Spierling U, Iurgel I (2003) 'Just talking about art'—creating virtual storytelling experiences in mixed reality. In Balet O, Subsol G, Torguet P (eds) Virtual storytelling. Using virtual reality technologies for storytelling. ICVS 2003. Lecture notes in computer science, vol 2897. Springer, Berlin

Sylaiou S, Gavalas D, Kasapakis V, Djardanova E (2020) Avatars as storytellers: affective narratives in virtual museums. Pers Ubiquit Comput. https://doi.org/10.1007/s00779-019-01358-2

Sylaiou S, Mania K, Paliokas I, Pujol-Tost L, Killintzis V, Liarokapis F (2017) Exploring the educational impact of diverse technologies in online virtual museums. Int J Arts Technol 10(1):58–84

Truong K, Hayes G, Abowd G (2006) Storyboarding: an empirical determination of best practices and effective guidelines, pp 12–21

Usher R (2001) Telling a story about research and research as story-telling. In: Paechter et al (eds) Knowledge power and learning. SAGE Publications Ltd, London

Watson TJ (2000) Ethnographic Fiction Science: Making Sense of Managerial Work and Organizational Research Processes with Caroline and Terry. Organization 7(3):489–510

Wyman B, Smith S, Meyers D, Godfrey M (2011a) Digital storytelling in museums: observations and best practices. Curator Mus J 54(4):461–468

Wyman B, Smith S, Meyers D, Godfrey M (2011) Digital storytelling in museums: observations and best practices. Curator Mus J 54(4):461–468

What is Storytelling? National Storytelling Network. https://storynet.org/what-is-storytelling/

Museum Stories 1: A definition of storytelling. http://www.svegliamuseo.com/en/raccontare-il-museo-storytelling/

Storycenter. https://www.storycenter.org

International Conference on Interactive Digital Storytelling (ICIDS). http://icids.org/

Center for Digital Storytelling. http://storycenter.org/about-us/

Patel S, A Framework for digital storytelling in museums. https://www.museumnext.com/insight/digital_storytelling_in_museums/

Saroj Ghose, Rethinking museums: the emerging face of storytelling. http://www.maltwood.uvic.ca/cam/publications/other_publications/Text_of_Rethinking_Museums.pdf

Aristotle, Poetics. http://classics.mit.edu/Aristotle/poetics.mb.txt

Aristotle on Storytelling in User Experience. https://www.interaction-design.org/literature/article/aristotle-on-storytelling-in-user-experience

Zengin M (2016) An introduction to intertextuality as a literary theory: definitions, axioms and the originators. Pamukkale Univ J Soc Sci Inst 2016(50):299–327

Part VI
Preservation and Reconstruction

Chapter 20
Analyzing Spatial Distribution of Photographs in Cultural Heritage Applications

Florian Niebling, Jonas Bruschke, Heike Messemer, Markus Wacker and Sebastian von Mammen

Abstract Digitized historical photographs are invaluable sources and key items for scholars in Cultural Heritage (CH) research. Properties of photographic items, such as position and orientation of the camera, can be automatically estimated using Structure from Motion (SfM) algorithms to enable spatial queries on image repositories. Interactive spatial and temporal browsing of photographs of architecture and corresponding 3D models allows historians to gain knowledge about the development of a city, as well as about the changing interest of photographers in depicting particular buildings over time. In this chapter, we present a classification of phenomena modeling the statistical distribution of historical photographic depictions of architecture. This classification serves the design of specialized visualization methods that show statistical aggregation of photographs in spatial contexts, thus supporting research workflows of art and architectural historians.

F. Niebling (✉) · J. Bruschke
Human-Computer Interaction, Julius-Maximilians-Universität Würzburg,
Am Hubland, 97074 Würzburg, Germany
e-mail: florian.niebling@uni-wuerzburg.de

J. Bruschke
e-mail: jonas.bruschke@uni-wuerzburg.de

H. Messemer
Institute of Art History, Julius-Maximilians-Universität Würzburg,
Am Hubland, 97074 Würzburg, Germany
e-mail: heike.messemer@uni-wuerzburg.de

M. Wacker
Faculty of Informatics/Mathemathics, University of Applied Sciences Dresden,
Friedrich-List-Platz 1, 01069 Dresden, Germany
e-mail: wacker@informatik.htw-dresden.de

S. von Mammen
Games Engineering, Julius-Maximilians-Universität Würzburg,
Am Hubland, 97074 Würzburg, Germany
e-mail: sebastian.von.mammen@uni-wuerzburg.de

© Springer Nature Switzerland AG 2020
F. Liarokapis et al. (eds.), *Visual Computing for Cultural Heritage*, Springer Series
on Cultural Computing, https://doi.org/10.1007/978-3-030-37191-3_20

20.1 Introduction

Historical photographs are important research objects by themselves. They are also invaluable resources for research about the situations they depict. Over the last decades, large amounts of according documents have been digitized and made available to researchers by means of online repositories. These photo collections provide access to the captured data but they also provide a greater infrastructure that allows to evolve specific research efforts.

Archives and image repositories containing historical media are usually accessible to the broad public and for a variety of purposes. However, Sweetnam et al. provide an overview of the users of such archives, which summarizes the target groups as professional researchers, apprentice investigators, informed users, and the general public (Sweetnam et al. 2012). The typical motivations for accessing the archives and repositories are scientific research, pedagogical application, and the study of historical sites. The collections' interfaces need to support these goals and be tailored to the different target groups (Münster et al. 2020).

Accessing the collections, one primary challenge of the users is finding relevant data. To this end, metadata is of great help, as descriptions, classifications, annotations of data items allow the user to identify objects of interest much quicker, if concrete target criteria can be formulated. In addition to browsing online collections using metadata, progress has recently been made by embedding the documents into spatial and temporal contexts and, thus, to provide natural access to these vast online resources (Niebling et al. 2018c, d). These methods also support scientists to tackle research questions aiming at spatiotemporal relationships, such as where photographs have been predominantly taken during a specific time span. The basis for creating according interfaces to large-scale image repositories is the aggregation of data in a spatial and temporal model, employing methods of photogrammetry to spatialize historical photographs with respect to specific building situations.

Our main research objective is to explore methods of interactive visualization of spatial properties and relationships within this model, especially by means of statistical aggregation of positions and orientations of historical photographs. To this end, we have analyzed spatial distributions of historical photographs of the city of Dresden. They have been made available online as part of the Deutsche Fotothek,[1] an online media repository containing more than 1.8 million freely accessible historical documents. Our analysis aimed at the aforementioned applicability of visualization methods from a user's perspective.

In this chapter, we provide an overview of *imaging situations* that occur in these data.

In particular, we focus on the explicit distribution of locations and orientations of the photographers' points of view when taking photographs of specific architectural sites. We have translated these explicit imaging situations into *imaging phenomena*, i.e. abstract formulations of imaging situations with similar properties (Fig. 20.1).

---

[1]http://www.deutschefotothek.de.

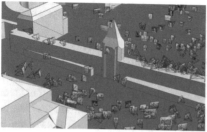
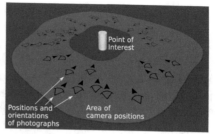

(a) A concrete imaging situation   (b) Corresponding imaging phenomenon

Fig. 20.1 Imaging situation and corresponding imaging phenomenon instantiated with concrete photo positions and orientations

Current methods of visualization for spatial distributions of images (e.g. heat maps) are mainly concerned with the *position* of images. We present first adaptations of visualization methods from other application domains that also address *orientation*, towards offering supporting tools to historians with corresponding spatial research questions. The introduced differentiation of *imaging phenomena* can be used to evaluate the effectiveness of deployed visualization methods in empirical user studies.

20.2   Related Work

Today, photographs are increasingly taken by means of mobile devices capable of automatically geo-tagging the stored files (Luo et al. 2011). The willingness to share these images online led to the situation that billions of contemporary images are publicly available on the Internet. Popular platforms like *Google Maps* or *Flickr* enable the users to spatially browse those geo-referenced images (Torniai et al. 2007).

On a much smaller scale, there are platforms like *Historypin* (2019), where the general public can upload and locate historical images on a map. Similar platforms are driven and curated by archives, e.g., *PhillyHistory* (2019). Although their focus is on historical images, they utilize 2D map providers like *Google Maps* or *OpenStreetMap*, which contain only contemporary map material.

Snavely et al. (2006) introduced a 3D exploration method to browse large, unstructured photo collections. By employing photogrammetric methods, in particular Structure from Motion (SfM), they could detect 2D feature points in each image and match them with features in other images. By relating similar features in multiple images, the relative camera motion can be estimated between the respective images, as well as 3D points of the depicted objects forming a sparse 3D point cloud. In their approach, Snavely et al. mapped the relative positions to absolute coordinates interactively. The user could either navigate the 3D point cloud itself, or leap from one image to its closest neighboring image in a specified direction. Later, Agarwal et al. (2011)

demonstrated 3D reconstruction of whole cities applying the same photogrammetric methods to contemporary, high-quality, touristic online photos.

This success relies on the rich data sets which are often unavailable in historic contexts. In particular, the limitations of historic data sets, and thus, the insufficiency of Snavely et al.'s approach is due to two observations. (1) Way fewer photographs were taken in the past. As a result, there are often not enough images with overlapping areas available for processing. (2) Historical photographic data often exhibits low image quality and do not share facts about camera parameters such as their focal length. In combination, detecting corresponding features across several images becomes a rather difficult problem. Varying lighting conditions and changes in depicted structures make the processing even more challenging. So far, 3D reconstructions from old, monochromatic photographs were only successful in case of very few selected data sets (Maiwald et al. 2017). Nevertheless, various CH projects are working on 4D reconstruction combining contemporary images with historical photographs. Ioannides et al. (2013) as well as Kyriakaki et al. (2014) propose scalable reconstruction approaches of 4D visual content from web retrieved images. Voulodimos et al. (2016) combine close range with airborne photogrammetry and terrestrial laser scanning to create more precise 3D models.

Schindler and Daellert (2010) explored the use of SfM in the context of historical image analysis more extensively. They managed to detect changes in the cityscape and thus were able to infer the temporal order of images. But their aim to automatically reconstruct a 4D, spatiotemporal, city model could only be partially achieved (Schindler and Dellaert 2012). Due to the observed limitations of historical image data sets, only very few structures could be partially 3D reconstructed and only for images taken after 1950. Therefore, Schindler & Daellert had to switch to a manual approach to reconstruct 3D models and to manually position and orientate photos with respect to these models. The images could then be browsed within the 4D city model.

Périnaud et al. (2015) did not pursue an automatic reconstruction of historical buildings based on 2D images. Instead, they implemented a historical geographic information system (4D GIS) incorporating 3D buildings with a low level of detail. Their main research objective was to describe urban transformation processes by means of existing standardized storage models and to attach the corresponding historical records, including historical photographs (Samuel et al. 2016). While navigating the resulting 3D city model, the documents were visualized floating above the respective buildings. In order to realize such a spatial association, algorithms need to be crafted that do not only position these documents but also prevent occlusions between images and 3D models (Chagnaud et al. 2016).

The research group *Urban History 4D* builds upon these approaches to make historical photographs available for spatial browsing. As the architectural situation depicted in historical images is changing over time, the corresponding images are placed within a 3D city model that has been obtained from city authorities and extended by 3D models of historical buildings. Little can be done about the sparse documentation of historical buildings in general. However, there is ongoing research to overcome the shortcomings of photogrammetric methods in combination with historical photographs (Maiwald et al. 2018; Maiwald 2019). Its main goal is to eventually be able to automatically spatialize the respective historical data sets and even generate historical 3D geometries in some cases. The 3D content and the spatialized images are the basis for further applications for browsing photographs (Niebling et al. 2018a) and disseminating cultural heritage information (Niebling et al. 2018b; Maiwald et al. 2019). A web-based 4D browser environment (Bruschke et al. 2017, 2018a) targets an expert community, i.e., art historians, and offers advanced features for spatial browsing and visualization of statistical documentation properties (see Sect. 20.4).

In order to display the statistical spatial distribution of geo-located photos with unknown orientation, the shot locations are traditionally aggregated in so-called heat maps—2D maps where higher frequencies result in higher color intensities—that are mapped onto the floor plane. Heat maps have also been employed to show which areas are depicted most often in a collection of images. Chippendale et al. (Chippendale et al. 2008) use heat maps on mountains to visualize the attractiveness of peaks and other features according to the number of depictions of the respective area in a collection of photos downloaded from an online media repository.

As the visualization of orientation of photos is not yet widely explored, adapting methods from other disciplines is a viable next step. For visualizing fluid dynamics, for example, the location and orientation of virtual particles is tracked over time. Sequences of sample points can be rendered as curves or arrows whose thickness reflects the speed, etc. In addition to glyph-based visualization of the direction of flow, e.g. rendering arrows at discrete grid points (Borgo et al. 2013), advected particles and their trails, dense texture-based approaches (Laramee et al. 2004), as well as deformation of geometric shapes (Schroeder et al. 1991) can be employed to visualize orientation. Laidlaw et al. performed a user study to compare the performance of users in analyzing various characteristics of flow fields employing different methods of visualization (Laidlaw et al. 2005). They caution against methods of visualization that directly support only specific user tasks, arguing towards more generalized methods.

Numerous existing tools for research platforms and applications concerning media repositories stem from computer science, and neither support the functional needs of scholars from the humanities, nor consider their usage patterns and skill sets (Dudek et al. 2015). In addition, interfaces to repositories of historical photos often only allow queries on metadata, and are focused on the individual documents, not on the repository as a dataset itself. As a result, scientific research questions concerning spatial properties in general, and distributions of spatial positions and orientations in particular, are hard to answer with available tools. Although there are many approaches to visualize spatial properties in other scientific domains, there are currently no adaptations of these methods to the statistical visualization of spatial photo repositories for CH research.

20.3 Research Use Cases in Art and Architectural History

For art and architectural historians, image repositories are important research tools for retrieving historical photographs and for gaining background information. They often focus on the discussion of the historical sources, while a main research interest lies in the development of a personal information topography (Bakewell et al. 1988). In current image repositories, the search workflow usually starts by typing keywords in a search form which yields lists of accordingly annotated items. Browsing the findings might reveal photographs relevant to one's research questions. Facilitating this process, frequently used categories of metadata, including names, dates, or places, may be made available as presets to choose from in a search toolbar menu. In this way, prior selections of images can also be filtered and refined. The outlined search process relies on metadata and is not performed on the actual photographs. As a consequence, the results are highly dependent on the quality and quantity of metadata and keywords, but also on the user's knowledge and expertise concerning the specific annotations of the dataset. For a person conducting an image search concerning architecture, it is often not easy to verbalize queries, especially if only vague idea of where the building of interest once stood guide the search (Friedrichs et al. 2018).

Another challenge is the presentation of search results, which is currently realized as a one-dimensional list in most image repositories. Although results can be sorted alphabetically, chronologically, or via search related aspects such as the names of the photographer or architect of a given building, these presentations do not enable the user to acquire an overview of the whole set of results, and therefore make it hard to refine one's queries.

Spatial search that is not driven by mere metadata but actual depiction of spatial relationships in spatial contexts is currently missing from prevalent repositories despite its potential benefits across all target groups—from amateurs to professionals (Bruschke et al. 2018a). Next to enhancing searching image repositories, spatializing historical photographs can also provide answers to spatially motivated questions, such as:

- Which buildings were photographed more (or less) often than others? In which time period does this change?
- Are there certain areas in the city, which were in focus more frequently than others? And in which time periods can this be recognized?
- From which directions has a point of interest been photographed? Is there one main direction?
- Do there exist any favored places from which photographers depicted the surrounding architecture?
- Are there architectural details which are depicted in photographs more often than the building itself?

To answer these questions, a time and space oriented visualization of the search results is necessary, contributing to an all-encompassing impression of the city at a certain point in time. To this end, we developed a catalog of imaging phenomena to propose a categorization for spatialized photographs.

20.4 Spatiotemporal Browsing in 3D Web Environments

As stated in the previous section, conventional interfaces of image repositories have limited possibilities to support spatiotemporal research questions. Furthermore, the existing mechanisms lead to an inefficient and inexpedient usage (Beaudoin and Brady 2011; Kamposiori 2012). We have compared an extensive amount of online repositories and also interviewed a large number of art historians to identify desiderata of different target groups and to derive requirements of users dealing with such repositories (Friedrichs et al. 2018). On this basis, we created a web-based prototype of a research environment. We extended basic search features introduced in Sect. 20.3 with a 3D viewport and a timeline to enable spatial and temporal browsing (Fig. 20.2).

The images in our dataset are spatially oriented within the 3D city model. This facilitates a better understanding of the distribution of the images as well as the spatial context of the photographer regarding the surrounding buildings (Schindler and Dellaert 2012). The user is able to take the photographer's perspective and blend between photograph and 3D model to detect changes in the cityscape. When dealing with hundreds or thousands of images, displaying all images at their individual positions can lead to substantial overdraw, limiting the usefulness of the resulting visualization. To improve lucidity and usability, we dynamically cluster images in relation to the user's distance using a single-linkage hierarchical clustering method (Fig. 20.2).

Fig. 20.2 Web-based, prototypical research environment implementing conventional as well as spatial and temporal searching techniques

Spatial browsing offers further prospects to narrow down the image search results. By projecting spatialized images onto the geo-located 3D models, it can be determined which buildings or parts of buildings are depicted in which photographs. Using this established linkage between buildings and photographs, we allow search results to be filtered by selecting or deselecting 3D models.

20.5 Analysis and Modeling of Phenomena

Definition 1 (*Imaging Situation*) We define an *Imaging Situation* as specific positions, shapes and surroundings of buildings, and a collection of associated photographic images which are spatialized, i.e. the exact position and orientation of the camera are known.

Definition 2 (*Imaging Phenomenon*) An *Imaging Phenomenon* is an abstraction of *Imaging Situations* with similar properties, i.e. the relations of buildings are corresponding, and also positions and orientations of cameras are similar with respect to the architecture.

The spatial analysis of historical photographs yields recurring patterns with respect to points of view, urban environments, and concrete buildings. We refer to these as different imaging phenomena. In order to automatically classify imaging phenomena, we derived distinctive features which include a recognizable orientation of the images and the arrangements of building geometries. A basic model of imaging phenomena considers a small number of primitives: *Areas of camera positions*, i.e. a polygon to describe the area where photographers were standing when taking photos, *points of interest* (POI), i.e. areas of varying extent that the photographers were trying to capture, and additional building geometry and other items that potentially blocked the photographer's view (Fig. 20.3). The orientations of photos in a particular area of camera positions yield one or more average directions of camera views, pointing to the various points of interest.

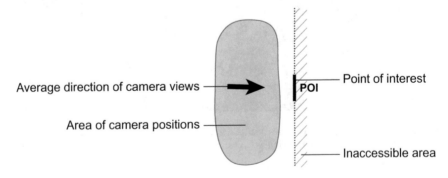

Fig. 20.3 Schematic of an imaging phenomenon using the example of a facade with a single POI

Exploring the dataset of historical images within the 3D city model, several recurring imaging situations could be identified. Analyzing these urban imaging phenomena, we could reduce them to six scenarios that include *Detached* shots, shots of *Facades*, *Corners*, *Town Squares*, *Galleries*, and *Bridges*. The target object of *Detached* shots may be monuments, fountains, statues, or even a freestanding building like a church. The category *Gallery* describes an architectural situation where photographers are taking images of a point of interest further down the road, with buildings on both sides. *Bridge* resembles situations where points of interests are captured from more distant spots, e.g., a city skyline that is photographed from a bridge or from an opposite river bank.

For each category, different arrangements are possible that affect the number, size, and position of the POIs as well as the corresponding areas of camera positions. The most basic set-up is a single POI photographed from a single area of camera positions. A single POI may also be photographed from multiple areas. This may be due to the arrangement of streets or footpaths. Multiple POIs may be close to each other, so that the areas from which they are captured may intersect or be reasonably close to each other. This also includes fore-/background scenarios, e.g., a statue in front of a building. Multiple POIs can also be considered as competing in attracting the photographer. This especially becomes visible when the POIs are in opposite directions of each other, with respect to a joint or overlapping area of camera positions. Broad or fuzzy POIs are not focusing a specific object, but depict a broader scene. For instance, this can be a city skyline, an assembly of houses at a town square, a wide wall painting, or a streetscape.

We arranged the observed categories in a two-dimensional matrix according to their described urban scenario as well as to the arrangement of POIs and area of camera positions (Figs. 20.4 and 20.5). The categories were extended by phenomena that were not observed in our current data basis but describe viable alternatives. Some combinations of observed features resemble others, e.g. *Facade—Single POI* and *Town Square—Single POI*. Others are not meaningful and are therefore left blank in the matrix. For instance, it is not possible to encounter opposite points of interest when looking at a single facade, POIs at opposite facades are already covered within the town square category.

Since many phenomena feature common parameters, such as the number of POIs or area of camera positions, they can also be hierarchically sorted (Fig. 20.6). This results in an additional, simplified categorization and allows to focus on single parameters. Besides, it reveals that the number of phenomena featuring a single area of camera positions and multiple POIs appear above average. The *Single broad (fuzzy) POI* category is omitted in this hierarchy due to the special characteristic of the POI.

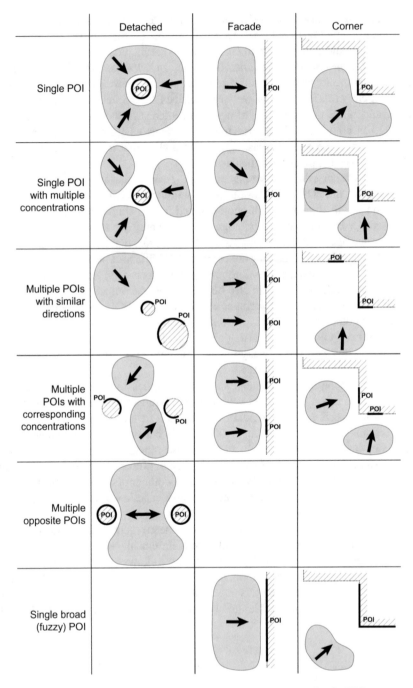

Fig. 20.4 Catalog of phenomena for detached, facade, and corner scenarios for POIs

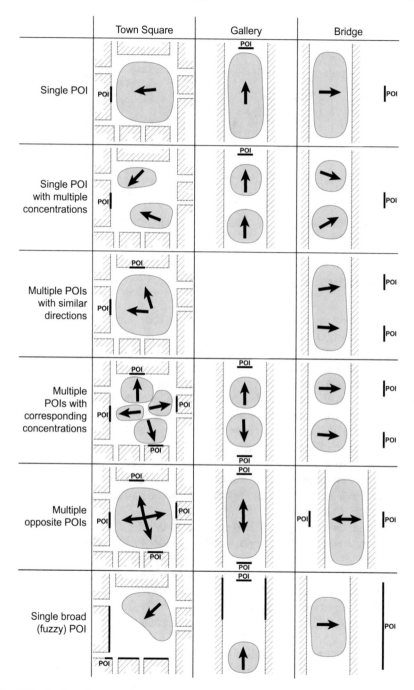

Fig. 20.5 Catalog of phenomena for town square, gallery, and bridge scenarios for POIs

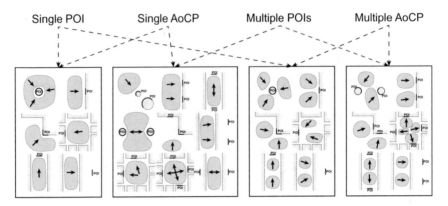

Fig. 20.6 Hierarchical arrangement of phenomena by number of POI and area of camera positions (AoCP). *Single broad (fuzzy) POI* is omitted

20.6 Statistical Visualization Methods

Spatial visualization and browsing of photos can offer additional insights into the spatial and temporal distribution of items in the image repository, and the relationships between architecture and corresponding depictions of these buildings. In the prototypical research environment that we introduced in Sect. 20.4, users cannot only browse spatialized photographs in 3D reconstructed environments. Instead, we also offer means to spatially interact with various aspects of the imaging phenomena to reveal further relationships. For instance, selecting a POI, all its linked photographs are highlighted with a common color. Upon inquiry, we also provide statistical data at a glance, such as the number of items linked to an object. With comprehensive photo repositories, further aggregation of images is neccessary to enable users to gain an overview of spatial and temporal properties of the complete dataset or of complex search results, such as the development of positions and orientations of photographers over time.

From a group of images, additional data can be extracted to expose statistical information, such as the distribution of camera positions with respect to a 3D building model. We employ heat maps (Fig. 20.7a) to allow users to identify clusters of images in the data set. For each point of the heat map, the number of images within a certain radius is determined and mapped to a color obtained from a color palette. The radii of the clustering can be adjusted to maintain visibility from different distances. A smaller radius results in more, smaller hot spots whereas a big radius yields fewer hot spots spanning a greater area (Fig. 20.8).

However, such heat map visualizations only reflect positions but omit orientations. In order to get an initial grasp of orientation of a set of photographs, surface heat maps can be employed. These heat maps on surface of buildings can be used to visualize the number of photographs that depict certain parts of an object, and thus, to identify attractive building parts (Fig. 20.7b). To generate these *surface heat maps*,

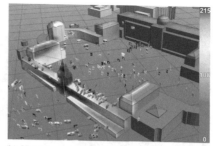

(a) Conventional heat map visualizing aggregations of photographs. The color at each point of the ground correlates with the number of images within a certain radius.

(b) Heat map projected onto a POI's surface to detect interesting architectural details. The color of each point of the building correlates with the number of images that contain the respective spot.

Fig. 20.7 Different types of heat map visualizations

(a)   **(b)**

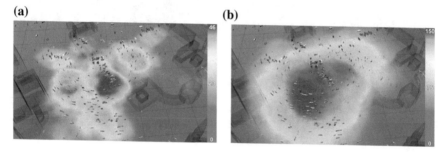

Fig. 20.8 Heat maps with a sample radius of **a** 20 m and **b** 50 m

a set of texture coordinates for the 3D models is computed depending on the user's view. Each pixel in a photo is translated to a geo-referenced world position using ray tracing determining the pixel's position on the object's surface. Incorporating the camera frustum and hence the orientation information of the images as well as occlusion by other buildings, the number of images that see this point can then be traced and represented in the surface texture of the respective building.

This visualization method, however, does not show the origin of the photographs. To overcome this issue, ground and surface heat maps can be combined (Fig. 20.9). But there are still several shortcomings: (1) The relations between hot spots on the ground heat map and those of the surface heat map are not clear or can be ambiguous. (2) The orientations of the images are not explicitly shown. (3) Parts of the ground heat map are occluded by the building in favor of displaying the surface heat map. At this point, more advanced visualization methods need to be developed. They need to integrate the orientation of images so that the user will be able to easily comprehend where clusters of photographs are oriented towards. First approaches that adopt methods from flow visualization have already been presented (Bruschke et al. 2018b).

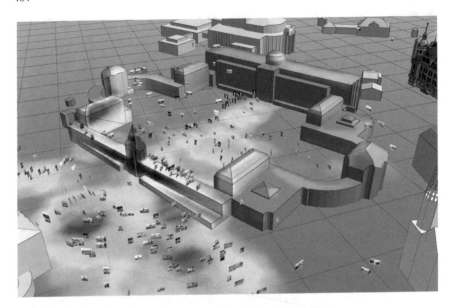

Fig. 20.9 Combination of ground heat map and surface heat map

The classification of imaging phenomena established in Sect. 20.5 provides a basis for the development and evaluation of visualization methods adapted to the requirements and workflows of art and architectural historians.

20.7 Discussion and Conclusion

We develop a research environment implementing spatial and temporal search, providing visualization methods to visualize spatial properties of repositories containing historical photographs, to enable art and architectural historians to answer their spatial and temporal research questions. Towards this end, we have analyzed imaging phenomena in the spatialized subset of the media repository Deutsche Fotothek, i.e. spatial distributions of points of view and orientations of photographers with respect to the architecture existing at the respective time.

Analyzing our current dataset of spatialized images, several imaging situations were identified exposing distinctive features, such as conspicuous orientation of images with respect to the arrangement of the surrounding architecture. We have classified the observed imaging situations into abstract imaging phenomena, organized in two dimensions according to the described urban scenario, arrangement of POIs and area of camera positions. Combination of features in the matrix also produces phenomena that are plausible, but could not be directly observed in the limited dataset, resulting in more than thirty phenomena. The matrix of phenomena presents possible patterns, indicating from which perspectives the city was perceived by photographers. For art and architectural historians, this is especially relevant in combination with temporal information, as they are able to trace typical imaging situations over certain time periods.

The described existing visualization methods are able to reveal statistical information about sets of photographs. However, the different methods are rather limited to specific use cases, in particular to research questions that are primarily concerned with positions of images. Traditional ground heat maps allow to easily identify spatial aggregations of images. They cannot be used to directly convey information about depicted buildings, since orientations of the cameras are not contained in the visualization. In contrast, surface heat maps can be used to reveal which parts of a building have been depicted most often. Unfortunately, these parts might be photographed from completely different view points, which is not deducible from the visualization. The combination of both methods results in ambiguous relations between hot spots, that users have to draw by themselves. Nevertheless, this visualization method offers a new view on architecture for art and architectural historians.

To support research questions concerning orientation, such as *from which side has a building been preferably photographed?*, advanced methods to visualize spatial information contained in the images need to be developed. Particularly, camera directions as well as their statistical distribution need to be emphasized in visualizations. First ideas have already been presented to visualize orientation, including approaches building on methods from flow visualization (Bruschke et al. 2018b).

In future work, the categorization of phenomena will lay the basis for extensive evaluations of visualization methods which can be applied to datasets of spatialized photographs. In particular, the observed imaging phenomena can be employed to assess the performance of users in detecting the various properties contained in the classification with the use of different visualization methods: the existence and positions of POIs in a given imaging situation, the areas of camera positions, as well as the predominant orientation of photographers in these areas. In addition, the established phenomena might also be used to automatically detect imaging situations in large image repositories, enabling the users to browse the dataset by phenomena.

Acknowledgements The work presented in this paper has been funded by the German Federal Ministry of Education and Research (BMBF) as part of the research project "HistStadt4D—Multimodale Zugänge zu historischen Bildrepositorien zur Unterstützung stadt- und baugeschichtlicher Forschung und Vermittlung", grant identifier 01UG1630A/B.

References

Agarwal S, Furukawa Y, Snavely N, Simon I, Curless B, Seitz SM, Szeliski R (2011) Buidling rome in a day. Commun ACM 54(10):105–112. https://doi.org/10.1145/2001269.2001293
Bakewell E, Beeman WO, Reese CM (1988) Object, image, inquiry: the art historian at work. Getty Publications

Beaudoin JE, Brady JE (2011) Finding visual information: a study of image resources used by archaeologists, architects, art historians, and artists. Art Doc: J Art Libr Soc N Am 30(2):24–36. https://doi.org/10.1086/adx.30.2.41244062

Borgo R, Kehrer J, Chung DHS, Maguire E, Laramee RS, Hauser H, Ward M, Chen M (2013) Glyph-based visualization: foundations, design guidelines, techniques and applications. In: Sbert M, Szirmay-Kalos L (eds) Eurographics 2013 - state of the art reports. The Eurographics Association. https://doi.org/10.2312/conf/EG2013/stars/039-063

Bruschke J, Niebling F, Maiwald F, Friedrichs K, Wacker M, Latoschik ME (2017) Towards browsing repositories of spatially oriented historic photographic images in 3D web environments. In: Proceedings of the 22nd international conference on 3D web technology (Web3D '17). ACM. https://doi.org/10.1145/3055624.3075947

Bruschke J, Maiwald F, Münster S, Niebling F (2018a) Browsing and experiencing repositories of spatially oriented historic photographic images. SDH 2(2), 138–149. https://doi.org/10.14434/sdh.v2i2.24460

Bruschke J, Niebling F, Wacker M (2018b) Visualization of orientations of spatial historical photographs. In: Sablatnig R, Wimmer M (eds) Eurographics workshop on graphics and cultural heritage, pp 189–192. The Eurographics Association. https://doi.org/10.2312/gch.20181359

Chagnaud C, Samuel J, Servigne S, Gesquiére G (2016) Visualization of documented 3D cities. In: Eurographics workshop on urban data modelling and visualisation. The Eurographics Association. https://doi.org/10.2312/udmv.20161425

Chippendale P, Zanin M, Andreatta C (2008) Spatial and temporal attractiveness analysis through geo-referenced photo alignment. In: 2008 IEEE international geoscience and remote sensing symposium, vol 2, pp 1116–1119. https://doi.org/10.1109/IGARSS.2008.4779195

City of Philadelphia (2019) PhillyHistory – The philadelphia city archive. https://www.phillyhistory.org. Accessed 05 July 2019

Dudek I, Blaise JY, De Luca L, Bergerot L, Renaudin N (2015) How was this done? an attempt at formalising and memorising a digital asset's making-of. In: 2015 digital heritage, vol 2, pp 343–346. IEEE. https://doi.org/10.1109/DigitalHeritage.2015.7419519

Friedrichs K, Münster S, Kröber C, Bruschke J (2018) Creating suitable tools for art and architectural research with historic media repositories. In: Münster S, Friedrichs K, Niebling F, Seidel-Grzesińska A (eds) Digital research and education in architectural heritage, pp 117–138. Springer International Publishing, Cham. https://doi.org/10.1007/978-3-319-76992-9_8

Historypin (2019) Connecting communities with local history. https://www.historypin.org. Accessed 05 July 2019

Ioannides M, Hadjiprocopi A, Doulamis N, Doulamis A, Protopapadakis E, Makantasis K, Santos P, Fellner D, Stork A, Balet O et al (2013) Online 4D reconstruction using multi-images available under open access. ISPRS annals of the photogrammetry, Remote sensing and saptial information sciences, II-5 W 1, 169–174

Kamposiori C (2013) Digital infrastructure for art historical research: thinking about user needs. In: Proceedings from the electronic visualisation and the arts (EVA 2012) conference, pp 245–253

Kyriakaki G, Doulamis A, Doulamis N, Ioannides M, Makantasis K, Protopapadakis E, Hadjiprocopis A, Wenzel K, Fritsch D, Klein M et al (2014) 4D reconstruction of tangible cultural heritage objects from web-retrieved images. Int J Herit Digit Era 3(2):431–451

Laidlaw DH, Kirby RM, Jackson CD, Davidson JS, Miller TS, da Silva M, Warren WH, Tarr MJ (2005) Comparing 2D vector field visualization methods: a user study. IEEE Trans Vis Comput Graph 11(1):59–70. https://doi.org/10.1109/TVCG.2005.4

Laramee RS, Hauser H, Doleisch H, Vrolijk B, Post FH, Weiskopf D (2004) The state of the art in flow visualization: dense and texture-based techniques. Comput Graph Forum 23(2):203–221. https://doi.org/10.1111/j.1467-8659.2004.00753.x

Luo J, Joshi D, Yu J, Gallagher A (2011) Geotagging in multimedia and computer vision–a survey. Multimed Tools Appl 51(1):187–211. https://doi.org/10.1007/s11042-010-0623-y

Maiwald F (2019) Generation of a benchmark dataset using historical photographs for an automated evaluation of different feature matching methods. Int Arch Photogramm, Remote Sens Spat Inf Sci XLII-2/W13, 87–94. https://doi.org/10.5194/isprs-archives-XLII-2-W13-87-2019

Maiwald F, Henze F, Bruschke J, Niebling F (2019) Geo-information technologies for a multimodal access on historical photographs and maps for research and communication in urban history. Int. Arch. Photogramm. Remote Sens Spat Inf Sci 42(2/W11)

Maiwald F, Schneider D, Henze F, Münster S, Niebling F (2018) Feature matching of historical images based on geometry of quadrilaterals. Int Arch Photogramm, Remote Sens Spat Inf Sci XLII-2, 643–650. https://doi.org/10.5194/isprs-archives-XLII-2-643-2018

Maiwald F, Vietze T, Schneider D, Henze F, Münster S, Niebling F (2017) Photogrammetric analysis of historical image repositories for virtual reconstruction in the field of digital humanities. ISPRS Int Arch Photogramm Remote Sens Spatial Inf Sci XLII-2/W3, 447–452. https://doi.org/10.5194/isprs-archives-XLII-2-W3-447-2017

Münster S, Niebling F, Bruschke J, Barthel K, Friedrichs K, Kröber C, Maiwald F (2020) Urban history research and discovery in the age of digital repositories. A report about users and requirements. In: Digital Cultural Heritage, pp 63–84. Springer, Berlin

Niebling F, Bruschke J, Latoschik ME (2018a) Browsing spatial photography for dissemination of cultural heritage research results using augmented models. In: Sablatnig R, Wimmer M (eds) Eurographics workshop on graphics and cultural heritage, pp 185–188. The Eurographics Association. https://doi.org/10.2312/gch.20181358

Niebling F, Maiwald F, Barthel K, Latoschik ME (2018b) 4D Augmented city models, photogrammetric creation and dissemination. In: Münster S, Friedrichs K, Niebling F, Seidel-Grzesińska A (eds) Digital research and education in architectural heritage, pp 196–212. Springer International Publishing, Cham. https://doi.org/10.1007/978-3-319-76992-9_12

Niebling F, Maiwald F, Münster S, Bruschke J, Henze F (2018c) Accessing urban history using spatial historical photographs. In: 2018 3rd digital heritage international congress (DigitalHERITAGE) held jointly with 2018 24th international conference on virtual systems & Multimedia (VSMM). IEEE, pp 1–8

Niebling F, Münster S, Bruschke J, Maiwald F, Friedrichs K (2018d) Stadtgeschichtliche Forschung anhand räumlich- und zeitlich verorteter Photographien. In: Burghardt M, Müller-Birn C (eds) INF-DH-2018. Gesellschaft für Informatik e.V, Bonn

Périnaud C, Gay G, Gesquière G (2015) Exploration of the changing structure of cities: challenges for temporal city models. In: 2015 digital heritage, vol 2. IEEE, pp 73–76. https://doi.org/10.1109/DigitalHeritage.2015.7419455

Samuel J, Prinaud C, Servigne S, Gay G, Gesquière G (2016) Representation and visualization of urban fabric through historical documents. In: Catalano CE, De Luca L (eds) 14th eurographics workshop on graphics and cultural heritage. The Eurographics Association. https://doi.org/10.2312/gch.20161399

Schindler G, Dellaert F (2010) Probabilistic temporal inference on reconstructed 3D scenes. In: 2010 IEEE conference on computer vision and pattern recognition (CVPR). IEEE, pp 1410–1417. https://doi.org/10.1109/CVPR.2010.5539803

Schindler G, Dellaert F (2012) 4D cities: analyzing, visualizing, and interacting with historical urban photo collections. J Multimed 7(2):124–131. https://doi.org/10.4304/jmm.7.2.124-131

Schroeder WJ, Volpe CR, Lorensen WE (1991) The stream polygon: a technique for 3d vector field visualization. In: Proceeding visualization '91. IEEE, pp 126–132. https://doi.org/10.1109/VISUAL.1991.175789

Snavely N, Seitz SM, Szeliski R (2006) Photo tourism: exploring photo collections in 3D. ACM Trans Graph (SIGGRAPH Proceedings) 25(3):835–846. https://doi.org/10.1145/1141911.1141964

Sweetnam MS, Agosti M, Orio N, Ponchia C, Steiner CM, Hillemann EC, Ó Siochrú M, Lawless S (2012) User needs for enhanced engagement with cultural heritage collections. In: Theory and practice of digital libraries. Springer Berlin Heidelberg, pp 64–75. https://doi.org/10.1007/978-3-642-33290-6_8

Torniai C, Battle S, Cayzer S (2007) Sharing, discovering and browsing geotagged pictures on the world wide web. In: Scharl A, Tochtermann K (eds) The geospatial web. Springer, London, pp 159–170. https://doi.org/10.1007/978-1-84628-827-2_15

Voulodimos A, Doulamis N, Fritsch D, Makantasis K, Doulamis A, Klein M (2016) Four-dimensional reconstruction of cultural heritage sites based on photogrammetry and clustering. J Electron Imaging 26(1):011013

Chapter 21
Relict–Interpolated–Extrapolated– Speculative: An Approach to Degrees of Accuracy in Virtual Heritage Reconstruction

Marleen de Kramer

Abstract The London Charter for the Computer-Based Visualisation of Cultural Heritage (2009) lays out best-practice guidelines for producing reconstructions of ruined buildings but does not mandate specific tools, workflows, or data formats, acknowledging that technology will change over time. Their implementation is left up to the individual researcher. The approach described here is designed to produce a virtual 3D model for public consumption within the scope of a small, individual research project. It allows the user to query metadata and understand degrees of accuracy without sacrificing a photorealistic, immersive experience. Recognising that accuracy is dependent on the level of detail at which the reconstruction is to be made and viewed, it is presented as a matrix rather than a linear scale. This allows elements of the reconstruction to be sorted into 12 discrete categories of accuracy. The goal is a scientifically validated virtual reconstruction that can be used to teach a non-professional audience about the metadata that goes into such work.

21.1 Introduction

In 1964, the Venice Charter for the Conservation and Restoration of Monuments and Sites specified that ruined monuments are not to be reconstructed, and any parts added or rebuilt must be clearly recognisable as such and not be built in the style of the original. That risks faking history—as the new material weathers, future generations will be unable to tell what is authentic and what has been reproduced, thereby eroding its value as an historic document. However, attempting to preserve a monument in a perpetual state of ruin not only presents technical challenges, but precludes many uses, including, presumably, that for which it was built, so most are restored to a degree, then supplemented with new architecture.

According to these foundational standards for international heritage conservation, it is also not acceptable to peel away later additions to restore a previous state, except

M. de Kramer (✉)
C2DH - Luxembourg Centre for Contemporary and Digital History and Institute for History, University of Luxembourg, Esch-sur-Alzette, Luxembourg
e-mail: marleen.dekramer@uni.lu

© Springer Nature Switzerland AG 2020
F. Liarokapis et al. (eds.), *Visual Computing for Cultural Heritage*, Springer Series on Cultural Computing, https://doi.org/10.1007/978-3-030-37191-3_21

in very specific circumstances where the historical and artistic value of the old far outweigh the new—buildings change over time. Their structure, their use, and their decoration changes.

As medievalist Dr. Sara Uckelman wrote in response to the fire in Notre Dame Cathedral in April 2019:

> [...]churches live. They are not static monuments to the past. They are built, they get burned, they are rebuilt, they are extended, they get ransacked, they get rebuilt, they collapse because they were not built well, they get rebuilt, they get extended, they get renovated, they get bombed, they get rebuilt. It is the continuous presence, not the original structure, that matters. (Uckelman 2019)

So how do we reconcile this with our desire to know what structures looked like at different points in their history? How they were used, and how they related to their environment? How do we communicate this knowledge with different disciplines, and with the general public, that might not have the skills to imagine a complete three-dimensional structure from ruins and old drawings?

Historically, communicating these theories has relied on drawings and architectural scale models. Now, we can use digital tools to create models not reliant on physical constraints, which can be presented as films, as still images, but also on interactive screens and in immersive virtual environments, which give a realistic impression of a space, complete with authentic-looking materials, sounds, and lighting.

This hyper-realism can make it hard for the viewer to separate fact from fiction or archaeological evidence from speculation, which is reinforced by the "museum effect" (Putnam 2001, p. 34)—something being exhibited in a museum or displayed in relation to a heritage site gives it an aura of importance and authenticity, independently of its actual provenance. This effect, described by Lawrence Weschler as the "Voice of Institutional Authority" (Weschler 1996, p. 101) comes with a responsibility to ensure that the viewer understands the meaning and the limits behind visualisations. All too often, such concerns are dismissed with the addition of the qualifier "artist's impression" in the description of the image or model.

21.2   Scientific Reconstructions

What's the difference between a reconstruction and an artist's impression? Merely that the latter doesn't imply scientific accuracy. This phrase is often used in an attempt to bypass the issue of explaining how a reconstruction was validated, how and by whom design decisions were made, and how conflicting theories were reconciled. This process is time-consuming to document—but very necessary if the finished model is to be a scientific document in its own right, in which "the foundations of evidence for the reconstructed elements, and the reasoning around them, are made not only explicit and interrogable but also can be updated, extended and reused by other researchers in future work" (Bruseker et al. 2015).

As any good science, a virtual model shows a hypothesis, but gives the viewer the data needed to make the experiment reproducible—meaning that by following the same steps, the researcher will arrive at similar conclusions—and provides for new data to be introduced, potentially changing the results. This is also an important step towards providing sustainability for a virtual model. Often, this word is used to describe issues with data storage, file interoperability, project responsibilities and other practical concerns, but it must extend beyond them to include an output whose underlying structure is available to other researchers and which they can update independently of the original author (Champion and Rahaman 2019).

The ICOMOS Charter for the Interpretation and Presentation of Cultural Heritage Sites specifies that *"visual reconstructions [...]should be based upon detailed and systematic analysis of environmental, archaeological, architectural, and historical data, including analysis of written, oral and iconographic sources, and photography. The information sources on which such visual renderings are based should be clearly documented and alternative reconstructions based on the same evidence, when available, should be provided for comparison"* (ICOMOS 2007). Best-practice guidelines for producing such models are laid out in the London Charter for the Computer-Based Visualisation of Cultural Heritage. They encompass the key areas of "intellectual integrity, reliability, documentation, sustainability and access" (Denard 2009), but do not mandate specific tools, workflows, or data formats, acknowledging that technology will change over time.

Putting these guidelines into practice is, therefore, left to the individual researcher. Many current scholarly proposals rely on a dedicated database in a suitable format to be in place, so the data can be mapped to CIDOC-CRM, a cultural-heritage-specific ontology (Doerr 2003), and published as Linked (Open) Data. However, from a standpoint of finances, expertise, and time, this is outside the scope of many individual projects. At best, reconstructions are given a brief text description or labelled using percentages of accuracy—which look scientific, but include no explanation of how they were calculated or indeed what an accuracy of "50%" means.

21.3 Case Study: Larochette Castle

My own work is a proposal toward addressing this problem in practice, seeking to fulfil the demands of the aforementioned Charters. As these documents represent a consensus reached through long debate between interdisciplinary groups seeking to establish digital cultural heritage as a recognised science, they are a good basis on which to build this type of scholarly work.

The case study for this approach is a virtual reconstruction of the castle in Larochette, Luxembourg, at its fullest extent in the 16th century, shortly before it was largely destroyed by fire in 1565 (Zimmer 1990, p. 14). This model is to serve as a vehicle to demonstrate to the viewer how such reconstructions are made, the nature of the metadata, paradata, and decision-making processes behind them, and that they represent a hypothesis rather than absolute fact. This requires a system that is, in its

Fig. 21.1 This model at Larochette lacks all useful metadata—it does not indicate which building or year it depicts, the scale, its creator or its year of creation

display, simple and intuitive, and which can be used to document knowledge provenance and visualise the problems of uncertainty and lack of data in architectural reconstructions (compare Fig. 21.1).

In essence, the creation of the virtual model follows the standard series of steps laid out by Bruseker, Guillem, and Carboni: commissioning, documentation research, proposition identification, function hypothesis assumption, global geometric volume reasoning, in situ element reconstruction, ex situ element reconstruction, and visual representation production (Bruseker et al. 2015), following a similar looped reasoning process. As the model is constructed, the decisions behind the drawing are entered into a table that records the decision made, the reasoning behind the decision, which part of the building and which aspect it concerns, its estimated accuracy, the data sources and their types, experts involved, and whether this decision conflicts with any other data. As a simple CSV file, this table is a sustainable way to document the project's metadata and paradata as it is machine readable by a variety of software. By attaching unique identifiers to each part of the model and entering them in the table, it serves as a simple relational database that can later be queried to display the metadata alongside the model based on parameters chosen by the user.

21.4 Accuracy

To make "accuracy" a useful metric, it must be defined in relation to the project. In its simplest form, it is binary: something is either accurate, or it is not, it is "factual" or "hypothetical". This oversimplifies the matter, making it unclear how much data is needed to count as "factual". Moreover, the level of accuracy can fluctuate simply by level of detail—it is easy to say that the existence of Larochette castle is "factual", since its ruins are clearly visible, but the paint colour on an individual wall that's no longer standing is entirely a matter of conjecture and therefore "hypothetical". To this end, I have designed an accuracy matrix rather than a linear scale. The first axis has four categories, in decreasing order of estimated accuracy, which are intentionally broad and chosen to be reasonably self-explanatory:

Relict–Interpolated–Extrapolated–Speculative

"Relict" covers elements for which evidence survives from the time of their creation—this could be archaeological evidence, but also covers contemporary drawings or descriptions. "Interpolated" refers to elements reconstructed by consulting several "relict" data points, e.g. filling a gap in a wall along an existing foundation. Where this "interpolated" result is a line between two points, an "extrapolated" one is a vector, using a solid point of reference augmented with secondary and tertiary sources—for example, continuing the battlements along a wall at the level of the remaining ones, because a wall such as this would have been embattled. "Speculative" results are obtained using only secondary and tertiary sources, e.g. placing a window in a wall because an inventory mentions a curtain there, but not knowing where exactly in the room it was located (Fig. 21.2).

The second dimension in the matrix is level of detail (LoD). This concept is widely used in architecture and building information modelling (BIM), with many computer aided design suites offering adaptive display depending on the architectural scale selected. Different architectural scales are associated with different levels of detail because they are normally used to display different types of information, a convention derived from the days of manual drafting when drawings were constrained by the physical size of the paper (ArchDaily 2018).

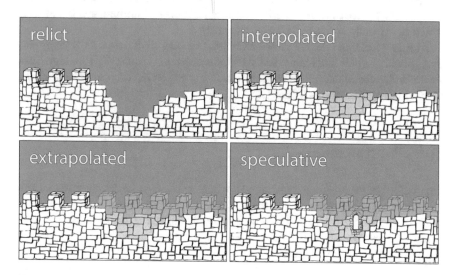

Fig. 21.2 The four degrees of accuracy

Fig. 21.3 Accuracy versus
level of detail

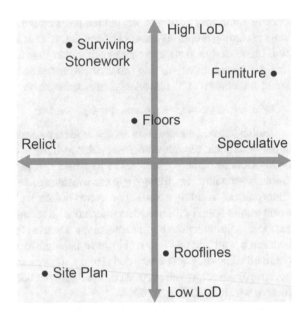

Low, medium, and high levels of detail, as used here, correspond to the conventions of site, building, and detail scales. At a site scale of approximately 1:200, architectural plans deal with a building's general shape and volume, roof lines, access points, and relationships between different elements. At a building scale of about 1:100, doors, windows, and relative wall thicknesses are shown, and the overall flow and composition of the floor plan and facade are drawn. At a detailed scale of around 1:50 or less, the focus is on materials, surface treatments, furniture, and the internal structures of walls, roofs, and other components.

At a low LoD, the degree of accuracy may be very high, with the location and dimensions of a building known based historic maps, etc., while at a very high LoD, such as individual rooms, all conclusions may be speculative, with no trace remaining of the original furnishings (Fig. 21.3).

21.5 Segmentation

This system relies on a segmented model whose granularity increases with its LoD, controlled by attribute tables attached to the segments. This means that while at a low level of detail, a space may simply be filled with a single monolithic block named "keep", the same space could be occupied by dozens of individual stones, beams, and furnishings at a detail scale.

The display of these elements can then be adapted dynamically, e.g. showing anything with an accuracy of "interpolated" or better at a medium level of detail, along with the metadata linked to individual elements. As new data are found or new conclusions reached, individual segments can be updated or their classification changed without invalidating the model entirely, though the changes may perpetuate through higher levels of detail.

This approach requires re-modelling the same building up to three times to provide geometries for all levels, which can be a very time-consuming process. Therefore, a maximum level of detail for each element can be selected depending on its function in the finished model. This does not necessarily have to correlate to the level of data available for each section—it is entirely possible to build a detailed speculative model of an important area, while only roughly sketching in a background that could be researched in depth.

Furthermore, geometry is not the only way to convey more detailed information. When modelling geometries, a balance must be struck between an accurate representation and a low polygon count—the more detailed the geometry, the larger the load on the graphics processor, meaning that better computer hardware is needed to display the model. Instead, as often seen in computer gaming, a detailed texture can be overlaid on a reduced geometry to give it the appearance of more detail. Especially in architectural applications, many elements have simple basic geometries—flat walls, beams, doors, etc.—that can easily be made more complex with a simple swap of texture, e.g. showing individual roof tiles instead of flat colour. The higher polygon counts can then be reserved for areas where geometric detail is important, i.e. showing "relict"-level architectural stonework or making areas that the viewer will see close up more realistic.

21.6 Maximum Levels of Detail by Area

The castle of Larochette and its surrounding town were closely linked—especially after the castle's owners decided to remove parts of the castle wall to allow more living space, relying on the city walls for defence (legal contract 1415, in Hardt 1849). Meanwhile, the location of the castle and the shape of the town are determined by the landscape around it, contained by steep cliffs and a meandering river. Therefore, the castle cannot be understood without its geographic context, and those areas need to be included in the model. A preliminary landscape study was carried out, cross-validating historic maps with microtoponyms and historic representations (de Kramer et al. 2018).

The focus remains on the castle, so the level of detail of its surroundings can be much lower than that of the castle itself. Consequently, the town was modelled at a low level of detail (Fig. 21.4) corresponding to a "site" scale, showing building heights, footprints, and roof lines, but not doors, windows, chimneys, or other "building" scale details. The landscape, taken from official LiDAR scan data, has had its geometric level of detail reduced outside the immediate area of the castle. Still, in order to support the realistic aesthetic of the model, they have been given photographic textures that give an impression of the colour and material of their original facades.

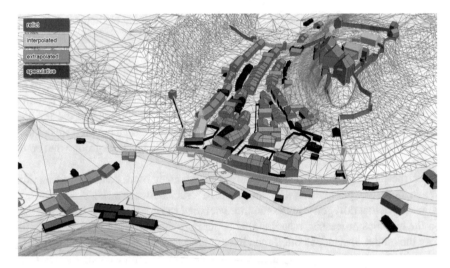

Fig. 21.4 A volumetric reconstruction of the town, castle and landscape at a low level of detail, with accuracies segmented by building

Within the castle itself, the focus will be on the Criechinger Haus, a building situated at the north-eastern corner of the castle (Fig. 21.5). As this is the only part of the castle to have been physically reconstructed, it is the only one that visitors

Fig. 21.5 The Criechinger Haus, partially reconstructed

can enter and walk around at the appropriate floor levels, and it contains interesting details in the stonework and chapel. However, it has not had its furnishings, wall coverings, etc. restored. Therefore, I decided to reproduce this building at a detailed, if speculative scale to allow users a direct comparison—and, entirely pragmatically, for ease of access in making photogrammetric models of the architectural details.

The rest of the castle—its walls, gate house, keep, living quarters and outbuildings—will be represented at a medium Level of Detail, a building scale. While no more or less accurate than the Criechinger Haus, they will only be viewed from the exterior, and are not intended for closer inspection.

21.7 Examples

With three levels of detail and four degrees of accuracy, 12 different combinations are possible, the more interesting of which are explained below.

High LoD, relict: in essence, the rest of the model can be seen as a frame to showcase these parts, which combine good detail with high accuracy. These are elements that still survive, and which can be closely measured and modelled, like photogrammetric scans of architectural details in lintels and columns (Fig. 21.6).

High LoD, speculative: The living quarters are filled with reproduction furniture of the period to showcase its use, though no actual furniture, nor depictions of furniture or inventories survive.

Medium LoD, interpolated or extrapolated: This category makes up the bulk of the model, containing wooden floors evidenced by beam holes, gaps filled in sections of wall, missing stairs replaced, etc.

Fig. 21.6 An example of a high-LoD relict element, a photogrammetric model of a surviving door in the Criechinger Haus

Low LoD, relict: This category is perhaps the most fruitful for future researchers to develop, as it contains many elements that still exist, but have not been studied in greater detail because they are not the focus of the model, such as the Roman watchtower on the hill to the south.

Low LoD, speculative: This category contains the "infill" needed to complete the insignificant areas of the model—for example, the outbuildings behind the houses in the town, which add to the complete picture but whose location, dimensions and density are not known.

21.8 Conflicting Data

A good example of a place where data conflicts and a decision has to be made is the eastern gate of the city walls. In his seminal work on the castles of Luxembourg, *Die Burgen des Luxemburger Landes*, John Zimmer includes a map of the historic town and castle (Zimmer 1996), which he asserts is based on archaeological evidence[1] and old maps. It shows a small, *rectangular* building on the *northern* side of the bridge, where the road crosses the river and runs into the town.

In contrast, the Ferraris map (de Ferraris 1778), one of the oldest maps of the region, shows a protrusion on the *southern* side of the bridge—coloured in red to indicate that it was surveyed, rather than estimated. The first cadastral map of the region, produced in 1824, shows a small building of somewhat *ambiguous shape* on the *northern* side of the bridge, attached to the larger municipal building behind it.

This disparity can perhaps be explained by the fact that the river meanders and may change its course from time to time, necessitating a new wooden bridge, but matters are further complicated by the introduction of a third data point. In 1845, the Dutch artist Barend Cornelis Koekkoek sketched the town as a preliminary study for a series of landscape paintings. His view of the eastern gate shows a remnant of city wall, several recognisable buildings still present in both the maps and the modern town, a wooden bridge—and on its *northern* side, the stump of a *round* tower. Koekkoek was, in his own words, prone to "assembling real elements into an artistic whole that does not exist in this form in reality" for his landscape paintings, which he called "pretty lies" (Pelgrom 2012). However, his sketches are generally considered to be meticulous studies, and his Luxembourgish paintings are closer to the truth than his usual style.

All these points combine to make an interesting conundrum—which source should we believe? John Zimmer, who sees things with a modern engineer's eye and includes scholarly citations in his work? One or the other of the historic maps, whose makers surveyed the structures when they were still standing? The sketch by an artist who is carefully studying shapes in preparation for his work?

---

[1]Unfortunately, official reports on the findings of the rescue excavations are not available, so all data on archaeological evidence is second hand.

Fig. 21.7 A map combining different data sources

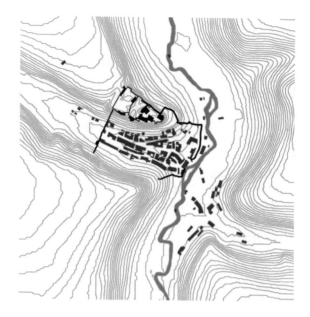

Unless new evidence comes to light, it is not possibly to conclusively reconcile these different sources (Fig. 21.7). Instead, they can be used as an example of how to deal with dependencies.

21.9   Dependencies

Making a decision about the shape and the location of the gatehouse will affect other decisions, from the rendering of the building itself to the precise location of the bridge, the path the road takes once it passes through the wall, and even how reliable the sources that gave the conflicting data are considered to be in relation to other decisions. Therefore, the decisions themselves, the reasons one solution was chosen over alternatives, the data supporting each one and how this decision relates to the overall process must be recorded.

This issue is far from trivial, and requires detailed mapping, preferably using an ontology like CIDOC-CRM—which would be far too complex to present to the public. Instead, users should be made aware of this type of issues and the changes they can perpetuate across the model without naming them all explicitly. Meanwhile, not all possible variants must be fully mapped out; instead, documenting where they would branch, and which branch was pursued allows future researchers to add their own data.

21.10   Interactivity

The model will be presented in an interactive, immersive app that allows the user to control their environment, either in virtual reality or on a screen. It offers a choice of a bird's-eye or an interior view in which to explore the model. On load, the model will be presented at a maximum level of detail and with photorealistic textures to provide an impression of its state ca. 1550.

Using simple sliders, the user can choose to dynamically adapt the display to reveal which parts have which levels of accuracy at different levels of detail. All parts below the chosen combination are faded out, turning semi-transparent and removing their textures to highlight the higher-quality parts, but still offer a context for them.

Selecting individual building elements will let users view the associated metadata stored in the underlying table. Similar elements can be grouped for this purpose to avoid excessive repetition—for example, it can be given all at once for the beams in a certain floor.

Since an explorable model will not, by itself, be enough to give the user a deeper understanding of the connections between data and metadata and how decisions in reconstructions affect other parts of the model, mini-games can be introduced to demonstrate particular aspects.

The first of these is based on our initial landscape study and serves to pique interest in linguistics and historical geography alongside the architectural reconstruction. It places the user in an interactive educational environment that rewards them for engaging with the content, and allows natural movement and intuitive interaction prompted by curiosity (Fig. 21.8).

Fig. 21.8   A screenshot from the microtoponym learning game

By combining building blocks with symbols for place name elements and placing them on the map, the user progressively makes representations of those place names appear in the landscape below, connecting microtoponyms, their meanings, their place in the landscape and the history of the town. Learning how place names connect to history is implicit, but not presented as the major goal (Morse and de Kramer 2019).

Dependencies can be demonstrated in a "choose your own adventure" storytelling format, allowing the user to make decisions about which sources to trust; this influences which options are available later in the story and can be compared to the outcomes of choosing different options.

21.11 Conclusion

Though it does not have the resources that can be devoted to a larger team effort, this project seeks to fulfil the key points of "intellectual integrity, reliability, documentation, sustainability and access" in a way that is manageable alongside its other requirements. Documentation cannot overshadow the reconstruction process itself, but neither can it be ignored—it is an integral part of any scientific endeavour. Communicating this to the public is as important as communicating the results themselves.

The Charter of Venice demands that "[restoration] must stop at the point where conjecture begins" (ICOMOS 1964), but virtual reconstruction allows us to speculate freely without affecting the original structure. Still, as researchers, we have a responsibility to document our knowledge and conjecture, to allow and encourage criticism of our results, and not to sell our hypotheses as the absolute truth.

Acknowledgements I would like to thank the Centre for Contemporary and Digital History (C[2]DH), the Institute for History (IHIST), and the Luxembourg National Research Fund (FNR) (10929115) for their support. Thanks also to my colleagues, Sam Mersch and Christopher Morse for their collaboration in the initial landscape study, and to all reviewers for their useful comments. All images author's own.

References

Bruseker G, Guillem A, Carboni N (2015) Semantically documenting virtual reconstruction: building a path to knowledge provenance. ISPRS Ann Photogramm Remote Sens Spat Inf Sci II-5/W3:33–40. https://doi.org/10.5194/isprsannals-II-5-W3-33-2015

Cadastral Map of Larochette, 1824, administration du cadastre et de la topographie, Luxembourg

Champion E, Rahaman H (2019) 3D digital heritage models as sustainable scholarly resources. Sustainability 11(8):2425. https://doi.org/10.3390/su11082425

de Ferraris J (1778) Map of the Austrian Netherlands, scale 1/11.520, 1778, sheet 242, via 'The Ferraris Map • KBR', KBR. https://www.kbr.be/en/the-ferraris-map/. Accessed 1 July 2019 de Kramer M, Mersch S, Morse C (2018) Reconstructing the historic landscape of Larochette, Luxembourg. In: Ioannides M et al (eds) Digital heritage. Progress in cultural heritage: documentation, preservation, and protection. EuroMed 2018. Lecture notes in computer science, vol 11197. Springer, Cham

Denard H (2009) The London charter for the computer-based visualisation of cultural heritage, v 2.1. King's College London. http://www.londoncharter.org

Doerr M (2003) The CIDOC CRM—an ontological approach to semantic interoperability of metadata. AI Mag AIM 24

Hardt M (1849) Burgfrieden von Uren und Fels - ein diplomatischer Beitrag zur Untersuchung luxemburgischer Urkunden. Publications de la Section historique de l'Institute grand-ducal de Luxembourg, 1849V, Deuxieme Partie. Luxembourg, 1850

ICOMOS (1964) The Venice Charter-1964, 2nd international congress of architects and technicians of historic monuments, Venice

ICOMOS (2007) The Ename Charter—The ICOMOS Charter for the interpretation and presentation of cultural heritage sites

Morse CM, de Kramer M (2019) What's in a name: gamifying the intangible history of Larochette, Luxembourg. In: CHNT conference proceedings, Vienna

Pelgrom A (2012) 'Domänen der Kunst - B.C. Koekkoek und seine luxemburgischen Landschaften für König Wilhelm II' in Gemalt für den König - B.C. Koekkoek und die luxemburgische Landschaft, 13–38, Musée national d'histoire et d'art Luxembourg

Putnam J (2001) Art and artifact: the museum as medium. Thames & Hudson, London

Uckelman S (2019) Churches have been bombed, burned and ransacked for centuries. And then they are brought back to life I opinion. Miami Herald. https://www.miamiherald.com/opinion/op-ed/article229346624.html. Accessed 1 July 2019

Understanding and using architectural scales. ArchDaily, 2018. https://www.archdaily.com/904882/understanding-and-using-architectural-scales. Accessed 1 July 2019

Weschler L (1996) Mr. Wilson's Cabinet of Wonder: pronged ants, horned humans, mice on toast, and other marvels of jurassic technology. Random House, New York

Zimmer J (1990) Die Burg Fels: Ihre Baugeschichte (éd. Les amis du château de Larochette). Sankt Paulus-Druckerei, Luxembourg

Zimmer J (1996) Die Burgen des Luxemburger Landes, 1. Band. Imprimerie Saint-Paul s.a., Luxembourg

Chapter 22
Preserving and Presenting Cultural Heritage Using Off-the-Shelf Software

Eike Falk Anderson, David John, Richard Mikulski, Adam Redford
and Mario Romero

Abstract The preservation and presentation of cultural heritage (CH) encompasses many domains and disciplines and ranges from tangible CH, traditionally taking the form of museum exhibits and historical sites that are open to the public to intangible CH, focussing on human and societal aspects of CH, as opposed to physical artefacts. The use of computer graphics (CG) and related techniques such as interactive virtual environments since the 1990s has had a profound impact on the presentation of and public engagement with CH, allowing virtual reconstruction of archaeological/historical sites as well as the virtual (re-)construction of culturally and historically relevant artefacts. These are frequently implemented using bespoke or proprietary systems, often explicitly created with a CH application in mind, which may require specialist expertise or significant investment. There exist, however, alternative approaches that can simplify and improve the uptake of CG for CH. In this chapter we discuss how off-the-shelf CG systems such as developer and artists' tools for the entertainment industries, which are comparatively inexpensive, usually provide open developer licenses, and sometimes are even available free of charge, or affordable consumer-level hardware, can be used for the preservation and presentation of tangible and intangible CH, the application of which we illustrate with a set of case studies.

E. F. Anderson (✉) · A. Redford
The National Centre for Computer Animation, Bournemouth University, Poole, UK
e-mail: eanderson@bournemouth.ac.uk

A. Redford
e-mail: aredford@bournemouth.ac.uk

D. John
Department of Creative Technology, Bournemouth University, Poole, UK
e-mail: djohn@bournemouth.ac.uk

R. Mikulski
Department of Archaeology & Anthropology, Bournemouth University, Poole, UK
e-mail: rmikulski@bournemouth.ac.uk

M. Romero
Department of Computational Science and Technology, KTH Royal Institute of Technology, Stockholm, Sweden
e-mail: marior@kth.se

© Springer Nature Switzerland AG 2020
F. Liarokapis et al. (eds.), *Visual Computing for Cultural Heritage*, Springer Series on Cultural Computing, https://doi.org/10.1007/978-3-030-37191-3_22

22.1 Introduction

In recent years, the use of CG and related techniques, e.g. for virtual reconstructions and 3D digital imaging, have become increasingly recognized as tools with significant potential for the documentation, analysis and presentation (Addison 2000) of all aspects of CH and material culture (Berndt and Carlos 2000), facilitating the development of novel presentation formats for raising public awareness of CH, bringing history "alive" and attracting new audiences to museums. Their combination with new media (the web and computer/video games) and novel interaction techniques have enabled the proliferation of CG and related techniques for CH, providing an important approach to the preservation and presentation of CH. These technologies have been used by museums, providing new approaches to the curation of artefacts, aided archaeologists in the analysis of sites and artefacts, been applied to formal and informal education settings, and they have enabled the development of novel presentation formats such as virtual museums or serious games for raising public awareness of CH (Anderson et al. 2010). They have also benefited from the development and spread of multi-modal user interfaces and mobile devices, opening up new avenues to the digitization of tangible CH, the authoring and capture of intangible CH as well as representations of CH using augmented reality (AR) and mixed reality (MR), facilitating novel paradigms for interaction with CH.

Serious games and similar interactive virtual environments (VEs) allow audiences to experience tangible and intangible CH—in this context sometimes referred to as Virtual Heritage (VH)—either on-site, often using a kiosk-style presentation system, AR with mobile devices, or on-line. Over the past decade, MR interfaces related to these, have also shown a potential to enhance the audience's experiences of virtual worlds and VH. Recently it has been demonstrated that game engines used for interactive VEs can also be used for animation production (Bąk and Wojciechowska 2020) as a more affordable alternative to conventional tools.

Until a few years ago, CG systems for CH were often created with bespoke hard- and software, almost always expensive to acquire and time-consuming to develop. Only fairly recently has there been a trend to replace proprietary systems with off-the-shelf solutions and once expensive professional systems are being subsumed by affordable consumer-level systems, reducing up-front costs and greatly simplifying development of CH applications. In this chapter we first provide an overview of the preservation and presentation of CH, followed by a set of recent case studies, illustrating and discussing how affordable off-the-shelf CG systems—developer and artists' tools from the entertainment industries—can be employed to achieve this.

22.2 Preserving and Presenting Cultural Heritage Using CG

The potential of CG methods and techniques for the preservation and presentation of CH has been known for decades, but before the advent of consumer-grade high-performance hard- and software its uptake was limited due to a lack of tools and visual realism (Addison 2001). Great advances in CG hardware, methods and related techniques, such as recent developments in VR and multi-modal user interfaces, have popularized the use of CG as such and consequently increased the use of CG for CH (Berndt and Carlos 2000; Anderson 2013). This increased use of CG in CH has driven technological, methodological and conceptual developments ranging from the development of production pipelines reaching from the digitization of CH artefacts to their public presentation (Bruno et al. 2010), to the development of internationally recognized principles concerning the digitization and visualisation of CH as set out in the "London Charter" (Beacham et al. 2009).

There are many CG methods and techniques that are suitable for application to the preservation and presentation of CH, a detailed taxonomy and discussion of was presented by Foni et al. (2010). As a first step, most of these CH approaches require the 3D construction or reconstruction of CH objects, which other than by means of manual modelling or procedural generation (Haegler et al. 2009) would require some form of 3D acquisition technique (Pavlidis et al. 2007) for digitizing the CH artefact or site. While there are many different methods and techniques to achieve this (Vilbrandt et al. 2004), the best results tend to be achieved when different techniques are combined (Núñez Andrés et al. 2012). Other than straightforward visualisations, CH applications implemented using interactive VEs as used in video games have not only facilitated the virtual (re-)construction of culturally and historically relevant artefacts in serious games for education (Anderson et al. 2010), but they have also been used by museums, providing new approaches for the promotion of knowledge transfer and supporting public outreach and they have enabled the development of novel presentation formats for raising public awareness of CH. Such VH systems can take the form of physical installations, e.g. kiosk-style systems located in museums, or of web-based on-line applications. Examples for these are "Colonia3D", a virtual reconstruction of Roman Cologne (Trapp et al. 2012) in the "Romano-Germanic Museum" of Cologne (Germany) or the on-line only "Virtual Viipuri", a virtual reconstruction of the formerly Finnish city of Vyborg before it was lost to the Soviet Union (Wells 2019).

Interactive VEs and related technologies and techniques are especially interesting for the emerging application area concerned with the preservation, presentation and dissemination of intangible CH, which in recent years has been highlighted by the UNESCO (2003), which is concerned with human and societal aspects of CH. The recording or capturing and consecutive visualisation of intangible CH, as it literally concerns the intangible, provides both conceptual and practical challenges that interactive VEs are ideally suited to address, as audiences are immersed in and interact with the VE, allowing them to subjectively experience the heritage artefact. Their employment in the preservation of heritage artefacts such as rituals and stories can be combined with the application of novel interaction methods (Anderson 2013), and MR presentations such as the Egyptian Oracle (Gillam and Jacobson 2015), where a public performance is enhanced with an interactive VE, are another possibility for the presentation of intangible CH.

A large number of CH applications created over the past decades have been developed using proprietary soft- and hardware systems, however, in many cases the development of such applications can be improved, sped-up and/or simplified through the use of appropriate off-the-shelf solutions. In general, among the main benefits for the use of off-the-shelf hardware and software are often considerable cost savings (Weinberg and Harsham 2009), and this is equally true for any hardware employed in CH applications, starting with the underlying computing platform. For example, in 2000 an interactive visualisation of the Siena Cathedral (Italy) was deployed on a highly specialized 3D graphics platform (SGI ONYX2-InfiniteReality3) (Behr et al. 2001), costing a six figure USD value. Less specialized off-the-shelf hardware such as a workstation computer with a consumer-grade graphics card can be just as effective and should be considered for CH applications before a much more expensive specialized solution is used—with the benefit of hindsight, one could argue that higher-end off-the-shelf hardware of the time could have achieved similar results for the Siena Cathedral, at a fraction of the costs.

Regarding the creation of interactive VEs and virtual reality systems for CH, Champion (2015) highlighted "infrastructure issues" that result in huge expenses incurred through the development of proprietary systems, which can be much simplified through the use of game engines as used in the entertainment industry. The use of game engines as visualisation infrastructure in projects that do not have entertainment as their primary objective, e.g. in scientific research, is not new (Lewis and Jacobson 2002). In CH contexts, games technology and game engines—as mentioned above—have been used for the creation of CH serious games (Anderson et al. 2010; Mortara et al. 2014), however, the commercial game engines used in popular entertainment games have often been too expensive to be employed for CH purposes, and their use has frequently been limited to the creation of so-called "Mods" (modifications) for existing commercial entertainment games (Kushner 2003), such as the "History Game Canada" (Rockwell and Kee 2011). Recent changes in the licensing terms and costs for game engines, however, have made these software systems considerably more attractive for developers in many different domains, including the preservation and presentation of CH, greatly simplifying the selection of a suitable system infrastructure, for which established methodologies can be employed (Anderson et al. 2013). This can be observed in the development of the Egyptian Oracle mentioned above, itself based on the earlier Virtual Egyptian Temple VH experience (Troche and Jacobson 2010), which over several iterations evolved from a proprietary software system that was replaced with a Mod of a commercial entertainment game (Unreal Tournament 2004), which was subsequently ported to the low-cost Unity game engine (Jacobson et al. 2019).

22.3 Case Studies

To demonstrate the effectiveness of using off-the-shelf CG systems for CH we explore a number of successful case studies employing such visual computing methods, techniques and technologies in CH contexts, i.e. different manners in which CG has and can be applied to the interpretation of CH objects, aiding their digital and physical preservation as well as their dissemination. These include applications of affordable interactive VE infrastructure (game engines and graphics and visualisation libraries) to support different CH presentation formats, as well as museum exhibits and the digitization of archaeological human remains.

22.3.1 The "Exercise Smash" Virtual Heritage Experience

VH presentations that allow users to experience the past by directly immersing them in an interactive VE at the time and place of a historical event have the potential to engage audiences in a similar way as computer games. As such they need to be able to provide a similar interface and visual quality to entertainment games (Anderson et al. 2010). Computer game engines, as used in these entertainment games, provide an ideal infrastructure for interactive VEs, implementing VH presentations. In this first case study we present a synthesis of tangible and intangible heritage based on maritime archaeology that was implemented using an off-the-shelf game engine and created using affordable 3D content creation programs usually employed in the entertainment industry.

22.3.1.1 Exercise Smash

"Exercise Smash" was a military exercise conducted in Studland Bay on England's south coast on the 4th of April 1944 as preparation for the D-Day landings. During this live-fire landing exercise several amphibious tanks that were launched from landing craft sank before reaching the beach with the loss of six crew members' lives. While several of the wrecks were popular targets for sports divers, over time, the exact locations of all of the tank wrecks were lost until in 2014 an archaeological search and survey by Maritime Archaeologists from Bournemouth University (BU), UK (Manousos 2014) resulted in their rediscovery, followed up by a photogrammetric survey in 2018, when 3D scans of the tank wrecks were created.

22.3.1.2 A Snapshot in Time

The aim of the "Exercise Smash" project was to develop a VH experience that provides audiences who may not be able to dive and visit the actual wrecks with a

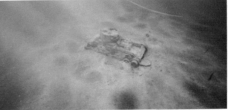

Fig. 22.1 The two parts of the VH experience. Left: taking part in the 1944 amphibious landing exercise; Right: exploring the submerged tank wrecks in a present-day virtual dive

means to experience the underwater archaeology that is more engaging than existing "virtual dive trails" (James 2018), which tend to limit their visualisation to little more than an interactive 3D model viewer for 3D scans of the archaeological remains (frequently annotated with additional information) without depicting the surrounding environment. One of the main aims of this project was therefore to provide a more immersive VE that provides "visitors" of the virtual dive trail with the impression of viewing the archaeological remains in situ, i.e. under water, within a complete VE that resembles the actual site.

In the "Exercise Smash" VH experience, the archaeological remains are being presented in two modes within two fully interactive VEs (Fig. 22.1). Firstly, as a snapshot in time that allows audiences to experience the historical event that created the archaeological remains, and secondly as a virtual dive that allows audiences to experience the remains as they exist now (Anderson and Cousins 2019). Specifically, in the first part, audiences get to take part in the landing exercise, where they have to try to 'swim' one of the tanks from a landing craft to the beach. The second part is a virtual diving expedition in which participants can take a boat to the locations of the submerged tank wrecks, dive down to the wrecks and explore them.

To create this VH experience, Unreal Engine 4 (UE4; free for non-commercial projects) was used as the interactive VE infrastructure, with 3D assets (models and textures) resulting from photogrammetric surveys of the wreck sites processed and additional 3D assets created using Autodesk Maya and Adobe Photoshop, with additional work on textures performed using Substance Painter. All of these are affordable standard software packages used in game development. An initial version of the VH experience was unveiled to visitors of The Tank Museum in Bovington (Dorset, UK) during the June 2019 "Tankfest" event, where it was well received.

22.3.2 Creating Visualisations Using Game Engines for the New Forest Heritage Mapping Project

The New Forest is a National Park in the south of England covering 566 square kilometres of pasture and heathland, containing many well-preserved archaeological sites dating from the Neolithic up to the Second World War. In 2011, a Lidar (Light Detection and Ranging) survey of the entire forest was commissioned to produce an accurate ground level 3D map of the forest, stripped of trees and foliage. This map was examined to search for features in the landscape that may indicate archaeological remains. Before the scheme, 1000 archaeological sites had been recorded throughout the forest, but after examining the Lidar images, over 3,000 had been identified (New Forest National Park Authority 2019). As part of the effort to engage the public with the heritage of the forest and promote conservation Games Technology students from BU created interactive virtual reality visualisations, bringing to life several of the historic sites. These environments have been exhibited at various public events including a four-month exhibition at the New Forest Visitor Centre, Lyndhurst (September 2015–January 2016), that attracted over 30,000 visitors and other shorter events (Shaw et al. 2016; John et al. 2017, 2018).

Visualisations were created for a range of sites covering a wide spread of historic periods including a Neolithic long barrow, Bronze Age round barrows, Iron Age hillforts, Rockbourne Roman villa, a medieval hunting lodge, Tudor coastal defence forts, Buckler's Hard Georgian shipbuilding yard, Fritham Victorian gunpowder factory, airfields from the First and Second World Wars, Matley First World War training trenches and Yew Tree Heath Anti-Aircraft Battery. Game engines (Unity and UE4) were used to create the environments to make use of the pre-existing functionality and graphical capabilities that enable the user to explore the environment at a human scale from a first-person perspective, at a low cost.

A major consideration for the development of the VEs was the intended platform, ideally including a VR headset and a computer with high graphics capabilities. However, it was not possible to commit expensive hardware for long-running exhibitions, where only iPad tablets with limited storage capacity and restricted processing power were available. It was possible to create flythrough videos of the VEs with full detail and visual effects to display on large TV screens and projections at the event. VR headsets were available only at special events.

The landscapes were the largest features in the VEs and used a large percentage of the available processing resources. There was a trade-off between maximising the size of the landscape and optimising the environment to suit the available resources. Some environment details were lost, but background images could be used to show distant hills, and a fog effect could be applied to reduce clarity of the horizon and keep the user's focus on the immediate environment. An exception to this approach was the Beaulieu Second World War airfield environment (Fig. 22.2a) that allowed users to fly at an angle that prevented the landscape's edges from being hidden.

Accurate landscape terrains were generated from heightmaps that were exported from the Lidar data and imported into the game engine. The Lidar survey had a resolution of one vertex every 50 cm. UE4 imported this data, placing one vertex per metre, so the X and Y axes were scaled by half for the correct dimensions. The height (Z axis) had to be manually adjusted, as UE4 imports height values as a percentage of the minimum and maximum of the range in the heightmap, rather than an absolute value. When a map texture that shows the height contours is overlaid, it is possible

(a)						(b)						(c)

(d)						(e)						(f)

(g)						(h)						(i)

Fig. 22.2 Examples of the New Forest virtual visualisations (running left to right, top to bottom); **a** Beaulieu Airfield, **b** Hurst Castle, **c** Buckland Rings, **d** Rockbourne Roman Villa, **e** Fritham Gunpowder Factory, **f** Medieval Hunting Lodge at Telegraph Hill, **g** Stoney Cross airfield, **h** East Boldre airfield, **i** Frankenbury Hillfort

to measure the distance between contours and to adjust the height until the distance between these contours matches the scale.

Once the heightmap has been imported, the terrain often required additional clean-up. There may be unwanted terrain features, such as outlines of modern roads and unintended bumps caused by cars or dense bushes. Features such as buildings and taller trees are removed from the heightmap by the Lidar processing software (identified by a sudden change in height values), creating holes in the imported landscape terrain. These unwanted bumps and holes need to be manually corrected by using the landscape editing tools. Fixing unwanted features in the terrain can be a long and tedious process, but only needs to be done in places where the defects are visible in the environment and cannot be covered by meshes or foliage. Other implications for the implementation of landscape textures arise from the choice of target platform: the iPads have a limit on the number of textures that can be applied to landscapes, which affects how different layers are rendered. Single layer satellite images can be used as textures, but these are unsuitable for viewing from close range.

Different approaches can be taken for creating 3D models for use in the environment. The Hurst Castle environment (Fig. 22.2b) used a single large model for the castle. Similarly, the Buckler's Hard environment contained one highly-detailed ship model, surrounded by less-detailed buildings. This approach allows the main 3D models and textures to be more complex and natural lighting to be applied, whereas, the greater the complexity of the main model, the less detail can be added to other objects in the scene, making the environment less believable for users. An alternative approach is to create smaller objects that can be repeated multiple times, such as the roundhouses, wicker fences and palisades in the Rockbourne Villa (Fig. 22.2d) and Iron Age Hill fort environments (Fig. 22.2c). For 3D models that are viewed at a distance it was more efficient to add detail to the textures and normal maps instead of the 3D objects. Due to hardware limitations, many effects that make the game graphics visually appealing (including foliage, atmospheric fog and post processing volumes) could not be reproduced accurately by the iPads, for instance, the Medieval Hunting Lodge environment (Fig. 22.2f) contained a large number of trees that could not be rendered on an iPad and even mid-range game development computers struggled to display the environment with a reasonable frame-rate.

An important feature within the VEs was the display of information about the site to the user. When navigation is controlled with mouse and keyboard, it is relatively simple to assign keys or buttons to toggle the display of information on and off (as in the Gunpowder Factory environment—Fig. 22.2e). A keyboard is not easily available for the iPad presentation, and consequently, all control has to be provided through the touch screen using the default navigation controls or on-screen buttons. For the Rockbourne and Neolithic Long Barrow environments, information is displayed on information boards (Fig. 22.2d) that appear when the user overlaps with a box trigger, and that are hidden when the user leaves the trigger area. It can be difficult to read text written on objects within the environment when the user is oriented at a wrong angle to an information board. The board itself can potentially obstruct the users' movement. For example, it was possible for the user to be lifted up by an information board and become stuck inside the Neolithic Barrow. An alternative strategy was to display the information directly on the screen, either above the top of the scene (as in the Gunpowder Factory—Fig. 22.2e—and the Medieval Hunting Lodge—Fig. 22.2f— environments) or covering the scene (as in the East Boldre—Fig. 22.2h—and Stoney Cross—Fig. 22.2g—environments).

It is important to consider how to help users navigating the environment, especially in light of the conflict between allowing them to freely explore the virtual world and the definition of a predetermined path around the environment. A total of 20 information boards were hidden throughout the Rockbourne environment, however, it is easy for users to miss the display of important information. An evaluation of 30 participants discovered that while free-exploration of the VE was more popular than reading a guide book, it was the readers who absorbed more knowledge (John et al. 2017). In an effort to guide users to areas of interest, the information boards in the Gunpowder Factory environment were left visible at all times. Similarly, floating icons were used to draw attention to areas where information was available in the Medieval Hunting Lodge (Fig. 22.2f) and Stoney Cross Airfield (Fig. 22.2g) environments, although these were always prominent in the environment. An objective marker system that displayed diamond shapes was used in the East Boldre (Fig. 22.2h) environment to indicate where areas of interest were located. For the Frankenbury Iron Age Fort environment (Fig. 22.2i), icons were moved from the environment to a permanently displayed overhead mini-map on the bottom left side of the screen.

The project demonstrated that game engines can be employed successfully as a tool for creating VR environments for use in public engagement activities. There are a number of technical challenges that need to be overcome when using Lidar for creating landscapes, and different strategies have to be followed for implementing the display of information and other interactive features. Furthermore, the amount of detail and visual effects that can be displayed depends on the intended presentation platform. Other findings of the "New Forest Heritage Mapping Project" are that a presentation using VR headsets rates higher as an immersive experience than iPads, but where it is not possible to supervise these activities iPads can provide an engaging experience. Visitors will not find an iPad touch screen more difficult to navigate than using a keyboard and mouse. There may be differences in the strength of opinion between participants, depending on their previous experience of VR or knowledge of the site being visualised, but overall feedback has been positive.

22.3.3 Poole Museum—Town Cellars Visualisation

Game engines are not limited to the creation of games or similar artefacts involving interactive VEs but can also be applied in situations where more traditional solutions are unsuitable, e.g. because of time constraints, and the creation of 3D animated films and videos can be very time consuming in terms of 3D rendering (the process of synthesizing animation frames from 3D assets).

In certain situations, the image quality achievable with modern game engines can closely match the image quality of expensive production-rendering systems, making them a viable alternative to such systems. An example for a project in which this was successfully done is our second case study, the "Town Cellars Visualisation" project for Poole Museum, a local heritage museum in Poole (Dorset, UK) (Anderson et al. 2018).

This project involved a mixture of architectural and heritage visualisation, based on documented archaeological findings as well as on-site collected photographic references (using a consumer DSLR—digital single-lens reflex—camera) and manual measurements, resulting in the "town cellars transformation", showing a transition of the Grade I listed town cellars building that is part of the museum in its current state to a planned restoration closely matching its original state (Fig. 22.3).

The virtual reconstruction was carried out over a 3-week period, mainly within the UE4 game engine environment, with some 3D models created using Maya and texture assets created with Photoshop and Substance Painter. UE4 was then also used for the rendering of the animation frames, with the resulting video edited with Adobe Premiere, aiming to provide visual aids for stakeholders and funders as well as providing information about the developments to the general public.

The end results are of a quality that is comparable to that achievable with common 3D modelling and animation systems employing a built-in or 3rd party off-line rendering solution, demonstrating both the versatility of modern computer game engines and their suitability for all aspects of cultural heritage visualisation.

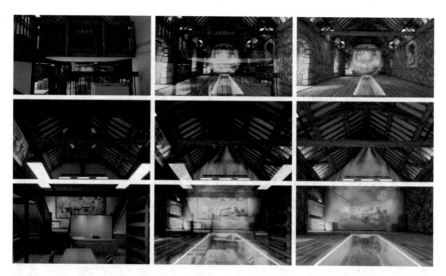

Fig. 22.3 Returning Poole Town Cellars closer to their original state (left to right)

22.3.4   Tidebanan: Visualizing the History of the Stockholm Metro

Transportation is central for urban design. Roads, railways, and metro lines determine city shape and culture. People search for neighbourhoods largely based on accessibility, which predominantly determines property value and area services. This section presents Tidebanan, a project aiming at visualizing the demographic and cultural events in Stockholm during the creation of its metro system.

Tidebanan began as a student project in the Information Visualization course at KTH, Royal Institute of Technology, Stockholm. The aim of the project was to provide an interactive visualisation of the metro system across space, the map of Stockholm, and time, the period beginning in 1949 when the system opened the first lines and stations[1] (Fig. 22.4). It is a Geographic Information System (GIS) that includes several layers. The cultural heritage (CH) explored is the history of the metro system, facts about the design, construction and operation of its 100 stations, images and videos of inaugurations, and historical changes in population density. Users can pan and zoom across a city map and scrub across time (Fig. 22.5). The visualisation shows annual population density since 1950 as a layered choropleth map.

The original student project only had content available online. After a demonstration, the Director of the Transport Museum of Stockholm urged the students to transform the project into an exhibit. The students collaborated with museum staff to curate deeper and novel content. They searched through unpublished museum

---

[1]For a sample exploration of Tidebanan, please visit https://people.kth.se/~edahls/Tidebanan/. For a video demonstration of the original project, please visit https://vimeo.com/135973471.

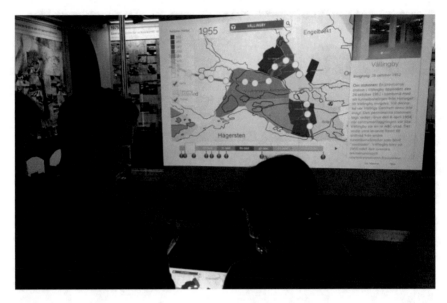

Fig. 22.4 Visitors interacting with Tidebanan, a visualisation of the history of the Stockholm metro system (1949–2016), a permanent exhibit at the Transport Museum of Stockholm

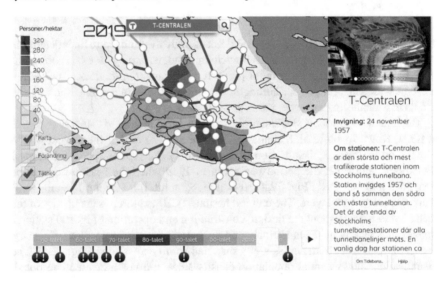

Fig. 22.5 Tidebanan shows data starting from the 1950s. Users navigate the timeline by scrubbing the horizontal bar, pan and zoom the map on the central panel and select information layers with the checkboxes on the left. The right panel presents content about each station

1957 år ett annat viktigt år i tunnelbanans historia. Då invigdes nämligen T-Centralen och tunnelbanans södra och västra sträckningar bands nu samman. Nu kunde stockholmare åka med "gröna faran" från tex Högdalen i söder till Vällingby i väster, och det utan att byta tåg. Samma år började också tunnelbanans stationer att smyckas med konst.

Fig. 22.6   King Gustaf VI Adolf of Sweden inaugurating T-centralen, 1957, one of the never-before published images digitized from museum archives

material and carefully selected, digitized and restored never-before-published photographs and films dating back to 1950 (Fig. 22.6). The students placed the content at the appropriate spatio-temporal locations on the visualization and provided navigation techniques, including overviewing, zooming, filtering, scrubbing, panning, and clicking for details on points of interest (Shneiderman 2003) (Fig. 22.5).

The equipment consisted of off-the-shelf hardware: a personal computer, a touchscreen display, and a projector. The touchscreen, computer, cables, projector, and projection screen were mounted on sturdy frames to withstand the extensive usage of museum exhibits. Staff jokingly called this "museum-strength" development. The touchscreen was placed horizontally on a tailor-made wooden box to allow one or more visitors to interactively explore the visualisation, while the projector opened the experience to a larger audience. The system used standard touch gesture libraries including one-finger touch and release for clicking, two-finger stretching and pinching for zooming in and out respectively, and one-finger swiping for panning and scrubbing. The system also used off-the-shelf open source software which consisted of D3.js, Javascript, HTML 5, jQuery, and CSS. D3 (Data-Driven Documents) is a high-level Javascript library for interactively visualizing data using web standards. jQuery is a JavaScript library to easily traverse and manipulate trees in HTML DOM (Document Object Model). The maps, demographic data, and facts about each station were open data sourced from Wikidata and Wikipedia. The media content started as open data in Wikidata, and, as stated before, after careful curation it included never-before published images and film held at the museum archives.

From this perspective, all the components of the system were either free of charge or very inexpensive. The project's only cost to the museum were two student internships, the site license and the hardware (combined, approximately 20 thousand euros). For the students, the first compensation was in academic credits and learning. Then, the site license and internships compensated their efforts beyond the course project. For the course leaders, their time while on the course project was covered by their salaries for teaching. The time supporting and researching the work beyond the course project was a contribution from the course leaders financed by open researching funding. The rewards include collaborating in a museum exhibit, providing new and engaging experiences to a large audience of museum visitors, increasing the public visibility of the museum and the university as institutions for collaborative innovation, evidence for future external funding, and learning from the on-site longitudinal research of its deployment, which affords the current report as this work has not been previously published.

The exhibit opened in September 2015 and ran uninterrupted for two years, until the museum closed for relocation in 2017. The museum and exhibit are planned to reopen in 2020. It is important to note that the system did not crash during that time and that it did not require hardware or software maintenance. While on exhibit, we observed and interviewed visitors interacting with the visualisation. The most enthusiastic visitors were children and older adults. The children enjoyed the digital interaction and understood the content and effects of their actions with relative ease. They learned about the history, planning, and impact of the metro system. They also enjoyed the anecdotal content. Older adults, on the other hand, enjoyed remembering the events depicted in the visualisation. For them, it was a trip through their own history and relationship to the city.

The visualisation includes historical photos and films that had never been seen as they were in storage. Each metro station has content associated to it. For example, the 1957 opening of the central station T-centralen, connecting the south and north lines (Fig. 22.6). The same year, the metro stations also began to be decorated with art.

Each station has images and text describing its history and art. Important events are signalled with exclamation points over the period and place where they happened. The visualisation has two more layers of information. It displays choropleth maps of the population density of Stockholm divided into its parishes and the population change since 1950. These layers, coupled with the temporal slider and the creation of the metro lines, support an informal analysis of the impact the metro system has had on the population density of the city.

22.3.4.1 Lessons Learned

We conclude this section with a synthesis of the lessons learned while designing the course project and transitioning it into the exhibit. While each museum exhibit is unique, our aim is to provide pointers for future students, educators, researchers, designers and curators for expediting their processes and ensuring a more permanent and engaging experience for visitors.

1. **Stay connected**: collaborating with local museums and institutions is critical for the serendipitous development of projects like Tidebanan. The course leaders

had collaborated with the museum director and it was relatively simple to present the student project to start the collaboration.

2. **Give creative freedom**: course leaders allow students to explore and create their own projects. Students are free to choose content and are evaluated on their ability to justify their design choices on solid technical and theoretical frameworks.

3. **Do not retain intellectual property**: Swedish universities do not make a claim on the intellectual property (IP) of student or research projects. Course leaders chose to not claim IP on the course projects. Thus, all the IP remained with students, allowing for independent negotiations with the museum.

4. **Carefully review software licenses**: Tidebanan uses free open source licenses. When packaging a software system, it is critical to review what is possible to sell and what must remain free and open.

5. **Distinguish course rewards from project remuneration**: students who worked on the course project received academic credit and achieved learning objectives. The compensation ends there for the entire team. Only some members of the team went on to improve the project to be able to sell a license and only two worked in internships. It is critical to be clear about compensation. If the recompense is not clear, projects like Tidebanan never become exhibits as students and other stakeholders are not able to reach an agreement.

6. **Build for museum strength**: successful museum exhibits experience phenomenal usage. Both hardware and software must be robust and durable. All system components must be designed, developed and tested using rigorous engineering practices. Museum staff do not have the resources, time or competence to regularly maintain or repair exhibits. Once an exhibit is down, there is a very high likelihood it will remain down for a long period, particularly for informal projects with thin financing. More damagingly, exhibits that are out of order deface the museum. Exhibits must be built to last. In the words of our museum colleagues, they must have "museum strength".

7. **Let the museum bring out the big guns!**: most student projects that reach the level of excellence required for a top grade would be considered merely a curiosity by museum curators. Students lack the competence and content for producing long-lasting experiences that engage museum visitors. More importantly, these goals are beyond course learning objectives. It is only after meticulous collaboration with museum curators that the project reached the levels required for becoming an exhibit. The curators contributed novel and exciting content and subtle story-telling techniques that made all the difference for visitors.

22.3.5 Virtual Reconstructions of Cranial and Postcranial Fragments Using Photogrammetry

Archaeological human remains, most often encountered in a skeletal state, are a fundamental element of the archaeological record and as such constitute a unique repository of information concerning the individuals and/or group they represent. As part of teaching collections, they perform an essential role in medical and anatomical education; they also contribute to museum displays and general education, and they form an important focus for public engagement. This case study involved the digitization of skull fragments from a single individual found in the "Crusaders' pit" (Haber et al. 2019), a 13th century mass burial of Crusaders killed in battle that was recovered during archaeological research excavations in Sidon (Lebanon) between 2009 and 2010.

Skeletal remains are often fragile and individual in nature (human skeletal remains derived from archaeological excavations are often recovered in a fragmented state), presenting a finite physical resource requiring careful management and conservation (Caffell et al. 2001). Preserving such remains and fragments, which retain evidence of identity, trauma and pathological processes, is an important on-going concern, as these are typically the elements that garner most interest and consequently are subject to more handling and greater risk of damage and loss. 3D imaging techniques represent important opportunities to create detailed, objective records of such skeletal remains of which, ultimately, only dust will remain.

Within bioanthropology, digital 3D reconstructions have tended to employ computed tomography and laser scanning for data acquisition, however, Katz and Friess (2014) reported minimal deviation between models created by surface laser scanning and 3D photogrammetry, concluding that the latter afforded reduced costs and greater portability. Our case study formed part of a pilot study to demonstrate how fragmented human skeletal material could be reconstructed to demonstrate the nature of skeletal injuries and their location/distribution in a format more readily accessible than traditional 2D images/other formats. Specifically, the study aimed to evaluate the validity and potential usefulness of digital 3D reconstructions of bone fragments using digital photogrammetric techniques combined with standard manual 3D asset creation techniques more commonly used in the feature film visual effects industry, to virtually reconstruct partial cranial and postcranial bone fragments suitable both for public presentation as well as for academic researchers intending to analyse and interpret these fragments.

For the academic researcher, a useful 3D model requires a high resolution of at least 1 mm, if not 0.5 mm. A lay audience, e.g. a member of the general public at a museum display with no in-depth knowledge or experience, will have quite different needs. In the latter case, a reduced resolution is likely to be sufficient for highlighting major changes such as gross pathological changes or severe trauma. Specific to the two skull fragments that were modelled and refitted virtually here, the cranial remains show multiple sharp force trauma to the head of one individual. A single heavy blade wound has partially penetrated the posterior left parietal bone, whilst a second heavy blade cut has fully penetrated the inferior posterior aspect of the right side of the head, involving multiple bones. Together, these lesions represent evidence for perimortem trauma from interpersonal or inter-group violence.

22.3.5.1 Model Acquisition and Reconstruction

The first step in the process of creating the virtual version of the cranial fragment is taking a number of photographs of the fragment and processing the photographs with appropriate photogrammetry software. There are a number of constraints to take into consideration when photographing an object for photogrammetry, and failure to adhere to these constraints could result in the software being unable to process the images correctly. The first constraint is that the object must not be moved, i.e. it must remain still, in place, with the camera moving around it, so it is not possible to use a stationary camera with the object on a turntable. Consequently, more physical space is required to allow moving the camera (and possibly tripod) around the object in 360°. The second constraint is that there needs to be visual overlap between each of the photographs, meaning that it is necessary to move the camera in approximately 5° increments around the object.

For this project, 40–50 photographs of the skull fragment from different elevations were taken using a Canon EOS 5D Mk. III DSLR camera. The software used was Autodesk Recap Photo (although this can create a fairly accurate mesh from low-resolution photographs, best results are achieved using as high resolution photographs as possible). After the photographs had been taken, they were processed to produce a 3D mesh with a basic UV layout and textures applied.

The next step of the virtual reconstruction of the cranial fragment combined the output from the photogrammetry with manual asset creation methods from the feature film visual effects industry. This first required mesh clean-up and the creation of an improved UV layout, for which Maya (using the Maya LT feature set) was used. For best texture resolution and detail, textures were re-projected onto this UV layout from a sample of the source photographs, using the virtual cameras created by Recap Photo (Fig. 22.7a). Mari (by The Foundry) was used for this projection of the photographs onto the UV layout.

As even lighting on all sides of the subject during photography from different angles for photogrammetry is difficult to achieve, usually there will be slight variations in object colour and lighting. Mari was also used for the final steps of the

(a)   **(b)**

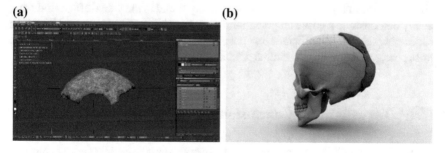

Fig. 22.7 Digitizing cranial and postcranial skull fragments; left—**a** texture projection onto the 3D skull fragment in Mari; right—**b** integration of digitized bones with a generic skull model to contextualize multiple partial cranial fragments

Fig. 22.8 Results from the photogrammetry process alone (left), compared to the combined process (right)

process of cleaning up and balancing brightness, contrast, and colour of the projection images to match one another. As a benefit, this method produces far higher quality results than the output from the photogrammetry process alone (Fig. 22.8).

22.3.5.2 Visualisation Results

To help viewers to quickly identify and locate a bone fragment which they might otherwise be unable to relate to their own body, due to limited anatomical knowledge, the resulting skull fragments were integrated with a generic skull model, showing the skull fragments in their correct position (Fig. 22.7b). This is similar to the common practice employed by museum curators for displaying physical bone fragments: the fragments are placed on the appropriate location of a clay model, demonstrating how the part fits on the whole. The results indicate that challenges remain when attempting to digitally reconstruct smaller-scale bones or bone fragments with specific micro-morphological characteristics by using the 3D photogrammetric methods described. More specifically, it may be extremely difficult to reconstruct accurate models of smaller-scale features, such as fracture surfaces (often including complex trabecular bone) or cortical fracture surface texture, both of which are important factors when interpreting fractures and how they have propagated/been generated. Despite these limitations, 3D models, such as those created using the described processes, employing affordable CG solutions more usually found in the visual effects industry, clearly demonstrate significant potential for use in public engagement activities. The achieved resolution is sufficient for models to clearly represent bone elements and gross changes and/or severe trauma affecting them.

22.4 Discussion and Conclusions

The proliferation of CG through new media over the past three decades, e.g. through the use of CG on the world-wide-web, means that CG is ubiquitous, and has found its way into many different domains, including CH. There it offers novel approaches to the preservation and presentation of (tangible and intangible) CH, where in particular, CG applications offer new levels of interaction. While interactive museum exhibits have existed for several decades, the advent of digital technologies provides potential for fundamentally deeper, richer, more complex and engaging interaction. Ranging from hands-on exploration and discovery to non-linear and non-deterministic story-telling, this creates paradigmatic shifts in active learning, from home, in educational institutions, in museums or at CH sites. This engagement with CH can extend from keyboard and mouse interaction to fully-immersive see-through AR experiences with whole-body interaction. Similarly, such CH applications afford richer and deeper levels of immersion. Studies have correlated immersion with learning, and while well-curated museums, by definition, provide immersive experiences to their visi-tors, the level of immersive reality and interactive experiences afforded by digital technologies does not yet have a clear precedent.

Levels of documentation have also improved far beyond what was considered pos-sible only two to three decades ago. Home photography and film (and later video) have existed for almost a century. The vast pervasiveness of digital tools and devices over recent years has not only led to improvements of existing methods and tech-niques (e.g. better visual quality), but also opened up new avenues of recording and documenting CH with much greater fidelity than previously possible, allowing, for instance, fully-immersive VR exploration of content.

The same is true for the level of communication facilitated by digital technologies and new media. Museums and CH sites have employed a number of mechanisms to communicate across time and different kinds of people, such as guest books recording visitors' comments. Digital technologies and new media, however, afford much richer and nuanced communication platforms. They provide a means through which groups of people across the world can communicate, learn together and share experiences without the necessity of being present in the same space, at the same time. These communication mechanisms are unique to the digital infrastructure provided by today's ubiquitous off-the-shelf, mobile-networked and sensor-rich devices.

The majority of the case studies described in this chapter were created with the participation of university students (undergraduate and postgraduate), with most of the development work carried out by those students. The involvement of students in CH projects involving CG is frequently practiced, e.g. students created the majority of the 3D models for the Colonia 3D project mentioned in Sect. 22.2 (Trapp et al. 2012), but it presents a number of challenges (see Sect. 22.3.4.1). For example, the project duration will likely extend beyond the course during which it was created, so students will have to commit their personal time even after their course has concluded. Generated IP is another issue, especially if the project includes commercialisation of the work, as the Swedish university practice of making no claim on IP derived from student or research projects is not ubiquitous. A useful consideration is to keep project briefs involving students fairly open to allow exploration and experimentation. As digital CH presentations are often created to engage younger audiences, like the students themselves, giving them the creative freedom to build a CH system that would engage them, will most likely benefit the whole project.

A driving factor for the rapid spread of VH applications in recent years has been the considerable improvement of visual quality in real-time CG and interactive techniques. Itself driven by major advances in computer games technologies, these, in turn, have helped to bring forth standardisation of methods and techniques, and subsequent integration with standardised hard- and software systems. This has driven down costs, which in combination with their widespread acceptance has resulted in the creation of affordable off-the-shelf, consumer-level hard- and software systems.

The intended presentation platform that an interactive CH application is built on directly influences its potential features in terms of graphics capabilities and interaction interfaces. One therefore needs to keep in mind that this does not only present benefits, but also potential drawbacks as the use of off-the-shelf systems means that CH systems based on these will share their limitations. For wider public engagement purposes, whether online, through a mobile app, or within a museum display or educational resource, context is clearly important. Different audiences have differing needs and require varying amounts and/or types of information to interpret digital 3D models, therefore, the provision of appropriate contextual information is essential for the success of visualisation as a resource/tool. The application of VH infrastructure and techniques can provide this, and using of off-the-shelf systems creates affordable solutions.

To conclude, in this chapter we have presented a set of case studies that demonstrate how off-the-shelf CG systems, such as inexpensive developer and artists' tools from the entertainment industries and consumer-level hardware, can be used for the creation of CG systems for the preservation and presentation of CH.

Acknowledgements and Credits The authors would like to acknowledge those who contributed to the case studies detailed in this chapter. *Case Study 3.1*—Joseph Adams, Eike Falk Anderson, Arran Bidwell, Tom Cousins, Dawid Kupisinski, Alexander Lechev, Manuella Nagiel and Radu Rosca. *Case Study 3.2*—Matthew Archer, Paul Cheetham, Christopher Becket, Michaela Blakeburn, Anthony Bossom, Daniel Dean, Karl Gosling, Jacob Halford, Charles Hunt, David Hurst, Harrison Jerreat, David John, Harry Manley, Jack Masterman, Robert Moseley, Lawrence Shaw, Jamie Sheridan, Aaron Stone, Taylor Strudwick, Adrian Tarranowicz and Richard Wilkinson. *Case Study 3.3*—Eike Falk Anderson, Lucy Cole, Isabella "Izzy" Deacon, Miguel Correia Jamal Pinto Goncalves, Rachel Martin, Claudia Moore, Michael Spender and David Watkins. *Case Study 3.4*—Anders Bea, Dan Cariño, Erik Dahlström, Niclas Ericsson, Julia Gerhardsen, Evert Lagerberg, Mario Romero, Christoffer Sandahl, Fiona Stewart and Björn Thuresson. *Case Study 3.5*—Adam Redford and Richard Mikulski.

References

Addison AC (2000) Emerging trends in virtual heritage. IEEE Multimed 7(2):22–25
Addison AC (2001) Virtual heritage: technology in the service of culture. In: 2001 conference on virtual reality, archaeology, and cultural heritage, VAST '01, pp 343–354 (2001)
Anderson EF (2013) Computer games technology and serious games for the preservation of cultural heritage. In: 3rd international conference of young folklorists: vernacular expressions and analytic categories—abstracts. University of Tartu, pp 11–12

Anderson EF, Cousins T (2019) Interactive presentation of archaeology in the historical context and the present—virtual heritage experiences that blend tangible and intangible cultural heritage. In: UK chapter of computer applications and quantitative methods in archaeology

Anderson EF, McLoughlin L, Liarokapis F, Peters C, Petridis P, de Freitas S (2010) Developing serious games for cultural heritage: a state-of-the-art review. Virtual Real 14(4):255–275

Anderson EF, McLoughlin L, Watson J, Holmes S, Jones P, Pallett H, Smith B (2013) Choosing the infrastructure for entertainment and serious computer games—a whiteroom benchmark for game engine selection. In: 2013 5th international conference on games and virtual worlds for serious applications (VS-GAMES)

Anderson EF, Cole L, Deacon I, Goncalves M, Moore C (2018) Poole Museum—our museum project visualisation: town cellars transformation. Poole Museum. https://www.youtube.com/watch?v=E8L1U0HNhRo

Bąk A, Wojciechowska M (2020) Using the game engine in the animation production process. In: Huk M, Maleszka M, Szczerbicki E (eds) Intelligent information and database systems: recent developments. Springer International Publishing, Cham, pp 209–220

Beacham R, Niccolucci F, Denard H (2009) London charter for the computer-based visualisation of cultural heritage. http://www.londoncharter.org. Version 2.1

Behr J, Fröhlich T, Knöpfle C, Kresse W, Lutz B, Reiners D, Schöffel F (2001) The digital cathedral of Siena—innovative concepts for interactive and immersive presentation of cultural heritage sites. In: International cultural heritage informatics meeting, pp 57–71

Berndt E, Carlos J (2000) Cultural heritage in the mature era of computer graphics. IEEE Comput Graphics Appl 20(1):36–37

Bruno F, Bruno S, De Sensi G, Luchi ML, Mancuso S, Muzzupappa M (2010) From 3D reconstruction to virtual reality: a complete methodology for digital archaeological exhibition. J Cult Herit 11(1):42–49

Caffell AC, Roberts CA, Janaway RC, Wilson AS (2001) Pressures on osteological collections: the importance of damage limitation. In: Human remains: conservation, retrieval and analysis, British archaeological reports, international series. Archaeopress, pp 187–197

Champion E (2015) Critical gaming: interactive history and virtual heritage. Ashgate

Foni AE, Papagiannakis G, Magnenat-Thalmann N (2010) A taxonomy of visualization strategies for cultural heritage applications. J Comput Cult Herit 3(1):1:1–1:21

Gillam R, Jacobson J (eds) (2015) The Egyptian oracle project: ancient ceremony in augmented reality. Bloomsbury Publishing

Haber M, Doumet-Serhal C, Scheib CL, Xue Y, Mikulski R, Martiniano R, Fischer-Genz B, Schutkowski H, Kivisild T, Tyler-Smith C (2019) A transient pulse of genetic admixture from the crusaders in the near east identified from ancient genome sequences. Am J Hum Genet 104(5):977–984

Haegler S, Müller P, Van Gool L (2009) Procedural modeling for digital cultural heritage. EURASIP J Image Video Process 2009(1)

Jacobson J, Gillam R, Hopkins D (2019) Virtual Egyptian temple: credits. http://publicvr.org/html/EgyptCredits.txt

James A (2018) Review of the virtual dive trails scheme (7374): a big splash or a damp squib? Report for historic England. https://historicengland.org.uk/content/docs/getinvolved/dive-trails-review-pdf

John D, Shaw L, Cheetham P, Manley H, Stone AA, Blakeburn M, Gosling K (2017) Educational virtual reality visualisations of heritage sites. In: Eurographics workshop on graphics and cultural heritage

John D, Hurst D, Cheetham P, Manley H (2018) Visualising Dudsbury Hillfort: using immersive virtual reality to engage the public with cultural heritage. In: Eurographics workshop on graphics and cultural heritage

Katz D, Friess M (2014) Technical note: 3D from standard digital photography of human crania—a preliminary assessment. Am J Phys Anthropol 154(1):152–158

Kushner D (2003) It's a mod, mod world. IEEE Spectr 40(2):56–57

Lewis M, Jacobson J (2002) Introduction. Commun ACM 45(1):27–31

Manousos O (2014) An assessment of the submerged archaeology of exercise 'Smash I' in Studland Bay. MSc Maritime Archaeology, Bournemouth University

Mortara M, Catalano CE, Bellotti F, Fiucci G, Houry-Panchetti M, Petridis P (2014) Learning cultural heritage by serious games. J Cult Herit 15(3):318–325

New Forest National Park Authority: how laser mapping is used (2019). https://www.newforestnpa. gov.uk/conservation/preserving-history-and-culture/heritagemapping/laser-mapping-used/

Núñez Andrés A, Buill Pozuelo F, Regot Marimón J, de Mesa Gisbert A (2012) Generation of virtual models of cultural heritage. J Cult Herit 13(1):103–106

Pavlidis G, Koutsoudis A, Arnaoutoglou F, Tsioukas V, Chamzas C (2007) Methods for 3D digitization of cultural heritage. J Cult Herit 8(1):93–98

Rockwell GM, Kee K (2011) The leisure of serious games: a dialogue. Game Stud 11(2)

Shaw L, John D, Manley H, Underwood G (2016) More than just a pretty picture: a review of the use of 3D printing, touch tables and virtual environments to engage the public with lidar and the archaeology of the new forest. In: Conference of computer applications and quantitative methods in archaeology

Shneiderman B (2003) The eyes have it: a task by data type taxonomy for information visualizations. In: The craft of information visualization. Elsevier, pp 364–371

Trapp M, Semmo A, Pokorski R, Herrmann CD, Döllner J, Eichhorn M, Heinzelmann M (2012) Colonia 3D communication of virtual 3D reconstructions in public spaces. Int J Herit Digit Era 1(1):45–74

Troche J, Jacobson J (2010) An exemplar of ptolemaic egyptian temples. In: Conference of computer applications and quantitative methods in archaeology

UNESCO (2003) Convention for the safeguarding of the intangible cultural heritage

Vilbrandt C, Pasko G, Pasko A, Fayolle PA, Vilbrandt T, Goodwin JR, Goodwin JM, Kunii TL (2004) Cultural heritage preservation using constructive shape modeling. Comput Graph Forum 23(1):25–41

Weinberg G, Harsham B (2009) Developing a low-cost driving simulator for the evaluation of in-vehicle technologies. Tech. Rep. TR2009-064, Mitsubishi Electric Research

Wells C (2019) "Vyborg is ours": the collective memory of a lost Finnish city. In: Creating the city. Identity, memory and participation. Conference proceedings. Malmö University Publications in Urban Studies, pp 194–215

Printed in the United States
by Baker & Taylor Publisher Services